Reviewer Acclaim for Je
Applied Microsoft .NET Framew

D0127614

"The time Jeffrey spent with the .NET Framework is evident in this well-written and informative book."

Eric Rudder (senior vice president,
developer and platform evangelism, Microsoft)

"Jeff has worked directly with the folks who built the CLR [common language runtime] on a daily basis and has written the finest book on the internals of the CLR that you'll find anywhere."

Dennis Angeline (lead program manager,
CLR, Microsoft)

"Jeff brings his years of Windows programming experience and insight to explain how the .NET Framework really works, why we built it the way we did, and how you can get the most out of it."

Brad Abrams (lead program manager,
.NET Framework, Microsoft)

"Jeff Richter brings his well-known flair for explaining complicated material clearly, concisely, and accurately to the new areas of the C# language, the .NET Framework, and the .NET common language runtime. This is a must-have book for anyone wanting to understand the whys and hows behind these important new technologies."

Jim Miller (lead program manager,
CLR kernel, Microsoft)

"Easily the best book on the common language runtime. The chapter on the CLR garbage collector [Chapter 19] is awesome. Jeff not only describes the theory of how the garbage collector works but also discusses aspects of finalization that every .NET developer should know."

Mahesh Prakriya (lead program manager,
CLR team, Microsoft)

"This book is an accurate, in-depth, yet readable exploration of the common language runtime. It's one of those rare books that seems to anticipate the reader's question and supply the answer in the very next paragraph. The writing is excellent."

Jim Hogg (program manager, CLR team, Microsoft)

"Just as *Programming Applications for Microsoft Windows* became the must-have book for Win32 programmers, *Applied Microsoft .NET Framework Programming* promises to be the same for serious .NET Framework programmers. This book is unique in its bottom-up approach to understanding .NET Framework programming. By providing the reader with a solid understanding of lower-level CLR concepts, Jeff provides the groundwork needed to write solid, secure, high-performing managed code applications quickly and easily."

Steven Pratschner (program manager, CLR team, Microsoft)

"Jeff Richter, he the MAN!"

Anonymous (program manager, CLR, Microsoft)

"I don't care what it says; whenever Jeffrey authors a book, I immediately rush out and get it and add it to my shelf of his computer books."

Arlene Richter (Jeff's mom)

"A must-read for massage therapists everywhere!"

Kristin Trace (Jeff's wife)

"Meow! Meow!"

Max (Jeff's cat)

"If I write only two .NET Framework books, this is the second one."

Jeffrey Richter (himself)

Microsoft®

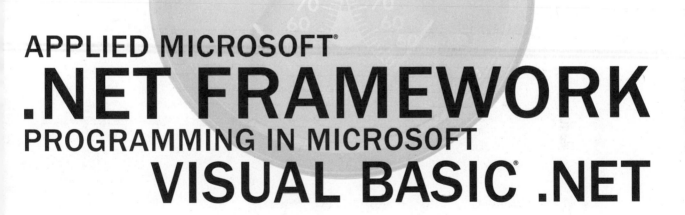

APPLIED MICROSOFT®
.NET FRAMEWORK
PROGRAMMING IN MICROSOFT
VISUAL BASIC® .NET

Jeffrey Richter
Francesco Balena

Microsoft®
.net™

PUBLISHED BY
Microsoft Press
A Division of Microsoft Corporation
One Microsoft Way
Redmond, Washington 98052-6399

Library of Congress Cataloging-in-Publication Data
Richter, Jeffrey.
    Applied Microsoft .NET Framework Programming in Microsoft Visual Basic .NET/
Jeffrey Richter, Francesco Balena.
       p. cm.
    Includes index.
    ISBN 0-7356-1787-2
    1. Microsoft.net framework.   2. Internet programming.   3. Microsoft Visual BASIC.   I.
Balena, Francesco, 1960– II. Title.

QA76.625 .R533 2002
005.2'76--dc21   2002069254

Printed and bound in the United States of America.

1 2 3 4 5 6 7 8 9   QWE   7 6 5 4 3 2

Distributed in Canada by H.B. Fenn and Company Ltd.

A CIP catalogue record for this book is available from the British Library.

Microsoft Press books are available through booksellers and distributors worldwide. For further information about international editions, contact your local Microsoft Corporation office or contact Microsoft Press International directly at fax (425) 936-7329. Visit our Web site at www.microsoft.com/mspress. Send comments to *mspinput@microsoft.com*.

Acquisitions Editor: Anne Hamilton
Project Editor: Sally Stickney

Body Part No. X08-81846

To Kristin

I want to tell you how much you mean to me.
Your energy and exuberance always lift me higher.
Your smile brightens my every day.
Your zest makes my heart sing.
I love you.

—J.R.

To my parents, who taught me to pursue my goals,
however distant they seemed to be.

—F.B.

Contents at a Glance

Table of Contents

Part III   Designing Types

Acknowledgments

I couldn't have written this book without the help and technical assistance of many people. In particular, a special thank you goes to my Wintellect colleague Francesco Balena, who worked with me in transforming the original book to meet the needs of Visual Basic developers.

I'd also like to thank the following people:

- **Members of the Microsoft Press team** Grant Duers, Teresa Fagan, Don Fowley, Anne Hamilton, Elizabeth Hansford, Michael Kloepfer, Aaron Lavin, Lisa Pawlewicz, and Sally Stickney.

- **Members of the Microsoft .NET Framework team** Fred Aaron, Brad Abrams, Mark Anders, Chris Anderson, Dennis Angeline, Keith Ballinger, Sanjay Bhansali, Mark Boulter, Christopher Brown, Chris Brumme, Kathleen Carey, Ian Carmichael, Rajesh Chandrashekaran, Yann Christensen, Suzanne Cook, Krzysztof Cwalina, Shajan Dasan, Peter de Jong, Blair Dillaway, Patrick Dussud, Erick Ellis, Bill Evans, Michael Fanning, Greg Fee, Kit George, Peter Golde, Will Greg, Bret Grinslade, Brian Grunkemeyer, Eric Gunnerson, Simon Hall, Jennifer Hamilton, Brian Harry, Michael Harsh, Jonathan Hawkins, Anders Hejlsberg, Jim Hogg, Paul Johns, Gopal Kakivaya, Sonja Keserovic, Abhi Khune, Loren Kornfelder, Nikhil Kothari, Tim Kurtzman, Brian LaMacchia, Sebastian Lange, Serge Lidin, Francois Liger, Yung-Shin "Bala" Lin, Mike Magruder, Rudi Martin, Erik Meijer, Gene Milener, Jim Miller, Anthony Moore, Vance Morrison, David Mortenson, Yuval Neeman, Lance Olson, Srivatsan Parthasarathy, Mahesh Prakriya, Steven Pratchner, Susan Radke-Sproul, Jayanth Rajan, Dmitry Robsman, Jay Roxe, Dario Russi, Craig Schertz, Alan Shi, Craig Sinclair, Greg Singleton, Ralph Squillace, Paul Stafford, Larry Sullivan, Dan Takacs, Ryley Taketa, David Treadwell, Sean Trowbridge, Nate Walker, Sara Williams, Jason Zander, and Eric Zinda. If I've forgotten anyone, please forgive me.

- **Reviewers**   Keith Ballinger, Tom Barclay, Lars Bergstrom, Stephen Butler, Jeffrey Cooperstein, Robert Corstanje, Tarek Dawoud, Sylvain Dechatre, Ash Dhanesha, Shawn Elliott, Chris Falter, Lakshan Fernando, Manish Godse, Eric Gunnerson, Brian Harry, Chris Hockett, Dekel Israeli, Paul Johns, Jeanine Johnson, Jim Kieley, Alex Lerner, Richard Loba, Kerry Loynd, Rob Macdonald, Darrin Massena, John Noss, Piet Obermeyer, Peter Plamondon, Keith Pleas, Mahesh Prakriya, Doug Purdy, Kent Sharkey, Alan Shi, Dan Vallejo, Scott Wadsworth, Beth Wood, and Steven Wort.

- **Wintellectuals**   Jim Bail, Doug Boling, Jason Clark, Paula Daniels, Dino Esposito, Lewis Frazer, John Lam, Jeff Prosise, John Robbins, Kenn Scribner, and Chris Shelby.

Introduction

Over the years, our computing lifestyles have changed. Today, everyone sees the value of the Internet, and our computing lifestyle is becoming more and more dependent on Web-based services. Personally, I love to shop, get traffic conditions, compare products, buy tickets, and read product reviews all via the Internet.

However, I'm finding that there are still many things I'd like to do using the Internet that aren't possible today. For example, I'd like to find restaurants in my area that serve a particular cuisine. Furthermore, I'd like to be able to ask if the restaurant has any seating for, say, 7:00 p.m. that night. Or if I had my own business, I might like to know which vendor has a particular item in stock. If multiple vendors can supply me with the item, I'd like to be able to find out which vendor offers the least expensive price for the item or maybe which vendor can deliver the item to me the fastest.

Services like these don't exist today for two main reasons. The first reason is that no standards are in place for integrating all this information. After all, vendors today each have their own way of describing what they sell. The emerging standard for describing all types of information is Extensible Markup Language (XML). The second reason these services don't exist today is the complexity of developing the code necessary to integrate such services.

Microsoft has a vision in which selling services is the way of the future—that is, companies will offer services and interested users can consume these services. Many services will be free; others will be available through a subscription plan, and still others will be charged per use. You can think of these services as the execution of some business logic. Here are some examples of services:

- Validating a credit card purchase
- Getting directions from point A to point B
- Viewing a restaurant's menu
- Booking a flight on an airline, a hotel room, or a rental car
- Updating photos in an online photo album
- Merging your calendar and your children's calendars to plan a family vacation
- Paying a bill from a checking account
- Tracking a package being shipped to you

I could go on and on with ideas for services that any company could implement. Without a doubt, Microsoft will build some of these services and offer them in the near future. Other companies (like yours) will also produce services, some of which might compete with Microsoft in a free market.

So how do we get from where we are today to a world in which all these services are easily available? And how do we produce applications—HTML-based or otherwise—that use and combine these services to produce rich features for the user? For example, if restaurants offered the service of retrieving their menu, an application could be written to query every restaurant's menu, search for a specific cuisine or dish, and then present only those restaurants in the user's own neighborhood in the application.

> **Note** To create rich applications like these, businesses must offer a programmatic interface to their business logic services. This programmatic interface must be callable remotely using a network, like the Internet. This is what the Microsoft .NET initiative is all about. Simply stated, the .NET initiative is all about connecting information, people, and devices.

Let me explain it this way: Computers have peripherals—mouse, monitor, keyboard, digital cameras, and scanners—connected to them. An operating system, such as Microsoft Windows, provides a development platform that abstracts the application's access to these peripherals. You can even think of these peripherals as services, in a way.

In this new world, the services (or peripherals) are now connected to the Internet. Developers want an easy way to access these services. Part of the Microsoft .NET initiative is to provide this development platform. The following diagram shows an analogy. On the left, Windows is the development platform that abstracts the hardware peripheral differences from the application developer. On the right, the Microsoft .NET Framework is the development platform that abstracts the XML Web service communication from the application developer.

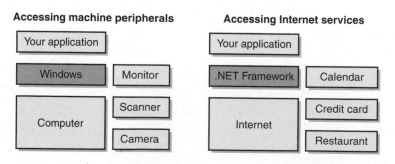

Although a leader in the development and definition of the standards involved in making this new world possible, Microsoft doesn't own any of the standards. Client machines describe a server request by creating specially formatted XML and then sending it (typically using HTTP) over an intranet or the Internet. Servers know how to parse the XML data, process the client's request, and return the response as XML back to the client. *Simple Object Access Protocol* (SOAP) is the term used to describe the specially formatted XML when it is sent using HTTP.

The following figure shows a bunch of XML Web services all communicating with one another using SOAP with its XML payload. The figure also shows clients running applications that can talk to Web services and even other clients via SOAP (XML). In addition, the figure shows a client getting its results via HTML from a Web server. Here the user probably filled out a Web form, which was sent back to the Web server. The Web server processed the user's request (which involved communicating with some Web services), and the results are ultimately sent back to the user via a standard HTML page.

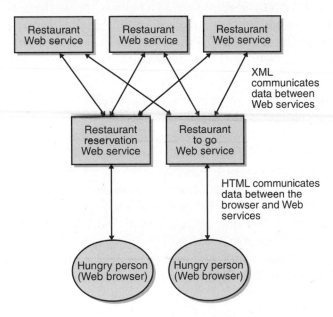

In addition, the computers providing the services must be running an operating system that is listening for these SOAP requests. Microsoft hopes that this operating system will be Windows, but Windows isn't a requirement. Any operating system that can listen on a TCP/IP socket port and read/write bytes to the port is good enough. In the not too distant future, mobile phones, pagers, automobiles, microwave ovens, refrigerators, watches, stereo equipment, game consoles, and all kinds of other devices will also be able to participate in this new world.

On the client or application side, an operating system must be running that can read/write to a socket port to issue service requests. The client's computer must also be capable of supporting whatever features the user's application desires. If the user's application wants to create a window or a menu, the operating system must provide this functionality or the application developer must implement it manually. Of course, Microsoft hopes that people will write applications that take advantage of the rich feature set in Windows, but again, Windows is a recommendation, not a necessity.

What I'm trying to say is that this new world will happen whether Microsoft is a part of it or not. Microsoft's .NET initiative is all about making it really easy for developers to create and access these services.

Today, we could all go write our own operating systems and create our own custom Web servers to listen for and manually process SOAP requests if we wanted to, but it would be really difficult and would take a long time. Microsoft has taken on all this hard work for us, and we can just leverage Microsoft's efforts to greatly simplify our own development efforts. Now we, as application developers, can concentrate and focus on our business logic and services, leaving all the communication protocols and plumbing to Microsoft (who has a lot of developers that just love to do this nitty-gritty stuff).

What Makes Up the Microsoft .NET Initiative

I've been working with Microsoft and its technologies for many years now. Over the years, I've seen Microsoft introduce all kinds of new technologies and initiatives: MS-DOS, Windows, Windows CE, OLE, COM, ActiveX, COM+, Windows DNA, and so on. When I first started hearing about Microsoft's .NET initiative, I was surprised at how solid Microsoft's story seemed to be. It really seemed to me that they had a vision and a plan and that they had rallied the troops to implement the plan.

I contrast Microsoft's .NET platform to ActiveX, which was just a new name given to good old COM to make it seem more user friendly. ActiveX didn't mean much (or so many developers thought), and the term, along with ActiveX controls, never really took off. I also contrast Microsoft's .NET initiative to Windows DNA (Distributed InterNet Architecture), which was another marketing label that Microsoft tacked onto a bunch of already existing technologies. But I really believe in the Microsoft .NET initiative, and to prove it, I've written two books: this one and the one that preceded it, *Applied Microsoft .NET Framework Programming*. So, what exactly constitutes the Microsoft .NET initiative? Well, there are several parts to it, and I'll describe each one in the following sections.

An Underlying Operating System: Windows

Because these Web services and applications that use Web services run on computers and because computers have peripherals, we still need an operating system. Microsoft suggests that people use Windows. Specifically, Microsoft is adding XML Web service–specific features to its Windows line of operating systems, and Windows XP and the servers in the Windows .NET Server Family will be the versions best suited for this new service-driven world.

Specifically, Windows XP and the Windows .NET Server Family products have integrated support for the Microsoft .NET Passport XML Web service. Passport is a service that authenticates users. Many Web services will require user authentication to access information securely. When users log on to a computer running Windows XP or one of the servers from the Windows .NET Server Family, they are effectively logging on to every Web site and Web service that uses Passport for authentication. This means that users won't have to enter usernames and passwords as they access different Internet sites. As you can imagine, Passport is a huge benefit to users: one identity and password for everything you do, and you have to enter it only once!

In addition, Windows XP and the Windows .NET Server Family products have some built-in support for loading and executing applications implementing the .NET Framework. Finally, Windows XP and the Windows .NET Server Family operating systems have a new, extensible instant messaging notification application. This application allows third-party vendors (such as Expedia, the United States Postal Service, and many others) to communicate with users seamlessly. For example, users can receive automatic notifications when their flights are delayed (from Expedia) and when a package is ready to be delivered (from the U.S. Postal Service).

I don't know about you, but I've been hoping for services like these for years—I can't wait!

Helpful Products: The .NET Enterprise Servers

As part of the .NET initiative, Microsoft is providing several products that companies can choose to use if their business logic (services) finds them useful. Here are some of Microsoft's enterprise server products:

- Microsoft Application Center 2000
- Microsoft BizTalk Server 2000
- Microsoft Commerce Server 2000
- Microsoft Exchange 2000

- Microsoft Host Integration Server 2000

- Microsoft Internet Security and Acceleration (ISA) Server 2000

- Microsoft Mobile Information Server 2002

- Microsoft SQL Server 2000

It's likely that each of these products will eventually have a ".NET" added to its name for marketing purposes. But I'm also sure that over time, these products will integrate more .NET features into them as Microsoft continues the initiative.

The Development Platform: The .NET Framework

Some of Microsoft's XML Web services (like Passport) exist today. These services run on Windows and are built using technologies such as C/C++, ATL, Win32, COM, and so on. As time goes on, these services and new services will ultimately be implemented using newer technologies, such as C# (pronounced "C sharp") and the .NET Framework.

> **Important** Even though this entire introduction is geared toward building Internet applications and Web services, the .NET Framework is capable of a lot more. All in all, the .NET Framework development platform allows developers to build the following kinds of applications: XML Web services, Web Forms, Win32 GUI applications, Win32 CUI (console UI) applications, services (controlled by the Service Control Manager), utilities, and stand-alone components. The material presented in this book is applicable to any and all of these application types.

The .NET Framework consists of two parts: the common language runtime (CLR) and the Framework Class Library (FCL). The .NET Framework is the part of the initiative that makes developing services and applications really easy. And, most important, this is what this book is all about: developing applications and XML Web services for the .NET Framework.

Initially, Microsoft will make the CLR and FCL available in the various versions of Windows, including Windows 98, Windows 98 Second Edition, and Windows Me as well as Windows NT 4, Windows 2000, and both 32-bit and 64-bit versions of Windows XP and the Windows .NET Server Family servers. A "lite" version of the .NET Framework, called the .NET Compact Framework, is also available for PDAs (such as Windows CE and Palm) and appliances (small devices). On December 13, 2001, the European Computer Manufacturers Association (ECMA) accepted the C# programming language, portions of the CLR, and portions of the FCL as standards. It won't be long before ECMA-compliant versions of these technologies appear on a wide variety of operating systems and CPUs.

> **Note**   Windows XP (both Home Edition and Professional) doesn't ship with the .NET Framework "in the box." However, the .NET Framework is included in Windows XP Service Pack 1 (SP1). In addition, the Windows .NET Server Family (Windows .NET Web Server, Windows .NET Standard Server, Windows .NET Enterprise Server, and Windows .NET Datacenter Server) will include the .NET Framework. In fact, this is how the Windows .NET Server Family got its name. The next version of Windows (code-named "Longhorn") will include the .NET Framework in all editions. For now, you'll have to redistribute the .NET Framework with your application, and your setup program will have to install it. Microsoft does make a .NET Framework redistribution file that you're allowed to freely distribute with your application: *http://go.microsoft.com/fwlink/?LinkId=5584*.

Almost all programmers are familiar with runtimes and class libraries. As a Visual Basic programmer, you've surely dabbled with the Visual Basic runtime library, and if you've written code in C++, you're familiar with the C-runtime library, the standard template library (STL), the Microsoft Foundation Class library (MFC), and the Active Template Library (ATL). And, of course, Java programmers are familiar with the Java virtual machine and its class library. In fact, the Windows operating system itself can be thought of as a runtime engine and library. Runtime engines and libraries offer services to applications, and we programmers love them because they save us from reinventing the same algorithms over and over again.

The Microsoft .NET Framework allows developers to leverage technologies more than any earlier Microsoft development platform did. Specifically, the .NET Framework really delivers on code reuse, code specialization, resource management, multilanguage development, security, deployment, and administration. While designing this new platform, Microsoft also felt it was necessary to improve on some of the deficiencies of the current Windows platform. The following list gives you just a small sampling of what the CLR and the FCL provide:

- **Consistent programming model** Unlike today, when some operating system facilities are accessed via dynamic-link library (DLL) functions and other facilities are accessed via COM objects, all application services are offered via a common object-oriented programming model.

- **Simplified programming model** The CLR seeks to greatly simplify the plumbing and arcane constructs required by Win32 and COM. Specifically, the CLR frees the developer from having to understand any of the following concepts: the registry, globally unique identifiers (GUIDs), `IUnknown`, `AddRef`, `Release`, `HRESULT`s, and so on. The CLR doesn't just abstract these concepts away from the developer; these concepts simply don't exist, in any form, in the CLR. Of course, if you want to write a .NET Framework application that interoperates with existing, non-.NET code, you must still be aware of these concepts.

- **Run once, run always** All Windows developers are familiar with "DLL hell" versioning problems. This situation occurs when components being installed for a new application overwrite components of an old application, causing the old application to exhibit strange behavior or to stop functioning altogether. The architecture of the .NET Framework now isolates application components so that an application always loads the components that it was built and tested with. If the application runs after installation, then the application should always run. This slams shut the gates of "DLL hell."

- **Simplified deployment** Today, Windows applications are incredibly difficult to set up and deploy. Several files, registry settings, and shortcuts usually need to be created. In addition, completely uninstalling an application is nearly impossible. With Windows 2000, Microsoft introduced a new installation engine that helps with all these issues, but it's still possible that a company authoring a Microsoft installer package might fail to do everything correctly. The .NET Framework seeks to banish these issues into history. The .NET Framework components (known simply as *types*) are not referenced by the registry. In fact, installing most .NET Framework applications requires no more than copying the files to a directory and adding a shortcut to the Start menu, desktop, or Quick Launch bar. Uninstalling the application is as simple as deleting the files.

- **Wide platform reach** When compiling source code for the .NET Framework, the compilers produce common intermediate language (CIL) instead of the more traditional CPU instructions. At run time, the CLR translates the CIL into native CPU instructions. Because the translation to native CPU instructions is done at run time, the translation is done for the host CPU. This means that you can deploy your .NET Framework application on any machine that has an ECMA-compliant version of the CLR and FCL running on it. These machines can be x86, IA64, Alpha, PowerPC, and so on. Users will immediately appreciate the value of this broad execution if they ever change their computing hardware or operating system.

■ **Programming language integration**   COM allows different programming languages to *interoperate* with one another. The .NET Framework allows languages to be *integrated* with one another so that you can use types of another language as if they are your own. For example, the CLR makes it possible to create a class in C++ that derives from a class implemented in Visual Basic. The CLR allows this because it defines and provides a Common Type System (CTS) that all programming languages that target the CLR must use. The Common Language Specification (CLS) describes what compiler implementers must do in order for their languages to integrate well with other languages. Microsoft is itself providing several compilers that produce code targeting the runtime: Visual Basic .NET (which now subsumes Visual Basic Scripting Edition, or VBScript, and Visual Basic for Applications, or VBA), Managed Extensions for C++, C#, and JScript. In addition, companies other than Microsoft and academic institutions are producing compilers for other languages that also target the CLR.

■ **Simplified code reuse**   Using the mechanisms described earlier, you can create your own classes that offer services to third-party applications. This makes it extremely simple to reuse code and also creates a large market for component (type) vendors.

■ **Automatic memory and management (garbage collection)** Programming requires great skill and discipline, especially when it comes to managing the use of resources such as files, memory, screen space, network connections, database resources, and so on. One of the most common bugs is neglecting to free one of these resources, ultimately causing the application to perform improperly at some unpredictable time. The CLR automatically tracks resource usage, guaranteeing that your application never leaks resources. In fact, there is no way to explicitly "free" memory. In Chapter 19, "Automatic Memory Management (Garbage Collection)," I explain exactly how garbage collection works.

- **Type-safe verification** The CLR can verify that all your code is type-safe. Type safety ensures that allocated objects are always accessed in compatible ways. Hence, if a method input parameter is declared as accepting a 4-byte value, the CLR will detect and trap attempts to access the parameter as an 8-byte value. Similarly, if an object occupies 10 bytes in memory, the application can't coerce the object into a form that will allow more than 10 bytes to be read. Type safety also means that execution flow will transfer only to well-known locations (that is, method entry points). There is no way to construct an arbitrary reference to a memory location and cause code at that location to start executing. Together, these measures ensure type safety eliminating many common programming errors and classic system attacks (for example, exploiting buffer overruns).

- **Rich debugging support** Because the CLR is used for many programming languages, it is now much easier to implement portions of your application using the language best suited to a particular task. The CLR fully supports debugging applications that cross language boundaries.

- **Consistent method failure paradigm** One of the most aggravating aspects of Windows programming is the inconsistent style that functions use to report failures. Some functions return Win32 status codes, some functions return HRESULTs, and some functions throw exceptions. (Earlier versions of Visual Basic use error codes but actually work with HRESULTs.) In the CLR, all failures are reported via exceptions—period. Exceptions allow the developer to isolate the failure recovery code from the code required to get the work done. This separation greatly simplifies writing, reading, and maintaining code. In addition, exceptions work across module and programming language boundaries. And, unlike status codes and HRESULTs, exceptions can't be ignored. The CLR also provides built-in stack-walking facilities, making it much easier to locate any bugs and failures. If you've worked with Visual Basic 6, you'll see that you catch exceptions much like you trapped old-style errors. So even though the syntax of Visual Basic .NET is different than it was in earlier versions, you should have no trouble understanding how to properly handle errors.

- **Security** Traditional operating system security provides isolation and access control based on user accounts. This model has proven useful, but at its core it assumes that all code is equally trustworthy. This assumption was justified when all code was installed from physical media (for example, CD-ROM) or trusted corporate servers. But with the increasing reliance on mobile code such as Web scripts, applications downloaded over the Internet, and e-mail attachments, we need ways to control the behavior of applications in a more code-centric manner. Code access security provides a means to do this.

■ **Interoperability**   Microsoft realizes that developers already have an enormous amount of existing code and components. Rewriting all this code to take full advantage of the .NET Framework platform would be a huge undertaking and would prevent the speedy adoption of this platform. So the .NET Framework fully supports the ability for the developers to access their existing COM components as well as call Win32 functions in existing DLLs. If you've followed a component-based approach in designing your existing Visual Basic 6 applications, you can easily call these components from Visual Basic .NET applications and reuse your existing code.

Users won't directly appreciate the CLR and its capabilities, but they will certainly notice the quality and features of applications that utilize the CLR. In addition, users and your company's bottom line will appreciate how the CLR allows applications to be developed and deployed more rapidly and with less administration than Windows has ever allowed in the past.

The Development Environment: Visual Studio .NET

The last part of the .NET initiative that I want to mention is Visual Studio .NET. Visual Studio .NET is Microsoft's development environment. Microsoft has been working on it for many years and has incorporated a lot of .NET Framework–specific features into it. Visual Studio .NET runs on Windows NT 4, Windows 2000, Windows XP, and the Windows .NET Server Family servers, and it will run on future versions of Windows. Of course, the code produced by Visual Studio .NET will run on all these Windows platforms plus Windows 98, Windows 98 Second Edition, and Windows Me.

Like any good development environment, Visual Studio .NET includes a project manager; a source code editor; UI designers; lots of wizards, compilers, linkers, tools, and utilities; documentation; and debuggers. It supports building applications for both the 32-bit and 64-bit Windows platforms as well as for the new .NET Framework platform. Another important improvement is that there is now just one integrated development environment for all programming languages.

Microsoft also provides a .NET Framework SDK. This free SDK includes all the language compilers, a bunch of tools, and a lot of documentation. Using this SDK, you can develop applications for the .NET Framework without using Visual Studio .NET. You'll just have to use your own editor and project management system. You also don't get drag-and-drop Web Forms and Windows

Forms building. I use Visual Studio .NET regularly and will refer to it throughout this book. However, this book is mostly about programming in general, so Visual Studio .NET isn't required to learn, use, and understand the concepts I present in each chapter.

Goal of This Book

The purpose of this book is to explain how to develop applications for the .NET Framework. Specifically, this means that I intend to explain how the CLR works and the facilities it offers. I'll also discuss various parts of the FCL. No book could fully explain the FCL—it contains literally thousands of types, and this number is growing at an alarming rate. So, here I'm concentrating on the core types that every developer needs to be aware of. And while this book isn't specifically about Windows Forms, XML Web services, Web Forms, and so on, the technologies presented in the book are applicable to all these application types.

With this book, I'm not attempting to teach you the Visual Basic .NET programming language, and I don't assume that you're an experienced Visual Basic 6 developer, even though in some cases I compare Visual Basic .NET with earlier versions of Visual Basic. I do assume, however, that you're familiar with object-oriented programming concepts such as data abstraction, inheritance, and polymorphism. A good understanding of these concepts is critical because all .NET Framework features are offered via an object-oriented paradigm. If you're not familiar with these concepts, I strongly suggest you first find a book that teaches these concepts.

Although I don't intend to teach programming, I will spend time on various programming topics that are specific to the .NET Framework. All .NET Framework developers must be aware of these topics, which I explain and use throughout this book.

I provide lots of code examples in the book to show how things really work. The best language for me to use to explain how the .NET Framework's CLR works would be IL (intermediate language) assembly language. IL is the only programming language that the CLR understands. All language compilers compile source code to IL, which is later processed by the CLR. Using IL, you can access every feature offered by the CLR.

However, using IL assembly language is a pretty low-level way to write programs and isn't an ideal way to demonstrate programming concepts. In my *Applied Microsoft .NET Framework Programming* book (Microsoft Press, 2002), I decided to use C# as the programming language of choice for all examples. I chose C# because it is the language Microsoft designed specifically for developing code for the .NET Framework. After *Applied Microsoft .NET Framework Programming* shipped, I heard from a number of Visual Basic developers that they'd like to understand the CLR and its abilities from the perspective of Visual Basic .NET. Because the CLR's behavior is identical regardless of the programming language being used, I assumed that modifying my book for Visual Basic .NET would be a fairly straightforward task. There was just one problem: I wasn't familiar with Visual Basic .NET and had even less knowledge of Visual Basic 6 and what issues Visual Basic programmers would run into as they adopted the .NET Framework development platform. So I did a very smart thing: I contacted my friend and fellow Wintellectual Francesco Balena. Francesco has been working with Visual Basic for many years and has been aggressively learning about the Visual Basic .NET language. Francesco edited every chapter, keeping the Visual Basic developer in mind at all times. His edits included many comparisons with Visual Basic 6, and he also added explanations for many of the features offered by Visual Basic .NET. As I reviewed Francesco's chapters, I learned quite a bit about Visual Basic .NET as well as gained respect for it.

Many developers believe that Visual Basic .NET is a subset of C# in terms of functionality. However, this is not true. Visual Basic .NET offers parameterful properties, exception filtering, more flexible ways to implement interface methods, method static variables, optional parameters and default arguments, and easier creation and handling of events, just to name a few of its strengths. All these new topics are discussed in this book.

Occasionally, this book does address features of the CLR that are not exposed by Visual Basic .NET. For these few features (such as operator overloading and unsafe code), Francesco and I agreed to explain the CLR feature anyway even though Visual Basic .NET programmers won't be able to use it. To explain or demonstrate these features, code is shown in C# or Managed Extensions for C++. This way, you'll understand what the CLR can do, and if you really need a particular feature, you can implement some of your application code using a different programming language. Also, Visual Basic .NET is evolving, and future versions of the language will probably gain support for these features. Understanding what the CLR is capable of (regardless of programming language) will really help you as you work with the .NET Framework development platform.

System Requirements

The .NET Framework will install on Windows 98, Windows 98 Second Edition, Windows Me, Windows NT 4 (all editions), Windows 2000 (all editions), Windows XP (all editions), and the Windows .NET Server Family servers. You can download it from *http://go.microsoft.com/fwlink/?LinkId=5584.*

The .NET Framework SDK and Visual Studio .NET will install on Windows NT 4 (all editions), Windows 2000 (all editions), Windows XP (all editions), and the servers in the Windows .NET Server Family. You can download the .NET Framework SDK from *http://go.microsoft.com/fwlink/?LinkId=77*. You have to buy Visual Studio .NET, of course.

You can download the code associated with this book from *http://www.Wintellect.com*.

This Book Has No Mistakes

This section's title clearly states what I want to say. But we all know that it is a flat-out lie. My editors and I have worked hard to bring you the most accurate, up-to-date, in-depth, easy-to-read, painless-to-understand, bug-free information. Even with the fantastic team assembled, things inevitably slip through the cracks. If you find any mistakes in this book (especially bugs), I would greatly appreciate it if you would send the mistakes to me at *http://www.Wintellect.com*.

Support

Every effort has been made to ensure the accuracy of this book. Microsoft Press provides corrections for books through the World Wide Web at the following address:

http://www.microsoft.com/mspress/support/

To connect directly to the Microsoft Press Knowledge Base and enter a query regarding a question or an issue that you may have, go to

http://www.microsoft.com/mspress/support/search.asp

If you have comments, questions, or ideas regarding this book, please send them to Microsoft Press using either of the following methods:

Postal Mail:
Microsoft Press
Attn: *Applied Microsoft .NET Framework Programming with Visual Basic .NET* Editor
One Microsoft Way
Redmond, WA 98052-6399

E-Mail:
MSPINPUT@MICROSOFT.COM

Please note that product support is not offered through the above mail addresses. For support information regarding C#, Visual Studio, or the .NET Framework, visit the Microsoft Product Standard Support Web site at

http://support.microsoft.com

Part I

Basics of the Microsoft .NET Framework

1

The Architecture of the .NET Framework Development Platform

The Microsoft .NET Framework introduces many new concepts, technologies, and terms. My goal in this chapter is to give you an overview of how the .NET Framework is architected, introduce you to some of the new technologies the framework includes, and define many of the terms you'll be seeing when you start using it. I'll also take you through the process of building your source code into an application or a set of redistributable components (types) and then explain how these components execute.

Compiling Source Code into Managed Modules

OK, so you've decided to use the .NET Framework as your development platform. Great! Your first step is to determine what type of application or component you intend to build. Let's just assume that you've completed this minor detail, everything is designed, the specifications are written, and you're ready to start development.

Now you must decide what programming language to use. This task is usually difficult because different languages offer different capabilities. For example, in unmanaged C/C++, you have pretty low-level control of the system. You can manage memory exactly the way you want to, create threads easily if you need to, and so on. Visual Basic 6, on the other hand, allows you to build UI applications very rapidly and makes it easy for you to control COM objects and databases.

3

> **Note**   This book is about the .NET Framework's common language runtime (CLR) as seen through the eyes of the Microsoft Visual Basic .NET developer. The CLR offers many features that Visual Basic and other programming languages do not expose. Since this book is really about the CLR, I've chosen to describe CLR features that are not available to Visual Basic programmers using other programming languages such as C#, Managed Extensions for C++, and even IL assembly language. This way, you will know what the CLR's capabilities are, giving you a better understanding of what the CLR is and what it can do. With this knowledge, you may decide to write parts of your application using other programming languages; as you'll see this is very easy to do and offers you a lot of flexibility. As time marches on, Microsoft will be adding more and more features to Visual Basic and the other compilers to expose more of the CLR's features to developers using these higher-level programming languages.

The common language runtime (CLR) is just what its name says it is: a runtime that is usable by different and varied programming languages. The features of the CLR are available to any and all programming languages that target it—period. If the runtime uses exceptions to report errors, then all languages get errors reported via exceptions. If the runtime allows you to create a thread, then any language can create a thread.

In fact, at runtime, the CLR has no idea which programming language the developer used for the source code. This means that you should choose whatever programming language allows you to express your intentions most easily. You can develop your code in any programming language you desire as long as the compiler you use to compile your code targets the CLR.

So, if what I say is true, what is the advantage of using one programming language over another? Well, I think of compilers as syntax checkers and "correct code" analyzers. They examine your source code, ensure that whatever you've written makes some sense, and then output code that describes your intention. Different programming languages allow you to develop using different syntax. Don't underestimate the value of this choice. For mathematical or financial applications, expressing your intentions using APL syntax can save many days of development time when compared to expressing the same intention using Perl syntax, for example.

Microsoft is creating several language compilers that target the runtime: Visual Basic, Managed Extensions for C++, C# (pronounced "C sharp"), JScript, J# (a Java language compiler), and an intermediate language (IL) assembler. In addition to Microsoft, several other companies are creating compilers that produce code that targets the CLR. I'm aware of compilers for Alice, APL, COBOL, Component Pascal, Eiffel, Fortran, Haskell, Mercury, ML, Mondrian, Oberon, Perl, Python, RPG, Scheme, and Smalltalk.

Figure 1-1 shows the process of compiling source code files. As the figure shows, you can create source code files using any programming language that supports the CLR. Then you use the corresponding compiler to check the syntax and analyze the source code. Regardless of which compiler you use, the result is a *managed module*. A managed module is a standard Microsoft Windows portable executable (PE) file that requires the CLR to execute. In the future, other operating systems may use the PE file format as well. Table 1-1 describes the parts of a managed module.

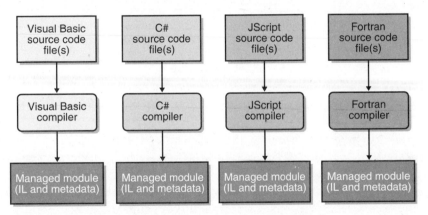

Figure 1-1   Compiling source code into managed modules

Most compilers of the past produced code targeted to a specific CPU architecture, such as x86, IA64, Alpha, or PowerPC. All CLR-compliant compilers produce IL code instead. (I'll go into more detail about IL code later in this chapter.) IL code is sometimes referred to as *managed code* because the CLR manages its lifetime and execution.

Table 1-1   Parts of a Managed Module

Part	Description
PE header	The standard Windows PE file header, which is similar to the Common Object File Format (COFF) header. This header indicates the type of file: GUI, CUI, or DLL, and it also has a timestamp indicating when the file was built. For modules that contain only IL code, the bulk of the information in the PE header is ignored. For modules that contain native CPU code, this header contains information about the native CPU code.
CLR header	Contains the information (interpreted by the CLR and utilities) that makes this a managed module. The header includes the version of the CLR required, some flags, the MethodDef metadata token of the managed module's entry point method (**Main** method), and the location/size of the module's metadata, resources, strong name, some flags, and other less interesting stuff.
Metadata	Every managed module contains metadata tables. There are two main types of tables: tables that describe the types and members defined in your source code and tables that describe the types and members referenced by your source code.
Intermediate language (IL) code	Code that the compiler produced as it compiled the source code. The CLR later compiles the IL into native CPU instructions.

In addition to emitting IL, every compiler targeting the CLR is required to emit full *metadata* into every managed module. In brief, metadata is simply a set of data tables that describe what is defined in the module, such as types and their members. In addition, metadata has tables indicating what the managed module references, such as imported types and their members. Metadata is a superset of older technologies such as type libraries and interface definition language (IDL) files. The important thing to note is that CLR metadata is far more complete. And, unlike type libraries and IDL, metadata is always associated with the file that contains the IL code. In fact, the metadata is always embedded in the same EXE/DLL as the code, making it impossible to separate the two. Because the compiler produces the metadata and the code at the same time and binds them into the resulting managed module, the metadata and the IL code it describes are never out of sync with one another.

Metadata has many uses. Here are some of them:

- Metadata removes the need for header and library files when compiling since all the information about the referenced types/members is contained in the file that has the IL that implements the type/members. Compilers can read metadata directly from managed modules.

- Microsoft Visual Studio .NET uses metadata to help you write code. Its IntelliSense feature parses metadata to tell you what methods a type offers and what parameters that method expects.

- The CLR's code verification process uses metadata to ensure that your code performs only "safe" operations. (I'll discuss verification shortly.)

- Metadata allows an object's fields to be serialized into a memory block, remoted to another machine, and then deserialized, re-creating the object and its state on the remote machine.

- Metadata allows the garbage collector to track the lifetime of objects. For any object, the garbage collector can determine the type of the object and, from the metadata, know which fields within that object refer to other objects.

In Chapter 2, I'll describe metadata in much more detail.

Microsoft's Visual Basic, C#, JScript, J#, and the IL Assembler always produce managed modules that require the CLR to execute. End-users must have the CLR installed on their machine in order to execute any managed modules, in the same way that they must have the Microsoft Foundation Class (MFC) library or Visual Basic DLLs installed to run MFC or Visual Basic 6 applications.

By default, Microsoft's C++ compiler builds unmanaged modules: the EXE or DLL files that we're all familiar with. These modules don't require the CLR in order to execute. However, by specifying a new command-line switch, the C++ compiler can produce managed modules that do require the CLR to execute. Of all the Microsoft compilers mentioned, C++ is unique in that it is the only language that allows the developer to write both managed and unmanaged code and have it emitted into a single module. This can be a great feature because it allows developers to write the bulk of their application in managed code (for type safety and component interoperability) but continue to access their existing unmanaged C++ code.

Combining Managed Modules into Assemblies

The CLR doesn't actually work with modules; it works with *assemblies*. An assembly is an abstract concept that can be difficult to grasp initially. First, an assembly is a logical grouping of one or more managed modules or resource files. Second, an assembly is the smallest unit of reuse, security, and versioning. Depending on the choices you make with your compilers or tools, you can produce a single-file or a multifile assembly.

In Chapter 2, I'll go over assemblies in great detail, so I don't want to spend a lot of time on them here. All I want to do now is make you aware that there is this extra conceptual notion that offers a way to treat a group of files as a single entity.

Figure 1-2 should help explain what assemblies are about. In this figure, some managed modules and resource (or data) files are being processed by a tool. This tool produces a single PE file that represents the logical grouping of files. What happens is that this PE file contains a block of data called the *manifest*. The manifest is simply another set of metadata tables. These tables describe the files that make up the assembly, the publicly exported types implemented by the files in the assembly, and the resource or data files that are associated with the assembly.

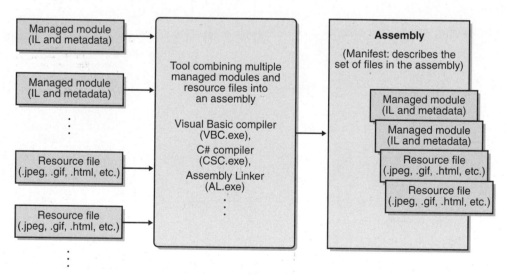

Figure 1-2   Combining managed modules into assemblies

By default, compilers actually do the work of turning the emitted managed module into an assembly; that is, the Visual Basic .NET compiler emits a managed module that contains a manifest. The manifest indicates that the assembly consists of just the one file. So for projects that have just one managed module and no resource (or data) files, the assembly will be the managed module and you don't have any additional steps to perform during your build process. If you want to group a set of files into an assembly, you'll have to be aware of more tools (such as the Assembly Linker, AL.exe) and their command-line options. I'll explain these tools and options in Chapter 2.

An assembly allows you to decouple the logical and physical notions of a reusable, deployable, versionable component. How you partition your code and resources into different files is completely up to you. For example, you could put rarely used types or resources in separate files that are part of an assembly. The separate files could be downloaded from the Web as needed. If the files are never needed, they're never downloaded, saving disk space and reducing installation time. Assemblies allow you to break up the deployment of the files while still treating all the files as a single collection.

An assembly's modules also include information, including version numbers, about referenced assemblies. This information makes an assembly *self-describing*. In other words, the CLR knows everything about what an assembly needs in order to execute. No additional information is required in the registry or in Active Directory. Because no additional information is needed, deploying assemblies is much easier than deploying unmanaged components.

Loading the Common Language Runtime

Each assembly that you build can be either an executable application or a DLL containing a set of types (components) for use by an executable application. Of course, the CLR is responsible for managing the execution of code contained within these assemblies. This means that the .NET Framework must be installed on the host machine. Microsoft has created a redistribution package that you can freely ship to install the .NET Framework on your customers' machines. Eventually, the .NET Framework will be packaged with future versions of Windows so that you won't have to ship it with your assemblies.

You can tell whether the .NET Framework has been installed by looking for the MSCorEE.dll file in the %windir%\system32 directory. The existence of this file tells you that the .NET Framework is installed. However, several versions of the .NET Framework can be installed on a single machine simultaneously. If you want to determine exactly which versions of the .NET Framework are installed, examine the subkeys under the following registry key:

```
HKEY_LOCAL_MACHINE\SOFTWARE\Microsoft\.NETFramework\policy
```

When you build an EXE assembly, the compiler/linker emits some special information into the resulting assembly's PE file header and the file's **.text** section. When the EXE file is invoked, this special information causes the CLR to load and initialize. The CLR then locates the application's entry point method and allows the application to start executing.

Similarly, if an unmanaged application calls **LoadLibrary** to load a managed assembly, the DLL's entry point function knows to load the CLR in order to process the code contained within the assembly.

For the most part, you don't need to know about or understand how the CLR gets loaded. For most programmers, this special information allows the application to just run, and there's nothing more to think about. For the curious, however, I'll spend the remainder of this section explaining how a managed EXE or DLL starts the CLR. If you're not interested in this subject, feel free to skip to the next section. Also, if you're interested in building an unmanaged application that hosts the CLR, see Chapter 20.

Figure 1-3 summarizes how a managed EXE loads and initializes the CLR.

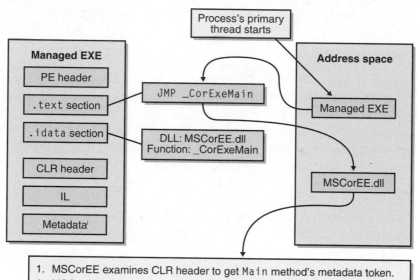

Figure 1-3   Loading and initializing the CLR

When the compiler/linker creates an executable assembly, the following 6-byte x86 stub function is emitted into the PE file's `.text` section:

```
JMP _CorExeMain
```

Because the **_CorExeMain** function is imported from Microsoft's MSCorEE.dll dynamic-link library, MSCorEE.dll is referenced in the assembly file's import (`.idata`) section. MSCorEE.dll stands for *Microsoft Component Object Runtime Execution Engine*. When the managed EXE file is invoked, Windows treats it just like any normal (unmanaged) EXE file: the Windows loader loads the file and examines the `.idata` section to see that MSCorEE.dll should be loaded into the process's address space. Then the loader obtains the address of the **_CorExeMain** function inside MSCorEE.dll and fixes up the stub function's **JMP** instruction in the managed EXE file.

The process's primary thread begins executing this x86 stub function, which immediately jumps to **_CorExeMain** in MSCorEE.dll. **_CorExeMain** initializes the CLR and then looks at the executable assembly's CLR header to determine what managed entry point method should execute. The IL code for the method is then compiled into native CPU instructions, and the CLR jumps to the native code (using the process's primary thread). At this point, the managed application's code is running.

The situation is similar for a managed DLL. When building a managed DLL, the compiler/linker emits a similar 6-byte x86 stub function in the PE file's `.text` section for a DLL assembly:

```
JMP _CorDllMain
```

The **_CorDllMain** function is also imported from MSCorEE.dll, causing the DLL's `.idata` section to reference MSCorEE.dll. When Windows loads the DLL, it will automatically load MSCorEE.dll (if it isn't already loaded), obtain the address of the **_CorDllMain** function, and fix up the 6-byte x86 **JMP** stub in the managed DLL. The thread that called **LoadLibrary** to load the managed DLL now jumps to the x86 stub in the managed DLL assembly, which immediately jumps to the **_CorDllMain** function in MSCorEE.dll. **_CorDllMain** initializes the CLR (if it hasn't already been initialized for the process) and then returns so that the application can continue executing as normal.

These 6-byte x86 stub functions are required to run managed assemblies on Windows 98, Windows 98 Second Edition, Windows Me, Windows NT 4, and Windows 2000 because all these operating systems shipped long before the CLR became available. Note that the 6-byte stub function is specifically for x86 machines. This stub doesn't work properly if the CLR is ported to run on other CPU architectures. Because Windows XP and the Windows .NET Server Family support both the x86 and the IA64 CPU architectures, Windows XP and the Windows .NET Server Family loaders were modified to look specifically for managed assemblies.

On Windows XP and the Windows .NET Server Family, when a managed assembly is invoked (typically via `CreateProcess` or `LoadLibrary`), the OS loader detects that the file contains managed code by examining directory entry 14 in the PE file header. (See `IMAGE_DIRECTORY_ENTRY_COM_DESCRIPTOR` in WinNT.h.) If this directory entry exists and is not 0, the loader ignores the file's import (`.idata`) section and automatically loads MSCorEE.dll into the process's address space. Once loaded, the OS loader makes the process's thread jump directly to the correct function in MSCorEE.dll. The 6-byte x86 stub functions are ignored on machines running Windows XP and the Windows .NET Server Family.

One last note on managed PE files: they always use the 32-bit PE file format, not the 64-bit PE file format. On 64-bit Windows systems, the OS loader detects the managed 32-bit PE file and automatically knows to create a 64-bit address space.

Executing Your Assembly's Code

As mentioned earlier, managed modules contain both metadata and intermediate language (IL). IL is a CPU-independent machine language created by Microsoft after consultation with several external commercial and academic language/compiler writers. IL is much higher level than most CPU machine languages. IL understands object types and has instructions that create and initialize objects, call virtual methods on objects, and manipulate array elements directly. It even has instructions that throw and catch exceptions for error handling. You can think of IL as an object-oriented machine language.

Usually, developers will program in a high-level language, such as Visual Basic or C#. The compilers for these high-level languages produce IL. However, like any other machine language, IL can be written in assembly language, and Microsoft does provide an IL Assembler, ILAsm.exe. Microsoft also provides an IL Disassembler, ILDasm.exe.

Keep in mind that any high-level language will most likely expose only a subset of the facilities offered by the CLR. However, using IL assembly language allows a developer access to all the CLR's facilities. So, should your programming language of choice hide a facility the CLR offers that you really want to take advantage of, you can choose to write that portion of your code in IL assembly or perhaps another programming language that exposes the CLR feature you seek.

The only way for you to know what facilities the CLR offers is to read documentation specific to the CLR itself. In this book, I try to concentrate on CLR features and how they are exposed or not exposed by the Visual Basic language. I suspect that most other books and articles will present the CLR via a language perspective and that most developers will come to believe that the CLR offers only what the developer's chosen language exposes. As long as your language allows you to accomplish what you're trying to get done, this blurred perspective isn't a bad thing.

Important   I think that this ability to switch programming languages easily with rich integration between languages is an awesome feature of the CLR. Unfortunately, I also believe that developers will often overlook this feature. Programming languages such as Visual Basic and C# are excellent languages for doing I/O operations. APL is a great language for doing advanced engineering or financial calculations. Through the CLR, you can write the I/O portions of your application using Visual Basic and then write the engineering calculations part using APL. The CLR offers a level of integration between these languages that is unprecedented and really makes mixed-language programming worthy of consideration for many development projects. Another important point to keep in mind about IL is that it isn't tied to any specific CPU platform. This means that a managed module containing IL can run on any CPU platform as long as the operating system running on that CPU platform hosts a version of the CLR. Although the initial release of the CLR runs only on 32-bit Windows platforms, developing an application using managed IL sets up a developer to be more independent of the underlying CPU architecture.

Even though today's CPUs can't execute IL instructions directly, CPUs of the future might have this capability. To execute a method, its IL must first be converted to native CPU instructions. This is the job of the CLR's JIT (just-in-time) compiler.

IL and Protecting Your Intellectual Property

Some people are concerned that IL doesn't offer enough intellectual property protection for their algorithms. In other words, they think you could build a managed module and someone else could use a tool, such as IL Disassembler, to easily reverse engineer exactly what your application's code does.

Yes, it's true that IL code is higher level than most other assembly languages and that, in general, reverse engineering IL code is relatively simple. However, when implementing an XML Web service or a Web Forms application, your managed module resides on your server. Because no one outside your company can access the module, no one outside your company can use any tool to see the IL—your intellectual property is completely safe.

If you're concerned about any of the managed modules that you do distribute, you can obtain an obfuscator utility from a third-party vendor. These utilities "scramble" the names of all the private symbols in your managed module's metadata. It will be difficult for someone to "unscramble" the names and understand the purpose of each method. Note that these obfuscators can provide only a little protection since the IL must be available at some point in order for the CLR to process it.

If you don't feel that an obfuscator offers the kind of intellectual property protection that you desire, you can consider implementing your more sensitive algorithms in some unmanaged module that will contain native CPU instructions instead of IL and metadata. Then you can use the CLR's interoperability features to communicate between the managed and unmanaged portions of your application. Of course, this assumes that you're not worried about people reverse engineering the native CPU instructions in your unmanaged code.

Figure 1-4 shows what happens the first time a method is called.

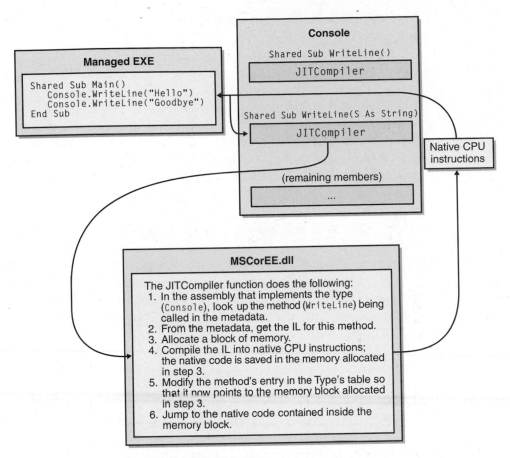

Figure 1-4   Calling a method for the first time

Just before the **Main** method executes, the CLR detects all the types that are referenced by **Main**'s code. This causes the CLR to allocate an internal data structure that is used to manage access to the referenced type. In Figure 1-4, the **Main** method refers to a single type, **Console**, causing the CLR to allocate a single internal structure. This internal data structure contains an entry for each method defined by the type. Each entry holds the address where the method's implementation can be found. When initializing this structure, the CLR sets each entry to an internal, undocumented function contained inside the CLR itself. I call this function `JITCompiler`.

When `Main` makes its first call to `WriteLine`, the `JITCompiler` function is called. The `JITCompiler` function is responsible for compiling a method's IL code into native CPU instructions. Because the IL is being compiled "just in time," this component of the CLR is frequently referred to as a *JITter* or a *JIT compiler*.

When called, the `JITCompiler` function knows what method is being called and what type defines this method. The `JITCompiler` function then searches the defining assembly's metadata for the called method's IL. `JITCompiler` next verifies and compiles the IL code into native CPU instructions. The native CPU instructions are saved in a dynamically allocated block of memory. Then, `JITCompiler` goes back to the type's internal data structure and replaces the address of the called method with the address of the block of memory containing the native CPU instructions. Finally, `JITCompiler` jumps to the code in the memory block. This code is the implementation of the `WriteLine` method (the version that takes a `String` parameter). When this code returns, it returns to the code in `Main`, which continues execution as normal.

`Main` now calls `WriteLine` a second time. This time, the code for `WriteLine` has already been verified and compiled. So the call goes directly to the block of memory, skipping the `JITCompiler` function entirely. After the `WriteLine` method executes, it returns to `Main`. Figure 1-5 shows what the situation looks like when `WriteLine` is called the second time.

A performance hit is incurred only the first time a method is called. All subsequent calls to the method execute at the full speed of the native code: verification and compilation to native code are not performed again.

The JIT compiler stores the native CPU instructions in dynamic memory. This means that the compiled code is discarded when the application terminates. So, if you run the application again in the future or if you run two instances of the application simultaneously (in two different operating system processes), the JIT compiler will have to compile the IL to native instructions again.

For most applications, the performance hit incurred by JIT compiling isn't significant. Most applications tend to call the same methods over and over again. These methods will take the performance hit only once while the application executes. It's also likely that more time is spent inside the method than calling the method.

Standardizing the .NET Framework

In October 2000, Microsoft (along with Intel and Hewlett-Packard as co-sponsors) proposed a large subset of the .NET Framework to the ECMA (the European Computer Manufacturer's Association) for the purpose of standardization. The ECMA accepted this proposal and created a technical committee (TC39) to oversee the standardization process. The technical committee is charged with the following duties:

- **Technical Group 1** Develop a dynamic scripting language standard (ECMAScript). Microsoft's implementation of ECMA-Script is JScript.

- **Technical Group 2** Develop a standardized version of the C# programming language.

- **Technical Group 3** Develop a Common Language Infrastructure (CLI) based on a subset of the functionality offered by the .NET Framework's CLR and class library. Specifically, the CLI will define a file format, a common type system, an extensible metadata system, an intermediate language (IL), and access to the underlying platform (P/Invoke). In addition, the CLI will define a factorable (to allow for small hardware devices) base class library designed for use by multiple programming languages.

In October 2001, TG2 and TG3 submitted their documents describing the first version of C# and the CLI. With version 1 of the standard complete, they have been contributed to ISO/IEC JTC 1 (Information Technology) in hopes of becoming an international standard. Now that version 1 is complete, the technical groups continue to investigate further directions for CLI, C#, and ECMAScript as well as entertain proposals for any complementary or additional technology. For more information about ECMA, see *http://www.ECMA.ch* and *http://MSDN.Microsoft.com/Net/ECMA*.

Now that the CLI, C#, and ECMAScript have been standardized, Microsoft doesn't "own" any of these technologies. Microsoft will simply be one company of many (hopefully) that are producing implementations of these technologies. Certainly Microsoft hopes that their implementation will be the best in terms of performance and customer-demand-driven features. This is what will help sales of Windows, since the Microsoft "best of breed" implementation will run only on Windows. However, other companies may implement these standards, compete against Microsoft, and possibly win.

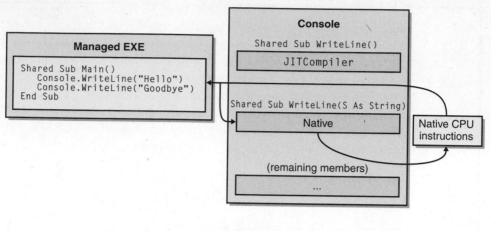

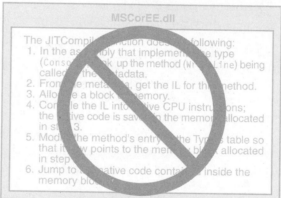

Figure 1-5 Calling a method for the second time

You should also be aware that the CLR's JIT compiler optimizes the native code just as the back-end of an unmanaged C++ compiler does. Again, it might take more time to produce the optimized code, but the code will execute with much better performance than if it hadn't been optimized.

For those developers coming with experience of traditional compiled languages (unmanaged languages), such as Visual Basic 6 or C/C++, you're probably thinking about the performance ramifications of all this. After all, unmanaged code is compiled for a specific CPU platform and, when invoked, the code can simply execute. In this managed environment, compiling the code is accomplished in two phases. First, the compiler passes over the source code, doing as much work as possible in producing IL. But to execute the code, the IL itself must be compiled into native CPU instructions at run time, requiring more memory to be allocated and requiring additional CPU time to do the work.

Believe me, since I approached the CLR from a C/C++ background myself, I was quite skeptical and concerned about this additional overhead. My coauthor, an experienced Visual Basic developer, had some of the same concerns. The truth is that this second compilation stage that occurs at run time does hurt performance and it does allocate dynamic memory. However, Microsoft has done a lot of performance work to keep this additional overhead to a minimum.

If you too are skeptical, you should certainly build some applications and test the performance for yourself. In addition, you should run some nontrivial managed applications Microsoft or others have produced and measure their performance. I think you'll be surprised at how good the performance actually is.

In fact, you'll probably find this hard to believe, but many people (including me) think that managed applications could actually outperform unmanaged applications. There are many reasons to believe this. For example, when the JIT compiler compiles the IL code into native code at run time, the compiler knows more about the execution environment than an unmanaged compiler would know. Here are some ways that managed code could outperform unmanaged code:

- A JIT compiler could detect that the application is running on a Pentium 4 and produce native code that takes advantage of any special instructions offered by the Pentium 4. Usually, unmanaged applications are compiled for the lowest-common-denominator CPU and avoid using special instructions that would give the application a performance boost over newer CPUs.

- A JIT compiler could detect that a certain test is always false on the machine that it is running on. For example, consider a method with code like this:

```
If NumberOfCPUs > 1 Then
    ⋮
End If
```

This code could cause the JIT compiler not to generate any CPU instructions if the host machine has only one CPU. In this case, the native code has been fine-tuned for the host machine: the code is smaller and executes faster.

- The CLR could profile the code's execution and recompile the IL into native code while the application runs. The recompiled code could be reorganized to reduce incorrect branch predictions depending on the observed execution patterns.

These are only a few of the reasons why you should expect future managed code to execute better than today's unmanaged code. As I said, the performance is currently quite good for most applications, and it promises to improve as time goes on.

If your experiments show that the CLR's JIT compiler doesn't offer your application the kind of performance it requires, you may want to take advantage of the NGen.exe tool that ships with the .NET Framework SDK. This tool compiles all of an assembly's IL code into native code and saves the resulting native code to a file on disk. At run time, when an assembly is loaded, the CLR automatically checks to see whether a precompiled version of the assembly also exists, and if it does, the CLR loads the precompiled code so that no compilation at run time is required. Note that NGen.exe must be conservative about the assumptions it makes about the actual execution environment, and for this reason, the code produced by NGen.exe won't be as highly optimized as the JIT compiler–produced code.

IL and Verification

IL is stack-based, which means that all its instructions push operands onto an execution stack and pop results off the stack. Because IL offers no instructions to manipulate registers, compiler developers have an easy time producing IL code; they don't have to think about managing registers, and fewer IL instructions are needed (since none exist for manipulating registers).

IL instructions are also typeless. For example, IL offers an **add** instruction that adds the last two operands pushed on the stack; there are not separate 32-bit and 64-bit **add** instructions. When the **add** instruction executes, it determines the types of the operands on the stack and performs the appropriate operation.

In my opinion, the biggest benefit of IL isn't that it abstracts away the underlying CPU. The biggest benefit is application robustness. While compiling IL into native CPU instructions, the CLR performs a process called *verification*. Verification examines the high-level IL code and ensures that everything it does is "safe." For example, verification checks that no memory is read from without having previously been written to, that every method is called with the correct number of parameters and that each parameter is of the correct type, that every method's return value is used properly, that every method has a return statement, and so on.

The managed module's metadata includes all the method and type information used by the verification process. If the IL code is determined to be "unsafe," then a `System.Security.VerificationException` exception is thrown, preventing the method from executing.

Is Your Code Safe?

Microsoft's Visual Basic compiler always produces *safe code*. Safe code is code that is verifiably safe. That is, the CLR can analyze safe code and ensure that there are no mistakes in the code with regards to reading memory or writing memory. However, sometimes unsafe code is useful, and while Visual Basic doesn't support it, some other languages, like C#, do. For example, walking through a block of memory looking for some byte sequence and using unsafe code can sometimes improve performance, as demonstrated in the "Fast Array Access" section in Chapter 14.

By default, the Microsoft C# compiler produces safe code. However, using the **unsafe** keyword in C# or other languages (such as Managed Extensions for C++ or IL assembly language), it's possible to produce code that can't be verifiably safe. The code might, in fact, be safe, but the CLR is unable to prove this by examining the IL.

To ensure that all your managed module's methods contain verifiably safe IL, you can use the PEVerify utility (PEVerify.exe) that ships with the .NET Framework SDK. When Microsoft tests their Visual Basic and C# compilers, they run the resulting module through PEVerify to ensure that the compiler always produces verifiably safe code. If PEVerify detects unsafe code, Microsoft fixes the compiler.

You may want to consider running PEVerify on your own modules before you package and ship them. If PEVerify detects a problem, then there is a bug in the compiler and you should report it to Microsoft (or whatever company produces the compiler you're using). If PEVerify doesn't detect any unverifiable code, you know that your code will run without throwing a **VerificationException** on the end-user's machine.

You should be aware that verification requires access to the metadata contained in any dependant assemblies. So when you use PEVerify to check an assembly, it must be able to locate and load all referenced assemblies. Because PEVerify uses the CLR to locate the dependant assemblies, the assemblies are located using the same binding and probing rules that would normally be used when executing the assembly. (I'll discuss these binding and probing rules in Chapter 2 and Chapter 3.)

Note that an administrator can elect to turn off verification (using the Microsoft .NET Framework Configuration administrative tool). With verification off, the JIT compiler will compile unverifiable IL into native CPU instructions; however, the administrator is taking full responsibility for the code's behavior.

In Windows, each process has its own virtual address space. Separate address spaces are necessary because you can't trust the application's code. It is entirely possible (and unfortunately, all too common) that an application will read from or write to an invalid memory address. By placing each Windows process in a separate address space, you gain robustness: one process can't adversely affect another process.

By verifying the managed code, however, you know that the code doesn't improperly access memory that it shouldn't and you know that the code can't adversely affect another application's code. This means that you can run multiple managed applications in a single Windows virtual address space.

Because Windows processes require a lot of operating system resources, having many of them can hurt performance and limit available resources. Reducing the number of processes by running multiple applications in a single OS process can improve performance, require fewer resources, and be just as robust. This is another benefit of managed code as compared to unmanaged code.

The CLR does, in fact, offer the ability to execute multiple managed applications in a single OS process. Each managed application is called an *App-Domain*. By default, every managed EXE will run in its own, separate address space that has just the one AppDomain. However, a process hosting the CLR (such as Internet Information Services [IIS] or a future version of SQL Server) can decide to run AppDomains in a single OS process. I'll devote part of Chapter 20 to a discussion of AppDomains.

The .NET Framework Class Library

Included with the .NET Framework is a set of .NET Framework Class Library (FCL) assemblies that contains several thousand type definitions, where each type exposes some functionality. All in all, the CLR and the FCL allow developers to build the following kinds of applications:

- **XML Web services**   Methods that can be accessed over the Internet very easily. XML Web services are, of course, the main thrust of Microsoft's .NET initiative.

- **Web Forms**   HTML-based applications (Web sites). Typically, Web Forms applications will make database queries and Web service calls, combine and filter the returned information, and then present that information in a browser using a rich HTML-based user interface. Web Forms provides a Visual Basic 6 and Visual InterDev style development environment for Web applications written in any CLR language.

- **Windows Forms**   Rich Windows GUI applications. Instead of using a Web Forms page to create your application's UI, you can use the more powerful, higher performance functionality offered by the Windows desktop. Windows Forms applications can take advantage of controls, menus, and mouse and keyboard events, and they can talk directly to the underlying operating system. Like Web Forms applications, Windows Forms applications also make database queries and call XML Web services. Windows Forms provides a Visual Basic 6–like development environment for GUI applications written in any CLR language.

- **Windows console applications**   For applications with very simple UI demands, a console application provides a quick and easy way to build an application. Compilers, utilities, and tools are typically implemented as console applications.

- **Windows services**   Yes, it is possible to build service applications controllable via the Windows Service Control Manager (SCM) using the .NET Framework.

- **Component library**   The .NET Framework allows you to build stand-alone components (types) that can be easily incorporated into any of the previously mentioned application types. Because the FCL contains literally thousands of types, a set of related types is presented to the developer within a single namespace. For example, the **System** namespace (which you should become most familiar with) contains the **Object** base type, from which all other types ultimately derive. In addition, the **System** namespace contains types for integers, characters, strings, exception handling, and console I/O as well as a bunch of utility types that convert safely between data types, format data types, generate random numbers, and perform various math functions. All applications will use types from the **System** namespace.

To access any of the platform's features, you need to know which namespace contains the types that expose the facilities you're after. If you want to customize any type's behavior, you can simply derive your own type from the desired FCL type. The object-oriented nature of the platform is how the .NET Framework presents a consistent programming paradigm to software developers. Also, developers can easily create their own namespaces containing their own types. These namespaces and types merge seamlessly into the programming paradigm. Compared to Win32 programming paradigms, this new approach greatly simplifies software development.

Most of the namespaces in the FCL present types that can be used for any kind of application. Table 1-2 lists some of the more general namespaces and briefly describes what the types in that namespace are used for.

Table 1-2   Some General FCL Namespaces

Namespace	Description of Contents
System	All the basic types used by every application
System.Collections	Types for managing collections of objects; includes the popular collection types, such as stacks, queues, hash tables, and so on
System.Data	Types for accessing a database. Collectively, the types in this namespace are referred to as ADO.NET.
System.Diagnostics	Types to help instrument and debug applications
System.Drawing	Types for manipulating 2-D graphics; typically used for Windows Forms applications and for creating images that are to appear in a Web Forms page
System.EnterpriseServices	Types for managing transactions, queued components, object pooling, JIT activation, security, and other features to make the use of managed code more efficient on the server
System.Globalization	Types for National Language Support (NLS), such as string compares, formatting, and calendars
System.IO	Types for doing stream I/O, walking directories and files
System.Management	Types used for managing other computers in the enterprise via Windows Management Instrumentation (WMI)
System.Net	Types that allow for network communications
System.Reflection	Types that allow the inspection of metadata and late binding to types and their members
System.Resources	Types for manipulating external data resources
System.Runtime.InteropServices	Types that allow managed code to access unmanaged OS platform facilities such as COM components and functions in Win32 DLLs

(continued)

Table 1-2   Some General FCL Namespaces   *(continued)*

Namespace	Description of Contents
System.Runtime.Remoting	Types that allow for types to be accessed remotely
System.Runtime.Serialization	Types that allow for instances of objects to be persisted and regenerated from a stream
System.Security	Types used for protecting data and resources
System.Text	Types to work with text in different encodings, such as ASCII or Unicode
System.Threading	Types used for asynchronous operations and synchronizing access to resources
System.Xml	Types used for processing XML schemas and data

This book is about the CLR and about the general types that interact closely with the CLR (which are most of the namespaces listed in Table 1-2). So the content of this book is applicable to all .NET Framework programmers, regardless of the type of application they're building.

In addition to the more general namespaces, the FCL also offers namespaces whose types are used for building specific application types. Table 1-3 lists some of the application specific namespaces in the FCL.

Table 1-3   Some Application-Specific FCL Namespaces

Namespace	Application Type
System.Web.Services	Types used to build XML Web services
System.Web.UI	Types used to build Web Forms
System.Windows.Forms	Types used to build Windows GUI applications
System.ServiceProcess	Types used to build a Windows service controllable by the SCM

I expect many good books will be published that explain how to build specific application types (such as Windows services, Web Forms, and Windows Forms). These books will give you an excellent start at helping you build your application. I tend to think of these application-specific books as helping you learn from the top down because they concentrate on the application type and not on the development platform. In this book, I'll offer information that will help you learn from the bottom up. After reading this book and an application-specific book, you should be able to easily and proficiently build any kind of .NET Framework application you desire.

The Common Type System

By now, it should be obvious to you that the CLR is all about types. Types expose functionality to your applications and components. Types are the mechanism by which code written in one programming language can talk to code written in a different programming language. Because types are at the root of the CLR, Microsoft created a formal specification—the Common Type System (CTS)—that describes how types are defined and how they behave.

The CTS specification states that a type can contain zero or more members. In Part III, I'll cover all these members in great detail. For now, I just want to give you a brief introduction to them:

■   **Field**   A data variable that is part of the object's state. Fields are identified by their name and type.

■   **Method**   A function that performs an operation on the object, often changing the object's state. Methods have a name, a signature, and modifiers. The signature specifies the calling convention, the number of parameters (and their sequence), the types of the parameters, and the type of value returned by the method.

■   **Property**   To the caller, this member looks like a field. But to the type implementer, it looks like a method (or two). Properties allow an implementer to validate input parameters and object state before accessing the value and/or calculate a value only when necessary. They also allow a user of the type to have simplified syntax. Finally, properties allow you to create read-only or write-only "fields."

■   **Event**   An event allows a notification mechanism between an object and other interested objects. For example, a button could offer an event that notifies other objects when the button is clicked.

The CTS also specifies the rules for type visibility and for access to the members of a type. For example, marking a type as *public* (using the `Public` keyword in Visual Basic) exports the type, making it visible and accessible to any assembly. On the other hand, marking a type as *assembly* (called `Friend` in Visual Basic) makes the type visible and accessible to code within the same assembly only. Thus, the CTS establishes the rules by which assemblies form a boundary of visibility for a type, and the CLR enforces the visibility rules.

Regardless of whether a type is visible to a caller, the type gets to control whether the caller has access to its members. The following list shows the valid options for controlling access to a method or a field:

- **Private**   The method is callable only by other methods in the same class type.

- **Family**   The method is callable by derived types, regardless of whether they are within the same assembly. Note that many languages (such as Visual Basic) refer to family as `Protected`.

- **Family and assembly**   The method is callable by derived types, but only if the derived type is defined in the same assembly. Many languages (such as Visual Basic and C#) don't offer this access control. Of course, IL assembly language makes it available.

- **Assembly**   The method is callable by any code in the same assembly. Visual Basic refers to this as `Friend` while some other languages, such as C#, refer to *assembly* as `internal`.

- **Family or assembly**   The method is callable by derived types in any assembly. The method is also callable by any types in the same assembly. Visual Basic refers to *family or assembly* as `Protected Friend` while some other languages, like C#, return to this accessibility as `internal protected`.

- **Public**   The method is callable by any code in any assembly.

In addition, the CTS defines the rules governing type inheritance, virtual functions, object lifetime, and so on. These rules have been designed to accommodate the semantics expressible in modern-day programming languages. In fact, you won't even need to learn the CTS rules per se since the language you choose will expose its own language syntax and type rules in the same way you're familiar with today and will map the language-specific syntax into the "language" of the CLR when it emits the managed module.

When I first started working with the CLR, I soon realized that it's best to think of the language and the behavior of your code as two separate and distinct things. Using Visual Basic, you can define your own types with their own members. Of course, you could have used C# or C++ to define the same type with the same members. Sure, the syntax you use for defining this type is different depending on the language you choose, but the behavior of the type will be absolutely identical regardless of the language because the CLR's CTS defines the behavior of the type.

To help clarify this idea, let me give you an example. The CTS supports single inheritance only. So, while the C++ language supports types that inherit from multiple base types, the CTS can't accept and operate on any such type. To help the developer, the Microsoft Visual C++ compiler reports an error if it detects that you're attempting to create managed code that includes a type inherited from multiple base types.

Here's another CTS rule. All types must (ultimately) inherit from a predefined type: `System.Object`. As you can see, `Object` is the name of a type defined in the `System` namespace. This `Object` is the root of all other types and therefore guarantees every type instance has a minimum set of behaviors. Specifically, the `System.Object` type allows you to do the following:

- Compare two instances for equality

- Obtain a hash code for the instance

- Query the true type of an instance

- Perform a shallow (bitwise) copy of the instance

- Obtain a string representation of the instance's current state

The Common Language Specification

COM allows objects created in different languages to communicate with one another. On the other hand, the CLR now integrates all languages and allows objects created in one language to be treated as equal citizens by code written in a completely different language. This integration is possible because of the CLR's standard set of types, self-describing type information (metadata), and common execution environment.

While this language integration is a fantastic goal, the truth of the matter is that programming languages are very different from one another. For example, some languages don't treat symbols with case-sensitivity or don't offer unsigned integers, operator overloading, or methods that support a variable number of parameters.

If you intend to create types that are easily accessible from other programming languages, you need to use only features of your programming language that are guaranteed to be available in all other languages. To help you with this, Microsoft has defined a *Common Language Specification* (CLS) that details for compiler vendors the minimum set of features that their compilers must support if these compilers are to target the CLR.

The CLR/CTS supports a lot more features than the subset defined by the CLS, so if you don't care about interlanguage operability, you can develop very rich types limited only by the language's feature set. Specifically, the CLS defines rules that externally visible types and methods must adhere to if they are to be accessible from any CLS-compliant programming language. Note that the CLS rules don't apply to code that is accessible only within the defining assembly. Figure 1-6 summarizes the ideas expressed in this paragraph.

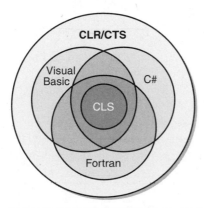

Figure 1-6   Languages offer a subset of the CLR/CTS and a superset of the CLS (but not necessarily the same superset).

As Figure 1-6 shows, the CLR/CTS offers a set of features. Some languages expose a large subset of the CLR/CTS. A programmer willing to write in IL assembly language, for example, is able to use all the features the CLR/CTS offers. Most other languages, such as Visual Basic, C#, and Fortran, expose a subset of the CLR/CTS features to the programmer. The CLS defines the minimum set of features that all languages must support.

If you're designing a type in one language and you expect that type to be used by another language, you shouldn't take advantage of any features that are outside the CLS. Doing so would mean that your type's members might not be accessible by programmers writing code in other programming languages.

The Visual Basic compiler considers everything to be CLS-compliant so I have to use another programming language to demonstrate how to define a CLS-compliant type. In the following code, a CLS-compliant type is being defined in C#. However, the type has a few non-CLS-compliant constructs causing the C# compiler to complain about the code.

```
using System;

// Tell compiler to check for CLS compliance
[assembly:CLSCompliant(true)]

// Errors appear because the class is public
public class App {

    // Error: Return type of 'App.Abc()' is not CLS-compliant
    public  UInt32 Abc() { return 0; }

    // Error: Identifier 'App.abc()' differing
    // only in case is not CLS-compliant
    public  void    abc() { }

    // No error: Method is private
    private UInt32 ABC() { return 0; }
}
```

In this code, the `[assembly:CLSCompliant(true)]` attribute is applied to the assembly. This attribute tells the compiler to ensure that any publicly exposed type doesn't have any construct that would prevent the type from being accessed from any other programming language. When this code is compiled, the C# compiler emits two errors. The first error is reported because the method **Abc** returns an unsigned integer; Visual Basic and some other languages can't manipulate unsigned integer values. The second error is because this type exposes two public methods that differ only by case and return type: **Abc** and **abc**. Visual Basic and some other languages can't call both these methods.

Interestingly, if you were to delete `public` from in front of `'class App'` and recompile, both errors would go away. The reason is that the **App** type would default to `internal` and would therefore no longer be exposed outside the assembly. For a complete list of CLS rules, refer to the "Cross-Language Interoperability" section in the .NET Framework SDK documentation.

Let me distill the CLS rules to something very simple. In the CLR, every member of a type is either a field (data) or a method (behavior). This means that every programming language must be able to access fields and call methods. Certain fields and certain methods are used in special and common ways. To ease programming, languages typically offer additional abstractions to make coding these common programming patterns easier. For example, some languages expose concepts such as enums, arrays, properties, indexers, delegates, events, constructors, destructors, operator overloads, conversion operators, and so on. When a compiler comes across any of these things in your source code, it must translate these constructs into fields and methods so that the CLR and any other programming language can access the construct.

Consider the following type definition, which contains a constructor, a destructor, some overloaded operators, a property, an indexer, and an event. Note that the code shown is there just to make the code compile; it doesn't show the correct way to implement a type. Also note that this example is in C# because Visual Basic doesn't currently support destructors and overloaded operators.

```csharp
using System;

class Test {
   // Constructor
   public Test() {}

   // Destructor
   ~Test() {}

   // Operator overload
   public static Boolean operator == (Test t1, Test t2) {
      return true;
   }
   public static Boolean operator != (Test t1, Test t2) {
      return false;
   }

   // An operator overload
   public static Test operator + (Test t1, Test t2) { return null; }

   // A property
   public String AProperty {
      get { return null; }
      set { }
   }

   // An indexer
   public String this[Int32 x] {
      get { return null; }
      set { }
   }

   // An event
   event EventHandler AnEvent;
}
```

When the compiler compiles this code, the result is a type that has a number of fields and methods defined in it. You can easily see this using the IL Disassembler tool (ILDasm.exe) provided with the .NET Framework SDK to examine the resulting managed module, which is shown in Figure 1-7.

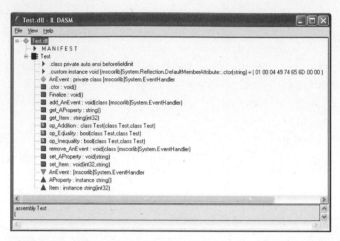

Figure 1-7 ILDasm showing Test type's fields and methods (obtained from metadata)

Table 1-4 shows how the programming language constructs got mapped to the equivalent CLR fields and methods.

Table 1-4 Test Type's Fields and Methods (obtained from metadata)

Type Member	Member Type	Equivalent Programming Language Construct
AnEvent	Field	Event; the name of the field is **AnEvent** and its type is **System.EventHandler**
.ctor	Method	Constructor
Finalize	Method	Destructor
add_AnEvent	Method	Event **add** accessor method
get_AProperty	Method	Property **get** accessor method
get_Item	Method	Indexer **get** accessor method
op_Addition	Method	**+** operator
op_Equality	Method	**==** operator
op_Inequality	Method	**!=** operator
remove_AnEvent	Method	Event **remove** accessor method
set_AProperty	Method	Property **set** accessor method
set_Item	Method	Indexer **set** accessor method

The additional nodes under the `Test` type that aren't mentioned in Table 1-4—`.class`, `.custom`, `AnEvent`, `AProperty`, and `Item`—identify additional metadata about the type. These nodes don't map to fields or methods; they just offer some additional information about the type that the CLR, programming languages, or tools can get access to. For example, a tool can see that the `Test` type offers an event, called `AnEvent`, which is exposed via the two methods (`add_AnEvent` and `remove_AnEvent`).

Interoperability with Unmanaged Code

The .NET Framework offers a ton of advantages over other development platforms. However, very few companies can afford to redesign and reimplement all of their existing code. Microsoft realizes this and has constructed the CLR so that it offers mechanisms that allow an application to consist of both managed and unmanaged parts. Specifically, the CLR supports three interoperability scenarios:

- **Managed code can call an unmanaged function in a DLL**   Managed code can easily call functions contained in DLLs using a mechanism called P/Invoke (for Platform Invoke). After all, many of the types defined in the FCL internally call functions exported from Kernel32.dll, User32.dll, and so on. Many programming languages will expose a mechanism that makes it easy for managed code to call out to unmanaged functions contained in DLLs. For example, a Visual Basic or C# application can call the `Create-Semaphore` function exported from Kernel32.dll.

- **Managed code can use an existing COM component (server)**   Many companies have already implemented a number of unmanaged COM components. Using the type library from these components, a managed assembly can be created that describes the COM component. Managed code can access the type in the managed assembly just like any other managed type. See the TlbImp.exe tool that ships with the .NET Framework SDK for more information. At times, you might not have a type library or you might want to have more control over what TlbImp.exe produces. In these cases, you can manually build a type in source code that the CLR can use to achieve the proper interoperability. For example, you could use DirectX COM components from a Visual Basic or C# application.

■ **Unmanaged code can use a managed type (server)**   A lot of existing unmanaged code requires that you supply a COM component for the code to work correctly. It's much easier to implement these components using managed code so that you can avoid all the code having to do with reference counting and interfaces. For example, you could create an ActiveX control or a shell extension in Visual Basic or C#. See the TlbExp.exe and RegAsm.exe tools that ship with the .NET Framework SDK for more information.

In addition to these three scenarios, Microsoft's Visual C++ compiler (version 13) supports a new **/clr** command-line switch. This switch tells the compiler to emit IL code instead of native x86 instructions. If you have a large amount of existing C++ code, you can recompile the code using this new compiler switch. The new code will require the CLR to execute, and you can now modify the code over time to take advantage of the CLR-specific features.

The **/clr** switch can't compile to IL any methods that contain inline assembly language (via the **__asm** keyword), accept a variable number of arguments, call **setjmp**, or contain intrinsic routines (such as **__enable**, **__disable**, **_ReturnAddress**, and **_AddressOfReturnAddress**). For a complete list of the constructs that the C++ compiler can't compile into IL, refer to the documentation for the Visual C++ compiler. When the compiler can't compile the method into IL, it compiles the method into x86 so that the application still runs.

Keep in mind that although the IL code produced is managed, the data is not; that is, data objects are not allocated from the managed heap and they are not garbage collected. In fact, the data types don't have metadata produced for them, and the types' method names are mangled.

The following C code calls the standard C runtime library's **printf** function and also calls the **System.Console WriteLine** method. The **System.Console** type is defined in the FCL. So, C/C++ code can use libraries available to C/C++ as well as managed types.

```
#include <stdio.h>        // For printf

#using <mscorlib.dll>     // For managed types defined in this assembly
using namespace System;   // Easily access System namespace types

// Implement a normal C/C++ main function
void main() {

    // Call the C runtime library's printf function.
    printf("Displayed by printf.\r\n");
```

```
// Call the FCL's System.Console's WriteLine method.
Console::WriteLine("Displayed by Console::WriteLine.");
}
```

Compiling this code couldn't be easier. If this code were in a MgdCApp.cpp file, you'd compile it by executing the following line at the command prompt:

```
cl /clr MgdCApp.cpp
```

The result is a MgdCApp.exe assembly file. If you run MgdCApp.exe, you'll see the following output:

```
C:\>MgdCApp
Displayed by printf.
Displayed by Console::WriteLine.
```

If you use ILDasm.exe to examine this file, you'll see the output shown in Figure 1-8.

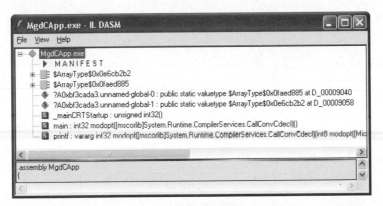

Figure 1-8 ILDasm showing MgdCApp.exe assembly's metadata

In Figure 1-8, you see that ILDasm shows all the global functions and global fields defined within the assembly. Obviously, the compiler has generated a lot of stuff automatically. If you double-click the **Main** method, ILDasm will show you the IL code:

```
.method public static int32
        modopt([mscorlib]System.Runtime.CompilerServices.CallConvCdecl)
        main() cil managed
{
  .vtentry 1 : 1
  // Code size       28 (0x1c)
  .maxstack  1
```

(continued)

```
IL_0000:  ldsflda    valuetype
                     $ArrayType$0x0faed885 '?A0x44d29f64.unnamed-global-0'
IL_0005:  call       vararg int32
   modopt([mscorlib]System.Runtime.CompilerServices.CallConvCdecl)
   printf(int8
   modopt([Microsoft.VisualC]Microsoft.VisualC.NoSignSpecifiedModifier)
   modopt([Microsoft.VisualC]Microsoft.VisualC.IsConstModifier)*)
IL_000a:  pop
IL_000b:  ldsflda    valuetype
                     $ArrayType$0x0e6cb2b2 '?A0x44d29f64.unnamed-global-1'
IL_0010:  newobj     instance void [mscorlib]System.String::.ctor(int8*)
IL_0015:  call       void [mscorlib]System.Console::WriteLine(string)
IL_001a:  ldc.i4.0
IL_001b:  ret
} // end of method 'Global Functions'::main
```

What we see here isn't pretty because the compiler generates a lot of special code to make all this work. However, from this IL code, you can see that **printf** and the **Console.WriteLine** method are both called.

2

Building, Packaging, Deploying, and Administering Applications and Types

Before we get into the chapters that explain how to develop programs for the Microsoft .NET Framework, let's discuss the steps required to build, package, and deploy your applications and their types. In this chapter, I'll focus on the basics of how to build components that are for your application's sole use. In Chapter 3, I'll cover the more advanced concepts you'll need to understand, including how to build and use assemblies containing components that are to be shared by multiple applications. In both chapters, I'll also talk about the ways an administrator can use information to affect the execution of an application and its types.

Today, applications consist of several types. (In the .NET Framework, a *type* is called a *component*, but in this book, I'll avoid the term *component* and use *type* instead.) Applications typically consist of types created by you and Microsoft as well as several other organizations. If these types are developed using any language that targets the common language runtime (CLR), they can all work together seamlessly; a type can even use another type as its base class, regardless of what languages the types are developed in.

In this chapter, I'll also explain how these types are built and packaged into files for deployment. In the process, I'll take you on a brief historical tour of some of the problems that the .NET Framework is solving.

.NET Framework Deployment Goals

Over the years, Windows has gotten a reputation for being unstable and complicated. This reputation, whether deserved or not, is the result of many different factors. First, all applications use dynamic-link libraries (DLLs) from Microsoft or other vendors. Because an application executes code from various vendors, the developer of any one piece of code can't be 100 percent sure how someone else is going to use it. This situation can potentially cause all kinds of trouble, but in practice, problems don't typically arise from this kind of interaction because applications are tested and debugged before they are deployed.

Users, however, frequently run into problems when one company decides to update its code and ships new files to them. These new files are supposed to be "backward compatible" with the previous files, but who knows for sure? In fact, when one vendor updates its code, retesting and debugging all the already shipped applications to ensure that the changes have had no undesirable effect is usually impossible.

I'm sure that everyone reading this book has experienced some variation of this problem: when installing a new application, you discover that it has somehow corrupted an already installed application. This predicament is known as "DLL hell." This type of instability puts fear into the hearts and minds of the typical computer user. The end result is that users have to carefully consider whether to install new software on their machines. Personally, I've decided not to try out certain applications for fear of some application I really rely on being adversely affected.

The second reason that has contributed to the reputation of Windows is installation complexities. Today, when most applications are installed, they affect all parts of the system. For example, installing an application causes files to be copied to various directories, updates registry settings, and installs shortcut links on your desktop, Start menu, and Quick Launch toolbar. The problem with this is that the application isn't isolated as a single entity. You can't easily back up the application since you must copy the application's files and also the relevant parts of the registry. In addition, you can't easily move the application from one machine to another; you must run the installation program again so that all files and registry settings are set properly. Finally, you can't easily uninstall or remove the application without having this nasty feeling that some part of the application is still lurking on your machine.

The third reason has to do with security. When applications are installed, they come with all kinds of files, many of them written by different companies. In addition, "Web applications" frequently have code that is downloaded over the wire in such a way that users don't even realize that code is being installed on their machines. Today, this code can perform any operation, including deleting files or sending e-mail. Users are right to be terrified of installing new applications because of the potential damage they can cause. To make users comfortable, security must be built into the system so that users can explicitly allow or disallow code developed by various companies to access the system resources.

The .NET Framework addresses the "DLL hell" issue in a big way, as you'll see as you read this chapter and Chapter 3. It also goes a long way toward fixing the problem of having an application's state scattered all over a user's hard disk. For example, unlike COM, components no longer require settings in the registry. Unfortunately, applications still require shortcut links, but future versions of Windows may solve this problem. As for security, the .NET Framework includes a new security model called *code access security*. Whereas Windows security is based around a user's identity, code access security is based around an assembly's identity. So a user could decide to trust all assemblies published by Microsoft or not to trust any assemblies downloaded from the Internet. As you'll see, the .NET Framework enables users to control their machines, what gets installed, and what runs more than Windows ever did.

Building Types into a Module

In this section, I'll show you how to turn your source file, containing various types, into a file that can be deployed. Let's start by examining the following simple application:

```
Public Class App
    Public Shared Sub Main()
        System.Console.WriteLine("Hi")
    End Sub
End Class
```

This application defines a type, called **App**. This type has a single static (referred to as **Shared** in Visual Basic), public method called **Main**. Inside **Main** is a reference to another type called **System.Console**. **System.Console** is a type implemented by Microsoft, and the intermediate language (IL) code that implements this type's methods is in the MSCorLib.dll file. So, our application defines a type and also uses another company's type.

To build this sample application, put the preceding code into a source code file, say App.vb, and then execute the following command line:

```
vbc.exe /out:App.exe /t:exe /r:MSCorLib.dll App.vb
```

This command line tells the Visual Basic compiler to emit an executable file called App.exe (`/out:App.exe`). The type of file produced is a Win32 console application (`/t[arget]:exe`).

When the Visual Basic compiler processes the source file, it sees that the code references the `System.Console` type's `WriteLine` method. At this point, the compiler wants to ensure that this type exists somewhere, that it has a `WriteLine` method, and that it checks that the types of the arguments that `WriteLine` expects match up with what the program is supplying. To make the Visual Basic compiler happy, you must give it a set of assemblies that it can use to resolve references to external types. (I'll define assemblies shortly, but for now you can think of an assembly as a set of one or more DLL files.) In the preceding command line, I've included the `/r[eference]:MSCorLib.dll` switch telling the compiler to look for external types in the assembly identified by the MSCorLib.dll file.

MSCorLib.dll is a special file in that it contains all the core types, such as bytes, integers, characters, strings, and so on. In fact, these types are so frequently used that the Visual Basic compiler automatically references this assembly. In other words, the following command line (with the `/r` switch omitted) gives the same results as the line shown earlier:

```
vbc.exe /out:App.exe /t:exe App.vb
```

> **Note**   When compiling Visual Basic source code, the VBC.exe compiler can emit code that references helper classes and methods. These helper classes and methods are defined in the Microsoft.Visual-Basic.dll assembly, which is installed with the .NET Framework. For this reason, the Visual Basic compiler always references the Microsoft.VisualBasic.dll assembly as well as the MSCorLib.dll assembly.

Furthermore, because the `/out:App.exe` and the `/t:exe` command-line switches also match what the Visual Basic compiler would choose as defaults, the following command line gives the same results too:

```
vbc.exe App.vb
```

Now let's take a closer look at the App.exe file produced by the Visual Basic compiler. What exactly is this file? Well, for starters, it's a standard PE (portable executable) file. This means that a machine running 32-bit or 64-bit

Windows should be able to load this file and do something with it. Windows supports two types of applications, those with a console user interface (CUI) and those with a graphical user interface (GUI). Because I specified the /t:exe switch, the Visual Basic compiler produced a CUI application. You'd use the /t:winexe switch to have the Visual Basic compiler produce a GUI application.

Now we know what kind of PE file we've created. But what exactly is in the App.exe file? A managed PE file has four main parts: the PE header, the CLR header, the metadata, and the IL. The PE header is the standard information that Windows expects. The CLR header is a small block of information that is specific to modules that require the CLR (managed modules). The header includes the major and minor version numbers of the metadata that the module was built with, some flags, a MethodDef token (described later) indicating the module's entry point method if this module is a CUI or GUI executable, and an optional strong name digital signature (discussed in Chapter 3). Finally, the header contains the size and offsets of certain metadata tables contained within the module. You can see the exact format of the CLR header by examining the IMAGE_COR20_HEADER defined in the CorHdr.h header file.

The metadata is a block of binary data that consists of several tables. There are three categories of tables: definition tables, reference tables, and manifest tables. Table 2-1 describes some of the more common definition tables that exist in a module's metadata block.

Table 2-1   Common Definition Metadata Tables

Metadata Definition Table Name	Description
ModuleDef	Always contains one entry that identifies the module. The entry includes the module's filename and extension (without path) and a module version ID (in the form of a GUID created by the compiler). This allows the file to be renamed while keeping a record of its original name. However, renaming a file is strongly discouraged and can prevent the CLR from locating an assembly at runtime—don't do this.
TypeDef	Contains one entry for each type defined in the module. Each entry includes the type's name, base type, and flags (i.e., public, private, etc.) and points to the methods it owns in the MethodDef table, the fields it owns in the FieldDef table, the properties it owns in the PropertyDef table, and the event it owns in the EventDef table.

(continued)

Table 2-1   Common Definition Metadata Tables *(continued)*

Metadata Definition Table Name	Description
MethodDef	Contains one entry for each method defined in the module. Each entry includes the method's name, flags (private, public, virtual, abstract, static, final, etc.), signature, and offset within the module where IL code can be found. Each entry can also refer to a ParamDef table entry where more information about the method's parameters can be found.
FieldDef	Contains one entry for every field defined in the module. Each entry includes a name, flags (i.e., private, public, etc.), and type.
ParamDef	Contains one entry for each parameter defined in the module. Each entry includes a name and flags (in, out, retval, etc.).
PropertyDef	Contains one entry for each property defined in the module. Each entry includes a name, flags, type, and backing field (which can be null).
EventDef	Contains one entry for each event defined in the module. Each entry includes a name and flags.

As a compiler compiles your source code, everything that your code defines causes an entry to be created in one of the tables described in Table 2-1. As the compiler compiles the source code, it also detects the types, fields, methods, properties, and events that the source code references. The metadata includes a set of reference tables that keep a record of this stuff. Table 2-2 shows some of the more common reference metadata tables.

Table 2-2   Common Reference Metadata Tables

Metadata Reference Table Name	Description
AssemblyRef	Contains one entry for each assembly referenced by the module. Each entry includes the information necessary to bind to the assembly: the assembly's name (without path and extension), version number, culture, and public key token (normally a small hash value, generated from the publisher's public key, identifying the referenced assembly's publisher). Each entry also contains some flags and a hash value. This hash value was intended to be a checksum of the referenced assembly's bits. The CLR completely ignores this hash value and will probably continue to do so in the future.

(continued)

Table 2-2   Common Reference Metadata Tables   *(continued)*

Metadata Reference Table Name	Description
ModuleRef	Contains one entry for each PE module that implements types referenced by this module. Each entry includes the module's filename and extension (without path). This table is used to bind to types that are implemented in different modules of the calling assembly's module.
TypeRef	Contains one entry for each type referenced by the module. Each entry includes the type's name and a reference to where the type can be found. If the type is implemented within another type, then the reference indicates a TypeRef entry. If the type is implemented in the same module, then the reference indicates a ModuleDef entry. If the type is implemented in another module within the calling assembly, then the reference indicates a ModuleRef entry. If the type is implemented in a different assembly, then the reference indicates an AssemblyRef entry.
MemberRef	Contains one entry for each member (fields and methods, as well as property and event methods) referenced by the module. Each entry includes the member's name and signature, and points to the TypeRef entry for the type that defines the member.

There are many more tables than what I list in Table 2-1 and Table 2-2, but I just wanted to give you a sense of the kind of information that the compiler emits to produce the metadata information. Earlier I mentioned that there is also a set of manifest metadata tables; I'll discuss these a little later in the chapter.

Various tools allow you to examine the metadata within a managed PE file. My personal favorite is ILDasm.exe, the IL Disassembler. To see the metadata tables, execute the following command line:

```
ILDasm /Adv App.exe
```

This causes ILDasm.exe to run, loading the App.exe assembly. The **/Adv** switch tells ILDasm to make some "advanced" menu items available. (For more information about ILDasm.exe's advanced switch, see the ILDasmAdvancedOptions.doc file that comes with the .NET Framework SDK.) These advanced menu items can be found on the View menu. To see the metadata in a nice, human-readable form, select the View.MetaInfo.Show! menu item (or press Ctrl+M). This causes the following information to appear:

```
ScopeName : App.exe
MVID      : {C738E9C9-9F61-4A14-8A00-ECE785571B41}
===============================================================
Global functions
-------------------------------------------------------------

Global fields
-------------------------------------------------------------

Global MemberRefs
-------------------------------------------------------------

TypeDef #1
-------------------------------------------------------------
    TypDefName: App  (02000002)
    Flags     : [Public] [AutoLayout] [Class] [AnsiClass]  (00000001)
    Extends   : 01000001 [TypeRef] System.Object
    Method #1
    -----------------------------------------------------------
        MethodName: .ctor (06000001)
        Flags     : [Public] [ReuseSlot] [SpecialName] [RTSpecialName] [.ctor]
                    (00001806)
        RVA       : 0x00002050
        ImplFlags : [IL] [Managed]  (00000000)
        CallCnvntn: [DEFAULT]
        hasThis
        ReturnType: Void
        No arguments.

    Method #2 [ENTRYPOINT]
    -----------------------------------------------------------
        MethodName: Main (06000002)
        Flags     : [Public] [Static] [ReuseSlot]  (00000016)
        RVA       : 0x00002058
        ImplFlags : [IL] [Managed]  (00000000)
        CallCnvntn: [DEFAULT]
        ReturnType: Void
        No arguments.
        CustomAttribute #1 (0c000001)
        -------------------------------------------------------
            CustomAttribute Type: 0a000003
            CustomAttributeName: System.STAThreadAttribute ::
                        instance void .ctor()
            Length: 4
            Value : 01 00 00 00
            ctor args: ()
```

```
TypeRef #1 (01000001)
-----------------------------------------------------------
Token:              0x01000001
ResolutionScope:    0x23000001
TypeRefName:        System.Object
    MemberRef #1
    -------------------------------------------------------

        Member: (0a000001) .ctor:
        CallCnvntn: [DEFAULT]
        hasThis
        ReturnType: Void
        No arguments.


TypeRef #2 (01000002)
-----------------------------------------------------------
Token:              0x01000002
ResolutionScope:    0x23000001
TypeRefName:        System.Console
    MemberRef #1
    -------------------------------------------------------

        Member: (0a000002) WriteLine:
        CallCnvntn: [DEFAULT]
        ReturnType: Void
        1 Arguments
            Argument #1:  String


TypeRef #3 (01000003)
-----------------------------------------------------------
Token:              0x01000003
ResolutionScope:    0x23000001
TypeRefName:        System.STAThreadAttribute
    MemberRef #1
    -------------------------------------------------------

        Member: (0a000003) .ctor:
        CallCnvntn: [DEFAULT]
        hasThis
        ReturnType: Void
        No arguments.


Assembly
-----------------------------------------------------------
    Token: 0x20000001
    Name : App
    Public Key    :
    Hash Algorithm : 0x00008004
    Major Version: 0x00000000
    Minor Version: 0x00000000
```

(continued)

```
    Build Number: 0x00000000
    Revision Number: 0x00000000
    Locale: <null>
    Flags : [SideBySideCompatible]  (00000000)

AssemblyRef #1
-------------------------------------------------------------
    Token: 0x23000001
    Public Key or Token: b7 7a 5c 56 19 34 e0 89
    Name: mscorlib
    Major Version: 0x00000001
    Minor Version: 0x00000000
    Build Number: 0x00000ce4
    Revision Number: 0x00000000
    Locale: <null>
    HashValue Blob:
    Flags: [none] (00000000)

AssemblyRef #2
-------------------------------------------------------------
    Token: 0x23000002
    Public Key or Token: b0 3f 5f 7f 11 d5 0a 3a
    Name: Microsoft.VisualBasic
    Major Version: 0x00000007
    Minor Version: 0x00000000
    Build Number: 0x00000ce4
    Revision Number: 0x00000000
    Locale: <null>
    HashValue Blob:
    Flags: [none] (00000000)

User Strings
-------------------------------------------------------------
70000001 : ( 2) L"Hi"
```

Fortunately, ILDasm processes the metadata tables and combines information where appropriate so that you don't have to parse the raw table information. For example, in the dump above, you see that when ILDasm shows a TypeDef entry, the corresponding member definition information is shown with it before the first TypeRef entry is displayed.

You don't need to fully understand everything you see here. The important thing to remember is that App.exe contains a TypeDef whose name is **App**. This type identifies a public class that is derived from **System.Object** (a type referenced from another assembly). The **App** type also defines two methods: **Main** and **.ctor** (a constructor).

Main is a static (**Shared**), public method whose code is IL (vs. native CPU code, such as x86). **Main** has a **void** return type and takes no arguments. The constructor method (always shown with a name of **.ctor**) is public and its code is also IL. The constructor has a **void** return type and has no arguments but has a **this** pointer (referred to as **Me** in Visual Basic), which refers to the object's memory that is to be constructed when the method is called.

I strongly encourage you to experiment using ILDasm. It can show you a wealth of information, and the more you understand what you're seeing, the better you'll understand the common language runtime and its capabilities. As you'll see, I use ILDasm quite a bit more in this book.

Just for fun, let's look at some statistics about the App.exe assembly. When you select ILDasm's View.Statistics menu item, the following information is displayed:

```
File size             : 3072
PE header size        : 512 (496 used)   (16.67%)
PE additional info    : 903              (29.39%)
Num.of PE sections    : 3
CLR header size       : 72               ( 2.34%)
CLR meta-data size    : 516              (16.80%)
CLR additional info   : 0                ( 0.00%)
CLR method headers    : 2                ( 0.07%)
Managed code          : 18               ( 0.59%)
Data                  : 812              (26.43%)
Unaccounted           : 237              ( 7.71%)

Num.of PE sections    : 3
    .text    - 1024
    .rsrc    - 1024
    .reloc   - 512

CLR meta-data size    : 516
    Module        -     1 (10 bytes)
    TypeDef       -     2 (28 bytes)      0 interfaces, 0 explicit layout
    TypeRef       -     3 (18 bytes)
    MethodDef     -     2 (28 bytes)      0 abstract, 0 native, 2 bodies
    MemberRef     -     3 (18 bytes)
    CustomAttribute-    1 (6 bytes)
    Assembly      -     1 (22 bytes)
    AssemblyRef   -     2 (40 bytes)
    Strings       -   115 bytes
    Blobs         -    40 bytes
    UserStrings   -     8 bytes
    Guids         -    16 bytes
    Uncategorized -   167 bytes
```

(continued)

```
CLR method headers : 2
   Num.of method bodies   - 2
   Num.of fat headers     - 0
   Num.of tiny headers    - 2

Managed code : 18
   Ave method size - 9
```

Here you can see the size (in bytes) of the file and the size (in bytes and percentages) of the various parts that make up the file. For this very small App.vb application, the PE header and the metadata occupy the bulk of the file's size. In fact, the IL code occupies just 18 bytes. Of course, as an application grows, it will reuse most of its types and references to other types and assemblies, causing the metadata and header information to shrink considerably as compared to the overall size of the file.

Combining Modules to Form an Assembly

The App.exe file discussed in the previous section is more than just a PE file with metadata; it is also an *assembly*. An assembly is a collection of one or more files containing type definitions and resource files. One of the assembly's files is chosen to hold a *manifest*. The manifest is another set of metadata tables that basically contain the names of the files that are part of the assembly. They also describe the assembly's version, culture, publisher, publicly exported types, and all the files that comprise the assembly.

The CLR operates on assemblies; that is, the CLR always loads the file that contains the manifest metadata tables first and then uses the manifest to get the names of the other files that are in the assembly. Here are some characteristics of assemblies that you should remember:

■   An assembly defines the reusable types.

■   An assembly is marked with a version number.

■   An assembly can have security information associated with it.

An assembly's individual files don't have these attributes—except for the file that contains the manifest metadata tables.

To package, version, secure, and use types, you must place them in modules that are part of an assembly. In most cases, an assembly consists of a single file, as the preceding App.exe example does. However, an assembly can also consist of multiple files: some PE files with metadata and some resource files such as .gif or .jpg files. It might help you to think of an assembly as a logical EXE or a DLL.

I'm sure that many of you reading this are wondering why Microsoft has introduced this new assembly concept. The reason is that an assembly allows you to decouple the logical and physical notions of reusable types. For example, an assembly can consist of several types. You could put the frequently used types in one file and the less frequently used types in another file. If your assembly is deployed by downloading it via the Internet, the file with the infrequently used types might not ever have to be downloaded to the client if the client never accesses the types. For example, an ISV specializing in UI controls might choose to implement Active Accessibility types in a separate module (to satisfy Microsoft's Logo requirements). Only users who require the additional accessibility features would require that this module be downloaded.

You configure an application to download assembly files by specifying a `codeBase` element (discussed in Chapter 3) in the application's configuration file. The `codeBase` element identifies a URL where all of an assembly's files can be found. When attempting to load an assembly's file, the CLR obtains the `codeBase` element's URL and checks the machine's download cache to see if the file is present. If it is, the file is loaded. If the file isn't in the cache, the CLR downloads the file from the URL into the cache. If the file can't be found, the CLR throws a `FileNotFoundException` exception at run time.

I've identified three reasons to use multifile assemblies:

■ You can partition your types among separate files, allowing for files to be incrementally downloaded as described in the Internet download scenario. Partitioning the types into separate files also allows for partial or piecemeal packaging and deployment for "shrink-wrapped" scenarios.

■ You can add resource or data files to your assembly. For example, you could have a type that calculates some insurance information. This type might require access to some actuarial tables to make its computations. Instead of embedding the actuarial tables in your source code, you could use a tool (such as the Assembly Linker [AL.exe], discussed later) so that the data file is considered to be part of the assembly. By the way, this data file can be in any format: a text file, a Microsoft Excel spreadsheet, a Microsoft Word table, or whatever you like—as long as your application knows how to parse the file's contents.

■   You can create assemblies consisting of types implemented in different programming languages. When you compile Visual Basic source
code, the compiler produces a module. When you compile C#
source code, the compiler produces a separate module. You can
implement some types in Visual Basic, some types in C#, and other
types in other languages. You can then use a tool to combine all
these modules into a single assembly. To developers using the
assembly, the assembly just contains a bunch of types; developers
won't even know that different programming languages were used.
By the way, if you prefer, you can run ILDasm.exe on each of the
modules to obtain an IL source code file. Then you can run
ILAsm.exe and pass it all the IL source code files. ILAsm.exe will produce a single file containing all the types. This technique requires
that your source code compiler produces IL-only code, so you can't
use this technique with Visual C++, for example.

Important   To summarize, an assembly is a unit of reuse, versioning,
and security. It allows you to partition your types and resources into
separate files so that you and consumers of your assembly get to
determine which files to package together and deploy. Once the CLR
loads the file containing the manifest, it can determine which of the
assembly's other files contain the types and resources that the application is referencing. Anyone consuming the assembly is required to
know only the name of the file containing the manifest; the file partitioning is then abstracted away from the consumer and can change in
the future without breaking the application's behavior.

To build an assembly, you must select one of your PE files to be the
keeper of the manifest. Or you can create a separate PE file that contains nothing but the manifest. Table 2-3 shows the manifest metadata tables that turn a
managed module into an assembly.

Table 2-3 Manifest Metadata Tables

Manifest Metadata Table Name	Description
AssemblyDef	Contains a single entry if this module identifies an assembly. The entry includes the assembly's name (without path and extension), version (major, minor, build, and revision), culture, flags, hash algorithm, and the publisher's public key (which can be null).
FileDef	Contains one entry for each PE and resource file that is part of the assembly. The entry includes the file's name and extension (without path), hash value, and flags. If this assembly consists only of its own file, the FileDef table has no entries.
ManifestResourceDef	Contains one entry for each resource that is part of the assembly. The entry includes the resource's name, flags (public, private), and an index into the FileDef table indicating the file that contains the resource file or stream. If the resource isn't a stand-alone file (such as a .jpeg or a .gif), the resource is a stream contained within a PE file. For an embedded resource, the entry also includes an offset indicating the start of the resource stream within the PE file.
ExportedTypesDef	Contains one entry for each public type exported from all the assembly's PE modules. The entry includes the type's name, an index into the FileDef table (indicating which of this assembly's files implements the type), and an index into the TypeDef table. *Note*: To save file space, types exported from the file containing the manifest are not repeated in this table because the type information is available using the metadata's TypeDef table.

The existence of a manifest provides a level of indirection between consumers of the assembly and the partitioning details of the assembly and makes assemblies self-describing. Also, note that the file containing the manifest knows which files are part of the assembly, but the individual files themselves aren't aware that they are part of an assembly.

> **Note** The assembly file that contains the manifest also has an AssemblyRef table in it. This table contains an entry for all the assemblies referenced by all the assembly's files. This allows tools to open an assembly's manifest and see its set of referenced assemblies without having to open the assembly's other files. Again, the entries in the AssemblyRef table exist to make an assembly self-describing.

The Visual Basic compiler produces an assembly when you specify any of the following command-line switches: `/t[arget]:exe`, `/t[arget]:winexe`, or `/t[arget]:library`. All these switches cause the compiler to generate a single PE file that contains the manifest metadata tables. The resulting file is either a CUI executable, a GUI executable, or a DLL, respectively.

In addition to these switches, the Visual Basic compiler supports the `/t[arget]:module` switch. This switch tells the compiler to produce a PE file that doesn't contain the manifest metadata tables. The PE file produced is always a DLL PE file, and this file must be added to an assembly before the types within it can be accessed. When you use the `/t:module` switch, the Visual Basic compiler, by default, names the output file with an extension of .netmodule.

> **Important**   Unfortunately, the Visual Studio .NET integrated development environment (IDE) doesn't natively support the ability for you to create multifile assemblies. If you want to create multifile assemblies, you must resort to using command-line tools.

There are many ways to add a module to an assembly. If you're using the Visual Basic compiler to build a PE file with a manifest, you can use the `/addmodule` switch. To understand how to build a multifile assembly, let's assume that we have two source code files:

- RUT.vb, which contains rarely used types
- FUT.vb, which contains frequently used types

Let's compile the rarely used types into their own module so that users of the assembly won't need to deploy this module if they never access the rarely used types:

```
vbc /t:module RUT.vb
```

This line causes the Visual Basic compiler to create a RUT.netmodule file. This file is a standard DLL PE file, but, by itself, the CLR can't load it.

Next let's compile the frequently used types into their own module. We'll make this module the keeper of the assembly's manifest because the types are used so often. In fact, because this module will now represent the entire assembly, I'll change the name of the output file to JeffTypes.dll instead of calling it FUT.dll:

```
vbc /out:JeffTypes.dll /t:library /addmodule:RUT.netmodule FUT.vb
```

This line tells the Visual Basic compiler to compile the FUT.vb file to produce the JeffTypes.dll file. Because **/t:library** is specified, a DLL PE file containing the manifest metadata tables is emitted into the JeffTypes.dll file. The **/addmodule:RUT.netmodule** switch tells the compiler that RUT.netmodule is a file that should be considered part of the assembly. Specifically, the **/addmodule** switch tells the compiler to add the file to the FileDef manifest metadata table and to add RUT.netmodule's publicly exported types to the ExportedTypesDef manifest metadata table.

Once the compiler has finished all its processing, the two files shown in Figure 2-1 are created. The module on the right contains the manifest.

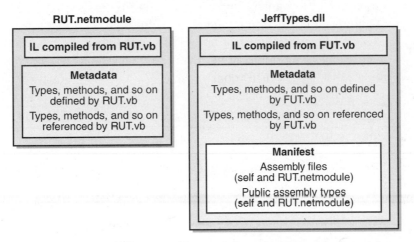

Figure 2-1   A multifile assembly consisting of two managed modules, one with a manifest

The RUT.netmodule file contains the IL code generated by compiling RUT.vb. This file also contains metadata tables that describe the types, methods, fields, properties, events, and so on that are defined by RUT.vb. The metadata tables also describe the types, methods, and so on that are referenced by RUT.vb. The JeffTypes.dll is a separate file. Like RUT.netmodule, this file includes the IL code generated by compiling FUT.vb and also includes similar definition and reference metadata tables. However, JeffTypes.dll contains the additional manifest metadata tables, making JeffTypes.dll an assembly. The additional manifest metadata tables describe all the files that make up the assembly (the JeffTypes.dll file itself and the RUT.netmodule file). The manifest metadata tables also include all the public types exported from JeffTypes.dll and RUT.netmodule.

Once the JeffTypes.dll assembly is built, you can use ILDasm.exe to examine the metadata's manifest tables to verify that the assembly file does in fact have references to the RUT.netmodule file's types. If you build this project and then use ILDasm.exe to examine the metadata, you'll see the FileDef and ExportedTypesDef tables included in the output.

> **Note** In reality, the manifest metadata tables don't actually include the types that are exported from the PE file that contains the manifest. The purpose of this optimization is to reduce the number of bytes required by the manifest information in the PE file. So statements like, "The manifest metadata tables also include all the public types exported from JeffTypes.dll and RUT.netmodule" aren't 100 percent accurate. However, this statement does accurately reflect what the manifest is logically exposing.

Here's what those tables look like:

```
File #1
----------------------------------------------------------
    Token: 0x26000001
    Name : rut.netmodule
    HashValue Blob : 75 70 8f 79 fe b4 fc 09  df 1a ce 70 f1 7f 7d 0b
                     cb b5 83 ca
    Flags : [ContainsMetaData]  (00000000)

ExportedType #1
----------------------------------------------------------
    Token: 0x27000001
    Name: ARarelyUsedType
    Implementation token: 0x26000001
    TypeDef token: 0x02000002
    Flags     : [Public] [AutoLayout] [Class] [AnsiClass]  (00000001)
```

From this, you can see that RUT.netmodule is a file considered to be part of the assembly. From the ExportedType table, you can see that there is a publicly exported type, **ARarelyUsedType**. The implementation token for this type is 0x26000001, which indicates that the type's IL code is contained in the RUT.netmodule file.

> **Note**   For the curious, metadata tokens are 4-byte values. The high byte indicates the type of token (0x01=TypeRef, 0x02=TypeDef, 0x26=FileRef, 0x27=ExportedType). For the complete list, see the `CorTokenType` enumerated type in the CorHdr.h file included with the .NET Framework SDK. The low three bytes of the token simply identify the row in the corresponding metadata table. For example, the implementation token 0x26000001 refers to the first row of the FileRef table. (Rows are numbered starting with 1, not 0.)

Any client code that consumes the JeffTypes.dll assembly's types must be built using the **/r[eference]:JeffTypes.dll** compiler switch. This switch tells the compiler to load the JeffTypes.dll assembly and all the files listed in its File-Def table. The compiler requires that all the assembly's files are installed and accessible. If you were to delete the RUT.netmodule file, the Visual Basic compiler would produce the following error:

```
C:\Net_Projects\ConsoleApplication1\rut.netmodule : error BC31011
Unable to load referenced library 'rut.netmodule': The system cannot
find the file specified.
vbc : error BC30142: Unable to generate a reference to file 'JeffTypes.dll'
(use TLBIMP utility to reference COM DLLs):
Error importing module 'rut.netmodule' of assembly 'JeffTypes.dll' --
The system cannot find the file specified.
```

This means that to build a new assembly, all the files from a referenced assembly *must* be present.

As the client code executes, it calls methods. When a method is called for the first time, the CLR detects what types the method references. The CLR then attempts to load the referenced assembly's file that contains the manifest. If the type being accessed is in this file, the CLR performs its internal bookkeeping, allowing the type to be used. If the manifest indicates that the referenced type is in a different file, the CLR attempts to load the necessary file, performs its internal bookkeeping, and allows the type to be accessed. The CLR loads assembly files only when a method referencing a type is called. This means that to run an application, all the files from a referenced assembly *do not* need to be present.

Adding Assemblies to a Project Using the Visual Studio .NET IDE

If you're using the Visual Studio .NET IDE to build your project, you'll have to add any assemblies you want to reference to your project. To do so, open the Solution Explorer window, right-click on the project you want to add a reference to, and select the Add Reference menu item. This causes the Add Reference dialog box, shown in Figure 2-2, to appear.

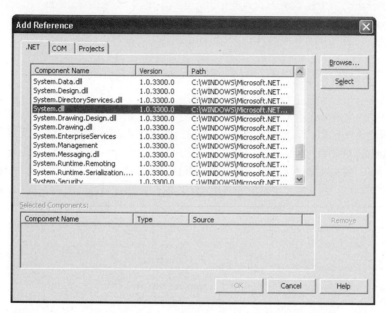

Figure 2-2   Add Reference dialog box in Visual Studio .NET

To have your project reference a managed assembly, select the desired assembly from the list. If the assembly you want isn't in the list, select the Browse button to navigate to the desired assembly (file containing a manifest) to add the assembly reference. The COM tab on the Add Reference dialog box allows an unmanaged COM server to be accessed from within managed source code. The Projects tab allows the current project to reference an assembly that is created by another project in the same solution.

To make your own assemblies appear in the .NET tab's list, add the following subkey to the registry:

```
HKEY_LOCAL_MACHINE\SOFTWARE\Microsoft\.NETFramework\
AssemblyFolders\MyLibName
```

MyLibName is a unique name that you create—Visual Studio doesn't display this name. After creating the subkey, change its default string value so that it refers to a directory path (such as "C:\Program Files\MyLibPath") containing your assembly's files.

Using the Assembly Linker

Instead of using the Visual Basic compiler, you might want to create assemblies using the Assembly Linker utility, AL.exe. The Assembly Linker is useful if you want to create an assembly consisting of modules built from different compilers (if your compiler doesn't support the equivalent of Visual Basic's **/addmodule** switch) or perhaps if you just don't know your assembly packaging requirements at build time. You can also use AL.exe to build resource-only assemblies (called *satellite* assemblies, which I'll talk about again later in the chapter), which are typically used for localization purposes.

The AL.exe utility can produce an EXE or a DLL PE file that contains nothing but a manifest describing the types in other modules. To understand how AL.exe works, let's change the way the JeffTypes.dll assembly is built:

```
vbc /t:module RUT.vb
vbc /t:module FUT.vb
al  /out:JeffTypes.dll /t:library FUT.netmodule RUT.netmodule
```

Figure 2-3 shows the files that result from executing these statements.

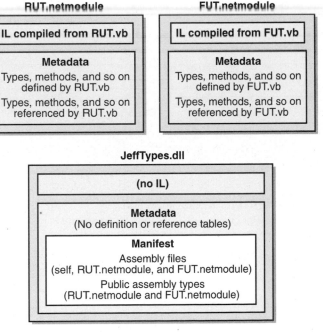

Figure 2-3   A multifile assembly consisting of three managed modules, one with a manifest

In this example, two separate modules, RUT.netmodule and FUT.netmodule, are created that are not themselves assemblies (because they don't contain manifest metadata tables). Then a third file is produced: JeffTypes.dll, which is a small DLL PE file (because of the **/t[arget]:library** switch) that contains no IL code but has manifest metadata tables indicating that RUT.netmodule and FUT.netmodule are part of the assembly. The resulting assembly consists of three files: JeffTypes.dll, RUT.netmodule, and FUT.netmodule. The Assembly Linker has no way to combine multiple files into a single file.

The AL.exe utility can also produce CUI and GUI PE files (using the **/t[arget]:exe** or **/t[arget]:winexe** command-line switch), but this is very unusual since it would mean that you'd have an EXE PE file with just enough IL code in it to call a method in another module. The Assembly Linker generates this IL code when you call AL.exe using the **/main** command-line switch.

```
vbc /t:module /r:JeffTypes.dll App.vb
al  /out:App.exe /t:exe /main:App.Main app.netmodule
```

Here the first line builds the App.vb file into a module. The second line produces a small App.exe PE file that contains the manifest metadata tables. In addition, there is a small global function emitted by AL.exe because of the **/main:App.Main** switch. This function, **__EntryPoint**, contains the following IL code:

```
.method privatescope static void __EntryPoint() il managed
{
  .entrypoint
  // Code size       8 (0x8)
  .maxstack  8
  IL_0000:  tail.
  IL_0002:  call       void [.module 'App.mod']App::Main()
  IL_0007:  ret
} // end of method 'Global Functions::__EntryPoint'
```

As you can see, this code simply calls the **Main** method contained in the **App** type defined in the App.netmodule file.

The **/main** switch in AL.exe isn't that useful because it's unlikely that you'd ever create an assembly for an application where the application's entry point isn't in the PE file that contains the manifest metadata tables. I mention the switch here only to make you aware of its existence.

Including Resource Files in the Assembly

When using AL.exe to create an assembly, you can add resource files (non-PE files) to the assembly by using the **/embed[resource]** switch. This switch takes a file (any file) and embeds the file's contents into the resulting PE file. The manifest's ManifestResourceDef table is updated to reflect the existence of the resources.

AL.exe also supports a **/link[resource]** switch, which also takes a file containing resources. However, the **/link[resource]** switch updates the manifest's ManifestResourceDef and FileDef tables, indicating that the resource exists and identifying which of the assembly's files contain it. The resource file is not embedded into the assembly PE file; it remains separate and must be packaged and deployed with the other assembly files.

Like AL.exe, VBC.exe also allows you to combine resources into an assembly produced by the Visual Basic compiler. The Visual Basic compiler's **/resource** switch embeds the specified resource file into the resulting assembly PE file, updating the ManifestResourceDef table. The compiler's **/linkresource** switch adds an entry to the ManifestResourceDef and the FileDef manifest tables to refer to a stand-alone resource file.

One last note about resources: it's possible to embed standard Win32 resources into an assembly. You can do this easily by specifying the pathname of a .res file with the **/win32res** switch when using either AL.exe or VBC.exe. In addition, you can quickly and easily embed a standard Win32 icon resource into an assembly file by specifying the pathname of an .ico file with the **/win32icon** switch when using either AL.exe or VBC.exe. The typical reason that an icon is embedded is so that Explorer can show an icon for a managed executable file.

Assembly Version Resource Information

When AL.exe or VBC.exe produces a PE file assembly, it also embeds into the PE file a standard Win32 Version resource. Users can examine this resource by viewing the file's properties. Figure 2-4 shows the Version page of the Jeff-Types.dll Properties dialog box.

Figure 2-4   Version tab of the JeffTypes.dll Properties dialog box

In addition, you can use the resource editor in Visual Studio .NET, shown in Figure 2-5, to view/modify the version resource fields.

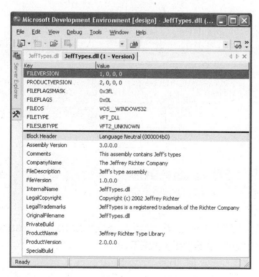

Figure 2-5   Resource editor in Visual Studio .NET

When building an assembly, you should set the version resource fields using custom attributes that you apply at the assembly level in your source code. Here's what the code that produced the version information in Figure 2-5 looks like:

```
Imports System.Reflection

' Set the version CompanyName, LegalCopyright, and LegalTrademarks fields.
<Assembly:AssemblyCompany("The Jeffrey Richter Company")>
<Assembly:AssemblyCopyright("Copyright (c) 2002 Jeffrey Richter")>
<Assembly:AssemblyTrademark( _
    "JeffTypes is a registered trademark of the Richter Company")>

' Set the version ProductName and ProductVersion fields.
<Assembly:AssemblyProduct("Jeffrey Richter Type Library")>
<Assembly:AssemblyInformationalVersion("2.0.0.0")>

' Set the version FileVersion, AssemblyVersion,
' FileDescription, and Comments fields.
<Assembly:AssemblyFileVersion("1.0.0.0")>
<Assembly:AssemblyVersion("3.0.0.0")>
<Assembly:AssemblyTitle("Jeff's type assembly")>
<Assembly:AssemblyDescription("This assembly contains Jeff's types")>

' Set the culture (discussed in the "Culture" section later in this chapter).
<Assembly:AssemblyCulture("")>
```

Table 2-4 shows the version resource fields and the custom attributes that correspond to them. If you're using AL.exe to build your assembly, you can use command-line switches to set this information instead of using the custom attributes. The second column in Table 2-4 shows the AL.exe command-line switch that corresponds to each version resource field. Note that the Visual Basic compiler doesn't offer these command-line switches and that, in general, using custom attributes is the preferred way to set this information.

Important   When you create a new Visual Basic project in Visual Studio .NET, an AssemblyInfo.vb file is automatically created for you. This file contains all the assembly attributes described in this section plus a few additional attributes that I'll cover in Chapter 3. You can simply open the AssemblyInfo.vb file and modify your assembly-specific information. The file that Visual Studio .NET creates for you has some problems that I'll go over later in this chapter. In a real production project, you must modify the contents of this file.

Table 2-4   Version Resource Fields and Their Corresponding AL.exe Switches and Custom Attributes

Version Resource	AL.exe Switch	Custom Attribute/Comment
FILEVERSION	`/fileversion`	`System.Reflection.AssemblyFileVersion-Attribute`
PRODUCTVERSION	`/productversion`	`System.Reflection.AssemblyInformationalVersionAttribute`
FILEFLAGSMASK	(none)	Always set to **VS_FFI_FILEFLAGSMASK** (defined in WinVer.h as 0x0000003F)
FILEFLAGS	(none)	Always 0
FILEOS	(none)	Currently always **VOS__WINDOWS32**
FILETYPE	`/target`	Set to **VFT_APP** if **/target:exe** or **/target:winexe** is specified; set to **VFT_DLL** if **/target:library** is specified
FILESUBTYPE	(none)	Always set to **VFT2_UNKNOWN** (This field has no meaning for **VFT_APP** and **VFT_DLL**.)
AssemblyVersion	`/version`	`System.Reflection.AssemblyVersionAttribute`
Comments	`/description`	`System.Reflection.AssemblyDescription-Attribute`
CompanyName	`/company`	`System.Reflection.AssemblyCompanyAttribute`
FileDescription	`/title`	`System.Reflection.AssemblyTitleAttribute`
FileVersion	`/version`	`System.Reflection.AssemblyVersionAttribute`
InternalName	`/out`	Set to the name of the output file specified (without the extension)
LegalCopyright	`/copyright`	`System.Reflection.AssemblyCopyrightAttribute`
LegalTrademarks	`/trademark`	`System.Reflection.AssemblyTrademarkAttribute`
OriginalFilename	`/out`	Set to the name of the output file (without a path)
PrivateBuild	(none)	Always blank
ProductName	`/product`	`System.Reflection.AssemblyProductAttribute`
ProductVersion	`/productversion`	`System.Reflection.AssemblyInformationalVersionAttribute`
SpecialBuild	(none)	Always blank

Version Numbers

In the previous section, you saw that several version numbers can be applied to an assembly. All these version numbers have the same format: each consists of four period-separated parts, as shown in Table 2-5.

Table 2-5   Format of Version Numbers

Part	Major Number	Minor Number	Build Number	Revision Number
Example:	2	5	719	2

Table 2-5 shows an example of a version number: 2.5.719.2. The first two numbers make up the "public perception" of the version. The public will think of this example as version 2.5 of the assembly. The third number, 719, indicates the build of the assembly. If your company builds its assembly every day, you should increment the build number each day as well. The last number, 2, indicates the revision of the build. If for some reason your company has to build an assembly twice in one day, maybe to resolve a hot bug that is halting other work, then the revision number should be incremented.

Microsoft uses this version-numbering scheme, and it's simply a recommendation; you're welcome to devise your own number-versioning scheme if you prefer. The only assumption the CLR makes is that bigger numbers indicate later versions.

You'll notice that an assembly has three version numbers associated with it. This is very unfortunate and leads to a lot of confusion. Let me explain each version number's purpose and how it is expected to be used:

- **AssemblyFileVersion**   This version number is stored in the Win32 version resource. This number is informational only; the CLR doesn't examine or care about this version number in any way. Typically, you set the major and minor parts to represent the version you want the public to see. Then you increment the build and revision parts each time a build is performed. Ideally, Microsoft's tool (such as VBC.exe or AL.exe) would automatically update the build and revision numbers for you (based on the data/time when the build was performed), but unfortunately it doesn't. This version number can be seen when using Windows Explorer and is used to determine exactly when an assembly file was built.

- **AssemblyInformationalVersionAttribute** This version number is also stored in the Win32 version resource, and again, this number is informational only; the CLR doesn't examine or care about it in any way. This version number exists to indicate the version of the product that includes this assembly. For example, Version 2.0 of MyProduct might contain several assemblies; one of these assemblies is marked as Version 1.0 since it's a new assembly that didn't ship in Version 1.0 of MyProduct. Typically, you set the major and minor parts of this version number to represent the public version of your product. Then you increment the build and revision parts each time you package a complete product with all its assemblies.

- **AssemblyVersion** This version number is stored in the AssemblyDef manifest metadata table. The CLR uses this version number when binding to strongly named assemblies (discussed in Chapter 3). This number is extremely important and is used to uniquely identify an assembly. When starting to develop an assembly, you should set the major, minor, build, and revision numbers and shouldn't change them until you're ready to begin work on the next deployable version of your assembly. When you build an assembly, this version number in the referenced assembly is embedded in the AssemblyRef table's entry. This means that an assembly is tightly bound to a specific version of a reference assembly.

Important   The VBC.exe and AL.exe tools support the ability to automatically increment the assembly version number with each build. This feature is a bug and shouldn't be used because changing the assembly version number will break any assemblies that reference this assembly. The AssemblyInfo.vb file that Visual Studio .NET automatically creates for you when you create a new project is in error: it sets the `AssemblyVersion` attribute so that its major and minor parts are 1.0 and that the build and revision parts are automatically updated by the compiler. You should definitely modify this file and hard-code all four parts of the assembly version number.

Culture

Like version numbers, assemblies also have a culture as part of their identity. For example, I could have an assembly that is strictly for German, another assembly for Swiss German, another assembly for U.S. English, and so on. Cultures are identified via a string that contains a primary and a secondary tag (as described in RFC1766). Table 2-6 shows some examples.

Table 2-6   Examples of Assembly Culture Tags

Primary Tag	Secondary Tag	Culture
de	(none)	German
de	AT	Austrian German
de	CH	Swiss German
en	(none)	English
en	GB	British English
en	US	U.S. English

In general, if you create an assembly that contains code, you don't assign a culture to it. This is because code doesn't usually have any culture-specific assumptions built into it. An assembly that isn't assigned a culture is referred to as being *culture neutral*.

If you're designing an application that has some culture-specific resources to it, Microsoft highly recommends that you create one assembly that contains your code and your application's default (or fallback) resources. When building this assembly, don't specify a specific culture. This is the assembly that other assemblies will reference to create and manipulate types.

Now you can create one or more separate assemblies that contain only culture-specific resources—no code at all. Assemblies that are marked with a culture are called *satellite assemblies*. For these satellite assemblies, assign a culture that accurately reflects the culture of the resources placed in the assembly. You should create one satellite assembly for each culture you intend to support.

You'll usually use the AL.exe tool to build a satellite assembly. You won't use a compiler because the satellite assembly should have no code contained within it. When using AL.exe, you specify the desired culture using the `/c[ulture]:text` switch, where text is a string such as "en-US" representing

U.S. English. When you deploy a satellite assembly, you should place it in a subdirectory whose name matches the culture text. For example, if the application's base directory is C:\MyApp, then the U.S. English satellite assembly should be placed in the C:\MyApp\en-US subdirectory. At run time, you access a satellite assembly's resources using the `System.Resources.Resource-Manager` class.

> **Note** Although strongly discouraged, it is possible to create a satellite assembly that contains code. If you prefer, you can specify the culture using the `System.Reflection.AssemblyCultureAttribute` custom attribute instead of using AL.exe's `/culture` switch, for example, as shown here:
>
> ```
> ' Set assembly's culture to Swiss German.
> <assembly:AssemblyCulture("de-CH")>
> ```
>
> Normally, you shouldn't build an assembly that references a satellite assembly. In other words, an assembly's AssemblyRef entries should all refer to culture-neutral assemblies. If you want to access types or members contained in a satellite assembly, you should use reflection techniques as discussed in Chapter 20.

Simple Application Deployment (Privately Deployed Assemblies)

Throughout this chapter, I've explained how you build modules and how you combine those modules into an assembly. At this point, I'm ready to package and deploy all the assemblies so that users can run the application.

Assemblies don't dictate or require any special means of packaging. The easiest way to package a set of assemblies is simply to copy all the files directly. For example, you could put all the assembly files on a CD-ROM disk and ship it to the user with a batch file setup program that just copies the files from the CD to a directory on the user's hard drive. Because the assemblies include all the dependent assembly references and types, the user can just run the application and the CLR will look for referenced assemblies in the application's directory. No modifications to the registry or to Active Directory are necessary for the application to run. To uninstall the application, just delete all the files—that's it!

Of course, you can package and install the assembly files using other mechanisms, such as .cab files (typically used for Internet download scenarios to compress files and reduce download times). You can also package the assembly files into an MSI file for use by the Windows Installer service (MSIExec.exe). Using MSI allows assemblies to be installed on demand the first time the CLR attempts to load the assembly. This feature isn't new to MSI; it can perform the same demand-load functionality for unmanaged EXE and DLL files as well.

> **Note**   Using a batch file or some other simple "installation software" will get an application onto the user's machine; however, you'll need more sophisticated installation software to create shortcut links on the user's desktop, Start menu, and Quick Launch toolbar. Also, you can easily back up and restore the application or move it from one machine to another, but the various shortcut links will require special handling. Future versions of Windows may improve this story.

Assemblies that are deployed to the same directory as the application are called *privately deployed assemblies* because the assembly files aren't shared with any other application (unless it's also deployed to the same directory). Privately deployed assemblies are a big win for developers, end-users, and administrators because they can simply be copied to an application's base directory and the CLR will load them and execute the code in them. In addition, an application can be uninstalled by simply deleting the assemblies in its directory. This allows simple backup and restore to work as well.

This simple install/move/uninstall story is possible because each assembly has metadata indicating which referenced assembly should be loaded; no registry settings or Active Directory settings are required.

In addition, the referencing assembly scopes every type. This means that an application always binds to the exact type that it was built and tested with; the CLR can't load a different assembly that just happens to provide a type with the same name. This is different from COM, where types are recorded in the registry, making them available to any application running on the machine.

In Chapter 3, I'll discuss how to deploy shared assemblies that are accessible by multiple applications.

Simple Administrative Control (Configuration)

The end-user or the administrator can best determine some aspects of an application's execution. For example, an administrator might decide to move an assembly's files on the user's hard disk or to override information contained in the assembly's manifest. Other scenarios also exist related to versioning and remoting; I'll talk about some of these in Chapter 3.

To allow administrative control over an application, a configuration file can be placed in the application's directory. An application's publisher can create and package this file. The setup program would then install this configuration file in the application's base directory. In addition, the machine's administrator or an end-user could create or modify this file. The CLR interprets the content of this file to alter its policies for locating and loading assembly files.

These configuration files contain XML and can be associated with an application or with the machine. Using a separate file (vs. registry settings) allows the file to be easily backed up and also allows the administrator to copy the application to another machine: just copy the necessary files and the administrative policy is copied too.

In Chapter 3, we'll explore this configuration file in more detail. But I want to give you a taste of it now. Let's say that the publisher of an application wants its application deployed with the JeffTypes assembly files in a different directory than the application's assembly file. The desired directory structure looks like this:

```
AppDir directory (contains the application's assembly files)
   App.exe
   App.exe.config (discussed below)

   AuxFiles subdirectory (contains JeffTypes' assembly files)
      JeffTypes.dll
      FUT.netmodule
      RUT.netmodule
```

Since the JeffTypes files are no longer in the application's base directory, the CLR won't be able to locate and load these files; running the application will cause a **System.IO.FileNotFoundException** exception to be thrown. To fix this, the publisher creates an XML configuration file and deploys it to the application's base directory. The name of this file must be the name of the application's main assembly file with a .config extension: App.exe.config, for this example. This configuration file should look like this:

```
<?xml version="1.0" encoding="utf-8" ?>
<configuration>
   <runtime>
      <assemblyBinding xmlns="urn:schemas-microsoft-com:asm.v1">
```

```
      <probing privatePath="AuxFiles" />
    </assemblyBinding>
  </runtime>
</configuration>
```

Whenever the CLR attempts to locate an assembly file, it always looks in the application's directory first, and if it can't find the file there, it looks in the AuxFiles subdirectory. You can specify multiple semicolon-delimited paths for the probing element's **privatePath** attribute. Each path is considered relative to the application's base directory. You can't specify an absolute or a relative path identifying a directory that is outside the application's base directory. The idea is that an application can control its directory and its subdirectories but has no control over other directories.

By the way, you can write code that opens and parses the information contained in a configuration file. This allows your application to define settings that an administrator or an end-user can create and persist in the same file as all the application's other settings. You use the classes defined in the **System.Configuration** namespace to manipulate a configuration file at run time. The name and location of this XML configuration is different depending on the application type.

■   For executable applications (EXEs), the configuration file must be in the application's base directory and it must be the name of the EXE file with ".config" appended to it.

■   For ASP.NET Web Forms and XML Web service applications, the file must be in the Web application's virtual root directory and is always named Web.config. In addition, subdirectories can also contain their own Web.config file and the configuration settings are inherited. For example, a Web application located at *http://www.Wintellect.com /Training* would use the settings in the Web.config files contained in the virtual root directory and in its Training subdirectory.

■   For assemblies containing client-side controls hosted by Microsoft Internet Explorer, the HTML page must contain a link tag whose **rel** attribute is set to "Configuration" and whose **href** attribute is set to the URL of the configuration file, which can be given any name. Here's an example: <LINK REL=Configuration HREF=http:// www.Wintellect.com/Controls.config>. For more information, see the .NET Framework documentation.

Probing for Assembly Files

When the CLR needs to locate an assembly, it scans several subdirectories. Here is the order in which directories are probed for a culture-neutral assembly:

```
AppBase\AsmName.dll
AppBase\AsmName\AsmName.dll
AppBase\privatePath1\AsmName.dll
AppBase\privatePath1\AsmName\AsmName.dll
AppBase\privatePath2\AsmName.dll
AppBase\privatePath2\AsmName\AsmName.dll
⋮
```

In the earlier example, no configuration file would be needed if the JeffTypes assembly files were deployed to a subdirectory called JeffTypes since the CLR would automatically scan for a subdirectory whose name matches the name of the assembly being searched for.

If the assembly can't be found in any of the preceding subdirectories, the CLR starts all over, using an .exe extension instead of a .dll extension. If the assembly still can't be found, a `FileNotFoundException` is thrown.

For satellite assemblies, the same rules are followed except that the assembly is expected to be in a subdirectory of the application base directory whose name matches the culture. For example, if AsmName.dll has a culture of "en-US" applied to it, the following directories are probed:

```
AppBase\en-US\AsmName.dll
AppBase\en-US\AsmName\AsmName.dll
AppBase\en-US\privatePath1\AsmName.dll
AppBase\en-US\privatePath1\AsmName\AsmName.dll
AppBase\en-US\privatePath2\AsmName.dll
AppBase\en-US\privatePath2\AsmName\AsmName.dll
⋮
```

Again, if the assembly can't be found in any of the subdirectories listed here, the CLR checks the same set of assemblies looking for an .exe file instead of a .dll file.

As mentioned at the beginning of this section, configuration settings apply to a particular application and to the machine. When you install the .NET Framework, it creates a Machine.config file. There is one Machine.config file per version of the CLR you have installed on the machine. In the future, it will be possible to have multiple versions of the .NET Framework installed on a single machine simultaneously.

The Machine.config file is located in the following directory:

```
C:\WINDOWS\Microsoft.NET\Framework\version\CONFIG
```

Of course, C:\WINDOWS identifies your Windows directory, and *version* is a version number identifying a specific version of the .NET Framework.

Settings in the Machine.config file override settings in an application-specific configuration file. An administrator can create a machine-wide policy by modifying a single file. Normally, administrators and users should avoid modifying the Machine.config file because this file has many settings related to various things, making it much more difficult to navigate. Plus, you want the application's settings to be backed up and restored, and keeping an application's settings in the application-specific configuration file enables this.

Because editing an XML configuration file is a little unwieldy, Microsoft's .NET Framework team produced a GUI tool to help. The GUI tool is implemented as a Microsoft Management Console (MMC) snap-in, which means that it isn't available when running on a Windows 98, Windows 98 Second Edition, or Windows Me machine. You can find the tool by opening Control Panel, selecting Administrative Tools, and then selecting the Microsoft .NET Framework Configuration tool. In the window that appears, you can traverse the tree's nodes until you get to the Applications node, as shown in Figure 2-6.

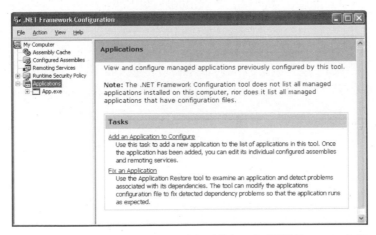

Figure 2-6   Applications node of the Microsoft .NET Framework Configuration tool

From the Applications node, you can select the Add An Application To Configure link that appears in the right-hand pane. This will invoke a wizard that will prompt you for the pathname of the executable file you want to create an XML configuration file for. After you've added an application, you can also use this to alter its configuration file. Figure 2-7 shows the tasks that you can perform to an application.

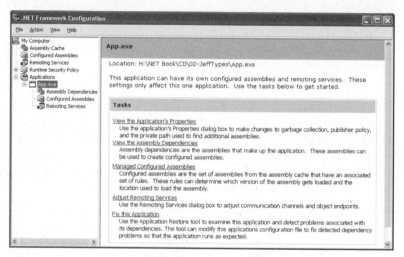

Figure 2-7   Configuring an application using the Microsoft .NET Framework Configuration tool

I'll discuss configuration files a bit more in Chapter 3.

3

Shared Assemblies

In Chapter 2, I talked about the steps required to build, package, and deploy an assembly. I focused on what's called *private deployment*, where assemblies are placed in the application's base directory (or a subdirectory thereof) for the application's sole use. Deploying assemblies privately gives a company a large degree of control over the naming, versioning, and behavior of the assembly.

In this chapter, I'll concentrate on creating assemblies that multiple applications can access. The assemblies that ship with the Microsoft .NET Framework are an excellent example of globally deployed assemblies because almost all managed applications use types defined by Microsoft in the .NET Framework Class Library (FCL).

As I mentioned in Chapter 2, Windows has a reputation for being unstable. The main reason for this reputation is the fact that applications are built and tested using code implemented by someone else. After all, when you write an application for Windows, your application is calling into code written by Microsoft developers. Also, a large number of companies out there make controls that application developers can incorporate into their own applications. In fact, the .NET Framework encourages this, and lots more control vendors will likely pop up over time.

As time marches on, Microsoft developers and control developers modify their code: they fix bugs, add features, and so on. Eventually, the new code makes its way onto the user's hard disk. The user's applications that were previously installed and working fine are no longer using the same code that the applications were built and tested with. As a result, the applications' behavior is no longer predictable, which contributes to the instability of Windows.

File versioning is a very difficult problem to solve. In fact, I assert that if you take a file and change just one bit in the file from a 0 to a 1 or from a 1 to a 0, there's absolutely no way to guarantee that code that used the original file will now work just as well if it uses the new version of the file. One of the reasons why this statement is true is that a lot of applications exploit bugs—either knowingly or unknowingly. If a later version of a file fixes a bug, the application no longer runs as expected.

So here's the problem: How do you fix bugs and add features to a file and also guarantee that you don't break some application? I've given this question a lot of thought and have come to one conclusion: it's just not possible. But, obviously, this answer isn't good enough. Files will ship with bugs, and developers will always want to add new features. There must be a way to distribute new files with the hope that the applications will work just fine. And if the application doesn't work fine, there has to be an *easy* way to restore the application to its "last-known good state."

In this chapter, I'll explain the infrastructure that the .NET Framework has in place to deal with versioning problems. Let me warn you: what I'm about to describe is complicated. I'm going to talk about a lot of algorithms, rules, and policies that are built into the common language runtime (CLR). I'm also going to mention a lot of tools and utilities that the application developer must use. This stuff is complicated because, as I've mentioned, the versioning problem is difficult to address and to solve.

Two Kinds of Assemblies, Two Kinds of Deployment

The .NET Framework supports two kinds of assemblies: *weakly named assemblies* and *strongly named assemblies*.

> **Important**   By the way, you won't find the term *weakly named assembly* in any of the .NET Framework documentation. Why? Because I made it up. In fact, the documentation has no term to identify a weakly named assembly. I decided to coin the term so that I can talk about assemblies without any ambiguity as to what kind of assembly I'm referring to.

Weakly named assemblies and strongly named assemblies are structurally identical—that is, they use the same portable executable (PE) file format, PE header, CLR header, metadata, and manifest tables that we examined in Chapter 2. And you use the same tools, such as the Visual Basic compiler and AL.exe, to build both kinds of assemblies. The real difference between weakly named and strongly named assemblies is that a strongly named assembly is signed with a publisher's public/private key pair that uniquely identifies the assembly's publisher. This key pair allows the assembly to be uniquely identified, secured, and versioned, and it allows the assembly to be deployed anywhere on the user's hard disk or even on the Internet. This ability to uniquely identify an assembly allows the CLR to enforce certain "known to be safe" policies when an application tries to bind to a strongly named assembly. This chapter is dedicated to explaining what strongly named assemblies are and what policies the CLR applies to them.

An assembly can be deployed in two ways: privately or globally. A privately deployed assembly is an assembly that is deployed in the application's base directory or one of its subdirectories. A weakly named assembly can be deployed only privately. I talked about privately deployed assemblies in Chapter 2. A globally deployed assembly is an assembly that is deployed into some well-known location that the CLR knows to look in when it's searching for an assembly. A strongly named assembly can be deployed privately or globally. I'll explain how to create and deploy strongly named assemblies in this chapter. Table 3-1 summarizes the kinds of assemblies and the ways that they can be deployed.

Table 3-1 How Weakly and Strongly Named Assemblies Can Be Deployed

Kind of Assembly	Can Be Privately Deployed?	Can Be Globally Deployed?
Weakly named	Yes	No
Strongly named	Yes	Yes

Giving an Assembly a Strong Name

If multiple applications are going to access an assembly, the assembly must be placed in a well-known directory and the CLR must know to look in this directory automatically when a reference to the assembly is detected. However, we have a problem: two (or more) companies could produce assemblies that have the same filename. Then, if both of these assemblies get copied into the same well-known directory, the last one installed wins and all the applications that were using the old assembly no longer function as desired. (This is exactly why DLL hell exists today in Windows.)

Obviously, differentiating assemblies simply by using a filename isn't good enough. The CLR needs to support some mechanism that allows assemblies to be uniquely identified. This is what the term *strongly named assembly* refers to. A strongly named assembly consists of four attributes that uniquely identify the assembly: a filename (without an extension), a version number, a culture identity, and a public key token (a value derived from a public key). The following strings identify four completely different assembly files:

```
"MyTypes,Version=1.0.8123.0,Culture=neutral,PublicKeyToken=b77a5c561934e089"
```

```
"MyTypes,Version=1.0.8123.0,Culture="en-US",PublicKeyToken=b77a5c561934e089"
```

```
"MyTypes,Version=2.0.1234.0,Culture=neutral,PublicKeyToken=b77a5c561934e089"
```

```
"MyTypes,Version=1.0.8123.0,Culture=neutral,PublicKeyToken=b03f5f7f11d50a3a"
```

The first string identifies an assembly file called MyTypes.dll. The company producing the assembly is creating version 1.0.8123.0 of this assembly, and nothing in the assembly is sensitive to any one culture because `Culture` is set to `neutral`. Of course, any company could produce a MyTypes.dll assembly that is marked with a version number of 1.0.8123.0 and a neutral culture.

There must be a way to distinguish this company's assembly from another company's assembly that happens to have the same attributes. For several reasons, Microsoft chose to use standard public/private key cryptographic technologies instead of any other unique identification technique, such as GUIDs, URLs, or URNs. Specifically, cryptographic techniques provide a way to check the integrity of the assembly's bits as they are installed on a hard drive, and they also allow permissions to be granted on a per-publisher basis. (I'll discuss these techniques more later in this chapter.)

So, a company that wants to uniquely mark its assemblies must acquire a public/private key pair. Then the public key can be associated with the assembly. No two companies should have the same public/private key pair, and this distinction is what allows two companies to create assemblies that have the same name, version, and culture without causing any conflict.

> **Note**   The `System.Reflection.AssemblyName` class is a helper class that makes it easy for you to build an assembly name and to obtain the various parts of an assembly's name. The class offers several public instance properties, such as `CultureInfo`, `FullName`, `KeyPair`, `Name`, and `Version`. The class also offers a few public instance methods, such as `GetPublicKey`, `GetPublicKeyToken`, `SetPublicKey`, and `SetPublicKeyToken`.

In Chapter 2, I showed you how to name an assembly file and how to apply an assembly version number and a culture. A weakly named assembly can have assembly version and culture attributes embedded in the manifest metadata; however, the CLR always ignores the version number and uses only the culture information when it's probing subdirectories looking for the satellite assembly. Because weakly named assemblies are always privately deployed, the CLR simply uses the name of the assembly (tacking on a .dll or an .exe extension) when searching for the assembly's file in the application's base directory or any of the subdirectories specified in the XML configuration file's probing element's **privatePath** attribute.

A strongly named assembly has a filename, an assembly version, and a culture. In addition, a strongly named assembly is signed with the publisher's private key.

The first step in creating a strongly named assembly is to obtain a key by using the Strong Name Utility, SN.exe, that ships with the .NET Framework SDK and Visual Studio .NET. This utility offers a whole slew of features depending on the command-line switch you specify. Note that all SN.exe's command-line switches are case-sensitive. To generate a public/private key pair, you run SN.exe as follows:

```
SN -k MyCompany.keys
```

This line tells SN.exe to create a file called MyCompany.keys. This file will contain the public and private key numbers persisted in a binary format.

Public key numbers are very big. If you want to, after creating the file that contains the public and private key, you can use the SN.exe utility again to see the actual public key. To do this, you must execute the SN.exe utility twice. First you invoke SN.exe with the **–p** switch to create a file that contains only the public key (MyCompany.PublicKey):

```
SN -p MyCompany.keys MyCompany.PublicKey
```

Then you invoke SN.exe, passing it the **–tp** switch and the file that contains just the public key:

```
SN -tp MyCompany.PublicKey
```

When I execute the command above, I get the following output:

```
Microsoft (R) .NET Framework Strong Name Utility  Version 1.0.3705.0
Copyright (C) Microsoft Corporation 1998-2001. All rights reserved.

Public key is
0024000004800000940000000602000000240000525341310004000001000100b52a8330e2024a
841e162230bfb25ba52cb768859288ca5f71026a2f47cdccb81b0b73e59749326245e61b9aad1a
```

(continued)

```
ebc1b95b302dcc4a03f3ac289fc36ef21ac59fc4d12fd1e2c1cc56c9e3697eacafdf9a71248aab
893b01b576171351b621a626f7c17c4bc920310d0eb5aa760dbd1429ceeddc63cae6e351bedf5c
1e966aa6
```

```
Public key token is df230cf39ded0e3c
```

The SN.exe utility doesn't offer any way for you to display the private key.

The size of public keys makes them difficult to work with. To make things easier for the developer (and for end-users too), *public key tokens* were created. A public key token is a 64-bit hash of the public key. SN.exe's **–tp** switch shows the public key token that corresponds to the complete public key at the end of its output.

Now that you know how to create a public/private key pair, creating a strongly named assembly is simple. You just apply an instance of the **System.Reflection.AssemblyKeyFileAttribute** attribute to your source code:

```
<Assembly:AssemblyKeyFile("MyCompany.keys")>
```

When a compiler sees this attribute in your source code, the compiler opens the specified file (MyCompany.Keys), signs the assembly with the private key, and embeds the public key in the manifest. Note that you sign only the assembly file that contains the manifest; the assembly's other files can't be signed explicitly.

Important When Visual Studio .NET builds a project, the working directory isn't necessarily the directory that contains your project's files. This means that the compiler might not be able to find the MyCompany.keys file. If the compiler can't find this file, it issues the following error: "vbc : error BC30140: Error creating assembly manifest: Error reading key file 'MyCompany.keys'—The system cannot find the file specified." To correct this problem, you must modify your source code so that the `AssemblyKeyFile` attribute refers to the full pathname of the MyCompany.keys file.

Here's what it means to sign a file: When you build a strongly named assembly, the assembly's FileDef manifest metadata table includes the list of all the files that make up the assembly. As each file's name is added to the manifest, the file's contents are hashed, and this hash value is stored along with the file's name in the FileDef table. You can override the default hash algorithm used with AL.exe's **/algid** switch or the assembly level **System.Reflection.AssemblyAlgorithmIdAttribute** custom attribute. By default, a SHA-1 algorithm is used, and this should be sufficient for almost all applications.

After the PE file containing the manifest is built, the PE file's entire contents are hashed, as shown in Figure 3-1. The hash algorithm used here is always SHA-1 and can't be overridden. This hash value—typically around 100 or 200 bytes in size—is signed with the publisher's private key, and the resulting RSA digital signature is stored in a reserved section (not included in the hash) within the PE file. The CLR header of the PE file is updated to reflect where the digital signature is embedded within the file.

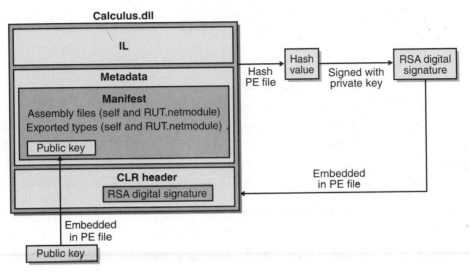

Figure 3-1   Signing an assembly

The publisher's public key is also embedded into the AssemblyDef manifest metadata table in this PE file. The combination of the filename, the assembly version, the culture, and the public key gives this assembly a strong name, which is guaranteed to be unique. There is no way that two companies could produce a "Calculus" assembly with the same public key (assuming that the companies don't share this key pair with each other).

At this point, the assembly and all its files are ready to be packaged and distributed.

As described in Chapter 2, when you compile your source code, the compiler detects the types and members that your code references. You must specify the referenced assemblies to the compiler. For the Visual Basic compiler, you use the **/reference** command-line switch. Part of the compiler's job is to emit an AssemblyRef metadata table inside the resulting managed module. Each entry in the AssemblyRef metadata table indicates the referenced assembly's name (without path and extension), version number, culture, and public key information.

> **Note** Strongly named assemblies can refer only to other strongly named assemblies; they can't reference any weakly named assemblies. The reason for this is that the weakly named assembly can't be installed into the global assembly cache (GAC). The weakly named assemblies would have to be loaded from the application's base directory, which would be different for every application.

> **Important** Because public keys are such large numbers and a single assembly might reference many assemblies, a large percentage of the resulting file's total size would be occupied with public key information. To conserve storage space, Microsoft hashes the public key and takes the last 8 bytes of the hashed value. This reduced value has been determined to be statistically unique and is therefore safe to pass around the system. These reduced public key values—known as public key tokens—are what are actually stored in an AssemblyRef table. In general, developers and end-users will see public key token values much more frequently than full public key values.

Following is the AssemblyRef metadata information for the JeffTypes.dll file that I discussed in Chapter 2:

```
AssemblyRef #1
-------------------------------------------------------
    Token: 0x23000001
    Public Key or Token: b7 7a 5c 56 19 34 e0 89
    Name: mscorlib
    Major Version: 0x00000001
    Minor Version: 0x00000000
    Build Number: 0x00000ce4
    Revision Number: 0x00000000
    Locale: <null>
    HashValue Blob: 3e 10 f3 95 e3 73 0b 33 1a 4a 84 a7 81 76 eb 32 4b
                    36 4d a5
    Flags: [none] (00000000)
```

From this, you can see that JeffTypes.dll references a type that is contained in an assembly matching the following attributes:

```
"MSCorLib,Version=1.0.3300.0,Culture=neutral,PublicKeyToken=b77a5c561934e089"
```

Unfortunately, ILDasm.exe uses the term *Locale* when it really should be using *Culture* instead. Microsoft says that they'll fix the term in a future version of the tool.

If you look at JeffTypes.dll's AssemblyDef metadata table, you see the following:

```
Assembly
-------------------------------------------------------------
    Token: 0x20000001
    Name : JeffTypes
    Public Key   :
    Hash Algorithm : 0x00008004
    Major Version: 0x00000001
    Minor Version: 0x00000000
    Build Number: 0x00000253
    Revision Number: 0x00005361
    Locale: <null>
    Flags : [SideBySideCompatible]  (00000000)
```

This is equivalent to the following:

```
"JeffTypes,Version=1.0.595.21345,Culture=neutral,PublicKeyToken=null"
```

In this line, no public key token is specified because in Chapter 2 the Jeff-Types.dll assembly wasn't signed with a public key, making it a weakly named assembly.

If I had used SN.exe to create a key file, added the **AssemblyKeyFile-Attribute** to the source code, and then recompiled, the resulting assembly would be signed. If you're using AL.exe to build the assembly, you specify its **/keyfile** switch instead of using the **AssemblyKeyFileAttribute**. If I had used ILDasm.exe to explore the new assembly's metadata, the AssemblyDef entry would have bytes appearing after the Public Key field and the assembly would be strongly named. By the way, the AssemblyDef entry always stores the full public key, not the public key token. The full public key is necessary to ensure that the file hasn't been tampered with. I'll explain the tamper resistance of strongly named assemblies later in this chapter.

The Global Assembly Cache

Now that you know how to create a strongly named assembly, it's time to learn how to deploy this assembly and how the CLR uses the information to locate and load the assembly.

If an assembly is to be accessed by multiple applications, the assembly must be placed into a well-known directory and the CLR must know to look in this directory automatically when a reference to the assembly is detected. This well-known location is called the *global assembly cache* (GAC), which can usually be found in the following directory:

```
C:\Windows\Assembly\GAC
```

Note By default, the CLR looks for the GAC in C:\Windows\Assembly\GAC. You can override where the CLR looks for the GAC, however, by performing a series of easy steps. For example, to move the GAC to a shared server, do the following:

- On a server machine (which I'll call "MyServer" for this example), create a new directory; you can name this directory anything you like, such as "SharedGAC".

- In this new directory, create a subdirectory, which must be called "Assembly".

- Copy all the files in an existing GAC to the new "Assembly" directory using XCOPY. For example,

```
XCOPY C:\Windows\Assembly C:\SharedGAC\Assembly /s /e
```

- Share the directory created in step 1. You can use any name for the share. I'll use "SharedGAC" for this example.

- To make a machine use the new, shared GAC, open RegEdit.exe and navigate to the HKEY_LOCAL_MACHINE\Software\Microsoft\Fusion subkey. Then add a `String` value called `CacheLocation` and set this value to the desired path: "\\MyServer\SharedGAC" in my example. Do this on every machine you want to share this one GAC.

After you've run some applications and are sure they're loading assemblies from the new GAC, you can delete the original GAC directory and its subdirectories by executing the following command:

```
rd C:\Windows\Assembly /s
```

The GAC directory is structured: it contains many subdirectories, and an algorithm is used to generate the names of these subdirectories. You should never manually copy assembly files into the GAC; instead, you should use tools to accomplish this task. These tools know the GAC's internal structure and how to generate the proper subdirectory names.

While developing and testing, the most common tool for installing a strongly named assembly into the GAC is GACUtil.exe. Running this tool without any command-line arguments yields the following usage:

```
Microsoft (R) .NET Global Assembly Cache Utility. Version 1.0.3415.0
Copyright (C) Microsoft Corporation 1998-2001. All rights reserved.

Usage: Gacutil <option> [<parameters>]
 Options:
  /i
    Installs an assembly to the global assembly cache. Include the
    name of the file containing the manifest as a parameter.
    Example:  /i myDll.dll

  /if
    Installs an assembly to the global assembly cache and forces
    overwrite if assembly already exists in cache. Include the
    name of the file containing the manifest as a parameter.
    Example:  /if myDll.dll

  /ir
    Installs an assembly to the global assembly cache with traced
    reference. Include the name of file containing manifest,
    reference scheme, ID and description as parameters.
    Example:  /ir myDll.dll FILEPATH c:\apps\myapp.exe MyApp

 /u[ngen]
    Uninstalls an assembly. Include the name of the assembly to
    remove as a parameter. If ngen is specified, the assembly is
    removed from the cache of ngen'd files, otherwise the assembly
    is removed from the global assembly cache.
    Examples:.
      /ungen myDll
      /u myDll,Version=1.1.0.0,Culture=en,PublicKeyToken=874e23ab874e23ab

  /ur
    Uninstalls an assembly reference. Include the name of the
    assembly, type of reference, ID and data as parameters.
    Example: /ur myDll,Version=1.1.0.0,Culture=en,
             PublicKeyToken=874e23ab874e23ab
             FILEPATH c:\apps\myapp.exe MyApp
```

(continued)

```
/uf
    Forces uninstall of an assembly by removing all install references.
    Include the full name of the assembly to remove as a parameter.
    Assembly will be removed unless referenced by Windows Installer.
    Example:  /uf myDll,Version=1.1.0.0,Culture=en,
              PublicKeyToken=874e23ab874e23ab

/l
    Lists the contents of the global assembly cache. Allows optional
    assembly name parameter to list matching assemblies only.

/lr
    Lists the contents of the global assembly cache with traced
    reference information. Allows optional assembly name parameter
    to list matching assemblies only.

/cdl
    Deletes the contents of the download cache

/ldl
    Lists the contents of the downloaded files cache

/nologo
    Suppresses display of the logo banner

/silent
    Suppresses display of all output
```

As you can see, you can invoke GACUtil.exe specifying the **/i** switch to install an assembly into the GAC, and you can use GACUtil.exe's **/u** switch to uninstall an assembly from the GAC. Note that you can't ever place a weakly named assembly into the GAC. If you pass the filename of a weakly named assembly to GACUtil.exe, it displays the following error message:

"Failure adding assembly to the cache: Attempt to install an assembly without a strong name."

> **Note** By default, the GAC is installed under the system's Windows directory: C:\Windows. Usually, the security applied to this directory allows only Administrators the ability to install and remove files. Be aware that GACUtil.exe will fail to install or uninstall an assembly if the user invoking the utility doesn't have sufficient security access.

Using GACUtil.exe's /i switch is very convenient for developer testing. However, if you use GACUtil.exe to deploy an assembly in a production environment, it's recommended that you use GACUtil.exe's /ir switch instead and its /ur switch to uninstall the assembly. The /ir switch integrates the installation with the Windows install and uninstall engine. Basically, it tells the system which application requires the assembly and then ties the application and the assembly together.

> **Note**   If a strongly named assembly is packaged in a cabinet (.cab) file or is compressed in some way, the assembly's file must first be decompressed to temporary files before you use GACUtil.exe to install the assembly's files into the GAC. Once the assembly's files have been installed, the temporary files can be deleted.

The GACUtil.exe tool doesn't ship with the end-user .NET Framework redistributable package. If your application includes some assemblies that you want deployed into the GAC, you must use the Windows Installer (MSI) version 2 or later because MSI is the only tool that is guaranteed to be on end-user machines and capable of installing assemblies into the GAC. (You can determine which version of the Windows Installer is installed by running MSIExec.exe.)

> **Important**   Globally deploying assembly files into the GAC is a form of registering the assembly, although the actual Windows registry isn't affected in any way. Installing assemblies into the GAC breaks the goal of simple application installation, backup, restore, moving, and uninstall. So really, you get only the "simple" story when you avoid global deployment and use private deployment exclusively.

What is the purpose of "registering" an assembly in the GAC? Well, say two companies each produce a Calculus assembly consisting of one file: Calculus.dll. Obviously, both these files can't go in the same directory because the last one installed would overwrite the first one, surely breaking some application. When you use a tool to install an assembly into the GAC, the tool creates subdirectories under the C:\Windows\Assembly\GAC directory and copies the assembly files into this subdirectory.

Normally, no one examines the GAC's subdirectories, so the structure of the GAC shouldn't really matter to you. As long as the tools and the CLR know the structure, all is good. Just for fun, I'll describe the internal structure of the GAC in the next section.

When you install the .NET Framework, an Explorer shell extension (ShFusion.dll) is installed. This shell extension also knows the structure of the GAC, and it displays the GAC's contents in a nice, user-friendly fashion. When I use Explorer and navigate to my C:\Windows\Assembly directory, I see what's shown in Figure 3-2: the assemblies installed into the GAC. Each row shows the assembly's name, type, version number, culture (if any), and public key token.

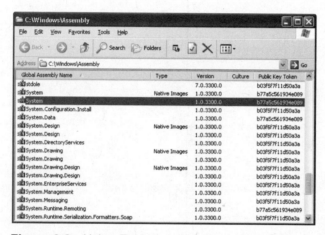

Figure 3-2   Using Explorer's shell extension to see the assemblies installed into the GAC

You can select an entry and click the secondary mouse button to display a context menu. The context menu contains Delete and Properties menu items. Obviously, the Delete menu item deletes the selected assembly's files from the GAC and fixes up the GAC's internal structure. Selecting the Properties menu item displays a property dialog box that looks like the one shown in Figure 3-3. The Last Modified timestamp indicates when the assembly was added to the GAC. Selecting the Version tab reveals the property dialog box shown in Figure 3-4.

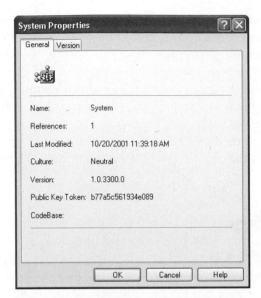

Figure 3-3   General tab of the System Properties dialog box

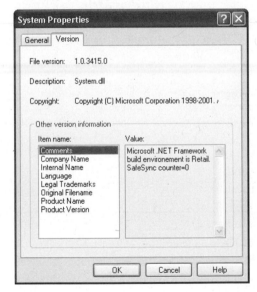

Figure 3-4   Version tab of the System Properties dialog box

Last but not least, you can drag an assembly file that contains a manifest and drop the file in Explorer's window. When you do this, the shell extension installs the assembly's files into the GAC. For some developers, this is an easier way to install assemblies into the GAC for testing instead of using the GACUtil.exe tool.

If you want to use Explorer to examine the GAC's native directory structure you can disable the ShFusion.dll shell extension via registry settings. Just open RegEdit.exe and navigate to HKEY_LOCAL_MACHINE\Software\Microsoft\Fusion subkey. Then, add a DWORD value called DisableCache-Viewer and set this value to 1.

The Internal Structure of the GAC

Simply stated, the purpose of the GAC is to maintain a relationship between a strongly named assembly and a subdirectory. Basically, the CLR has an internal function that takes an assembly's name, version, culture, and public key token. This function then returns the path of a subdirectory where the specified assembly's files can be found.

If you go to a command prompt and change into the C:\Windows\Assembly\GAC directory, you'll see several subdirectories, one for each assembly that has been installed into the GAC. Here's what my GAC directory looks like (with some of the directories deleted to save trees):

```
 Volume in drive C has no label.
 Volume Serial Number is 94FA-5DE7

 Directory of C:\WINDOWS\assembly\GAC

07/15/2002  05:07 PM    <DIR>          .
07/15/2002  05:07 PM    <DIR>          ..
07/15/2002  03:09 PM    <DIR>          Accessibility
07/15/2002  05:06 PM    <DIR>          ADODB
07/03/2002  04:54 PM    <DIR>          CRVsPackageLib
07/15/2002  05:06 PM    <DIR>          Microsoft.ComCtl2
07/15/2002  05:06 PM    <DIR>          Microsoft.ComctlLib
07/15/2002  05:05 PM    <DIR>          Microsoft.JScript
07/15/2002  05:07 PM    <DIR>          Microsoft.mshtml
07/15/2002  05:06 PM    <DIR>          Microsoft.MSMAPI
07/15/2002  05:06 PM    <DIR>          Microsoft.MSMask
07/15/2002  05:07 PM    <DIR>          Microsoft.MSRDC
07/15/2002  05:07 PM    <DIR>          Microsoft.MSWinsockLib
07/15/2002  05:07 PM    <DIR>          Microsoft.MSWLess
07/15/2002  05:07 PM    <DIR>          Microsoft.PicClip
07/15/2002  05:07 PM    <DIR>          Microsoft.RichTextLib
07/15/2002  05:06 PM    <DIR>          Microsoft.StdFormat
```

```
07/15/2002  05:07 PM    <DIR>          Microsoft.SysInfoLib
07/15/2002  05:07 PM    <DIR>          Microsoft.TabDlg
07/15/2002  05:05 PM    <DIR>          Microsoft.VisualBasic
07/15/2002  03:09 PM    <DIR>          System
07/15/2002  03:09 PM    <DIR>          System.Configuration.Install
07/15/2002  03:09 PM    <DIR>          System.Data
07/15/2002  03:09 PM    <DIR>          System.Design
07/15/2002  03:09 PM    <DIR>          System.DirectoryServices
07/15/2002  03:09 PM    <DIR>          System.Drawing
07/15/2002  03:09 PM    <DIR>          System.Drawing.Design
07/15/2002  03:08 PM    <DIR>          System.EnterpriseServices
07/15/2002  03:09 PM    <DIR>          System.Management
07/15/2002  03:09 PM    <DIR>          System.Messaging
07/15/2002  03:09 PM    <DIR>          System.Runtime.Remoting
07/15/2002  03:08 PM    <DIR>          System.Security
07/15/2002  03:09 PM    <DIR>          System.ServiceProcess
07/15/2002  03:09 PM    <DIR>          System.Web
07/15/2002  03:09 PM    <DIR>          System.Web.RegularExpressions
07/15/2002  03:09 PM    <DIR>          System.Web.Services
07/15/2002  03:09 PM    <DIR>          System.Windows.Forms
07/15/2002  03:09 PM    <DIR>          System.Xml
               0 File(s)              0 bytes
              95 Dir(s)  14,798,938,112 bytes free
```

If you change into one of these directories, you'll see one or more additional subdirectories. My System directory looks like this:

```
Volume in drive C has no label.
 Volume Serial Number is 94FA-5DE7

 Directory of C:\WINDOWS\assembly\GAC\System

07/15/2002  03:09 PM    <DIR>          .
07/15/2002  03:09 PM    <DIR>          ..
07/15/2002  03:09 PM    <DIR>          1.0.3300.0__b77a5c561934e089
               0 File(s)              0 bytes
               3 Dir(s)  14,798,929,920 bytes free
```

The System directory contains one subdirectory for every System.dll assembly installed on the machine. In my case, just one version of the System.dll assembly is installed:

```
"System,Version=1.0.3300.0,Culture=neutral,PublicKeyToken=b77a5c561934e089"
```

The attributes are separated by underscore characters and are in the form of *"(Version)_(Culture)_(PublicKeyToken)"*. In this example, there is no culture information, making the culture neutral. Inside this subdirectory are the files (such as System.dll) making up this strongly named version of the System assembly.

> **Important**   It should be obvious that the whole point of the GAC is to hold multiple versions of an assembly. For example, the GAC can contain version 1.0.0.0 and version 2.0.0.0 of Calculus.dll. If an application is built and tested using version 1.0.0.0 of Calculus.dll, the CLR will load version 1.0.0.0 of Calculus.dll for that application even though a later version of the assembly exists and is installed into the GAC. This is the CLR's default policy in regard to loading assembly versions, and the benefit of this policy is that installing a new version of an assembly won't affect an already installed application. You can affect this policy in a number of ways that I'll discuss later in this chapter.

Building an Assembly That References a Strongly Named Assembly

Whenever you build an assembly, the assembly will have references to other strongly named assemblies. This is true if only because `System.Object` is defined in MSCorLib.dll. However, it's likely that an assembly will reference types in other strongly named assemblies published either by Microsoft, by a third party, or by your own organization.

In Chapter 2, I showed you how to use VBC.exe's `/reference` command-line switch to specify the assembly filenames you want to reference. If the filename is a full path, VBC.exe loads the specified file and uses its metadata information to build the assembly. If you specify a filename without a path, VBC.exe attempts to find the assembly by looking in the following directories (in order of their presentation here):

1. The working directory.

2. The directory that contains the CLR that the compiler itself is using to produce the resulting assembly. MSCorLib.dll is always obtained from this directory. This directory has a path similar to the following:

   C:\WINDOWS\Microsoft.NET\Framework\v1.0.3427

3. Any directories specified using VBC.exe's `/libpath` command-line switch.

4. Any directories specified by the `LIB` environment variable.

So if you're building an assembly that references Microsoft's System.Drawing.dll, you can specify the `/reference:System.Drawing.dll` switch when invoking VBC.exe. The compiler will examine the directories shown earlier and will find the System.Drawing.dll file in the directory that contains the CLR that the compiler itself is using to produce the assembly. Even though this is the directory where the assembly is found at compile time, this isn't the directory where the assembly will be loaded from at run time.

You see, when you install the .NET Framework, it installs two copies of Microsoft's assembly files. One set is installed into the CLR directory, and another set is installed into the GAC. The files in the CLR directory exist so that you can easily build your assembly. The copies in the GAC exist so that they can be loaded at run time.

The reason that VBC.exe doesn't look in the GAC for referenced assemblies is because you'd have to specify a long, ugly path to the assembly file—something like C:\WINDOWS\Assembly\GAC\System.Drawing\ 1.0.3300.0__b03f5f7f11d50a3a\System.Drawing.dll. Alternatively, VBC.exe could allow you to specify a still long but slightly nicer-looking string, such as "System.Drawing, Version=1.0.3300.0, Culture=neutral, PublicKey-Token=b03f5f7f11d50a3a". Both of these solutions were deemed worse than having the assembly files installed twice on the user's hard drive.

Before leaving this section, I should also talk about *response files*. A response file is a text file that contains a set of compiler command-line switches. When you execute VBC.exe, the compiler opens response files and uses any switches that are specified in them as though the switches were passed on the command line. You instruct the compiler to use a response file by specifying its name on the command line prepended by an @ sign. For example, you could have a response file called MyProject.rsp that contains the following text:

```
/out:MyProject.exe
/target:winexe
```

To have VBC.exe use these settings, you'd invoke it as follows:

```
vbc.exe @MyProject.rsp CodeFile1.vb CodeFile2.vb
```

This tells the Visual Basic compiler what to name the output file and what kind of target to create. As you can see, response files are very convenient because you don't have to manually express the desired command-line arguments each time you want to compile your project.

Strongly Named Assemblies Are Tamper-Resistant

Signing a file with a private key ensures that the holder of the corresponding public key produced the assembly. When the assembly is installed into the GAC, the system hashes the contents of the file containing the manifest and compares the hash value with the RSA digital signature value embedded within the PE file (after unsigning it with the public key). If the values are identical, the file's contents haven't been tampered with and you know that you have the public key that corresponds to the publisher's private key. In addition, the system hashes the contents of the assembly's other files and compares the hash values with the hash values stored in the manifest file's FileDef table. If any of the hash values don't match, at least one of the assembly's files has been tampered with and the assembly will fail to install into the GAC.

> **Important**   This mechanism ensures only that a file's contents haven't been tampered with; the mechanism doesn't allow you to tell who the publisher is unless you're absolutely positive that the publisher produced the public key you have and you're sure that the publisher's private key was never compromised. If the publisher wants to associate its identity with the assembly, the publisher must use Microsoft's Authenticode technology in addition.

When an application needs to bind to an assembly, the CLR uses the referenced assembly's properties (name, version, culture, and public key) to locate the assembly in the GAC. If the referenced assembly can be found, its containing subdirectory is returned and the file holding the manifest is loaded. Finding the assembly this way assures the caller that the assembly loaded at run time came from the same publisher that built the assembly the code was compiled against. This assurance comes because the public key token in the referencing assembly's AssemblyRef table corresponds to the public key in the referenced assembly's AssemblyDef table. If the referenced assembly isn't in the GAC, the CLR looks in the application's base directory and then in any of the private paths identified in the application's configuration file; then, if the application was installed using MSI, the CLR asks MSI to locate the assembly. If the assembly can't be found in any of these locations, the bind fails and a `System.IO.FileNotFoundException` exception is thrown.

When strongly named assembly files are loaded from a location other than the GAC (for example, via the AppBase directory or via a `codeBase` element in a configuration file), the CLR compares hash values when the assembly is loaded. In other words, a hash of the file is performed every time an application executes. This performance hit is required to be certain that the assembly file's content hasn't been tampered with. When the CLR detects mismatched hash values at run time, it throws a `System.IO.FileLoadException` exception.

Delayed Signing

Earlier in this chapter, I discussed how the SN.exe tool can produce public/private key pairs. This tool generates the keys by making calls into the Crypto API provided by Windows. These keys can be stored in files or other "storage devices." For example, large organizations (such as Microsoft) will maintain the returned private key in a hardware device that stays locked in a safe; only a few people in the company have access to the private key. This precaution prevents the private key from being compromised and ensures the key's integrity. The public key is, well, public and freely distributed.

When you're ready to package your strongly named assembly, you'll have to use the secure private key to sign it. However, while developing and testing your assembly, gaining access to the secure private key can be a hassle. For this reason, the .NET Framework supports *delayed signing*, sometimes referred to as *partial signing*. Delayed signing allows you to build an assembly using only your company's public key; the private key isn't necessary. Using the public key allows assemblies that reference your assembly to embed the correct public key value in their AssemblyRef metadata entries. It also allows the assembly to be placed in the GAC's internal structure appropriately. If you don't sign the file with your company's private key, you lose all the tampering protection afforded to you because the assembly's files won't be hashed and a digital signature won't be embedded in the file. This loss of protection shouldn't be a problem, however, because you use delayed signing only while developing your own assembly, not when you're ready to package and deploy the assembly.

Basically, you get your company's public key value in a file and pass the filename to whatever utility you use to build the assembly. (You can use SN.exe's –p switch to extract a public key from a file that contains a public/private key pair.) You must also tell the tool that you want the assembly to be delay signed, meaning that you're not supplying a private key. In source code, you can apply the `AssemblyKeyFileAttribute` and `DelaySignAttribute` attributes to specify these things. If you're using AL.exe, you can specify the `/keyf[ile]` and `/delay[sign]` command-line switches.

When the compiler or AL.exe detects that you're delay signing an assembly, it will emit the assembly's AssemblyDef manifest entry and this entry will contain the assembly's public key. Again, the presence of the public key allows the assembly to be placed in the GAC. It also allows you to build other assemblies that reference this assembly; the referencing assemblies will have the correct public key in their AssembyRef metadata table entries. When creating the resulting assembly, space is left in the resulting PE file for the RSA digital signature. (The utility can determine how much space is necessary from the size of the public key.) Note that the file's contents won't be hashed at this time either.

At this point, the resulting assembly doesn't have a valid signature. Attempting to install the assembly into the GAC will fail because a hash of the file's contents hasn't been done—the file appears to have been tampered with. To install the assembly into the GAC, you must prevent the system from verifying the integrity of the assembly's files. To do this, you use the SN.exe utility specifying the –**Vr** command-line switch. Executing SN.exe with this switch also tells the CLR to skip checking hash values for any of the assembly's files when loaded at run time.

When you're finished developing and testing the assembly, you'll need to officially sign it so that you can package and deploy it. To sign the assembly, use the SN.exe utility again, this time with the –**R** switch and the name of the file that contains the actual private key. The –**R** switch causes SN.exe to hash the file's contents, sign it with the private key, and embed the RSA digital signature in the file where the space for it had previously been reserved. After this step, you can deploy the fully signed assembly. You can also turn verification of this assembly back on by using SN.exe's –**Vu** or –**Vx** command-line switch.

The following list summarizes the steps discussed in this section to develop your assembly by using the delay signing technique:

1. While developing an assembly, obtain a file that contains only your company's public key and add the following two attributes to your source code:

    ```
    ' Specify the full pathname for the file if using Visual Studio .NET
    <Assembly:AssemblyKeyFile("MyCompanyPublicKey.keys")>
    <Assembly:DelaySign(True)>
    ```

2. After building the assembly, execute the following line so that you can install it in the GAC, build other assemblies that reference the assembly, and test the assembly. Note that you have to do this only once; it's not necessary to perform this step each time you build your assembly.

    ```
    SN.exe -Vr MyAssembly.dll
    ```

3. When ready to package and deploy the assembly, obtain your company's private key and execute the following line:

```
SN.exe -R MyAssembly.dll MyCompanyPrivateKey.keys
```

4. To test, turn verification back on by executing the following line:

```
SN -Vu MyAssembly.dll
```

At the beginning of this section, I mentioned how organizations keep their key pairs in a hardware device, such as a smart card. To keep these keys secure, you must make sure the key values are never persisted in a disk file. Cryptographic service providers (CSPs) offer "containers" that abstract the location of these keys. Microsoft, for example, uses a CSP that has a container that, when accessed, grabs the private key from a smart card.

If your public/private key pair is in a CSP container, don't use the **AssemblyKeyFileAttribute** attribute or AL.exe's **/keyf[ile]** switch. Instead, use the **System.Reflection.AssemblyKeyNameAttribute** attribute or AL.exe's **/keyn[ame]** switch. When using SN.exe to add the private key to the delay signed assembly, you specify the **–Rc** switch instead of the **–R** switch. SN.exe offers additional switches that allow you to perform operations with a CSP.

> **Important** Delay signing is useful whenever you want to perform some other operation to an assembly before you deploy it. For example, because an assembly is just a normal Windows PE file, you might want to consider rebasing the load address for the file. To do this, you can use the normal Rebase.exe tool that ships with the Microsoft Win32 Platform SDK. You can't rebase a file after it's been fully signed because the hash values will be incorrect. So, if you want to rebase an assembly file or do any other type of post-build operation, you should use delay signing, perform the post-build operation, and then run SN.exe with the –R or –Rc switch to complete the signing of the assembly with all its hashing.

Here's the AssemInfo.vb file I use for all my personal projects:

```vb
'***************************************************************************
' Module:  AssemInfo.vb
' Notices: Copyright (c) 2003 Jeffrey Richter
'***************************************************************************/

Imports System.Reflection

'///////////////////////////////////////////////////////////////////////////

' Set the version CompanyName, LegalCopyright, and LegalTrademarks fields.
<Assembly:AssemblyCompany("The Jeffrey Richter Company")>
<Assembly:AssemblyCopyright("Copyright (c) 2002 Jeffrey Richter")>
<Assembly:AssemblyTrademark( _
    "JeffTypes is a registered trademark of the Richter Company")>

'///////////////////////////////////////////////////////////////////////////

' Set the version ProductName and ProductVersion fields.
<Assembly:AssemblyProduct("Jeffrey Richter Type Library")>
<Assembly:AssemblyInformationalVersion("2.0.0.0")>

'///////////////////////////////////////////////////////////////////////////

' Set the version FileVersion, AssemblyVersion,
' FileDescription, and Comments fields.
<Assembly:AssemblyFileVersion("1.0.0.0")>
<Assembly:AssemblyVersion("3.0.0.0")>
<Assembly:AssemblyTitle("Jeff's type assembly")>
<Assembly:AssemblyDescription("This assembly contains Jeff's types")>

'///////////////////////////////////////////////////////////////////////////

' Set the assembly's culture (""=neutral).
<Assembly:AssemblyCulture("")>

'///////////////////////////////////////////////////////////////////////////

#If Not StronglyNamedAssembly Then

' Weakly named assemblies are never signed.
<Assembly:AssemblyDelaySign(False)>

#Else

' Strongly named assemblies are usually delay signed while building and
' completely signed using SN.exe's -R or -Rc switch.
<Assembly:AssemblyDelaySign(True)>

    #If Not SignedUsingACryptoServiceProvider Then
```

```
' Give the name of the file that contains the public/private key pair.
' If delay signing, only the public key is used.
<Assembly:AssemblyKeyFile("MyCompany.keys")>

' Note: If AssemblyKeyFile and AssemblyKeyName are both specified,
' here's what happens...
' 1) If the container exists, the key file is ignored.
' 2) If the container doesn't exist, the keys from the key
'    file are copied into the container and the assembly is signed.

#Else

' Give the name of the cryptographic service provider (CSP) container
' that contains the public/private key pair.
' If delay signing, only the public key is used.
<Assembly:AssemblyKeyName("")>

#End If

#End If

'//////////////////////////// End of File ////////////////////////////////
```

When you create a new project with Visual Studio .NET, it automatically creates a new AssemblyInfo.vb file that is similar to the set of attributes shown here in my file. I prefer my file because my comments better describe what's going on and how the attributes map to the version resource information. In addition, the Visual Studio .NET AssemblyInfo.vb file initializes the **Assembly-Version** attribute incorrectly to "1.0.*", telling VBC.exe to generate build and revision version numbers automatically with each build. Having a different version for each build of your assembly prevents the CLR from loading your assembly when any previously built assemblies that reference an older version number need it.

Privately Deploying Strongly Named Assemblies

Installing assemblies into the GAC offers several benefits. The GAC enables many applications to share assemblies, reducing physical memory usage on a whole. In addition, it's easy to deploy a new version of the assembly into the GAC and have all applications use the new version via a publisher policy (described later in this chapter). The GAC also provides side-by-side management for an assembly's different versions. However, the GAC is usually secured so that only an administrator can install an assembly into it. Also, installing into the GAC breaks the simple copy deployment story.

While strongly named assemblies can be installed into the GAC, they certainly don't have to be. In fact, it's recommended that you deploy assemblies into the GAC only if the assembly is intended to be shared by many applications. If an assembly isn't intended to be shared, it should be deployed privately. Deploying privately preserves the "simple" copy install deployment story and better isolates the application and its assemblies. Also, the GAC isn't intended to be the new C:\Windows\System32 dumping ground for common files. The reason is because new versions of assemblies don't overwrite each other; they are installed side by side, eating up disk space.

> **Note**   When a strongly named assembly is installed into the GAC, the system ensures that the file containing the manifest hasn't been tampered with. This check occurs only once: at installation time. On the other hand, when a strongly named assembly is loaded from a directory other than the GAC, the CLR verifies the assembly's manifest file to ensure that the file's contents have not been tampered with. This additional performance hit occurs every time this file is loaded.

In addition to deploying a strongly named assembly in the GAC or privately, a strongly named assembly can be deployed to some arbitrary directory that a small set of applications know about. For example, you might be producing three applications, all of which want to share a strongly named assembly. Upon installation, you can create three directories: one for each application and an additional directory for the assembly you want shared. When you install each application into its directory, also install an XML configuration file and have the shared assembly's **codeBase** element indicate the path of the shared assembly. Now, at run time, the CLR will know to look in the strongly named assembly's directory for the shared assembly. For the record, this technique is rarely used and is somewhat discouraged because no single application controls when the assembly's files should be uninstalled.

Note   The configuration file's `codeBase` element actually identifies a URL. This URL can refer to any directory on the user's hard disk or to a Web address. In the case of a Web address, the CLR will automatically download the file and store it in the user's download cache (a subdirectory under C:\Documents and Settings\UserName\Local Settings\Application Data\Assembly\DL). When referenced in the future, the CLR will load the assembly from this directory rather than access the URL. An example of a configuration file containing a `code-Base` element is shown later in this chapter.

For example, on my machine, I have a downloaded assembly contained in the following path: c:\Documents and Settings\ JeffreyR\Local Settings\Application Data\Assembly\DL\ 3e8fa4cf1271d8f20dbc6c1fc577516c\92e54152\80ecc145_8fb6c101. The first subdirectory under DL is a cryptographically generated random string that only the CLR is aware of. This string is randomly generated to prevent malicious code from determining the exact location of the download assembly cache. (In a future version of the CLR, two subdirectories will be used for the random string since a single directory isn't as secure when you consider that there is an 8.3 equivalent for the long directory name.) The second subdirectory under DL is a hash value generated from the source URL. The third subdirectory under DL represents the timestamp when the assembly file's bits were last modified; the CLR uses this to ensure that all files of an assembly are placed in a single directory.

By default, a user's download cache can contain files occupying up to 50,000 KB. When adding files into the user's download cache, the CLR checks this quota, and if the quota is reached, the CLR deletes files by using a least-recently-used (LRU) algorithm. You can adjust the quota size by creating or modifying a DownloadCache-QuotaInKB DWORD registry value. This value can exist under the following two registry subkeys:

```
HKEY_LOCAL_MACHINE\SOFTWARE\Microsoft\Fusion
HKEY_CURRENT_USER\Software\Microsoft\Fusion
```

If the DownloadCacheQuotaInKB registry value exists in both registry subkeys, the CLR uses the smaller value of the two values.

Side-by-Side Execution

The strong versioning story presented here means that an assembly, App.exe, could bind to version 2.0.0.0 of a Calculus.dll assembly and version 3.0.0.0 of an AdvMath.dll assembly. The AdvMath.dll assembly could in turn bind to version 1.0.0.0 of a Calculus.dll assembly. Take a look at Figure 3-5.

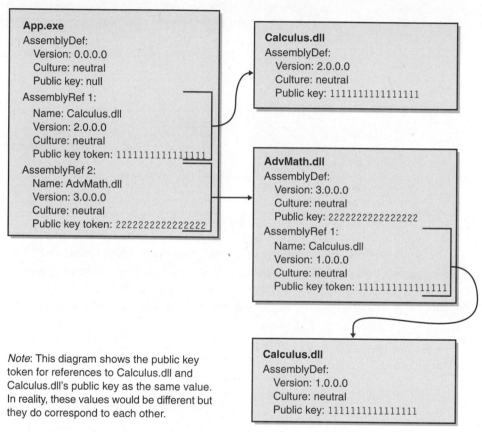

Note: This diagram shows the public key token for references to Calculus.dll and Calculus.dll's public key as the same value. In reality, these values would be different but they do correspond to each other.

Figure 3-5 An application that requires different versions of the Calculus.dll assembly in order to run

The CLR has the ability to load multiple files with the same name but with different paths into a single address space. This is called *side-by-side execution*, a key component for solving the Windows DLL hell problem.

> **Important** The ability to execute DLLs side by side is awesome because it allows you to create new versions of your assembly that don't have to maintain backward compatibility. Not having to maintain backward compatibility reduces coding and testing time for a product and allows you to get the product to market faster.

The developer must be aware of this side-by-side mechanism so that subtle bugs don't appear. For example, an assembly could create a named Win32 file-mapping kernel object and use the storage provided by this object. Another version of the assembly could also get loaded and attempt to create a file-mapping kernel object with the same name. This second assembly won't get new storage but will instead access the same storage allocated by the first assembly. If not carefully coded, the two assemblies will stomp all over each other's data and the application will perform unpredictably.

How the Runtime Resolves Type References

At the beginning of Chapter 2, you saw the following source code:

```
Public Class App
    Public Shared Sub Main()
        System.Console.WriteLine("Hi")
    End Sub
End Class
```

This code is compiled and built into an assembly, say App.exe. When you run this application, the CLR loads and initializes. Then the CLR reads the assembly's CLR header looking for the MethodDefToken that identifies the application's entry point method (**Main**). From the MethodDef metadata table, the offset within the file for the method's IL code is located and JIT-compiled into native code, which includes having the code verified for type safety, and the native code starts executing. Following is the IL code for the **Main** method. To obtain this output, I ran ILDasm.exe, selected the View menu's Show Bytes menu item, and double-clicked the **Main** method in the tree view.

```
.method public static void  Main() cil managed
// SIG: 00 00 01
{
  .entrypoint
  .custom instance void [mscorlib]System.STAThreadAttribute::.ctor() =
      ( 01 00 00 00 )
  // Method begins at RVA 0x2058
  // Code size       11 (0xb)
  .maxstack  8
  IL_0000:  /* 72  | (70)000001      */ ldstr      "Hi"
  IL_0005:  /* 28  | (0A)000002      */
call         void [mscorlib]System.Console::WriteLine(string)
  IL_000a:  /* 2A  |                 */ ret
} // End of method App::Main
```

When JIT-compiling this code, the CLR detects all references to types and members and loads their defining assemblies (if not already loaded). As you can see, the IL code above has a reference to **System.Console.WriteLine**. Specifically, the IL **call** instruction references metadata token 0A000002. This token identifies an entry in the MemberRef metadata table. The CLR looks up this MemberRef entry and sees that one of its fields refers to an entry in a Type-Ref table (the **System.Console** type). From the TypeRef entry, the CLR is directed to an AssemblyRef entry: "MSCorLib, Version=1.0.3300.0, Culture="neutral", PublicKeyToken=b77a5c561934e089". At this point, the CLR knows which assembly it needs. Now the CLR must locate the assembly in order to load it.

When resolving a referenced type, the CLR can find the type in one of three places:

■ **Same file**   Access to a type that is in the same file is determined at compile time (sometimes referred to as *early bound*). The type is loaded out of the file directly, and execution continues.

■ **Different file, same assembly**   The CLR ensures that the file being referenced is, in fact, in the assembly's FileRef table of the current assembly's manifest. The CLR then looks in the directory where the assembly's manifest file was loaded. The file is loaded, its hash value is checked to ensure the file's integrity, the type's member is found, and execution continues.

■ **Different file, different assembly**   When a referenced type is in a different assembly's file, the CLR loads the file that contains the referenced assembly's manifest. If this file doesn't contain the type, the appropriate file is loaded. The type's member is found, and execution continues.

> **Note**   The ModuleDef, ModuleRef, and FileDef metadata tables refer to files using the file's name and its extension. However, the AssemblyRef metadata table refers to assemblies by filename, without an extension. When binding to an assembly, the system automatically appends .dll and .exe file extensions while attempting to locate the file by probing the directories as mentioned in the section "Simple Administrative Control (Configuration)" in Chapter 2.

If any errors occur while resolving a type reference—file can't be found, file can't be loaded, hash mismatch, and so on—an appropriate exception is thrown.

In the previous example, the CLR sees that `System.Console` is implemented in a different assembly than the caller. The CLR must search for the assembly and load the PE file that contains the assembly's manifest. The manifest is then scanned to determine the PE file that implements the type. If the manifest file contains the referenced type, all is well. If the type is in another of the assembly's files, the CLR loads the other file and scans its metadata to locate the type. The CLR then creates its internal data structures to represent the type, and the JIT compiler completes the compilation for the `Main` method. Finally, the `Main` method can start executing.

Figure 3-6 illustrates how type binding occurs.

> **Important**   Strictly speaking, the example just described isn't 100 percent correct. For references to methods and types defined in an assembly other than MSCorLib.dll, the discussion is correct. However, MSCorLib.dll is closely tied to the version of the CLR that's running. Any assembly that references MSCorLib.dll (with the ECMA public key token of "b77a5c561934e089") always binds to the version of MSCorLib.dll that is in the same directory that contains the CLR itself. So in the previous example, the reference to `System.Console`'s `WriteLine` method binds to whatever version of MSCorLib.dll matches the version of the CLR, regardless of what version of MSCorLib.dll is referenced in the assembly's AssemblyRef metadata table.

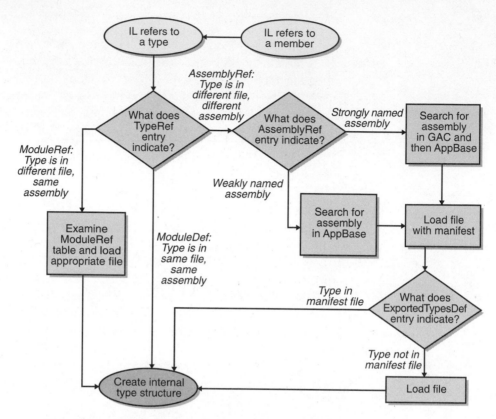

Figure 3-6   Flowchart showing how the CLR uses metadata to locate the proper assembly file that defines a type, given IL code that refers to a method or type

In this section, you saw how the CLR locates an assembly when using default policies. However, an administrator or the publisher of an assembly can override the default policy. In the next two sections, I'll describe how to alter the CLR's default binding policy.

Advanced Administrative Control (Configuration)

In the section "Simple Administrative Control (Configuration)" in Chapter 2, I gave a brief introduction to how an administrator can affect the way the CLR searches and binds to assemblies. In that section, I demonstrated how a referenced assembly's files can be moved to a subdirectory of the application's base directory and how the CLR uses the application's XML configuration file to locate the moved files.

Having discussed only the probing element's **privatePath** attribute in Chapter 2, I'm going to discuss the other XML configuration file elements in this section. Following is an XML configuration file:

```xml
<?xml version="1.0" encoding="utf-8" ?>
<configuration>
   <runtime>
      <assemblyBinding xmlns="urn:schemas-microsoft-com:asm.v1">
         <probing privatePath="AuxFiles;bin\subdir" />

         <dependentAssembly>

            <assemblyIdentity name="JeffTypes"
               publicKeyToken="32ab4ba45e0a69a1" culture="neutral"/>

            <bindingRedirect
               oldVersion="1.0.0.0" newVersion="2.0.0.0" />

            <codeBase version="2.0.0.0"
               href="http://www.Wintellect.com/JeffTypes.dll" />

         </dependentAssembly>

         <dependentAssembly>

            <assemblyIdentity name="FredTypes"
               publicKeyToken="1f2e74e897abbcfe" culture="neutral"/>

            <bindingRedirect
               oldVersion="3.0.0.0-3.5.0.0" newVersion="4.0.0.0" />

            <publisherPolicy apply="no" />

         </dependentAssembly>

      </assemblyBinding>
   </runtime>
</configuration>
```

This XML file gives a wealth of information to the CLR. Here's what it says:

■ **probing element** Look in the application base directory's AuxFiles and bin\subdir subdirectories when trying to find a weakly named assembly. For strongly named assemblies, the CLR looks in the GAC or in the URL specified by the **codeBase** element. The CLR looks in the application's private paths for a strongly named assembly only if no `codeBase` element is specified.

- **First `dependentAssembly`, `assemblyIdentity`, and `bindingRedirect` elements** When attempting to locate version 1.0.0.0 of the neutral culture JeffTypes assembly published by the organization that controls the `32ab4ba45e0a69a1` public key token, locate version 2.0.0.0 of the same assembly instead.

- **`codeBase` element** When attempting to locate version 2.0.0.0 of the neutral culture JeffTypes assembly published by the organization that controls the `32ab4ba45e0a69a1` public key token, try to find it at the following URL: http://www.Wintellect.com/JeffTypes.dll. Although I didn't mention it in Chapter 2, a `codeBase` element can also be used with weakly named assemblies. In this case, the assembly's version number is ignored and should be omitted from the XML's `codeBase` element. Also, the `codeBase` URL must refer to a directory under the application's base directory.

- **Second `dependentAssembly`, `assemblyIdentity`, and `bindingRedirect` elements** When attempting to locate version 3.0.0.0 through version 3.5.0.0 inclusive of the neutral culture FredTypes assembly published by the organization that controls the `1f2e74e897abbcfe` public key token, locate version 4.0.0.0 of the same assembly instead.

- **`publisherPolicy` element** If the organization that produces the FredTypes assembly has deployed a publisher policy file (described in the next section), the CLR should ignore this file.

When compiling a method, the CLR determines the types and members being referenced. Using this information, the CLR determines—by looking in the referencing assembly's AssemblyRef table—what assembly was originally referenced when the calling assembly was built. The CLR then looks up the assembly in the application's configuration file and applies any version number redirections.

If the `publisherPolicy` element's `apply` attribute is set to `yes`—or if the element is omitted—the CLR examines the GAC and applies any version number redirections that the publisher of the assembly feels is necessary. I'll talk more about publisher policy in the next section.

The CLR then looks up the assembly in the machine's Machine.config file and applies any version number redirections there. Finally, the CLR knows the version of the assembly that it should load, and it attempts to load the assembly from the GAC. If the assembly isn't in the GAC and if there is no `codeBase` element, the CLR probes for the assembly as I described in Chapter 2. If the configuration file that performs the last redirection also contains a `codeBase` element, the CLR attempts to load the assembly from the `codeBase` element's specified URL.

Using these configuration files, an administrator can really control what assembly the CLR decides to load. If an application is experiencing a bug, the administrator can contact the publisher of the errant assembly. The publisher can send the administrator a new assembly that the administrator can install. By default, the CLR won't load this new assembly since the already built assemblies don't reference the new version. However, the administrator can modify the application's XML configuration file to instruct the CLR to load the new assembly.

If the administrator wants all applications on the machine to pick up the new assembly, the administrator can modify the machine's Machine.config file instead and the CLR will load the new assembly whenever an application refers to the old assembly.

If the new assembly doesn't fix the original bug, the administrator can delete the binding redirection lines from the configuration file and the application will behave as it did before. It's important to note that the system allows the use of an assembly that doesn't exactly match the assembly version recorded in the metadata. This extra flexibility is very handy. Later in this chapter, I'll go into more detail about how an administrator can easily repair an application.

The .NET Framework Configuration Tool

If you don't like manually editing XML text files—and who does?—you can use the .NET Framework Configuration tool, which ships with the .NET Framework. Open Control Panel, select Administrative Tools, and then select the Microsoft .NET Framework Configuration tool. While in the tool, you can select Configure An Assembly, which causes an assembly's Properties dialog box to pop up. From within this dialog box, you can set all of the XML configuration information. Figures 3-7, 3-8, and 3-9 show different pages of an assembly's Properties dialog box.

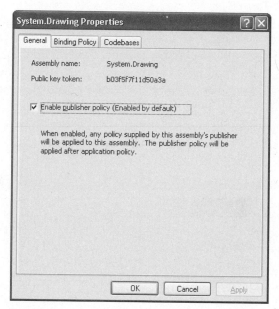

Figure 3-7   General tab of the System.Drawing Properties dialog box

The .NET Framework Configuration Tool   *(continued)*

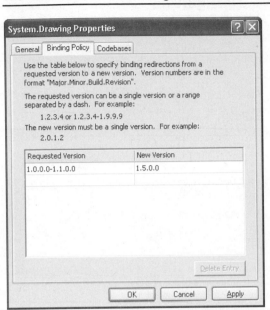

Figure 3-8   Binding Policy tab of the System.Drawing Properties dialog box

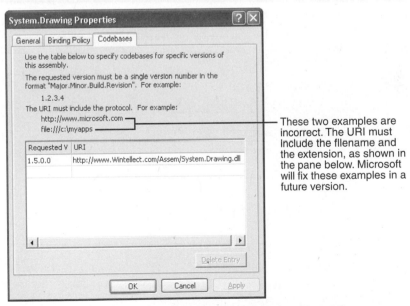

These two examples are incorrect. The URI must include the filename and the extension, as shown in the pane below. Microsoft will fix these examples in a future version.

Figure 3-9   Codebases tab of the System.Drawing Properties dialog box

Publisher Policy Control

In the scenario described in the previous section, the publisher of an assembly simply sent a new version of the assembly to the administrator, who installed the assembly and manually edited the application's or machine's XML configuration files. In general, when a publisher fixes a bug in an assembly, she would like an easy way to package and distribute the new assembly to all the users. But she also needs a way to tell each user's CLR to use the new assembly version instead of the old assembly version. Sure, each user could modify his application's or machine's XML configuration file, but this is terribly inconvenient and is error-prone. What the publisher needs is a way to create "policy information" that is installed on the user's computer when the new assembly is installed. In this section, I'll show how an assembly's publisher can create this policy information.

Let's say you're a publisher of an assembly and that you've just created a new version of your assembly that fixes some bugs. When you package your new assembly to send out to all your users, you should also create an XML configuration file. This configuration file looks just like the configuration files we've been talking about. Here's an example file (called JeffTypes.config) for the Jeff-Types.dll assembly:

```
<configuration>
   <runtime>
      <assemblyBinding xmlns="urn:schemas-microsoft-com:asm.v1">
         <dependentAssembly>

            <assemblyIdentity name="JeffTypes"
               publicKeyToken="32ab4ba45e0a69a1" culture="neutral"/>

            <bindingRedirect
               oldVersion="1.0.0.0" newVersion="2.0.0.0" />

            <codeBase version="2.0.0.0"
               href="http://www.Wintellect.com/JeffTypes.dll" />

         </dependentAssembly>
      </assemblyBinding>
   </runtime>
</configuration>
```

Of course, a publisher can set policy only for the assemblies that it itself creates. In addition, the elements shown here are the only elements that can be specified in a publisher policy configuration file; you can't specify the **probing** or **publisherPolicy** elements, for example.

This configuration file tells the CLR to load version 2.0.0.0 of the JeffTypes assembly whenever version 1.0.0.0 of the assembly is referenced. Now you, the publisher, can create an assembly that contains this publisher policy configuration file. You create the publisher policy assembly by running AL.exe as follows:

```
AL.exe /out:policy.1.0.JeffTypes.dll
       /version:1.0.0.0
       /keyfile:MyCompany.keys
       /linkresource:JeffTypes.config
```

Let me explain the meaning of AL.exe's command-line switches:

- **The /out switch**   This switch tells AL.exe to create a new PE file, called Policy.1.0.JeffTypes.dll, which contains nothing but a manifest. The name of this assembly is very important. The first part of the name, Policy, tells the CLR that this assembly contains publisher policy information. The second and third parts of the name, 1.0, tell the CLR that this publisher policy assembly is for any version of the Jeff-Types assembly that has a major and minor version of 1.0. Publisher policies apply to the major and minor version numbers of an assembly only; you can't create a publisher policy that is specific to individual builds or revisions of an assembly. The fourth part of the name, JeffTypes, indicates the name of the assembly that this publisher policy corresponds to. The fifth and last part of the name, dll, is simply the extension given to the resulting assembly file.

- **The /version switch**   This switch identifies the version of the publisher policy assembly; this version number has nothing to do with the JeffTypes assembly itself. You see, publisher policy assemblies can also be versioned. Today, the publisher might create a publisher policy redirecting version 1.0.0.0 of JeffTypes to version 2.0.0.0. In the future, the publisher might want to direct version 1.0.0.0 of JeffTypes to version 2.5.0.0. The CLR uses this version number so that it knows to pick up the latest version of the publisher policy assembly.

- **The /keyfile switch**   This switch causes AL.exe to sign the publisher policy assembly using the publisher's public/private key pair. This key pair must also match the key pair used for all versions of the JeffTypes assembly. After all, this is how the CLR knows that the same publisher created both the JeffTypes assembly and this publisher policy file.

■ **The /linkresource switch** This switch tells AL.exe that the XML configuration file is to be considered a separate file of the assembly. The resulting assembly consists of two files, both of which must be packaged and deployed to the users along with the new version of the JeffTypes assembly. By the way, you can't use AL.exe's **/embed-resource** switch to embed the XML configuration file into the assembly file, making a single file assembly, because the CLR requires that the XML file be contained in its own, separate file.

Once this publisher policy assembly is built, it can be packaged together with the new JeffTypes.dll assembly file and deployed to users. The publisher policy assembly must be installed into the GAC. While the JeffTypes assembly can also be installed into the GAC, it doesn't have to be. It could be deployed into an application's base directory or some other directory identified by a **codeBase** URL.

Important A publisher should create a publisher policy assembly only when deploying a bug fix or a service pack version of an assembly. When installing an application "out of the box," no publisher policy assemblies should be installed.

I want to make one last point about publisher policy. Say that a publisher distributes a publisher policy assembly and for some reason the new assembly introduces more bugs than it fixes. If this happens, the administrator would like to tell the CLR to ignore the publisher policy assembly. To have the CLR do this, the administrator can edit the application's configuration file and add the following **publisherPolicy** element:

```
<publisherPolicy apply="no"/>
```

This element can be placed in the application's configuration file so that it applies to all assemblies, or it can be placed in the application's configuration file to have it apply to a specific assembly. When the CLR processes the application's configuration file, it will see that the GAC shouldn't be examined for the publisher policy assembly. So, the CLR will continue to operate using the older version of the assembly. Note, however, that the CLR will still examine and apply any policy specified in the Machine.config file.

> **Important**   A publisher policy assembly is a way for a publisher to make a statement about the compatibility of different versions of an assembly. If a new version of an assembly isn't intended to be compatible with an earlier version, the publisher shouldn't create a publisher policy assembly. In general, use a publisher policy assembly when you build a new version of your assembly that fixes a bug. You should test the new version of the assembly for backward compatibility. On the other hand, if you're adding new features to your assembly, you should consider the assembly to have no relationship to a previous version and you shouldn't ship a publisher policy assembly. In addition, there's no need to do any backward compatibility testing with such an assembly.

Repairing a Faulty Application

When a console or Windows Forms application is running under a user account, the CLR keeps a record of the assemblies that the application actually loads; a record isn't kept for ASP.NET Web Forms or XML Web services applications. This assembly load information is accumulated in memory and is written to disk when the application terminates. The files that contain this information are written to the following directory:

```
C:\Documents and Settings\UserName\Local Settings\
    Application Data\ApplicationHistory
```

UserName identifies the name of the logged-on user.

If you look in this directory, you'll see files like this:

```
Volume in drive C has no label.
 Volume Serial Number is 94FA-5DE7

 Directory of C:\Documents and Settings\v-
jeffrr\Local Settings\ApplicationHistory

07/23/2002  10:46 AM    <DIR>          .
07/23/2002  10:46 AM    <DIR>          ..
07/22/2002  04:14 PM             1,014 App.exe.c4bc1771.ini
07/23/2002  10:46 AM             2,845 ConfigWizards.exe.c4c8182.ini
07/14/2002  05:51 PM             9,815 devenv.exe.49453f8d.ini
07/22/2002  02:25 PM             3,226 devenv.exe.7dc18209.ini
07/23/2002  10:46 AM             3,368 mmc.exe.959a7e97.ini
07/15/2002  03:06 PM             2,248 RegAsm.exe.18b34bd3.ini
               6 File(s)         22,516 bytes
               2 Dir(s)  14,698,717,184 bytes free
```

Each file identifies a particular application. The hexadecimal number is a hash value identifying the file's path and is needed to distinguish two files with the same name residing in different subdirectories.

As an application runs, the CLR maintains a "snapshot" of the set of assemblies loaded by the application. When the application terminates, this information is compared with the information in the application's corresponding .ini file. If the application loaded the same set of assemblies that it loaded previously, the information in the .ini file matches the information in memory and the in-memory information is discarded. If on the other hand the in-memory information differs from the information in the .ini file, the CLR appends the in-memory information to the .ini file. By default, the .ini file is able to store up to five snapshots.

Basically, the CLR is keeping a record of the assemblies that an application used. Now, let's say that you install some new assemblies and maybe some new publisher policy assembly gets installed too. A week later, you run an application and all of a sudden the application isn't performing correctly. What can you do? Historically, in Windows, the best thing to do would be to reinstall the failing application and hope that the reinstall wouldn't break some other application (which would be likely).

Fortunately for the end-user, the CLR keeps a historical record of the assemblies that an application uses. All you have to do is build an XML configuration file for the application where the elements tell the CLR to use the same assemblies that were loaded when the application was in a last-known good state.

To make creating or modifying an application configuration file easy, you can use the .NET Framework Configuration tool. Run the tool, right-click on the Application node in the tree pane, and select the Fix An Application menu item. This causes the dialog box in Figure 3-10 to appear.

> **Note**   The .NET Framework Configuration tool is a Microsoft Management Console (MMC) snap-in and, therefore, isn't installed on Windows 98, Windows 98 Second Edition, or Windows Me. However, on these operating systems, you can use the .NET Framework Wizards utility to do what I describe in this section. You can invoke this tool from the Start menu by clicking Program Files, then Administrative Tools, and then .NET Framework Wizards.

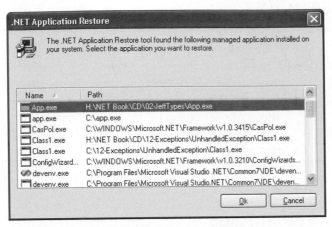

Figure 3-10   .NET Application Configuration tool showing all applications that have had assembly load information recorded at one time or another

The dialog box in Figure 3-10 shows the applications about which the CLR has accumulated assembly load information. Basically, an entry appears here for every .ini file in the ApplicationHistory subdirectory. Once you select an application, the dialog box in Figure 3-11 appears.

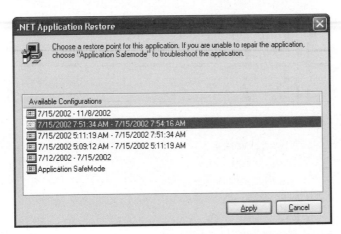

Figure 3-11   The .NET Application Configuration tool showing the dates when loaded assemblies differed

Each entry in this dialog box represents the set of assemblies that were loaded by the application. The user can select a date range during which the application was working correctly, and the tool will create or modify the application's XML configuration file so that the CLR will now load the last-known good set of assemblies for the application. The Application SafeMode entry ensures that the application loads with the same exact set of assemblies that it was built and tested with; it prevents the CLR from redirecting an assembly to a different version.

Changes to the application's XML configuration file can be identified by surrounding comment elements that contain ".NET Application Restore Begin-Block" and ".NET Application Restore EndBlock". The ".NET Application Restore RollBackBlock" contains the original XML configuration prior to restoring to a specific snapshot. Here's an example:

```xml
<configuration>
   <runtime>
      <assemblyBinding xmlns="urn:schemas-microsoft-com:asm.v1">
         <dependentAssembly>

            <!--.NET Application Restore BeginBlock #1 29437104.-387708080
               7/24/2002 6:48:25 PM-->

            <assemblyIdentity name="JeffTypes"
               publicKeyToken="32ab4ba45e0a69a1" culture="neutral" />

            <bindingRedirect
               oldVersion="1.0.0.0" newVersion="2.0.0.0" />

            <publisherPolicy apply="no"/>
            <!--.NET Application Restore EndBlock #1-->

            <!--.NET Application Restore RollBackBlock #1
                7/24/2002 6:48:25 PM<assemblyIdentity name="JeffTypes"
                publicKeyToken="32ab4ba45e0a69a1" culture=""/>-->

         </dependentAssembly>
      </assemblyBinding>
   </runtime>
</configuration>
```

Part II

Working with Types and the Common Language Runtime

4

Type Fundamentals

In this chapter, I'm going to introduce the information that is fundamental to working with types and the common language runtime (CLR). In particular, I'll discuss the minimum set of behaviors that you can expect every type to have. I'll also describe type safety and the various ways you can cast objects from one type to another. Finally, I'll talk about namespaces and assemblies.

All Types Are Derived from `System.Object`

The CLR requires that every object ultimately be derived from the **System.Object** type. This means that the following two type definitions (shown using Microsoft Visual Basic) are identical:

```
' Implicitly derive from Object
Class Employee
    ⋮
End Class

' Explicitly derive from Object
Class Employee
    Inherits System.Object
    ⋮
End Class
```

Because all object types are ultimately derived from **System.Object**, you are guaranteed that every object of every type has a minimum set of methods. Specifically, the **System.Object** class offers the public instance methods listed in Table 4-1.

Table 4-1   Public Methods of `System.Object`

Public Method	Description
`Equals`	Returns **True** if two objects have the same value. For more information about this method, see Chapter 6.
`GetHashCode`	Returns a hash code for this object's value. A type should override this method if its objects are to be used as a key in a hash table. The method should provide a good distribution for its objects. For more information about this method, see Chapter 6.
`ToString`	By default, returns the full name of the type (**Me.Get-Type().FullName.ToString()**). However, it is common to override this method so that it returns a **String** object containing a string representation of the object's state. For example, the core types, such as **Boolean** and **Int32**, override this method to return a string representation of their values. It is also common to override this method for debugging purposes: you can call it and get a string showing the values of the object's fields. Note that **ToString** is expected to be aware of the **Culture-Info** associated with the calling thread. Chapter 6 discusses **ToString** in greater detail.
`GetType`	Returns an instance of a **Type**-derived object that identifies the type of this object. The returned **Type** object can be used with the Reflection classes to obtain metadata information about the type. Reflection is discussed in Chapter 20. The **GetType** method is nonvirtual, which prevents a class from overriding the method and lying about its type, violating type safety.

In addition, types that derive from **System.Object** have access to the protected methods listed in Table 4-2.

Table 4-2   Protected Methods of `System.Object`

Protected Method	Description
`MemberwiseClone`	This nonvirtual method creates a new instance of the type and sets the new object's fields to be identical to the **Me** object's fields. A reference to the new instance is returned. For more information about this method, see Chapter 6.
`Finalize`	This virtual method is called when the garbage collector determines that the object is garbage but before the memory for the object is reclaimed. Types that require cleanup when collected should override this method. I'll talk about this important method in much more detail in Chapter 19.

The CLR requires that all objects be created using the **New** operator (which emits the **newobj** IL instruction). The following line shows how to create an **Employee** object:

```
Dim e As Employee = New Employee("ConstructorParam1")
```

which can also be shortened as

```
Dim e As New Employee("ConstructorParam1")
```

Here's what the **New** operator does:

1. It allocates memory for the object by allocating the number of bytes required for the specified type from the managed heap.

2. It initializes the object's overhead members. Every object instance has two additional members associated with the instance that the CLR uses to manage the object. The first member is the object's pointer to the type's method table, and the second member is a SyncBlockIndex.

3. The type's instance constructor is called, passing it any parameters (the string "**ConstructorParam1**", in the preceding example) specified in the call to **New**. Although most languages compile constructors so that they call the base type's constructor, the CLR doesn't require this call.

After **New** has performed all these operations, it returns a reference to the newly created object. In the preceding code example, this reference is saved in the variable **e**, which is of type **Employee**.

By the way, the **New** operator has no complementary operator; that is, there is no way to explicitly free the memory allocated for an object. The CLR imposes a garbage-collected environment (described in Chapter 19) that automatically detects when objects are no longer being used or accessed and frees the object's memory automatically.

Visual Basic Standard Modules

Visual Basic 6 and earlier versions allow developers to define global variables and methods. Although Visual Basic .NET requires that all fields and methods be defined within a type, it offers a mechanism that allows developers to believe that they are defining global variables and methods. This mechanism is called the *standard module*. The following code demonstrates how to declare a standard module that contains a "global" variable and a global "method" in Visual Basic .NET:

```
Imports System

' Define a standard module named "MyStdMod".
Module MyStdMod

    ' x appears as a global variable.
    Dim x as Int32

    ' Main appears as a global method.
    Sub Main()
      ⋮
    End Sub

End Module
```

If you were to compile this Visual Basic source code module and examine the metadata using ILDasm.exe, you'd see the following type definition entry:

```
TypeDef #1
----------------------------------------------------------------

    TypDefName: MyStdMod  (02000002)
    Flags     : [NotPublic] [AutoLayout] [Class] [Sealed] [AnsiClass] (00000100)
    Extends   : 01000001 [TypeRef] System.Object
    Field #1
    ----------------------------------------------------------------

        Field Name: x (04000001)
        Flags     : [Private] [Static]  (00000011)
        CallCnvntn: [FIELD]
        Field type: I4


    Method #1 [ENTRYPOINT]
    ----------------------------------------------------------------

        MethodName: Main (06000001)
        Flags     : [Public] [Static] [ReuseSlot]  (00000016)
        RVA       : 0x00002050
        ImplFlags : [IL] [Managed]  (00000000)
        CallCnvntn: [DEFAULT]
        ReturnType: Void
        No arguments.
        CustomAttribute #1 (0c000001)
        ----------------------------------------------------------------

            CustomAttribute Type: 0a000002
            CustomAttributeName: System.STAThreadAttribute ::
                    instance void .ctor()
            Length: 4
            Value : 01 00 00 00

            ctor args: ()
```

```
CustomAttribute #1 (0c000002)
-------------------------------------------------------
    CustomAttribute Type: 0a000001
    CustomAttributeName: Microsoft.VisualBasic.CompilerServices.StandardModul
eAttribute ::
  instance void .ctor()
    Length: 4
    Value : 01 00 00 00                                          >
<

    ctor args: ()
```

After examining this metadata, it's easy to see that declaring a Visual Basic **Module** is exactly like declaring a class with the following characteristics:

■ The class is always sealed and is immediately derived from **System.Object**. The class cannot implement any interfaces. By default, this class has **Friend** accessibility, meaning that the members defined within the class are accessible only to code contained within the same assembly. However, you can override this default by explicitly marking the module with **Public** or **Friend** accessibility.

■ The class never contains an instance constructor, preventing instances of this class from being created. However, **Shared** (static) constructors (also known as *type constructors*) are allowed. Type constructors are discussed in Chapter 9.

■ All methods defined in the module are **Shared**; it's not possible to define any instance methods in a module. By default, methods are marked as **Public**; however, you can override this default by explicitly marking a method as **Public**, **Friend**, or **Private**.

■ All variables defined in the module are considered **Shared** fields; it's not possible to define any instance fields in a module. By default, fields declared with the **Dim** statement are marked as **Private**; however, you can override this default by explicitly marking a field as **Public**, **Friend**, or **Private**.

At this point, you might be asking yourself this question: "Since a module is really just a class, what good is a module?" Well, Visual Basic offers simple syntax for code defined outside the module to access the members within a module. The following code demonstrates this syntax:

```
Imports System

Class Foo
   Public Sum As Int32

   ' A Public constructor
   Public Sub New()
      ' This line calls AnotherStdMod's Shared Add method.
      Sum = AnotherStdMod.Add(1, 2)

      ' This line demonstrates the simplified syntax allowed
      ' because Add is defined within a standard module.
      ' Add "looks like" a global function.
      Sum = Add(1, 2)
   End Sub
End Class

Module AnotherStdMod
   ' Application EntryPoint method
   Sub Main()
      Dim o As New Foo()
      Console.WriteLine(o.Sum)
   End Sub

   ' "Global" Public Add method
   Public Function Add(ByVal x As Int32, ByVal y As Int32)
      Return x + y
   End Function
End Module
```

In **Foo**'s constructor (the **New** method), the first call to **Add** compiles correctly and causes **AnotherStdMod**'s **Shared Add** method to execute. This shouldn't be surprising since **Add** is a public, shared method defined within a class named **AnotherStdMod**. This first call to **Add** doesn't show off the "feature" of modules, so in **Foo**'s constructor, I also show a second call to **Add**. In this second call, **Add** is referred to without being qualified with the module's name: **AnotherStdMod**. It looks like **Add** is a global method.

Normally, when you define a class in Visual Basic, code outside the class must reference the class's members using qualified names. How does the Visual Basic compiler know to allow the simplified syntax when accessing members inside a module? The answer is that module classes have the **Microsoft.VisualBasic.CompilerServices.StandardModuleAttribute** applied to them. (Custom attributes are discussed in Chapter 16.) You can see this line at the bottom of the metadata shown earlier. When the Visual Basic compiler sees code referring to a member or field that it can't resolve, it checks whether the member or field is defined within a class marked with the **StandardModuleAttribute**

attribute and generates code that refers to the fully qualified member or field name.

By the way, Visual Basic allows you to define multiple modules in a single assembly. If you have code that refers to a member that exists in multiple modules, the Visual Basic compiler issues an error because it can't determine which member the code really intends to access. To resolve the ambiguity, you must modify the source code and make it reference the member using a fully qualified name.

The `StandardModuleAttribute` attribute is specific to the Visual Basic compiler. So to access a public member defined in a public module, code written in another language (such as C#) must qualify the member with the class name. Even though you might not be programming in Visual Basic, it's possible to define a public class containing public static methods and fields and apply the `Microsoft.VisualBasic.CompilerServices.StandardModuleAttribute` attribute to the class. Of course, you'll have to reference the Microsoft.VisualBasic.dll assembly to build the code. If you apply this attribute to your own class, Visual Basic programmers will be able to treat the members of your class as global members.

The `StandardModuleAttribute` attribute is used for many classes in the `Microsoft.VisualBasic` namespace, which has been designed to ease the migration of code written in earlier versions of Visual Basic. This namespace contains classes such as `DateAndTime`, `Information`, `Interaction`, and `Strings`, which in turn contain static methods such as `DateAdd`, `UBound`, `MsgBox`, and `InStr`. Because these classes are flagged with the `StandardModuleAttribute` attribute, you can omit the class's name when you use these methods, which therefore appear to be functions (as they were in Visual Basic 6 and previous versions).

```
' This code works because the Microsoft.VisualBasic namespace
' is imported by default in all Visual Basic programs.

Dim arr(10) As Integer
Console.WriteLine(UBound(arr))                    ' Displays "10"
' The following statement reaches the same result but is more verbose.
Console.WriteLine(Information.UBound(arr))
```

Even though these shared methods can make your transition to Visual Basic .NET easier, you should make an effort to use classes and methods from the **System** namespace (and its child namespaces) exclusively in your applications because they are generally faster and more flexible than the Visual Basic–specific methods that exist solely to help migrate code written for previous versions of Visual Basic.

Casting Between Types

One of the most important features of the CLR is its type safety. At run time, the CLR always knows what type an object is. You can always discover an object's exact type by calling the `GetType` method. Because this method is nonvirtual, it is impossible for a type to spoof another type. For example, the `Employee` type can't override the `GetType` method and have it return a type of `SpaceShuttle`.

Developers frequently find it necessary to cast an object to various types. The CLR allows you to cast an object to its type or to any of its base types. Your programming language of choice decides how to expose casting operations to the developer. For example, Visual Basic doesn't require any special syntax to cast an object to any of its base types because casts to base types are considered safe implicit conversions. However, things become more complicated when you cast an object to any of its derived types because such a cast could fail. The exact behavior of Visual Basic depends on the `Option Strict` setting for the source file containing the statement. If `Option Strict` is off, Visual Basic .NET behaves as a weakly typed language, allowing code that doesn't contain explicit casts to compile; this setting improves compatibility with Visual Basic 6, but I strongly discourage it because bugs in your code could appear only at run time; it's always better to catch bugs at compile time. If `Option Strict` is on, Visual Basic .NET behaves as a strongly typed language and requires that the code contain explicit casts when assigning an object to a variable of a more derived type. Unfortunately, Microsoft decided that `Option Strict Off` is the default setting, so I suggest that you turn it on whenever you start a new project. You can enable or disable the `Option Strict` setting in one of the following ways:

- If compiling from the command line, you can use the `/optionstrict` or `/optionstrict+` switch to enable it, or `/optionstrict-` to disable it.

- If working in Visual Studio, you can select the desired option in the Build page of the Project Properties dialog box.

- In either case, you can override the project-level setting by inserting an `Option Strict On` or `Option Strict Off` statement at the top of a source file. (`Option Strict` by itself turns the setting off.)

> **Note**   The Option Strict setting affects the behavior of the compilers in ways other than just allowing implicit casts to a derived type. When Option Strict is on, all the assignment statements that might throw an exception at run time require an explicit conversion operation, for example, converting an Int32 to an Int16, a Double to a Single, a String to a Char, and from any numeric type to a Boolean. Additionally, the Option Strict On statement prevents assignments from a Boolean to any numeric type in a measure to tighten type safety. Finally, when Option Strict is on, you can't perform late-bound method calls, which might fail at run time; you can't use the \division operator with floating-point values because it silently converts its operands to Int64; and you must explicitly convert the result of the ^ operator if the target isn't a Double variable.

Visual Basic provides two operators for performing a cast: **DirectCast** and **CType**. Of the two, **DirectCast** is preferred because it usually produces more efficient code and because it is better about preserving type safety. However, **DirectCast** can be used only to cast a reference type (described in Chapter 5) to some other type (a reference type or a value type). On the other hand, the **CType** operator (described in the next section) can be used to cast reference types or value types (also described in Chapter 5) to some other type (a reference type or a value type), The following code demonstrates casting to base and derived types using the **DirectCast** operator:

```
' This type is implicitly derived from System.Object.
Class Employee
   ⋮
End Class

Class App
   Public Shared Sub Main()
      ' No cast is needed because New returns an Employee object
      ' and Object is a base type of Employee.
      Dim o As Object = New Employee()

      ' A cast is required because Employee is derived from Object.
      ' This cast isn't required if Option Strict is off.
      Dim e As Employee = DirectCast(o, Employee)
   End Sub
End Class
```

This example shows what is necessary for the compiler to compile your code. Now I'll explain what happens at run time. At run time, the CLR checks casting operations to ensure that casts are always to the object's actual type or any of its base types. For example, the following code will compile (regardless of the current **Option Strict** setting), but at run time, an **InvalidCastException** exception will be thrown:

```
Class Manager
    Inherits Employee
    ⋮
End Class

Class App
    Public Shared Sub Main()
        ' Construct a Manager object and pass it to PromoteEmployee.
        ' A Manager IS-A Object: PromoteEmployee runs OK.
        Dim m As Manager = New Manager()
        PromoteEmployee(m)

        ' Construct a DateTime object and pass it to PromoteEmployee.
        ' A DateTime is NOT derived from Employee: PromoteEmployee
        ' throws a System.InvalidCastException exception.
        Dim newYears As DateTime = New DateTime(2001, 1, 1)
        PromoteEmployee(newYears)
    End Sub

    Public Shared Sub PromoteEmployee(ByVal o As Object)
        ' At this point, the compiler doesn't know exactly what
        ' type of object o refers to. So the compiler allows the
        ' code to compile. However, at run time, the CLR does know
        ' what type o refers to (each time the cast is performed) and
        ' it checks whether the object's type is Employee or any type
        ' that is derived from Employee.
        Dim e As Employee = DirectCast(o, Employee)
        ⋮
    End Sub
End Class
```

In the **Main** method, a **Manager** object is constructed and passed to **PromoteEmployee**. This code compiles and executes because **Manager** is derived from **Object**, which is what **PromoteEmployee** expects. Once inside **PromoteEmployee**, the CLR confirms that **o** refers to an object that is either an **Employee** or a type that is derived from **Employee**. Because **Manager** is derived from **Employee**, the CLR performs the cast and allows **PromoteEmployee** to continue executing.

After **PromoteEmployee** returns, **Main** constructs a **DateTime** object and passes it to **PromoteEmployee**. Again, **DateTime** is derived from **Object**, so the compiler compiles the code that calls `PromoteEmployee`. However, inside `PromoteEmployee`, the CLR checks the cast and detects that **o** refers to a `DateTime` object and is therefore not an `Employee` or any type derived from `Employee`. At this point, the CLR can't allow the cast and throws a `System.InvalidCastException` exception.

If the CLR allowed the cast, there would be no type safety and the results would be unpredictable, including the possibility of application crashes and security breaches caused by the ability of types to easily spoof other types. Type spoofing is the cause of many security breaches and compromises an application's stability and robustness. Type safety is therefore an extremely important part of the Microsoft .NET Framework.

By the way, the proper way to prototype the `PromoteEmployee` method would be to have it take an `Employee` instead of an `Object` as a parameter. I used `Object` so that I could demonstrate how the compilers and the CLR deal with casting.

Casting with the `CType` Operator

As mentioned in the preceding section, the `DirectCast` operator can be used only to cast a reference type object to a reference type or a value type. If you want to cast an instance of a value type—an Int64 to an `Int32`, for example—to another type, you can't use the `DirectCast` operator. Instead, you must use the `CType` operator. The only "problem" with the `CType` operator is that it is very aggressive about type conversions. For example, the following line will actually cast the string "123" to an `Int32` whose value is 123:

```
Dim i As Int32 = CType("123", Int32)
```

While in some situations this aggressive casting is very nice and convenient, it can be a potential type-safety hazard since the preceding code is allowing you to easily treat a string value as an integer value. When compiling code that uses the `CType` operator, if the compiler detects that the two types are numeric primitive types (as discussed in Chapter 5), it produces very efficient code to perform the cast. On the other hand, if at least one of the types is not a numeric primitive type, the compiler calls methods defined by types in the `Microsoft.VisualBasic.CompilerServices` namespace to aggressively convert one type to another.

These methods typically take advantage of the `IConvertible` interface (as described in Chapter 12), but these methods employ additional means as well in an effort to make the conversion happen. For example, when casting the string "123" to an `Int32` (as shown earlier), the Visual Basic compiler generates a call to `Microsoft.VisualBasic.CompilerServices.IntegerType`'s `FromString` method. Internally, this method examines the string to determine whether it contains an octal, decimal to hexadecimal number. The method might also call a **Parse** method (described in Chapter 12) and perform rounding operations. Here's an example of what types of problem this behavior can cause:

```
' You might expect that the following statement throws an exception,
' but it doesn't because &H123 is a valid number in hex notation.
Console.WriteLine(CType("&H123", Int32))    ' Displays "291"

' This statement works because CType automatically rounds the result.
Console.WriteLine(CType("123.67", Int32))   ' Displays "124"
```

What you should take away from this discussion is that **CType** is aggressive about casting and that this casting can cause several methods to be called, which hurts performance. In addition, playing fast and loose with casting hurts compile-time type safety, meaning that more of your application's bugs will show up at run time.

Don't let me scare you off completely from using the **CType** operator. But whenever possible, you should avoid using it. If you must use it—such as when you need to cast a value type to another type—go ahead and use it. Just be aware that the cast might not give you the result you expect and that some casts require a lot of code to execute.

Using the **CType** operator to cast an object to a primitive type is so useful and common that Visual Basic offers some additional cast operators to simplify coding. Here are the convenient cast operators: **CBool** casts an object to a **Boolean**, **CByte** casts an object to a **Byte**, **CChar** casts an object to a **Char**, **CDate** casts an object to a **DateTime**, **CDbl** casts an object to a **Double**, **CDec** casts an object to a **Decimal**, **CInt** casts an object to an **Int32**, **CLng** casts an object to an **Int64**, **CObj** casts an object to an **Object**, **CShort** casts an object to an **Int16**, **CSng** casts an object to a **Single**, and **CStr** casts an object to a **String**.

For example, the **CInt** operator can be used to cast a string to an **Int32**:

```
' Identical to CType('123', Int32)
Dim i As Int32 = CInt("123")
```

As with the **DirectCast** operator, if the **CType** operator (or one of its convenient cast operators) can't find some way to cast the specified object to the desired type, an **InvalidCastException** exception will be thrown.

Testing an Object's Type with the `TypeOf...Is` Expression

The **DirectCast** and **CType** operators attempt to cast an object from one type to another. If a compatible cast can't be made, an **InvalidCastException** exception is thrown. To ensure that an application recovers gracefully from an exception, the developer must take advantage of exception handling mechanisms, as described in Chapter 18.

If you prefer to avoid using exception handling code, you can take advantage of Visual Basic's **TypeOf...Is** expression. The **TypeOf...Is** expression checks whether an object is compatible with a specified type, and the result of the evaluation is a **Boolean**: **True** or **False**. The **TypeOf...Is** expression will never throw an exception. The following code demonstrates:

```
Dim o As System.Object = New System.Object()
Dim b1 As System.Boolean = (TypeOf o Is System.Object)   ' b1 is True.
Dim b2 As System.Boolean = (TypeOf o Is Employee)        ' b2 is False.
```

If the object reference is **Nothing**, the **TypeOf...Is** expression always returns **False** because there is no object available to check its type. The **TypeOf...Is** expression is typically used as follows:

```
If TypeOf o Is Employee Then
    Dim e As Employee = DirectCast(o, Employee)
    ' Use e within the 'If' statement.
End If
```

In this code, the object referred to by **o** is checked to see whether it is an **Employee** (or any type derived from **Employee**). If the object is compatible with **Employee**, **DirectCast** is used to cast the reference to an **Employee** reference. In this case, the **DirectCast** will always succeed and an **InvalidCastException** exception will never be thrown.

Unfortunately, there is a performance problem with the preceding code: the CLR is actually checking the object's type twice: the **TypeOf...Is** expression first checks to see whether **o** is compatible with the **Employee** type. If it is, then inside the **If** statement, the CLR again verifies that **o** refers to an **Employee** when performing the cast. Some languages, such as C#, offer another cast operator (the **as** operator) so that the CLR has to check the type of an object only once. Unfortunately, because Visual Basic doesn't offer such an operator, there's no way to improve the performance of the previous code example when using Visual Basic.

To make sure you understand everything just presented, take the following quiz. Assume that these two class definitions exist:

```
Class B
    Public x As Int32
End Class

Class D
    Inherits B
    Public y As Int32
End Class
```

Now examine the lines of Visual Basic code in Table 4-3. For each line, decide whether the line would compile and execute successfully (marked OK below), cause a compile-time error (CTE) if **Option Strict** is on, or cause a run-time error (RTE).

Table 4-3   Type-Safety Quiz

Statement	OK	CTE	RTE
`Dim o1 As System.Object = New System.Object()`	✓		
`Dim o2 As System.Object = New B()`	✓		
`Dim o3 As System.Object = New D()`	✓		
`Dim o4 As System.Object = o3`	✓		
`Dim b1 As B = New B()`	✓		
`Dim b2 As B = New D()`	✓		
`Dim d1 As D = New D()`	✓		
`Dim b3 As B = New System.Object()`		✓	
`Dim d3 As D = New System.Object()`		✓	
`Dim b4 As B = d1`	✓		
`Dim d2 As D = b2`		✓	
`Dim d4 As D = DirectCast(d1, D)`	✓		
`Dim d5 As D = DirectCast(b2, D)`	✓		
`Dim d6 As D = DirectCast(b1, D)`			✓
`Dim b5 As B = DirectCast(o1, B)`			✓
`Dim b6 As B = DirectCast(b2, D)`	✓		

Namespaces and Assemblies

Namespaces allow for the logical grouping of related types, and developers typically use them to make it easier to locate a particular type. For example, the **System.Collections** namespace defines a bunch of collection types, and the **System.IO** namespace defines a bunch of types for performing I/O operations. Here's some code that constructs a **System.IO.FileStream** object and a **System.Collections.Queue** object:

```
Class App
   Shared Sub Main()
      ' Construct a System.IO.FileStream object, assigning its address to fs.
      Dim fs As System.IO.FileStream = New System.IO.FileStream(...)

      ' Construct a System.Collections.Queue object, assigning its
      ' address to q. Notice the more convenient syntax.
      Dim q As New System.Collections.Queue()
   End Sub
End Class
```

As you can see, the code is pretty verbose; it would be nice if there were some shorthand way to refer to the **FileStream** and **Queue** types to reduce typing. Fortunately, many compilers do offer mechanisms to reduce programmer typing. The Visual Basic compiler provides this mechanism via the **Imports** statement, and C# provides it via the **using** directive. The following code is identical to the previous example:

```
' Import some namespaces in my Visual Basic application:
Imports System.IO            ' Try prepending "System.IO."
Imports System.Collections   ' Try prepending "System.Collections."

Class App
   Shared Sub Main()
      ' Construct a System.IO.FileStream object, assigning its address to fs.
      Dim fs As FileStream = New FileStream(...)

      ' Construct a System.Collections.Queue object, assigning its
      ' address to q. Notice the more convenient syntax.
      Dim q As New Queue()
   End Sub
End Class
```

To the compiler, a namespace is simply an easy way of making a type's name longer and more likely to be unique by preceding the name with some symbols separated by dots. So the compiler interprets the reference to

`FileStream` in this example to mean `System.IO.FileStream`. Similarly, the compiler interprets the reference to `Queue` to mean `System.Collections.Queue`.

Using Visual Basic's `Imports` statement or C#'s `using` directive is entirely optional; you're always welcome to type out the fully qualified name of a type if you prefer. These directives instruct the compiler to "try" prepending different prefixes to a type name until a match is found.

> **Important**   The CLR doesn't know anything about namespaces. When you access a type, the CLR needs to know the full name of the type and which assembly contains the definition of the type so that it can load the proper assembly, find the type, and manipulate it.

In the previous code example, the compiler needs to ensure that every type referenced exists and that my code is using that type in the correct way: calling methods that exist, passing the right number of arguments to these methods, ensuring that the arguments are the right type, using the method's return value correctly, and so on. If the compiler can't find a type with the specified name in the source files or in any referenced assemblies, it tries prepending "`System.IO.`" to the type name and checks whether the generated name matches an existing type. If the compiler still can't find a match, it tries prepending "`System.Collections.`" to the type's name. The two `Imports` directives shown earlier allow me to simply type "`FileStream`" and "`Queue`" in my code—the compiler automatically expands the references to "`System.IO.FileStream`" and "`System.Collections.Queue`". I'm sure you can easily imagine how much typing this saves.

In addition to Visual Basic's `Imports` directive, the VBC.exe compiler also supports a `/imports` command-line switch. This switch simply allows you to import a set of comma-separated namespaces without adding `Imports` directives in your source code. Adding `Imports` directives to your source code is preferred to using the command-line switch because the code is more likely to build correctly since it's less dependent on build settings. When compiling from inside Microsoft Visual Studio, you can also leverage the ability to define project-wide imports from the Imports page in the Project Properties dialog box. When you create a new project, Visual Studio automatically Imports a few project-wide namespaces for you—for example, console application projects automatically import the following namespaces: `Microsoft.VisualBasic`, `System`, `System.Collections`, `System.Data`, and `System.Diagnostics`—but you can add other namespaces if you need to.

When checking for a type's definition, the compiler must be told which assemblies to examine. The compiler will scan all the assemblies it knows about, looking for the type's definition. Once the compiler finds the proper assembly, the assembly information and the type information are emitted into the resulting managed module's metadata. To get the assembly information, you must pass the assembly that defines any referenced types to the compiler. The Visual Basic compiler, by default, automatically looks in the MSCorLib.dll assembly even if you don't explicitly tell it to. The MSCorLib.dll assembly contains the definitions of all the core .NET Framework Class Library (FCL) types, such as `Object`, `Int32`, `String`, and so on.

> **Note** When Microsoft first started working on the .NET Framework, MSCorLib.dll was an acronym for Microsoft Common Object Runtime Library. Once ECMA started to standardize the CLR and parts of the FCL, MSCorLib.dll officially became the acronym for Multilanguage Standard Common Object Runtime Library.

As you might imagine, there are some potential problems with the way that compilers treat namespaces: it's possible to have two (or more) types with the same name in different namespaces. Microsoft strongly recommends that you define unique names for types. However, in some cases, it's simply not possible. The CLR encourages the reuse of components. Your application might take advantage of a component that Microsoft created and another component that Wintellect created. These two companies might both offer a type named `Widget`—Microsoft's `Widget` does one thing, and Wintellect's `Widget` does something entirely different. In this scenario, you have no control over the naming of the types, so you can differentiate between the two widgets by using their fully qualified names when referencing them. To reference Microsoft's `Widget`, you would use `Microsoft.Widget`, and to reference Wintellect's `Widget`, you would use `Wintellect.Widget`.

In the following code, the reference to `Widget` is ambiguous and the Visual Basic compiler generates the following: "error BC30561: 'Widget' is ambiguous, imported from the namespaces or types 'Wintellect, Microsoft'":

```
Imports Microsoft        ' Try prepending "Microsoft."
Imports Wintellect       ' Try prepending "Wintellect."

Class App
   Shared Sub Main()
      Dim w As Widget = New Widget     ' An ambiguous reference
   End Sub
End Class
```

To remove the ambiguity, you must explicitly tell the compiler which `Widget` you want to create:

```
Imports Microsoft        ' Try prepending "Microsoft."
Imports Wintellect       ' Try prepending "Wintellect."

Class App
   Shared Sub Main()
      Dim w As Wintellect.Widget = New Wintellect.Widget     ' Not ambiguous
   End Sub
End Class
```

There's another form of the Visual Basic `Imports` directive that allows you to create an alias for a single type or namespace. This is handy if you have just a few types that you use from a namespace and don't want to pollute the global namespace with all of a namespace's types. The following code demonstrates another way to solve the ambiguity problem shown in the preceding code:

```
Imports Microsoft        ' Try prepending "Microsoft."
Imports Wintellect       ' Try prepending "Wintellect."

' Define WintellectWidget symbol as an alias to Wintellect.Widget.
Imports WintellectWidget = Wintellect.Widget

Class App
   Shared Sub Main()
      Dim w As WintellectWidget = New WintellectWidget     ' No error now
   End Sub
End Class
```

These methods of disambiguating a type are useful, but in some scenarios, you need to go further. Imagine that the Australian Boomerang Company (ABC) and the Alaskan Boat Corporation (ABC) are each creating a type, called `BuyProduct`, which they intend to ship in their respective assemblies. It's likely that both companies would create a namespace called `ABC` that contains a type called `BuyProduct`. Anyone who tries to develop an application that needs to buy both boomerangs and boats would be in for some trouble unless the programming language provides a way to programmatically distinguish between the assemblies, not just between the namespaces.

Unfortunately, the Visual Basic **Imports** directive only supports namespaces; it doesn't offer any way to specify an assembly. However, in the real world, this problem doesn't come up very often and is rarely an issue. If you're designing component types that you expect third parties to use, you should define these types in a namespace so that compilers can easily disambiguate types. In fact, to reduce the likelihood of conflict, you should use your full company name (not an acronym) as your top-level namespace name. Referring to the .NET Framework SDK documentation, you can see that Microsoft uses a namespace of "Microsoft" for Microsoft-specific types. (See the **Microsoft.VisualBasic**, **Microsoft.CSharp**, and **Microsoft.Win32** namespaces as examples.)

Creating a namespace is simply a matter of writing a namespace declaration into your code as follows (in Visual Basic):

```
Namespace CompanyName       ' CompanyName
    Class A                 ' CompanyName.A
        ⋮
        Class B             ' CompanyName.A.B
        ⋮
        End Class
    End Class

    Namespace X             ' CompanyName.X
        Class C             ' CompanyName.X.C
        ⋮
        End Class
    End Namespace
End Namespace
```

Some compilers don't support namespaces at all, and other compilers are free to define what "namespace" means to a particular language. In Visual Basic, namespaces are implicitly public and you can't change this by using any access modifiers. However, Visual Basic does allow you to define types within a namespace that are internal (can't be used outside the assembly) or public (can be accessed by any assembly).

In addition to Visual Basic's **Namespace** statement, the VBC.exe compiler also supports a **/rootnamespace** command-line switch. This switch simply prepends the specified string (and a period) to all types defined in your source code modules. This switch is a quick and dirty way to make all the types part of a top-level namespace so that your source code appears less cluttered without a **Namespace** statement. When compiling from inside Visual Studio, you can define the root namespace in the General page of the Project Properties dialog box.

How Namespaces and Assemblies Relate

Be aware that a namespace and an assembly (the file that implements a type) aren't necessarily related. In particular, the various types belonging to a single namespace might be implemented in multiple assemblies. For example, the `System.IO.FileStream` type is implemented in the MSCor-Lib.dll assembly, and the `System.IO.FileSystemWatcher` type is implemented in the System.dll assembly. In fact, there is no System.Collections.dll assembly.

A single assembly can house types in different namespaces. For example, the `System.Int32` and `System.Collections.ArrayList` types are both in the MSCorLib.dll assembly.

When you look up a type in the .NET Framework SDK documentation, the documentation will clearly indicate the namespace that the type belongs to and also what assembly the type is implemented in. In the Requirements section in Figure 4-1, you can see that the `ResXFileRef` type belongs in the `System.Resources` namespace but is implemented in the System.Windows.Forms.dll assembly. To compile code that references the `ResXFileRef` type, you'd add an `Imports System.Resources` directive to your source code and you'd use the `/r:System.Windows.Forms.dll` compiler switch.

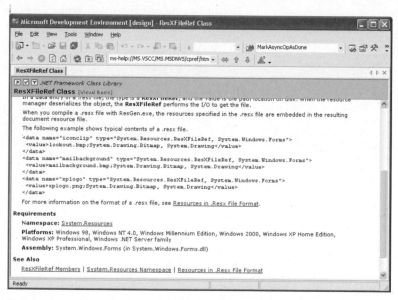

Figure 4-1 Requirements section showing namespace and assembly information for a type.

5

Primitive, Reference, and Value Types

In this chapter, I'll discuss the different kinds of types that you'll run into as a Microsoft .NET Framework developer. It is crucial that all developers be familiar with the different behaviors that these types exhibit. When I was first learning the .NET Framework, I didn't fully understand the difference between primitive, reference, and value types. This lack of clarity led me to unwittingly introduce subtle bugs and performance issues into my code. By explaining the differences between the types here, I'm hoping to save you some of the headaches I experienced while getting up to speed.

Programming Language Primitive Types

Certain data types are so commonly used that many compilers allow code to manipulate them using simplified syntax. For example, you could allocate an integer using the following syntax:

```
Dim a As System.Int32 = New System.Int32()
```

But I'm sure you'd agree that declaring and initializing an integer using this syntax is rather cumbersome. Fortunately, many compilers (including Visual Basic) allow you to use syntax similar to the following instead:

```
Dim a As Integer = 0
```

This syntax certainly makes the code more readable, and, of course, the intermediate language (IL) generated is identical no matter which syntax is used. Any data types the compiler directly supports are called *primitive types*. Primitive types map directly to types existing in the .NET Framework Class Library (FCL). For example, in Visual Basic, an `Integer` maps directly to the `System.Int32` type. Because of this, the following four lines of code all compile correctly and produce the same result: an integer initialized to 0:

```
Dim a As Integer = 0                       ' Most convenient syntax
Dim a As System.Int32 = 0                  ' Convenient syntax
Dim a As Integer = New Integer()           ' Inconvenient syntax
Dim a As System.Int32 = New System.Int32   ' Inconvenient syntax
```

Table 5-1 shows the FCL types that have corresponding primitives in Visual Basic. For the types that are compliant with the Common Language Specification (CLS), other languages will offer similar primitive types. However, languages aren't required to offer any support for the non-CLS-compliant types.

Microsoft documentation states, "As a matter of style, use of the keyword is favored over use of the complete system type name." I disagree with this statement; I prefer to use the FCL type names and completely avoid the primitive type names. In fact, I wish that compilers didn't even offer the primitive type names and forced developers to use the FCL type names instead. Here are my reasons:

- I've seen a number of developers confused, not knowing whether to use `Integer` or `Int32` in their code. Because in Visual Basic the `Integer` (a keyword) maps exactly to `System.Int32` (a FCL type), there is no difference and either can be used.

- In Visual Basic, `Long` maps to `System.Int64`, but in a different programming language, `Long` could map to an `Int16` or `Int32`. In fact, Managed Extensions for C++ treats `long` (lowercase) as an `Int32`. Someone reading source code in one language could easily misinterpret the code's intention if the person was used to programming in a different programming language. In fact, most languages won't even treat `Long` as a keyword and won't compile code that uses it.

- The FCL has many types with methods that have type names as part of their method names. For example, the `BinaryReader` type offers methods such as `ReadBoolean`, `ReadInt32`, `ReadSingle`, and so on, and the `System.Convert` type offers methods such as `ToBoolean`, `ToInt32`, `ToSingle`, and so on. Although it's legal to write the following code, the line with `Integer` feels very unnatural to me, and it's not obvious that the line is correct:

```
Dim br As New BinaryReader(...)
Dim val As Integer = br.ReadInt32()     ' OK, but feels unnatural
Dim val2 As Int32 = br.ReadInt32()      ' OK and feels good
```

For all these reasons, I'll use the FCL type names throughout this book.

In many programming languages, you would expect the following code to compile and execute correctly:

```
Dim i As Int32 = 5        ' A 32-bit value
Dim l As Int64 = I        ' Implicit cast to a 64-bit value
```

Table 5-1   FCL Types with Corresponding Visual Basic Primitives

Visual Basic Primitive Type	FCL Type	CLS-Compliant	Description
Byte	System.Byte	Yes	Unsigned 8-bit value
Short	System.Int16	Yes	Signed 16-bit value
Integer	System.Int32	Yes	Signed 32-bit value
Long	System.Int64	Yes	Signed 64-bit value
Char	System.Char	Yes	16-bit Unicode character (**char** never represents an 8-bit value as it would in unmanaged C++.)
Single	System.Single	Yes	IEEE 32-bit **float**
Double	System.Double	Yes	IEEE 64-bit **float**
Boolean	System.Boolean	Yes	A **True/False** value. In Visual Basic, casting a **Boolean** whose value is **True** to a numeric type results in a value of −**1**. Note that many other languages cast a **Boolean** value of **True** to +**1**.
Decimal	System.Decimal	Yes	A 128-bit high-precision floating-point value commonly used for financial calculations where rounding errors can't be tolerated. Of the 128 bits, 1 bit represents the sign of the value, 96 bits represent the value itself, and 8 bits represent the power of 10 to divide the 96-bit value by (can be anywhere from 0 to 28). The remaining bits are unused.
Object	System.Object	Yes	Base type of all types
String	System.String	Yes	An array of characters

However, based on the casting discussion presented in Chapter 4, you wouldn't expect this code to compile. After all, `System.Int32` and `System.Int64` are different types. Well, you'll be happy to know that the Visual Basic compiler does compile this code correctly and it runs as expected. Why?

The reason is that the Visual Basic compiler has intimate knowledge of primitive types and applies its own special rules when compiling the code. In other words, your compiler of choice recognizes common programming patterns and produces the necessary IL to make the written code work as expected. Specifically, compilers typically support patterns related to casting, literals, and operators, as shown in the following examples.

First, the compiler is able to perform implicit or explicit casts between primitive types like these:

```
Dim i As Int32 = 5                    ' Implicit cast from Int32 to Int32
Dim l As Int64 = i                    ' Implicit cast from Int32 to Int64
Dim s As Single = i                   ' Implicit cast from Int32 to Single
Dim b As Byte = CType(i, Byte)        ' Explicit cast from Int32 to Byte
Dim v As Int16 = CType(s, Int16)      ' Explicit cast from Single to Int16
```

(As I explain in Chapter 4, Visual Basic also offers specific operators for conversion between primitive types, such as `CInt`, `CStr`, and the new `CShort` and `CChar`.) Visual Basic allows implicit casts if the conversion is "safe," that is, no loss of data is possible, such as converting an `Int32` to an `Int64`. But with `Option Strict` turned on, Visual Basic requires explicit casts if the conversion is potentially unsafe. For numeric types, "unsafe" means that you could lose precision or magnitude as a result of the conversion. For example, converting from `Int32` to `Byte` requires an explicit cast because precision might be lost from large `Int32` numbers; converting from `Single` to `Int16` requires a cast because `Single` can represent numbers of a larger magnitude than `Int16` can.

Be aware that different compilers can generate different code to handle these cast operations. For example, when casting a `Single` with a value of 6.8 to an `Int32`, some compilers could generate code to put a 6 in the `Int32`, and others could perform the cast by rounding the result up to 7. By the way, Visual Basic uses a technique called *bankers rounding*, which works like this: if the fractional part is less than .5, the fractional part of the number is truncated; if the fractional part is higher than .5, the number is rounded up; and if the fractional part is exactly .5, the number is rounded down if the integer part is an even number and rounded up if the integer part is an odd number. You can avoid bankers rounding by using Visual Basic's `Fix` and `Int` functions instead of casting.

> **Note** If you find yourself working with types that your compiler of choice doesn't support as primitive types, you might be able to use the static methods of the `System.Convert` type to help you cast between objects of different types. The `Convert` type knows how to convert between objects within the various core types in the FCL: `Boolean`, `Char`, `SByte`, `Byte`, `Int16`, `UInt16`, `Int32`, `UInt32`, `Int64`, `UInt64`, `Single`, `Double`, `Decimal`, `DateTime`, and `String`. The `Convert` type also offers a static `ChangeType` method that allows an object to be converted from one type to another arbitrary type as long as the type of the source object implements the `IConvertible` interface and specifically the `ToType` method. Visual Basic's `CType` operator takes advantage of `Convert`'s methods internally to help it cast objects from one type to another.

In addition to casting, primitive types can be written as literals, as shown here:

```
Console.WriteLine(123.ToString() & 456.ToString())  ' "123456"
```

Also, if you have an expression consisting of literals, the compiler is able to evaluate the expression at compile time, improving the application's performance.

```
Dim found As Boolean = False    ' Generated code sets found to 0.
Dim x As Int32 = 100 + 20 + 3   ' Generated code sets x to 123.
Dim s As String = "a " & "bc"   ' Generated code sets s to "a bc".
```

Visual Basic supports typed constants too, using the **Const** keyword:

```
Const ONE As Short = 1
Const USERNAME As String = "Jeff"
```

By default, all integer numbers that appear in code are **Int32** constants and all floating-point numbers are **Double** constants, but you can change their type by appending a character suffix:

```
Dim sh As Int16 = 1S       ' S is for Short.
Dim i As Int32 = 2%        ' % is for Integer.
Dim l As Int64 = 3&        ' & is for Long.
Dim si As Single = 4.0!    ' ! is for Single.
Dim do As Double = 5.0#    ' # is for Double.
Dim de As Decimal = 6@     ' @ is for Decimal.
```

Finally, the compiler automatically knows how to interpret operators (such as **+**, **-**, *****, **/**, **&**, **^**, **=**, **<>**, **>**, **<**, **>=**, **<=**, and so on) when used in code:

```
Dim x As Int32 = 10
Dim y As Int32 = x + 23
Dim lessThanFifty As Boolean = (y < 50)
```

Checked and Unchecked Primitive Type Operations

Programmers are well aware that many arithmetic operations on primitives could result in an overflow:

```
Dim b As Byte = 100
b = CType(b + 200, Byte)        ' This throws an overflow.
```

> **Important**   The CLR performs arithmetic operations on 32-bit and 64-bit values only. So, b and 200 are first converted to 32-bit values and then added together. The result is a 32-bit value that must be cast to a `Byte` before the result can be stored back in the variable b. Visual Basic doesn't perform this cast for you implicitly, which is why the `Byte` cast on the second line of the preceding code is required.

Different languages handle overflows in different ways. C and C++ don't consider overflows to be an error and allow the value to wrap; the application continues running with its fingers crossed. On the other hand, by default, Visual Basic considers integer overflows as errors and throws an exception when it detects an overflow.

The CLR offers IL instructions that allow the compiler to choose the desired behavior. The CLR has an instruction called **add** that adds two values together. The **add** instruction performs no overflow checking. The CLR also has an instruction called **add.ovf** that adds two values together. However, **add.ovf** throws a `System.OverflowException` exception if an overflow occurs. In addition to these two IL instructions for the add operation, the CLR also has similar IL instructions for subtraction (**sub/sub.ovf**), multiplication (**mul/mul.ovf**), and data conversions (**conv/conv.ovf**).

Visual Basic allows the programmer to decide how overflows should be handled. By default, overflow checking is turned on. This means that the compiler generates IL code using the versions of the add, subtract, multiply, and conversion instructions that include overflow checking. As a result, the code runs slowly—but developers can be assured that all overflows will correctly throw an exception.

You can get the Visual Basic compiler to ignore overflows using VBC.exe's **/removeintchecks+** command-line switch (or by selecting the Remove Integer Overflow Checks check box in Visual Studio's Optimizations page in the Project Properties dialog box). This switch tells the compiler to generate code using the versions of the add, subtract, multiply, and conversion IL instructions that don't check for overflows. The code executes faster because the CLR isn't checking these operations to see whether an overflow will occur. If an overflow does occur, the result will be incorrect (it will wrap over the highest or lowest allowed limit for the target data type) but no **OverflowException** exception will be thrown. In some cases, the wrapping behavior isn't a problem or is even desired, for example, when calculating a hash value or a checksum.

Note that the **/removeintchecks+** command-line switch affects only integer overflows. Floating-point operations never throw an overflow exception. Instead, they store the special infinity value in the target variable:

```
Dim d As Double = 1E100
d = d ^ 4                          ' Causes an overflow
Console.WriteLine(d)               ' Displays "Infinity"
```

You can test whether a floating-point value is equal to infinity by means of the **IsPositiveInfinity** and **IsNegativeInfinity** shared methods of the **System.Single** and **System.Double** classes, or you can just compare a value with the **PositiveInfinity** or **NegativeInfinity** constants as demonstrated here:

```
' Continuing previous code snippet
Console.WriteLine(Double.IsPositiveInfinity(d))    ' Displays "True"
Console.WriteLine(d = Double.PositiveInfinity)     ' Displays "True"
```

Infinite values follow the usual algebra rules. For example, adding two positive infinite values gives a positive infinity; adding two negative infinite values gives a negative infinity (shown as **−Infinity**); dividing any number by a positive or negative infinite value returns 0. Most other operations on infinite values, such as divisions between infinite numbers, aren't defined and return a **NaN** (Not-a-Number) value, which can be tested with **System.Single** and **System.Double** class's shared **IsNan** method.

Rather than have overflow checking turned on or off globally, programmers are much more likely to want to decide case by case whether to have overflow checking. Although C# allows this flexibility by offering **checked** and **unchecked** operators, Visual Basic is missing this feature.

Important   The System.Decimal type is a very special type. Although many programming languages (Visual Basic and C# included) consider Decimal a primitive type, the CLR does not. This means that the CLR doesn't have IL instructions that know how to manipulate a Decimal value. If you look up the Decimal type in the .NET Framework documentation, you'll see that it has public, static methods called Add, Subtract, Multiply, Divide, and so on. In addition, the Decimal type provides operator overload methods for +, -, *, /, and so on.

When you compile code using Decimal values, the compiler generates code to call Decimal's members to perform the actual operation. This means that manipulating Decimal values is slower than manipulating CLR primitive values. Also, because there are no IL instructions for manipulating Decimal values, VBC.exe's /removeintchecks+ command-line switch has no effect. Operations on Decimal values always throw an OverflowException exception if the operation can't be performed safely.

Reference Types and Value Types

The CLR supports two kinds of types: reference types and value types. Of the two, you'll run into reference types much more often. *Reference types* are always allocated from the managed heap, and the Visual Basic **New** operator returns the memory address of the object—the memory address refers to the object's bits. You need to bear in mind some performance considerations when you're working with reference types. First consider these facts:

■ The memory must be allocated from the managed heap.

■ Each object allocated on the heap has some additional overhead members associated with it that must be initialized.

■ Allocating an object from the managed heap could force a garbage collection to occur.

If every type were a reference type, an application's performance would suffer greatly. Imagine how poor performance would be if every time you used an Int32 value, a memory allocation occurred! To improve performance for simple, frequently used types, the CLR offers "lightweight" types called *value types*. Value type instances are usually allocated on a thread's stack (although they can also be embedded in a reference type object). The variable representing the instance doesn't contain a pointer to an instance; the variable contains the fields of the instance itself. Because the variable contains the instance's fields, a pointer doesn't have to be dereferenced to manipulate the instance. Value type instances don't come under the control of the garbage collector, thus reducing pressure in the managed heap and reducing the number of collections an application requires over its lifetime.

The .NET Framework Reference documentation clearly indicates which types are reference types and which are value types. When looking up a type in the documentation, any type called a *class* is a reference type. For example, the `System.Object` class, the `System.Exception` class, the `System.IO.FileStream` class, and the `System.Random` class are all reference types. On the other hand, the documentation refers to each value type as a *structure* or an *enumeration*. For example, the `System.Int32` structure, the `System.Boolean` structure, the `System.Decimal` structure, the `System.TimeSpan` structure, the `System.DayOf-Week` enumeration, the `System.IO.FileAttributes` enumeration, and the `System.Drawing.FontStyle` enumeration are all value types.

If you look more closely at the documentation, you'll notice that all the structures are immediately derived from the `System.ValueType` type. `System.ValueType` is itself immediately derived from the `System.Object` type. By definition, all value types must be derived from `System.ValueType`.

> **Note**   All enumerations are derived from `System.Enum`, which is itself derived from `System.ValueType`. The CLR and all programming languages give enumerations special treatment. For more information about enumerated types, refer to Chapter 13.

Even though you can't choose a base type when defining your own value type, a value type can implement one or more interfaces if you choose. In addition, the CLR doesn't allow a value type to be used as a base type for any other reference type or value type. So, for example, it's not possible to define any new types using `Boolean`, `Char`, `Int32`, `Int64`, `Single`, `Double`, `Decimal`, and so on as base types.

The following code and Figure 5-1 demonstrate how reference types and value types differ:

```vb
' Reference type (because of 'Class')
Class SomeRef
    Public x As Int32
End Class

' Value type (because of 'Structure')
Structure SomeVal
    Public x As Int32
End Structure

Class App
    Public Shared Sub Main()
        Dim r1 As New SomeRef()     ' Allocated in heap
        Dim v1 As New SomeVal()     ' Allocated on stack
        r1.x = 5                    ' Pointer dereference
        v1.x = 5                    ' Changed on stack
        Console.WriteLine(r1.x)     ' Displays "5"
        Console.WriteLine(v1.x)     ' Also displays "5"
        ' The left side of Figure 5-1 reflects the situation
        ' after the lines above have executed.

        Dim r2 As SomeRef = r1      ' Copies reference (pointer) only
        Dim v2 As SomeVal = v1      ' Allocates on stack and copies members
        r1.x = 8                    ' Changes r1.x and r2.x
        v1.x = 9                    ' Changes v1.x, not v2.x
        Console.WriteLine(r1.x)     ' Displays "8"
        Console.WriteLine(r2.x)     ' Displays "8"
        Console.WriteLine(v1.x)     ' Displays "9"
        Console.WriteLine(v2.x)     ' Displays "5"
        ' The right side of Figure 5-1 reflects the situation
        ' after ALL the lines above have executed.
    End Sub
End Class
```

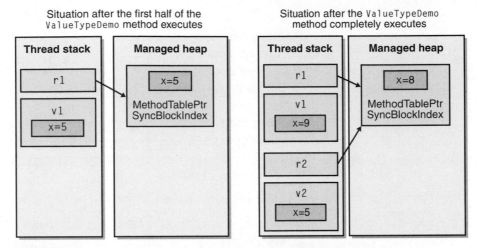

Figure 5-1   Memory layout differences between reference and value types

In this code, the **SomeVal** type is declared using **Structure** instead of the more common **Class**. In Visual Basic, types declared using **Structure** are value types, and types declared using **Class** are reference types. As you can see, the behavior of reference types and value types differ quite a bit. As you use types in your code, you must be aware of whether the type is a reference type or a value type because it can greatly affect how you express your intentions in the code.

> **Note**   Other languages can have different syntaxes for describing value types versus reference types. For example, C# uses the **struct** keyword, and Managed Extensions for C++ uses the **__value** modifier.

In the preceding code, you saw this line:

```
Dim v1 As New SomeVal()      ' Allocated on stack
```

The way this line is written makes it look like a **SomeVal** instance will be allocated on the managed heap. However, the Visual Basic compiler knows that **SomeVal** is a value type and produces code that allocates the **SomeVal** instance on the thread's stack. Visual Basic also ensures that all the fields in the value type instance are zeroed.

The preceding line could have been written like this instead:

```
Dim v1 As SomeVal    ' Allocated on stack
```

This line also produces IL that allocates the instance on the thread's stack and zeroes the fields.

When designing your own types, consider carefully whether to define them as value types instead of reference types. In some situations, value types can give better performance. In particular, you should declare a type as a value type if *all* the following statements are true:

- The type acts like a primitive type.

- The type doesn't need to inherit from any other type.

- The type won't have any other types derived from it.

- Instances of the type aren't frequently passed as method parameters. By default, parameters are passed by value, which causes the fields in value type instances to be copied, frequently hurting performance.

- Instances of the type aren't frequently returned from methods. Again, a method that returns a value type causes the fields in the instance to be copied into memory allocated by the caller when the method returns, hurting performance.

- Instances of the type aren't frequently used in collections such as **ArrayList**, **Hashtable**, and so on. Classes that manage a set of generic objects require that value type instances be boxed. Boxing causes additional memory to be allocated, and additional memory copy operations hurt performance. (I'll explain boxing and unboxing in more detail in the next section.)

The main advantage of value types is that they're not allocated in the managed heap. Of course, value types have several limitations of their own when compared to reference types. Here are some of the ways in which value types and reference types differ:

- Value type objects have two representations: an *unboxed* form and a *boxed* form (discussed in the next section). Reference types are always in a boxed form.

- Value types are derived from **System.ValueType**. This type offers the same methods as defined by **System.Object**. However, **System.Value-Type** overrides the **Equals** method so that it returns **True** if the values of the two object's fields match. In addition, **System.ValueType** overrides the **GetHashCode** method so that it produces a hash code value using an algorithm that takes into account the values in the object's instance fields. When defining your own value types, you should override and provide explicit implementations for the **Equals** and **GetHashCode** methods. I'll cover the **Equals** and **GetHashCode** methods in Chapter 6.

■ Because you can't declare a new value type or a new reference type using a value type as a base class, you shouldn't introduce any new virtual methods into a value type. No methods can be abstract, and all methods are implicitly sealed (can't be overridden).

■ Reference type variables contain the memory address of objects in the heap. By default, when a reference type variable is created, it is initialized to **Nothing**, indicating that the reference type variable doesn't currently point to a valid object. Attempting to use a **Nothing** reference type variable causes a **NullReferenceException** exception to be thrown. By contrast, value type variables always contain a value of the underlying type, and all members of the value type are initialized to 0. It's not possible to generate a **NullReferenceException** exception when accessing a value type.

■ When you assign a value type variable to another value type variable, a field-by-field copy is made. When you assign a reference type variable to another reference type variable, only the memory address is copied.

■ Because of the previous point, two or more reference type variables can refer to a single object in the heap, allowing operations on one variable to affect the object referenced by the other variable. On the other hand, value type variables each have their own copy of the "object's" data, and it's not possible for operations on one value type variable to affect another.

■ Because unboxed value types aren't allocated on the heap, the storage allocated for them is freed as soon as the method that defines an instance of the type is no longer active. This means that a value type instance doesn't receive a notification (via a **Finalize** method) when its memory is reclaimed.

> **Note** In fact, it would be quite odd to define a value type with a
> `Finalize` method since the method would be called only on boxed
> instances. For this reason, many compilers (including C#) don't allow
> you to define `Finalize` methods on value types. Although the CLR
> allows a value type to define a `Finalize` method, the CLR won't call
> this method when a boxed instance of the value type is garbage col-
> lected. The Visual Basic compiler accepts `Finalize` methods on value
> types, but this method is never called.

How the CLR Controls the Layout of a Type's Fields

To improve performance, the CLR is capable of arranging the fields of a
type any way it chooses. For example, the CLR might reorder fields in
memory so that object references are grouped together and data fields are
properly aligned and packed. However, when you define a type, you can
tell the CLR whether it must keep the type's fields in the same order the
developer specified them or whether it can reorder as it sees fit.

You tell the CLR what to do by applying the `System.Run-`
`time.InteropServices.StructLayoutAttribute` attribute on the class or
structure you're defining. To this attribute's constructor, you can pass `Lay-`
`outKind.Auto` to have the CLR arrange the fields or `LayoutKind.Sequen-`
`tial` to have the CLR preserve your field layout. If you don't explicitly
specify the `StructLayoutAttribute` on a type that you're defining, your
compiler selects whatever layout it thinks best.

You should be aware that Microsoft's Visual Basic and C# compilers
select `LayoutKind.Auto` for reference types (classes) and `Layout-`
`Kind.Sequential` for value types (structures). It is obvious that these two
compiler teams feel that structures are commonly used when interoperating
with unmanaged code, and for this to work, the fields must stay in the order
defined by the programmer. However, if you're creating a value type that
has nothing to do with interoperability with unmanaged code, you probably
want to override the Visual Basic compiler's default. Here's an example:

How the CLR Controls the Layout of a Type's Fields   *(continued)*

```
Imports System
Imports System.Runtime.InteropServices

' Let the CLR arrange the fields to improve performance for
' this value type.
<StructLayout(LayoutKind.Auto)> _
Structure Point
    Public x, y As Int32
End Structure
```

Boxing and Unboxing Value Types

Value types are lighter weight than reference types because they are not allocated in the managed heap, not garbage collected, and not referred to by pointers. However, in many cases, you must get a reference to an instance of a value type. For example, let's say that you wanted to create an **ArrayList** object (a type defined in the **System.Collections** namespace) to hold a set of **Point** structures. The code might look like this:

```
' Declare a value type.
Structure Point
    Public x, y As Int32
End Structure

Class App
    Shared Sub Main()
        Dim a As New ArrayList()
        Dim p As Point                 ' Allocate a Point (not in the heap).
        Dim i As Int32
        For i = 0 To 9
            p.x = i                    ' Initialize the members in the value type.
            p.y = i
            a.Add(p)                   ' Box the value type and add the
                                       ' reference to the ArrayList.
        Next
        ⋮
    End Sub
End Class
```

With each iteration of the loop, a **Point** value type's fields are initialized. Then the **Point** is stored in the **ArrayList**. But let's think about this for a moment. What is actually being stored in the **ArrayList**? Is it the **Point** structure, the address of the **Point** structure, or something else entirely? To get the answer, you must look up **ArrayList**'s **Add** method and see what type its parameter is defined as. In this case, the **Add** method is prototyped as follows:

```
Public Overridable Function Add(ByVal value As Object) As Int32
```

From this, you can plainly see that **Add** takes an **Object** as a parameter, indicating that **Add** requires a reference (or pointer) to an object on the managed heap as a parameter. But in the preceding code, I'm passing **p** a **Point** value type. For this code to work, the **Point** value type must be converted into a true heap-managed object and a reference to this object must be obtained.

It's possible to convert a value type to a reference type using a mechanism called *boxing*. Internally, here's what happens when an instance of a value type is boxed:

1. Memory is allocated from the managed heap. The amount of memory allocated is the size the value type requires plus any additional overhead to consider this value type to be a true object. The additional overhead includes a method table pointer and a SyncBlock-Index.

2. The value type's fields are copied to the newly allocated heap memory.

3. The address of the object is returned. This address is now a reference to an object; the value type is now a reference type.

Some language compilers, like Visual Basic and C#, automatically produce the IL code necessary to box a value type instance, but you still need to understand what's going on under the covers so that you're aware of code size and performance issues.

In the preceding code, the Visual Basic compiler detected that I was passing a value type to a method that requires a reference type, and it automatically emitted code to box the object. So at run time, the fields currently residing in the **Point** value type (**p**) are copied into the newly allocated **Point** object. The address of the boxed **Point** object (now a reference type) is returned and is then passed to the **Add** method. The **Point** object will remain in the heap until it is garbage collected. The **Point** value type variable (**p**) can be reused or freed since the **ArrayList** never knows anything about it. Note that the lifetime of the boxed value type extends beyond the lifetime of the unboxed value type.

Many languages designed for the CLR (for example, Visual Basic and C#) automatically emit the code necessary to box value types into reference types when necessary. However, some languages (such as Managed Extensions for C++) require that the programmer write code to explicitly box value types when necessary.

Now that you know how boxing works, let's talk about unboxing. Let's say that in another piece of code you want to grab the first element out of the **ArrayList**:

```
Dim p As Point = DirectCast(a(0), Point)
```

Here you're taking the reference (or pointer) contained in element 0 of the **ArrayList** and trying to put it into a **Point** value type, **p**. For this to work, all the fields contained in the boxed **Point** object must be copied into the value type variable, **p**, which is on the thread's stack. The CLR accomplishes this copying in two steps. First the address of the **Point** fields in the boxed **Point** object is obtained. This process is called *unboxing*. Then the values of these fields are copied from the heap to the stack-based value type instance.

Unboxing is *not* the exact opposite of boxing. The unboxing operation is much less costly than boxing. Unboxing is really just the operation of obtaining a pointer to the raw value type (data fields) contained within an object. So, unlike boxing, unboxing doesn't involve the copying of any bytes in memory. However, an unboxing operation is typically followed by copying the fields, making these two operations the exact opposite of a boxing operation.

Obviously, boxing and unbox/copy operations hurt your application's performance in terms of both speed and memory, so you should be aware of when the compiler generates code to perform these operations automatically and try to write code that minimizes this code generation.

Internally, here's exactly what happens when a reference type is unboxed:

1. If the reference is **Nothing**, a **NullReferenceException** exception is thrown.

2. If the reference doesn't refer to an object that is a boxed value of the desired value type, an **InvalidCastException** exception is thrown.

A pointer to the value type contained inside the object is returned. The value type that this pointer refers to doesn't know anything about the usual overhead associated with a true object: a method table pointer and a SyncBlockIndex.

In effect, the pointer refers to the unboxed portion in the boxed object. The second item means that the following code will *not* work as you might expect:

```
Shared Sub Main()
   Dim x As Int32 = 5
   Dim o As Object = x                   ' Box x; o refers to the boxed
                                         ' object.
   Dim y As Int16 = DirectCast(o, Int16) ' Throws an InvalidCastException
End Sub
```

Logically, it makes sense to take the boxed **Int32** that **o** refers to and cast it to an **Int16**. However, when unboxing an object, the cast must be to the unboxed type—**Int32** in this case. Here's the correct way to write this code:

```
Shared Sub Main()
   Dim x As Int32 = 5
   Dim o As Object = x             ' Box x; o refers to the boxed object.
   ' Unbox to the correct type, and then cast.
   Dim y As Int16 = CType(DirectCast(o, Int32), Int16)
End Sub
```

However, the **CType** operator, being aggressive in its effort to cast values, allows you to unbox the value and cast it in a single operation:

```
Dim y As Int16 = CType(o, Int16)
```

Even though, strictly speaking, an unboxing operation doesn't copy any fields, it is frequently followed immediately by a field copy, which does copy the fields from the heap to the stack. In fact, in Visual Basic, an unbox operation is always followed by a field copy. Let's take a look at some Visual Basic code demonstrating that unbox and copy operations always work together:

```
Shared Sub Main()
   Dim p As Point
   p.x = 1: p.y = 1
   Dim o As Object = p         ' Boxes p; o refers to the boxed object.
   p = DirectCast(o, Point)    ' Unboxes o AND copies fields from
                               ' object to stack
End Sub
```

On the last line of code, the Visual Basic compiler emits an IL instruction to unbox **o** (get the address of the fields in the object) and another IL instruction to copy the fields from the heap to the stack-based variable **p**.

Now look at this code:

```
Shared Sub Main()
   Dim p As Point
   p.x = 1
   p.y = 1
   Dim o As Object = p         ' Boxes p; o refers to the boxed object.
```

```
' The lines below change Point's x field to 2.
p = DirectCast(o, Point)   ' Unboxes o AND copies fields from
                           ' object to stack
p.x = 2
o = p
End Sub
```

The code at the bottom of this fragment just wants to change **Point**'s **x** field from 1 to 2. To do this, an unbox operation must be performed, followed by a field copy, followed by changing the field (on the stack), followed by a boxing operation (which creates a whole new object in the managed heap). Hopefully, you see the impact that boxing and unboxing/copying operations have on your application's performance.

Some languages, like Managed Extensions for C++, allow you to unbox a boxed value type without copying the fields. Unboxing returns the address of the unboxed portion of a boxed object (ignoring the object's method table pointer and SyncBlockIndex overhead). You can now use this pointer to manipulate the unboxed instance's fields (which happen to be in a boxed object on the heap). For example, the previous code would be much more efficient if written in Managed Extensions for C++ because you could change the value of **Point**'s **x** field within the already boxed **Point** object. This would avoid both allocating a new object on the heap and copying all the fields twice!

Important   If you're the least bit concerned about your application's performance, you must be aware of when the compiler produces the code that performs these operations. Some languages, such as Managed Extensions for C++, require the programmer to explicitly write code to box and unbox value types. Managed Extensions for C++ offers the **__box** operator and `dynamic_cast` operator to do boxing and unboxing operations, respectively. This requirement makes the developer's job harder because he must write the necessary code; on the plus side, though, the developer will know exactly when boxing and unboxing operations are occurring. However, many languages (such as Visual Basic and C#) will automatically emit the IL code necessary to box and unbox value types. Although this built-in functionality makes the code look nicer and eases the burden on the developer, it also means that it's not obvious to the developer when boxing and unboxing operations are occurring.

Let's look at a few more examples that demonstrate boxing and unboxing:

```
Sub Main()
   Dim v As Int32 = 5        ' Create an unboxed value type variable.
   Dim o As Object = v       ' o refers to a boxed Int32 containing 5.
   v = 123                   ' Changes the unboxed value to 123
   Console.WriteLine(
      String.Concat(v, ", ", DirectCast(o, Int32))) ' Displays "123, 5"
End Sub
```

In this code, can you guess how many boxing operations occur? You might be surprised to discover that the answer is three! Let's analyze the code carefully to really understand what's going on. To help you understand, I've included the IL code generated for the **Main** method shown in the preceding code. I've commented the code so that you can easily see the individual operations.

```
.method public static void  Main() cil managed
{
  .entrypoint
  .custom instance void [mscorlib]System.STAThreadAttribute::.ctor() = ( 01 00
00 00 )
  // Code size       50 (0x32)
  .maxstack  3
  .locals init ([0] object o,
                [1] int32 v)

  // Load 5 into v.
  IL_0000:  ldc.i4.5
  IL_0001:  stloc.1

  // Box v, and store the reference pointer in o.
  IL_0002:  ldloc.1
  IL_0003:  box          [mscorlib]System.Int32
  IL_0008:  stloc.0

  // Load 123 into v.
  IL_0009:  ldc.i4.s   123
  IL_000b:  stloc.1

  // Box v, and leave the pointer on the stack for Concat.
  IL_000c:  ldloc.1
  IL_000d:  box          [mscorlib]System.Int32

  // Load the string on the stack for Concat.
  IL_0012:  ldstr        ", "

  // Unbox o: Get the pointer to the Int32's field on the stack.
  IL_0017:  ldloc.0
  IL_0018:  unbox        [mscorlib]System.Int32
```

```
// Copy the bytes from the boxed Int32 to the stack.
IL_001d:  ldobj      [mscorlib]System.Int32

// Box the Int32, and leave the pointer on the stack for Concat.
IL_0022:  box        [mscorlib]System.Int32

// Call Concat.
IL_0027:  call       string [mscorlib]System.String::Concat(object,
                                                            object,
                                                            object)

// The string returned by Concat is passed to Console.WriteLine.
IL_002c:  call       void [mscorlib]System.Console::WriteLine(string)
IL_0031:  ret
} // end of method Module1::Main
```

First an **Int32** unboxed value type (**v**) is created and initialized to 5. Then an **Object** reference type (**o**) is created, and it wants to point to **v**. But because reference types must always point to objects in the heap, Visual Basic generated the proper IL code to box **v** and store the address of the boxed "copy" of **v** in **o**. Now the value 123 is placed into the unboxed value type **v**; this has no effect on the boxed **Int32** value, which keeps its value of 5.

Next is the call to the **String.Concat** method, passing three parameters: an unboxed **Int32** value type (**v**), a **String** (which is a reference type), and a reference to a boxed **Int32** value type (**o**) that is being cast to an unboxed **Int32**. These must somehow be combined to create a **String**.

There are several overloaded versions of the **Concat** method; all of them perform identically—the only difference is in the number of parameters. Because a string is being created from the concatenation of three items, the **Concat** method called has the following signature:

```
Public Public Shared Function Concat(ByVal arg0 As Object, _
    ByVal arg1 As Object, ByVal arg2 As Object) As String
```

For the first parameter, **arg0**, **v** is passed. But **v** is an unboxed value parameter and **arg0** is an **Object**, so **v** must be boxed and the address to the boxed **v** is passed for **arg0**. For the **arg1** parameter, the "**,**" string is passed as a reference to a **String** object. Finally, for the **arg2** parameter, **o** (a reference to an **Object**) is cast to an **Int32**, creating a temporary instance of an **Int32** value type on the IL evaluation stack that receives a copy of the unboxed version of the value currently referred to by **o**. This temporary **Int32** value type must be boxed again with the memory address being passed for **Concat**'s **arg2** parameter.

The **Concat** method calls each of the specified object's **ToString** methods and concatenates each object's string representation. The **String** object returned from **Concat** is then passed to **WriteLine** to show the final result.

You can improve the previous code by calling **WriteLine** like this:

```
Console.WriteLine(String.Concat(v.ToString, ", ", o))   ' Displays "123, 5"
```

Now **ToString** is called on the unboxed value type **v** and a **String** is returned. String objects are already reference types and can simply be passed to the **Concat** method without requiring any boxing.

Let's look at yet another example that demonstrates boxing and unboxing:

```
Shared Sub Main()
    Dim v As Int32 = 5          ' Create an unboxed value type variable.
    Dim o As Object = v         ' o refers to the boxed version of v.

    v = 123                     ' Changes the unboxed value type to 123
    Console.WriteLine(v)        ' Displays "123"

    v = CType(o, Int32)         ' Unboxes o into v.
    Console.WriteLine(v)        ' Displays "5"
End Sub
```

How many boxing operations do you count in this code? The answer is one. The reason that there is only one boxing operation is that the **System.Console** class defines a **WriteLine** method that accepts an **Int32** as a parameter:

```
Public Shared Sub WriteLine(ByVal value As Int32)
```

In the two calls to **WriteLine** above, the variable **v**, an **Int32** unboxed value type, is passed by value. Now, it could be that **WriteLine** will box this **Int32** internally, but you have no control over that. The important thing is that you've done the best you could and have eliminated the boxing from your own code.

If you take a close look at the FCL, you'll notice many overloaded methods that differ based on their value type parameters. For example, the **System.Console** type offers several overloaded versions of the **WriteLine** method:

```
Public Shared Sub WriteLine(ByVal value As Boolean)
Public Shared Sub WriteLine(ByVal value As Char)
Public Shared Sub WriteLine(ByVal value As Int32)
Public Shared Sub WriteLine(ByVal value As UInt32)
Public Shared Sub WriteLine(ByVal value As Int64)
Public Shared Sub WriteLine(ByVal value As UInt64)
Public Shared Sub WriteLine(ByVal value As Single)
Public Shared Sub WriteLine(ByVal value As Double)
Public Shared Sub WriteLine(ByVal value As Decimal)
```

You'll also find a similar set of overloaded methods for **System.Console**'s **Write** method, **System.IO.BinaryWriter**'s **Write** method, **System.IO.Text-Writer**'s **Write** and **WriteLine** methods, **System.Runtime.Serialization.Seri-alizationInfo**'s **AddValue** method, **System.Text.StringBuilder**'s **Append** and

Insert methods, and so on. All these methods offer overloaded versions for the sole purpose of reducing the number of boxing operations for the common value types.

The fact that these overloaded methods exist clearly show that Microsoft felt it necessary to reduce boxing operations in order to improve overall performance. Certainly, you should write code that tries to reduce boxing whenever possible. Of course, there are times when boxing is necessary and it comes in quite handy. Basically, if you want a reference to an instance of a value type, the instance must be boxed. Usually this happens because you have a value type and you want to pass it to a method that requires a reference type. However, this situation isn't the only one in which you'll need to box an instance of a value type.

Recall that unboxed value types are lighter-weight types than reference types for two reasons:

- They are not allocated on the managed heap.

- They don't have the additional overhead members that every object on the heap has: a method table pointer and a SyncBlockIndex.

Because unboxed value types don't have a SyncBlockIndex, you can't have multiple threads synchronize their access to the instance using the methods of the **System.Threading.Monitor** type. Because unboxed value types don't have a method table pointer, you can't call inherited implementations of virtual methods using an unboxed instance of the value type. In addition, casting an unboxed instance of a value type to one of the type's interfaces requires that the instance be boxed because interfaces are always reference types. (I'll talk about interfaces in Chapter 15.) The following code demonstrates:

```
Imports System

Structure Point
    Implements ICloneable
    Public x, y As Int32

    ' Override the ToString method inherited from System.ValueType.
    Public Overrides Function ToString() As String
        Return String.Format("({0}, {1})", x, y)
    End Function

    ' Implementation of ICloneable's Clone method
    Public Function Clone() As Object Implements ICloneable.Clone
        Return MemberwiseClone()
    End Function
End Structure
```

(continued)

```
Class App
   Shared Sub Main()
      ' Create an instance of the Point value type on the stack.
      Dim p As Point

      ' Initialize the instance's fields.
      p.x = 10
      p.y = 20

      ' p does NOT get boxed to call ToString.
      Console.WriteLine(p.ToString())

      ' p DOES get boxed to call GetType.
      Console.WriteLine(p.GetType())

      ' p does NOT get boxed to call Clone.
      ' Clone returns an object that is unboxed,
      ' and its fields are copied into p2.
      Dim p2 As Point = DirectCast(p.Clone(), Point)

      ' p2 DOES get boxed, and the reference is placed in c.
      Dim c As ICloneable = p2

      ' c does NOT get boxed because it is already boxed.
      ' Clone returns a reference to an object that is saved in o.
      Dim o As Object = c.Clone()

      ' o is unboxed, and fields are copied into p.
      p = DirectCast(o, Point)
   End Sub
End Class
```

This code demonstrates several scenarios related to boxing and unboxing:

■ **Calling ToString** In the call to **ToString**, **p** doesn't have to be boxed. At first, you'd think that **p** would have to be boxed because **ToString** is a method that is inherited from the base type, **System.ValueType**. Normally, to call an inherited method, you'd need to have a pointer to the type's method table—and because **p** is an unboxed value type, there's no reference to **Point**'s method table. However, the Visual Basic compiler sees that **Point** overrides the **ToString** method, and it emits code that calls **ToString** directly. The compiler knows that polymorphism can't come into play here since **Point** is a value type and value types can't be used as the base type for any other type.

■ **Calling** GetType   In the call to GetType, p does have to be boxed. The reason is that the **Point** type doesn't implement GetType; it is inherited from **System.ValueType**. So to call GetType, you must have a pointer to **Point**'s method table, which can be obtained only by boxing **p**.

■ **Calling** Clone **(first time)**   In the first call to Clone, p doesn't have to be boxed because **Point** implements the Clone method and the compiler can just call it directly. Note that **Clone** returns an **Object**, which is a reference to a boxed **Point** object on the heap. This object must be unboxed and its fields copied to the unboxed value type **p2**.

■ **Casting to** ICloneable   When casting **p2** to a variable that is of an interface type, **p2** must be boxed because interfaces are reference types by definition. So, **p2** is boxed and the pointer to this boxed object is stored in the variable **c**.

■ **Calling** Clone **(second time)**   In the second call to Clone, no boxing occurs and the **Clone** method is called on the already boxed object residing in the heap. **Clone** creates a new object on the heap and returns a reference to this new object. This reference is saved in **o** (a reference type).

■ **Casting to** Point   When casting **o** to a **Point**, the object on the heap referred to by **o** is unboxed and its fields are copied from the heap to **p**, an instance of the **Point** type residing on the stack.

I realize that all this information about reference types, values types, and boxing might be overwhelming at first. However, a solid understanding of these concepts is critical to any .NET Framework developer's long-term success. Trust me: having a solid grasp of these concepts will allow you to build efficient applications faster and easier.

6

Common Object Operations

In this chapter, I'll describe how to properly implement the operations that all objects must exhibit. Specifically, I'll talk about object equality, identity, hash codes, and cloning.

Object Equality and Identity

The **System.Object** type offers a virtual method, named **Equals**, whose purpose is to return **True** if two objects have the same "value." The Microsoft .NET Framework Class Library (FCL) includes many methods, such as **System.Array**'s **IndexOf** method and **System.Collections.ArrayList**'s **Contains** method, that internally call **Equals**. Because **Equals** is defined by **Object** and because every type is ultimately derived from **Object**, every instance of every type offers the **Equals** method. For types that don't explicitly override **Equals**, the implementation provided by **Object** (or the nearest base class that overrides **Equals**) is inherited. The following code shows how **System.Object**'s **Equals** method is implemented:

```
Class Object
    Public Overridable Function Equals(ByVal obj As Object) As Boolean
        ' If both refer nces point to the same
        ' object, they must be equal.
        If Me Is obj Then
            Return True
        Else
            Return False
        End If
    End Function
    ⋮
End Class
```

As you can see, this method takes the simplest approach possible: if the two references being compared point to the same object, **True** is returned; in any other case, **False** is returned. If you define your own types and you want to compare their fields for equality, **Object**'s default implementation won't be sufficient for you; you must override **Equals** and provide your own implementation.

When you implement your own **Equals** method, you must ensure that it adheres to the four properties of equality:

- **Equals** must be reflexive; that is, **x.Equals(x)** must return **True**.

- **Equals** must be symmetric; that is, **x.Equals(y)** must return the same value as **y.Equals(x)**.

- **Equals** must be transitive; that is, if **x.Equals(y)** returns **True** and **y.Equals(z)** returns **True**, then **x.Equals(z)** must also return **True**.

- **Equals** must be consistent. Provided that there are no changes in the two values being compared, **Equals** should consistently return **True** or **False**.

If your implementation of **Equals** fails to adhere to all these rules, your application will behave in strange and unpredictable ways.

Unfortunately, implementing your own version of **Equals** isn't as easy and straightforward as you might expect. You must do a number of operations correctly, and, depending on the type you're defining, the operations are slightly different. Fortunately, there are only three different ways to implement **Equals**. Let's look at each pattern individually.

Implementing Equals for a Reference Type Whose Base Classes Don't Override Object's Equals

The following code shows how to implement **Equals** for a type that directly inherits **Object**'s **Equals** implementation:

```
' This is a reference type (because of 'Class').
Class MyRefType
    Inherits BaseType
    Dim refobj As RefType     ' This field is a reference type.
    Dim valobj As ValType     ' This field is a value type.

    Public Overrides Overloads Function Equals(ByVal obj As Object) As Boolean
        ' Because 'Me' isn't Nothing, if obj is Nothing,
        ' then the objects can't be equal.
        If obj Is Nothing Then Return False
```

```
      ' If the objects are of different types, they can't be equal.
      If Not (obj.GetType() Is Me.GetType()) Then Return False

      ' Cast obj to this type to access fields. NOTE: This cast can't
      ' fail because you know that the objects are of the same type.
      Dim other As MyRefType = DirectCast(obj, MyRefType)

      ' To compare reference fields, do this:
      If Not Object.Equals(refobj, other.refobj) Then Return False

      ' To compare value fields, do this:
      If Not valobj.Equals(other.valobj) Then Return False

      Return True    ' Objects are equal.
   End Function
End Class
```

This version of **Equals** starts out by comparing **obj** against **Nothing**. If the object being compared is not **Nothing**, then the types of the two objects are compared. If the objects are of different types, then they can't be equal. If both objects are the same type, then you cast **obj** to **MyRefType**, which can't possibly throw an exception because you know that both objects are of the same type. Finally, the fields in both objects are compared, and **True** is returned if all fields are equal.

You must be very careful when comparing the individual fields. The preceding code shows two different ways to compare the fields based on what types of fields you're using.

■   **Comparing reference type fields**   To compare reference type fields, you should call **Object**'s static **Equals** method. **Object**'s static **Equals** method is just a little helper method that returns **True** if two reference objects are equal. Here's how **Object**'s static **Equals** method is implemented internally:

```
Public Overloads Shared Function Equals(ByVal objA As Object, _
   ByVal objB As Object) As Boolean
   ' If objA and objB refer to the same object, return True.
   If objA Is objB Then Return True

   ' If objA or objB is Nothing, they can't be equal; return False.
   If (objA Is Nothing) OrElse (objB Is Nothing) Then Return False

   ' Ask objA if objB is equal to it, and return the result.
   Return objA.Equals(objB)
End Function
```

You use this method to compare reference type fields because it's legal for them to have a value of **Nothing**. Certainly, calling **refobj.Equals(other.refobj)** will throw a **NullReferenceException** if **refobj** is **Nothing**. **Object**'s static **Equals** helper method performs the proper checks against **Nothing** for you.

- **Comparing value type fields**   To compare value type fields, you should call the field type's **Equals** method to have it compare the two fields. You shouldn't call **Object**'s static **Equals** method because value types can never be **Nothing** and calling the static **Equals** method would box both value type objects.

Implementing Equals for a Reference Type When One or More of Its Base Classes Overrides Object's Equals

The following code shows how to implement **Equals** for a type that inherits an implementation of **Equals** other than the one **Object** provides:

```
' This is a reference type (because of 'Class').
Class MyRefType
   Inherits BaseType
   Dim refobj As RefType      ' This field is a reference type.
   Dim valobj As ValType      ' This field is a value type.

   Public Overloads Overrides Function Equals(ByVal obj As Object) As Boolean
      ' Let the base type compare its fields.
      If Not MyBase.Equals(obj) Then Return False

      ' All the code from here down is identical to
      ' that shown in the previous version.

      ' Because 'Me' isn't Nothing, if obj is Nothing,
      ' then the objects can't be equal.
      ' NOTE: This line can be deleted if you trust that
      ' the base type implemented Equals correctly.
      If obj Is Nothing Then Return False

      ' If the objects are of different types, they can't be equal.
      ' NOTE: This line can be deleted if you trust that
      ' the base type implemented Equals correctly.
      If Not (obj.GetType() Is Me.GetType()) Then Return False

      ' Cast obj to this type to access fields. NOTE: This cast
      ' can't fail because you know that the objects are of the same type.
      Dim other As MyRefType = DirectCast(obj, MyRefType)
```

```
      ' To compare reference fields, do this:
      If Not Object.Equals(refobj, other.refobj) Then Return False

      ' To compare value fields, do this:
      If Not valobj.Equals(other.valobj) Then Return False

      Return True     ' Objects are equal.
   End Function
End Class
```

This code is practically identical to the code shown in the previous section. The only difference is that this version also allows its base type to compare its fields. If the base type doesn't think the objects are equal, then they can't be equal.

It is very important that you do *not* call **MyBase.Equals** if doing so would result in calling the **Equals** method provided by **System.Object**. The reason is that **Object**'s **Equals** method returns **True** only if the references point to the same object. If the references don't point to the same object, then **False** will be returned and your **Equals** method will always return **False**!

Certainly, if you're defining a type that is directly derived from **Object**, you should implement **Equals** as shown in the previous section. If you're defining a type that isn't directly derived from **Object**, you must first determine if that type (or any of its base types, except **Object**) provides an implementation of **Equals**. If any of the base types provide an implementation of **Equals**, then call **MyBase.Equals** as shown in this section.

Implementing Equals for a Value Type

As I mentioned in Chapter 5, all value types are derived from **System.ValueType**. **ValueType** overrides the implementation of **Equals** offered by **System.Object**. Internally, **System.ValueType**'s **Equals** method uses reflection (covered in Chapter 20) to get the type's instance fields and compares the fields of both objects to see if they have equal values. This process is very slow, but it's a reasonably good default implementation that all value types will inherit. However, it does mean that reference types inherit an implementation of **Equals** that is really identity and that value types inherit an implementation of **Equals** that is value equality.

For value types that don't explicitly override **Equals**, the implementation provided by **ValueType** is inherited. The following code shows how **System.ValueType**'s **Equals** method is implemented:

```
Imports System.Reflection

Class ValueType
   Public Overloads Overrides Function Equals(ByVal obj As Object) As Boolean
```

(continued)

```vb
        ' Because 'Me' isn't Nothing, if obj is Nothing,
        ' then the objects can't be equal.
        If obj Is Nothing Then Return False

        ' Get the type of 'Me' object.
        Dim thisType As Type = Me.GetType()

        ' If 'Me' and 'obj' are different types, they can't be equal.
        If Not (thisType Is obj.GetType()) Then Return False

        ' Get the set of public and private instance
        ' fields associated with this type.
        Dim fields() As FieldInfo = thisType.GetFields(BindingFlags.Public _
           Or BindingFlags.NonPublic Or BindingFlags.Instance)

        ' Compare each instance field for equality.
        Dim i As Integer
        For i = 0 To fields.Length - 1
           ' Get the value of the field from both objects.
           Dim thisValue As Object = fields(i).GetValue(Me)
           Dim thatValue As Object = fields(i).GetValue(obj)

           ' If the values aren't equal, the objects aren't equal.
           If Not Object.Equals(thisValue, thatValue) Then Return False
        Next

        ' All the field values are equal, and the objects are equal.
        Return True
     End Function
       ⋮
End Structure
```

Even though **ValueType** offers a pretty good implementation for **Equals** that would work for most value types that you define, you should still provide your own implementation of **Equals**. The reason is that your implementation will perform significantly faster and will be able to avoid extra boxing operations.

The following code shows how to implement **Equals** for a value type:

```vb
' This is a value type (because of 'Structure').
Structure MyValType
    Dim refobj As RefType    ' This field is a reference type.
    Dim valobj As ValType    ' This field is a value type.

    Public Overloads Overrides Function Equals(ByVal obj As Object) As Boolean
        ' If obj is not your type, then the objects can't be equal.
        If Not (TypeOf obj Is MyValType) Then Return False
```

```
        ' Call the type-safe overload of Equals to do the work.
        Return Me.Equals(DirectCast(obj, MyValType))
    End Function

    ' Implement a strongly typed version of Equals.
    Public Overloads Function Equals(ByVal obj As MyValType) As Boolean
        ' To compare reference fields, do this:
        If Not Object.Equals(Me.refobj, obj.refobj) Then Return False

        ' To compare value fields, do this:
        If Not Me.valobj.Equals(obj.valobj) Then Return False

        Return True     ' Objects are equal.
    End Function
End Structure
```

For value types, the type should define a strongly typed version of **Equals**. This version takes the defining type as a parameter, giving you type safety and avoiding extra boxing operations. If you're writing your value type with a language that supports operator overloading (such as C#), you should also provide strongly typed operator overloads for the equality and inequality operators (== and !=, in C#). The following code demonstrates how to test two value types for equality:

```
Dim v1, v2 As MyValType

' The following line calls the strongly typed version of
' Equals (no boxing occurs).
If v1.Equals(v2) Then ...

' The following line calls the version of
' Equals that takes an object (4 is boxed).
If v1.Equals(4) Then ...
```

Inside the strongly typed **Equals** method, the code compares the fields in exactly the same way that you'd compare them for reference types. Keep in mind that the code doesn't do any casting, doesn't compare the two instances to see if they're the same type, and doesn't call the base type's **Equals** method. These operations aren't necessary because the method's parameter already ensures that the instances are of the same type. Also, because all value types are immediately derived from **System.ValueType**, you know that your base type has no fields of its own that need to be compared.

You'll notice in the **Equals** method that takes an **Object** that I used the **TypeOf…Is** expression to check the type of **obj**. I used **TypeOf…Is** instead of

GetType because calling GetType on an instance of a value type requires that the instance be boxed. I demonstrated this in the "Boxing and Unboxing Value Types" section in Chapter 5.

Summary of Implementing Equals and the Equality and Inequality Operators

In this section, I summarize how to implement equality for your own types:

- **Compiler primitive types** Your compiler will provide implementations of the = and <> operators for types that it considers primitives. For example, the Visual Basic compiler knows how to compare Object, Boolean, Char, Int16, Int32, Int64, Single, Double, Decimal, and so on for equality. In addition, these types provide implementations of Equals, so you can call this method as well as use operators.

- **Reference types** For reference types you define, override the Equals method and in the method do all the work necessary to compare object states and return. If your type doesn't inherit Object's Equals method, call the base type's Equals method.

- **Value types** For your value types, define a type-safe version of Equals that does all the work necessary to compare object states and return. Implement the type-unsafe version of Equals by having it call the type-safe Equals internally.

Identity

The purpose of a type's Equals method is to compare two instances of the type and return True if the instances have equivalent states or values. However, it's sometimes useful to see whether two references refer to the same, identical object. To do this, System.Object offers a static method called ReferenceEquals, which is implemented as follows:

```
Class Object
    Public Shared Function ReferenceEquals(ByVal objA As Object, _
        ByVal objB As Object) As Boolean
        Return (objA Is objB)
    End Function
End Class
```

As you can plainly see, ReferenceEquals simply uses the Is operator to compare the two references. In fact, the Is operator requires that both operands be reference types; if you specify a value type, the compiler issues an error.

If you're writing Visual Basic code, you could use the **Is** operator instead of calling **Object**'s **ReferenceEquals** method if you prefer. Here's some code demonstrating how to use **ReferenceEquals** and the **Is** operator:

```
Shared Sub Main()
    ' Construct a reference type object.
    Dim r1 As RefType = New RefType()

    ' Make another variable point to the reference object.
    Dim r2 As RefType = r1

    ' Do r1 and r2 point to the same object?
    Console.WriteLine(Object.ReferenceEquals(r1, r2))   ' "True"
    Console.WriteLine(r1 Is r2)                          ' "True"

    ' Construct another reference type object.
    r2 = New RefType()

    ' Do r1 and r2 point to the same object?
    Console.WriteLine(Object.ReferenceEquals(r1, r2))  ' "False"
    Console.WriteLine(r1 Is  r2)                         ' "False"

    ' Create an instance of a value type.
    Dim x As Int32 = 5

    ' Do x and x point to the same object?
    Console.WriteLine(Object.ReferenceEquals(x, x))    ' "False"
    ' "False" is displayed because x is boxed twice
    ' into two different objects.

    ' The line below must be commented out because the
    ' Is operator can't be used with value type operands.
    ' Console.WriteLine(x Is x)                          ' "False"

End Sub
```

Object Hash Codes

The designers of the FCL decided that it would be incredibly useful if any instance of any object could be placed into a hash table collection. To this end, **System.Object** provides a virtual **GetHashCode** method so that an **Int32** hash code can be obtained for any and all objects.

If you define a type and override the **Equals** method, you should also override the **GetHashCode** method. The reason why a type should define both **Equals** and **GetHashCode** is that the implementation of the **System.Collections.Hashtable** type requires that any two objects that are equal must have the same hash code value. So if you override **Equals**, you should override **Get-HashCode** to ensure that the algorithm you use for calculating equality corresponds to the algorithm you use for calculating the object's hash code.

Basically, when you add a key/value pair to a **Hashtable** object, a hash code for the key object is obtained first. This hash code indicates what "bucket" the key/value pair should be stored in. When the **Hashtable** object needs to look up a key, it gets the hash code for the specified key object. This code identifies the "bucket" that is now searched looking for a stored key object that is equal to the specified key object. Using this algorithm of storing and looking up keys means that if you change a key object that is in a **Hashtable**, the **Hashtable** will no longer be able to find the object. If you intend to change a key object in a hash table, you should first remove the original object/value pair, next modify the key object, and then add the new key object/value pair back into the hash table.

Defining a **GetHashCode** method can be easy and straightforward. But, depending on your data types and the distribution of data, it can be tricky to come up with a hashing algorithm that returns a well-distributed range of values. Here's a simple example that will probably work just fine for **Point** objects:

```
Class Point
    Public x, y As Int32
    Public Overrides Function GetHashCode() As Int32
      Return x Xor y
    End Function
    ⋮
End Class
```

When selecting an algorithm for calculating hash codes for instances of your type, try to follow these guidelines:

■ Use an algorithm that gives a good random distribution for the best performance of the hash table.

■ Your algorithm can also call the base type's **GetHashCode** method, including its return value in your own algorithm. However, you don't generally want to call **Object**'s or **ValueType**'s **GetHashCode** method because the implementation in either method doesn't lend itself to high-performance hashing algorithms.

■ Your algorithm should use at least one instance field.

■ Ideally, the fields you use in your algorithm should be immutable; that is, the fields should be initialized when the object is constructed and they should never again change during the object's lifetime.

- Your algorithm should execute as quickly as possible.

- Objects with the same value should return the same code. For example, two **String** objects with the same text should return the same hash code value.

System.Object's implementation of the **GetHashCode** method doesn't know anything about its derived type and any fields that are in the type. For this reason, **Object**'s **GetHashCode** method returns a number that is guaranteed to uniquely identify the object within the AppDomain; this number is guaranteed not to change for the lifetime of the object. After the object is garbage collected, however, its unique number can be reused as the hash code for a new object.

System.ValueType's implementation of **GetHashCode** uses reflection and returns the hash code of the first instance field defined in the type. This is a naïve implementation that might be good for some value types, but I still recommend that you implement **GetHashCode** yourself. Even if your hash code algorithm returns the hash code for the first instance field, your implementation will be faster than **ValueType**'s implementation. Here's what **ValueType**'s implementation of **GetHashCode** looks like:

```
Class ValueType
    Public Overrides Function GetHashCode() As Int32

        ' Get this type's public/private instance fields.
        Dim fields() As FieldInfo = Me.GetType().GetFields( _
            BindingFlags.Instance Or BindingFlags.Public Or _
            BindingFlags.NonPublic)

        If fields.Length > 0 Then
            ' Return the hash code for the first non-null field.
            Dim i As Integer
            For i = 0 To fields.Length - 1
                Dim obj As Object = fields(i).GetValue(Me)
                If Not (obj Is Nothing) Then Return obj.GetHashCode()
            Next
        End If

        ' No non-null fields exist; return a unique value for the type.
        ' NOTE: GetMethodTablePtrAsInt is an internal, undocumented method.
        Return GetMethodTablePtrAsInt(Me)
    End Function
End Class
```

If you're implementing your own hash table collection for some reason or you're implementing any piece of code where you'll be calling **GetHashCode**, you should never persist hash code values. The reason is that hash code values are subject to change. For example, a future version of a type might use a different algorithm for calculating the object's hash code.

Object Cloning

At times, you want to take an existing object and make a copy of it. For example, you might want to make a copy of an `Int32`, a `String`, an `ArrayList`, a `Delegate`, or some other object. For some types, however, cloning an object instance doesn't make sense. For example, it doesn't make sense to clone a `System.Threading.Thread` object since creating another `Thread` object and copying its fields doesn't create a new thread. Also, for some types, when an instance is constructed, the object is added to a linked list or some other data structure. Simple object cloning would corrupt the semantics of the type.

A class must decide whether or not it allows instances of itself to be cloned. If a class wants instances of itself to be cloneable, the class should implement the `ICloneable` interface, which is defined as follows. (I'll talk about interfaces in depth in Chapter 15.)

```
Public Interface ICloneable
    Function Clone() As Object
End Interface
```

This interface defines just one method, `Clone`. Your implementation of `Clone` is supposed to construct a new instance of the type and initialize the new object's state so that it is identical to the original object. The `ICloneable` interface doesn't explicitly state whether `Clone` should make a shallow copy of its fields or a deep copy. So you must decide for yourself what makes the most sense for your type and then clearly document what your `Clone` implementation does.

> **Note** For those of you who are unfamiliar with the term, a *shallow copy* is when the values in an object's fields are copied but what the fields refer to is not copied. For example, if an object has a field that refers to a string and you make a shallow copy of the object, then you have two objects that refer to the same string. On the other hand, a *deep copy* is when you make a copy of what an object's fields refer to. So if you made a deep copy of an object that has a field that refers to a string, you'd be creating a new object and a new string—the new object would refer to the new string. The important thing to note about a deep copy is that the original and the new object share nothing; modifying one object has no effect on the other object.

Many developers implement **Clone** so that it makes a shallow copy. If you want a shallow copy made for your type, implement your type's **Clone** method by calling **System.Object**'s protected **MemberwiseClone** method, as demonstrated here:

```
Class MyType
    Implements ICloneable
    Public Function Clone() As Object Implements ICloneable.Clone
        Return MemberwiseClone()
    End Function
End Class
```

Internally, **Object**'s **MemberwiseClone** method allocates memory for a new object. The new object's type matches the type of the object referred to by the **Me** reference. **MemberwiseClone** then iterates through all the instance fields for the type (and its base types) and copies the bits from the original object to the new object. Note that no constructor is called for the new object—its state will simply match that of the original object.

Alternatively, you can implement the **Clone** method entirely yourself, and you don't have to call **Object**'s **MemberwiseClone** method. Here's an example:

```
Class MyType
    Implements ICloneable

    Dim al As ArrayList

    ' Private constructor called by Clone
    Private Sub New(ByVal al As ArrayList)
        ' Refer to a shallow copy of the ArrayList passed.
        Me.al = DirectCast(al.Clone(), ArrayList)
    End Sub

    Public Function Clone() As Object Implements ICloneable.Clone
        ' Construct a new MyType object, passing it the
        ' ArrayList used by the original object.
        Return New MyType(al)
    End Function
End Class
```

You might have realized that the discussion in this section has been geared toward reference types. I concentrated on reference types because instances of value types always support making shallow copies of themselves. After all, the system has to be able to copy a value type's bytes when boxing it. The following code demonstrates the cloning of value types:

```
Shared Sub Main()
    Dim x As Int32 = 5
    Dim y As Int32 = x    ' Copy the bytes from x to y.
    Dim o As Object = x   ' Boxing x copies the bytes from x to the heap.
    y = CType(o, Int32)   ' Unbox o, and copy bytes from the heap to y.
End Sub
```

Of course, if you're defining a value type and you'd like your type to support deep cloning, then you should have the value type implement the **ICloneable** interface as shown earlier. (Don't call **MemberwiseClone**, but rather, allocate a new object and implement your deep copy semantics.)

Part III
Designing Types

7

Type Members and Their Accessibility

In Part II, I focused on types and what operations are guaranteed to exist on all instances of any type. I also explained the different types that you can create: reference types and value types. In this chapter and the subsequent ones in this part, I'll show you how to design types using the different kinds of members that can be defined within a type. In Chapters 8 through 11, I'll discuss the various members in detail.

Type Members

A type can define zero or more of the following members:

- **Constants (Chapter 8)** A *constant* is a symbol that identifies a never-changing data value. These symbols are typically used to make code more readable and maintainable. Constants are always associated with a type, not an instance of a type. In a sense, constants are always static.

- **Fields (Chapter 8)** A *field* represents a read-only or read/write data value. A field can be static, in which case the field is considered part of the type's state. A field can also be instance (nonstatic), in which case it's considered part of an object's state. I strongly encourage you to make fields private so that the state of the type or object can't be corrupted by code outside of the defining type. A value type designed in Visual Basic must contain at least one instance field or event declaration.

- **Instance constructors (Chapter 9)** An *instance constructor* is a method used to initialize a new object's instance fields to a good initial state.

- **Type constructors (Chapter 9)** A *type constructor* is a method used to initialize a type's static fields to a good initial state.

- **Methods (Chapter 9)** A *method* is a function that performs operations that change or query the state of a type (static method) or an object (instance method). Methods typically read and write to the fields of the type or object.

- **Operator overloads (Chapter 9)** An *operator overload* is a method that defines how an object should be manipulated when certain operators are applied to the object. Because some programming languages (including Visual Basic) don't support operator overloading, operator overload methods are not part of the Common Language Specification (CLS).

- **Conversion operators (Chapter 9)** A *conversion operator* is a method that defines how to implicitly or explicitly cast or convert an object from one type to another type. As with operator overload methods, some programming languages (including Visual Basic) don't support conversion operators, so they're not part of the CLS.

- **Properties (Chapter 10)** A *property* is a method that allows a simple, fieldlike syntax for setting or querying part of the logical state of a type or object while ensuring that the state doesn't become corrupt.

- **Events (Chapter 11)** A *static event* is a mechanism that allows a type to send a notification to a listening type or a listening object. An *instance* (nonstatic) *event* is a mechanism that allows an object to send a notification to a listening type or a listening object. Events are usually raised in response to a state change occurring in the type or object offering the event. Behind the scenes, an *event* consists of two methods that allow types or objects ("listeners") to register and unregister interest in the "event." In addition to the two methods, events typically use a delegate field to maintain the set of registered listeners.

- **Types** A *type* can define other types nested within it. This approach is typically used to break a large, complex type down into smaller building blocks to simplify the implementation.

Again, the purpose of this chapter isn't to describe these various members in detail but to set the stage and explain what these various members all have in common.

Regardless of the programming language you're using, the corresponding compiler must process your source code and produce metadata for each kind of member in the preceding list and IL code for each method member. The format of the metadata is identical regardless of the source programming language you use, and this feature is what makes the CLR a *common language* runtime. The metadata is the common information that all languages produce and consume, enabling code in one programming language to seamlessly access code written in a completely different programming language.

This common metadata format is also used by the CLR, which determines how constants, fields, constructors, methods, properties, and events all behave at run time. Simply stated, metadata is the key to the whole Microsoft .NET Framework development platform; it enables the seamless integration of languages, types, and objects.

The following Visual Basic code shows a type definition that contains an example of all the possible members. The code shown here will compile (with warnings), but it isn't representative of a type that you'd normally create: most of the methods do nothing of any real value. Right now, I just want to show you how the compiler translates this type and its members into metadata. Once again, I'll discuss the individual members in the next few chapters.

```vb
Imports System

Class SomeType                                              1

    ' Nested class
    Class SomeNestedType                                    2
    End Class

    ' Constant, read-only, and static read/write field
    Const SomeConstant As Int32 = 1                         3
    ReadOnly SomeReadOnlyField As Int32 = 2                 4
    Shared SomeReadWriteField As Int32 = 3                  5

    ' Type constructor
    Shared Sub New()                                        6
    End Sub

    ' Instance constructors
    Public Sub New()                                        7
    End Sub
```

(continued)

```
Public Sub New(ByVal x As Int32)                              8
End Sub

' Static and instance methods

Function InstanceMethod() As String                           9
End Function
Shared Sub Main()                                            10
End Sub

' Instance property
Property SomeProp() As Int32                                 11
   Get                                                       12
       Return 0
   End Get
   Set(ByVal Value As Int32)                                13
   End Set
End Property

' Instance default property
Default Public Property Item(ByVal s As String) As Int32     14
   Get                                                       15
       Return 0
   End Get
   Set(ByVal Value As Int32)                                16
   End Set
End Property

' Instance event
Event SomeEvent as EventHandler                              17
End Class
```

If you were to compile the type just defined and examine the metadata in ILDasm.exe, you'd see the output shown in Figure 7-1.

Notice that all the members defined in the source code cause the compiler to emit some metadata. In fact, some of the members (the event, 17) cause the compiler to generate additional members (a field and two methods) as well as additional metadata. I don't expect you to fully understand what you're seeing here now. But as you read the next few chapters, I encourage you to look back to this example to see how the member is defined and what effect that has on the metadata produced by the compiler.

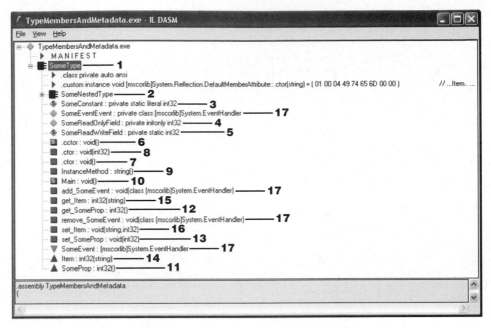

Figure 7-1   ILDasm.exe output showing metadata from preceding code

Accessibility Modifiers and Predefined Attributes

In this section, I'll summarize the accessibility modifiers and predefined attributes that can be placed on types, fields, and methods (including properties and events). The accessibility modifiers indicate which types and members can be legally referenced from code. The predefined attributes fine-tune this accessibility and allow you to change a member's semantics.

The CLR defines the set of possible accessibility modifiers, but each programming language chooses the syntax and term it wants to use to expose the modifier to developers. For example, the CLR uses the term *Assembly* to indicate that a member is accessible to any code within the same assembly. However, Visual Basic and C# call it `Friend` and `internal`, respectively.

Table 7-1 shows the accessibility modifiers that can be applied to a type, field, or method. *Private* is the most restrictive, and *Public* is the least restrictive.

Table 7-1   Accessibility Modifiers for Types, Fields, or Methods

CLR Term	Visual Basic Term	C# Term	Description
Private	Private	private	Accessible only by methods in the defining type (or any of its nested types)
Family	Protected	protected	Accessible only by methods in this type (or any of its nested types) or one of its derived types without regard to assembly
Family and Assembly	(not supported)	(not supported)	Accessible only by methods in this type (or any of its nested types) and by derived types in the defining assembly
Assembly	Friend	internal	Accessible only by methods in the defining assembly
Family or Assembly	Protected Friend	protected internal	Accessible only by methods in this type, any derived type, or any type defined in the defining assembly
Public	Public	public	Accessible to all methods in all assemblies

When designing a type or a member, you can select only one accessibility modifier. So, for example, you can't mark a method as both *Assembly* and *Public*. Nested types (which are considered members) can be marked with any of the six accessibility modifiers. However, unnested types can be marked only with *Public* or *Assembly* accessibility because the other accessibility modifiers just don't make sense. If an unnested type isn't explicitly marked, Visual Basic and C# both default to *Assembly* (Friend/internal).

In addition to the accessibility modifiers, types and members can also be marked with some predefined attributes. The CLR defines the set of predefined attributes, but each programming language might choose different names for these attributes.

Type Predefined Attributes

Table 7-2 shows the predefined attributes that can be applied to a type.

Table 7-2   Predefined Attributes for Types

CLR Term	Visual Basic Term	C# Term	Description
Abstract	`MustInherit`	`abstract`	The type can't be instantiated. The type can be used as a base type for another type. If the derived type is is not abstract, instances of it can be constructed
Sealed	`NotInheritable`	`sealed`	The type can't be used as a base type.

The CLR allows types to be marked as *Abstract* or as *Sealed* but not both. I think this restriction is unfortunate because a number of types don't allow instances of themselves to be created and can't be used as a base type.

For example, it doesn't make sense to construct an instance of the `Console` or `Math` type because these types contain only static methods. It also doesn't make sense to use either of these types as a base type for defining a new type. I think it would be nice to mark these types as *Abstract* (no instances can be created) and as *Sealed* (can't be used as a base type).

Because the CLR doesn't support this marking, if you're designing your own type that contains only static members, you should mark the type as *Sealed* and define a private, parameterless constructor that is never called. Defining the private constructor stops the Visual Basic and C# compilers from automatically producing a public, parameterless constructor. Because code outside the type can't access a constructor, no instances of the type can be created.

Field Predefined Attributes

Table 7-3 shows the predefined attributes that can be applied to a field.

The CLR allows fields to be marked as *Static*, *InitOnly*, or both *Static* and *InitOnly*. Note that constants (discussed in Chapter 8) are always considered *Static* and can't be marked with *InitOnly*.

Table 7-3 **Predefined Attributes for Fields**

CLR Term	Visual Basic Term	C# Term	Description
Static	`Shared`	`static`	The field is part of the type's state as opposed to being part of an object's state.
Instance	(default)	(default)	The field is associated with an instance of the type, not the type itself.
InitOnly	`ReadOnly`	`readonly`	The field can be written to only by code contained in a constructor method.

Method Predefined Attributes

Table 7-4 shows the predefined attributes that can be applied to a method.

Table 7-4 **Predefined Attributes for Methods**

CLR Term	Visual Basic Term	C# Term	Description
Static	`Shared`	`static`	The method is associated with the type itself, not an instance of the type. Static methods can't access instance fields or methods defined within the type because the static method isn't aware of any object.
Instance	(default)	(default)	The method is associated with an instance of the type, not the type itself. The method can access instance fields and methods as well as static fields and methods.
Virtual	`Overridable`	`virtual`	The most-derived method is called even if the object is cast to a base type. Applies only to instance (nonstatic) methods.
Newslot	`Shadows`	`new`	The method should not override an instance method defined by its base type; the method hides the inherited method. Applies only to instance methods.

(continued)

Table 7-4   **Predefined Attributes for Methods**   *(continued)*

CLR Term	Visual Basic Term	C# Term	Description
Override	`Overrides`	`override`	Explicitly indicates that the method is overriding a virtual method defined by its base type. Applies only to derived methods.
Abstract	`MustOverride`	`abstract`	Indicates that a deriving type must implement a method with a signature matching this abstract method. A type with an abstract method is an abstract type. Applies only to virtual methods.
Final	`NotOverridable`	`sealed`	A derived type can't override this method. Applies only to derived methods.

In Chapter 9, I'll describe some of these attributes in detail. Any polymorphic instance method can be marked as either *Abstract* or *Final* but not both. Marking a virtual method as *Final* means that no more derived types can override the method—but this is an uncommon thing to want to do.

When compiling code, the language compiler is responsible for checking that the code is referencing types and members correctly. If the code references some type or member incorrectly, the language compiler has the responsibility of emitting the appropriate error message. In addition, the JIT compiler ensures that references to fields and methods are legal when compiling IL code into native CPU instructions. For example, if the verifier detects code that is improperly attempting to access a private field or method, the JIT compiler throws a `FieldAccessException` exception or a `MethodAccessException` exception, respectively. Verifying the IL code ensures that the accessibility modifiers and predefined attributes are properly honored at run time, even if a language compiler chose to ignore them and generated an otherwise-valid assembly.

8

Constants and Fields

In this chapter, I'll show you how to add data members to a type. Specifically, we'll look at constants and fields.

Constants

A constant is a symbol that has a never-changing value. When defining a constant symbol, its value must be determinable at compile time. The compiler then saves the constant's value in the module's metadata. This means that you can define a constant only for types that your compiler considers as primitive types. Another point to remember is that constants are always considered part of a type, not part of an instance; this is fine since a constant's value never changes.

> **Note** In Visual Basic, the following types are primitives and can be used to define constants: `Boolean`, `Char`, `Byte`, `Decimal`, `Int16` (`Short`), `Int32` (`Integer`), `Int64` (`Long`), `Single`, `Double`, and `String`. Enumerated types that have a primitive as an underlying type can also be used as constants.

When using a constant symbol, compilers look up the symbol in the metadata of the module that defines the constant, extract the constant's value, and embed the value in the emitted IL code. This means that constants don't have a good cross-module versioning story, so you should use them only when you know that the value of a symbol will never change. (Defining `MaxInt16` as `32767` is a good example.) Let me demonstrate exactly what I mean. First take the following code and compile it into a DLL assembly:

```
Imports System

Public Class Component
    ' NOTE: Visual Basic doesn't allow Shared to be specified for
    ' constants because constants are always implicitly shared.
    Public Const MaxEntriesInList As Int32 = 50
End Class
```

Then use the following code to build an application:

```
Imports System

Class App
    Shared Sub Main()
        Console.WriteLine("Max entries supported in list: " _
            & Component.MaxEntriesInList)
    End Sub
End Class
```

You'll notice that this application code references the `MaxEntriesInList` constant. When the compiler builds the application code, it sees that `MaxEntriesInList` is a constant literal with a value of `50` and embeds the `Int32` value of `50` right inside the application's IL code. In fact, after building the application code, the DLL assembly isn't even loaded at run time and can be deleted from the disk.

This example should make the versioning problem obvious to you. If the developer changes the `MaxEntriesInList` constant to `1000` and rebuilds the DLL assembly, the application code isn't affected. For the application to pick up the new value, it would have to be recompiled as well. You can't use constants if you need to have a value in one module picked up by another module at run time (instead of compile time). Instead, you can use read-only fields, which I'll discuss later in this chapter.

When Is a Constant Not Always a Constant?

Because a constant's value is embedded directly in IL code, constants don't require any memory allocated for them at run time. Because no memory is allocated, many languages (such as C#) don't allow you to write code that gets the memory address of a constant, nor do they allow you to call a method passing a constant by reference.

Visual Basic, however, offers some special treatment for constants. In Visual Basic, when you write code that attempts to modify a constant variable, the compiler generates code that creates a temporary (not constant) variable, copies the constant value to the temporary variable, and allows your code to manipulate the temporary variable. This behavior gives you the impression that you're changing the constant value even though you're really not. The following code demonstrates this:

```
Option Strict On
Option Explicit On

Imports System

Class App
    Const X As Int32 = 5

    Shared Sub Main()
        ' The compiler creates a temporary Int32 variable here
        ' and copies the constant X (5) into it. The address of
        ' the temporary variable is passed to Foo (which adds 5
        ' to the temporary variable).
        Foo(X)

        ' The constant value 5 is passed to WriteLine. The temporary
        ' variable isn't used here since X is supposed to be a constant.
        Console.WriteLine(X)     ' Displays "5"
    End Sub

    Shared sub Foo(ByRef Y as Int32)
        Y = Y + 5
        Console.WriteLine(Y)     ' Displays "10"
    End Sub
End Class
```

If you build and run this code, you'll see the following output:

```
10
5
```

Personally, I find this behavior to be dangerous because the results aren't necessarily what you expect. After all, the preceding code calls **Foo**, and **Foo** adds 5 to the value passed (by reference) to it. So when **Foo** returns, the value in **X** should be **10** and yet **Main**'s call to **WriteLine** displays **5**. If you were to write the preceding code in C#, the compiler would issue an error and simply not compile the code, reinforcing the idea that **X** is a constant and that it is illegal for code to change its value.

Of course, if you change the declaration of X so that it is not a constant:

```
Shared X As Int32 = 5
```

and then rebuild and run the application, the output would be quite different and what most programmers would expect:

```
10
10
```

Fields

A field is a data member that holds an instance of a value type or a reference to a reference type. The CLR supports both type (static) and instance (nonstatic) fields. For type fields, the dynamic memory to hold the field is allocated when the type is loaded into an AppDomain (see Chapter 20), which typically happens the first time any method that references the type is JIT compiled. For instance fields, the dynamic memory to hold the field is allocated when an instance of the type is constructed.

Because fields are stored in dynamic memory, their value can be obtained at run time only. Fields also solve the versioning problem that exists with constants. In addition, a field can be of any data type, so you don't have to restrict yourself to your compiler's built-in primitive types (as you do for constants).

The CLR supports read-only fields and read/write fields. Most fields are read/write fields, meaning that the field's value might change multiple times as the code executes. However, read-only fields can be written to only within a constructor method (which is called only once, when an object is first created). Compilers and verification ensure that read-only fields are not written to by any method other than a constructor.

Let's take the example from the "Constants" section and fix the versioning problem by using a static read-only field. Here's the new version of the DLL assembly's code:

```
Imports System

Public Class Component
    ' The Shared keyword is required to associate the field with the type.
    Public Shared ReadOnly MaxEntriesInList As Int32 = 50
End Class
```

This is the only change you have to make; the application code doesn't have to change at all, although you must rebuild it to see the new behavior. Now, when the application's **Main** method runs, the CLR will load the DLL assembly (so this assembly is now required at run time) and grab the value of the `MaxEntriesIn-List` field out of the dynamic memory that was allocated for it. Of course, the value will be `50`.

Let's say that the developer of the DLL assembly changes the `50` to `1000` and rebuilds the assembly. When the application code is re-executed, it will automatically pick up the new value: `1000`. In this case, the application code doesn't have to be rebuilt—it just works (although its performance is adversely affected). A caveat: this scenario assumes that the new version of the DLL assembly is not strongly named or that the versioning policy of the application is such that the CLR loads this new version.

The preceding example shows how to define a read-only static field that is associated with the type itself. You can also define read/write static fields and read-only and read/write instance fields. When declaring a field in Visual Basic, the compiler will assume that the field has `Private` scope unless you explicitly specify a different access modifier, such as `Public`, `Protected Friend`, `Friend`, or `Protected` (as discussed in Table 7-1 in Chapter 7). Also, when declaring a field, Visual Basic allows you to omit the `Dim` keyword when you explicitly specify any access modifier or when you explicitly specify `Shared` or `ReadOnly`. For some reason, Visual Basic *requires* that you omit the `Dim` keyword when using the `Const` keyword. Here is some code demonstrating the different ways to declare fields:

```
Imports System

Public Class SomeType
    ' A Private constant
    Const A As Int32 = 1

    ' Compiler error: 'Dim' is not valid on a constant declaration.
    Const Dim B As Int32 = 1

    ' This is a public, shared (static) read-only field; its value
    ' is calculated and stored in memory when this class is initialized
    ' at run time. Note that 'Dim' can be omitted.
    Public Shared ReadOnly Rand As Random = New Random()

    ' This is a private, shared (static) read/write field.
    Shared NumberOfWrites As Int32 = 0

    ' This is a private, instance read-only field.
    ReadOnly Pathname As String = "Untitled"

    ' This is a private, instance read/write field.
    Dim Count as Int32
```

(continued)

```
        ' This is also a private, instance read/write field.
        ' Note: 'Dim' can be omitted if 'Private' is specified.
        Private Count2 as Int32

        ' This is a public, instance read/write field.
        Public fs As System.IO. FileStream

        Sub New(ByVal Pathname As String)
            ' This line changes a read-only field.
            ' This is OK because the code is in a constructor.
            Me.Pathname = Pathname
        End Sub

        Function DoSomething() As String
            ' This line reads and writes to the static read/write field.
            NumberOfWrites = NumberOfWrites + 1

            ' This line reads the read-only instance field.
            Return Pathname
        End Function
End Class
```

In this code, many of the fields are initialized inline. Visual Basic allows you to use this convenient inline initialization syntax to initialize a class's constants, read/write, and read-only fields. As you'll see in Chapter 9, Visual Basic treats initializing a field inline as shorthand syntax for initializing the field in a constructor.

9

Methods

In this chapter, I'll talk about the different kinds of methods a type can define and the various issues related to methods. Specifically, I'll show you how to define constructor methods (both instance and type), how to pass parameters by reference to a method and how to define methods that accept a variable number of parameters, how to use optional parameters, and how to use static variables in methods. In addition, I'll cover how Microsoft Visual Basic programmers can work with operator overload methods and type conversion methods that have been defined by types implemented in other programming languages (such as C#). Finally, I'll explain the virtual method versioning mechanism that exists to stop the potential for application instability when a base class's programming interface has changed.

Instance Constructors

Constructors are methods that allow an instance of a type to be initialized to a good state. For code to be verifiable, the common language runtime (CLR) requires that every class (reference type) have at least one constructor defined within it. (This constructor can be private if you want to prevent code outside your class from creating any instances of the class.) When creating an instance of a reference type, memory is allocated for the instance, the object's overhead fields (method table pointer and SyncBlockIndex) are initialized, and the type's instance constructor is called to set the initial state of the object.

When constructing a reference type object, the memory allocated for the object is always zeroed out before the type's instance constructor is called. Any fields that the constructor doesn't explicitly overwrite are guaranteed to have a value of `0` or `Nothing`.

By default, many compilers (including Visual Basic and C#) define a public, parameterless constructor (often called a *default constructor*) for reference types when you don't explicitly define your own constructor. For example, the following type has a public, parameterless constructor, allowing any code that can access the type to construct an instance of the type.

```
Class SomeType
    ' Visual Basic automatically defines a default public,
    ' parameterless constructor.
End Class
```

The preceding type definition is identical to the following type definition:

```
Class SomeType
    Public Sub New()
    End Sub
End Class
```

A type can define several instance constructors. Each constructor must have a different signature, and each can have different accessibility. For verifiable code, a class's instance constructor must call its base class's constructor before accessing any of the inherited fields of the base class. Many compilers, including Visual Basic's, generate the call to the base class's default constructor—if it has one—automatically, so you typically don't have to worry or think about this at all. Ultimately, **System.Object**'s public, parameterless constructor gets called. This constructor does nothing—it simply returns.

In a few situations, an instance of a type can be created without an instance constructor being called. In particular, calling **Object**'s **MemberwiseClone** method allocates memory, initializes the object's overhead fields, and then copies the source object's bytes to the new object. Also, a constructor usually isn't called when deserializing an object.

Visual Basic offers a simple syntax that allows the initialization of fields when a reference type object is constructed:

```
Class SomeType
    Dim x As Int32 = 5
End Class
```

When a **SomeType** object is constructed, its **x** field will be initialized to **5**. How does this happen? Well, if you examine the intermediate language (IL) for **SomeType**'s constructor method (also called **.ctor**), you'll see the code in Figure 9-1.

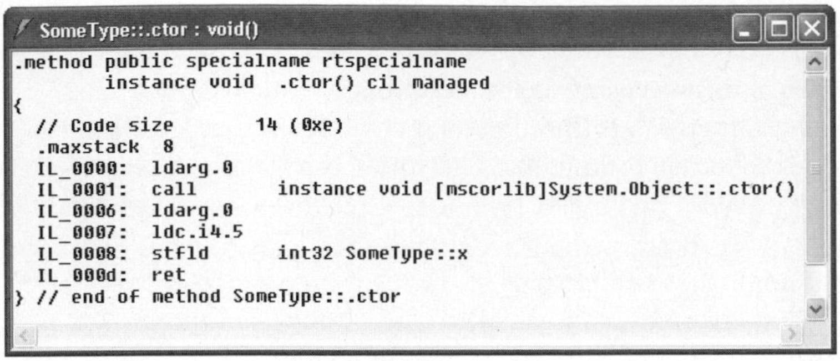

```
 SomeType::.ctor : void()                                    _ □ ✕

.method public specialname rtspecialname
        instance void  .ctor() cil managed
{
  // Code size         14 (0xe)
  .maxstack  8
  IL_0000:  ldarg.0
  IL_0001:  call          instance void [mscorlib]System.Object::.ctor()
  IL_0006:  ldarg.0
  IL_0007:  ldc.i4.5
  IL_0008:  stfld         int32 SomeType::x
  IL_000d:  ret
} // end of method SomeType::.ctor
```

Figure 9-1   The IL code for **SomeType**'s constructor method

In Figure 9-1, you see that **SomeType**'s constructor contains code to call the base class's constructor followed by code that stores a **5** into **x**. In other words, the Visual Basic compiler allows the convenient syntax that lets you initialize the instance fields inline and translates this to code in the constructor method to perform the initialization. This means that you should be aware of code explosion. Imagine the following class:

```
Class SomeType
    Dim x As Int32 = 5
    Dim s As String = "Hi there"
    Dim d As Double = 3.14159
    Dim b As Byte

    ' Here are some constructors.
    Public Sub New()
       ⋮
    End Sub
    Public Sub New(ByVal x As Int32)
       ⋮
    End Sub
    Public Sub New(ByVal s As String)
       ⋮
       d = 10
    End Sub
End Class
```

When the compiler generates code for the three constructor methods, each method includes the code to initialize **x**, **s**, and **d**. After this initialization code, the compiler appends to the method the code that appears in the constructor methods. For example, the code generated for the constructor that takes a **String** parameter includes the code to initialize **x**, **s**, and **d** and then overwrites **d** with the value **10**. Note that the CLR guarantees that **b** is initialized to **0** even though no code exists to explicitly initialize it.

Because there are three constructors in the preceding class, the compiler generates the code to initialize **x**, **s**, and **d** three times—once per constructor. If you have several initialized instance fields and a lot of overloaded constructor methods, you should consider defining the fields without the initialization, creating a single constructor that performs the common initialization, and having each constructor explicitly call the common initialization constructor. This approach will reduce the size of the generated code.

```
Class SomeType
   ' No code here to explicitly initialize the fields
   Dim x As Int32
   Dim s As String
   Dim d As Double
   Dim b As Byte

   ' All the other constructors must call this constructor.
   ' This constructor contains the code to initialize the fields.
   Public Sub New()
      x = 5
      s = "Hi there"
      d = 3.14159
   End Sub

   ' This constructor calls the default constructor first.
   Public Sub New(ByVal x As Int32)
      Me.New()
      Me.x = x
   End Sub

   ' This constructor calls the default constructor first.
   Public Sub New(ByVal s As String)
      Me.New()
      Me.s = s
   End Sub
End Class
```

Value type constructors work quite differently from reference type constructors. First, the CLR doesn't require value types to have any constructor methods defined within them. In fact, many compilers (including Visual Basic and C#) don't give value types default parameterless constructors. The reason for the difference is that value types can be implicitly created. Examine the following code:

```
Structure Point
    Public x, y As Int32
End Structure

Class Rectangle
    Public topLeft, bottomRight As Point
End Class
```

To construct a **Rectangle**, the **New** operator must be used and a constructor must be specified. In this case, the constructor automatically generated by the Visual Basic compiler is called. When memory is allocated for the **Rectangle**, the memory includes the two instances of the **Point** value type. For performance reasons, the CLR doesn't attempt to call a constructor for each value type contained within the reference type. But as I mentioned earlier, the CLR guarantees that the fields of the value types are initialized to **0**/**Nothing**.

The CLR does allow you to define constructors on value types. The only way that these constructors will execute is if you write code to explicitly call one of them, as in **Rectangle**'s constructor shown here:

```
Structure Point
    Public x, y As Int32

    Public Sub New(ByVal x As Int32, ByVal y As Int32)
        Me.x = x
        Me.y = y
    End Sub
End Structure

Class Rectangle
    Public topLeft, bottomRight As Point

    Sub New()
        ' In Visual Basic, New on a value type just calls a constructor
        ' to initialize the value type's already allocated memory.
        topLeft = New Point(1, 2)
        bottomRight = New Point(100, 200)
    End Sub
End Class
```

A value type's instance constructor is executed only when explicitly called. So if **Rectangle**'s constructor didn't initialize its **topLeft** and **bottomRight** fields using the **New** operator to call **Point**'s constructor, the **x** and **y** fields in both **Point** fields would be **0**.

In the **Point** value type defined earlier, no default parameterless constructor is defined. However, let's rewrite that code as follows:

```
Structure Point
    Public x, y As Int32

    Public Sub New()
        Me.x = 5
        Me.y = 5
    End Sub
End Structure

Class Rectangle
    Public topLeft, bottomRight As Point

    Sub New()
    End Sub
End Class
```

Now when a new **Rectangle** is constructed, what do you think the **x** and **y** fields in the two **Point** fields, **topLeft** and **bottomRight**, would be initialized to: **0** or **5**? (Hint: This is trick question.)

Many developers (especially those with a C++ background) would expect the Visual Basic compiler to emit code in **Rectangle**'s constructor that automatically calls **Point**'s default parameterless constructor for the **Rectangle**'s two fields. However, to improve the run-time performance of the application, the Visual Basic compiler doesn't automatically emit this code. In fact, many compilers will never emit code to call a value type's default constructor automatically, even if the value type offers a parameterless constructor. To have a value type's parameterless constructor execute, the developer must add explicit code to call a value type's constructor.

Based on the information in the preceding paragraph, you should expect the **x** and **y** fields in **Rectangle**'s two **Point** fields to be initialized to **0** in the code shown earlier because there are no explicit calls to **Point**'s constructor anywhere in the code.

However, I did say that my original question was a trick question. The "trick" part is that Visual Basic doesn't allow a value type to define a parameterless constructor. So the previous code won't actually compile. The Visual Basic compiler produces the following error when attempting to compile that code: "error BC30629: Structures cannot declare a non-shared 'Sub New' with no parameters."

Visual Basic purposely disallows value types to define parameterless constructors to remove any confusion a developer might have about when that constructor gets called. If the constructor can't be defined, the compiler can never generate code to call it automatically. Without a parameterless constructor, a value type's fields are always initialized to 0/Nothing.

> **Note** Strictly speaking, the CLR guarantees that a value type's fields are initialized to 0/Nothing only when the value type is a field nested within a reference type. However, stack-based value type fields are not guaranteed to be 0/Nothing. For verifiability, any stack-based value type field must be written to prior to being read. If code could read a value type's field prior to writing to the field, a security breach is possible. Visual Basic and other compilers that produce verifiable code ensure that all stack-based value types have their fields zeroed out or at least written to before being read so that a verification exception won't be thrown at run time. For the most part, this means that you can assume that your value types have their fields initialized to 0 and you can completely ignore everything in this note.

Keep in mind that although Visual Basic doesn't allow value types with parameterless constructors, the CLR does. So if the unobvious behavior described earlier doesn't bother you, you can use another programming language (such as IL assembly language) to define your value type with a parameterless constructor.

Because Visual Basic doesn't allow value types with parameterless constructors, compiling the following type produces the following error: "error BC31049: Initializers on structure members are valid only for constants."

```
Structure SomeValType
    Dim x As Int32 = 5
End Structure
```

As I mentioned in the preceding note, verifiable code requires that all of a value type's fields be initialized prior to being read. So when you write code to explicitly call a value type's constructor, the Visual Basic compiler generates code that allocates a temporary instance of the value type and initializes all its fields to 0/Nothing. The compiler then generates code to call the specified constructor; this constructor operates on the temporary instance. When the constructor returns, all fields in the temporary instance are copied to the variable that you declared in your code. Unfortunately, the result of all this is that your method requires more memory and runs a little slower because of the additional allocation, initialization, and field copy.

Not all compilers adopt this behavior. For example, the C# compiler avoids this performance hit, but it requires that you manually initialize all the fields of a structure from inside its constructor.

> **Important**   In Visual Basic source code, the developer defines a constructor by creating a method named `New`. This means that in Visual Basic, a developer can define a method whose name matches the name of the type. However, you should avoid this practice because the methods won't be callable from some other programming languages (like C#). In fact, defining a member whose name matches the name of the type itself is considered non-CLS-compliant for this very reason. For the same reason, a C# developer should avoid defining a method named `New` (a legal method name in C#) because Visual Basic developers can't invoke it.

Type Constructors

In addition to instance constructors, the CLR also supports type constructors (also known as *static constructors*, *class constructors*, or *type initializers*). A type constructor can be applied to interfaces (although Visual Basic doesn't allow this), reference types, and value types. Just as instance constructors are used to set the initial state of an instance of a type, type constructors are used to set the initial state of a type. By default, types don't have a type constructor defined within them. If a type has a type constructor, it can have no more than one. In addition, type constructors never have parameters. In Visual Basic, here's how to define a reference type and a value type that have type constructors:

```
Class SomeRefType
    Shared Sub New()
        ' This executes the first time a SomeRefType is accessed.
    End Sub
End Class

Structure SomeValType
    ' In Visual Basic, a structure must define at least one field.
    Dim x As Int32

    ' Visual Basic does allow value types to define
    ' parameterless type constructors.
```

```
Shared Sub New()
    ' This executes the first time a SomeValType is accessed.
End Sub
End Structure
```

You'll notice that you define type constructors just as you would parameterless instance constructors except that you must mark them as **Shared**. Also, type constructors should always be private; Visual Basic makes them private for you automatically. In fact, if you explicitly mark a type constructor as private (or anything else) in your source code, the Visual Basic compiler issues the following error: "error BC30480: Shared 'Sub New' cannot be declared 'Private'."

Type constructors should be private to prevent any developer-written code from calling them; the CLR is always capable of calling a type constructor. In addition, the CLR exercises freedom as to when it decides to call the type constructor. The CLR calls a type constructor at either of the following times:

■ Just before the first instance of the type is created or just before the first access to a noninherited field or member of the class is accessed. This is called *precise* semantics because the CLR will call the type constructor at exactly the right time.

■ Sometime before the first access of a noninherited static field. This is called *before-field-init* semantics because the CLR guarantees only that the static constructor will run sometime before the static field is accessed; it could run much earlier.

By default, compilers choose which of these semantics makes the most sense for the type you're defining and informs the CLR of this choice by setting the **beforefieldinit** metadata flag. Once executed, the type constructor will never be called again for the lifetime of that AppDomain. Because the CLR is responsible for calling type constructors, you should always avoid writing any code that requires type constructors to be called in a specific order.

The CLR guarantees only that a type constructor has started execution—it can't guarantee that the type constructor has completed execution. This behavior was necessary to avoid deadlocks in the unusual case when two type constructors reference each other.

Finally, if a type constructor throws an unhandled exception, the CLR considers the type to be unusable. Attempting to access any fields or methods of the type will cause a **System.TypeInitializationException** to be thrown.

The code in a type constructor has access only to a type's static fields, and its usual purpose is to initialize those fields. As it does with instance fields, Visual Basic offers a simple syntax that allows you to initialize a type's static fields.

```
Class SomeType
    Shared x As Int32 = 5
End Class
```

When this code is built, the compiler automatically generates a type constructor for **SomeType**. It's as if the source code had originally been written as follows:

```
Class SomeType
    Shared x As Int32
    Shared Sub New()
        x = 5
    End Sub
End Class
```

Using ILDasm.exe, it's easy to verify what the compiler actually produced by examining the IL for the type constructor, shown in Figure 9-2. Type constructor methods are always called **.cctor** (for class constructor) in a method definition metadata table.

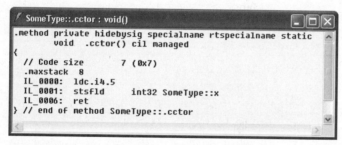

Figure 9-2 The IL code for **SomeType**'s type constructor method

In Figure 9-2, you see that the **.cctor** method is private and static. In addition, notice that the code in the method does in fact load a **5** into the static field **x**.

Type constructors shouldn't call a base type's type constructor. Such a call isn't necessary because none of a type's shared fields are inherited from its base type.

Finally, assume that you have this code:

```
Class SomeType
    Shared x As Int32 = 5
    Shared Sub New()
        x = 10
    End Sub
End Class
```

In this case, the Visual Basic compiler generates a single type constructor method. This constructor first initializes **x** to **5** and then initializes **x** to **10**. In other words, when the compiler generates IL code for the type constructor, it first emits the code required to initialize the static fields followed by the explicit code contained in your type constructor method. Emitting the code in this order is exactly the way it works for instance constructors too.

Note   Some languages, like Java, expect that accessing a type causes its type constructor and all its base type's type constructors to be called. In addition, interfaces implemented by the types must also have their type constructors called. The CLR doesn't offer this semantic. However, the CLR does offer compilers and developers the ability to provide this semantic via the `RunClassConstructor` method offered by the `System.Runtime.CompilerServices.RuntimeHelpers` type. Any language that requires this semantic would have its compiler emit code into a type's type constructor that calls this method for all base types and interfaces. When attempting to call a type constructor, the CLR knows if the type constructor has executed previously and, if it has, doesn't call it again.

Important   Occasionally, developers ask me if there's a way to get some code to execute when a type is unloaded. You should first know that types are unloaded only when the AppDomain shuts down. When the AppDomain shuts down, the object that identifies the type becomes unreachable and the garbage collector reclaims the type object's memory. This behavior leads many developers to believe that they could add a static `Finalize` method to the type, which will automatically get called when the type is unloaded. Unfortunately, the CLR doesn't support static `Finalize` methods. All is not lost, however. If you want some code to execute when an AppDomain shuts down, you can register a callback method with the `System.AppDomain` type's `DomainUnload` event.

Passing Parameters by Reference to a Method

By default, the CLR assumes that all method parameters are passed by value. When reference type objects are passed, the reference (or pointer) to the object is passed (by value) to the method. This means that the method can modify the referenced object and the caller will see the change. For value type instances, a copy of the instance is passed to the method. This means that the method gets its own private copy of the value type and the instance in the caller isn't affected.

> **Important**   In a method, you must know whether each parameter passed is a reference type or a value type because the code you write to manipulate the parameter could be markedly different.

The CLR allows you to pass parameters by reference instead of by value. In Visual Basic, you do this by using the **ByRef** keyword. This keyword tells the Visual Basic compiler to emit metadata indicating that this designated parameter is passed by reference, and the compiler uses this to generate code to pass the address of the parameter rather than the parameter itself.

Reference types and value types behave very differently when passed by reference. Let's look at using **ByRef** with value types first:

```
Imports System

Class App
    Shared Sub Main()
        Dim x As Int32        ' x is initialized to 0.
        x = 5                 ' x is set to 5.
        SetVal(x)             ' The address of x is passed to SetVal.
        Console.WriteLine(x)  ' Displays "12"
    End Sub

    Shared Sub AddVal(ByRef v As Int32)
        ' Add 7 to the Int32 residing on the caller's stack.
        v = v + 7
    End Sub
End Class
```

In this code, **x** is declared on **Main**'s stack and is initialized to **5**. The address of **x** is then passed to **AddVal**. **AddVal**'s **v** is a pointer to an **Int32** value type. Inside **AddVal**, the **Int32** that **v** points to can be modified any way the

AddVal method desires. In this example, **AddVal** simply adds **7** to the value in the **Int32**. When **AddVal** returns, **Main**'s **x** will have a value of **12**, which is what gets displayed on the console. Using **ByRef** with value types is efficient because it prevents instances of the value type's fields from being copied when making method calls.

Using **ByRef** with value types gives you the same behavior that you already get when passing reference types by value. With value types, **ByRef** allows a method to manipulate a single value type instance. The caller must allocate the memory for the instance, and the callee manipulates that memory. With reference types, the caller allocates memory for a pointer to a reference object and the callee manipulates this pointer. Because of this behavior, using **ByRef** with reference types is useful only when the method is going to "return" a reference to an object that it knows about. The following code demonstrates:

```
Imports System
Imports System.IO

Class App
    Public Shared Sub Main()
        Dim fs As FileStream

        ' Open the first file to be processed.
        StartProcessingFiles(fs)

        ' Continue while there are more files to process.
        Do Until fs Is Nothing
            fs.Read(...)
            ContinueProcessingFiles(fs)
        Loop
    End Sub

    Shared Sub StartProcessingFiles(ByRef fs As FileStream)
        fs = New FileStream(...)
    End Sub

    Shared Sub ContinueProcessingFiles(ByRef fs As FileStream)
        fs.Close()          ' Close the last file worked on.

        ' Open the next file; if there are no more files, return Nothing.
        If noMoreFilesToProcess Then
            fs = Nothing
        Else
            fs = new FileStream(...)
        End If
    End Sub
End Class
```

As you can see, the big difference with this code is that the methods that have **ByRef** reference type parameters are constructing an object and the pointer to the new object is returned to the caller. You'll also notice that the **ContinueProcessingFiles** method can manipulate the object being passed into it before returning a new object.

Here's another example that demonstrates how to use the **ByRef** keyword to implement a method that swaps two reference types:

```
Public Shared Sub Swap(ByRef a As Object, ByRef b As Object)
    Dim t As Object = b
    b = a
    a = t
End Sub
```

To swap references to two **String** objects, you'd probably think that you could write code like this:

```
Public Shared Sub SomeMethod()
    Dim s1 As String = "Jeffrey"
    Dim s2 As String = "Richter"
    ⋮
    Swap(s1, s2)
    Console.WriteLine(s1)   ' Displays "Richter"
    Console.WriteLine(s2)   ' Displays "Jeffrey"
End Sub
```

However, this code won't compile if **Option Strict** is on. The problem is that variables passed by reference to a method must be the same type. In other words, **Swap** expects two references to an **Object** type, not two references to a **String** type. To swap the two **String** references, you must do this:

```
Public Shared Sub Main()
  Dim s1 As String = "Jeffrey"
  Dim s2 As String = "Richter"

  ' Variables that are passed by reference
  ' must match what the method expects.
  Dim o1 As Object = s1
  Dim o2 As Object = s2
  Swap(o1, o2)

  ' Now cast the objects back to strings.
  s1 = DirectCast(o1, String)
  s2 = DirectCast(o2, String)

  Console.WriteLine(s1)   ' Displays "Richter"
  Console.WriteLine(s2)   ' Displays "Jeffrey"
End Sub
```

This version of **SomeMethod** does compile and execute as expected, even if **Option Strict** is on. The reason why the parameters passed must match the parameters the method expects is to ensure that type safety is preserved. The following code, which thankfully won't compile, shows how type safety could be compromised.

```
Option Strict On

Imports System
Imports System.IO

Class SomeType
    Public val As Int32
End Class

Class App
    Public Shared Sub Main()
        Dim st As SomeType

        ' The following line generates error BC30512: Option Strict On
        ' disallows implicit conversions from 'System.Object' to 'SomeType'.
        GetAnObject(st)

        Console.WriteLine(st.val)
    End Sub

    Shared Sub GetAnObject(ByRef o As Object)
        o = New String("X"c, 100)
    End Sub
End Class
```

In this code, **Main** clearly expects **GetAnObject** to return a **SomeType** object. However, because **GetAnObject**'s signature indicates a reference to an **Object**, **GetAnObject** is free to initialize **o** to an object of any type. In this example, when **GetAnObject** returned to **Main**, **st** would refer to a **String**, which is clearly not a **SomeType** object, and the call to **Console.WriteLine** would certainly fail. Fortunately, the Visual Basic compiler won't compile the preceding code because **st** is a reference to **SomeType** but **GetAnObject** requires a reference to an **Object**.

Passing a Variable Number of Parameters to a Method

It's sometimes convenient for the developer to define a method that can accept a variable number of parameters. For example, the **System.String** type offers methods allowing an arbitrary number of strings to be concatenated together and methods allowing the caller to specify a set of strings that are to be formatted together.

To declare a method that accepts a variable number of arguments, you declare the method as follows:

```
Shared Function Add(ByVal ParamArray values() As Int32) As Int32
   ' NOTE: It is possible to pass the values
   ' array to other methods if you want to.

   Dim x As Int32
   Dim sum As Int32 = 0
   For x = 0 To values.Length - 1
      sum += values(x)
   Next
   Return sum
End Function
```

As you can see, this **Add** method takes a single parameter: a reference to an array of **Int32** values. Inside the method, **sum** is initialized to **0** and each element in the array is added to **sum**. At the end of the method, **sum** is returned to the caller.

Because **Add**'s parameter is an array, code can call this method as follows:

```
Public Shared Sub Main()
   ' Displays "15"
   Console.WriteLine(Add(New Int32() {1, 2, 3, 4, 5}))
End Sub
```

It's clear that the array can easily be initialized with an arbitrary number of elements and then passed off to **Add** for processing. Although the preceding code would compile and work correctly, it is a little ugly. As developers, we would certainly prefer to have written the call to **Add** as follows:

```
Public Shared Sub Main()
   ' Displays "15"
   Console.WriteLine(Add(1, 2, 3, 4, 5))
End Sub
```

You'll be happy to know that we can do this because of the **ParamArray** keyword. The **ParamArray** keyword tells the compiler to apply an instance of the **System.ParamArrayAttribute** custom attribute to the parameter. (I discuss custom attributes in Chapter 16.) Because the **ParamArray** keyword is just shorthand for this attribute, the **Add** method's prototype could have been defined like this:

```
' Notice that you must specify either "ParamArrayAttribute" or
' [ParamArray], because ParamArray is a Visual Basic keyword.
Shared Function Add(<ParamArrayAttribute()> ByVal values() As Int32) As Int32
   :
End Function
```

When the Visual Basic compiler detects a call to a method, the compiler checks all the methods with the specified name, where no parameter has the `ParamArrayAttribute` attribute applied. If a method exists that can accept the call, the compiler generates the code necessary to call the method. However, if the compiler can't find a match, it looks for methods that have a `ParamArray-Attribute` attribute to see whether the call can be satisfied. If the compiler finds a match, it emits code that constructs an array and populates its elements before emitting the code that calls the selected method.

In the previous example, no **Add** method is defined that takes five **Int32**-compatible arguments; however, the compiler sees that the source code has a call to **Add** that is being passed a list of **Int32** values and that there is an **Add** method whose array-of-**Int32** parameter is marked with the `ParamArray-Attribute` attribute. So the compiler considers this a match and generates code that coerces the parameters into an **Int32** array and then calls the **Add** method. The result is that you can write the code easily passing a bunch of parameters to **Add**, but the compiler generates code as though you'd written the first version that explicitly constructs and initializes the array.

Only the last parameter to a method can be marked with the `ParamArray` keyword (or the `ParamArrayAttribute` attribute). This parameter must also identify a single-dimension array of any type. It's legal to pass **Nothing** or a reference to an array of **0** entries as the last parameter to the method. The following call to **Add** compiles fine, runs fine, and produces a resulting sum of **0** (as expected):

```
Public Shared Sub Main()
   ' Displays "0"
   Console.WriteLine(Add())
End Sub
```

So far, all the examples have shown how to write a method that takes an arbitrary number of **Int32** parameters. How would you write a method that takes an arbitrary number of parameters where the parameters could be any type? The answer is very simple: just modify the method's prototype so that it takes an array of **Object**s instead of an array of **Int32s**. Here's a method that displays the **Type** of every object passed to it:

```
Class App
   Public Shared Sub Main()
      DisplayTypes(New Object(), New Random(), "Jeff", 5)
   End Sub

   Shared Sub DisplayTypes(ByVal ParamArray objects() As Object)
      Dim o As Object
      For Each o In objects
```

(continued)

```
            Console.WriteLine(o.GetType().ToString())
        Next
    End Sub
End Class
```

Running this code yields the following output:

```
System.Object
System.Random
System.String
System.Int32
```

> **Note** The `ParamArray` keyword exists in previous versions of Visual Basic. However, its behavior in Visual Basic .NET is slightly different. First, a Visual Basic 6 `ParamArray` argument can only be an array of `Variant`s, and the caller can even omit one or more items on the argument list. (The callee can detect this case with the `IsMissing` function.) In earlier versions of Visual Basic, you can't pass a real array to a `ParamArray` argument, as you can do in Visual Basic .NET: the array the callee receives is just a pseudo-array; you can check its bounds with the `LBound` and `UBound` functions, but you can't pass it to another method. Finally, a `ParamArray` argument can be passed only with `ByRef` in Visual Basic 6, whereas it can be passed only with `ByVal` in Visual Basic .NET.

Optional Arguments

Visual Basic .NET supports optional arguments, that is, arguments that the caller can omit when invoking the method. Here's an example:

```
Class App
    Public Shared Sub Main()
        Console.WriteLine(Max(15, 3))       ' Displays "15"
        Console.WriteLine(Max(15, 3, 22))   ' Displays "22"
    End Sub

    Shared Function Max(ByVal d1 As Double, ByVal d2 As Double, _
        Optional ByVal d3 As Double = Double.NegativeInfinity) As Double
        If d1 > d2 Then
            Max = d1
        Else
            Max = d2
```

```
        End If
        If d3 > Max Then Max = d3
    End Function
End Class
```

A method can take any number of optional parameters, provided that they come after all the mandatory ones. Also, you can't mix the **Optional** and the **ParamArray** keywords in the same method definition. Unlike earlier versions of Visual Basic, for Visual Basic .NET, you must specify an optional argument's default value. The default value indicates the value of the argument if the caller omits it.

You should use optional arguments only if the caller of the method can easily anticipate the optional argument's default value and if the default value doesn't affect the outcome. For example, in the preceding **Max** method, the optional argument's default value is set to **Double.NegativeInfinity**. If the caller doesn't specify the optional argument, **Double.NegativeInfinity**, which never affects the maximum value for a list of numbers, is assumed. Similarly, you might use the value **0** when evaluating a sum of numbers or **1** when evaluating their product.

If you can't think of an innocuous default value, you should choose a value that is clearly invalid. This way, the method can detect that the caller didn't specify a value for the default argument and the method can execute accordingly. For example, I could rewrite the preceding **Max** method like this:

```
Shared Function Max(ByVal d1 As Double, ByVal d2 As Double, ⌐
    Optional ByVal d3 As Double = Double.NaN) As Double
    If d1 > d2 Then
        Max = d1
    Else
        Max = d2
    End If
    If Not Double.IsNaN(d3) AndAlso d3 > Max Then Max = d3
End Function
```

Optional arguments provide some convenience for a method's caller, but they also have some shortcomings that you must be aware of:

■   Using optional parameters doesn't make your code faster. In fact, when the compiler detects an absent optional argument, the compiler looks up the default value (out of the assembly's metadata tables) and emits IL code that calls the method passing it the default value. In other words, optional arguments are a feature that is exposed at the source code level but not at the IL level.

- Because IL always calls a method passing a complete set of arguments, the value of an absent argument is determined at compile time, not at run time. This has versioning consequences. For example, say a ComponentAssembly.dll assembly contains a method that has an optional **Int32** argument whose default value is **5**. Now imagine an AppAssembly.exe assembly that contains a call to this method and the optional argument isn't specified. When compiling AppAssembly.exe, the compiler emits IL code that passes **5** to the method. Let's say that the method in ComponentAssembly.dll has its optional parameter's default value changed to **123** and the assembly is rebuilt. If the AppAssembly.exe assembly isn't rebuilt, then at run time, **5** is passed to the method—the new default value (**123**) isn't passed to the method unless the code in AppAssembly.exe is also recompiled.

- Optional arguments aren't CLS-compliant. In other words, many languages (like C# and Managed Extensions for C++) don't support optional arguments and therefore can't take advantage of them. Programmers using these languages must always specify all arguments when calling a method. For this reason, an optional parameter's default value must be clearly specified in any documentation that accompanies the component. I highly recommended that you not use optional arguments in public methods of public types.

- Because an optional argument's default value is looked up and emitted into IL code at compile time, you can use primitive types only for optional arguments (**Byte**, **Int16**, **Int32**, **Int64**, **Single**, **Double**, **String**, and so on).

- Finally, a method has no way to know for sure if the caller has omitted an optional argument.

The last point requires further explanation. For example, you might believe that using a **Double.NaN** default value for a **Double** argument and then testing for this default value inside the method is safe enough to ascertain that the optional argument has been passed or omitted. Unfortunately, the client can still pass the **Double.NaN** value, either intentionally or accidentally, as in the following code snippet:

```
' The last argument is evaluated to Double.NaN.
Console.WriteLine(Max(15, 3, Math.Sqrt(-1)))
```

To avoid all these shortcomings, you should avoid optional arguments entirely and use overloaded methods, which don't suffer from versioning problems and can deliver better performance. Here's how you can overload the **Max** function to support two or three arguments:

```
Shared Function Max(ByVal d1 As Double, ByVal d2 As Double) As Double
    If d1 > d2 Then
        Max = d1
    Else
        Max = d2
    End If
End Function

Shared Function Max(ByVal d1 As Double, ByVal d2 As Double, _
    ByVal d3 As Double) As Double
    Max = Max(d1, Max(d2, d3))
End Function
```

Speaking of method overloading, remember that you can't have two methods that differ only by their optional arguments because the compiler wouldn't know which method to choose if the caller omitted the optional arguments.

Static Variables in a Method

Visual Basic allows a method to declare static variables. Unlike regular local variables, static variables aren't allocated on the stack and preserve their value between calls to the method, as this code demonstrates:

```
Imports System

Class App
    Shared Sub Main()
        SomeMethod()
        SomeMethod()
        SomeMethod()
    End Sub

    Shared Sub SomeMethod()
        Static count As Int32 = 0
        count += 1
        Console.WriteLine("SomeMethod called {0} time(s).", count)
    End Sub
End Class
```

When you run this code, you see the following output in the console window:

```
SomeMethod called 1 time(s).
SomeMethod called 2 time(s).
SomeMethod called 3 time(s).
```

The CLR doesn't actually support static variables. When compiling your code, the Visual Basic compiler translates this high-level Visual Basic construct into IL code that the CLR can understand in order to provide you shared variable functionality. Basically, the Visual Basic compiler examines the previous source and internally translates it into something like this:

```
Imports System
Imports System.Threading
Imports Microsoft.VisualBasic.CompilerServices

Class App
    Private Shared _STATIC_SomeMethod_001_count_Init As _
        New StaticLocalInitFlag()
    Private Shared _STATIC_SomeMethod_001_count As Int32

    Shared Sub Main()
        SomeMethod()
        SomeMethod()
        SomeMethod()
    End Sub

    Shared Sub SomeMethod()

        ' Is this the first time this method is called?
        If Not _STATIC_SomeMethod_001_count_Init.State = 1 Then

            ' Yes; ensure that only one thread at a time can execute this code.
            Monitor.Enter(_STATIC_SomeMethod_001_count_Init)
            Try
                ' Is this the first time this method is called?
                If _STATIC_SomeMethod_001_count_Init.State = 0 Then
                    ' Setting Init.State to 2 means that initialization
                    ' has started.
                    _STATIC_SomeMethod_001_count_Init.State = 2

                    ' Initialize the static variable to 0
                    ' (as in the original source code).
                    _STATIC_SomeMethod_001_count = 0
                Else
                    ' Did initialization start but not complete?
                    If _STATIC_SomeMethod_001_count_Init.State = 2 Then
                        ' Yes; throw an IncompleteInitializationException.
```

```
                Throw New IncompleteInitialization()
            End If
        End If
    Finally
        ' Setting Init.State to 1 means that initialization
        ' has completed.
        _STATIC_SomeMethod_001_count_Init.State = 1

        ' Wake up any other threads attempting to execute this method.
        Monitor.Exit(_STATIC_SomeMethod_001_count_Init)
    End Try
End If

' Here is the real code for the method.

' Increment "count" by 1.
_STATIC_SomeMethod_001_count += 1

' Display the string (including the value in "count").
Console.WriteLine("SomeMethod called {0} time(s).", _
    _STATIC_SomeMethod_001_count)
    End Sub
End Class
```

As you can see, the compiler generates a lot of code when you use static variables. In particular, the compiler renamed the shared **count** field to **_STATIC_SomeMethod_001_count** and defined a new, private, shared field (**_STATIC_SomeMethod_001_count_Init**). When the **SomeType** type is first accessed, its type constructor is called, which constructs an instance of a **Microsoft.VisualBasic.CompilerServices.StaticLocalInitFlag** class. This class contains a single public field, **State**, that indicates whether a method's static fields have been initialized. When constructed, the **State** field is initialized to **0** by the CLR.

Inside **SomeMethod** is where you see the extra code the compiler generates. First, the code examines **_STATIC_SomeMethod_001_count_Init**'s **State** field and sees that it's set to **0**, meaning that this is the first time the method has ever been called. If the method has never been called before, the code initializes the static variable to the value indicated in the original source code (**0**). But this initialization must be performed in a thread-safe manner, which is why **Monitor.Enter** is called before initializing **_STATIC_SomeMethod_001_count**.

After **_STATIC_SomeMethod_001_count** is initialized, the code in the **Finally** block executes. This code sets **_STATIC_SomeMethod_001_count_Init**'s **State** field to 1 to indicate that the "static variable" has been initialized. Future calls to this method will now bypass the initialization code and execute the code that corresponds to **SomeMethod**'s original source code.

Note that if the static **count** variable had been declared in an instance method (vs. a shared method), the compiler would have declared the **_STATIC_ SomeMethod_001_count** field and the **_STATIC_SomeMethod_001_count_Init** field as instance fields instead of shared fields. In other words, a static field in an instance method maintains its value on a per-object rather than a per-type basis.

Operator Overload Methods

Some programming languages allow a type to define how operators should manipulate instances of the type. For example, a lot of types (such as **System.String**) overload the equality (**==** in C#) and inequality (**!=** in C#) operators. The CLR doesn't know anything about operator overloading because it doesn't even know what an operator is. Your programming language defines what each operator symbol means and what code should be generated when these special symbols appear.

For example, in C#, applying the **+** symbol to primitive numbers causes the compiler to generate code that adds the two numbers together. When the **+** symbol is applied to strings, the C# compiler generates code that concatenates the two strings together. For inequality, C# uses the **!=** symbol, while Visual Basic uses the **<>** symbol. Finally, the **^** symbol means exclusive OR (XOR) in C#, but it means exponent in Visual Basic.

Although the CLR doesn't know anything about operators, the CLR specifications do indicate how languages should expose operator overloads so that they can be readily consumed by code written in a different programming language. Each programming language gets to decide for itself whether it will support operator overloads and, if it does, the syntax for expressing and using them. As far as the CLR is concerned, operator overloads are simply methods.

Your programming language of choice chooses whether or not to support operator overloading and what the syntax looks like. When you compile your source code, the compiler produces a method that identifies the behavior of the operator. For example, say that you define a class like this (in C#):

```
class Complex {
   public static Complex operator+(Complex c1, Complex c2) { ... }
}
```

The compiler emits a method definition for a method named **op_Addition**; the method definition entry also has the **specialname** flag set, indicating that this is a "special" method. When language compilers (including the C# compiler) see a **+** operator specified in source code, they look to see if one of the operand's types defines a **specialname** method named **op_Addition** whose parameters are compatible with the operand's types. If this method exists, the compiler emits code to call this method. If no such method exists, a compilation error occurs.

Table 9-1 shows the set of standard C# operator symbols and the corresponding recommended method name that compilers should emit and consume. I'll explain the table's third column in the next section.

Table 9-1   C# Operators and Their CLS-Compliant Method Names

C# Operator Symbol	Special Method Name	Suggested CLS-Compliant Method Name
+	op_UnaryPlus	Plus
-	op_UnaryNegation	Negate
~	op_OnesComplement	OnesComplement
++	op_Increment	Increment
--	op_Decrement	Decrement
(none)	op_True	IsTrue { get; }
(none)	op_False	IsFalse { get; }
+	op_Addition	Add
+=	op_AdditionAssignment	Add
-	op_Subtraction	Subtract
-=	op_SubtractionAssignment	Subtract
*	op_Multiply	Multiply
*=	op_MultiplicationAssignment	Multiply
/	op_Division	Divide
/=	op_DivisionAssignment	Divide
%	op_Modulus	Mod
%=	op_ModulusAssignment	Mod
^	op_ExclusiveOr	Xor
^=	op_ExclusiveOrAssignment	Xor
&	op_BitwiseAnd	BitwiseAnd
&=	op_BitwiseAndAssignment	BitwiseAnd
|	op_BitwiseOr	BitwiseOr
|=	op_BitwiseOrAssignment	BitwiseOr
&&	op_LogicalAnd	And
||	op_LogicalOr	Or
!	op_LogicalNot	Not
<<	op_LeftShift	LeftShift

(continued)

Table 9-1   C# Operators and Their CLS-Compliant Method Names   *(continued)*

C# Operator Symbol	Special Method Name	Suggested CLS-Compliant Method Name
<<=	op_LeftShiftAssignment	LeftShift
>>	op_RightShift	RightShift
>>=	op_RightShiftAssignment	RightShift
(none)	op_UnsignedRightShiftAssignment	RightShift
==	op_Equality	Equals
!=	op_Inequality	Compare
<	op_LessThan	Compare
>	op_GreaterThan	Compare
<=	op_LessThanOrEqual	Compare
>=	op_GreaterThanOrEqual	Compare
=	op_Assign	Assign

Important   If you examine the core Microsoft .NET Framework Class Library (FCL) types (Int32, Int64, UInt32, and so on), you'll see that they don't define any operator overload methods. The reason they don't is that the CLR offers IL instructions to directly manipulate instances of these types. If the types were to offer methods and if compilers were to emit code to call these methods, a run-time performance cost would be associated with the method call. Plus, the method would ultimately have to execute some IL instructions to perform the expected operation anyway. This is the reason that the core FCL types don't define any operator overload methods. Here's what this means to you: because Visual Basic doesn't support unsigned numeric types, you won't be able to perform any operations on instances of that.

Operators and Programming Language Interoperability

Operator overloading can be a very useful tool, allowing developers to express their thoughts with succinct code. However, as you know, not all programming languages (including Visual Basic and Java) support operator overloading. So when a Visual Basic developer applies the **+** operator to a type that Visual Basic doesn't consider to be a primitive, the compiler generates an error and won't compile the code. So here's the problem that needs to be solved: How can a Visual Basic developer call the operator methods defined by a type that was written in a language that supports operator overloading?

Visual Basic doesn't offer special syntax that allows a type to define an overload for the + operator. In addition, Visual Basic doesn't know how to translate code using a + symbol to call the **op_Addition** method. However, Visual Basic (like all languages) does support the ability to call a type's methods. So in Visual Basic, you can call an **op_Addition** method that was generated by a type built with the C# compiler.

Given that information, you'd likely believe that you could also define a type in Visual Basic that offers an **op_Addition** method that would be callable by C# code using the + operator. However, you'd be wrong. When the C# compiler detects the + operator, it looks for an **op_Addition** method that has the **specialname** metadata flag associated with it so that the compiler knows for sure that the **op_Addition** method is intended to be an operator overload method. Because the **op_Addition** method produced by Visual Basic won't have the **specialname** flag associated with it, the C# compiler will produce a compilation error. Of course, code in any language can explicitly call a method that just happens to be named **op_Addition**, but the compilers won't translate a usage of the + symbol to call this method.

The following source code files summarize this discussion. The first one is a Visual Basic type (defined in a library) that offers an **op_Addition** method. Again, the code isn't implemented correctly, but it compiles and demonstrates what I've been talking about.

```
Imports System

Public Class VBType

    ' Define an op_Addition method that adds two VBType objects together.
    ' This is NOT a true overload of the + operator because the Visual Basic
    ' compiler won't associate the specialname metadata flag with this method.
    Public Shared Function op_Addition(a as VBType, b as VBType) As VBType
        Return Nothing
    End Function
End Class
```

The second one is a C# application that adds two instances of **VBType**:

```
using System;

public class CSharpApp {
    public static void Main() {
```

(continued)

```
      // Construct an instance of VBType.
      VBType vb = new VBType();

      // When not commented out, the following line produces a
      // compiler error because VBType's op_Addition method is missing
      // the specialname metadata flag.
      // vb = vb + vb;

      // The following line compiles and runs; it just doesn't look nice.
      vb = VBType.op_Addition(vb, vb);
   }
}
```

As you can see from the preceding code, the C# code can't use the **+** symbol to add two **VBType** objects together. However, it can add the objects together by explicitly calling **VBType**'s **op_Addition** method.

Now let's reverse the example and build a Visual Basic application that uses a C# type. Here's a C# type (defined in a library) that offers an overload of the **+** operator:

```
using System;

public class CSharpType {

   // Overload the + operator.
   public static CSharpType operator+(CSharpType a, CSharpType b) {
      return null;
   }
}
```

And here's a Visual Basic application that adds two instances of the **CSharpType**:

```
Imports System

Public Class VBApp
   Public Shared Sub Main()

      ' Construct an instance of the CSharpType.
      Dim cs as new CSharpType()

      ' When uncommented, the following line produces a
      ' compiler error because Visual Basic doesn't know how to translate
      ' the + symbol to call CSharpType's op_Addition method.
      ' cs = cs + cs

      ' The following line compiles and runs; it just doesn't look nice.
      cs = CSharpType.op_Addition(cs, cs)
   End Sub
End Class
```

Here the Visual Basic code can't use the **+** symbol to add two **CSharpType** objects together because Visual Basic doesn't know to translate the **+** symbol to call the **op_Addition** method. However, the Visual Basic code can add the objects together by explicitly calling **CSharpType**'s **op_Addition** method (even though this method has the **specialname** metadata flag associated with it).

Jeff's Opinion About Microsoft's Operator Method Name Rules

I'm sure that all these rules about when you can and can't call an operator overload method seem very confusing and overly complicated. If compilers that supported operator overloading just didn't emit the **specialname** metadata flag, the rules would be a lot simpler and programmers would have an easier time working with types that offer operator overload methods. Languages that support operator overloading would support the operator symbol syntax, and all languages would support calling the various **op_** methods explicitly. I can't come up with any reason why Microsoft made this so difficult, and I hope they'll loosen these rules with future versions of their compilers.

For a type that defines operator overload methods, Microsoft recommends that the type also define friendlier public instance methods that call the operator overload methods internally. For example, a public friendly named method, called **Add**, should be defined by a type that overloads the **op_Addition** or **op_AdditionAssignment** method. The third column in Table 9-1 lists the recommended friendly name for each operator. So the **Complex** type shown earlier should be defined like this:

```
class Complex {
    public static Complex operator+(Complex c1, Complex c2) { ... }
    public Complex Add(Complex c) { return(this + c); }
}
```

Certainly, code written in any programming language can call any of the friendly operator methods, such as **Add**. Microsoft's guideline that types offer these friendly method names complicates the story even more. I feel that this additional complication is unnecessary and that calling these friendly named methods would cause an additional performance hit unless the JIT compiler is able to inline the code in the friendly named method. Inlining the code would cause the JIT compiler to optimize the code, removing the additional method call and boosting run-time performance.

Conversion Operator Methods

Occasionally, you need to convert an object from one type to an object of a different type. For example, I'm sure you've had to convert a **Byte** to an **Int32** at some point in your life. When the source type and the target type are a compiler's primitive types, the compiler knows how to emit the necessary code to convert the object.

However, if neither type is one of the compiler's primitive types, the compiler won't know how to perform the conversion. For example, imagine that the FCL included a **Rational** data type. It might be convenient to convert an **Int32** object or a **Single** object to a **Rational** object. Moreover, it also might be nice to convert a **Rational** object to an **Int32** or a **Single** object.

To make these conversions, the **Rational** type should define public constructors that take a single parameter: an instance of the type that you're converting from. You should also define public instance **ToXxx** methods that take no parameters (just like the very popular **ToString** method). Each method will convert an instance of the defining type to the **Xxx** type. Here's how to correctly define conversion constructors and methods for a **Rational** type:

```
Class Rational
    ' Constructs a Rational from an Int32
    Public Sub New(ByVal numerator As Int32)
        ⋮
    End Sub

    ' Constructs a Rational from a Single
    Public Sub New(ByVal value As Single)
        ⋮
    End Sub

    ' Converts a Rational to an Int32
    Public Function ToInt32() As Int32
        ⋮
    End Function

    ' Converts a Rational to a Single
    Public Function ToSingle() As Single
        ⋮
    End Function
End Class
```

By invoking these constructors and methods, a developer using any programming language can convert an **Int32** to a **Single** object to a **Rational** object and convert a **Rational** object to an **Int32** or a **Single** object. The ability to do these conversions can be quite handy, and when designing a type, you should seriously consider what conversion constructors and methods make sense for your type.

I should point out that some programming languages (like C#) offer conversion operator overloading in addition to the constructors and methods discussed. *Conversion operators* are shared methods that convert an object from one type to another type. Unfortunately, Visual Basic doesn't allow you to access conversion operator methods that types implemented in these other languages might define.

How Virtual Methods Are Called

Methods represent code that performs some operation on the type (shared methods) or an instance of the type (nonshared methods). All methods have a name, a signature, and a return value. A type can have multiple methods with the same name as long as each method has a different set of parameters or a different return value. So it's possible to define two methods with the same name and the same parameters as long as the methods have a different return type. However, except for IL assembly language, I'm not aware of any language that takes advantage of this "feature"; most languages require that methods differ by parameters and ignore a method's return type when determining uniqueness.

By examining metadata, the CLR can determine whether a nonshared method is a virtual or nonvirtual method. However, the CLR doesn't use this information when calling a method. Instead, the CLR offers two IL instructions for calling a method: `call` and `callvirt`. The `call` IL instruction calls a method based on the type of the reference, and the `callvirt` IL instruction calls a method based on the type of the object referred to. When compiling your source code, the compiler knows whether or not you're calling a virtual method and emits the proper `call` or `callvirt` IL instruction. This means that it's possible to call a virtual method nonvirtually, an approach that is commonly used when your code calls a virtual method defined in your type's base class, as shown here:

```
Class SomeClass
    ' ToString is a virtual method defined in the base class: Object.
    Public Overrides Function ToString() As String
        ' Compiler uses the 'call' IL instruction to call
        ' Object's ToString method nonvirtually.

        ' If the compiler were to use 'callvirt' instead of 'call', this
        ' method would call itself recursively until the stack overflowed.
        Return MyBase.ToString()
    End Function
End Class
```

Compilers also typically emit the `call` IL instruction when calling a virtual method using a reference to a sealed type. Emitting `call` instead of `callvirt` improves performance because the CLR doesn't have to check the actual type of the object being referenced. In addition, for value types (which are always sealed), using `call` prevents the boxing of the value type, which reduces memory and CPU usage.

Regardless of whether `call` or `callvirt` is used to call an instance method, all instance methods always receive a hidden **Me** pointer as the method's first parameter. The **Me** pointer refers to the object being operated on.

Virtual Method Versioning

Back in the old days, a single company was responsible for all the code that made up an application. Today, many different companies often contribute parts to help construct another company's application. For example, lots of applications today use components created by other companies—in fact, the COM(+) and .NET technologies encourage this practice. When applications consist of many parts created and distributed by different companies, many versioning issues come up.

I talked about some of these versioning issues in Chapter 3 when I explained strongly named assemblies and discussed how an administrator can ensure that an application binds to the assemblies that it was built and tested with. However, other versioning issues cause source code compatibility problems. For example, you must be very careful when adding or modifying members of a type if that type is used as a base type. Let's look at some examples.

CompanyA has designed the following type, **Phone**:

```
Namespace CompanyA
    Class Phone
        Public Sub Dial()
            Console.WriteLine("Phone.Dial")
            ' Do work to dial the phone here.
        End Sub
    End Class
End Namespace
```

Now imagine that CompanyB defines another type, **BetterPhone**, which uses CompanyA's **Phone** type as its base:

```
Namespace CompanyB
    Class BetterPhone
        Inherits CompanyA.Phone
```

```
      Public Sub Dial()
         Console.WriteLine("BetterPhone.Dial")
         EstablishConnection()
         MyBase.Dial()
      End Sub

      Protected Overridable Sub EstablishConnection()
         Console.WriteLine("BetterPhone.EstablishConnection")
         ' Do work to establish the connection.
      End Sub
   End Class
End Namespace
```

When CompanyB attempts to compile its code, the Visual Basic compiler issues the following warning: "warning BC40004: sub 'Dial' conflicts with sub 'Dial' in the base class 'Phone' and so should be declared 'Shadows'." This warning is notifying the developer that **BetterPhone** is defining a **Dial** method, which will hide the **Dial** method defined in **Phone**. This new method could change the semantic meaning of **Dial** (as defined by CompanyA when it originally created the **Dial** method).

It's a very nice feature of the compiler to warn you of this potential semantic mismatch. The compiler also tells you how to remove the warning by adding the **Shadows** keyword before the definition of **Dial** in the **BetterPhone** class. Here's the fixed **BetterPhone** class:

```
Namespace CompanyB
   Class BetterPhone
      Inherits CompanyA.Phone

      ' This Dial method has nothing to do with Phone's Dial method.
      Public Shadows Sub Dial()
         Console.WriteLine("BetterPhone.Dial")
         EstablishConnection()
         MyBase.Dial()
      End Sub

      Protected Overridable Sub EstablishConnection()
         Console.WriteLine("BetterPhone.EstablishConnection")
         ' Do work to establish the connection.
      End Sub
   End Class
End Namespace
```

At this point, CompanyB can use **BetterPhone** in its application. Here's some sample code that CompanyB might write:

```
Class App
   Shared Sub Main()
      Dim phone As New CompanyB.BetterPhone()
      phone.Dial()
   End Sub
End Class
```

When this code runs, the following output is displayed:

```
BetterPhone.Dial
BetterPhone.EstablishConnection
Phone.Dial
```

This output shows that CompanyB is getting the behavior it desires. The call to **Dial** is calling the new **Dial** method defined by **BetterPhone**, which calls the virtual **EstablishConnection** method and then calls the **Phone** base type's **Dial** method.

Now let's imagine that several companies have decided to use CompanyA's **Phone** type. Let's further imagine that these other companies have decided that the ability to establish a connection in the **Dial** method is a really useful feature. This feedback is given to CompanyA, who now goes and revises its **Phone** class:

```
Namespace CompanyA
   Class Phone
      Public Sub Dial()
         Console.WriteLine("Phone.Dial")
         EstablishConnection()
         ' Do work to dial the phone here.
      End Sub

      Protected Overridable Sub EstablishConnection()
         Console.WriteLine("Phone.EstablishConnection")
         ' Do work to establish the connection.
      End Sub
   End Class
End Namespace
```

Now when CompanyB compiles its **BetterPhone** type (derived from this new version of CompanyA's **Phone**), the compiler issues this warning: "warning BC40005: sub 'EstablishConnection' shadows an overridable method in a base class. To override the base method, this method must be declared 'Overrides'."

The compiler is alerting you to the fact that both **Phone** and **BetterPhone** offer an **EstablishConnection** method and that the semantics of both might not be identical: simply recompiling **BetterPhone** can no longer give the same behavior as it did when using the first version of the **Phone** type.

If CompanyB decides that the **EstablishConnection** methods are not semantically identical in both types, then CompanyB can tell the compiler that the `Dial` and `EstablishConnection` methods defined in `BetterPhone` are the "correct" methods to use and that they have no relationship with the `Dial` and `EstablishConnection` methods defined in the `Phone` base type. CompanyB informs the compiler by keeping `Shadows` on the `Dial` method and by adding `Shadows` to the `EstablishConnection` method:

```
Namespace CompanyB
    Class BetterPhone
        Inherits CompanyA.Phone

        ' Keep 'Shadows' to mark this method as having no
        ' relationship to the base type's Dial method.
        Public Shadows Sub Dial()
            Console.WriteLine("BetterPhone.Dial")
            EstablishConnection()
            MyBase.Dial()
        End Sub

        ' Add 'Shadows' to mark this method as having no
        ' relationship to the base type's EstablishConnection method.
        Protected Overridable Shadows Sub EstablishConnection()
            Console.WriteLine("BetterPhone.EstablishConnection")
            ' Do work to establish the connection.
        End Sub
    End Class
End Namespace
```

In this code, the `Shadows` keyword tells the compiler to emit metadata, making it clear to the CLR that `BetterPhone`'s `Dial` and `EstablishConnection` methods are intended to be treated as new functions that are introduced by the `Better-Phone` type. The CLR will know that there is no relationship between `Phone`'s and `BetterPhone`'s methods.

> **Note**   Without the `Shadows` keyword, the developer of `BetterPhone` couldn't use the method names `Dial` and `EstablishConnection`. This would most likely cause a ripple effect of changes throughout the entire source code base, breaking source and binary compatibility. This type of pervasive change is usually undesirable, especially in any moderate to large project. However, if changing the method name causes only moderate updates in the source code, you should change the name of the methods so that the two different meanings of `Dial` and `EstablishConnection` don't confuse other developers.

When the same application code (in the `Main` method) executes, the output is as follows:

```
BetterPhone.Dial
BetterPhone.EstablishConnection
Phone.Dial
Phone.EstablishConnection
```

This output shows that `Main`'s call to `Dial` calls the new `Dial` method defined by `BetterPhone`. `Dial` then calls the virtual `EstablishConnection` method that is also defined by `BetterPhone`. When `BetterPhone`'s `EstablishConnection` method returns, `Phone`'s `Dial` method is called. `Phone`'s `Dial` method calls `EstablishConnection`, but because `BetterPhone`'s `EstablishConnection` is marked with `Shadows`, `BetterPhone`'s `EstablishConnection` method isn't considered an override of `Phone`'s virtual `EstablishConnection` method. As a result, `Phone`'s `Dial` method calls `Phone`'s `EstablishConnection` method—this is the desired behavior.

Alternatively, CompanyB could have gotten the new version of CompanyA's `Phone` type and decided that `Phone`'s semantics of `Dial` and `EstablishConnection` are exactly what it's been looking for. In this case, CompanyB would modify its `BetterPhone` type by removing its `Dial` method entirely. In addition, because CompanyB now wants to tell the compiler that `BetterPhone`'s `EstablishConnection` method is related to `Phone`'s `EstablishConnection` method, the `Shadows` keyword must be removed. Simply removing the `Shadows` keyword isn't enough, though, because now the compiler can't tell exactly what the intention is of `BetterPhone`'s `EstablishConnection` method. To express his intent exactly, the CompanyB developer must also add the `Overrides` keyword to the `BetterPhone`'s `EstablishConnection` method. (Note that you must also delete the `Overridable` keyword because the `Overrides` keyword makes a method implicitly overridable.) The following code shows the new version of `BetterPhone`:

```
Namespace CompanyB
    Class BetterPhone
        Inherits CompanyA.Phone

        ' Delete the Dial method (inherit Dial from base).

        ' Remove 'Shadows' and add 'Overrides' to
        ' mark this method as having a relationship to the base
        ' type's EstablishConnection method. Note that marking a
        ' method with 'Overrides' makes it overridable as well.
        Protected Overrides Sub EstablishConnection()
```

```
        Console.WriteLine("BetterPhone.EstablishConnection")
        ' Do work to establish the connection.
    End Sub
  End Class
End Namespace
```

Now when the same application code (in the **Main** method) executes, the output is as follows:

```
Phone.Dial
BetterPhone.EstablishConnection
```

This output shows that **Main**'s call to **Dial** calls the **Dial** method defined by **Phone** and inherited by **BetterPhone**. Then when **Phone**'s **Dial** method calls the virtual **EstablishConnection** method, **BetterPhone**'s **EstablishConnection** method is called because it overrides the virtual **EstablishConnection** method defined by **Phone**.

10

Properties

In this chapter, I'll talk about properties. Properties allow source code to call a method using a simplified syntax. The common language runtime (CLR) offers two kinds of properties: parameterless properties, which are called *properties*, and parameterful properties, which are called different names by different programming languages. For example, C# calls parameterful properties *indexers*, and Managed Extensions for C++ calls them *indexed properties*. Visual Basic uses the term *property* to refer to both parameterless and parameterful properties. However, Visual Basic also offers a feature called *default properties*, which is a special way to use a parameterful property. I'll discuss default properties later in this chapter.

Parameterless Properties

Many types define state information that can be retrieved or altered. Frequently, this state information is implemented as field members of the type. For example, here's a type definition that contains two fields:

```
Public Class Employee
    Public Name As String       ' The employee's name
    Public Age As Int32         ' The employee's age
End Class
```

If you were to create an instance of this type, you could easily get or set any of this state information with code similar to the following:

```
Dim e As New Employee()
e.Name = "Jeffrey Richter"     ' Set the employee's Name.
e.Age = 35                     ' Set the employee's Age.

Console.WriteLine(e.Name)      ' Displays "Jeffrey Richter"
```

Querying and setting an object's state information in the way I just demonstrated is very common. However, I would argue that the preceding code should never be implemented as it's shown. One of the covenants of object-oriented design and programming is *data encapsulation*. Data encapsulation means that your type's fields should never be publicly exposed because it's too easy to write code that improperly uses the fields, corrupting the object's state. For example, a developer could easily corrupt an **Employee** object with code like this:

```
e.Age = -5      ' How could someone be -5 years old?
```

There are additional reasons for encapsulating access to a type's data field. For example, you might want access to a field to execute some side effect, cache some value, or lazily create some internal object. You might also want access to the field to be thread-safe. Or perhaps the field is a logical field whose value isn't represented by bytes in memory but whose value is instead calculated using some algorithm.

For any of these reasons, when designing a type, I strongly suggest that all your fields be private or at least protected—never public. Then, to allow a user of your type to get or set state information, you expose methods for that specific purpose. Methods that wrap access to a field are typically called *accessor methods*. These accessor methods can optionally perform sanity checking and ensure that the object's state is never corrupted. For example, I'd rewrite the previous class as follows:

```
Public Class Employee
    Private Name As String      ' Field is now private.
    Private Age As Int32        ' Field is now private.

    Public Function GetName() As String
        Return Name
    End Function

    Public Sub SetName(ByVal value As String)
        Name = value
    End Sub

    Public Function GetAge() As Int32
        Return Age
    End Function

    Public Sub SetAge(ByVal value As Int32)
        If value < 0 Then
            Throw New ArgumentOutOfRangeException( _
                "Age must be greater than or equal to 0")
        End If
        Age = value
    End Sub
End Class
```

Although this is a simple example, you should still be able to see the enormous benefit you get from encapsulating the data fields. You should also be able to see how easy it is to make read-only or write-only properties: just don't implement one of the accessor methods.

Encapsulating the data as shown earlier has two disadvantages. First, you have to write more code because you now have to implement additional methods. Second, users of the type must now call methods rather than simply refer to a single field name.

```
e.SetAge(35)      ' Updates the age
e.SetAge(-5)      ' Throws ArgumentOutOfRangeException
```

Personally, I think these disadvantages are quite minor. Nevertheless, the CLR offers a mechanism, properties, that alleviates the first disadvantage a little and removes the second disadvantage entirely.

The class shown here uses properties and is functionally identical to the class shown earlier:

```
Public Class Employee
    Private _Name As String  ' Prepending "_" avoids name conflict.
    Private _Age As Int32     ' Prepending "_" avoids name conflict.

    Public Property Name() As String
        Get
            Return _Name
        End Get
        Set(ByVal value As String)      ' 'value' identifies the new value.
            _Name = value
        End Set
    End Property

    Public Property Age() As Int32
        Get
            Return _Age
        End Get
        Set(ByVal value As Int32)       ' 'value' identifies the new value.
            If value < 0 Then
                Throw New ArgumentOutOfRangeException( _
                    "Age must be greater than or equal to 0")
            End If
            _Age = value
        End Set
    End Property
End Class
```

As you can see, properties complicate the definition of the type slightly, but the fact that they allow you to write your code as follows more than compensates for the extra work:

```
e.Age = 35      ' Updates the age
e.Age = -5      ' Throws ArgumentOutOfRangeException
```

You can think of properties as *smart fields*: fields with additional logic behind them. The CLR supports shared (static), instance, and virtual properties. In addition, properties can be marked with any accessibility modifier (discussed in Chapter 7) and defined within an interface (discussed in Chapter 15).

Each property has a name and a type. It isn't possible to overload parameterless properties (that is, have two properties with the same name if their types are different). When you define a property, you typically specify both a **Get** and a **Set** method. However, you can leave out the **Set** method to define a read-only property or leave out the **Get** method to define a write-only property. When you omit a **Set** accessor method, you must specify the **ReadOnly** modifier as in the following example:

```
Public Class Person
    Private _Name As String  ' Prepending "_" avoids name conflict.

    ' ReadOnly is required here since no Set method is defined.
    Public ReadOnly Property Name() As String
        Get
            Return _Name
        End Get
    End Property
End Class
```

Similarly, if you want to define a write-only property, you would omit a **Get** accessor method and include the **WriteOnly** modifier on the **Property** statement.

It's also quite common for the property's **Get/Set** methods to manipulate a private field defined within the type. This field is commonly referred to as the *backing field*. The **Get** and **Set** methods don't have to access a backing field, however. For example, the **System.Threading.Thread** type offers a **Priority** property that communicates directly with the operating system; the **Thread** object doesn't maintain a field for a thread's priority. Another example of properties without backing fields are those read-only properties calculated at run time—for example, the length of a zero-terminated array or the area of a rectangle when you have its height and width.

When you define a property, the compiler emits up to three things into the resulting managed module:

■   A method representing the property's **Get** accessor method. This is emitted only if you define a **Get** accessor method for the property.

■   A method representing the property's **Set** accessor method. This is emitted only if you define a **Set** accessor method for the property.

■   A property definition in the managed module's metadata. This is always emitted.

Refer to the **Employee** type shown earlier. As the compiler compiles this type, it comes across the **Name** and **Age** properties. Because both properties have **Get** and **Set** accessor methods, the compiler emits four method definitions into the **Employee** type. It's as though the original source were written as follows:

```
Public Class Employee
    Private _Name As String   ' Prepending "_" avoids name conflict.
    Private _Age As Int32     ' Prepending "_" avoids name conflict.

    Public Function get_Name() As String
       Return _Name
    End Function

    Public Sub set_Name(ByVal value As String)
       _Name = value
    End Sub

    Public Function get_Age() As Int32
       Return _Age
    End Function

    Public Sub set_Age(ByVal value As Int32)
       If value < 0 Then
          Throw New ArgumentOutOfRangeException( _
             "Age must be greater than or equal to 0")
       End If
       _Age = value
    End Sub
End Class
```

The compiler automatically generates names for these methods by prepending **get_** or **set_** to the property name specified by the developer.

Visual Basic has built-in support for properties. When the Visual Basic compiler sees code that's trying to get or set a property, the compiler actually emits a call to one of these methods. If you're using a programming language that doesn't directly support properties, you can still access properties by calling the desired accessor method. The effect is exactly the same; it's just that the source code doesn't look as pretty.

In addition to emitting the accessor methods, compilers also emit a property definition entry into the managed module's metadata for each property defined in the source code. This entry contains some flags and the type of the property, and it refers to the **Get** and **Set** accessor methods. This information exists simply to draw an association between the abstract concept of a "property" and its accessor methods. Compilers and other tools can use this metadata, which can be obtained by using the **System.Reflection.PropertyInfo** class. The CLR doesn't use this metadata information, though, and requires only the accessor methods at run time.

You should use properties only for operations that execute quickly because the syntax for accessing a property is identical to the syntax for accessing a field. Code with this syntax traditionally doesn't take long to execute; use methods for operations that require more execution time. For example, calculating the area of a rectangle is fast, so it would make sense to use a read-only property. But calculating the number of elements in a linked-list collection can be quite slow, so you might want to use a method instead of a read-only property.

For simple **Get** and **Set** accessor methods, the JIT compiler *inlines* the code so that there's no run-time performance hit as a result of using properties rather than fields. Inlining is when the code for a method (or an accessor method, in this case) is compiled directly in the method that is making the call. This removes the overhead associated with making a call at run time at the expense of making the compiled method's code bigger. Because property accessor methods typically contain very little code, inlining them can make code smaller and can make it execute faster.

Parameterful Properties

In the previous section, the **Get** accessor methods for the properties accepted no parameters. For this reason, I called these properties *parameterless properties*. These properties are easy to understand because they have the feel of accessing a field. In addition to these fieldlike properties, the CLR also supports what I call *parameterful properties*, whose **Get** accessor methods accept one or more parameters. Different programming languages expose parameterful properties in different ways. Also, as I mentioned at the beginning of the chapter, languages use different terms to refer to parameterful properties: C# calls them *indexers*, and Managed Extensions for C++ calls them *index properties*. In this section, I'll focus on how Visual Basic exposes parameterful properties. In Visual Basic, parameterful properties are simply called *properties*.

A substantial difference between parameterless and parameterful properties is that you can mark a parameterful property with the **Default** keyword. In

Visual Basic, default properties can be accessed using an arraylike syntax. In other words, you can think of a default property as a way for the Visual Basic developer to overload the **()** operator. Here's an example of a **BitArray** type that allows arraylike syntax to index into the set of bits maintained by an instance of the type:

```
Public Class BitArray
    ' A Private byte array that holds the bits
    Private byteArray() As Byte
    Private numBits As Int32
    ' This array avoids a time-consuming 2^n operation.
    Private bitMask() As Byte = {1, 2, 4, 8, 16, 32, 64, 128}

    ' Constructor that allocates the byte array and sets all bits to 0
    Public Sub New(ByVal numBits As Int32)
        ' Validate arguments first.
        If numBits <= 0 Then
          Throw New ArgumentOutOfRangeException("numBits", _
              "numBits must be > 0")
        End If

        ' Save the number of bits.
        Me.numBits = numBits
        ' Allocate the bytes for the bit array.
        ReDim byteArray((numBits - 1) \ 8)
    End Sub

    ' This is the parameterful property.
    Default Public Property Item(ByVal bitPos As Int32) As Boolean
        ' This is the property's Get accessor method.
        Get
            ' Validate arguments first.
            If bitPos < 0 Or bitPos >= numBits Then
              Throw New IndexOutOfRangeException()
            End If
            ' Return the state of the indexed bit.
            Return CBool(byteArray(bitPos \ 8) And bitMask(bitPos Mod 8))
        End Get

        ' This is the property's Set accessor method.
        Set(ByVal Value As Boolean)
            If bitPos < 0 Or bitPos >= numBits Then
              Throw New IndexOutOfRangeException()
            End If
            If Value Then
              ' Turn on the indexed bit.
              byteArray(bitPos \ 8) = byteArray(bitPos \ 8) Or _
                  bitMask(bitPos Mod 8)
```

(continued)

```
        Else
            ' Turn off the indexed bit.
            byteArray(bitPos \ 8) = byteArray(bitPos \ 8) And _
                Not bitMask(bitPos Mod 8)
        End If
    End Set
  End Property
End Class
```

Notice the **Default** keyword in the definition of the **Item** property, which makes this parameterful property a default property. Thanks to this keyword, using the **BitArray** type's **Item** property is incredibly simple:

```
' Allocate a BitArray that can hold 14 bits.
Dim ba As New BitArray(14)
' Turn on all the even-numbered bits by calling the Set accessor method.
Dim x As Int32
For x = 0 To 13
   ba(x) = ((x Mod 2) = 0)
Next

' Show the state of all the bits by calling the Get accessor method.
For x = 0 To 13
   Console.WriteLine ("Bit {0} is {1}", x, ba(x))
Next
```

In the **BitArray** example, the **Item** default property takes one **Int32** parameter, **bitPos**. All default properties must have at least one parameter, but they can have more. These parameters (as well as the return type) can be of any type.

It's quite common to create a default property that takes an **Object** as a parameter to look up values in an associative array. In fact, the **System.Collections.Hashtable** type offers a default **Item** property that takes a key (of type **Object**) and returns the value associated with the key (also of type **Object**). Unlike parameterless properties, a type can offer multiple, overloaded default properties (or any property with parameters, for that matter) as long as their signatures differ.

Like a parameterless property's **Set** accessor method, a default property's **Set** accessor method must also have a parameter (called **Value** in the example above) that matches the type of the property itself. This parameter indicates the new value desired for the "indexed element."

The CLR doesn't differentiate parameterless properties and parameterful properties; to the CLR, each is simply a pair of methods defined within a type. The CLR allows static parameterless and parameterful properties. In Visual Basic, you make a property static by applying the **Shared** modifier to it. However, Visual Basic forbids applying the **Shared** modifier to default properties.

Because the CLR treats parameterful properties just as it does parameterless properties, the compiler emits the same three items into the resulting managed module:

■ A method representing the parameterful property's **Get** accessor method. This is emitted only if you define a **Get** accessor method for the property.

■ A method representing the parameterful property's **Set** accessor method. This is emitted only if you define a **Set** accessor method for the property.

■ A property definition in the managed module's metadata, which is always emitted. There's no special parameterful property metadata definition table because, to the CLR, parameterful properties are just properties.

When examining the .NET Framework Reference documentation, you can often tell if a type offers a default property by looking for a property named **Item**. For example, the **System.Collections.SortedList** type offers a public instance property named **Item**; this property is **SortedList**'s default property. The reason that "Item" was chosen as the name is because default properties are frequently used to access a single item managed by the owning object. By the way, C# supports only one parameterful property for a given type, and it is automatically converted to a pair of methods called **get_Item** and **set_Item**. The C# developer can change this behavior and select a name other than **Item** by applying a **System.Runtime.CompilerServices.IndexerName** attribute to a C# indexer. This attribute affects the name of the default method that other languages, such as Visual Basic, see, but it doesn't affect how a C# program uses the method because the C# language can reference a default property only by using the **[]** syntax, always omitting the method name.

Here's some C# code that demonstrates how to access the default **Item** property in the **BitArray** class:

```
// Construct an instance of the BitArray type.
BitArray ba = new BitArray(10);

// C# uses [] instead of () to specify array elements.
Console.WriteLine(ba[2]);      // Displays True or False
```

By the way, the **System.String** type is an example of a type that changed the name of its indexer. The name of **String**'s indexer is **Chars** instead of **Item**. This property allows you to get the individual characters within a string. For programming languages that don't use **[]** operator syntax to access this property, **Chars** was decided to be a more meaningful name.

Selecting the Primary Parameterful Property

C#'s limitations with respect to indexers—that is, the fact that only one property can take parameters—begs the following questions: What if a type is defined in Visual Basic or in a programming language that does allow the developer to define several parameterful properties? How can this type be consumed from C#? The answer is that a type must select one of the parameterful property method names to be the default property by applying an instance of `System.Reflection.DefaultMemberAttribute` to the class itself. For the record, `DefaultMemberAttribute` can be applied to a class, a structure, or an interface. In Visual Basic, this attribute is automatically inserted when one of the properties or methods in a type is marked with the `Default` keyword. This is the only parameterful property that C# will be able to access. Therefore, you should keep in mind that any nondefault parameterful property that you define in a Visual Basic type can't be used from C# (short of calling the `get_` and `set_` methods directly).

When the Visual Basic compiler sees code that is trying to get or set a default property, the compiler actually emits a call to one of these `get_` or `set_` accessor methods. To the CLR, there's no difference between parameterless properties and parameterful properties, so you use the same `System.Reflection.PropertyInfo` class to find the association between a parameterful property and its accessor methods. The JIT compiler is also free to inline an accessor method's code into the calling method's code.

11

Events

In this chapter, I'll talk about the last kind of member that a type can define: an event. A type that defines an event member allows the type (or instances of the type) to notify other objects that something special has happened. For example, the **Button** class defines an event called **Click**. When a **Button** object is clicked, several objects in the application might want to receive a notification and perform some action. Events are type members that allow for this interaction. Specifically, defining an event member means that a type is offering three capabilities:

- The capability for objects to register their interest in the event
- The capability for objects to unregister their interest in the event
- The capability for the object defining the event to maintain the set of registered objects and to notify these objects when something special happens

The CLR's event model is based on *delegates*. A delegate is a type-safe way to invoke a callback method. In this chapter, I'll be using delegates, but I won't fully explain the ins and outs of them until Chapter 17.

To help you fully understand the way events work within the common language runtime (CLR), I'll start by defining a scenario in which events are useful. Suppose you want to design an e-mail application. When an e-mail message arrives, the user might like the message to be forwarded to a fax machine or a pager. In architecting this application, let's say that you'll first design a type, called **MailManager**, which receives the incoming e-mail messages. **MailManager** will expose an event, called **MailMsg**. Other types (such as **Fax** and **Pager**) might register interest in this event. When **MailManager** receives a new e-mail message, it will fire the event, distributing the message to each of the registered objects. Each object can process the message any way it desires.

When the application initializes, let's instantiate just one instance of **Mail-Manager**—the application can then instantiate any number of **Fax** and **Pager** types. Figure 11-1 shows how the application initializes and what happens when a new e-mail message arrives.

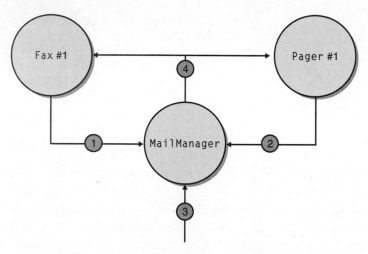

1. A Fax object registers interest with the MailManager's event.
2. A Pager object registers interest with the MailManager's event.
3. A new mail message arrives at MailManager.
4. The MailManager object fires the notification off to all the registered objects, which process the mail message as desired.

Figure 11-1   Architecting an application to use events

Here's how the application illustrated in Figure 11-1 works. The application initializes by constructing an instance of **MailManager**. **MailManager** offers a **MailMsg** event. When the **Fax** and **Pager** objects are constructed, they register themselves with **MailManager**'s **MailMsg** event so that **MailManager** knows to notify the **Fax** and **Pager** objects when new e-mail messages arrive. Now, when **MailManager** receives a new e-mail message (sometime in the future), it will fire the **MailMsg** event, giving all the registered objects an opportunity to process the new message any way they want.

Designing a Type That Exposes an Event

Let's look at the type definition for **MailManager** to really understand all the steps you must take to properly define an event member using Microsoft's recommended design pattern:

```
Class MailManager
    ' The MailMsgEventArgs type is defined within the MailManager type.
    Public Class MailMsgEventArgs
        Inherits EventArgs

        ' 1. Type defining information passed to receivers of the event
        Public Sub New(ByVal from As String, ByVal dest As String, _
            ByVal subject As String, ByVal body As String)

            Me.from = from
            Me.dest = dest
            Me.subject = subject
            Me.body = body
        End Sub


        Public ReadOnly from, dest, subject, body As String
    End Class

    ' 2. Delegate type defining the prototype of the callback method
    '    that receivers must implement
    Public Delegate Sub MailMsgEventHandler(ByVal sender As Object, _
        ByVal args As MailMsgEventArgs)

    ' 3. The event itself
    Public Event MailMsg As MailMsgEventHandler

    ' NOTE: Visual Basic lets you define the delegate implicitly by specifying
    ' a parameter signature in the Event declaration. The following
    ' (commented) event declaration is equivalent to steps 2 AND 3.
    ' Public Event MailMsg(ByVal sender As Object, _
    '        ByVal args As MailMsgEventArgs)

    ' 4. Protected, virtual method responsible for notifying registered
    '    objects of the event
    Protected Overridable Sub OnMailMsg(ByVal e As MailMsgEventArgs)
        ' Notify all the objects in the delegate linked list.
        RaiseEvent MailMsg(Me, e)
    End Sub

    ' 5. Method that translates the input into the desired event.
    '    This method is called when a new e-mail message arrives.
    Public Sub SimulateArrivingMsg(ByVal from As String, _
        ByVal dest As String, ByVal subject As String, ByVal body As String)
        ' Construct an object to hold the information you want
        ' to pass to the receivers of the notification.
        Dim e As New MailMsgEventArgs(from, dest, subject, body)
```

(continued)

```
        ' Call the virtual method notifying the object that the event
        ' occurred. If no derived type overrides this method, the object
        ' will notify all the registered listeners.
        OnMailMsg(e)
    End Sub
End Class
```

All the work related to implementing this architecture is the responsibility of the developer who is designing the **MailManager** type. The developer must define the following items.

1. **Define a type that will hold any additional information that should be sent to receivers of the event notification**   By convention, types that hold event information are derived from **System.EventArgs**, and the name of the type should end with **EventArgs**. In this example, the **MailMsgEventArgs** type has fields identifying who sent the message (from), who is receiving the message (dest), the subject of the message (subject), and the message text itself (body).

Note   The **EventArgs** type is defined in the .NET Framework Class Library (FCL) and looks like this:

```
<Serializable()> _
Public Class EventArgs
    Public Shared ReadOnly Empty As EventArgs = New EventArgs()
    Public Sub New()
        ' Empty procedure
    End Sub
End Class
```

As you can see, this type is nothing to write home about. It simply serves as a base type from which other types can derive. Many events don't have any additional information to pass on. For example, when a **Button** notifies its registered receivers that the button has been clicked, just invoking the callback method is enough information. When you're defining an event that doesn't have any additional data to pass on, just use **EventArgs.Empty** rather than constructing a new **EventArgs** object.

---

2. **Define a delegate type specifying the prototype of the method that will be called when the event fires**   By convention, the name of the delegate should end with `EventHandler`. Also by convention, the prototype should be a subroutine (versus a function) and take two parameters (although some event handlers in the FCL, such as `System.ResolveEventHandler`, violate this convention). The first parameter is an `Object` that refers to the object sending the notification, and the second parameter is an `EventArgs`-derived type containing any additional information that receivers of the notification require.

   If you're defining an event that has no additional information that you want to pass to receivers of the event, you don't have to define a new delegate; you can use the FCL's `System.EventHandler` delegate and pass `EventArgs.Empty` for the second parameter. The prototype of `EventHandler` is as follows:

   ```
   Public Delegate Sub EventHandler(ByVal sender As Object,
                                    ByVal e As EventArgs)
   ```

3. **Define an event**   In this example, `MailMsg` is the name of the event. This event is of the `MailMsgEventHandler` type, meaning that all receivers of the event notification must supply a callback method whose prototype matches that of the `MailMsgEventHandler` delegate. Unlike other languages, such as C#, Visual Basic offers a simplified syntax that lets you define both the delegate type and the event in a single statement, by specifying the delegate syntax right after the name of the event in the **Event** statement, as in:

   ```
   Public Event MailMsg(ByVal sender As Object, _
                        ByVal args As MailMsgEventArgs)
   ```

   When you do this, Visual Basic automatically creates a delegate type whose name is determined by appending `EventHandler` to the name of the event. So if the event is called `MailMsg`, the delegate type's name will be `MailMsgEventHandler`.

4. **Define a protected, virtual method responsible for notifying registered objects of the event**   The `OnMailMsg` method is called when a new e-mail message arrives. This method receives an initialized `MailMsgEventArgs` object containing additional information about the event. This method should first check to see whether any objects have registered interest in the event, and if they have, fire the event.

   A type that uses `MailManager` as a base type is free to override the `OnMailMsg` method. This capability gives the derived type control over the firing of the event. The derived type can handle the new e-mail message in any way it sees fit. Usually, a derived type calls the base type's `OnMailMsg` method so that the registered object receives the notification. However, the derived type might decide not to have the event forwarded on.

5. **Define a method that translates the input into the desired event** Your type must have some method that takes some input and translates it into the firing of an event. In this example, the `Simulate-ArrivingMsg` method is called to indicate that a new e-mail message has arrived into `MailManager`. `SimulateArrivingMsg` accepts information about the message and constructs a new `MailMsgEventArgs` object, passing the message information to its constructor. `MailManager`'s own virtual `OnMailMsg` method is then called to formally notify the `MailManager` object of the new e-mail message. Normally, this causes the event to be fired by means of the `RaiseEvent` statement, notifying all the registered objects. (As mentioned before, a type using `MailManager` as a base type can override this behavior.)

Let's now take a closer look at what it really means to define the `MailMsg` event. When the compiler examines the source code, the compiler comes across the line that defines the event:

```
Public Event MailMsg As MailMsgEventHandler
```

The Visual Basic compiler translates this single line of source code into the following three constructs:

```
' 1. A PRIVATE delegate field that is initialized to Nothing
Private MailMsgEvent As MailMsgEventHandler = Nothing

' 2. A PUBLIC add_* method
'     Allows objects to register interest in the event
'     NOTE: The MethodImplAttribute type is defined in the
'     System.Runtime.CompilerServices namespace.
<MethodImplAttribute(MethodImplOptions.Synchronized)> _
Public Overridable Sub add_MailMsg(ByVal handler As MailMsgEventHandler)
    ' Delegate is a reserved Visual Basic keyword.
    MailMsgEvent = DirectCast([Delegate].Combine(MailMsgEvent, handler), _
      MailMsgEventHandler)
End Sub

' 3. A PUBLIC remove_* method
'     Allows objects to unregister interest in the event
<MethodImplAttribute(MethodImplOptions.Synchronized)> _
Public Overridable Sub remove_MailMsg(ByVal handler As MailMsgEventHandler)
    ' Delegate is a reserved Visual Basic keyword.
```

```
MailMsgEvent = DirectCast([Delegate].Remove(MailMsgEvent, handler), _
    MailMsgEventHandler)
End Sub
```

The first construct is simply a field of the appropriate delegate type; its name is assigned by appending **Event** to the name of the event. This field is a reference to the head of a linked list of delegates that want to be notified of this event. This field is initialized to **Nothing**, meaning that no listeners have registered interest in the event. When an object registers interest in the event, this field refers to an instance of the **MailMsgEventHandler** delegate. Each **MailMsgEventHandler** delegate instance has a pointer to yet another **MailMsg-EventHandler** delegate or to **Nothing** to mark the end of the linked list. When a listener registers interest in an event, the listener is simply adding an instance of the delegate type to the linked list. Obviously, unregistering means removing the delegate from the linked list.

You'll notice that the delegate field, **MailMsgEvent** in this example, is always private even though the original line of source code defines the event as public. The reason for making the delegate field private is to prevent code outside the defining type from manipulating it improperly. If the field were public, any code could assign to the field, wiping out all the delegates that have registered interest in the event.

The second construct the Visual Basic compiler generates is a method that allows other objects to register their interest in the event. The Visual Basic compiler automatically names this function by prepending **add_** to the event's name (**MailMsg**). The Visual Basic compiler automatically generates the code that is inside this method. The code always calls **System.Delegate**'s static **Combine** method, which adds the instance of a delegate to the linked list of delegates and returns the new head of the linked list. Because **Delegate** is a reserved Visual Basic keyword, you must call this method either as **System.Delegate.Combine** or as **[Delegate].Combine**.

The third and final construct the Visual Basic compiler generates is a method that allows an object to unregister its interest in the event. Again, the Visual Basic compiler automatically names this function by prepending **remove_** to the event's name (**MailMsg**). The code inside this method always calls **Delegate**'s static **Remove** method, which removes the instance of a delegate from the linked list of delegates and returns the new head of the linked list.

You should also notice that both the **add** and **remove** methods have a **System.Runtime.CompilerServices.MethodImplAttribute** attribute applied to them. More specifically, these methods are marked as synchronized, making them thread-safe: multiple listeners can register or unregister themselves with the event at the same time without corrupting the linked list.

In this example, the **add** and **remove** methods are public. The reason they are public is that the original line of source code declared the event to be public. If the event had been declared protected, the **add** and **remove** methods generated by the compiler would also have been declared protected. So, when you define an event in a type, the accessibility of the event determines what code can register and unregister interest in the event, but only the type itself can ever access the delegate field directly.

In addition to emitting the preceding three constructs, compilers also emit an event definition entry into the managed module's metadata. This entry contains some flags and the underlying delegate type, and it refers to the **add** and **remove** accessor methods. This information exists simply to draw an association between the abstract concept of an "event" and its accessor methods. Compilers and other tools can use this metadata, and certainly, this information can be obtained by using the **System.Reflection.EventInfo** class. However, the CLR itself doesn't use this metadata information and requires only the accessor methods at run time.

Designing a Type That Listens for an Event

The hard work is definitely behind you at this point. In this section, I'll show you how to define a type that uses an event provided by another type. Let's start off by examining the code for the **Fax** type:

```
Class Fax
   ' Pass the MailManager object to the constructor.
   Public Sub New(ByVal mm As MailManager)
      ' Construct an instance of the MailMsgEventHandler
      ' delegate that refers to the FaxMsg callback method.
      ' Register the callback method with MailManager's MailMsg event.
      AddHandler mm.MailMsg, _
         New MailManager.MailMsgEventHandler(AddressOf FaxMsg)
   End Sub

   ' This is the method that MailManager will call to
   ' notify the Fax object that a new e-mail message has arrived.
   Private Sub FaxMsg(ByVal sender As Object, _
      ByVal e As MailManager.MailMsgEventArgs)
      ' The 'sender' identifies the MailManager in case
      ' you want to communicate back to it.

      ' The 'e' identifies the additional event information
      ' that the MailManager wants to provide.

      ' Normally, the code here would fax the e-mail message. This test
      ' implementation displays the information on the console.
```

```
        Console.WriteLine("Faxing mail message:")
        ' Notice how you can embed carriage returns (CRs) and
        ' linefeeds (LFs) without using string concatenation.
        Console.WriteLine("   From: {0}{4}    To: {0}{4}    " _
            & "Subject: {2}{4}    Body: {3}{4}", _
            e.from, e.dest, e.subject, e.body, ControlChars.CrLf)
    End Sub

    Public Sub Unregister(ByVal mm As MailManager)
        ' Construct an instance of the MailMsgEventHandler
        ' delegate that refers to the FaxMsg callback method.
        RemoveHandler mm.MailMsg, _
            New MailManager.MailMsgEventHandler(AddressOf FaxMsg)
    End Sub
End Class
```

When the e-mail application initializes, it would first construct a **Mail-Manager** object and save the reference to this object in a variable. Then the application would construct a **Fax** object, passing the reference to the **MailManager** object as a parameter. In the **Fax** constructor, a new **MailManager.MailMsgEvent-Handler** delegate object is constructed. This new delegate object is a wrapper around the **Fax** type's **FaxMsg** method. You'll notice that the **FaxMsg** method is a subroutine (**Sub**) and takes the same two parameters as defined by the **Mail-Manager**'s **MailMsgEventHandler** delegate—this is required for the code to compile.

After constructing the delegate, the **AddHandler** statement causes the Visual Basic compiler to produce code that calls the **add_MailMsg** method. It's as though you had written the following line of code:

```
mm.add_MailMsg(New MailManager.MailMsgEventHandler(AddressOf FaxMsg))
```

Interestingly, you don't have to explicitly create a delegate object because the **AddressOf** operator does it for you. In other words, you can simplify the **Sub New** procedure as follows:

```
Public Sub New(ByVal mm As MailManager)
    ' Register the callback method with MailManager's MailMsg event.
    ' (There's no need to construct an instance of the MailMsgEventHandler
    ' delegate that refers to the FaxMsg callback method.)
    AddHandler mm.MailMsg, AddressOf FaxMsg
End Sub
```

Even if you're using a programming language that doesn't directly support events, you can still register a delegate with the event by calling the **add** accessor method explicitly. The effect is identical; it's just that the source code doesn't look as pretty. It's the **add** method that registers the delegate with the event by adding it to the event's linked list of delegates.

When **MailManager** fires the event, the **Fax** object's **FaxMsg** method gets called. The method is passed a reference to the **MailManager** object. Most of the time, this parameter is ignored, but it can be used if the **Fax** object wants to access fields or methods of the **MailManager** object in response to the event notification. The second parameter is a reference to a **MailMsgEventArgs** object. This object contains any additional information that **MailManager** thought would be useful to event receivers.

From the **MailMsgEventArgs** object, the **FaxMsg** method has easy access to the message's sender, the message's recipient, the message's subject, and the message's text. In a real **Fax** object, this information would be faxed to somewhere. In this example, the information is simply displayed in the console window.

When an object is no longer interested in receiving event notifications, it should unregister its interest. For example, the **Fax** object would unregister its interest in the **MailMsg** event if the user no longer wanted her e-mail forwarded to a fax. As long as an object stays registered with another object's event, the object can't be garbage collected. If your type implements **IDisposable**'s **Dispose** method, disposing of the object should cause it to unregister interest in all events. (See Chapter 19 for more information about **IDisposable**.)

Code that demonstrates how to unregister for an event is shown in **Fax**'s **Unregister** method. This method is practically identical to the code shown in the **Fax** type's constructor. The only difference is that this code uses **Remove-Handler** instead of **AddHandler**. When the Visual Basic compiler sees code using the **RemoveHandler** statement to unregister a delegate with an event, it emits a call to the event's **remove** method. Again, you don't need to explicitly create an instance of the delegate because the **AddressOf** operator does it for you, and you can simplify the **Unregister** method as follows:

```
Public Sub Unregister(ByVal mm As MailManager)
    RemoveHandler mm.MailMsg, AddressOf FaxMsg
End Sub
```

As with the **AddHandler** statement, even if you're using a programming language that doesn't directly support events, you can still unregister a delegate with the event by calling the **remove** accessor method explicitly. The **remove** method unregisters the delegate from the event by scanning the linked list for a delegate that wraps the same method as the callback passed in. If a match is found, the existing delegate is removed from the event's linked list of delegates. If a match isn't found, no error occurs and the linked list is unaltered.

By the way, Visual Basic requires that your code use the **AddHandler** and **RemoveHandler** statement to add and remove delegates from the linked list. If you try to call the **add** or **remove** method explicitly, the Visual Basic compiler produces a compiler error.

The `MailManager` sample application (which can be downloaded from *http://www.wintellect.com*) shows all the source code for the `MailManager` type, the `Fax` type, and the `Pager` type. You'll notice that the `Pager` type is implemented quite similarly to the `Fax` type.

A Simpler Way to Register and Unregister Interest in Events

Visual Basic offers a simplified syntax for registering and unregistering events. If a client stores a reference to an object in a field marked with the `WithEvents` keyword, there is no need to explicitly call the `AddHandler` and `RemoveHandler` statements. Storing a non-`Nothing` value in the field is all you need to start receiving events from the referenced objects; storing `Nothing` in the field immediately unregisters the client. Here's a short program that demonstrates how the `WithEvents` keyword works:

```
Class App
    Shared WithEvents mm As MailManager

    Shared Sub Main()
        ' This statement registers the client so that it can receive events.
        mm = New MailManager()
        ' Let MailManager fire an event.
        ' (At this point, the MailMsgHandler procedure is invoked.)
        mm.SimulateArrivingMsg("Joe", "Ann", "Greetings", "Hello, Ann")
        ' After the next statement, no more events can be received.
        mm = Nothing
    End Sub

    Shared Sub MailMsgHandler(ByVal sender As Object, _
        ByVal args As MailManager.MailMsgEventArgs) _
        Handles mm.MailMsg
        Console.WriteLine("The MailMsg event has been fired")
    End Sub
End Class
```

Notice that the `Handles` statement lets the compiler know that the `MailMsgHandler` procedure is to be called when the `MailMsg` event in the `MailManager` class fires. The `Handles` statement supports a comma-separated list of event names: they can be the same event from different instances of the `MailManager` class; they can even be different events from any instance of any class. The only requirement is that all the specified events define a delegate that mirrors the argument signature of the procedure to which `Handles` is applied.

So how can Visual Basic ensure that the application registers the client with **MailManager** as soon as you assign a non-**Nothing** value to the **mm** field and unregisters it as soon as you store **Nothing** in the **mm** field? A look at the metadata and IL produced by the previous code reveals that the **mm** field actually causes the compiler to emit a read/write property named **mm**. This property has **Get** and **Set** accessor methods that wrap a private field that has the same name as the original field except prepended by an underscore (**_mm**).

Whenever you have code that sets or gets the value in the **mm** "field," the compiler actually produces code to call the **mm** property's **Get** or **Set** method. (These methods appear as **get_mm** and **set_mm** in metadata.) The **get_mm** method's implementation simply returns the value of the **_mm** field. The **set_mm** method's implementation is where the magic happens. This method is effectively implemented as follows:

```
' Ensure that calls to this method are thread-safe.
<MethodImpl(Runtime.CompilerServices.MethodImplOptions.Synchronized)> _
Shared Sub set_mm(ByVal WithEventsValue As MailManager)

    ' If the current value in _mm is not Nothing, I am currently set
    ' up to receive events fired from the object referenced by _mm.
    ' Unregister my interest in these events.
    If Not _mm Is Nothing Then
        RemoveHandler _mm.MailMsg, AddressOf MailMsgHandler
    End If

    ' Remember the object from which I'm now interested in receiving events.
    _mm = WithEventsValue

    ' If the current value in _mm is not Nothing, register my interest
    ' in events fired from this object.
    If _mm Is Nothing Then
        AddHandler _mm.MailMsg, AddressOf MailMsgHandler
    End If
End Sub
```

As you can see, the **WithEvents** keyword exists just to simplify registering and unregistering interest in events. In the preceding example, it's hard to see the real value of the **WithEvents** keyword since the code is registering interest only in **MailManager**'s one **MailMsg** event. However, if the **MailManager** class defined several events and the **App** class wanted to register interest in multiple events, the **WithEvents** keyword greatly simplifies coding because the Visual Basic compiler will implement the **Set** property accessor method so that it automatically calls **AddHandler** and **RemoveHandler** for every method you write that has the **Handles** statement associated with it.

A Word About Performance

Interestingly, the IL inside the `set_mm` method doesn't check whether the value being assigned is the same as the current value in the `_mm` field, and it executes the two steps in all cases. The fact that the `mm` "field" is actually a property and that all accesses to it are translated into method calls means that you can expect accessing a `WithEvents` field to be slower than accessing a regular field. As a matter of fact, some informal benchmarks show that reading the `mm` field is about five times slower than reading a standard field. Even more astonishing is that assigning a value to the `mm` field is nearly 200 times slower than assigning a value to a regular field. The bottom line is this: if you care about performance, you should avoid frequent assignments to a `WithEvents` field.

Finally, you should be aware that passing a `WithEvents` field as a `ByRef` argument is remarkably slower than passing a regular field. Consider the following code:

```
Shared WithEvents mm As New MailManager

Shared Sub Main()
    ByRefProc(mm)
End Sub

Shared Sub ByRefProc(ByRef x As MailManager)
    ' Uses the x argument and possibly assigns a new value to it.
    ⋮
End Sub
```

Visual Basic can't simply pass the address of the value returned from the `get_mm` method to the `ByRef x` argument because any change inside the `ByRefProc` procedure wouldn't affect the field. Therefore, the Visual Basic compiler produces IL code that stores the return value of the `get_mm` method in a temporary variable, passes the address of this temporary variable to the `ByRefProc` procedure, and then passes the value of this temporary variable to the `set_mm` method. After the Visual Basic compiler compiles the `Main` subroutine, it's as if `Main` had been implemented like this:

```
Shared Sub Main()
    ' Create a temporary variable equal to the mm property.
    Dim temp As MailManager = get_mm()

    ' Call the subroutine, passing the address of the temporary variable.
    ByrefProc(temp)

    ' Assign the new value in the temporary variable to the mm property.
    set_mm(temp)
End Sub
```

Part IV
Essential Types

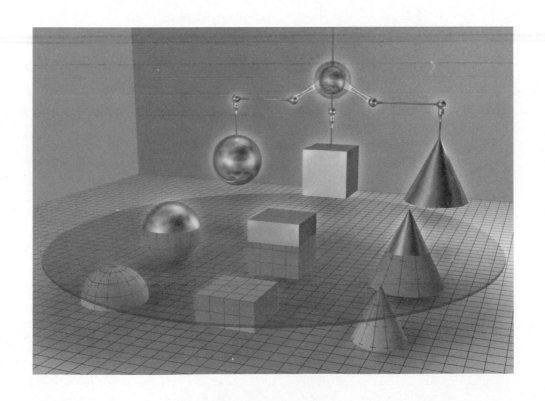

12

Working with Text

In this chapter, I'll explain the mechanics of working with individual characters and strings in the Microsoft .NET Framework. I'll start by talking about the **System.Char** structure and the various ways that you can manipulate a character. Then I'll go over the more useful **System.String** class, which allows you to work with immutable strings. (Once created, immutable strings can't be modified in any way.) After examining strings, I'll show you how to perform various operations efficiently to build a string dynamically via the **System.Text.StringBuilder** class. With the string basics out of the way, I'll then describe how to format objects into strings and how to efficiently persist or transmit strings using various encodings.

Characters

In the .NET Framework, characters are always represented in 16-bit Unicode code values, easing the development of global applications. A character is represented with an instance of the **System.Char** structure (a value type). The **System.Char** type is pretty simple. It offers two public read-only constant fields: **MinValue**, defined as &H0000, and **MaxValue**, defined as &HFFFF.

Given an instance of a **Char**, you can call the shared **GetUnicodeCategory** method, which returns a value of the **System.Globalization.UnicodeCategory** enumerated type. This value indicates whether the character is a control character, a currency symbol, a lowercase letter, an uppercase letter, a punctuation character, a math symbol, and so on (as defined by the Unicode 3.0 standard).

To ease developing, the **Char** type also offers several shared methods, such as **IsDigit**, **IsLetter**, **IsWhiteSpace**, **IsUpper**, **IsLower**, **IsPunctuation**, **IsLetterOrDigit**, **IsControl**, **IsNumber**, **IsSeparator**, **IsSurrogate**, and **IsSymbol**. All these methods call **GetUnicodeCategory** internally and simply return **True** or **False**. Note that all these methods take either a single character for a parameter or a **String** and the index of a character within the **String** as parameters.

In addition, you can convert a single character to its lowercase or upper-case equivalent by calling the shared **ToLower** or **ToUpper** method. The call to one of these methods converts the character using the culture information associated with the calling thread (which the methods obtain internally by querying **System.Threading.Thread**'s shared **CurrentCulture** property); or you can specify a particular culture by passing an instance of a **System.Globalization.CultureInfo** class to these methods. **ToLower** and **ToUpper** require culture information because letter casing is a culture-dependent operation. For example, Turkish considers the uppercase of U+0069 (LATIN SMALL LETTER I) to be U+0130 (LATIN CAPITAL LETTER I WITH DOT ABOVE), whereas other cultures consider the result to be U+0049 (LATIN CAPITAL LETTER I).

In addition to these shared methods, the **Char** type also offers a few instance methods of its own. The **Equals** method returns **True** if two **Char** instances represent the same 16-bit Unicode code point. The **CompareTo** method (defined by the **IComparable** interface) returns a comparison of two code points; this comparison is not culture-sensitive. Chapter 15 explains how the **IComparable** interface and its **CompareTo** method work. The **ToString** method returns a **String** consisting of a single character. The opposite of **ToString** is **Parse**, which takes a single-character **String** and returns the character.

The last method, **GetNumericValue**, returns the numeric equivalent of a character. The following code demonstrates:

```
Imports System
Imports Microsoft.VisualBasic

Class App
   Shared Sub Main()
      Dim d As Double

      ' "U+0033" is the "digit 3"
      d = Char.GetNumericValue(ChrW(&H33))
      Console.WriteLine(d.ToString())  ' Displays "3"

      ' "U+00BC" is the "vulgar fraction one quarter ('¼')"
      d = Char.GetNumericValue(ChrW(&HBC))
      Console.WriteLine(d.ToString())  ' Displays "0.25"

      ' 'A' is the "Latin capital letter A"
      d = Char.GetNumericValue("A"c)   ' An invalid numeric value
      Console.WriteLine(d.ToString())  ' Displays "-1"
   End Sub
End Class
```

Finally, four techniques allow you to convert between various numeric types to `Char` instances and vice versa. The techniques are listed here in order of preference:

- **Casting**   The easiest way to convert a `Char` to a numeric value such as an `Int32` is simply by casting. Of the four techniques, this is the most efficient because the compiler emits intermediate language (IL) instructions to do the conversion and no methods have to be called. In addition, some languages (such as C#) allow you to indicate whether the conversion should be done using checked or unchecked code (discussed in Chapter 5). This lets you decide whether you'd like a `System.OverflowException` thrown when converting a value causes a loss of data. Unfortunately, Visual Basic doesn't support casting a character to a numeric type or a numeric type to a character so you must use one of the techniques that follow.

- **Use the `Convert` type**   The `System.Convert` type offers several shared methods that know how to convert a `Char` to a numeric type and vice versa. All these methods perform the conversion as a checked operation, causing an `OverflowException` to be thrown should the conversion result in the loss of data.

- **Use the `IConvertible` interface**   The `Char` type and all the numeric types in the .NET Framework Class Library (FCL) implement the `IConvertible` interface. This interface defines methods such as `ToUInt16` and `ToChar`. This technique doesn't perform as well as the preceding technique because calling an interface method on a value type requires that the instance be boxed—`Char` and all the numeric types are value types. `IConvertible`'s methods throw exceptions if the type can't be converted (such as converting a `Char` to a `Boolean`) or if the conversion results in a loss of data. Note that many types (including the FCL's `Char` and numeric types) implement `IConvertible`'s methods as explicit interface member implementations (described in Chapter 15). This means that you explicitly have to cast the instance to an `IConvertible` before you can call any of the interface's methods.

- **Use `Microsoft.VisualBasic.Strings` type's `AscW` and `ChrW` methods**   The `AscW` method converts a `Char` to an `Int32` while the `ChrW` method converts an `Int32` to a `Char`. In addition to these methods, the `Strings` type also offers `Asc` and `Chr` methods, which operate on single-byte character set (SBSC) or multibyte character set (MBCS) characters. Internationalizing an application is much easier if you use the **AscW** and **ChrW** methods; these methods perform much better as well. In fact, in some cases, the Visual Basic compiler detects calls to the **AscW** and **ChrW** methods and inlines the code directly, avoiding the method call entirely. By the way, the **Strings** type has the **Microsoft.VisualBasic.CompilerServices.Standard-ModuleAttribute** attribute associated with it, allowing you to call the **AscW** and **ChrW** methods without having to qualify them with the class name (**Strings**). For more information about the **StandardModule-Attribute** attribute, see Chapter 4.

The following code demonstrates how to use the three techniques that are available in Visual Basic.

```
Imports System
Imports Microsoft.VisualBasic ' Needed for AscW and ChrW

Class App
   Shared Sub Main()
      Dim c As Char, n As Int32

      ' Convert number <-> character using AscW and ChrW
      c = ChrW(65)
      Console.WriteLine(c)                    ' Displays "A"

      n = AscW(c)
      Console.WriteLine(n)                    ' Displays "65"

      ' Convert number <-> character using Convert
      c = Convert.ToChar(65)
      Console.WriteLine(c)                    ' Displays "A"

      n = Convert.ToInt32(c)
      Console.WriteLine(n)                    ' Displays "65"

      ' This demonstrates Convert's range checking.
      Try
         c = Convert.ToChar(70000)            ' Too big for 16 bits
         Console.WriteLine(c)                 ' Doesn't execute

      Catch ex As OverflowException
         Console.WriteLine("Can't convert 70000 to a Char")
      End Try

      ' Convert number <-> character using IConvertible
      c = (CType(65, IConvertible)).ToChar(Nothing)
      Console.WriteLine(c)                    ' Displays "A"
```

```
      n = (CType(c, IConvertible)).ToInt32(Nothing)
      Console.WriteLine(n)                    ' Displays "65"
   End Sub
End Class
```

The `System.String` Type

Certainly, one of the most used types in any application is **System.String**. A **String** represents an immutable ordered set of characters. The **String** type is derived immediately from **Object**, making it a reference type. (No string ever lives on a thread's stack.) The **String** type also implements several interfaces (**IComparable**, **ICloneable**, **IConvertible**, and **IEnumerable**).

Constructing Strings

Many programming languages (including Visual Basic) consider **String** to be a primitive type—that is, the compiler lets you express literal strings directly in their source code. The compiler places these literal strings in the module's metadata, and they are accessed at run time using a mechanism called *string interning* (which I'll talk about later in this chapter).

In Visual Basic, you can use the **New** operator to construct a **String** object:

```
Imports System

Class App
   Shared Sub Main()
      Dim s As New String("Hi there.")
      Console.WriteLine(s)                    ' Displays "Hi there."
   End Sub
End Class
```

However, if you built this code and examined the IL, you'd see the following:

```
.method public static void  Main() cil managed
{
  .entrypoint
  .custom instance void [mscorlib]System.STAThreadAttribute::.ctor()
      = ( 01 00 00 00 )
  // Code size       23 (0x17)
  .maxstack  1
  .locals init (string V_0)
  IL_0000:  ldstr      "Hi there."
  IL_0005:  call       char[] [Microsoft.VisualBasic]Microsoft.VisualBasic.
     CompilerServices.CharArrayType::FromString(string)
```

(continued)

```
IL_000a:  newobj      instance void [mscorlib]System.String::.ctor(char[])
IL_000f:  stloc.0
IL_0010:  ldloc.0
IL_0011:  call        void [mscorlib]System.Console::WriteLine(string)
IL_0016:  ret
} // end of method App::Main
```

In this example, the string "Hi there." is first passed to the **Microsoft.Visual-Basic.CompilerServices.CharArrayType** type's **FromString** method. The **FromString** method converts the string to a **Char** array. This **Char** array is then passed to **System.String**'s constructor, which constructs a new **String** object; the constructor then returns the reference to this **String** object. This reference is saved in the local variable, which is then passed to **System.Console**'s **WriteLine** method.

If you spend some time thinking about this IL code, you'll realize that it's very inefficient. After all, the compiler started with a **String** object and then converted it to a **Char** array so that it could construct a **String** object. The Visual Basic compiler will work much more efficiently if you rewrite the source code using the following special simplified syntax:

```
Imports System

Class App
   Shared Sub Main()
      Dim s As String = "Hi there."
      Console.WriteLine(s)              ' Displays "Hi there."
   End Sub
End Class
```

If you were to compile this code and examine its IL (using ILDasm.exe), you'd see the following:

```
.method public static void  Main() cil managed
{
  .entrypoint
  .custom instance void [mscorlib]System.STAThreadAttribute::.ctor()
      = ( 01 00 00 00 )
  // Code size        13 (0xd)
  .maxstack  1
  .locals init (string V_0)
  IL_0000:  ldstr      "Hi there."
  IL_0005:  stloc.0
  IL_0006:  ldloc.0
  IL_0007:  call       void [mscorlib]System.Console::WriteLine(string)
  IL_000c:  ret
} // end of method App::Main
```

The IL instruction that constructs a new instance of an object is `newobj` (as seen in the first IL example). However, no `newobj` instruction appears in this second IL code example. The special `ldstr` (load string) IL instruction constructs a `String` object using a literal string obtained from metadata. This shows you that the CLR does, in fact, have a special, efficient way of constructing `String` objects.

In rare cases, you might need a `String` object that isn't constructed from a literal string contained in metadata. To accomplish this, you would use Visual Basic's `New` operator and call one of the constructors provided by the `String` type. The constructors that take `Char*` or `SByte*` parameters were designed to be callable from code written using Managed Extensions for C++. These constructors create a `String` object, initializing the string from an array of `Char` instances or signed bytes. The other constructors don't have any pointer parameters and can be called from any managed programming language. For example, you can initialize a `String` from a `Char` array (or a portion thereof) or by repeating a given `Char` the specified number of times.

A Visual Basic string constant is delimited by double quote characters. You can embed a double quote in the string by repeating it:

```
Console.WriteLine("A ""quoted"" word");    ' A "quoted" word
```

Visual Basic doesn't allow you to embed control characters inside a string constant. Instead, you can use the constants exposed by the `Microsoft.Visual-Basic ControlChars` class and insert them in the right position by using the `&` concatenation operator:

```
Dim s As String = "First line" & ControlChars.NewLine & "Second line"
```

The `ControlChars` class offers other useful constants, such as `NullChar`, `Back`, `Tab`, `VerticalTab`, `Cr`, and `Lf`. There is also a `CrLf` constant whose value is identical to `NewLine` when your code is running on Windows. However, you should avoid using the `CrLf` constant because some operating systems don't use a carriage-return/linefeed combination to produce a new line. Finally, the `System.Environment` type also offers a constant named `NewLine`. The value of this constant will always be identical to `ControlChars`' `NewLine` constant regardless of operating system, so you can use either class's `NewLine` in your code.

You can concatenate several strings to form a single string using Visual Basic's `&` operator as follows:

```
' Three literal strings concatenated to form a single literal string
Dim s As String = "Hi" & " " & "there."
```

In this code, because all the strings are literal strings, the compiler concatenates them at compile time and ends up placing just one string—"Hi there."—in the module's metadata. Using the **&** operator on nonliteral strings causes the con-catenation to be performed at run time. To concatenate several strings together at run time, don't use the **&** operator because it creates multiple string objects in the garbage collected heap. Instead, use the **System.Text.StringBuilder** type (which I'll explain later in this chapter).

Now that you've seen how to construct a string, let's talk about some of the operations you can perform on **String** objects.

Strings Are Immutable

The most important thing to know about a **String** object is that it is immutable; that is, once created, a string can never get longer, get shorter, or have any of its characters changed. Having immutable strings offers several benefits. First, it allows you to perform operations on a string without actually changing the string:

```
If s.ToLower().Substring(10, 20).EndsWith("exe") Then
  ⋮
End If
```

Here, **ToLower** returns a new string; it doesn't modify the characters of the string **s**. **SubString** operates on the string returned by **ToLower** and also returns a new string, which is then examined by **EndsWith**. The two temporary strings created by **ToLower** and **SubString** are not referenced long by the application code, and the garbage collector will reclaim their memory at the next collection. These short-lived objects are very quick to collect, and it's usually not worth investing time in your algorithm in an attempt to improve performance.

Having immutable strings also means that there are no thread synchroni-zation issues when accessing a string. In addition, it's possible for two **String** references to refer to the same string object instead of different string objects if the strings are identical. This can reduce the number of strings in the system, conserving memory usage, and it is what string interning (discussed later in the chapter) is all about.

For performance reasons, the **String** type is tightly integrated with the CLR. Specifically, the CLR knows the exact layout of the fields defined within the **String** type and accesses these fields directly. This performance and direct access come at a small development cost: the **String** class is sealed. If you were able to define your own type, using **String** as a base type, you could add your own fields, which would break the assumptions the CLR makes. In addition, you could break some assumptions that the CLR has made about **String** objects being immutable.

Comparing Strings

Comparing is probably the most common operation performed on strings. Fortunately, the **String** type offers several shared and instance methods that allow you to compare strings in very useful ways. Table 12-1 summarizes these methods.

Table 12-1   Methods for Comparing Strings

Member	Member Type	Description
Compare	Shared method	Returns how two strings should be sorted with respect to each other. Unlike the **CompareTo** method, this method gives you control over the culture used (via a **CultureInfo** object) and case sensitivity. If you need more advanced string comparison functionality, see the discussion of the **CompareInfo** class later in this section.
CompareTo	Instance method	Returns how two strings should be sorted with respect to each other. This method always uses the **CultureInfo** object associated with the calling thread.
StartsWith EndsWith	Instance method	Returns **True** if the string starts/ends with the specified string. The comparison is always case sensitive and uses the **CultureInfo** object associated with the calling thread. To perform the same operations with case insensitivity, use **Compare-Info**'s **IsPrefix** and **IsSuffix** methods.
CompareOrdinal	Shared method	Returns **True** if two strings have the same set of characters. Unlike the other compare methods, this method simply compares the code values of the characters in the string; it doesn't do a culturally aware comparison, and the comparison is always case sensitive. This method is faster than the other compare methods, but it shouldn't be used for sorting strings that are destined to be shown to a user since the resulting set of strings might not be ordered the way a user would expect. For example, **CompareOrdinal** will sort "a" after "A" since the code value of "a" is a larger value than the code value for "A".
Equals	Shared and instance methods	Returns **True** if two strings have the same set of characters. Internally, **Equals** calls **String**'s shared **CompareOrdinal** method. The shared **Equals** method first checks whether the two references refer to the same object; if they do, it returns **True** instead of comparing the string's individual characters. Comparing references improves performance greatly when using the interned string mechanism, which I'll describe shortly.
GetHashCode	Instance method	Returns a hash code for the string.

In addition to these methods, the **String** type provides overloads of the equality and inequality operators. Internally, these operator methods are implemented by calling **String**'s shared **Equals** method. Since Visual Basic doesn't support operator overloading, it never produces code to call these operator methods. In Visual Basic, when you compare strings using the = or <> operators, the compiler produces code that calls the **StrCmp** helper method defined within the **Microsoft.VisualBasic.CompilerServices.StringType** class. Internally, the **StrCmp** method calls **System.String**'s **CompareOrdinal** method.

There are two reasons to compare two strings with each other. The first is to determine whether the two strings represent essentially the same string. The second is to sort the strings, usually for presentation to a user. To determine whether two strings are equal, you can use the **CompareOrdinal** method. This method is fast because it compares only the code values in the strings. However, some strings are logically equal even though they might not have the same code values.

To determine whether these two strings are equal, you should call the **Compare** method instead. Internally, this method uses culture-specific sorting tables (as defined by the Unicode 3.1 standard) that are part of the .NET Framework itself. Because these tables are included in the .NET Framework, all versions of the .NET Framework (regardless of underlying operating system platform) will compare and sort the strings in the same way. When comparing two strings for equality, you can have the **Compare** method perform a case-sensitive or case-insensitive comparison depending on your application's needs.

Important   When comparing strings or converting strings to uppercase or lowercase, you should usually use **InvariantCulture**. For example, use **InvariantCulture** when comparing and converting pathnames and filenames, registry keys and values, reflection strings, XML tags and XML attribute names, and any other programmatic strings. In fact, you should use a noninvariant culture only when you're comparing and converting strings that are to be displayed to the user in a linguistically correct manner. And, of course, the culture you use should match the user's chosen language and optionally the user's country.

The following code demonstrates the difference between calling **Compare-Ordinal** and **Compare**:

```
Imports System
Imports System.Globalization

Class App
    Shared Sub Main()
        Dim s1 As String = "Strass"
        Dim s2 = "Straß"
        Dim x As Int32
        Dim res As String

        ' CompareOrdinal returns nonzero: strings have different values.
        x = String.CompareOrdinal(s1, s2)
        If x = 0 Then res = "equals" Else res = "does not equal"
        Console.WriteLine("CompareOrdinal: '{0}' {2} '{1}'", s1, s2, res)

        ' Compare returns zero: strings have the same value.
        x = New CultureInfo("de-DE").CompareInfo.Compare(s1, s2)
        If x = 0 Then res = "equals" Else res = "does not equal"
        Console.WriteLine("Compare: '{0}' {2} '{1}'", s1, s2, res)
    End Sub
End Class
```

Building and running this code produces the following output:

```
CompareOrdinal: 'Strass' does not equal 'Straß'
Compare: 'Strass' equals 'Straß'
```

You'd also use the **Compare** method to sort strings. However, you should always have **Compare** perform case-sensitive comparisons when comparing strings for sorting. The reason is that two strings that differ only by case are considered equal, and as you sort the strings in a list, the order of the "equal" strings could be different each time you run the application; this could confuse the user.

Internally, **String**'s **Compare** method obtains the **CurrentCulture** associated with the calling thread and then reads the **CurrentCulture**'s **CompareInfo** property. This property returns a reference to a **System.Globalization.Compare-Info** object. Because a **CompareInfo** object encapsulates a culture's character comparison tables, there's only one **CompareInfo** object per culture.

String's **Compare** method simply determines the culture's **CompareInfo** object and then calls the object's **Compare** method. **String**'s **Compare** method allows you to specify a case-sensitive or case-insensitive comparison. However, `CompareInfo`'s `Compare` method exposes richer control over the comparison, which is required for some applications. These applications will have to obtain a reference to the desired culture's `CompareInfo` object and call its `Compare` method directly.

Specifically, some overloads of `CompareInfo`'s `Compare` method take a `CompareOptions` enumerated type, which defines the following symbols: `IgnoreCase`, `IgnoreKanaType`, `IgnoreNonSpace`, `IgnoreSymbols`, `IgnoreWidth`, `None`, `Ordinal`, and `StringSort`. For a complete description of these symbols, consult the .NET Framework documentation.

The following code demonstrates how culture plays an important part when sorting strings:

```
Imports System
Imports System.Globalization
Imports System.Text
Imports System.Threading
Imports System.Windows.Forms

Class App
    Shared Sub Main()
        Dim sb As New StringBuilder()
        Dim sign() As String = {"<", "=", ">"}
        Dim x As Int32

        ' The following code demonstrates how strings compare
        ' for different cultures.
        Dim s1 As String = "coté"
        Dim s2 As String = "côte"

        ' Sorting strings for French in France
        x = New CultureInfo("fr-FR").CompareInfo.Compare(s1, s2)
        sb.AppendFormat("fr-FR Compare: {0} {2} {1}", s1, s2, sign(x + 1))
        sb.Append(Environment.NewLine)

        ' Sorting strings for Japanese in Japan
        x = New CultureInfo("ja-JP").CompareInfo.Compare(s1, s2)
        sb.AppendFormat("ja-JP Compare: {0} {2} {1}", s1, s2, sign(x + 1))
        sb.Append(Environment.NewLine)

        ' Sorting strings for the thread's culture
        x = Thread.CurrentThread.CurrentCulture.CompareInfo.Compare(s1, s2)
        sb.AppendFormat("{0} Compare: {1} {3} {2}", _
            Thread.CurrentThread.CurrentCulture.Name, s1, s2, sign(x + 1))
```

```
sb.Append(Environment.NewLine)
sb.Append(Environment.NewLine)

' The following code demonstrates how to use
' CompareInfo.Compare's advanced options with two Japanese
' strings. These strings represent the word "shinkansen"
' (the name for the Japanese high-speed train) in both
' hiragana and katakana.
    s1 = "しんかんせん"  ' ("\u3057\u3093\u304B\u3093\u305b\u3093")
    s2 = "シンカンセン"  ' ("\uff7c\uff9d\uff76\uff9d\uff7e\uff9d")

' Here's the result of a default comparison.
x = String.Compare(s1, s2, True, New CultureInfo("ja-JP"))
sb.AppendFormat("Simple ja-JP Compare: {0} {2} {1}", s1, s2, _
    sign(x + 1))
sb.Append(Environment.NewLine)

' Here's the result of a comparison that ignores Kana type.
Dim ci As CompareInfo = CompareInfo.GetCompareInfo("ja-JP")
x = ci.Compare(s1, s2, CompareOptions.IgnoreKanaType)
sb.AppendFormat("Advanced ja-JP Compare: {0} {2} {1}", s1, s2, _
    sign(x + 1))

MessageBox.Show(sb.ToString(), "StringSorting Results")
    End Sub
End Class
```

Building and running this code produces the output shown in Figure 12-1.

Figure 12-1   `StringSorting` results

In addition to **Compare**, the **CompareInfo** class offers **IndexOf**, **IsLastIndexOf**, **IsPrefix**, and **IsSuffix** methods. Because all these methods offer overloads that take a **CompareOptions** enumeration value as a parameter, they give you more control than the corresponding methods defined by the **String** class.

Japanese Characters

To see Japanese characters in the source code and in the message box, Windows must have the East Asian Language files installed (which use approximately 230 MB of disk space). To install these files, open the Regional And Language Options dialog box (shown in Figure 12-2) in Control Panel, select the Languages tab, check the Install Files For East Asian Languages check box, and press OK. This causes Windows to install the East Asian language fonts and Input Method Editor (IME) files.

Figure 12-2   Installing East Asian Language files using the Regional And Language Options Control Panel dialog box

Also, the source code file can't be saved in ANSI; I used UTF-8, which the Visual Studio .NET editor and Microsoft's Visual Basic compiler handle just fine.

String Interning

As I said in the preceding section, comparing strings is a common operation for many applications—it's also a task that can hurt performance significantly. The reason for the performance hit is that string comparisons require that each character in the string be checked, one by one, until two characters are determined to be different. To compare a string to see whether it contains the value "Hello", a loop must compare two characters five times. In addition, if you have several instances of the string "Hello" in memory, you're wasting memory because strings are immutable. You'll use memory much more efficiently if there is just one "Hello" string in memory and all references to the "Hello" string point to a single object.

If your application frequently compares strings for equality or if you expect to have many string objects with the same value, you can enhance performance substantially if you take advantage of the string interning mechanism in the CLR. To understand how the string interning mechanism works, examine the following code:

```
Dim s As String = "Hello"
Console.WriteLine(Object.ReferenceEquals("Hello", s))
```

Do you think this code displays "True" or "False"? Many people expect "False". After all, there are two "Hello" string objects and **ReferenceEquals** returns **True** only if the two references passed to it point to the same object. Build and run this code, however, and you'll see that "True" is displayed. The same happens if you use Visual Basic's **Is** operator:

```
Dim s As String = "Hello"
Console.WriteLine(s Is "Hello")
```

Let's see why.

When the CLR initializes, it creates an internal hash table in which the keys are strings and the values are references to string objects in the managed heap. Initially, the table is empty (of course). When the JIT compiler compiles this method, it looks up each literal string in the hash table. The compiler looks for the first "Hello" string and because it doesn't find one constructs a new **String** object in the managed heap (that refers to this string) and adds the "Hello" **String** and a reference to the object into the hash table. Then the JIT compiler looks up the second "Hello" string in the hash table. It finds this string, so nothing happens. Because there are no more literal strings in the code, the code can now execute.

When the code executes, it needs a reference to the "Hello" string. The CLR looks up "Hello" in the hash table, finds it, and returns a reference to the previously created **String** object. This reference is saved in the variable **s**. For the second line of code, the CLR again looks up "Hello" in the hash table and finds it. The reference to the same **String** object is passed along with **s** to **Object**'s shared **ReferenceEquals** method or to Visual Basic's **Is** operator, both of which return **True**.

All literal strings embedded in the source code are always added to the internal hash table when a method referencing the strings is JIT compiled. But what about strings that are dynamically constructed at run time? What do you expect the following code to display?

```
Dim s1 As String = "Hello"
Dim s2 As String = "Hel"
Dim s3 As String = s2 + "lo"
Console.WriteLine(Object.ReferenceEquals(s1, s3))
Console.WriteLine(s1.Equals(s3))
```

In this code, the string referred to by **s2** ("Hel") and the literal string ("lo") are concatenated. The result is a newly constructed string object, referred to by **s3**, that resides on the managed heap.

This dynamically created string does contain "Hello", but the string isn't added to the internal hash table. Therefore, **ReferenceEquals** returns **False** because the two references point to different string objects. However, the call to **Equals** produces a result of **True** because the strings do, in fact, represent the same set of characters. Obviously, **ReferenceEquals** performs much better than **Equals**, and an application's performance is greatly improved if all the string comparisons simply compare references instead of characters. Plus, an application requires fewer objects in the heap if there's a way to collapse dynamic strings with the same set of characters down to single objects in the heap.

Fortunately, the **String** type offers two shared methods that allow you to do this:

```
Public Shared Function Intern(ByVal str As String) As String
Public Shared Function IsInterned(ByVal str As String) As String
```

The first method, **Intern**, takes a **String** and looks it up in the internal hash table. If the string exists, a reference to the already existing **String** object is returned; otherwise, the string is added to the string pool and a reference to it is returned. If the application no longer holds a reference to the original **String** object, the garbage collector is able to free the memory of that string. The preceding code can now be rewritten using **Intern** as follows:

```
Dim s1 As String = "Hello"
Dim s2 As String = "Hel"
Dim s3 As String = s2 + "lo"
s3 = String.Intern(s3)
Console.WriteLine(Object.ReferenceEquals(s1, s3))
Console.WriteLine(s1.Equals(s3))
```

Now **ReferenceEquals** returns a value of **True** and the comparison is much faster. In addition, the **String** object that **s3** originally referred to is now free to be garbage collected. This code actually executes slower than the previous version because of the work that **String**'s **Intern** method must perform. You should intern strings only if you intend to compare a string multiple times in your application. Otherwise, you'll hurt performance instead of improve it.

Note that the garbage collector can't free the strings the internal hash table refers to because the hash table holds the reference to those **String** objects. **String** objects referred to by the internal hash table can't be freed until there are no AppDomains in the process that refer to the string object. Also note that string interning occurs on a per-process basis, meaning that a single string object can be accessed from multiple AppDomains, conserving memory usage. The capability of multiple AppDomains to access a single string also improves performance since strings never have to be marshaled across AppDomains within a single process; just the reference is marshaled.

As I mentioned earlier, the **String** type also offers a shared **IsInterned** method. Like the **Intern** method, the **IsInterned** method takes a **String** and looks it up in the internal hash table. If the string is in the hash table, **IsInterned** returns a reference to the interned string object. If the string isn't in the hash table, however, **IsInterned** returns **Nothing**; it doesn't add the string to the hash table.

The C# compiler uses the **IsInterned** method to allow **switch/case** statements to work efficiently on strings. Unfortunately, the Visual Basic compiler isn't as efficient, so you have to help it a little. Consider the following code:

```
Imports System

Class App
   Shared Sub Main()
      Lookup("Jeff", "Richter")
      Lookup("Fred", "Flintstone")
   End Sub

   Shared Sub Lookup(ByVal firstName As String, ByVal lastName As String)
      Select Case firstName + " " + lastName
         Case "Jeff Richter"
            Console.WriteLine("Jeff")
         Case "Joe Smith"
            Console.WriteLine("Joe")
         Case Else
            Console.WriteLine("Unknown")
      End Select
   End Sub
End Class
```

Because all the strings being tested in the various **Case** statements are constant strings, they have been stored in the string intern pool; therefore, you might improve the performance of the code by checking whether the concatenated string is also in the pool. Because you can't use the **Is** operator in a **Case** statement, you must convert the **Select Case** block into an **If…ElseIf** block:

```
Shared Sub Lookup(ByVal firstName As String, ByVal lastName As String)
   Dim tmp As String = String.IsInterned(firstName & " " & lastName)

   If tmp Is "Jeff Richter" Then
      Console.WriteLine("Jeff")
   ElseIf tmp Is "Joe Smith" Then
      Console.WriteLine("Joe")
   Else
      ' The concatenated string isn't in the pool (and therefore tmp
      ' is Nothing) or isn't one of the string constants in the
      ' original Case clauses.
      Console.WriteLine("Unknown")
   End If
End Sub
```

The important thing to notice in this code is that the code calls **IsInterned**, passing the string specified in the original **Select Case** statement. If **IsInterned** returns **Nothing**, the string can't match any of the original **Case** strings (that I had to translate into **If** or **ElseIf** statements), causing the **Else** code to execute: "Unknown" is displayed to the user. However, if **IsInterned** sees that the concatenated string does exist in the internal hash table, it returns a reference to the hash table's **String** object. The address of the interned string is then compared with the addresses of the interned literal strings specified by each **If** or **ElseIf** statement. Comparing the addresses is much faster than comparing all the characters in each string, and the code determines very quickly which **Console.WriteLine** statement to execute.

String Pooling

When compiling source code, your compiler must process each literal string and emit the string into the managed module's metadata. If the same literal string appears several times in your source code, then emitting all these strings into the metadata will bloat the size of the resulting file.

To remove this bloat, many compilers (including the Visual Basic compiler) write the literal string into the module's metadata only once. All code that references the string will be modified to refer to the one string in the metadata. This ability of a compiler to merge multiple occurrences of a single string into a single instance can reduce the size of a module substantially. This process is nothing new—C/C++ compilers have been doing it for years. (Microsoft's C/C++ compiler calls this *string pooling*.) Even so, string pooling is another way to improve the performance of strings and just one more piece of knowledge you should have in your repertoire.

Examining a String's Characters

Although comparing strings is useful for sorting them or for detecting equality, sometimes you just need to examine the characters within a string. The **String** type offers several methods to help you do this. Table 12-2 summarizes these methods.

Table 12-2   Methods for Examining String Characters

Member	Member Type	Description
Length	Instance read-only property	Returns the number of characters in the string
Chars	Instance read-only indexer property	Returns the character at the specified index within the string
GetEnumerator	Instance method	Returns an **IEnumerator** that can be used to iterate over all the characters in the string
ToCharArray	Instance method	Returns a **Char** array that contains a portion of the string's characters
IndexOf LastIndexOf	Instance methods	Returns the index of the first/last character/string matching a specified value
IndexOfAny LastIndexOfAny	Instance methods	Returns the index of the first/last character matching an array of specified characters

In reality, a **System.Char** represents a single 16-bit Unicode code value that doesn't necessarily equate to an abstract Unicode character. For example, some abstract Unicode characters are a combination of two code values. When combined, the U+0625 (Arabic letter Alef with Hamza below) and U+0650 (Arabic Kasra) characters form a single abstract character.

In addition, some Unicode abstract characters require more than a 16-bit value to represent them. These characters are represented using two 16-bit code values. The first code value is called the *high surrogate*, and the second code value is called the *low surrogate*. High surrogates have a value between U+D800 and U+DBFF, and low surrogates have a value between U+DC00 and U+DFFF. The use of surrogates allows Unicode to express more than a million different characters.

Surrogate characters are rarely used in the United States and Europe but are frequently used in East Asia. To properly work with abstract Unicode characters, you should use the **System.Globalization.StringInfo** type. You can call this type's shared **GetTextElementEnumerator** method to acquire a **System.Globalization.TextElementEnumerator** object that allows you to enumerate through all the abstract Unicode characters contained in the string.

Alternatively, you could call **StringInfo**'s shared **ParseCombiningCharacters** method to obtain an array of **Int32** values. The length of the array indicates how many abstract Unicode characters are contained in the string. Each element of the array identifies an index into the string where the first code value for the abstract Unicode character can be found.

The following code demonstrates how to properly use the **StringInfo**'s **GetTextElementEnumerator** and **ParseCombiningCharacters** methods to manipulate a string's abstract Unicode characters:

```
Imports System
Imports System.Text
Imports System.Windows.Forms
Imports System.Globalization

Class App
   Shared Sub Main()
      ' The following string contains combining characters.
      Dim s As String = "a" & ChrW(&H304) & ChrW(&H308) & "bc" & ChrW(&H327)
      MessageBox.Show(s)
      EnumTextElements(s)
      EnumTextElementIndexes(s)
   End Sub

   Shared Sub EnumTextElements(ByVal s As String)
      Dim sb As StringBuilder = New StringBuilder()

      Dim charEnum As TextElementEnumerator = _
         StringInfo.GetTextElementEnumerator(s)
      While (charEnum.MoveNext())
         sb.AppendFormat("Character at index {0} is '{1}'{2}", _
            charEnum.ElementIndex, charEnum.GetTextElement(), _
            Environment.NewLine)
      End While
      MessageBox.Show(sb.ToString(), "Result of GetTextElementEnumerator")
   End Sub

   Shared Sub EnumTextElementIndexes(ByVal s As String)
      Dim sb As StringBuilder = New StringBuilder()

      Dim textElemIndex() As Int32 = StringInfo.ParseCombiningCharacters(s)
      Dim i As Int32 = 0
      For i = 0 To textElemIndex.Length - 1
         sb.AppendFormat("Character {0} starts at index {1}{2}", _
            i, textElemIndex(i), Environment.NewLine)
      Next
      MessageBox.Show(sb.ToString(), "Result of ParseCombiningCharacters")
   End Sub
End Class
```

Building and running this code produces the message boxes shown in Figures 12-3 and 12-4.

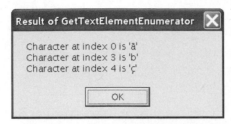

Figure 12-3   Result of `GetTextElementEnumerator`

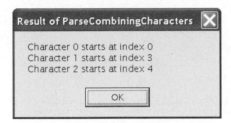

Figure 12-4   Result of `ParseCombiningCharacters`

> **Note**   To see the message box text in Figure 12-3 correctly, I had to open the Windows Display Properties dialog box and change the font used by message box text to Lucida Sans Unicode because this font contains glyphs for these combining characters. This is also why I don't have the code display the results to the console.

In this example, I'm calling `StringInfo`'s shared `GetTextElementEnumerator` method. I pass a `String` to this method and it returns a `TextElementEnumerator` object. I can now use this enumerator object as I would any other enumerator object. The `TextElementEnumerator` object also offers a read-only `ElementIndex` property that returns the index of the code value in the original string where the character begins and a `GetTextElement` method that returns a string consisting of all the code values necessary to make up the character.

In addition, `StringInfo` provides a shared `ParseCombiningCharacters` method that parses a string and returns an array of `Int32`s. Each element in the returned array is an index of a code-point unit that is the start of an abstract character. The .NET Framework SDK documentation shows an example of how to call this method. Note that the `StringInfo` class defines a public constructor, but this is a bug; there's never a reason to construct an instance of a `StringInfo`.

Other String Operations

The `String` type also offers methods that allow you to copy a string or parts of it. Table 12-3 summarizes these methods.

Table 12-3   Methods for Copying Strings

Member	Method Type	Description
`Clone`	Instance	Returns a reference to the same object (`Me`). This is OK because `String` objects are immutable. This method implements `String`'s `ICloneable` interface.
`Copy`	Shared	Returns a new string that is a duplicate of the specified string. This method is rarely used and exists to help applications that treat strings as tokens. Normally, strings with the same set of characters are interned to a single string. This method creates a new string object so that the references (pointers) are different even though the strings contain the same characters.
`CopyTo`	Instance	Copies a portion of the string's characters to an array of characters.
`SubString`	Instance	Returns a new string representing a portion of the original string.
`ToString`	Instance	Returns a reference to the same object (`Me`).

In addition to these methods, `String` offers many shared and instance methods that manipulate a string, such as `Insert`, `Remove`, `PadLeft`, `Replace`, `Split`, `Join`, `ToLower`, `ToUpper`, `Trim`, `Concat`, `Format`, and so on. Again, the important thing to remember about all these methods is that they return new string objects; because strings are immutable, once they're created, they can't be modified in any way.

Dynamically Constructing a String Efficiently

Because the `String` type represents an immutable string, the FCL provides another type, `System.Text.StringBuilder`, which allows you to perform dynamic operations with strings and characters to create a `String`. Think of

StringBuilder as a fancy constructor to create a **String** that can be used with the rest of the framework. In general, you should design methods that take **String** parameters, not **StringBuilder** parameters, unless you define a method that returns a string dynamically constructed by the method itself.

Internally, a **StringBuilder** object has a field that refers to an array of **Char** structures. **StringBuilder**'s members allow you to manipulate this character array, effectively shrinking the string or changing the characters in the string. If you grow the string past the allocated array of characters, the **StringBuilder** automatically allocates a new, larger array, copies the characters, and starts using the new array. The previous array is garbage collected.

When finished using the **StringBuilder** object to construct your string, "convert" the **StringBuilder**'s character array into a **String** simply by calling the **StringBuilder**'s **ToString** method. Internally, this method just returns a reference to the string field maintained inside the **StringBuilder**. This makes the **StringBuilder**'s **ToString** method very fast because the array of characters isn't copied.

The **String** returned from **StringBuilder**'s **ToString** method must be immutable. So if you ever call a method that attempts to modify the string field maintained by the **StringBuilder**, the **StringBuilder**'s methods know that **ToString** was called on it and they internally create and use a new character array, allowing you to perform manipulations without affecting the string returned by the previous call to **ToString**.

Constructing a StringBuilder Object

Unlike with the **String** class, the CLR has no special knowledge of the **StringBuilder** class. In addition, most languages (including Visual Basic) don't consider the **StringBuilder** class to be a primitive type. You construct a **StringBuilder** object as you would any other nonprimitive type:

```
Dim sb As New StringBuilder(...)
```

The **StringBuilder** type offers many constructors. The job of each constructor is to allocate and initialize the three internal fields maintained by each **StringBuilder** object:

■   **Maximum capacity**   An **Int32** field that specifies the maximum number of characters that can be placed in the string. The default is **Int32.MaxValue** (2 billion). It's unusual to change this value. However, you might specify a smaller maximum capacity to ensure that you never create a string over a certain length. Once constructed, a **StringBuilder**'s maximum capacity field can't be changed.

- **Capacity** An `Int32` field indicating the size of the character array field being maintained by the `StringBuilder`. The default is 16. If you have some idea how many characters you'll place in the `String-Builder`, you should use this number to set the capacity when constructing the `StringBuilder` object.

    When appending characters to the character array, the `String-Builder` detects whether the array is trying to grow beyond the array's capacity. If it is, the `StringBuilder` automatically doubles the capacity field, allocates a new array (the size of the new capacity), and copies the characters from the original array into the new array. The original array will be garbage collected in the future. Dynamically growing the array hurts performance; avoid this by setting a good initial capacity.

- **Character array** An array of `Char` structures that maintains the set of characters in the "string." The number of characters is always less than or equal to the capacity and maximum capacity fields. You can use the `StringBuilder`'s `Length` property to obtain the number of characters used in the array. The `Length` is always less than or equal to the `StringBuilder`'s capacity field. When constructing a `String-Builder`, you can pass a String to initialize the character array. If you don't specify a string, the array initially contains no characters—that is, the `Length` property returns `0`.

StringBuilder's Members

Unlike a `String`, a `StringBuilder` represents a mutable string. This means that most of `StringBuilder`'s members change the contents in the array of characters and don't cause new objects to be allocated in the managed heap. A `StringBuilder` allocates a new object on only two occasions:

- You dynamically build a string that is longer than the capacity you've set.

- You attempt to modify the array after `StringBuilder`'s `ToString` method has been called.

You should also be aware that in the interest of faster performance, `StringBuilder`'s methods are not thread-safe. This is usually fine since it's unusual for multiple threads to access a single `StringBuilder` object. If your application requires thread-safe manipulation of a `StringBuilder` object, you must explicitly add the thread synchronization code.

Table 12-4 summarizes `StringBuilder`'s members.

Table 12-4 `StringBuilder`'s **Members**

Member	Member Type	Description
MaxCapacity	Read-only property	Returns the largest number of characters that can be placed in the string.
Capacity	Read/write property	Gets or sets the size of the character array. Trying to set the capacity smaller than the string's length throws an `ArgumentOutOfRangeException` exception.
EnsureCapacity	Method	Guarantees that the character array is at least the size specified to this method. If the value passed is larger than the `StringBuilder`'s current capacity, the current capacity gets bigger. If the current capacity is already bigger than the value passed to this method, no change occurs.
Length	Read/write property	Gets the number of characters in the "string." This number will likely be smaller than the character array's current capacity. You can also use this property to set the number of characters in the string. When making the length shorter, the string is truncated to the specified length. When making the length longer, the end of the string is padded with &H0000 characters. If the specified length is greater than the current capacity, `Capacity` is set to the specified length.
ToString	Method	The parameterless version of this method returns a `String` representing the `StringBuilder`'s character array field. This method is efficient because it doesn't create a new `String` object. Any attempt to modify the `StringBuilder`'s array causes the `StringBuilder` to allocate and use a new array (initializing it from the old array). The version of `ToString` that takes `startIndex` and `length` parameters creates a new `String` object representing the desired portion of the `StringBuilder`'s string.
Chars	Read/write indexer property	Gets or sets the character at the specified index into the character array. Visual Basic developers can access this member by using default property syntax. Specifically, you can omit `Chars` from your code and access individual characters using array syntax.
Append Insert	Method	Appends or inserts a single object into the character array, growing the array if necessary. The object is converted to a string using the general format and the culture associated with the calling thread.

(continued)

Table 12-4   `StringBuilder`**'s Members**   *(continued)*

Member	Member Type	Description
`AppendFormat`	Method	Appends the specified objects into the character array, growing the array if necessary. The objects are converted to strings using the formatting and culture information provided by the caller. `AppendFormat` is one of the most common methods used with `StringBuilder` objects.
`Replace`	Method	Replaces one character with another or one string with another from within the character array.
`Remove`	Method	Removes a range of characters from the character array.
`Equals`	Method	Returns `True` only if both `StringBuilder` objects have the same maximum capacity, capacity, and characters in the array.

Most of `StringBuilder`'s methods return a reference to the same `String-Builder` object. This allows a convenient syntax to chain several operations together:

```
Dim sb As New StringBuilder
Dim s As String = sb.AppendFormat("{0} {1}", "Jeffrey", Richter"). _
    Replace(" ", "-").Remove(4, 3).ToString()
Console.WriteLine(s)      ' "Jeff-Richter"
```

You'll notice that the `String` and `StringBuilder` classes don't have full method parity; that is, `String` has `ToLower`, `ToUpper`, `EndsWiths`, `PadLeft`, `Trim`, and so on. The `StringBuilder` class doesn't offer any of these methods. On the other hand, the `StringBuilder` class offers a richer `Replace` method that allows you to replace characters or strings in a portion of the string (not the whole string). It's unfortunate that there isn't complete parity between these two classes because now you must convert between `String` and `StringBuilder` to accomplish certain tasks. For example, to build up a string, convert all characters to uppercase, and then insert a string requires code like this:

```
' Construct a StringBuilder to do string manipulations.
Dim sb As New StringBuilder()

' Perform some string manipulations using the StringBuilder.
sb.AppendFormat("{0} {1}", "Jeffrey", "Richter").Replace(" ", "-")

' Convert the StringBuilder to a String in order to make
' all the characters uppercase.
Dim s As String = sb.ToString().ToUpper()
```

```
' Clear the StringBuilder (allocates a new Char array).
sb.Length = 0

' Load the uppercase String into the StringBuilder,
' and do more manipulations.
sb.Append(s).Insert(8, "Marc-")

' Convert the StringBuilder back to a String.
s = sb.ToString()

' Display the String to the user.
Console.WriteLine(s)    ' "JEFFREY-Marc-RICHTER"
```

It's inconvenient to have to write this code just because **StringBuilder** doesn't offer all the operations that **String** does. In the future, I hope Microsoft will add more string operation methods to **StringBuilder** to make it a more complete class.

Obtaining a String Representation for an Object

You frequently need to obtain a string representation for an object. Usually this is necessary when you want to display a numeric type (such as **Byte**, **Int32**, **Single**, and so on) or a **DateTime** object to the user. Because the .NET Framework is an object-oriented platform, every type is responsible for providing code that converts an instance's "value" to a string equivalent. When designing how types should accomplish this, the designers of the FCL decided to devise a pattern that would be used consistently throughout. In this section, I'll describe this pattern.

You can obtain a string representation for any object by calling the **ToString** method. A public, parameterless **ToString** method is defined by **System.Object** and is therefore callable using an instance of any type. Semantically, **ToString** returns a string representing the object's current value, and this string should be formatted for the calling thread's current culture; that is, the string representation of a number should use the proper decimal separator, digit grouping symbol, and so on associated with the culture assigned to the calling thread.

System.Object's implementation of **ToString** simply returns the full name of the object's type. This value isn't particularly useful but is a reasonable default for the many types that can't offer a sensible string. For example, what should a string representation of a **FileStream** or a **Hashtable** object look like?

All types that want to offer a reasonable way to obtain a string representing the current value of the object should override the **ToString** method. For all base types built into the FCL (**Byte**, **Int32**, **UInt64**, **Double**, and so on), Microsoft has already overridden these types' **ToString** method and implemented it to return a culturally aware string.

Specific Formats and Cultures

The parameterless **ToString** method has two problems. First, the caller has no control over the formatting of the string. For example, an application might want to format a number into a currency string or a decimal string, or a percent string or a hexadecimal string. Second, the caller can't choose to format a string using a specific culture. This second problem is more troublesome for server-side application code than for client-side code. On rare occasions, an application needs to format a string using a culture different from the culture associated with the calling thread. To have more control over string formatting, you need a version of the **ToString** method that allows you to specify specific formatting and culture information.

Types that want to offer the caller a choice in formatting and culture implement the **System.IFormattable** interface:

```
Public Interface IFormattable
    Function ToString(ByVal format As String, _
        ByVal formatProvider As IFormatProvider) As String
End Interface
```

In the FCL, all the base types (**Byte**, **SByte**, **Int16/UInt16**, **Int32/UInt32**, **Int64/UInt64**, **Single**, **Double**, **Decimal**, and **DateTime**) implement this interface. Some other types, like **GUID**, also implement it. Finally, every enumerated type automatically implements the **IFormattable** interface to obtain a meaningful string symbol from the numeric value stored in an instance of an enumerated type.

IFormattable's **ToString** method takes two parameters. The first, **format**, is a string that tells the method how the object should be formatted. **ToString**'s second parameter, **formatProvider**, is an instance of a type that implements the **System.IFormatProvider** interface. This type supplies specific culture information to the **ToString** method. I'll discuss how shortly.

The type implementing the **IFormattable** interface's **ToString** method determines which format strings it's going to recognize. If you pass a format string that the type doesn't recognize, the type should throw a **System.Format-Exception** exception.

Many of the types that Microsoft has defined in the FCL recognize several formats. For example, the **DateTime** type supports "d" for short date, "D" for long date, "g" for general, "M" for month/day, "s" for sortable, "T" for time, "u" for universal time in ISO 8601 format, "U" for universal time in long date format, "Y" for year/month, and more. All enumerated types support "G" for general, "F" for flags, "D" for decimal, and "X" for hexadecimal. I'll cover formatting enumerated types in more detail in Chapter 13.

Also, all the built-in numeric types support "C" for currency, "D" for decimal, "E" for scientific (exponential), "F" for fixed-point, "G" for general, "N" for number, "P" for percent, "R" for round-trip, and "X" for hexadecimal. In fact, the numeric types also support picture format strings just in case the simple format strings don't offer you exactly what you're looking for. Picture format strings contain special characters that tell the type's `ToString` method exactly how many digits to show, exactly where to place a decimal separator, exactly how many digits to place after the decimal separator, and so on. For complete information about format strings, see "Formatting Strings" in the .NET Framework SDK.

Calling `ToString` passing `Nothing` for the format string is identical to calling `ToString` and passing "G" for the format string. In other words, objects format themselves using the "General format" by default. When implementing a type, choose a format that you think will be the most commonly used format; this format is the "General format." By the way, the `ToString` method that takes no parameters assumes that the caller wants the general format.

So now that format strings are out of the way, let's turn to culture information. By default, strings are formatted using the culture information associated with the calling thread. The parameterless `ToString` method certainly does this, and so does `IFormattable`'s `ToString` if you pass `Nothing` for the `format-Provider` parameter.

Culture-sensitive information applies when you're formatting numbers (including currency, integers, floating point, and percentages), dates, and times. A type that represents a GUID has a `ToString` method that just returns a string representing the GUID's value. There's no need to consider the thread's current culture when generating the GUID's string.

When formatting a number, the `ToString` method sees what you've passed for the `formatProvider` parameter. If `Nothing` is passed, `ToString` determines the culture associated with the calling thread by reading the `System.Threading.Thread.CurrentThread.CurrentCulture` property. This property returns an instance of the `System.Globalization.CultureInfo` type.

Using this object, `ToString` reads its `NumberFormat` or `DateTimeFormat` property, depending on whether a number or date/time is being formatted. These properties return an instance of `System.Globalization.NumberFormatInfo` or `System.Globalization.DateTimeFormatInfo`, respectively. The `NumberFormatInfo` type defines a bunch of properties, such as `CurrencyDecimalSeparator`, `CurrencySymbol`, `NegativeSign`, `NumberGroupSeparator`, and `PercentSymbol`. Likewise, the `DateTimeFormatInfo` type defines an assortment of properties, such as `Calendar`, `DateSeparator`, `DayNames`, `Long-`

DatePattern, **ShortTimePattern**, and **TimeSeparator**. **ToString** reads these properties when constructing and formatting a string.

When calling **IFormattable**'s **ToString** method, instead of passing **Nothing**, you can pass a reference to an object whose type implements the **IFormatProvider** interface:

```
Public Interface IFormatProvider
   Function GetFormat(ByVal formatType As Type) As Object
End Interface
```

Here's the basic idea behind the **IFormatProvider** interface: when a type implements this interface, it is saying that an instance of the type knows how to provide culture-specific formatting information and that the culture information associated with the calling thread should be ignored.

The **System.Globalization.CultureInfo** type is one of the very few types defined in the FCL that implements the **IFormatProvider** interface. If you want to format a string for, say, Vietnam, you'd construct a **CultureInfo** object and pass that object in as **ToString**'s **formatProvider** parameter. The following code obtains a string representation of a **Decimal** numeric value formatted as currency appropriate for Vietnam:

```
Dim price As Decimal = 123.54
Dim s As String = price.ToString("C", New CultureInfo("vi-VN"))
System.Windows.Forms.MessageBox.Show(s)
```

If you build and run this code, the message box shown in Figure 12-5 appears.

Figure 12-5   Numeric value formatted correctly to represent Vietnamese currency

Internally, **Decimal**'s **ToString** method sees that the **formatProvider** argument is not **Nothing** and calls the object's **GetFormat** method as follows:

```
Dim nfi As NumberFormat = DirectCast( _
   formatProvider.GetFormat(GetType(NumberFormatInfo)), NumberFormatInfo)
```

This is how **ToString** asks the (**CultureInfo**) object for the appropriate number formatting information. Number types (like **Decimal**) ask for only number formatting information. But other types (like **DateTime**) could call **GetFormat** like this:

```
Dim dtfi As NumberFormat = DirectCast( _
    formatProvider.GetFormat(GetType(DateTimeFormatInfo)), DateTimeFormatInfo)
```

Actually, since **GetFormat**'s parameter can identify any type, the method is flexible enough to allow any type of format information to be requested. The types in version 1 of the .NET Framework call **GetFormat** asking only for number or date/time information; in the future, other kinds of formatting information could be requested.

By the way, if you want to obtain a string for an object that isn't formatted for any particular culture, you should call **System.Globalization.CultureInfo**'s shared **InvariantCulture** property and pass the object returned as **ToString**'s **formatProvider** parameter:

```
Dim price As Decimal = 123.54
Dim s As String = price.ToString("C", CultureInfo.InvariantCulture)
System.Windows.Forms.MessageBox.Show(s)
```

If you build and run this code, the message box shown in Figure 12-6 appears. Notice the first character in the resulting string: ¤. This is the international sign for currency (U+00A4).

Figure 12-6   Numeric value formatted to represent a culture-neutral currency

Normally, you wouldn't display a string formatted using the invariant culture to a user. Typically, you'd just save this string in a data file so that it could be parsed later. Basically, the invariant culture allows you to pass understandable strings from culture to culture.

In the FCL, just three types implement the **IFormatProvider** interface. The first is **CultureInfo**, which I've already explained. The other two are **Number-FormatInfo** and **DateTimeFormatInfo**. When **GetFormat** is called on a **Number-FormatInfo** object, the method checks whether the type being requested is a **NumberFormatInfo**. If it is, **Me** is returned; if it's not, **Nothing** is returned. Similarly, calling **GetFormat** on a **DateTimeFormatInfo** object returns **Me** if a

`DateTimeFormatInfo` is requested and `Nothing` if it's not. These two types implement this interface simply as a programming convenience.

When trying to obtain a string representation of an object, the caller commonly specifies a format and uses the culture associated with the calling thread. For this reason, you often call `ToString`, passing a string for the format parameter and `Nothing` for the `formatProvider` parameter. To make calling `ToString` easier for you, many types offer several overloads of the `ToString` method. For example, the `Decimal` type offers four different `ToString` methods:

```
' This version calls ToString(Nothing, Nothing).
' Meaning: General format, thread's culture information
Function ToString() As String


' This version is where the actual implementation of ToString goes.
' This version implements IFormattable's ToString method.
' Meaning: Caller-specified format and culture information
Function ToString(ByVal format As String, _
   ByVal formatProvider As IFormatProvider) As String


' This version simply calls ToString(format, Nothing).
' Meaning: Caller-specified format, thread's culture information
Function ToString(ByVal format As String) As String


' This version simply calls ToString(Nothing, formatProvider).
' Meaning: General format, caller-specified culture information
Function ToString(ByVal formatProvider As IFormatProvider) As String
```

Formatting Multiple Objects into a Single String

So far, I've explained how an individual type formats its own objects. At times, however, you want to construct strings that consist of many formatted objects. For example, the following string has a date, a person's name, and an age:

```
Dim s As String = String.Format("On {0}, {1} is {2} years old.", _
   DateTime.Now, "Wallace", 35)
Console.WriteLine(s)
```

If you build and run this code on August 23, 2002, at 4:37 P.M., you'll see the following line of output:

```
On 8/23/2002 4:37:37 PM, Wallace is 35 years old.
```

`String`'s shared `Format` method takes a format string that identifies replaceable parameters using numbers in braces. The format string used in this example tells the `Format` method to replace "{0}" with the first parameter after the format string (the current date/time), replace "{1}" with the second parameter after the format string ("Wallace"), and replace "{2}" with the third parameter after the format string (35).

Internally, the **Format** method calls each object's **ToString** method to obtain a string representation for the object. Then the returned strings are all appended and the complete, final string is returned. This is all fine and good, but it means that all the objects are formatted using their general format and the calling thread's culture information.

You can have more control when formatting an object if you specify format information within braces. For example, the following code is identical to the previous example except that I've added formatting information to replaceable parameters 0 and 2:

```
String = String.Format("On {0:D}, {1} is {2:E} years old.", _
   DateTime.Now, "Wallace", 35)
Console.WriteLine(s)
```

If you build and run this code on August 23, 2002, at 4:37 P.M., you'll see the following line of output:

```
On Friday, August 23, 2002, Wallace is 3.500000E+001 years old.
```

When the **Format** method parses the format string, it sees that replaceable parameter 0 should have its **IFormattable** interface's **ToString** method passing "D" and **Nothing** for its two parameters. Likewise, **Format** calls replaceable parameter 2's **IFormattable ToString** method, passing "E" and **Nothing**. If the type doesn't implement the **IFormattable** interface, then **Format** calls its parameterless **ToString** method and the general format is appended into the resulting string.

The **String** class offers several overloads of the shared **Format** method. One version takes an object that implements the **IFormatProvider** interface so that you can format all the replaceable parameters using caller-specified culture information. Obviously, **Format** calls each object's **ToString** method, passing it whatever **IFormatProvider** object was passed to **Format**.

If you're using **StringBuilder** instead of **String** to construct a string, you can call **StringBuilder**'s **AppendFormat** method. This method works exactly like **String**'s **Format** method except that it formats a string and appends to the **StringBuilder**'s character array. Like **String**'s **Format**, **AppendString** takes a format string, and there's a version that takes an **IFormatProvider**.

System.Console offers **Write** and **WriteLine** methods that also take format strings and replaceable parameters. However, there are no overloads of **Console**'s **Write** and **WriteLine** methods that allow you to pass an **IFormatProvider**. If you want to format a string for a specific culture, you have to call **String**'s **Format** method, first passing the desired **IFormatProvider** object and then passing the resulting string to **Console**'s **Write** or **WriteLine** method. This shouldn't be a big deal since, as I said earlier, it's rare for client-side code to format a string using a culture other than the one associated with the calling thread.

Providing Your Own Custom Formatter

By now it should be clear that the formatting capabilities in the .NET Framework were designed to offer you a great deal of flexibility and control. However, we're not quite done. It's possible for you to define a method that **StringBuilder**'s **AppendFormat** method will call whenever any object is being formatted into a string. In other words, instead of calling **ToString** for each object, **AppendFormat** can call a function that you define, allowing you to format any or all of the objects any way you want. What I'm about to describe works only when calling **StringBuilder**'s **AppendFormat** method. **String**'s **Format** method doesn't support this mechanism.

Let me explain this mechanism by way of an example. Let's say that you're formatting HTML text that a user will view in an Internet browser. You want all **Int32** values to display in bold. To accomplish this, every time an **Int32** value is formatted into a **String**, you want to surround the string with HTML bold tags: **<B>** and **</B>**. The following code demonstrates how easy it is to do this:

```
Imports System
Imports System.Text
Imports System.Globalization
Imports System.Threading

Class BoldInt32s
   Implements IFormatProvider, ICustomFormatter

   Public Function GetFormat(ByVal formatType As Type) As Object _
      Implements IFormatProvider.GetFormat
      If formatType Is GetType(ICustomFormatter) Then Return Me
      Return Thread.CurrentThread.CurrentCulture.GetFormat(formatType)
   End Function

   Public Function Format(ByVal strFormat As String, ByVal arg As Object, _
      ByVal formatProvider As IFormatProvider) As String _
      Implements ICustomFormatter.Format
      Dim s As String

      If TypeOf arg Is IFormattable Then
         s = DirectCast(arg, IFormattable).ToString(strFormat, formatProvider)
      Else
         s = arg.ToString()
      End If
```

```
      If arg.GetType() Is GetType(Int32) Then
         Return "<B>" + s + "</B>"
      Else
         Return s
      End If
   End Function
End Class

Class App
   Shared Sub Main()
      Dim sb As New StringBuilder()
      sb.AppendFormat(New BoldInt32s(), "{0} {1} {2:M}", _
         "Jeff", 123, DateTime.Now)
      Console.WriteLine(sb)
   End Sub
End Class
```

When you compile and run this code, it displays the following output:

```
Jeff <B>123</B> January 23
```

In **Main**, I'm constructing an empty **StringBuilder** and then appending a formatted string into it. When I call **AppendFormat**, the first parameter is an instance of the **BoldInt32s** class. This class implements the **IFormatProvider** interface that I discussed earlier. In addition, this class implements the **ICustom-Formatter** interface:

```
Public Interface ICustomFormatter
   Function Format(ByVal strFormat As String, ByVal arg As Object, _
      ByVal ICustomFormatter As IFormatProvider) As String
End Interface
```

This interface's **Format** method is called whenever **StringBuilder**'s **AppendFormat** needs to obtain a string for an object. You can do some pretty clever things inside this method that give you a great deal of control over string formatting. Let's look inside the **AppendFormat** method to see exactly how it works. The following pseudocode shows how **AppendFormat** does its stuff:

```
Public Function AppendFormat(ByVal formatProvider As IFormatProvider, _
   ByVal format As String, ByVal ParamArray args() As Object) As StringBuilder

   ' If an IFormatProvider was passed, find out
   ' whether it offers an ICustomFormatter object.
   Dim cf As ICustomFormatter = Nothing
   If Not formatProvider Is Nothing Then
      cf = DirectCast(formatProvider.GetFormat(GetType(ICustomFormatter)), _
         ICustomFormatter)
   End If
```

(continued)

```
                       ' Keep appending literal characters (not shown in this pseudocode)
                       ' and replaceable parameters to the StringBuilder's character array.
                       While MoreReplaceableArgumentsToAppend
                          ' argFormat refers to the replaceable format string obtained
                          ' from the format parameter.
                             Dim argFormat As String = ...

                          ' argObj refers to the corresponding element
                          ' from the args array parameter.
                          Dim argObj As Object = ...

                          ' argStr will refer to the formatted string to be appended
                          ' to the final, resulting string.
                          Dim argStr As String = Nothing

                          ' If a custom formatter is available, let it format the argument.
                          If Not cf Is Nothing Then
                             argStr = cf.Format(argFormat, argObj, formatProvider)
                          End If

                          ' If there is no custom formatter or if it didn't format
                          ' the argument, try something else.
                          If argStr Is Nothing Then
                             ' Does the argument's type support rich formatting?
                             If TypeOf argObj Is IFormattable Then
                                ' Yes; pass the format string and provider to
                                ' the type's IFormattable ToString method.
                                argStr = DirectCast(argObj, IFormattable). _
                                   ToString(argFormat, formatProvider)
                             Else
                                ' No; get the general format using
                                ' the thread's culture information.
                                If Not argObj Is Nothing Then
                                   argStr = argObj.ToString()
                                Else
                                   argStr = String.Empty
                                End If
                             End If
                          End If
                          ' Append argStr's characters to the character array field member.
                          ⋮
                       End While
                    Return Me
                 End Function
```

When **Main** calls **AppendFormat**, **AppendFormat** calls my format provider's **GetFormat** method, passing it the **ICustomFormatter** type. The **GetFormat** method defined in my **BoldInt32s** type sees that the **ICustomFormatter** is being requested and returns a reference to its own object. If any other type is requested of **GetFormat**, I call the **GetFormat** method using the **CultureInfo** object associated with the calling thread.

Whenever **AppendFormat** needs to format a replaceable parameter, it calls **ICustomFormatter**'s **Format** method. In my example, this calls the **Format** method defined by my **BoldInt32s** type. In my **Format** method, I check whether the object being formatted supports rich formatting via the **IFormattable** interface. If the object doesn't, I call the simple, parameterless **ToString** method to format the object. If the object supports **IFormattable**, I call the rich **ToString** method, passing it the format string and the format provider.

Now that I have the formatted string, I check whether the object is an **Int32** type, and if it is, I wrap the formatting string in **<B>** and **</B>** HTML tags and return the new string. If the object is not an **Int32**, I simply return the formatted string without any further processing.

Parsing a String to Obtain an Object

In the preceding section, I explained how to take an object and obtain a string representation of that object. In this section, I'll talk about the opposite: how to take a string and obtain an object representation of it. Obtaining an object from a string isn't a very common operation, but it does occasionally come in handy. Microsoft felt it necessary to formalize a mechanism by which strings can be parsed into objects.

Any type that can parse a string offers a public, shared method named **Parse**. This method takes a **String** and returns an instance of the type; in a way, **Parse** acts like a constructor. In the FCL, a **Parse** method exists on all the numeric types as well as for **DateTime**, **TimeSpan**, and a few other types (like the SQL data types).

Let's look at how to parse a string into a numeric type. All the numeric types (**Byte**, **SByte**, **Int16/UInt16**, **Int32/UInt32**, **Int64/UInt64**, **Single**, **Double**, and **Decimal**) offer at least one **Parse** method. Here I'll show you just the **Parse** method defined by the **Int32** type. (The **Parse** methods for the other numeric types are identical.)

```
Public Shared Function Parse(ByVal s As String, _
   ByVal style As NumberStyles, ByVal provider As IFormatProvider) As Int32
```

Just from looking at the prototype, you should be able to guess exactly how this method works. The **String** parameter, **s**, identifies a string representation of a number you want parsed into an **Int32** object. The **System.Globalization.NumberStyles** parameter, **style**, is a set of bit flags that identify characters that **Parse** should expect to find in the string. And the **IFormatProvider** parameter, **provider**, identifies an object that the **Parse** method can use to obtain culture-specific information as discussed earlier in this chapter.

For example, the following code causes **Parse** to throw a **System.Format-Exception** exception because the string being parsed contains a leading space:

```
Dim x As Int32 = Int32.Parse(" 123", NumberStyles.None, Nothing)
```

To allow **Parse** to skip over the leading space, change the **style** parameter as follows:

```
Dim x As Int32 = Int32.Parse(" 123", NumberStyles.AllowLeadingWhite, Nothing)
```

Table 12-5 shows the bit symbols that the **NumberStyles** type defines.

Table 12-5 Bit Symbols Defined by the NumberStyles Type

Symbol	Value	Description
None	&H00000000	None of the special characters represented by any of the bits in the remaining rows in this table are allowed in the string.
AllowLeadingWhite AllowTrailingWhite	&H00000001 &H00000002	The string can contain leading/trailing whitespace characters (identified by the following Unicode code points: &H0009, &H000A, &H000B, &H000C, &H000D, and &H0020).
AllowLeadingSign AllowTrailingSign	&H00000004 &H00000008	The string can contain a valid leading/trailing sign character. **NumberFormatInfo**'s **PositiveSign** and **NegativeSign** properties determine valid leading-sign characters.
AllowParentheses AllowDecimalPoint	&H00000010 &H00000020	The string can contain parentheses. The string can contain a valid decimal-separator character. **NumberFormatInfo**'s **NumberDecimalSeparator** and **CurrencyDecimalSeparator** properties determine valid decimal-separator characters.
AllowThousands	&H00000040	The string can contain a valid grouping-separator character. **NumberFormatInfo**'s **NumberGroupSeparator** and **CurrencyGroupSeparator** properties determine valid grouping-separator characters. **NumberFormatInfo**'s **NumberGroupSizes** and **CurrencyGroupSizes** properties determine the number of digits in the group.
AllowExponent	&H00000080	The string can contain a number expressed in exponent format: {e | E} [{+ | -}] **n** where **n** is a number.

(continued)

Table 12-5   **Bit Symbols Defined by the** `NumberStyles` **Type**   *(continued)*

Symbol	Value	Description
`AllowCurrencySymbol`	&H00000100	The string can contain a valid currency symbol, which `NumberFormatInfo`'s `CurrencySymbol` property determines.
`AllowHexSpecifier`	&H00000200	The string can contain hex digits (0–9, A–F), and the string is considered to be a hex value.

In addition to the bit symbols in Table 12-5, the `NumberStyles` enumerated type also defines some symbols that represent common combinations of the individual bits. Table 12-6 shows these.

Table 12-6   **Symbols for** `NumberStyles`' **Bit Combinations**

Symbol	Bit Set		
Integer	`AllowLeadingWhite` `AllowLeadingSign`	`Or AllowTrailingWhite`	`Or`
Number	`AllowLeadingWhite` `AllowLeadingSign` `AllowDecimalPoint`	`Or AllowTrailingWhite` `Or AllowTrailingSign` `Or AllowThousands`	`Or` `Or`
Float	`AllowLeadingWhite` `AllowLeadingSign` `AllowExponent`	`Or AllowTrailingWhite` `Or AllowDecimalPoint`	`Or` `Or`
Currency	`AllowLeadingWhite` `AllowLeadingSign` `AllowParentheses` `AllowThousands`	`Or AllowTrailingWhite` `Or AllowTrailingSign` `Or AllowDecimalPoint` `Or AllowCurrencySymbol`	`Or` `Or` `Or`
HexNumber	`AllowLeadingWhite` `AllowHexSpecifier`	`Or AllowTrailingWhite`	`Or`
Any	`AllowLeadingWhite` `AllowLeadingSign` `AllowParentheses` `AllowThousands` `AllowExponent`	`Or AllowTrailingWhite` `Or AllowTrailingSign` `Or AllowDecimalPoint` `Or AllowCurrencySymbol`	`Or` `Or` `Or` `Or`

Here's a code fragment showing how to parse a hexadecimal number:

```
Dim x As Int32 = Int32.Parse("1A", NumberStyles.HexNumber, Nothing)
Console.WriteLine(x)     ' Displays "26"
```

This **Parse** method accepts three parameters. For convenience, many types offer additional overloads of **Parse** so that you don't have to pass as many arguments. For example, **Int32** offers four overloads of the **Parse** method:

```
' Passes NumberStyles.Integer for style
' and Nothing for provider parameters.
Public Shared Function Parse(ByVal s As String) As Int32

' Passes Nothing for the provider parameter.
Public Shared Function Parse(ByVal s As String, _
   ByVal style As NumberStyles) As Int32

' Passes NumberStyles.Integer for the style parameter.
Public Shared Function Parse(ByVal s As String, _
   ByVal provider As IFormatProvider) As Int32

' This is the method I've been talking about in this section.
Public Shared Function Parse(ByVal s As String, _
   ByVal style As NumberStyles, ByVal provider As IFormatProvider) As Int32
```

The **DateTime** type also offers a **Parse** method:

```
Public Shared Function Parse(ByVal s As String, _
   ByVal provider As IFormatProvier, _
   ByVal styles As DateTimeStyles) As DateTime
```

This method works just like the **Parse** method defined on the number types except that **DateTime**'s **Parse** method takes a set of bit flags defined by the **DateTimeStyles** enumerated type instead of the **NumberStyles** enumerated types. Table 12-7 shows the bit symbols that the **DateTimeStyles** type defines.

Table 12-7 Bit Symbols Defined by the DateTimeStyles Type

Symbol	Value	Description
None	&H00000000	None of the special characters represented by the bits in the remaining rows in this table are allowed in the string.
AllowLeadingWhite AllowTrailingWhite AllowInnerWhite	&H00000001 &H00000002 &H00000004	The string can contain leading/trailing/inner white-space characters (identified by the following Unicode code points: &H0009, &H000A, &H000B, &H000C, &H000D, and &H0020).
NoCurrentDateDefault AdjustToUniversal	&H00000008 &H00000010	When parsing a string that contains only a time (no date), set the date to January 1, 0001 instead of the current date. When parsing a string that contains a time-zone specifier ("GMT", "Z", "+xxxx", "-xxxx"), adjust the parsed time base to Greenwich Mean Time.

In addition to these bit symbols, the **DateTimeStyles** enumerated type also defines an **AllowWhiteSpaces** symbol that represents all the **White** symbols OR'd together (**AllowLeadingWhite Or AllowInnerWhite Or AllowTrailingWhite**).

For convenience, the **DateTime** type offers three overloads of the **Parse** method:

```
' Nothing for formatProvider and DateTimeStyles.None
Public Shared Function Parse(ByVal s As String) As DateTime


' DateTimeStyles.None
Public Shared Function Parse(ByVal s As String, _
    ByVal provider As IFormatProvider) As DateTime


' This is the method I've been talking about in this section.
Public Shared Function Parse(ByVal s As String, _
    ByVal provider As IFormatProvider, _
    ByVal styles As DateTimeStyles) As DateTime
```

Parsing dates and times is complex. Many developers have found **DateTime**'s **Parse** method too forgiving in that it sometimes parses strings that don't contain dates or times. For this reason, the **DateTime** type also offers a **ParseExact** method that accepts a picture format string that indicates exactly how the date/time string is formatted and how it should be parsed. For more information about picture format strings, see the **DateTimeFormatInfo** class in the .NET Framework SDK.

Encodings: Converting Between Characters and Bytes

In Win32, programmers all too frequently have to write code to convert Unicode characters and strings to multibyte character set (MBCS) characters and strings. I've certainly written my share of this code, and it's very tedious to write and error prone to use. In the CLR, all characters are represented as 16-bit Unicode code values and all strings are composed of 16-bit Unicode code values. This makes working with characters and strings easy at run time.

At times, however, you want to save strings to a file or transmit them over a network. If the strings consist mostly of characters readable by English-speaking people, then saving or transmitting a set of 16-bit values isn't very efficient because half of the bytes written would contain zeros. Instead, it would be more efficient to *encode* the 16-bit values into a compressed array of bytes and then *decode* the array of bytes back into an array of 16-bit values.

Encodings also allow a managed application to interact with strings created by non-Unicode systems. For example, if you want to produce a file readable by an application running on a Japanese version of Windows 95, you have to save the Unicode text using the Shift-JIS (code page 932) encoding. Likewise, you'd use a Shift-JIS encoding to read a text file produced on a Japanese Windows 95 system into the CLR.

Encoding is typically done when you want to send a string to a file or network stream using the `System.IO.BinaryWriter` or `System.IO.StreamWriter` type. Decoding is typically done when you want to read a string from a file or network stream using the `System.IO.BinaryReader` or `System.IO.StreamReader` type. If you don't explicitly select an encoding, all these types default to using UTF-8. (UTF stands for Unicode Transformation Format.) However, at times, you might want to encode or decode a string.

Fortunately, the FCL offers some types to make character encoding and decoding easy. The two most frequently used encodings are UTF-16 and UTF-8.

- UTF-16 encodes each 16-bit character as 2 bytes. It doesn't affect the characters at all, and no compression occurs—its performance is excellent. UTF-16 encoding is also referred to as *Unicode encoding*. UTF-16 can also be used to convert from little endian to big endian and vice versa.

- UTF-8 encodes some characters as 1 byte, some characters as 2 bytes, some characters as 3 bytes, and some characters as 4 bytes. Characters with a value below &H0080 are compressed to 1 byte, which works very well for characters used in the United States. Characters between &H0080 and &H07FF are converted to 2 bytes, which works well for European and Middle Eastern languages. Characters of &H0800 and above are converted to 3 bytes, which works well for East Asian languages. Finally, surrogate character pairs are written out as 4 bytes. UTF-8 is an extremely popular encoding, but it's less useful than UTF-16 if you encode many characters with values of &H0800 or above.

Although the UTF-16 and UTF-8 encodings are by far the most common, the FCL also supports some encodings that are used less frequently:

- UTF-7 encoding is typically used with older systems that work with characters that can be expressed using 7-bit values. You should avoid this encoding because it usually ends up expanding the data rather than compressing it. The Unicode Consortium has deprecated this encoding starting with the Unicode 3.0 standard.

- ASCII encodes the 16-bit characters into ASCII characters; that is, any 16-bit character with a value less than &H0080 is converted to a single byte. Any character with a value greater than &H007F can't be converted, and the character's value is lost. For strings consisting of characters in the ASCII range (&H00 to &H7F), this encoding compresses the data in half and is very fast (because the high byte is just chopped off). This encoding isn't good if you have characters outside the ASCII range because the character's values are lost.

Finally, the FCL also allows you to encode 16-bit characters to an arbitrary code page. Like the ASCII encoding, encoding to a code page is dangerous because any character whose value can't be expressed in the specified code page is lost. You should always use UTF-16 or UTF-8 encoding unless you must work with some legacy files or applications that already use one of the other encodings.

When you need to encode or decode a set of characters, you should obtain an instance of a class derived from **System.Text.Encoding**. **Encoding** is an abstract base class that offers several shared properties, each of which returns an instance of an **Encoding**-derived class. (Each encoding class is basically a wrapper around the **WideCharToMultiByte** and **MultiByteToWideChar** Win32 functions that you might be familiar with.)

Here's an example that encodes and decodes characters using UTF-8:

```vb
Imports System
Imports System.Text

Class App
    Shared Sub Main()
        ' This is the string I'm going to encode.
        Dim s As String = "Hi there."

        ' Obtain an Encoding-derived object that knows how
        ' to encode/decode using UTF-8.
        Dim encodingUTF8 As Encoding = System.Text.Encoding.UTF8

        ' Encode a string into an array of bytes.
        Dim encodedBytes() As Byte = encodingUTF8.GetBytes(s)

        ' Show the encoded byte values.
        Console.WriteLine("Encoded bytes: " & _
            BitConverter.ToString(encodedBytes))

        ' Decode the byte array back to a string.
        Dim decodedString As String = encodingUTF8.GetString(encodedBytes)

        ' Show the decoded string.
        Console.WriteLine("Decoded string: " + decodedString)
    End Sub
End Class
```

This code yields the following output:

```
Encoded bytes: 48-69-20-74-68-65-72-65-2E
Decoded string: Hi there.
```

In addition to the **UTF8** shared property, the **Encoding** class also offers the following shared properties: **Unicode**, **BigEndianUnicode**, **UTF7**, **ASCII**, and **Default**. The **Default** property returns an object that knows how to encode/decode using the user's code page as specified using the Regional And Language Options Control Panel applet in Windows. (See the **GetACP** Win32 function for more information.) However, using the **Default** property is discouraged.

In addition to these properties, **Encoding** also offers a shared **GetEncoding** method that allows you to specify a code page (by integer or by string) and returns an object that can encode/decode using the specified code page. You can call **GetEncoding** passing "Shift-JIS" or 932, for example.

When you first request an encoding object, the **Encoding** class's property or **GetEncoding** method constructs a single object for the requested encoding and returns this object. If an already requested encoding object is requested in the future, the encoding class simply returns the object it previously constructed; it doesn't construct a new object for each request. This efficiency reduces the number of objects in the system and puts less pressure in the garbage-collected heap.

Instead of calling one of **Encoding**'s shared properties or its **GetEncoding** method, you could also construct an instance of one of the following classes: **System.Text.UnicodeEncoding**, **System.Text.UTF8Encoding**, **System.Text.UTF7Encoding**, or **System.Text.ASCIIEncoding**. However, keep in mind that constructing any of these classes creates new objects in the managed heap, which hurts performance.

Three of these classes, **UnicodeEncoding**, **UTF8Encoding**, and **UTF7-Encoding**, offer multiple constructors allowing you more control over the encoding and byte order marks (BOMs). You might want to explicitly construct instances of these encoding types when working with a **BinaryWriter** or a **StreamWriter**. The **ASCIIEncoding** class has only a single constructor and therefore doesn't offer any more control over the encoding. If you need an **ASCIIEncoding** object, always obtain it by querying **Encoding**'s **ASCII** property; never construct an instance of the **ASCIIEncoding** class yourself.

Once you have an **Encoding**-derived object, you can convert an array of characters to an array of bytes by calling the **GetBytes** method. (Several overloads of this method exist.) To convert an array of bytes to an array of characters, call the **GetChars** method or the more useful **GetString** method. (Several overloads exist for both these methods.) The preceding code demonstrated calls to the `GetBytes` and `GetString` methods.

Although not that useful, all `Encoding`-derived types offer a `GetByteCount` method that obtains the number of bytes necessary to encode a set of characters without actually encoding. You could use this method to allocate an array of bytes. There's also a `GetCharCount` method that returns the number of characters that would be decoded without actually decoding. These methods are useful if you're trying to save memory and reuse an array.

The `GetByteCount`/`GetCharCount` methods aren't that fast because they must analyze the array of characters/bytes in order to return an accurate result. If you prefer speed to an exact result, you can call the `GetMaxByteCount` or `Get-MaxCharCount` method instead. Both methods take an integer specifying the number of characters or number of bytes and return a worst-case value.

Each `Encoding`-derived object offers a set of public read-only properties that you can query to obtain detailed information about the encoding. Table 12-8 briefly describes these properties.

Table 12-8   Properties of `Encoding`-Derived Classes

Property	Type	Description
EncodingName	String	Returns the encoding's human-readable name.
CodePage	Int32	Returns the encoding's code page.
WindowsCodePage	Int32	Returns the encoding's closest Windows code page.
WebName	String	Returns the IANA-registered name. (IANA stands for Internet Assigned Numbers Authority.) For more information, go to *http://www.iana.org*.
HeaderName	String	Returns mail agent header tag.
BodyName	String	Returns mail agent body tag.
IsBrowserDisplay	Boolean	Returns **True** if browser clients can use encoding for display purposes.
IsBrowserSave	Boolean	Returns **True** if browser clients can use encoding for saving purposes.
IsMailNewsDisplay	Boolean	Returns **True** if mail and news clients can use encoding for display purposes.
IsMailNewsSave	Boolean	Returns **True** if mail and news clients can use encoding for saving purposes.

To illustrate the properties and their meanings, I wrote the following program that displays these properties for several different encodings:

```vb
Imports System
Imports System.Text
Imports Microsoft.VisualBasic

Class App
   Shared Sub Main()
      Try
         Show(Encoding.Unicode)
         Show(Encoding.BigEndianUnicode)
         Show(Encoding.UTF8)
         Show(Encoding.UTF7)
         Show(Encoding.ASCII)
         Show(Encoding.Default)
         Show(Encoding.GetEncoding(0))      ' Same as Default
         Console.WriteLine()
         Console.WriteLine("Below are some specific code pages:")
         Show(Encoding.GetEncoding(437))
         Show(Encoding.GetEncoding(28595))
         Show(Encoding.GetEncoding(57008))
         Show(Encoding.GetEncoding(54936))
         Show(Encoding.GetEncoding(874))
      Catch e As ArgumentException
         Console.WriteLine(e.Message)
         Console.WriteLine( _
            "Use the Regional and Language Options Control Panel applet " & _
            "to install support for this code page.")
         Console.WriteLine( _
            "Specifically, you may need to select the Languages tab and " & _
            "turn on one or both of the following:")
         Console.WriteLine("   Install files for complex script and " & _
            "right-to-left languages")
         Console.WriteLine("   Install files for East Asian languages")
      End Try
   End Sub

   Shared Sub Show(ByVal e As Encoding)
      Console.WriteLine( _
         "{2}{1}" & _
         "{0}CodePage={3}, WindowsCodePage={4}{1}" & _
         "{0}WebName={5}, HeaderName={6}, BodyName={7}{1}" & _
         "{0}IsBrowserDisplay={8}, IsBrowserSave={9}{1}" & _
         "{0}IsMailNewsDisplay={10}, IsMailNewsSave={11}{1}", _
```

```
            ControlChars.Tab, Environment.NewLine, _
            e.EncodingName, _
            e.CodePage, e.WindowsCodePage, _
            e.WebName, e.HeaderName, e.BodyName, _
            e.IsBrowserDisplay, e.IsBrowserSave, _
            e.IsMailNewsDisplay, e.IsMailNewsSave)
    End Sub
End Class
```

Running this program yields the following output:

```
Unicode
    CodePage=1200, WindowsCodePage=1200
    WebName=utf-16, HeaderName=utf-16, BodyName=utf-16
    IsBrowserDisplay=False, IsBrowserSave=True
    IsMailNewsDisplay=False, IsMailNewsSave=False

Unicode (Big-Endian)
    CodePage=1201, WindowsCodePage=1200
    WebName=unicodeFFFE, HeaderName=unicodeFFFE, BodyName=unicodeFFFE
    IsBrowserDisplay=False, IsBrowserSave=False
    IsMailNewsDisplay=False, IsMailNewsSave=False

Unicode (UTF-8)
    CodePage=65001, WindowsCodePage=1200
    WebName=utf-8, HeaderName=utf-8, BodyName=utf-8
    IsBrowserDisplay=True, IsBrowserSave=True
    IsMailNewsDisplay=True, IsMailNewsSave=True

Unicode (UTF-7)
    CodePage=65000, WindowsCodePage=1200
    WebName=utf-7, HeaderName=utf-7, BodyName=utf-7
    IsBrowserDisplay=False, IsBrowserSave=False
    IsMailNewsDisplay=True, IsMailNewsSave=True

US-ASCII
    CodePage=20127, WindowsCodePage=1252
    WebName=us-ascii, HeaderName=us-ascii, BodyName=us-ascii
    IsBrowserDisplay=False, IsBrowserSave=False
    IsMailNewsDisplay=True, IsMailNewsSave=True

Western European (Windows)
    CodePage=1252, WindowsCodePage=1252
    WebName=Windows-1252, HeaderName=Windows-1252, BodyName=iso-8859-1
    IsBrowserDisplay=True, IsBrowserSave=True
    IsMailNewsDisplay=True, IsMailNewsSave=True
```

(continued)

```
Western European (Windows)
    CodePage=1252, WindowsCodePage=1252
    WebName=Windows-1252, HeaderName=Windows-1252, BodyName=iso-8859-1
    IsBrowserDisplay=True, IsBrowserSave=True
    IsMailNewsDisplay=True, IsMailNewsSave=True


Below are some specific code pages:
OEM United States
    CodePage=437, WindowsCodePage=1252
    WebName=IBM437, HeaderName=IBM437, BodyName=IBM437
    IsBrowserDisplay=False, IsBrowserSave=False
    IsMailNewsDisplay=False, IsMailNewsSave=False

Cyrillic (ISO)
    CodePage=28595, WindowsCodePage=1251
    WebName=iso-8859-5, HeaderName=iso-8859-5, BodyName=iso-8859-5
    IsBrowserDisplay=True, IsBrowserSave=True
    IsMailNewsDisplay=True, IsMailNewsSave=True

ISCII Kannada
    CodePage=57008, WindowsCodePage=57008
    WebName=x-iscii-ka, HeaderName=x-iscii-ka, BodyName=x-iscii-ka
    IsBrowserDisplay=False, IsBrowserSave=False
    IsMailNewsDisplay=False, IsMailNewsSave=False

Chinese Simplified (GB18030)
    CodePage=54936, WindowsCodePage=936
    WebName=GB18030, HeaderName=GB18030, BodyName=GB18030
    IsBrowserDisplay=True, IsBrowserSave=True
    IsMailNewsDisplay=True, IsMailNewsSave=True

Thai (Windows)
    CodePage=874, WindowsCodePage=874
    WebName=windows-874, HeaderName=windows-874, BodyName=windows-874
    IsBrowserDisplay=True, IsBrowserSave=True
    IsMailNewsDisplay=True, IsMailNewsSave=True
```

Table 12-9 completes the discussion of the methods offered by all **Encoding**-derived classes.

Table 12-9 **Methods of the** Encoding-**Derived Classes**

Method	Description
GetPreamble	Returns an array of bytes indicating what should be written to a stream before writing any encoded bytes. Frequently, these bytes are referred to as the byte order mark (BOM) byte. When you start reading from a stream, the BOM bytes automatically help detect what encoding was used when the stream was written so that the correct decoder can be used. For most **Encoding**-derived classes, this method returns an array of 0 bytes—that is, no preamble bytes. A **UTF8Encoding** object can be explicitly constructed so that this method returns a 3-byte array of &HEF, &HBB, &HBF. A **UnicodeEncoding** object can be explicitly constructed so that this method returns a 2-byte array of &HFE, &HFF for big endian encoding or a 2-byte array of &HFF, &HFE for little endian encoding.
Convert	Converts an array of bytes specified in a source encoding to an array of bytes specified by a destination encoding. Internally, this shared method calls the source encoding object's **GetChars** method and passes the result to the destination encoding object's **GetBytes** method. The resulting byte array is returned to the caller.
Equals	Returns **True** if two **Encoding**-derived objects represent the same code page and preamble setting.
GetHashCode	Returns the encoding object's code page.

Encoding/Decoding Streams of Characters and Bytes

Imagine that you're reading a UTF-16 encoded string via a **System.Net.Sockets.NetworkStream** object. The bytes will very likely stream in as chunks of data. In other words, you might first read 5 bytes from the stream, followed by 7 bytes. In UTF-16, each character consists of 2 bytes. So calling **Encoding**'s **GetString** method passing the first array of 5 bytes will return a string consisting of just two characters. If you later call **GetString** passing in the next 7 bytes that come in from the stream, **GetString** will return a string consisting of three characters and all the code points will have the wrong values!

This data corruption problem occurs because none of the **Encoding**-derived classes maintain any state in between calls to their methods. If you'll be encoding or decoding characters/bytes in chunks, you must do some additional work so that state is maintained between calls, preventing any loss of data.

To decode chunks of bytes, you should obtain a reference to an `Encoding`-derived object (as described in the previous section) and call its `GetDecoder` method. This method returns a reference to a newly constructed object whose type is derived from the `System.Text.Decoder` class. Like the `Encoding` class, the `Decoder` class is an abstract base class. If you look in the .NET Framework SDK documentation, you won't find any classes that represent concrete implementations of the `Decoder` class. However, the FCL does define a bunch of `Decoder`-derived classes, such as `UTF8Decoder`. These classes are all internal to the FCL, but the `GetDecoder` method can construct instances of these classes and return them to your application code.

All `Decoder`-derived classes offer two methods: `GetChars` and `GetChar-Count`. Obviously, these methods are used for decoding and work similarly to `Encoding`'s `GetChars` and `GetCharCount` methods, discussed earlier. When you call one of these methods, it decodes the byte array as much as possible. If the byte array doesn't contain enough bytes to complete a character, the leftover bytes are saved inside the decoder object. The next time you call one of these methods, the decoder object uses the leftover bytes plus the new byte array passed to it—this ensures that the chunks of data are decoded properly. `Decoder` objects are very useful when reading bytes from a stream.

An `Encoding`-derived type can be used for stateless encoding and decoding. However, a `Decoder`-derived type can be used only for decoding. If you want to encode strings in chunks, call `GetEncoder` instead of calling the `Encoding` object's `GetDecoder` method. `GetEncoder` returns a newly constructed object whose type is derived from the `System.Text.Encoder` class, which is also an abstract base class. Again, the .NET Framework SDK documentation doesn't contain any classes representing concrete implementations of the `Encoder` class. However, the FCL does define some `Encoder`-derived classes, such as `UTF8Encoder`. As with the `Decoder`-derived classes, these classes are all internal to the FCL, but the `GetEncoder` method can construct instances of these classes and return them to your application code.

All `Encoder`-derived classes offer two methods: `GetBytes` and `GetByte-Count`. On each call, the `Encoder`-derived object maintains any leftover state information so that you can encode data in chunks.

Base-64 String Encoding and Decoding

Today, the UTF-16 and UTF-8 encodings are becoming quite popular. Also gaining in popularity is the ability to encode a sequence of bytes to a base-64 string. The FCL does offer methods to do base-64 encoding and decoding, and you might expect that this would be accomplished via an **Encoding**-derived type. However, for some reason, base-64 encoding and decoding is done using some shared methods offered by the **System.Convert** type.

To encode a base-64 string as an array of bytes, you call **Convert**'s shared **FromBase64String** or **FromBase64CharArray** method. Likewise, to decode an array of bytes as a base-64 string, you call **Convert**'s shared **ToBase64String** or **ToBase64CharArray** method. The following code demonstrates how to use some of these methods:

```
Imports System

Class App
    Shared Sub Main()
        ' Get a set of 10 randomly generated bytes.
        Dim bytes(9) As Byte
        Dim rand As New Random()
        rand.NextBytes(bytes)

        ' Display the bytes.
        Console.WriteLine(BitConverter.ToString(bytes))

        ' Decode the bytes into a base-64 string, and show the string.
        Dim s As String = Convert.ToBase64String(bytes)
        Console.WriteLine(s)

        ' Encode the base-64 string back to bytes, and show the bytes.
        bytes = Convert.FromBase64String(s)
        Console.WriteLine(BitConverter.ToString(bytes))
    End Sub
End Class
```

Compiling this code and running the executable produces the following output. (Your output might vary from mine because of the randomly generated bytes.)

```
34-24-99-7A-66-BF-D1-5F-41-1C
NCSZema/0V9BHA==
34-24-99-7A-66-BF-D1-5F-41-1C
```

13

Enumerated Types and Bit Flags

In this chapter, I'll discuss enumerated types and bit flags. Since Windows has used these constructs for so many years, I'm sure that many of you are already familiar with how to use them. However, the common language runtime (CLR) and the .NET Framework Class Library (FCL) work together to make enumerated types and bit flags real object-oriented types that offer cool new features that I suspect most developers aren't familiar with. It's amazing to me how these new features, which are the focus of this chapter, make developing application code so much easier.

Enumerated Types

An enumerated type is a type that defines a set of symbolic names and value pairs. For example, the **Color** type shown here defines a set of symbols, with each symbol identifying a single color:

```
Enum Color
    Red         ' Assigned a value of 0
    Green       ' Assigned a value of 1
    Blue        ' Assigned a value of 2
    Orange      ' Assigned a value of 3
End Enum
```

Of course, programmers can always write a program using 0 to represent Red, 1 to represent Green, and so on. However, they shouldn't hard-code numbers into their code and should use an enumerated type instead, for at least two reasons:

- Enumerated types make the program much easier to write, read, and maintain. With enumerated types, the symbolic name is used throughout the code and the programmer doesn't have to mentally map that Red is 0 or that 0 means Red. Also, should a symbol's numeric value change, the code can simply be recompiled without requiring any changes to the source code. In addition, documentation tools and other utilities, such as a debugger, can show meaningful symbolic names to the programmer.

- Enumerated types are strongly typed. For example, the compiler will report an error if I attempt to pass `Color.Orange` as a value to a method requiring a `Fruit` enumerated type as a parameter.

In the CLR, enumerated types are more than just symbols that the compiler cares about. Enumerated types are treated as first-class citizens in the type system, which allows for very powerful operations that simply can't be done with enumerated types in other environments (such as in unmanaged C++, for example).

Every enumerated type inherits directly from `System.Enum`, which inherits from `System.ValueType`, which in turn inherits from `System.Object`. So, enumerated types are value types (described in Chapter 5) and can be represented in unboxed and boxed forms. However, unlike other value types, an enumerated type can't define any methods, properties, or events.

When an enumerated type is compiled, the Visual Basic compiler turns each symbol into a constant field of the type. For example, the compiler treats the `Color` enumeration shown earlier as if you had written code similar to the following:

```
Structure Color
    Inherits System.Enum

    Public Const Red    As Color = CType(0, Color)
    Public Const Green  As Color = CType(1, Color)
    Public Const Blue   As Color = CType(2, Color)
    Public Const Orange As Color = CType(3, Color)
End Structure
```

The Visual Basic compiler won't actually compile this code, but this example does give you an idea of what's happening internally. Basically, an enumerated type is just a structure that has a bunch of constant fields defined in it. The fields are emitted to the module's metadata and can be accessed via reflection. This means that you can get all the symbols and their values associated with an enumerated type at run time. It also means that you can convert a string symbol into its equivalent numeric value.

Important   Symbols defined by an enumerated type are constant values. This means that compilers convert code that references an enumerated type's symbol to a numeric value at compile time. Once this occurs, no reference to the enumerated type exists in metadata and the assembly that defines the enumerated type doesn't have to be available at run time. If you have code that references the enumerated type—rather than just having references to symbols defined by the type—the assembly that defines the enumerated type will be required at run time. Some versioning issues arise because enumerated type symbols are constants instead of read-only values. I explained these issues in Chapter 8.

To simplify these operations and make it so that you don't have to be familiar with reflection, the **System.Enum** base type offers several shared methods and instance methods that expose the special operations that can be performed on an instance of an enumerated type. I'll discuss some of these operations next.

For example, the **Enum** type has a shared method called **GetUnderlyingType**:

```
Shared Function GetUnderlyingType(ByVal enumType As Type) As Type
```

This method returns the core type used to hold an enumerated type's value. Every enumerated type has an underlying type, which can be **Byte**, **SByte**, **Int16**, **UInt16**, **Int32** (the most common and what Visual Basic chooses by default), **UInt32**, **Int64**, or **UInt64**. However, the Visual Basic compiler requires that you specify a primitive type when you define an **Enum** type, so you must use **Byte**, **Short**, **Integer** (the default), or **Long**; using a base class type (like **Int32**) generates an error. The following code shows how to declare an enumerated type with an underlying type of **Byte** (**System.Byte**) by using Visual Basic:

```
Enum Color As Byte
    Red
    Green
    Blue
    Orange
End Enum
```

With the **Color** enumerated type defined in this way, the following code shows what **GetUnderlyingType** will return:

```
' The following line displays "System.Byte".
' (Note that you must enclose Enum between square brackets
'  because it is a reserved keyword in Visual Basic.)
Console.WriteLine([Enum].GetUnderlyingType(GetType(Color)))
```

Given an instance of an enumerated type, it's possible to map that value to one of four string representations by using the **System.Enum.ToString** method:

```
Dim c As Color = Color.Blue
Console.WriteLine(c.ToString())      ' "Blue" (General format)
Console.WriteLine(c.ToString("G"))   ' "Blue" (General format)
Console.WriteLine(c.ToString("D"))   ' "2"    (Decimal format)
Console.WriteLine(c.ToString("X"))   ' "02"   (heX format)
```

Internally, the **ToString** method calls **System.Enum**'s shared **Format** method:

```
Public Shared Function Format(ByVal enumType As Type, _
   ByVal value As Object, ByVal strFormat As String)
```

Generally, I prefer to call the **ToString** method because it requires less code and it's easier to call. But using **Format** has one advantage over **ToString**. **Format** lets you pass a numeric value for the value parameter; you don't have to have an instance of the enumerated type. For example, the following code will display "Blue":

```
' The following line displays "Blue".
Console.WriteLine([Enum].Format(GetType(Color), CByte(2), "G"))
```

> **Note**   It's possible to declare an enumerated type that has multiple symbols all with the same numeric value. When converting a numeric value to a symbol, **Enum**'s methods return one of the symbols. However, there's no guarantee as to which symbol name is returned. Also, if no symbol is defined for the numeric value you're looking up, a string containing the numeric value is returned.

It's also possible to create an array that contains one element for each symbolic name in an enumerated type. You use **System.Enum**'s shared **GetValues** method:

```
Public Shared Function GetValues(ByVal enumType As Type) As Array
```

Using this method along with the **ToString** method, you can display all of an enumerated type's symbolic and numeric values, like so:

```
Dim colors() As Color = DirectCast([Enum].GetValues(GetType(Color)), Color())
Console.WriteLine("Number of symbols defined: {0}", colors.Length)
Console.WriteLine("Value{0}Symbol{1}-----{0}------", _
   ControlChars.Tab, Environment.NewLine)
Dim c As Color
For Each c In colors
```

```
' Display each symbol in Decimal and General format.
Console.WriteLine("{0,5:D}{1}{0:G}", c, ControlChars.Tab)
```

The previous code produces the following output:

```
Number of symbols defined: 4
Value    Symbol
-----    ------
    0    Red
    1    Green
    2    Blue
    3    Orange
```

This discussion shows some of the cool operations that can be performed on enumerated types. I suspect the **ToString** method with the general format will be used quite frequently to show symbolic names in a program's user interface, as long as the strings don't need to be localized (since enumerated types offer no support for localization). In addition to the **GetValues** method, the **Enum** type also offers the following two shared methods that return an enumerated type's symbols:

```
' Returns a String representation for the numeric value
Public Shared Function GetName(ByVal enumType As Type, _
   ByVal value As Object) As String


' Returns an array of Strings: one per symbol defined in the enum
Public Shared Function GetNames(ByVal enumType As Type) As String()
```

I've discussed a lot of methods that you can use to look up an enumerated type's symbol. But you also need a method that can look up a symbol's equivalent value, an operation that could be used to convert a symbol that a user enters into a text box, for example. Converting a symbol to an instance of an enumerated type is easily accomplished using **Enum**'s shared **Parse** method:

```
Public Shared Function Parse(ByVal enumType As Type, _
   ByVal value As String, ByVal ignoreCase As Boolean) As Object
```

Here's some code demonstrating how to use this method:

```
' Because Orange is defined as 3, 'c' is initialized to 3.
Dim c As Color = CType([Enum].Parse(GetType(Color), "orange", True), Color)

' Because Brown isn't defined, an ArgumentException is thrown.
c = CType([Enum].Parse(GetType(Color), "Brown", False), Color)

' Creates an instance of the Color enum with a value of 1
c = CType([Enum].Parse(GetType(Color), "1", False), Color)

' Creates an instance of the Color enum with a value of 23
c = CType([Enum].Parse(GetType(Color), "23", False), Color)
```

Finally, using **Enum**'s shared **IsDefined** method, you can determine whether a numeric value is legal for an enumerated type:

```
' Displays "True" because Color defines Green as 1
Console.WriteLine([Enum].IsDefined(GetType(Color), 1))

' Displays "True" because Color defines Red as 0
Console.WriteLine([Enum].IsDefined(GetType(Color), "Red"))

' Displays "False" because a case-sensitive check is performed
Console.WriteLine([Enum].IsDefined(GetType(Color), "red"))

' Displays "False" because Color doesn't have a symbol of value 10
Console.WriteLine([Enum].IsDefined(GetType(Color), 10))
```

The **IsDefined** method is frequently used to do parameter validation. Here's an example:

```
Public Sub SetColor(ByVal c As Color)
   If Not [Enum].IsDefined(GetType(Color), c) Then
      Throw New ArgumentOutOfRangeException("c", "Not a valid Color")
   End If
   ⋮
End Sub
```

The parameter validation is useful because someone could call **SetColor** like this:

```
SetColor(CType(547, Color))
```

Because no symbol has a corresponding value of 547, the **SetColor** method will throw an **ArgumentOutOfRangeException** exception, indicating which parameter was invalid and why.

Finally, the **System.Enum** type offers a set of shared **ToObject** methods that convert an instance of a **Byte**, **SByte**, **Int16**, **UInt16**, **Int32**, **UInt32**, **Int64**, or **UInt64** to an instance of an enumerated type.

Enumerated types are always used in conjunction with some other type. Typically, they're used for the type's method parameters, properties, and fields. A common question that arises is whether to define the enumerated type nested within the type that requires it or whether to define the enumerated type at the same level as the type that requires it. If you examine the FCL, you'll see that an enumerated type is usually defined at the same level as the class that requires it. The reason is simply to make the developer's life a little easier by reducing the amount of typing required. So, you should define your enumerated type at the same level unless you're concerned about name conflicts.

Bit Flags

Programmers frequently work with sets of bit flags. When you call the **System.IO.File** type's **GetAttributes** method, it returns an instance of a **FileAttributes** type. A **FileAttributes** type is an instance of an **Int32**-based enumerated type, where each bit reflects a single attribute of the file. The **FileAttributes** type is defined in the FCL as follows:

```
<Flags, Serializable> _
Public Enum FileAttributes
    [ReadOnly]          = &H0001    ' ReadOnly is a reserved keyword.
    Hidden              = &H0002
    System              = &H0004
    Directory           = &H0010
    Archive             = &H0020
    Device              = &H0040
    Normal              = &H0080
    Temporary           = &H0100
    SparseFile          = &H0200
    ReparsePoint        = &H0400
    Compressed          = &H0800
    Offline             = &H1000
    NotContentIndexed   = &H2000
    Encrypted           = &H4000
End Enum
```

To determine whether a file is hidden, you would execute code like this:

```
' This code assumes that you have used the following Imports statement:
'     Imports System.IO
Dim filename As String = "C:\Boot.ini"
Dim attributes As FileAttributes = File.GetAttributes(filename)
Console.WriteLine("Is {0} hidden? {1}", filename, _
    (attributes And FileAttributes.Hidden) <> 0)
```

And here's code demonstrating how to change a file's attributes to read-only and hidden:

```
File.SetAttributes("C:\Boot.ini", _
    FileAttributes.ReadOnly Or FileAttributes.Hidden)
```

As the **FileAttributes** type shows, it's common to use enumerated types to express the set of bit flags that can be combined. However, although enumerated types and bit flags are similar, they don't have exactly the same semantics. For example, enumerated types represent single numeric values, and bit flags represent a set of flags, some of which are on and some of which are off.

When defining an enumerated type that is to be used to identify bit flags, you should, of course, explicitly assign to each of the symbols numeric values that map to individual bits. It's also highly recommended that you apply the **System.FlagsAttribute** custom attribute type to the enumerated type, as shown here:

```
' The Visual Basic compiler allows either "Flags" or "FlagsAttribute".
<Flags> _
Enum Actions
    ' Bit-coded enums are usually initialized
    ' by using hex notation.
    Read   = &H0001
    Write  = &H0002
    Delete = &H0004
    Query  = &H0008
    Sync   = &H0010
End Enum
```

Because **Actions** is an enumerated type, you can use all the methods described in the previous section when working with bit flag enumerated types. However, it would be nice if some of those functions behaved a little differently. For example, let's say you had the following code:

```
Dim actions As Actions = actions.Read Or actions.Write ' &H0003
Console.WriteLine(actions.ToString)                    ' "Read, Write"
```

When **ToString** is called, it attempts to translate the numeric value into its symbolic equivalent. The numeric value is &H0003, which has no symbolic equivalent. However, the **ToString** method detects the existence of the **Flags** attribute on the **Actions** type, and **ToString** now treats the numeric value not as a single value but as a set of bit flags. Because the &H0001 and &H0002 bits are set, **ToString** generates the following string: "Read, Write". If you remove the **Flags** attribute from the **Actions** type, **ToString** would produce the following string: "3".

I discussed the **ToString** method in the previous section, and I showed that it offered three ways to format the output: "G" (general), "D" (decimal), and "X" (hex). When you're formatting an instance of an enumerated type by using the general format, the type is first checked to see whether the **Flags** attribute is applied to it. If this attribute is not applied, a symbol matching the numeric value is looked up and returned. If the **Flags** attribute is applied, a symbol matching each 1 bit is looked up and concatenated to a string; each symbol is separated by a comma.

If you prefer, you could define the **Actions** type without the **Flags** attribute and still get the correct string by using the "F" format:

```
' <Flags> _     ' Commented out now
Enum Actions
   Read   = &H0001
   Write  = &H0002
   Delete = &H0004
   Query  = &H0008
   Sync   = &H0010
End Enum

Dim actions As Actions = actions.Read Or actions.Write ' &H0003
Console.WriteLine(actions.ToString("F"))                ' "Read, Write"
```

As I mentioned in the previous section, the **ToString** method actually calls **System.Enum**'s shared **Format** method internally. This means that you can use the "F" format when calling the shared **Format** method. If the numeric value contains 1 bit with no matching symbols, the returned string will contain just a decimal number and none of the symbols will appear in the string.

The symbols you define in your enumerated type don't have to be pure powers of 2. For example, the **Actions** type could define a symbol called **All** with a value of &H001F. If an instance of the **Actions** type has a value of &H001F, formatting the instance will produce a string that contains "All". The other symbol strings won't appear.

So far, I've discussed how to convert numeric values into a string of flags. It's also possible to convert a string of comma-delimited symbols into a numeric value by calling **Enum**'s shared **Parse** method. Here's some code demonstrating how to use this method:

```
' Because Query is defined as 8, 'a' is initialized to 8.
Dim a As Actions = CType([Enum].Parse(GetType(Actions), "Query", True), _
   Actions)

' Because Query and Read are defined, 'a' is initialized to 9.
a = CType([Enum].Parse(GetType(Actions), "Query,Read", False), Actions)

' Creates an instance of the Actions enum with a value of 28
a = CType([Enum].Parse(GetType(Actions), "28", False), Actions)
Console.WriteLine(a.ToString)  ' "Delete, Query, Sync"

' Creates an instance of the Actions enum with a value of 333
a = CType([Enum].Parse(GetType(Actions), "333", False), Actions)
Console.WriteLine(a.ToString)  ' "333"
```

Again, when **Parse** is called, it checks whether the **Flags** custom attribute has been applied to the enumerated type. If the attribute exists, **Parse** splits the string into individual symbols, looks up each symbol, and bitwise-ORs the corresponding numeric value into the resulting instance of the enumerated type. See Chapter 16 for more information about custom attributes.

The **Flags** attribute affects how **ToString**, **Format**, and **Parse** behave. Compilers are also encouraged to look for this attribute and ensure that the enumerated type is being manipulated as a set of bit flags. For example, a compiler could allow only bit operations on the bit flag enumerated type and disallow other arithmetic operations, such as multiplication and division. The Visual Basic compiler ignores the **Flags** attribute completely; anything you can do with an enumerated type you can do with a bit flag enumerated type.

When using a Visual Studio .NET form designer, you can use a property window to make various settings at design time. If some of these settings are enumerated types, the form designer checks whether the **Flags** attribute is applied to the type and displays the possible values accordingly.

14

Arrays

Arrays are mechanisms that allow you to treat several items as a single collection. The Microsoft .NET common language runtime (CLR) supports single-dimension arrays, multidimension arrays, and jagged arrays (that is, arrays of arrays). All array types are implicitly derived from **System.Array**, which itself is derived from **System.Object**. This means that arrays are always reference types that are allocated on the managed heap and that your application's variable contains a reference to the array and not the array itself. In Visual Basic, you declare array reference variables and create arrays using the **Dim** and **ReDim** statements. The following code makes this clearer:

```
Dim myIntegers() As Int32      ' Declares a reference to an array
ReDim myIntegers(99)           ' Creates an array of 100 integers

Dim myLongs(99) As Int64       ' Declares and creates an array of 100 Longs
```

On the first line, **myIntegers** is a variable that's capable of pointing to a single-dimension array of **Int32**s. Initially, **myIntegers** will be set to **Nothing** because I haven't allocated an array. The second line of code allocates an array of 100 **Int32** values; all the **Int32**s are initialized to 0. For backward compatibility with Visual Basic 6 (but unlike in other languages, such as C#), the argument you pass when you create an array is the highest index available, not the number of elements. So the arrays created in the preceding code contain 100 elements, numbered 0 through 99. Even though **Int32**s are value types, the memory block large enough to hold these values is allocated from the managed heap. The memory block contains 100 unboxed **Int32** values. The address of this memory block is returned and saved in the variable **myIntegers**.

In a difference from previous versions of the language, Visual Basic .NET makes a clear distinction between the **Dim** and **ReDim** keywords. **Dim** is used to declare an array, its type, and its rank (or number of dimensions); optionally, you can create the elements of the array by passing a numeric value between the brackets. **ReDim** can be used only to create the elements of the array or to change the number of elements in an array that was created previously. Because you can't change either the rank of the array (as you could in Visual Basic 6) or the type of its elements, you must omit the **As** clause in Visual Basic .NET.

You can also create arrays of reference types:

```
Dim myControls() As Control       ' Declares a reference to an array
ReDim myControls(49) As Control   ' Creates an array of 50 Control
                                  ' references
```

On the first line, **myControls** is a variable capable of pointing to a single-dimension array of **Control** *references*. Initially, **myControls** will be set to **Nothing** because I haven't allocated an array. The second line allocates an array of 50 **Control** references; all of these references are initialized to **Nothing**. Because **Control** is a reference type, creating the array creates only references; the actual objects aren't created at this time. The address of this memory block is returned and saved in the variable **myControls**.

Figure 14-1 shows how arrays of value types and arrays of reference types look in the managed heap.

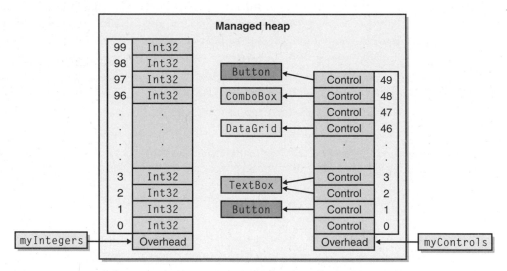

Figure 14-1   Arrays of value and reference types in the managed heap

In the figure, the **Controls** array shows the result after the following lines have executed:

```
myControls(1)  = New Button()
myControls(2)  = New TextBox()
myControls(3)  = myControls(2)    ' Two elements refer to the same object.
myControls(46) = New DataGrid()
myControls(48) = New ComboBox()
myControls(49) = New Button()
```

Common Language Specification (CLS) compliance requires that all arrays be zero-based. This allows a method written in Visual Basic to create an array and pass the array's reference to code written in another language, such as C#. In addition, because zero-based arrays are, by far, the most common arrays, Microsoft has spent a lot of time optimizing their performance. However, the CLR does support non-zero-based arrays even though their use is discouraged. For those of you who don't care about performance or cross-language portability, I'll demonstrate how to create and use non-zero-based arrays later in this chapter.

Notice in Figure 14-1 that each array has some additional overhead information associated with it. This information contains the rank of the array (number of dimensions), the lower bounds for each dimension of the array (almost always 0), and the length of each dimension. The overhead also contains the type of each element in the array. Shortly, I'll mention the methods that allow you to query this overhead information.

So far, I've shown examples demonstrating how to create single-dimension arrays. When possible, you should stick with single-dimension, zero-based arrays, sometimes referred to as *SZ arrays*, or *vectors*. Vectors give the best performance because you can use specific IL instructions—such as **newarr**, **ldelem**, **ldelema**, **ldlen**, and **stelem**—to manipulate them. However, if you prefer to work with multidimension arrays, you can. Here are some examples of multidimension arrays:

```
' Declare and create a two-dimension array of Doubles.
Dim myDoubles(9, 19) As Double


' Create a three-dimension array of Strings.
Dim myStrings(4, 2, 9) As String
```

Like previous versions of Visual Basic, Visual Basic .NET supports the **ReDim Preserve** statement for changing the number of elements in an array without clearing its current contents. If the array has more than one dimension, you can change only the rightmost dimension:

```
' (Continuing the previous example)
ReDim Preserve myStrings(4, 2, 99) As String


' The following statement throws a System.ArrayTypeMismatchException.
ReDim Preserve myStrings(4, 22, 9) As String
```

The CLR also supports jagged arrays. Zero-based, single-dimension jagged arrays have the same performance as normal vectors. However, accessing the elements of a jagged array means that two or more array accesses must occur. Note that jagged arrays are not CLS-compliant—because the CLS doesn't allow a `System.Array` object to be an element of an array—and can't be passed between code written in different programming languages. Fortunately, Visual Basic supports jagged arrays. Here are some examples of how to create an array of polygons, where each polygon consists of an array of `Point` instances:

```
' Create a one-dimension array of Point arrays.
Dim myPolygons(2)() As Point
' myPolygons(0) refers to an array of 10 Point instances.
ReDim myPolygons(0)(9)

' myPolygons(1) refers to an array of 20 Point instances.
ReDim myPolygons(1)(19)

' myPolygons(2) refers to an array of 30 Point instances.
ReDim myPolygons(2)(29)

' Display the Points in the second polygon.
Dim x As Int32
For x = 0 To myPolygons(1).Length - 1
    Console.WriteLine(myPolygons(1)(x))
Next
```

Note   The CLR verifies that an index into an array is valid. In other words, you can't create an array with 100 elements in it (numbered 0 through 99) and then try to access the element at index 100 or -5. Doing so will cause a `System.IndexOutOfRangeException` exception to be thrown. Allowing access to memory outside the range of an array would be a breach of type safety and a potential security hole, and the CLR doesn't allow verifiable code to do this. Usually, the performance associated with index checking is insubstantial because the JIT (just-in-time) compiler normally checks array bounds once before a loop executes instead of at each loop iteration. Some languages, like C#, support the ability to use unsafe techniques to access an array without bounds checking. The "Fast Array Access" section later in this chapter demonstrates how to do this. Unfortunately, Visual Basic doesn't support unsafe techniques, so there's no way to stop the CLR from performing array bounds checking.

All Arrays Are Implicitly Derived from `System.Array`

The `System.Array` type offers several static and instance members. Because all arrays are implicitly derived from `System.Array`, these members can be used to manipulate arrays of value types or reference types. Also note that **Array** implements several interfaces: `ICloneable`, `IEnumerable`, `ICollection`, and `IList`. These interfaces allow you to use arrays conveniently in many different scenarios.

Table 14-1 summarizes the methods offered by `System.Array` and the interfaces that it implements.

Table 14-1 **Members of** `System.Array`

Member	Member Type	Description
`Rank`	Read-only instance property	Returns the number of dimensions in the array.
`GetLength`	Instance method	Returns the number of elements in the specified dimension of the array.
`Length`	Read-only instance property	Returns the total number of elements in the array.
`GetLowerBound`	Instance method	Returns the lower bound of the specified dimension. This is almost always 0.
`GetUpperBound`	Instance method	Returns the upper bound of the specified dimension. This is almost always the number of elements in the dimension minus 1.
`IsReadOnly`	Read-only instance property	Indicates whether the array is read-only. For arrays, this is always **False**.
`IsSynchronized`	Read-only instance property	Indicates whether the array access is thread-safe. For arrays, this is always **False**.
`SyncRoot`	Read-only instance property	Retrieves an object that can be used to synchronize access to the array. For arrays, this is always a reference to the array itself.
`IsFixedSize`	Read-only instance property	Indicates whether the array is a fixed size. For arrays, this is always **True**.
`GetValue`	Instance method	Returns a reference to the element located at the specified position in the array. If the array contains value types, the return value refers to a boxed copy of the element. This rarely used method is required when you don't know at design time the number of dimensions in an array or when the lower bound of a single-dimension array is not zero.

(continued)

Table 14-1   Members of `System.Array`   *(continued)*

Member	Member Type	Description
`SetValue`	Instance method	Sets the element located at the specified position in the array. This rarely used method is required when you don't know at design time the number of dimensions in an array or when the lower bound of a single-dimension array is not zero.
`GetEnumerator`	Instance method	Returns an **IEnumerator** for the array. This allows using Visual Basic's **For Each…Next** statement (or an equivalent in another language). For multidimension arrays, the enumerator iterates through all the elements, with the rightmost dimension changing the fastest. *Note*: In Visual Basic 6, using the **For Each…Next** statement on a multidimension array iterates through all the elements, with the leftmost dimension changing the fastest, so you might need to revise your legacy code before porting it to Visual Basic .NET.
`Sort`	Static method	Sorts the elements in one array, in two arrays, or in a section of an array. The array element type must implement the **IComparer** interface or must pass an object whose type implements the **IComparer** interface.
`BinarySearch`	Static method	Searches the specified array for the specified element using a binary search algorithm. This method assumes that the array's elements are sorted. The array element type must implement the **IComparer** interface. You usually use the **Sort** method before calling **BinarySearch**.
`IndexOf`	Static method	Returns the offset of the first occurrence of a value in a one-dimension array or in a portion of it. The offset is from the array's lower bound. If the search fails, lower bound minus 1 is returned.
`LastIndexOf`	Static method	Returns the offset of the last occurrence of a value in a one-dimension array or in a portion of it. The offset is from the array's lower bound. If the search fails, lower bound minus 1 is returned.
`Reverse`	Static method	Reverses the order of the elements in the specified one-dimension array or in a portion of it.
`Clone`	Instance method	Creates a new array that's a shallow copy of the source array.
`CopyTo`	Instance method	Copies elements from one array to another array.
`Copy`	Static method	Copies a section of one array to another array, performing any appropriate casting required.

(continued)

Table 14-1 **Members of** `System.Array`   *(continued)*

Member	Member Type	Description
`Clear`	Static method	Sets a range of elements in the array to 0 or to a **Nothing** object reference.
`CreateInstance`	Static method	Creates an instance of an array. This rarely used method allows you to dynamically (at run time) define arrays of any type, rank, and bounds.
`Initialize`	Instance method	Calls the default constructor for each element in an array of value types. This method does nothing if the elements in the array are reference types. Visual Basic doesn't allow you to define default constructors for value types, so this method has no use for arrays of Visual Basic structures. This method is primarily for compiler vendors.

Casting Arrays

For arrays with reference type elements, the CLR allows you to implicitly cast the source array's element type to a target type. For the cast to succeed, both array types must have the same number of dimensions, and an implicit or explicit conversion from the source element type to the target element type must exist. The CLR doesn't allow the casting of arrays with value type elements to any other type. (However, by using the **Array.Copy** method, you can create a new array that has the desired effect.) The following code demonstrates how array casting works:

```
' Create a two-dimension FileStream array.
Dim fs2dim(4, 9) As FileStream

' Implicit cast to a two-dimension Object array
Dim o2dim(,) As Object = fs2dim

' Can't cast from a two-dimension array to a one-dimension array
' Compiler error BC30332: Value of type() '2-dimensional array of
' 'System.Object() ' cannot be converted to '1-dimensional array
' of System.IO.Stream' because 'System.Object' is not derived
' from() 'System.IO.Stream() '.
Dim s1dim() As Stream = CType (o2dim, Stream())

' Explicit cast to a two-dimension Stream array
Dim s2dim(,) As Stream = CType(o2dim, Stream(,))
```

(continued)

```
' Explicit cast to a two-dimension Type array;
' compiles but throws InvalidCastException at run time
Dim t2dim(,) As Type = CType(o2dim, Type(,))

' Create a one-dimension Int32 array (value types).
Dim i1dim(4) As Int32

' Can't cast from an array of value types to anything else
' Compile error BC30333: Value of type() '1-dimensional array of
'    Integer' cannot be converted to '1-dimensional array of
'    (System.Object) ' because 'Integer' is not a reference type.
Dim o1dim() As Object = CType(i1dim, Object())

' Array.Copy creates a new array, coercing each element in the source
' array to the desired type in the destination array. The following
' code creates an array of references to boxed Int32s.
ReDim o1dim(i1dim.Length - 1)
Array.Copy(i1dim, o1dim, i1dim.Length)
```

The **Array.Copy** method isn't just a method that speedily copies elements from one array to another. The **Copy** method is also capable of converting each array element as it's copied if conversion is required. The **Copy** method is capable of performing the following conversions.

■ Boxing value type elements to reference type elements, such as when copying an **Int32** array to an **Object** array

■ Unboxing reference type elements to value type elements, such as when copying an **Object** array to an **Int32** array

■ Widening CLR primitive value types, such as when copying an **Int32** array to a **Double** array

Here's another example showing the usefulness of **Copy**:

```
' Define a value type that implements an interface.
Structure MyValueType
   Implements ICloneable
   ⋮
End Structure

Class App
   Shared Sub Main()
      ' Create an array of 100 value types.
      Dim src(99) As MyValueType

      ' Create an array of ICloneable references.
      Dim dest(src.Length - 1) As ICloneable
```

```
        ' Initialize an array of ICloneable elements to refer to boxed
        ' versions of elements in the source array.
        Array.Copy(src, dest, src.Length)
    End Sub
End Class
```

As you might imagine, the .NET Framework Class Library (FCL) takes advantage of **Array**'s **Copy** method quite frequently.

Passing and Returning Arrays

Arrays are always passed by reference to a method. Because the CLR doesn't support the notion of constant parameters, the method is able to modify the elements in the array. If you don't want to allow this, you must make a copy of the array and pass the copy into the method. Note that the **Array.Copy** method performs a shallow copy, and, therefore, if the array's elements are reference types, the new array refers to the already existing objects.

To obtain a deep copy, you might want to clone the individual elements, but this requires that each object's type implements the **ICloneable** interface. Alternatively, you could serialize each object to a **System.IO.MemoryStream** and then immediately deserialize the memory stream to construct a new object. Depending on the object's types, the performance of these operations can be prohibitive, and not all types are serializable either.

Similarly, some methods return a reference to an array. If the method constructs and initializes the array, returning a reference to the array is fine. But if the method wants to return a reference to an internal array maintained by a field, you must decide whether you want the method's caller to have direct access to this array. If you do, just return the array's reference. But most often you won't want the method's caller to have such access, so the method should construct a new array and call **Array.Copy**, returning a reference to the new array. Again, you might want to clone each of the objects before returning the array reference.

If you define a method that is to return a reference to an array and if that array has no elements in it, your method can return either **Nothing** or a reference to an array with zero elements in it. When you're implementing this kind of method, Microsoft strongly recommends that you implement the method by having it return a zero-length array because doing so simplifies the code that a developer calling the method must write. The Visual Basic way for defining a zero-length array isn't very intuitive, though:

```
' This is an array with zero elements.
Dim myArray(-1) As String
```

If the method returns a zero-length array when it has no elements to return, the method's caller can write code as though it's processing elements, but the code also works correctly when there are no elements to process. The following easy-to-understand code runs correctly even if there are no appointments to iterate over:

```
' This code is easier to write and understand.
Dim appointments() As Appointment = GetAppointmentsForToday()
Dim a As Int32
For a = 0 To appointments.Length - 1
    ⋮
Next
```

The following code also runs correctly if there are no appointments to iterate over. However, this code is slightly more difficult to write and understand:

```
' This code is harder to write and understand.
Dim appointments() As Appointment = GetAppointmentsForToday()
If Not (appointments Is Nothing) Then
    Dim a As Int32
    For a = 0 To appointments.Length - 1
        ⋮
    Next
End If
```

If you design your methods so that they return arrays with zero elements instead of `Nothing`, callers of your methods will have an easier time working with them. By the way, you should do the same for fields. If your type has a field that's a reference to an array, you should always have the field refer to an array even if the array has no elements in it. Allowing the field to be `Nothing` will just make your type harder to use.

Creating Arrays That Have a Nonzero Lower Bound

Earlier I mentioned that it's possible to create and work with arrays that have nonzero lower bounds. You can dynamically create your own arrays by calling `Array`'s static `CreateInstance` method. Several overloads of this method exist, but they all allow you to specify the type of the elements in the array, the number of dimensions in the array, the lower bounds of each dimension, and the number of elements in each dimension. `CreateInstance` allocates memory for the array, saves the parameter information in the overhead portion of the array's memory block, and returns a reference to the array. You can cast the reference returned from `CreateInstance` to a variable so that it's easier for you to access the elements in the array.

Here's some code that demonstrates how to dynamically create a two-dimension array of **System.Decimal** values. The first dimension represents calendar years and goes from 1995 to 2004 inclusive. The second dimension represents quarters and goes from 1 to 4 inclusive.

```
' I want a two-dimension array [1995..2004][1..4]. Visual Basic 6
' version: Dim quarterlyRevenue(1995 to 2005, 1 to 4) As Decimal
Dim lowerBounds() As Int32 = {1995, 1}
Dim lengths() As Int32 = {10, 4}
' Declare the array.
Dim quarterlyRevenue(,) As Decimal
' Create the array, and cast the result.
quarterlyRevenue = DirectCast(Array.CreateInstance( _
   GetType(Decimal), lengths, lowerBounds), Decimal(,))
```

The following code iterates over all the elements in the dynamic array. I could have hard-coded the array's bounds into the code, which would have given better performance, but I decided to use some of **System.Array**'s **GetLowerBound** and **GetUpperBound** methods for demonstration purposes.

```
Dim firstYear As Int32 = quarterlyRevenue.GetLowerBound(0)
Dim lastYear As Int32 = quarterlyRevenue.GetUpperBound(0)
Console.WriteLine("{0,4}  {1,9}  {2,9}  {3,9}  {4,9}", _
   "Year", "Q1", "Q2", "Q3", "Q4")

Dim year As Int32
For year = firstYear To lastYear
   Console.Write(year & "  ")

   Dim quarter As Int32
   For quarter = quarterlyRevenue.GetLowerBound(1) To _
     quarterlyRevenue.GetUpperBound(1)
     Console.Write("{0,9:C}  ", quarterlyRevenue(year, quarter))
   Next
   Console.WriteLine()
Next
```

> **Note**   For single-dimension, non-zero-based arrays, Visual Basic doesn't allow the convenient syntax shown earlier, where you just index into the array. Instead, your code would have to call **Array**'s **GetValue** method, passing in the desired index.

Fast Array Access

Each time an element of an array is accessed, the CLR ensures that the index is within the array's bounds. This prevents you from accessing memory that is outside of the array, which would potentially corrupt other objects. If an invalid index is used to access an array element, the CLR throws a **System.IndexOutOf-RangeException** exception.

As you might expect, the CLR's index checking comes at a performance cost. If you have confidence in your code and if you don't mind resorting to nonverifiable (unsafe) code, you can access an array without having the CLR perform its index checking. Because Visual Basic doesn't support unsafe code, I'll use C# to demonstrate this technique:

```
using System;

class App {
   unsafe static void Main() {

      // Construct an array consisting of five Int32 elements.
      Int32[] arr = new Int32[] { 1, 2, 3, 4, 5 };

      // Obtain a pointer to the array's 0th element.
      fixed (Int32* element = &arr[0]) {

         // Iterate through each element in the array.
         // NOTE: The following code has a bug!
         for (Int32 x = 0, n = arr.Length; x <= n; x++) {
            Console.WriteLine(element[x]);
         }
      }
   }
}
```

To compile this code, enter the following at the command line (assuming the source is contained in a file named UnsafeArrayAccess.cs):

```
csc.exe /unsafe UnsafeArrayAccess.cs
```

After you build this small application, running it produces the following results:

```
1
2
3
4
5
0
```

Although you'd expect only five values to appear, six values actually appear because of a bug in the source code. In the **for** loop, the test expression should be x < n, not x <= n. You must be very careful when using unsafe code!

By the way, if you use ILDasm.exe to examine the intermediate language (IL) for **Main**, you'll see the following, which I've commented:

```
.method private hidebysig static void  Main() cil managed
{
  .entrypoint
  // Code size       58 (0x3a)
  .maxstack  3
  .locals ([0] int32[] arr,
           [1] int32& pinned element,
           [2] int32 x,
           [3] int32 n)

  // Construct an array of five Int32 elements.
  IL_0000:  ldc.i4.5
  IL_0001:  newarr      [mscorlib]System.Int32

  // Initialize the array's elements with values stored in metadata.
  IL_0006:  dup
  IL_0007:  ldtoken     field valuetype
    '<PrivateImplementationDetails>'/'$$struct0x6000001-1'
    '<PrivateImplementationDetails>'::'$$method0x6000001-1'
  IL_000c:  call
    void [mscorlib]System.Runtime.CompilerServices.RuntimeHelpers::
      InitializeArray(class [mscorlib]System.Array,
      valuetype [mscorlib]System.RuntimeFieldHandle)

  // Save the reference to the array in the arr variable.
  IL_0011:  stloc.0

  // Get the address of arr's 0th element and save it in element.
  IL_0012:  ldloc.0
  IL_0013:  ldc.i4.0
  IL_0014:  ldelema     [mscorlib]System.Int32
  IL_0019:  stloc.1

  // Initialize x to 0.
  IL_001a:  ldc.i4.0
  IL_001b:  stloc.2

  // Initialize n to the length of arr.
  IL_001c:  ldloc.0
  IL_001d:  ldlen
  IL_001e:  conv.i4
  IL_001f:  stloc.3
```

(continued)

```
// Branch to the for loop's test.
IL_0020:  br.s        IL_0032

// Calculate element + (4 * x) -- 4 is the number of bytes in an Int32.
IL_0022:  ldloc.1
IL_0023:  conv.i
IL_0024:  ldc.i4.4
IL_0025:  ldloc.2
IL_0026:  mul
IL_0027:  add

// Pass the value at this address to Console.WriteLine.
IL_0028:  ldind.i4
IL_0029:  call        void [mscorlib]System.Console::WriteLine(int32)

// Add 1 to x.
IL_002e:  ldloc.2
IL_002f:  ldc.i4.1
IL_0030:  add
IL_0031:  stloc.2

// for loop test: loop again if x <= n.
IL_0032:  ldloc.2
IL_0033:  ldloc.3
IL_0034:  ble.s       IL_0022

// End of loop: Put null in element (for safety).
IL_0036:  ldc.i4.0
IL_0037:  conv.u
IL_0038:  stloc.1

// Return from Main.
IL_0039:  ret
} // end of method App::Main
```

For comparison, here's a version that doesn't use unsafe code:

```
using System;

class App {
   static void Main() {

      Int32[] arr = new Int32[] { 1, 2, 3, 4, 5 };

      for (Int32 x = 0, n = arr.Length; x <= n; x++) {
         Console.WriteLine(arr[x]);
      }
   }
}
```

If you build this and use ILDasm.exe to examine the IL code, you'll see the following:

```
.method private hidebysig static void  Main() cil managed
{
  .entrypoint
  // Code size       43 (0x2b)
  .maxstack  3
  .locals init ([0] int32[] arr,
           [1] int32 x,
           [2] int32 n)

  // Construct an array of five Int32 elements.
  IL_0000:  ldc.i4.5
  IL_0001:  newarr     [mscorlib]System.Int32

  // Initialize the array's elements with values stored in metadata.
  IL_0006:  dup
  IL_0007:  ldtoken    field valuetype
    '<PrivateImplementationDetails>'/'$$struct0x6000001-1'
    '<PrivateImplementationDetails>'::'$$method0x6000001-1'
  IL_000c:  call
    void [mscorlib]System.Runtime.CompilerServices.RuntimeHelpers::
      InitializeArray(class [mscorlib]System.Array,
      valuetype [mscorlib]System.RuntimeFieldHandle)
  // Save the reference to the array in the arr variable.
  IL_0011:  stloc.0

  // Initialize x to 0
  IL_0012:  ldc.i4.0
  IL_0013:  stloc.1

  // Initialize n to the length of arr.
  IL_0014:  ldloc.0
  IL_0015:  ldlen
  IL_0016:  conv.i4
  IL_0017:  stloc.2

  // Branch to the for loop's test.
  IL_0018:  br.s       IL_0026

  // Pass the element in arr[x] to Console.WriteLine.
  IL_001a:  ldloc.0
  IL_001b:  ldloc.1
  IL_001c:  ldelem.i4
  IL_001d:  call       void [mscorlib]System.Console::WriteLine(int32)
```

(continued)

```
    // Add 1 to x.
    IL_0022:  ldloc.1
    IL_0023:  ldc.i4.1
    IL_0024:  add
    IL_0025:  stloc.1

    // for loop test: loop again if x < n.
    IL_0026:  ldloc.1
    IL_0027:  ldloc.2
    IL_0028:  ble.s       IL_001a

    // Return from Main.
    IL_002a:  ret
} // End of method App::Main
```

It's true that there's less IL code in the type-safe version. However, it's the type-safe version's `ldelem` instruction that causes the CLR to do index checking. The unsafe version uses the `ldind.i4` instruction, which simply obtains a 4-byte value from a memory address. Note that this unsafe array manipulation technique is usable with arrays whose elements are **SByte**, **Byte**, **Int16**, **UInt16**, **Int32**, **UInt32**, **Int64**, **UInt64**, **Char**, **Single**, **Double**, **Decimal**, **Boolean**, an enumerated type, or a value type structure whose fields are any of the aforementioned types.

Redimensioning an Array

Array's static **CreateInstance** method allows you to dynamically construct an array when you don't know at compile time the types of elements that the array is to maintain. The method is also useful when you don't know at compile time how many dimensions the array is to have and the bounds of those dimensions. In the section "Creating Arrays That Have a Nonzero Lower Bound," I demonstrated how to dynamically construct an array by using arbitrary bounds. You can also use the **CreateInstance** method to redimension an arbitrary array, like so:

```
Class App
   Shared Sub Main()
      ' Construct an array of three elements.
      Dim arr() As Int32 = {1, 2, 3}

      ' Display all the elements in the array.
      Dim x As Int32
      For Each x In arr
         Console.Write(x & " ")
      Next
      Console.WriteLine()
```

```
        ' Redimension the array so that it contains five elements.
        arr = DirectCast(ResizeArray(arr, 5), Int32())

        ' Display all the elements in the array.
        For Each x In arr
            Console.Write(x & " ")
        Next
        Console.WriteLine()

        ' Redimension the array so that it now contains two elements.
        arr = DirectCast(ResizeArray(arr, 2), Int32())

        ' Display all the elements in the array.
        For Each x In arr
            Console.Write(x & " ")
        Next
        Console.WriteLine()
    End Sub

    Public Shared Function ResizeArray (ByVal origArray As Array, _
        ByVal desiredSize As Int32) As Array
        ' Determine the type of each element.
        Dim t As Type = origArray.GetType().GetElementType()

        ' Construct a new array with the desired number of elements.
        ' The array's type must match the original array's type.
        Dim newArray As Array = Array.CreateInstance(t, desiredSize)

        ' Copy the elements from the original array into the new array.
        Array.Copy(origArray, 0, newArray, 0, _
            Math.Min(origArray.Length, desiredSize))

        ' Return the new array.
        Return newArray
    End Function
End Class
```

If you build and run this application, you'll see the following output:

```
1 2 3
1 2 3 0 0
1 2
```

Like previous versions of the language, Visual Basic .NET supports the **ReDim Preserve** statement, which can extend or shrink an array. However, the **ReDim Preserve** statement can change only the right-most dimension in a multi-dimension array, so the approach based on the **Array.CreateInstance** method is more generic because it can be adapted to arrays of any dimension. The following code shows how to use the **ReDim Preserve** statement:

```
Class App
   Shared Sub Main()
      ' Construct an array of three elements.
      Dim arr() As Int32 = {1, 2, 3}

      ' Display all the elements in the array.
      Dim x As Int32
      For Each x In arr
         Console.Write(x & " ")
      Next
      Console.WriteLine()

      ' Redimension the array so that it contains five elements.
      ReDim Preserve arr(5)

      ' Display all the elements in the array.
      For Each x In arr
         Console.Write(x & " ")
      Next
      Console.WriteLine()

      ' Redimension the array so that it now contains two elements.
      ReDim Preserve arr(2)

      ' Display all the elements in the array.
      For Each x In arr
         Console.Write(x & " ")
      Next
      Console.WriteLine()
   End Sub
End Class
```

If you build this and use ILDasm.exe to examine the IL code generated by the Visual Basic compiler, you'd see that each **ReDim Preserve** statement causes a sequence of IL instructions to be generated. For example, the first **ReDim Preserve** statement in the previous code example produces the following IL (which I've commented):

```
// Load arr on the stack.
IL_0050:  ldloc.0

// Cast arr to System.Array.
IL_0051:  castclass  [mscorlib]System.Array
```

```
// Load the size of the desired array (six elements) on the stack.
IL_0056:  ldc.i4.6

// Construct a new array of Int32s.
IL_0057:  newarr     [mscorlib]System.Int32

// Call a Visual Basic helper method to copy elements from the
// original array to the new array.
IL_005c:  call       class [mscorlib]System.Array [Microsoft.VisualBasic]
   Microsoft.VisualBasic.CompilerServices.Utils
      ::CopyArray(class [mscorlib]System.Array, class [mscorlib]System.Array)

// Cast the returned array to an array of the correct type.
IL_0061:  castclass  int32[]

// Store the new array reference back in the arr variable.
IL_0066:  stloc.0
```

Microsoft.VisualBasic.CompilerServices.Utils classes' shared **Copy-Array** method is a pretty big method. It contains a lot of error checking code (such as making sure that both arrays have the same number of dimensions and are of the same data type). If there are no errors, **CopyArray** ultimately calls **System.Array**'s **Copy** method to do the actual array element copying.

15

Interfaces

In this chapter, I'll explain how interfaces identify functionality that can be tacked onto a type. I'll then show you how a type can implement an interface to offer this well-defined functionality, allowing the type to be used in various scenarios easily. Finally, I'll demonstrate useful techniques for avoiding problems when you use interfaces—namely, duplication of member names and compromised compile-time type safety.

Interfaces and Inheritance

When programming, it's useful to think of an object as being of multiple types because the type of an object describes its capabilities and behavior. For example, you could design a **SortedList** type that maintains a set of objects in a sorted order. You could add any **System.Object**-derived type into the **SortedList** as long as the type supported the ability to compare itself to another type.

In a sense, the **SortedList** would like to accept only types that are derived from a hypothetical **System.Comparable** type. But many existing types aren't derived from **System.Comparable**. You can't add objects of these types to a **SortedList**, and a **SortedList** type becomes much less useful as a result.

Ideally, you'd want to take an existing **System.Object**-derived type and sometimes treat it as though it were a **System.Comparable**-derived type. The ability to treat an object as being of multiple types is frequently referred to as *multiple inheritance*. The common language runtime (CLR) supports single implementation inheritance and multiple interface inheritance.

The CLR allows a type to inherit from only one other type, which has **System.Object** as its root base type. This type of inheritance is called *implementation inheritance* because the derived type inherits all the behavior and capabilities of its base type: the derived type behaves exactly like the base type. Once the base type is inherited, however, the derived type can override the base type's behavior. This overriding of the base type's behavior (implementation) makes the new, derived type unique.

Interface inheritance means that a type inherits the method signatures of its interfaces but not their implementations. When a type inherits an interface, it is promising to provide its own implementations for the methods; if the type doesn't implement the interface's methods, the type is considered abstract and it won't be possible to construct an instance of the type.

Interfaces don't derive from any `System.Object`-derived type. An interface is simply an abstract type that consists of a set of virtual methods, each with its own name, parameters, and return type. Interface methods can't contain any implementation; hence, interface types are incomplete (abstract). Note that interfaces can also define events, parameterless properties, and parameterful properties because all of these are just syntax shorthands that map to methods anyway. The CLR also allows an interface to contain shared methods, shared fields, constants, and shared constructors. However, a CLS-compliant interface must not have any of these shared members because some programming languages aren't able to define or access them. In fact, Visual Basic prevents an interface from defining any shared members. In addition, the CLR doesn't allow an interface to contain any instance fields or instance constructors.

Here are the definitions of four interfaces that are defined in the .NET Framework Class Library (FCL):

```
Public Interface System.IComparable
    Function CompareTo(ByVal obj As Object) As Int32
End Interface

Public Interface System.Collections.IEnumerable
    Function GetEnumerator() As IEnumerator
End Interface

Public Interface System.Collections.IEnumerator
    Function MoveNext() As Boolean
    Sub Reset()
    ReadOnly Property Current() As Object          ' Read-only property
End Interface

Public Interface System.Collections.ICollection
    Inherits IEnumerable

    Sub CopyTo(ByVal arr As Array, ByVal index As Int32)
    ReadOnly Property Count() As Int32             ' Read-only property
```

```
    ReadOnly Property IsSynchronized() As Boolean  ' Read-only property
    ReadOnly Property SyncRoot() As Object         ' Read-only property
End Interface
```

By convention, the name of an interface type is prefixed with an uppercase I. An interface definition can be marked with modifiers—such as `Public`, `Protected`, `Friend`, and `Private`—in the same way that a class or structure can be marked. Of course, `Public` is used more than 99 percent of the time. These modifiers control the visibility of the interface definition and indicate which referents can see it.

> **Important**   Nonshared members of an interface are always considered public and virtual (`Overridable` in Visual Basic). This can't be changed. However, in Visual Basic, if you implement an interface method in a type and omit the `Overridable` keyword, the method is considered virtual *and* sealed—a type derived from the implementing type can't override the method.

Although an interface can't inherit another type's implementation, it can "inherit" the contract of other interfaces (as in the case of `ICollection` having `IEnumerable` as a base). In fact, an interface can include the contract of multiple interfaces. When a type "inherits" an interface, that type must implement all the methods defined by the interface and all the methods defined by any of the interface's "inherited" contracts as well. For example, any type that implements the `ICollection` interface must provide implementations for the `CopyTo`, `Count`, `IsSynchronized`, and `SyncRoot` members. In addition, the type must also provide an implementation for `IEnumerable`'s `GetEnumerator` method.

The `System.ICloneable` interface is defined (in MSCorLib.dll) as follows:

```
Public Interface ICloneable
    Function Clone() As Object
End Interface
```

The following code shows how to define a type that implements this interface and also shows code that clones an object:

```
Imports System

' Point is derived from System.Object and implements ICloneable.
Public NotInheritable Class Point
    Implements ICloneable
    Public x, y As Int32
```

(continued)

```vbnet
        Public Sub New(ByVal x As Int32, ByVal y As Int32)
            Me.x = x
            Me.y = y
        End Sub

        Public Overloads Overrides Function Equals(ByVal o As Object) As Boolean
            If TypeOf o Is Point Then
                Dim other As Point = DirectCast(o, Point)
                Return (other.x = Me.x) AndAlso (other.y = Me.y)
            End If
            Return False
        End Function

        ' This is the implementation for ICloneable's Clone method.
        Public Function Clone() As Object Implements ICloneable.Clone
            Return MemberwiseClone()
        End Function
End Class

Class App
    Public Shared Sub Main()
        Dim p1 As New Point(1, 2)

        ' Create another Point with the same values.
        Dim p2 As Point = DirectCast(p1.Clone, Point)

        ' p1 and p2 refer to two different objects: False is displayed.
        Console.WriteLine(Object.ReferenceEquals(p1, p2))

        ' p1 and p2 have the same value: True is displayed.
        Console.WriteLine(p1.Equals(p2))
    End Sub
End Class
```

As mentioned earlier, a type must inherit one type (even if it's **System.Object**, as in the preceding example). In addition, a type can implement zero or more interfaces. The FCL's **System.String** type, for example, inherits **System.Object**'s implementation and implements the **IComparable**, **ICloneable**, **IConvertible**, and **IEnumerable** interfaces. This means that the **String** type isn't required to implement the methods its **Object** base type offers. If the **String** type chooses not to implement **Object**'s methods explicitly, it simply inherits **Object**'s methods. However, the **String** type must implement the methods declared in all the interfaces; if it didn't, it would be an incomplete (abstract) type.

In Visual Basic, the **Implements** statement is used to tell the compiler which of the type's methods contains the code that implements an interface's method. The signature of the type's method must exactly match the signature of the interface's method. In the previous example, **Point**'s public **Clone** function contains the implementation for **ICloneable**'s **Clone** method. Here you see that the type's method (**Clone**) and the interface's method (**Clone**) have the exact same name and signature. When defining a type method whose job is to implement an interface's method, you should make sure that the type's method has the exact same name as the interface's method. Using the same method name reduces potential confusion for developers that use the type.

You should also define the type's methods as public so that users of the type can easily call the methods without first having to cast an instance of the type to a specific interface. For example, the **System.String** type inherits an implementation from **System.Object** and inherits the **IComparable**, **ICloneable**, **IConvertible**, and **IEnumerable** interfaces. Because **String** defines public methods whose names match the interface names, it is very easy to treat a **String** object as a **String** or as any of the interface types that it implements. See the following code for an example:

```
' Create a String object.
Dim s As String = "Jeffrey"
' Using s, I can call any method defined in String, Object, IComparable,
' ICloneable, IConvertible, or IEnumerable.

' Make an IComparable variable that references s.
Dim comparable As IComparable = s
' Using comparable, I can call any method declared by IComparable only.

' Make an ICloneable variable that references s.
Dim cloneable As ICloneable = s
' Using cloneable, I can call any method declared by ICloneable only.

' Make an IEnumerable variable that references s.
Dim enumerable As IEnumerable = DirectCast(cloneable, IEnumerable)
' You can cast a variable from one interface to another as long as
' the object's type implements both interfaces.
```

In this code, it doesn't matter which variable I use; I'm always affecting the **String** object identified by **s**. However, the variable's type indicates the legal actions that I can perform on that string object.

Let's return to the **SortedList** discussion. It's now possible to place a **String** object into the **SortedList** because it implements the **IComparable** interface. The only minor issue is that the **String** type is required to implement the **CompareTo** method (in **IComparable**), which needs to compare two **Object**s and return a value indicating which **Object** should come first.

IComparable's **CompareTo** method takes an **Object** parameter, not a **String** parameter. Any type implementing the **CompareTo** method must define the method so that its signature matches that of the interface's method. In the method, the code can do any casting necessary to perform the expected behavior. I'll address this "shortcoming" of interfaces in the upcoming section "Implementing Multiple Interfaces That Have the Same Method Name and Signature."

A `SortedList` type can successfully manage objects of any type (`String`, `DateTime`, `Int32`—whatever) as long as the types implement the `IComparable` interface.

> **Important**   Like a reference type, a value type can implement zero or more interfaces. However, when you cast an instance of a value type to an interface type, the value type instance must be boxed. This is because interfaces are always considered reference types, and the methods they define are always virtual (`Overridable` in Visual Basic). Recall that unboxed value types don't have a pointer to the type's method table. Boxing the value type allows the CLR to look up the type's method table so that the virtual method can be called.

I often hear the question, "Should I design a base type or an interface?" The answer isn't always clear-cut. Here are some guidelines that might help you:

- **IS-A vs. CAN-DO relationship**   A type can inherit only one implementation. If the derived type can't claim an IS-A relationship with the base type, then don't use a base type; use an interface. Interfaces imply a CAN-DO relationship. If the CAN-DO functionality feels like it belongs with various object types, use an interface.

- **Ease of use**   It's easier for you, as a developer, to define a new type derived from a base type than to create an interface. The base type can provide a lot of functionality, so the derived type probably needs only relatively small modifications to its behavior. If you supply an interface, the new type must implement all the members.

- **Consistent implementation**   No matter how well an interface contract is documented, it's very unlikely that everyone will implement the contract 100 percent correctly. In fact, COM suffers from this very problem, which is why some COM objects work correctly only with Microsoft Word or Microsoft Internet Explorer. By providing a base type with a good default implementation, you start off using a type that works and is well tested; you can then modify whatever parts need changing.

■   **Versioning**   If you add a method to the base type, the derived type inherits the new member's default implementation for free. In fact, the user's source code doesn't even have to be recompiled. Adding a new member to an interface forces the user of the interface to modify the source code before recompiling.

In the FCL, the classes related to streaming data use an implementation inheritance design. The `System.IO.Stream` class is an abstract base class. It provides a bunch of methods, such as `Read` and `Write`. Other classes—`System.IO.FileStream`, `System.IO.MemoryStream`, and `System.Net.Sockets.NetworkStream`—are derived from `Stream`. Microsoft chose an IS-A relationship between each of these three classes and the `Stream` class because it made implementing the concrete classes easier. For example, the derived classes need to implement only synchronous I/O operations; they inherit the ability to perform asynchronous I/O operations from the `Stream` base class.

Admittedly, choosing to use inheritance for the stream classes isn't an obvious decision; the `Stream` base class actually provides very little implementation. However, if you consider the Windows Forms control classes, where `Button`, `CheckBox`, `ListBox`, and all the other controls are derived from `System.Windows.Forms.Control`, it's easy to imagine all the code that `Control` implements, which the various control classes simply inherit to function correctly.

By contrast, Microsoft designed the FCL collections to be interface based. The `System.Collections` namespace defines several collection-related interfaces: `IEnumerable`, `ICollection`, `IList`, and `IDictionary`. Then Microsoft provided a number of concrete classes, such as `ArrayList`, `Hashtable`, `Queue`, `SortedList`, and so on, that implement combinations of these interfaces. Here the designers chose a CAN-DO relationship between the classes and the interfaces because the implementations of these various collection classes are radically different from one another. In other words, there isn't a lot of sharable code between an `ArrayList`, a `Hashtable`, and a `Queue`.

The operations that all these collection classes offer are, nevertheless, pretty consistent. For example, they all maintain a set of elements that can be enumerated, and they all allow adding and removing of elements. This consistency is the reason that making the collection classes interface based makes a lot of sense. If you have a reference to an object whose type implements the `IList` interface, you can write code to add elements, remove elements, and search for an element without having to know exactly what type of collection you're working with. This is a very powerful mechanism.

Designing an Application That Supports Plug-In Components

When you're building extensible applications, interfaces should be the centerpiece. Suppose, for example, that you're writing an application and you want others to be able to create types that your application can load and use seamlessly. Here's the way to design this application.

■   Create an assembly that defines an interface whose methods are used as the communication mechanism between the application and the plug-in components. When defining the parameters and return values for the interface methods, try to use other interfaces or types defined in MSCorLib.dll. If you want to pass and return your own data types, define them in this assembly too. Once you settle on your interface definitions, give this assembly a strong name (discussed in Chapter 3) and then package and deploy it to your partners and users. Consider this assembly immutable—that is, don't change its contents.

> **Note**   You can use types defined in MSCorLib.dll because the CLR always loads the version of MSCorLib.dll that matches the version of the CLR itself. Also, only a single version of MSCorLib.dll is ever loaded into a process. In other words, different versions of MSCorLib.dll never load side by side (as described in Chapter 3). As a result, you won't have any type version mismatches and your application will require less memory.

■   Create a separate assembly containing your application's types. This assembly will, obviously, reference the interface and types defined in the first assembly. Feel free to modify the code in this assembly to your heart's content. Because the plug-in developers won't reference this assembly, you can put out a new version of it every hour if you want to and not affect any of the plug-in developers.

■   The plug-in developers will, of course, define their own types in their own assembly. Their assembly will also reference the types in your interface assembly. The plug-in developers are also able to put out a new version of their assembly as often as they'd like, and the application will be able to consume the plug-in types without any problem whatsoever.

This small section contains some very important information. When using types across assemblies, you need to be concerned with assembly versioning issues. Take your time, and isolate the types that you use for communication across assembly boundaries into their own assembly. Avoid mutating or changing these type definitions—and don't change the version number of the assembly.

Also, avoid defining a type whose base type is defined in another assembly, even though the .NET Framework Design Guidelines encourage this; it's the wrong thing to do, because assemblies will be tied to specific versions of other assemblies. As a consequence of the CLR's side-by-side support, you'll end up pulling several different versions of an assembly into a single AppDomain. This can cause significant memory usage and severely hurt performance. It might also prevent—or at least make difficult—communication between the assemblies.

In addition, most compilers don't let you reference multiple versions of a specific assembly when building a managed module. This limitation can make it difficult for code to take advantage of new features (offered by a newer version of an assembly) and still communicate (via required types in an older version of an assembly).

Changing Fields in a Boxed Value Type Using Interfaces

Let's have some fun and see how well you understand value types, boxing, and unboxing. Examine the following code, and see whether you can figure out what it displays on the console:

```
Imports System

' Point is a value type.
Structure Point
    Public x, y As Int32

    Public Sub Change(ByVal x As Int32, ByVal y As Int32)
        Me.x = x
        Me.y = y
    End Sub

    Public Overrides Function ToString() As String
        Return String.Format("({0}, {1})", x, y)
    End Function
End Structure

Class App
    Public Shared Sub Main()
        Dim p As New Point()
```

(continued)

```
            p.x = 1
            p.y = 1
            Console.WriteLine(p)        ' Displays (1, 1)

            p.Change(2, 2)
            Console.WriteLine(p)        ' Displays (2, 2)

            Dim o As Object = p
            Console.WriteLine(o)        ' Displays (2, 2)

            CType(o, Point).Change(3, 3) ' Changes temporary Point on stack!
            Console.WriteLine(o)        ' Displays (2, 2)
        End Sub
End Class
```

Very simply, **Main** creates an instance of a **Point** value type on its stack and then changes its **x** and **y** fields to **1**. The first call to **WriteLine** calls **ToString** on the unboxed **Point**, and "(1, 1)" is displayed, as expected. Then, **p** is used to call the **Change** method, which changes the values of **p**'s **x** and **y** fields on the stack to **2**. The second call to **WriteLine** displays "(2, 2)", as expected.

Now, **p** is boxed, and **o** refers to the boxed **Point** object. The third call to **WriteLine** again shows "(2, 2)", which is also expected. Finally, I want to call the **Change** method to update the fields in the boxed **Point** object. However, **Object** (the type of the variable **o**) doesn't know anything about the **Change** method, so I must first cast **o** to a **Point**. Casting **o** to a **Point** unboxes **o** and copies the fields in the boxed **Point** to a temporary **Point** on the thread's stack. The **x** and **y** fields of this temporary point are changed to 3 and 3, but the boxed **Point** isn't affected by this call to **Change**. When **WriteLine** is called the fourth time, "(2, 2)" is displayed again. Many developers do *not* expect this.

If **Option Strict** is off, you can call the **Change** method directly from the **o** variable, without casting to a **Point** variable first. In this case, the two fields are correctly changed and "(3, 3)" is displayed. In most applications, however, you should avoid calling methods through late binding (or reflection) because the compiler can't check your code for type safety and the resulting code executes less efficiently.

Some languages, such as Managed Extensions for C++, let you change the fields in a boxed value type, but Visual Basic does not, short of using **Option Strict Off** and late binding as explained previously. However, even with **Option Strict On**, you can fool Visual Basic into changing the fields of the boxed value type by using an interface. The following code is a modified version of the previous code:

```
Option Strict On
Imports System
```

```vb
' Interface defining a Change method
Interface IChangeBoxedPoint
    Sub Change(ByVal x As Int32, ByVal y As Int32)
End Interface

' Point is a value type.
Structure Point
    Implements IChangeBoxedPoint

    Public x, y As Int32

    Public Sub Change(ByVal x As Int32, ByVal y As Int32) _
        Implements IChangeBoxedPoint.Change
        Me.x = x
        Me.y = y
    End Sub

    Public Overrides Function ToString() As String
        Return String.Format("({0}, {1})", x, y)
    End Function
End Structure

Class App
    Public Shared Sub Main()
        Dim p As New Point()

        p.x = 1
        p.y = 1
        Console.WriteLine(p)          ' Displays (1, 1)

        p.Change(2, 2)
        Console.WriteLine(p)          ' Displays (2, 2)

        Dim o As Object = p
        Console.WriteLine(o)          ' Displays (2, 2)

        CType(o, Point).Change(3, 3) ' Changes temporary Point on stack!
        Console.WriteLine(o)          ' Displays (2, 2)

        ' Boxes p; changes the boxed object and discards it
        CType(p, IChangeBoxedPoint).Change(4, 4)
        Console.WriteLine(p)          ' Displays (2, 2)

        ' Changes the boxed object and shows it
        CType(o, IChangeBoxedPoint).Change(5, 5)
        Console.WriteLine(o)          ' Displays (5, 5)
    End Sub
End Class
```

This code is almost identical to the previous version. The main difference is that the `Change` method is defined by the `IChangeBoxedPoint` interface, and the `Point` type now implements this interface. The `Change` method now belongs to both the class interface and the `IChangeBoxedPoint` interface, thanks to the `Implements` keyword at the end of the method signature. Inside `Main`, the first four calls to `WriteLine` are the same and produce the same results I had before (as expected). However, I've added two more examples to `Main` at the end.

In the first example, the unboxed `Point`, `p`, is cast to an `IChangeBoxed-Point`. This cast causes the value in `p` to be boxed. `Change` is called on the boxed value, which does change its `x` and `y` fields to 4 and 4, but after `Change` returns, the boxed object is immediately ready to be garbage collected. So the fifth call to `WriteLine` displays "(2, 2)"—many developers won't expect this result.

In the last example, the boxed `Point` referred to by `o` is cast to an `IChange-BoxedPoint`. No boxing is necessary here because `o` is already a boxed `Point`; in fact, I could replace the `CType` operator with the `DirectCast` operator, which works only on reference types. Then `Change` is called, which *does* change the boxed `Point`'s `x` and `y` fields. The interface method `Change` has allowed me to change the fields in a boxed `Point` object! Now when `WriteLine` is called, it displays "(5, 5)", as expected.

The purpose of this whole example is to demonstrate how an interface method is able to modify the fields of a boxed value type. In Visual Basic, this isn't possible without using an interface method.

Important   A number of developers reviewed the chapters of this book. After reading through some of my code samples (such as the preceding one), these reviewers would tell me that they've sworn off value types. I must say that these little value type nuances have cost me days of debugging time, which is why I spend time pointing them out in this book. I hope you'll remember some of these nuances and that you'll be prepared for them if and when they strike you and your code. Certainly, you shouldn't be scared of value types. They are useful types, and they have their place. After all, a program needs a little `Int32` love now and then. Just keep in mind that value types and reference types have very different behaviors, depending on how they're used. In fact, you should take the preceding code and declare the `Point` as a `Class` instead of a `Structure` to appreciate the results.

Implementing Multiple Interfaces That Have the Same Method Name and Signature

Defining a type that implements an interface is usually easy and straightforward. You simply implement methods in the type that match the methods and signatures defined by the interface and use Visual Basic's `Implements` statement to tell the compiler that the type's method contains the implementation for the interface's method. As stated earlier, you should define the methods as public and give the type's method the same name in order to reduce confusion for developers using the type.

Occasionally, you might find yourself defining a type that implements multiple interfaces that define methods with the same name and signature. For example, imagine that there are two interfaces defined as follows:

```
Public Interface IWindow
    Function GetMenu() As Object
End Interface

Public Interface IRestaurant
    Function GetMenu() As Object
End Interface
```

Let's say that you want to define a type that implements both these interfaces. If a single method can contain the implementation for both interface methods, you could code the type as follows:

```
' This type is derived from System.Object and
' implements the IWindow and IRestaurant interfaces.
Public Class GiuseppePizzeria
    Implements IWindow, IRestaurant

    ' This one method contains the implementation for both
    ' IWindow's and IRestaurant's GetMenu methods.
    Public Function GetMenu() As Object _
        Implements IWindow.GetMenu, IRestaurant.GetMenu
        ⋮
    End Function
End Class
```

In this example, the `GiuseppePizzeria` type defines just one public method named `GetMenu`. This method's `Implements` statement is followed by multiple *interfacename.methodname* elements because the method implements methods from different interfaces. Being able to specify multiple *interfacename.method-*

name elements is particularly handy when the method's purpose is simply to throw a `System.NotImplementedException` exception. Of course, when specifying multiple *interfacename.methodname* elements, all the interface methods must have identical parameters and return values.

The following code demonstrates all the scenarios in which `GiuseppePizzeria`'s `GetMenu` method executes:

```
Class App
   Shared Sub Main()
      ' Construct a GiuseppePizzeria object.
      Dim gp As GiuseppePizzeria = New GiuseppePizzeria()
      ' Calls the public GetMenu method
      Dim o1 As Object = gp.GetMenu()

      ' Calls the same GetMenu method
      Dim o2 As Object = DirectCast(gp, IWindow).GetMenu()

      ' Calls the same GetMenu method
      Dim o3 As Object = DirectCast(gp, IRestaurant).GetMenu()
   End Sub
End Class
```

This example shows how a single method can be implemented to handle several interface methods as long as the signatures of all the methods match. However, in real life, it's very unlikely that a single method implementation can suffice for multiple interface methods. For example, the code necessary to return a menu for a window and the code necessary to return a menu of food items will definitely require different implementations. So the `GiuseppePizzeria` type must implement two different methods. Because the CLR doesn't allow a type to define two methods with the same name and signature, we need to be creative to solve this problem. The following code demonstrates:

```
' This type is derived from System.Object and
' implements the IWindow and IRestaurant interfaces.
Public Class GiuseppePizzeria
   Implements IWindow, IRestaurant

   ' This method contains the implementation for IRestaurant's GetMenu method.
   Public Function GetMenu() As Object Implements IRestaurant.GetMenu
      ⋮
   End Function

   ' This method contains the implementation for IWindow's GetMenu method.
   Public Function IWindow_GetMenu() As Object Implements IWindow.GetMenu
      ⋮
   End Function
End Class
```

In this example, the `GiuseppePizzeria` type defines two methods: `GetMenu` and `IWindow_GetMenu`. The `GetMenu` method is public and contains the implementation for `IRestaurant`'s `GetMenu` method, whereas the `IWindow_GetMenu` method is private and contains the implementation for `IWindow`'s `GetMenu` method. The following code shows how a developer can use this type:

```
Class App
   Shared Sub Main()
      ' Construct a GiuseppePizzeria object.
      Dim gp As GiuseppePizzeria = New GiuseppePizzeria()
      ' Calls the public GetMenu method and returns
      ' the restaurant's menu of food items
      Dim o1 As Object = gp.GetMenu()
      ' Calls the public IWindow_GetMenu method and
      ' returns the window's menu
      Dim o2 As Object = gp.IWindow_GetMenu()

      ' Calls the public IWindow_GetMenu method and
      ' returns the window's menu
      Dim o3 As Object = DirectCast(gp, IWindow).GetMenu()

      ' Calls the public GetMenu method and returns
      ' the restaurant's menu of food items
      Dim o4 As Object = DirectCast(gp, IRestaurant).GetMenu()
   End Sub
End Class
```

In the previous example, `GiuseppePizzeria`'s `GetMenu` and `IWindow_GetMenu` methods are declared as `Public` methods. This allows the methods to be called using the `gp` variable (as shown in the `Main` method).

However, these methods don't have to be declared as `Public`. If you declared the methods as `Private`, for example, they wouldn't be callable using the `gp` variable. Instead, you'd have to cast the `gp` variable to an `IWindow` or `IRestaurant` interface first and then you could call the corresponding `GetMenu` method. Note that after you cast the `gp` variable to the desired interface, you always have the ability to call the methods that implement the interface's methods even if the methods are declared as `Private` methods within the type.

As I said, a type very rarely implements multiple interfaces that define methods with the same names and signatures, so you rarely need to do what I've done in the preceding code. However, this technique of defining methods whose names don't match the interface's method name is interesting and has other uses. In fact, I'll focus on this technique again in the next section.

Improving Type Safety and Reducing Boxing

Interfaces are great because they define a standard way for types to communicate with each other. However, this flexibility comes at the cost of compile-time type safety because most interface methods accept parameters of type `System.Object` or return a value whose type is `System.Object`. Look at the very common `IComparable` interface:

```
Public Interface IComparable
    Function CompareTo(ByVal other As Object) As Int32
End Interface
```

This interface defines one method that accepts a parameter of type `System.Object`. If I define my own type that implements this interface, the type definition might look like this:

```
Structure SomeValueType
    Implements IComparable
    Dim x As Int32

    Public Sub New(ByVal x As Int32)
        Me.x = x
    End Sub

    Public Function CompareTo(ByVal other As Object) As Int32 _
        Implements IComparable.CompareTo
        Return x - CType(other, SomeValueType).x
    End Function
End Structure
```

Using `SomeValueType`, I can now write the following code:

```
Public Shared Sub Main()
    Dim v As New SomeValueType(0)
    Dim o As New Object()
    Dim n As Int32 = v.CompareTo(o)
End Sub
```

In this code, I'm comparing apples and oranges. OK, I'm really comparing `SomeValueType`s and `Object`s, but you see that this code doesn't make a lot of sense because `Object` doesn't have an `x` field. The compiler can't detect the flaw in the logic, however, and it produces code—no warnings or errors are generated. But at run time, when `CompareTo` is called, an `InvalidCastException` is thrown when `other` is cast to `SomeValueType`.

As always, developers prefer compile-time errors to run-time errors, and you can get these compile-time errors to occur if you use some creativity when defining your type's methods. Let's modify `SomeValueType`'s method to see how we can obtain type safety:

```
Structure SomeValueType
    Implements IComparable
    Dim x As Int32

    Public Sub New(ByVal x As Int32)
        Me.x = x
    End Sub

    Public Function CompareTo(ByVal other As SomeValueType) As Int32
        Return x - other.x
    End Function

    ' Note that this method is marked as Private.
    Private Function IComparable_CompareTo(ByVal other As Object) _
        As Int32 Implements IComparable.CompareTo
        Return CompareTo(CType(other, SomeValueType))
    End Function
End Structure
```

Notice several things about this new version. First, it now has two methods that compare the current object to another object. The first **CompareTo** method is public, and it no longer takes an **Object** as a parameter; it now takes a **SomeValueType** instead. Because this parameter has changed, the code that casts **other** to **SomeValueType** is no longer necessary and has been removed. The resulting code is easier to maintain and is also type-safe at compile time. The following code demonstrates:

```
Option Strict On
  :
Dim v1 As New SomeValueType(1)
Dim v2 As New SomeValueType(2)
Dim n As Int32

n = v1.CompareTo(New Object())  ' Compile-time error
n = v1.CompareTo(v2)            ' Calls CompareTo
```

Changing the **CompareTo** method so that it's type-safe means that **SomeValueType** no longer adheres to the contract placed on it by implementing the **IComparable** interface. So **SomeValueType** must implement a **CompareTo** method that satisfies the **IComparable** contract. This is the job of the private **IComparable_CompareTo** method.

This **IComparable_CompareTo** method returns an **Int32** and accepts a **System.Object**, just like the method the **IComparable** interface defines. However, you need to keep in mind three characteristics of this **CompareTo** method. First, the name of this method doesn't matter at all: what matters is the **Implements IComparable.CompareTo** statement that follows its signature. This is very important. Basically, the name that follows the **Implements** keyword tells the CLR that

`IComparable_CompareTo` should be called only when using a reference to an `IComparable` object. To understand this constraint clearly, examine the following code:

```
Dim v1 As New SomeValueType(1)
Dim v2 As New SomeValueType(2)
Dim n As Int32

n = v1.CompareTo(v2)              ' Calls CompareTo
n = v2.CompareTo(v1)              ' Calls CompareTo

' NOTE: Getting an IComparable reference forces v1 to be boxed.
Dim comparable As IComparable = v1

' NOTE: This calls IComparable_CompareTo, which takes an Object as
' a parameter. This forces v2 to be boxed.
n = comparable.CompareTo(v2)
```

Second, `IComparable_CompareTo` is implemented by calling the other `CompareTo` method after casting `other` to a `SomeValueType`. This means that the existing code can be leveraged.

Finally, notice that the `IComparable_CompareTo` method is prefixed with a `Private` access modifier. The reason is that you never call this method through a `SomeValueType` variable, so it isn't necessary to have it appear in the class interface.

Using `v1` or `v2` from the preceding code, the only `CompareTo` method that is accessible is the type-safe version that takes a `SomeValueType` parameter. When you have a reference to an `IComparable` object, however, the `IComparable_CompareTo` method is accessible. In fact, it's the only method accessible because an `IComparable` reference variable can be used to call methods from the `IComparable` interface only. So the `IComparable_CompareTo` method is sometimes private and sometime public.

The purpose of defining the interface method privately is to provide for more type safety during application development. Although my example uses a value type, this mechanism can also be applied to reference types to improve their type safety. In addition to improving type safety, another beneficial side effect occurs when the interface method is defined privately on a value type, which `SomeValueType` happens to be.

Because `IComparable`'s `CompareTo` method takes an `Object` as a parameter, you can pass a value type for this parameter, but it must be boxed. As you know, boxing allocates memory from the heap, copies fields, and hurts performance, so avoid it whenever possible. Fortunately, the technique shown in this section allows you to get rid of unwanted boxing operations. To understand how, examine the following code:

```
Public Shared Sub Main()
    Dim v1 As New SomeValueType(1)
```

```
        Dim v2 As New SomeValueType(2)
        Dim n As Int32

        n = v1.CompareTo(v2)                     ' No boxing
        n = CType(v1, IComparable).CompareTo(v2) ' Boxes v1 and v2
End Sub
```

In this code, the first call to **CompareTo** calls the public, fully type-safe **CompareTo** method. Because this method isn't part of an interface and because it takes a **Some-ValueType** as a parameter, it can simply be called on the unboxed instance **v1**. In addition, **v2** doesn't have to be boxed and can be passed directly to the method.

On the second call to **CompareTo**, I first cast **v1** to an **IComparable**. This boxes **v1** and returns an **IComparable** reference, which I then use to call **IComparable_CompareTo**. This version of **CompareTo** is the private method, which takes a **System.Object** as a parameter. So **v2** must be boxed before **IComparable_CompareTo** can be called. Two boxing operations have occurred.

This technique is frequently used when implementing interfaces such as **ICloneable**, **IComparable**, **ICollection**, **IList**, and **IDictionary**. They let you create type-safe versions of these interface's methods, and they enable you to reduce boxing operations for value types.

Be Careful with Privately Defined Interface Methods

When examining the methods for a type in the .NET Framework reference documentation, privately defined interface methods do not appear. Their absence has confused many developers. For example, if you look up the **System.Int32** type in the reference documentation, you'll see that **Int32** implements the **IConvertible** interface. However, if you look at the "Int32 Members" help page, you won't see any of **IConvertible**'s methods (**ToBoolean**, **ToByte**, **ToChar**, **ToSingle**, and so on) listed. Why?

When the .NET Framework was in beta, Microsoft noticed that the **Int32** type offered around 20 methods and they were afraid that developers would quickly become overwhelmed when looking at the documentation for a "simple **Int32** type." So Microsoft decided not to show privately defined interface methods in the documentation to keep the documentation less cluttered. Then, of course, they had to change some of the type's methods to privately defined interface methods so that these methods wouldn't appear. For the **Int32** type, they chose to make the methods that implement the **IConvertible** interface privately defined methods. Because **IConvertible** defines 15 methods, the documentation for the **Int32** type

---

(continued)

Be Careful with Privately Defined Interface Methods   *(continued)*

now shows only 5 methods. This certainly makes the help look less cluttered and makes the `Int32` type look much more like a "simple type."

However, I've run into many developers who have just been confused by this decision. They see that the `Int32` type implements `IConvertible`, but the documentation doesn't reflect that these methods exist. And to make matters even worse, you can't call an `IConvertible` method on an `Int32` directly. For example, the following method won't compile:

```
Public Shared Sub Main()
    Dim x As Int32 = 5
    Dim s As Single = x.ToSingle(Nothing)
End Sub
```

When compiling this method, the Visual Basic compiler produces the following: "BC30456: 'ToSingle' is not a member of Integer". This error message confuses the developer even more because it's clearly stating that the `Int32` type doesn't define a `ToSingle` method when, in fact, it does.

To call `ToSingle` on an `Int32`, you must first cast the `Int32` to an `IConvertible`, as shown in the following method:

```
Public Shared Sub Main()
    Dim x As Int32 = 5
    Dim s As Single = CType(x, IConvertible).ToSingle(Nothing)
End Sub
```

Requiring this cast isn't obvious at all, and many developers won't figure this out on their own. But an even more troublesome problem exists: casting the `Int32` value type to an `IConvertible` also boxes the value type, wasting memory and hurting performance.

Was all this really necessary just to reduce documentation clutter? I don't think so. In my opinion, Microsoft should have left the documentation alone—it would have been accurate, complete, and less confusing, and the resulting code would be obvious and easier to write, and it would execute efficiently. Remember, my example here talks about the `Int32` type and how it implements `IConvertible` methods. But Microsoft chose to "hide documentation" for many types that implement various interfaces.

This discussion clearly shows you that you should use privately defined interface methods with great care. When many developers first learn about privately defined interface methods, they think they're cool and they start using them whenever possible. Don't do this! Privately defined interface methods are useful in some circumstances, but you should avoid them whenever possible since they make using a type much less obvious.

16

Custom Attributes

In this chapter, I'll discuss one of the most innovative features that the Microsoft .NET Framework has to offer: *custom attributes*. Custom attributes allow anyone (not just Microsoft) to define information that can be applied to almost any metadata table entry. This extensible metadata information can be queried at run time to dynamically alter the way code executes. As you use the various .NET Framework technologies (Windows Forms, Web Forms, XML Web services, and so on), you'll see that they all take advantage of custom attributes, allowing developers to express their intentions in code very easily. A solid understanding of custom attributes is necessary for any .NET Framework developer.

Using Custom Attributes

Attributes, such as **Public**, **Private**, **Shared**, and so on, can be applied to types and members. I think we'd all agree on the usefulness of applying attributes, but wouldn't it be even more useful if we could define our own attributes? For example, what if I could define a type and somehow indicate that the type can be remoted via serialization? Or maybe I could apply an attribute to a method to indicate that certain security permissions must be granted before the method can execute.

Of course, creating and applying user-defined attributes to types and methods would be great and convenient, but it would require the compiler to be aware of these attributes so that it could emit the attribute information into the resulting metadata. Because compiler vendors usually prefer not to release the source code for their compiler, Microsoft came up with another way to allow user-defined attributes. This mechanism, called *custom attributes*, is an incredibly powerful mechanism that's useful at both application design time and run time. Anyone can define and use custom attributes, and all compilers that target the common language runtime (CLR) must be designed to recognize custom attributes and emit them into the resulting metadata.

The first thing you should realize about custom attributes is that they're just a way to associate additional information with a target. The compiler emits this additional information into the managed module's metadata. Most attributes have no meaning for the compiler; the compiler simply detects the attributes in the source code and emits the corresponding metadata.

The .NET Framework Class Library (FCL) ships with many predefined attributes. For example, the `System.FlagsAttribute` attribute causes an enumerated type to act like a set of bit flags, the `System.SerializableAttribute` attribute allows a type's fields to be serialized and deserialized (typically used for remoting of a method's arguments and return value), several security-related attributes enable a method to ensure that it has a required privilege granted before attempting some particular kind of access, lots of interoperability-related attributes serve to allow managed code to call unmanaged code, and so on.

Following is some Visual Basic code with many attributes applied to it. It's not important to understand what this code does. I just want you to see what attributes look like.

```
<StructLayout(LayoutKind.Sequential, CharSet:=CharSet.Auto)> _
Class OSVERSIONINFO
    Sub New
        OSVersionInfoSize = CInt (Marshal.SizeOf(Me))
    End Sub

    Public OSVersionInfoSize As Int32 = 0
    Public MajorVersion As Int32 = 0
    Public MinorVersion As Int32 = 0
    Public BuildNumber As Int32 = 0
    Public PlatformId As Int32 = 0

    <MarshalAs(UnmanagedType.ByValTStr, SizeConst:=128)> _
    public CSDVersion As String = ""
End Class

Class AnotherClass
    <DllImport("Kernel32", CharSet:=CharSet.Auto, SetLastError:=True)> _
    Public Shared Function GetVersionEx( _
        <InAttribute(), Out ()> ByRef ver As OSVERSIONINFO) _
        As Boolean
        ' Nothing here
    End Function
End Class
```

In Visual Basic, you apply a custom attribute to a target by placing the attribute in angle brackets (<, >) immediately before the target. So in this case, the `StructLayout` attribute is applied to the `OSVERSIONINFO` class, the `MarshalAs` attribute is applied to the `CSDVersion` field, the `DllImport` attribute is applied to the `GetVersionEx` method, and the `InAttribute` and `OutAttribute` attributes are applied to `GetVersionEx`'s `ver` parameter. Every programming language defines the syntax that a developer must use in order to apply a custom attribute to a target. C#, for example, requires square brackets ([,]) instead of angle brackets.

The CLR allows attributes to be applied to just about anything that can be represented in a file's metadata. Most commonly, attributes are applied to entries in the following definition tables: TypeDef (class, structures, enum, interfaces, and delegates), MethodDef (including constructors), ParamDef, FieldDef, PropertyDef, EventDef, AssemblyDef, and ModuleDef. Although it's rare, attributes can also be applied to entries in reference tables, such as AssemblyRef, ModuleRef, TypeRef, and MemberRef. Finally, custom attributes can be applied to other pieces of metadata—such as security permissions, exported types, and resources.

Although the CLR allows custom attributes to be applied to any of these entities, most programming languages allow attributes to be applied only to entries in the various definition metadata tables. This is certainly true of Microsoft's Visual Basic and C# compilers. Specifically, Visual Basic allows you to apply an attribute only to source code that defines any of the following targets: assembly, module, type, field, method, method parameter, method return value, property, and event.

In general, Visual Basic requires that the attribute immediately precede the code entity it refers to. Attributes can also be applied to the current assembly or the current module, in which case there is no specific visible entity in source code. In these cases, you must prefix the attribute with `Assembly:` or `Module:`.

```
<Assembly: MyAttribute(1)>    ' Applied to the assembly
<Module: MyAttribute(2)>      ' Applied to the module
```

Now that you know how to apply a custom attribute, let's find out what an attribute really is. A custom attribute is simply an instance of a type. For Common Language Specification (CLS) compliance, custom attribute types must be derived, directly or indirectly, from `System.Attribute`. Visual Basic allows only CLS-compliant attributes. By examining the .NET Framework SDK documentation, you'll see that the following types (from the earlier example) are defined: `StructLayoutAttribute`, `MarshalAsAttribute`, `DllImportAttribute`, `InAttribute`, and `OutAttribute`. All these types happen to be defined in the `System.Runtime.InteropService` namespace, but attribute types can be defined in any namespace. Upon further examination, you'll notice that all these types are derived from **System.Attribute**, as all CLS-compliant attribute types must be.

As I mentioned, an attribute is an instance of a type. The type must have a public constructor to create an instance of it. So when you apply an attribute to a target, the syntax is similar to that for calling one of the type's instance constructors. In addition, a language might permit some special syntax that allows you to set any public fields or properties associated with the attribute type. Let's look at an example. Recall the application of the **DllImport** attribute as it was applied to the **GetVersionEx** method earlier:

```
<DllImport("Kernel32", CharSet:=CharSet.Auto, SetLastError:=True)>
```

The syntax of this line should look pretty strange to you because you could never use syntax like this when calling a constructor. If you examine the **DllImportAttribute** type in the documentation, you'll see that its constructor requires a single **String** parameter. In this example, "Kernel32" is being passed for this parameter. A constructor's parameters are called *positional parameters* and are mandatory: the parameter must be specified when the attribute is applied.

What are the other two "parameters"? This special syntax allows you to set any public fields or properties of the **DllImportAttribute** object after the object is constructed. In this example, when the **DllImportAttribute** object is constructed and "Kernel32" is passed to the constructor, the object's public instance fields, **CharSet** and **SetLastError**, are set to **CharSet.Auto** and **True**, respectively. The "parameters" that set fields or properties are called *named parameters* and are optional: the parameters don't have to be specified when you're applying an instance of the attribute. A little later on, I'll explain what causes an instance of the **DllImportAttribute** type to actually be constructed.

Also note that it's possible to apply multiple attributes to a single target. For example, the **GetVersionEx** method's **ver** parameter has both the **InAttribute** and **OutAttribute** attributes applied to it. When applying multiple attributes to a single target, be aware that the order of attributes has no significance. Also, in Visual Basic, multiple attributes must be comma-separated within a single set of angle brackets. The **Attribute** suffix is optional, unless dropping it would leave you with a reserved word (as in the case of **InAttribute**). If the attribute type's constructor takes no parameters, the parentheses are optional. The following lines behave identically and demonstrate some of the possible ways you can declare multiple attributes:

```
<Serializable(), Flags()>
<FlagsAttribute(), SerializableAttribute()>
<Serializable, Flags>
<FlagsAttribute, SerializableAttribute>
```

Defining Your Own Attribute

You know that an attribute is a type derived from **System.Attribute**, and you also know how to apply an attribute. Let's now look at how to define your own custom attributes. Say that you're the Microsoft employee responsible for adding the bit flag support to enumerated types. To accomplish this, the first thing you have to do is define a **FlagsAttribute** type:

```
Namespace System
    Public Class FlagsAttribute
        Inherits System.Attribute

        Sub New()

        End Sub
End Namespace
```

Notice that the **FlagsAttribute** type inherits from **System.Attribute**; this is what makes the **FlagsAttribute** type a CLS-compliant custom attribute. In addition, all nonabstract attributes must have **Public** accessibility, and by convention all attribute type names should end with "**Attribute**". Finally, all nonabstract attributes must contain at least one **Public** constructor, which you can omit in Visual Basic if you're satisfied with the default parameterless constructor that the compiler adds automatically. For example, the simple **FlagsAttribute** constructor takes no parameters and does absolutely nothing, so you can omit it if you want to.

So far, instances of the **FlagsAttribute** class can be applied to any target, but this attribute should really be applied to enumerated types only. It doesn't make sense to apply the attribute to a property or a method. To tell the compiler where this attribute can legally be applied, you apply an instance of the **System.AttributeUsageAttribute** class to the attribute type. Here's the new code:

```
Namespace System
    <AttributeUsage(AttributeTargets.Enum, Inherited:=False)> _
    Public Class FlagsAttribute
        Inherits System.Attribute

        Sub New()

        End Sub
End Namespace
```

In this new version, I've applied an instance of **AttributeUsageAttribute** to the attribute. After all, the attribute type is just a class and a class can have attributes applied to it. The **AttributeUsageAttribute** attribute is a simple type that allows you to indicate to a compiler where your custom attribute can legally be applied. All compilers have built-in support for this attribute and generate errors when a user-defined custom attribute is applied to an invalid target. In this example, the **AttributeUsage** attribute indicates that instances of the **Flags** attribute can be applied to enumerated type targets only.

Because all attributes are just types, you can easily understand the **AttributeUsageAttribute** type. Here's what the FCL source code for the type would look like if it were written in Visual Basic:

```
<AttributeUsage(AttributeTargets.Class, Inherited:=False), _
    Serializable()> _
Public NotInheritable Class AttributeUsageAttribute
    Inherits System.Attribute

    Friend m_attributeTarget As AttributeTargets = AttributeTargets.All
    Friend m_allowMultiple As Boolean = False
    Friend m_inherited As Boolean = False

    Public Sub New(ByVal validOn As AttributeTargets)
        m_attributeTarget = validOn
    End Sub

    ReadOnly Property ValidOn() As AttributeTargets
        Get
            Return m_attributeTarget
        End Get
    End Property

    Property AllowMultiple() As Boolean
        Get
            Return m_allowMultiple
        End Get
        Set(ByVal Value As Boolean)
            m_allowMultiple = Value
        End Set
    End Property

    Property Inherited() As Boolean
        Get
            Return m_inherited
        End Get
        Set(ByVal Value As Boolean)
            m_inherited = Value
        End Set
    End Property
End Class
```

As you can see, the **AttributeUsageAttribute** type has a constructor that allows you to pass bit flags indicating where your attribute can legally be applied. The **System.AttributeTargets** enumerated type is defined in the FCL as follows:

```
<Flags(), Serializable()> _
Public Enum AttributeTargets
    [Assembly]  = &H1
    [Module]    = &H2
    [Class]     = &H4
    [Struct]    = &H8
    [Enum]      = &H10
    Constructor = &H20
    Method      = &H40
    [Property]  = &H80
    Field       = &H100
    [Event]     = &H200
    [Interface] = &H400
    Parameter   = &H800
    [Delegate]  = &H1000
    ReturnValue = &H2000
    All = [Assembly] Or [Module] Or [Class] Or Struct Or [Enum] Or _
        Constructor Or Method Or [Property] Or Field Or [Event] Or _
        [Interface] Or Parameter Or [Delegate] Or ReturnValue
End Enum
```

The **AttributeUsageAttribute** class offers two additional public properties that can optionally be set when the attribute is applied to an attribute type: **AllowMultiple** and **Inherited**.

For most attributes, it makes no sense to apply them to a single target more than once. For example, nothing is gained by applying the **Flags** or **Serializable** attributes more than once to a single target. In fact, if you tried to compile the code below, the compiler would report the following: error BC30663: Attribute 'FlagsAttribute' cannot be applied multiple times:

```
<Flags(), Flags()>
Enum Color
    Red
End Enum
```

For a few attributes, however, it does make sense to apply the attribute multiple times to a single target. In the FCL, the **ConditionalAttribute** attribute class and lots of permission attribute classes (such as **EnvironmentPermissionAttribute**, **FileIOPermissionAttribute**, **ReflectionPermissionAttribute**, **RegistryPermissionAttribute**, and so on) allow multiple instances of themselves to be applied to a single target. If you don't explicitly set **AllowMultiple**, your attribute will get the default behavior, which allows it to be applied no more than once to a selected target.

AttributeUsageAttribute's other property, **Inherited**, indicates whether the purpose of the attribute should be considered to apply to derived classes or derived methods. Of all the attributes defined by the FCL, less than five have the **Inherited** property set to **True**. The following code demonstrates what it means for an attribute to be inherited:

```
<AttributeUsage(AttributeTargets.Class Or AttributeTargets.Method, _
    Inherited=True)>
Class TastyAttribute
    Inherits Attribute
End Class

<Tasty(), Serializable()> _
Public Class SomeType
    <Tasty()> Public Overridable Sub DoSomething()
    End Sub
End Class

Public Class AnotherType
    Inherits SomeType

    Public Overrides Sub DoSomething()
    End Sub
End Class
```

In this code, **AnotherType** and its **DoSomething** method are both considered **Tasty** because **Tasty** attributes are marked as inherited. However, **AnotherType** is not serializable because the FCL's **SerializableAttribute** type is marked as a noninherited attribute.

Be aware that the .NET Framework only considers targets of classes, methods, properties, events, and parameters to be inheritable. So when you're defining an attribute type, you should set **Inherited** to **True** only if your targets include any of these targets. Note that inherited attributes do not cause additional metadata to be emitted for the derived types into the managed module. I'll say more about this a little later in the section "Detecting the Use of a Custom Attribute."

> **Note** If you define your own attribute class and forget to apply an **AttributeUsage** attribute to your class, the compiler and the CLR will assume that your attribute can be applied to all targets, can be applied only once to a single target, and is inherited. These assumptions mimic the default field values in the **AttributeUsageAttribute** type.

Attribute Constructor and Field/Property Data Types

When defining your own custom attribute type, you can define a constructor that takes parameters that a developer applying an instance of your attribute type must specify. In addition, you can define nonstatic, public fields and properties in your type that identify settings a developer applying an instance of your attribute type can optionally specify.

When defining an attribute type's instance constructor, fields, and properties, you must restrict yourself to a small subset of data types. Specifically, the legal set of data types is limited to any of the following: **Boolean**, **Char**, **Byte**, **SByte**, **Int16** (**Short** in Visual Basic), **UInt16**, **Int32** (**Integer**), **UInt32**, **Int64** (**Long**), **UInt64**, **Single**, **Double**, **String**, **Type**, **Object**, or an enumerated type. (Of course, Visual Basic doesn't support signed bytes and unsigned integer types.) In addition, you can use a single-dimension, zero-based array of any of these types.

When applying an attribute, you must pass a compile-time constant expression that matches the type defined by the attribute class. Wherever the attribute class defines a **Type** parameter, **Type** field, or **Type** property, you must use Visual Basic's **GetType** operator as shown in the following code. Wherever the attribute class defines an **Object** parameter, **Object** field, or **Object** property, you can pass an **Int32**, a **String**, or any other constant expression. If the constant expression represents a value type, the value type will be boxed at run time when an instance of the attribute is constructed.

Here's an example of an attribute and an application of it:

```
<AttributeUsage(AttributeTargets.All)> _
Class SomeAttribute
    Inherits Attribute

    Sub New(ByVal name As String, ByVal o As Object, _
        ByVal types() As Type)
        ' 'name'  refers to a String.
        ' 'o' refers to one of the legal types (boxing if necessary).
        ' 'types' refers to a one-dimension, zero-based array of Type objects.
        :
    End Sub
End Class

<Some("Jeff", Color.Red, New Type(){GetType(Math), GetType(Console)})> _
Public Class SomeType
    :
End Class
```

Logically, when a compiler detects a custom attribute applied to a target, the compiler constructs an instance of the attribute type by calling its constructor, passing it any specified parameters. Then the compiler initializes any public fields and properties that have also been specified. Now that the custom attribute object is initialized, the compiler serializes the object out to the target's metadata table entry.

> **Important**   I've found that this is the best way for developers to think of custom attributes: instances of types that have been serialized to a byte stream that resides in metadata. Later, at run time, an instance of the type can be constructed by deserializing the bytes contained in the metadata.

> **Note**   Each parameter is written out with a 1-byte type ID followed by the value. After "serializing" the constructor's parameters, the compiler emits each of the specified field and property values by writing out the field/property name followed by a 1-byte type ID and then the value. For arrays, the count of elements is saved first, followed by each individual element.

Detecting the Use of a Custom Attribute

Defining an attribute type is useless by itself. Sure, you could define attribute types all you want and apply them all you want; but this would just cause additional metadata to be written out to the managed module—the behavior of your application code wouldn't change.

In Chapter 13, you saw that applying the `Flags` attribute to an enumerated type altered the behavior of `System.Enum`'s `ToString`, `Format`, and `Parse` methods. The reason these methods behave differently is that they check at run time whether the enumerated type they're operating on has the `Flags` attribute metadata associated with it. Code can look for the presence of attributes using a technology called *reflection*. I'll give some brief demonstrations of reflection here, but I'll discuss it fully in Chapter 20.

If you were the Microsoft employee responsible for implementing **Enum**'s **Format** method, you would implement it like this:

```
Shared Function Format(ByVal enumType As Type, ByVal value As Object, _
   ByVal format As String)

   ' Does the enumerated type have an instance of
   ' the FlagsAttribute type applied to it?
   If enumType.IsDefined(GetType(FlagsAttribute), False) Then
      ' Yes; execute code, treating value as a bit flag enumerated type.
      ⋮
   Else
      ' No; execute code, treating value as a normal enumerated type.
      ⋮
   End If
End Function
```

This code calls **Type**'s **IsDefined** method, effectively asking the system to look up the metadata for the enumerated type and see whether an instance of the **FlagsAttribute** type is associated with it. If **IsDefined** returns **True**, then an instance of **FlagsAttribute** is associated with the enumerated type and the **Format** method knows to treat the value as though it contained a set of bit flags. If **IsDefined** returns **False**, then **Format** treats the value as a normal enumerated type.

So if you define your own attribute types, you must also implement some code that checks for the existence of an instance of your attribute type (on some target) and then executes some alternate code path. This is what makes custom attributes so useful!

The FCL offers many ways to check for the existence of an attribute. If you're checking for the existence of an attribute via a **System.Type** object, you can use the **IsDefined** method as shown earlier. However, sometimes you want to check for an attribute on a target other than a type, such as an assembly, a module, or a method. For this discussion, let's concentrate on the methods defined by the **System.Attribute** type. You'll recall that all CLS-compliant attributes are derived from **System.Attribute**; this type defines three static methods for retrieving the attributes associated with a target: **IsDefined**, **GetCustomAttributes**, and **GetCustomAttribute**. Each of these functions has several overloaded versions. For example, each method has a version that works on type members (classes, structures, enums, interfaces, delegates, constructors, methods, properties, fields, events, and return types), parameters, modules, and assemblies. There are also versions that allow you to tell the system to walk up the derivation hierarchy to include inherited attributes in the results. Table 16-1 briefly describes what each method does.

**Table 16-1   System.Attribute's Methods That Reflect over Metadata
Looking for Instances of CLS-Compliant Custom Attributes**

Method	Description
IsDefined	Returns **True** if there is at least one instance of the specified **Attribute**-derived type associated with the target. This method is fast because it doesn't construct (deserialize) any instances of the attribute type.
GetCustomAttributes	Returns an array where each element is an instance of the specified attribute type that was applied to the target. Each instance is constructed (deserialized) using the parameters, fields, and properties specified during compilation. If the target has no instances of the specified attribute type, an empty array is returned. This method is typically used with attributes that have **AllowMultiple** set to **True**.
GetCustomAttribute	Returns an instance of the specified attribute type that was applied to the target. The instance is constructed (deserialized) using the parameters, fields, and properties specified during compilation. If the target has no instances of the specified attribute type, **Nothing** is returned. If the target has multiple instances of the specified attribute applied to it, a **System.Reflection.AmbiguousMatchException** exception is thrown. This method is typically used with attributes that have **AllowMultiple** set to **False**.

If you just want to see whether an attribute has been applied to a target, you should call **IsDefined** because it's much faster than the other two methods. However, you know that when an attribute is applied to a target, you can specify parameters to the attribute's constructor and you can also optionally set fields and properties. Using **IsDefined** won't construct an attribute object, call its constructor, or set its fields and properties.

If you want to construct an attribute object, you must call either **GetCustomAttributes** or **GetCustomAttribute**. Every time one of these methods is called, it constructs instances of the specified attribute type and sets each instance's fields and properties based on the values specified in the source code. These methods return references to fully constructed instances of the applied attribute types.

When you call any of these methods, internally, they must scan the managed module's metadata, performing string comparisons to locate the specified custom attribute class. Obviously, these operations take time. If you're performance conscious, you should consider caching the result of calling these methods rather than calling them repeatedly asking for the same information.

The `System.Reflection` namespace defines several types that allow you to examine the contents of a module's metadata: `Assembly`, `Module`, `Enum`, `ParameterInfo`, `MemberInfo`, `Type`, `MethodInfo`, `ConstructorInfo`, `FieldInfo`, `EventInfo`, `PropertyInfo`, and their respective `*Builder` types. All these types also offer `IsDefined` and `GetCustomAttributes` methods. Only `System.Attribute` offers the very convenient `GetCustomAttribute` method.

The version of `GetCustomAttributes` defined by the reflection types returns an array of `Object` types instead of an array of `Attribute` types. This is because the reflection types are able to return objects of non-CLS-compliant attribute types. You shouldn't be concerned about this inconsistency because non-CLS-compliant attributes are incredibly rare. In fact, in all the time I've been working with the .NET Framework, I've never seen one.

> **Note** Be aware that the methods on the reflection types consider only attributes on classes and methods to be inheritable; that is, if you call `IsDefined` or `GetCustomAttributes` using an `EventInfo`, a `PropertyInfo`, or a `ParameterInfo`, the `inherit` parameter is ignored and assumed to be `False`. Only the `Attribute` type's methods honor the `inherit` parameter for events, properties, and parameters.

There's just one more thing that you should be aware of: When you pass a type to `IsDefined`, `GetCustomAttribute`, or `GetCustomAttributes`, these methods search for the application of the attribute type you specify or any attribute type derived from the specified type. If your code is looking for a specific attribute type, you should perform an additional check on the returned value to ensure that what these methods returned is the exact type you're looking for. You might also want to consider defining your attribute type to be sealed to reduce potential confusion and eliminate this extra check. I must admit, all the attribute types I've ever seen inherit directly from `System.Attribute` so I've never run into this problem personally.

Here's some sample code that gets all the methods defined within a type and displays the attributes applied to each method. The code is for demonstration purposes; normally, you wouldn't apply these particular custom attributes to these targets as I've done here.

```vbnet
Imports System
Imports System.Diagnostics
Imports System.Reflection

<Assembly: CLSCompliant(True)>

<Serializable(), DefaultMember("Main")> _
Class App
   <Conditional("Debug"), Conditional("Release")> _
   Public Sub DoSomething()
   End Sub

   Sub New()
   End Sub

   <CLSCompliant(True), STAThread()> _
   Public Shared Sub Main()
      ' Display the type's name.
      Console.WriteLine("Attributes applied to: {0}", GetType(App))

      ' Get and show the set of attributes applied to this type.
      ShowAttributes(GetType(App).GetCustomAttributes(False))

      ' Get the set of methods associated with the type.
      Dim members() As MemberInfo = GetType(App).FindMembers( _
         MemberTypes.Constructor Or MemberTypes.Method, _
         BindingFlags.DeclaredOnly Or BindingFlags.Instance Or _
         BindingFlags.Public Or BindingFlags.Static, _
         Type.FilterName, "*")

      Dim member As MemberInfo
      For Each member In members
         ' Display the type's member name.
         Console.WriteLine("Attributes applied to: {0}", member.Name)

         ' Get and show the set of attributes applied to this member.
         ShowAttributes(member.GetCustomAttributes(False))
      Next
   End Sub

   Public Shared Sub ShowAttributes(ByVal attributes() As Object)
      Dim attribute As Object
      For Each attribute In attributes
         ' Display the type of each applied attribute.
         Console.Write("   {0}", attribute.GetType().ToString())
         If TypeOf attribute Is ConditionalAttribute Then
            Console.Write("  ({0})", DirectCast(attribute, _
               ConditionalAttribute).ConditionString)
         End If
```

```
        If TypeOf attribute Is CLSCompliantAttribute Then
            Console.Write("  ({0})", DirectCast(attribute, _
                CLSCompliantAttribute).IsCompliant)
        End If

        Console.WriteLine()
    Next

    If attributes.Length = 0 Then
        Console.WriteLine("   No attributes applied to this target.")
    End If

    Console.WriteLine()
    End Sub
End Class
```

Building and running this application yields the following output:

```
Attributes applied to: App
    System.Reflection.DefaultMemberAttribute

Attributes applied to: DoSomething
    System.Diagnostics.ConditionalAttribute   (Release)
    System.Diagnostics.ConditionalAttribute   (Debug)

Attributes applied to: Main
    System.STAThreadAttribute
    System.CLSCompliantAttribute   (True)

Attributes applied to: ShowAttributes
    No attributes applied to this target.

Attributes applied to: .ctor
    No attributes applied to this target.
```

Matching Two Attribute Instances Against Each Other

Now that your code knows how to check to see whether an instance of an attribute is applied to a target, it might want to check the fields of the attribute to see what values they have. One way to do this is to write code that checks the values of the type's fields. However, your attribute type could also override **System.Attribute**'s **Match** method. Then your code could construct an instance of the attribute type and call **Match** to compare it to the instance that was applied to the target. The following code demonstrates.

```vb
Imports System

<Flags()> _
Public Enum Accounts
    Savings = &H1
    Checking = &H2
    Brokerage = &H4
End Enum

<AttributeUsage(AttributeTargets.Class)> _
Public Class AccountsAttribute
    Inherits Attribute

    Dim accounts As Accounts

    Public Sub New(ByVal accounts As accounts)
        Me.accounts = accounts
    End Sub

    Public Overrides Function Match(ByVal obj As Object) As Boolean
        ' If the base class implements Match and the base class
        ' is not Attribute, then uncomment the line below.
        ' If Not (MyBase.Match(obj)) Then Return False

        ' Since "Me" isn't Nothing, if obj is Nothing,
        ' then the objects can't match.
        ' NOTE: You can delete this line if you trust that
        ' the base type implemented Match correctly.
        If (obj Is Nothing) Then Return False

        ' If the objects are of different types, they can't match.
        ' NOTE: You can delete this line if you trust that
        ' the base type implemented Match correctly.
        If Not (Me.GetType() Is obj.GetType()) Then Return False

        ' Cast obj to the type to access fields. NOTE: This cast
        ' can't fail because we know that the objects are of the same type.
        Dim other As AccountsAttribute = DirectCast(obj, _
            AccountsAttribute)

        ' Compare the fields.
        ' This example checks if 'Me' accounts is a subset
        ' of other's accounts.
        If ((other.accounts And accounts) <> accounts) Then Return False

        Return True    ' Objects match.
    End Function
```

```vb
Overloads Overrides Function Equals(ByVal obj As Object) As Boolean
    ' If the base class implements Equals and the base class
    ' is not Object, then uncomment the line below.
    ' If (Not MyBase.Equals(obj)) Then Return False

    ' Since "Me" isn't Nothing, if obj is Nothing,
    ' then the objects can't be equal.
    ' NOTE: You can delete this line if you trust that
    ' the base type implemented Equals correctly.
    ' If (obj Is Nothing) Then Return False

    ' If the objects are of different types, they can't be equal.
    ' NOTE: You can delete this line if you trust that
    ' the base type implemented Equals correctly.
    If Not (Me.GetType() Is obj.GetType()) Then Return False

    ' Cast obj to the type to access fields. NOTE: This cast
    ' can't fail because we know that the objects are of the same type.
    Dim other As AccountsAttribute = DirectCast(obj, _
        AccountsAttribute)

    ' Compare the fields to see if they have the same value.
    ' This example checks if "Me" accounts is the same
    ' as other's accounts.
    If (other.accounts <> accounts) Then Return False

    Return True     ' Objects are equal.
End Function

' Override GetHashCode since we override Equals.
Public Overrides Function GetHashCode() As Integer
    Return CInt(accounts)
End Function
End Class

<Accounts(Accounts.Savings)> _
Class ChildAccount
End Class

<Accounts(Accounts.Savings Or Accounts.Checking Or _
    Accounts.Brokerage)> _
Class AdultAccount
End Class

Class App
    Shared Sub Main()
        CanWriteCheck(New ChildAccount())
        CanWriteCheck(New AdultAccount())
```

(continued)

```
        ' This just demonstrates that the method works correctly on a
        ' type that doesn't have the AccountsAttribute applied to it.
        CanWriteCheck(New App())
    End Sub

    Public Shared Sub CanWriteCheck(ByVal obj As Object)
        ' Construct an instance of the attribute type and initialize it
        ' to what you are explicitly looking for.
        Dim checking As Attribute = _
            New AccountsAttribute(Accounts.Checking)

        ' Construct the attribute instance that was applied to the type.
        Dim validAccounts As Attribute = Attribute.GetCustomAttribute( _
            obj.GetType(), GetType(AccountsAttribute), False)

        ' If the attribute was applied to the type AND the
        ' attribute specifies the "Checking" account, write
        ' a check from this object.
        If (Not (validAccounts Is Nothing) AndAlso _
          checking.Match(validAccounts)) Then
            Console.WriteLine("{0} types can write checks.", _
                obj.GetType())
        Else
            Console.WriteLine("{0} types can NOT write checks.", _
                obj.GetType())
        End If
    End Sub
End Class
```

Building and running this application yields the following output:

```
ChildAccount types can NOT write checks.
AdultAccount types can write checks.
App types can NOT write checks.
```

You'll notice that the code for **Match** is almost identical to the code for **Equals** (discussed in Chapter 6); that is, in both, you must cast carefully and you must remember to call the base type's **Match** method if appropriate. If you define a custom attribute and you don't override the **Match** method, you'll inherit the implementation of **Attribute**'s **Match** method. This implementation simply calls **Equals**.

Pseudo-Custom Attributes

Certain Microsoft-defined attributes are used so frequently that emitting the full attribute information into the metadata would increase the size of the managed module significantly. These attributes get special treatment at compile time and are emitted into the metadata as bits. The CLR and the FCL know how to look in the metadata specifically for these *pseudo-custom attributes*. Examine the following code:

```
<Serializable()> _
Class SomeType
    ⋮
End Class
```

The FCL does offer a `System.SerializableAttribute` type, and an instance of this type is being applied to `SomeType`. Because the `Serializable` attribute is common, it is compiled into the metadata as a bit: the full metadata for an instance of the `Serializable` attribute won't be emitted to the metadata. This is why these attributes are called *pseudo*-custom attributes: they look like regular attributes, and you apply them in source code just as you do regular attributes, but they are persisted in a super-compressed way (as a bit).

The important point to remember about pseudo-custom attributes is that you can't detect their presence at run time in the same way you detect the presence of regular custom attributes. In an earlier code example, I applied the `Serializable` and `DefaultMemberAttribute` attributes to the `App` type. However, when the application runs, only the `DefaultMemberAttribute` is displayed. Methods such as `IsDefined`, `GetCustomAttributes`, and `GetCustomAttribute` don't work with pseudo-custom attributes.

Ideally, the .NET Framework team would have hidden the fact that pseudo-custom attributes are handled differently than regular attributes. And in future versions of the .NET Framework, they might. You can employ other means to detect the use of these pseudo-custom attributes. For example, `System.Type` offers read-only properties such as `IsSerializable`, `IsAutoLayout`, `IsExplicitLayout`, `IsLayoutSequential`, and more. And `System.Reflection.FieldInfo` offers read-only properties such as `IsNotSerialized`. However, for most pseudo-custom attributes, there are no types or methods defined in the FCL that allow you to detect the presence of a pseudo-custom attribute. (By the way, there is a way to detect pseudo-custom attributes if you resort to unmanaged code and access the CLR's COM interface directly.)

Here's a list of the .NET Framework–defined pseudo-custom attributes:

- `System.NonSerializedAttribute`
- `System.SerializableAttribute`
- `System.Diagnostics.DebuggableAttribute`
- `System.Runtime.CompilerServices.MethodImplAttribute`
- `System.Runtime.InteropServices.DllImportAttribute`
- `System.Runtime.InteropServices.InAttribute`
- `System.Runtime.InteropServices.ComImportAttribute`
- `System.Runtime.InteropServices.FieldOffsetAttribute`
- `System.Runtime.InteropServices.GuidAttribute`
- `System.Runtime.InteropServices.InterfaceTypeAttribute`
- `System.Runtime.InteropServices.OptionalAttribute`
- `System.Runtime.InteropServices.OutAttribute`
- `System.Runtime.InteropServices.PreserveSigAttribute`
- `System.Runtime.InteropServices.StructLayoutAttribute`
- `System.Runtime.InteropServices.MarshalAsAttribute`

17

Delegates

In this chapter, I talk about callback functions. Callback functions are an extremely useful programming mechanism that has been around for years. The Microsoft .NET Framework exposes a callback function mechanism using delegates. Unlike callback mechanisms used in other platforms, such as unmanaged C++, delegates offer much more functionality. For example, delegates ensure that the callback method is type-safe (in keeping with one of the most important goals of the common language runtime). Delegates also integrate the ability to call multiple methods serially and support the calling of static methods as well as instance methods.

A First Look at Delegates

The C runtime's **qsort** function takes a callback function to sort elements within an array. In Microsoft Windows, callback functions are required for window procedures, hook procedures, asynchronous procedure calls, and more. In the .NET Framework, callback methods are used for a whole slew of things. For example, you can register callback methods to get a variety of notifications, such as unhandled exceptions, window state changes, menu item selections, file system changes, and completed asynchronous operations.

In unmanaged C/C++, the address of a function is just a memory address. This address doesn't carry along any additional information, such as the number of parameters the function expects, the types of these parameters, the function's return value type, and the function's calling convention. In short, unmanaged C/C++ callback functions are not type-safe.

In the .NET Framework, callback functions are just as useful and pervasive as in unmanaged Windows programming. However, the .NET Framework provides a type-safe mechanism called *delegates*. I'll start off the discussion of delegates by showing you how to use them. The following code demonstrates how to declare, create, and use delegates.

```
Imports System
Imports System.Windows.Forms
Imports System.IO

Class ItemSet
    Private items() As Object

    Public Sub New(ByVal numItems As Int32)
        ReDim items(numItems - 1)
        Dim i As Int32
        For i = 0 To numItems - 1
            items(i) = i
        Next
    End Sub

    ' Define a Feedback type.
    ' NOTE: This type is nested within the ItemSet class.
    Public Delegate Sub Feedback(ByVal value As Object, _
        ByVal item As Int32, ByVal numItems As Int32)

    Public Sub ProcessItems(ByVal feedback As Feedback)
        Dim item As Int32
        For item = 0 To items.Length - 1
            If Not feedback Is Nothing Then
                ' If any callbacks are specified, call them.
                feedback(items(item), item + 1, items.Length)
            End If
        Next
    End Sub
End Class

Class App
    Public Shared Sub Main()
        StaticCallbacks()
        InstanceCallbacks()
    End Sub

    Shared Sub StaticCallbacks()
        ' Create an ItemSet object with five items in it.
        Dim setOfItems As New ItemSet(5)

        ' Process the items, but give no feedback.
        setOfItems.ProcessItems(Nothing)
        Console.WriteLine()
```

```vbnet
            ' Process the items, and give feedback to the console.
            setOfItems.ProcessItems(New ItemSet.Feedback( _
                AddressOf App.FeedbackToConsole))
            Console.WriteLine()

            ' Process the items, and give feedback to a message box.
            setOfItems.ProcessItems(New ItemSet.Feedback( _
                AddressOf App.FeedbackToMsgBox))
            Console.WriteLine()

            ' Process the items, and give feedback to the console
            ' AND to a message box.
            Dim fb As ItemSet.Feedback = Nothing
            fb = New ItemSet.Feedback(AddressOf App.FeedbackToConsole)
            fb = DirectCast( _
                [Delegate].Combine(fb, _
                    New ItemSet.Feedback(AddressOf App.FeedbackToMsgBox)), _
                ItemSet.Feedback)
            setOfItems.ProcessItems(fb)
            Console.WriteLine()
        End Sub

        Shared Sub FeedbackToConsole(ByVal value As Object, _
            ByVal item As Int32, ByVal numItems As Int32)
            Console.WriteLine("Processing item {0} of {1}: {2}.", _
                item, numItems, value)
        End Sub

        Shared Sub FeedbackToMsgBox(ByVal value As Object, _
            ByVal item As Int32, ByVal numItems As Int32)
            MessageBox.Show(String.Format("Processing item {0} of {1}: {2}.", _
                item, numItems, value))
        End Sub

        Shared Sub InstanceCallbacks()
            ' Create a set with five items in it.
            Dim setOfItems As New ItemSet(5)

            ' Process the items, and give feedback to a file.
            Dim appobj As New App()
            setOfItems.ProcessItems( _
                New ItemSet.Feedback(AddressOf appobj.FeedbackToFile))
            Console.WriteLine()
        End Sub

        Sub FeedbackToFile(ByVal value As Object, ByVal item As Int32, _
            ByVal numItems As Int32)
```

(continued)

```
        Dim sw As New StreamWriter("Status", True)
        sw.WriteLine("Processing item {0} of {1}: {2}.", item, numItems, value)
        sw.Close()
    End Sub
End Class
```

Now I'll describe what this code is doing. At the top, notice the **ItemSet** class. Pretend that this class contains a set of items that will be processed individually. When you create an **ItemSet** object, you pass the number of items it should manage to its constructor. The constructor then creates an array of **Object**s and initializes each object to an integer value.

The **ItemSet** class also defines a public delegate: **Feedback**. The delegate indicates the signature of a callback method. In this example, a **Feedback** delegate identifies a **Sub** method that takes three parameters (an **Object** and two **Int32**s).

The **ItemSet** class also defines a public method named **ProcessItems**. This method takes one parameter, **feedback**, which is a reference to a **Feedback** delegate object. **ProcessItems** iterates through all the elements of the array, and for each element, the callback method (specified by the **feedback** variable) is called. This callback method is passed the value of the item being processed, the item number, and the total number of items in the array. The callback method can process each item any way it chooses.

Using Delegates to Call Back Static Methods

Now that you understand how the **ItemSet** type is designed and how it works, let's see how to use delegates to call back static methods. The **StaticCallbacks** method that appears in the previous code sample is the focus of this section.

The **StaticCallbacks** method begins by constructing an **ItemSet** object, telling it to create an array of five objects. Then **ProcessItems** is called, passing it **Nothing** for its **feedback** parameter. **ProcessItems** represents a method that performs some action for every item managed by the **ItemSet** object. Because the **feedback** parameter is **Nothing** in this example, each item is processed without calling any callback methods.

For the second call to **ProcessItems**, a new **ItemSet.Feedback** delegate object is constructed. This delegate object is a wrapper around a method, allowing that method to be called back indirectly via the wrapper. To the **Feedback** type's constructor, the **AddressOf** operator followed by the name of a static method, **App.FeedbackToConsole** in this example, is passed; this indicates the method to be wrapped. The reference returned from the **New** operator is then passed to **ProcessItems**. Now when **ProcessItems** executes, it will call the **App** type's static **FeedbackToConsole** method for each item in the set. **FeedbackTo-Console** simply writes a string to the console indicating the item being processed and the item's value.

Visual Basic also supports a more concise syntax when creating a delegate: instead of explicitly calling the delegate's constructor, you can simply use the **AddressOf** operator followed by the name of the target method, as in the following statements:

```
' The following two statements are equivalent.
setOfItems.ProcessItems(New ItemSet.Feedback(AddressOf App.FeedbackToMsgBox))
setOfItems.ProcessItems(AddressOf App.FeedbackToConsole)

' The following two statements are equivalent.
fb = DirectCast([Delegate].Combine(fb, New ItemSet.Feedback( _
    AddressOf App.FeedbackToMsgBox)), ItemSet.Feedback)
fb = DirectCast([Delegate].Combine(fb, _
    AddressOf App.FeedbackToMsgBox), ItemSet.Feedback)
```

The Visual Basic compiler emits identical intermediate language (IL) code regardless of whether you use the full or the abbreviated delegate syntax. The emitted IL code always constructs an instance of the delegate class that wraps the specified method. Because the emitted IL code is identical, the abbreviated syntax is no more efficient than the full syntax. In this book, I'll use the full syntax exclusively because it accurately reflects what is actually happening and will therefore help you understand the common language runtime (CLR) better.

> **Note** The **FeedbackToConsole** method is defined as **Private** inside the **App** type, but the **ItemSet** type's **ProcessItems** method is able to call **App**'s private method. No security problem results here because **App**'s code explicitly decided to return a delegate wrapper over a private method.

The third call to **ProcessItems** is almost identical to the second call. The only difference is that the **Feedback** delegate object wraps the static **App.FeedbackToMsgBox** method. **FeedbackToMsgBox** builds a string indicating the item being processed and the item's value. This string is then displayed in a message box.

The fourth and final call to **ProcessItems** demonstrates how delegates can be linked together to form a chain. In this example, a reference variable to a **Feedback** delegate object, **fb**, is created and initialized to **Nothing**. This variable points to the head of a linked list of delegates. A value of `Nothing` indicates that there are no nodes in the linked list. Then a `Feedback` delegate object that wraps a call to `App`'s `FeedbackToConsole` method is constructed. The `fb` variable now refers to the head of the linked list.

Finally, another `Feedback` delegate object is constructed that wraps a call to `App`'s `FeedbackToMsgBox` method. The `System.Delegate` type's static `Combine` method is used to append a new delegate object to the linked list, and `fb` is updated to refer to the new head of the linked list. Now when `ProcessItems` is called, it is passed the head of the linked list of `Feedback` delegates. Inside `ProcessItems`, the line of code that calls the callback method actually ends up calling all the callback methods wrapped by the delegate objects in the linked list. In other words, for each item being iterated, `FeedbackToConsole` will be called immediately followed by `FeedbackToMsgBox`. I'll explain exactly how a delegate chain works later in this chapter.

Everything in this example is type-safe. For instance, when constructing a `Feedback` delegate object, the compiler ensures that `App`'s `FeedbackToConsole` and `FeedbackToMsgBox` methods have the exact prototype as defined by the `Feedback` delegate; that is, both methods must take three parameters (`Object` and two `Int32`s) and both methods must have the same return type (`void`). What would have happened if `FeedbackToConsole` had been prototyped like this?

```
Shared Sub FeedbackToConsole(ByVal value As Object, _
    ByVal item As Int32, ByVal numItems As Int32, ByVal s As String)
    ⋮
End Sub
```

The Visual Basic compiler wouldn't compile the code and would issue the following error: "error BC30408: Method 'Public Shared Sub FeedbackToConsole(value As Object, item As Integer, numItems As Integer, s As String)' does not have the same signature as delegate 'Delegate Sub Feedback(value As Object, item As Integer, numItems As Integer)'. "

Using Delegates to Call Back Instance Methods

In the code example near the beginning of the chapter, I explained how to use delegates to call static methods. You can also use delegates to call instance methods for a specific object. To understand how calling back an instance method works, look at the `InstanceCallbacks` method from the code shown earlier:

```
Shared Sub InstanceCallbacks()
    ' Create a set with five items in it.
    Dim setOfItems As New ItemSet(5)
```

```
' Process the items, and give feedback to a file.
Dim appobj As New App()
setOfItems.ProcessItems( _
   New ItemSet.Feedback (AddressOf appobj.FeedbackToFile))
Console.WriteLine()
End Sub
```

Notice that an **App** object is constructed after the **ItemSet** object is constructed. This **App** object doesn't have any fields or properties associated with it; I created it merely for demonstration purposes. When the new **Feedback** delegate object is constructed, its constructor is passed **appobj.FeedbackToFile**. This causes the delegate to wrap a reference to the **FeedbackToFile** method, which is an instance method (not a static method). When this instance method is called, the object that **appobj** refers to is the object being operated on (passed as the hidden **Me** parameter). The **FeedbackToFile** method works like the **FeedbackTo-Console** and **FeedbackToMsgBox** methods except that it opens a file and appends the processing item string to the end of the file.

Again, the purpose of this example is to demonstrate that delegates can wrap calls to instance methods as well as to static methods. For instance methods, the delegate needs to know the instance of the object that the method is going to operate on.

Demystifying Delegates

On the surface, delegates seem easy to use: you define them using Visual Basic's **Delegate** keyword, you construct instances of them using the familiar **New** operator, and you invoke the callback using familiar "method call" syntax (except that instead of a method name, you use the variable that refers to the delegate object).

However, what's really going on is quite a bit more complex than what the earlier examples illustrate. The compilers and the CLR do a lot of behind-the-scenes processing to hide the complexity. In this section, I'll focus on how the compiler and the CLR work together to implement delegates. Having this knowledge will improve your understanding of delegates and will teach you how to use them efficiently and effectively. I'll also touch on some additional features that delegates make available.

Let's start by reexamining this line of code:

```
Public Delegate Sub Feedback(ByVal value As Object, _
   ByVal item As Int32, ByVal numItems As Int32)
```

When it sees this line, the compiler defines a complete class definition that looks something like this:

```
Public Class Feedback
    Inherits System.MulticastDelegate
    ' Constructor
    Public Sub New(ByVal target As Object, ByVal methodPtr As Int32)

    ' Method with same prototype as specified by the source code
    Public Overridable Sub Invoke(ByVal value As Object, _
        ByVal item As Int32, ByVal numItems As Int32)

    ' Methods allowing the callback to be called asynchronously
    Public Overridable  BeginInvoke(ByVal value As Object, _
        ByVal item As Int32, ByVal numItems As Int32, _
        ByVal callback As AsyncCallback, ByVal object As Object) _
        As IAsyncResult

    Public Overridable Sub EndInvoke(result As IAsyncResult)
End Class
```

The class defined by the compiler has four methods: a constructor, **Invoke**, **BeginInvoke**, and **EndInvoke**. In this chapter, I'll concentrate on the constructor and **Invoke** methods.

You can verify that the compiler did indeed generate this class automatically by examining the resulting module with ILDasm.exe, as shown in Figure 17-1.

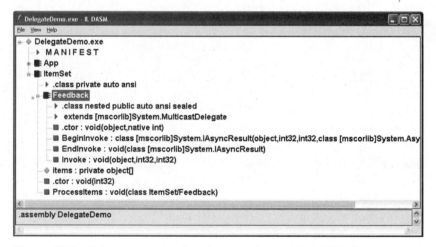

Figure 17-1   ILDasm.exe showing the metadata produced by the compiler for the delegate

In this example, the compiler has defined a class named **Feedback** that is derived from the **System.MulticastDelegate** type defined in the .NET Framework Class Library (FCL). (All delegate types are derived from **MulticastDelegate**.) The class is public because the delegate is declared as **Public** in the source code. If the source code had indicated `Private` or `Protected`, the `Feedback` class the compiler generated would also be private or protected, respectively. You should be aware that delegate types can be defined within a class (as in the example, `Feedback` is defined within the `ItemSet` class) or at global scope. Basically, because delegates are classes, a delegate can be defined anywhere a class can be defined.

Because all delegate types are derived from `MulticastDelegate`, they inherit `MulticastDelegate`'s fields, properties, and methods. Of all these members, three private fields are probably most significant. Table 17-1 describes these fields.

Table 17-1   `MulticastDelegate`'s **Significant Private Fields**

Field	Type	Description
_target	System.Object	Refers to the object that should be operated on when the callback method is called. This field is used for instance method callbacks.
_methodPtr	System.Int32	An internal integer that the CLR uses to identify the method that is to be called back.
_prev	System.MulticastDelegate	Refers to another delegate object. This field is usually `Nothing`.

Notice that all delegates have a constructor that takes two parameters: a reference to an object and an integer that refers to the callback method. If you examine the source code, however, you'll see that I'm passing in values such as `AddressOf App.FeedbackToConsole` or `AddressOf appobj.FeedbackToFile`.

As you might imagine, the compiler knows that a delegate is being constructed and parses the source code to determine which object and method are being referred to. A reference to the object is passed for the `target` parameter, and a special `Int32` value (obtained from a MethodDef or MethodRef metadata token) that identifies the method is passed for the `methodPtr` parameter. For static methods, `Nothing` is passed for the `target` parameter. Inside the constructor, these two parameters are saved in their corresponding private fields.

In addition, the constructor sets the `_prev` field to `Nothing`. This `_prev` field is used to create a linked list of `MulticastDelegate` objects. I'll ignore this field for now but cover it in detail later in the chapter, in the section "Delegate Chains."

So, each delegate object is really a wrapper around a method and an object to be operated on when the method is called. The `MulticastDelegate` class defines two read-only public instance properties: `Target` and `Method`.

Given a reference to a delegate object, you can query these properties. The `Target` property returns a reference to the object that will be operated on if the method is called back. If the method is a static method, `Target` returns `Nothing`. The `Method` property returns a `System.Reflection.MethodInfo` object that identifies the callback method.

You could use this information in several ways. For example, you could check to see whether a delegate object refers to an instance method of a specific type:

```
Function DelegateRefersToInstanceMethodOfType( _
    ByVal d As MulticastDelegate, ByVal type As Type) As Boolean
    Return Not (d.Target Is Nothing) AndAlso d.Target.GetType Is type
End Function
```

You could also write code to check whether the callback method has a specific name (such as `FeedbackToMsgBox`):

```
Function DelegateRefersToMethodOfName(ByVal d As MulticastDelegate, _
    ByVal methodName As String) As Boolean
    Return (d.Method.Name = methodName)
End Function
```

Now that you know how delegate objects are constructed, let's talk about how the callback method is invoked. For convenience, I've repeated the code to `ItemSet`'s `ProcessItems` here:

```
Public Sub ProcessItems(ByVal feedback As Feedback)
    Dim item As Int32
    For item = 0 To items.Length - 1
        If Not feedback Is Nothing Then
            ' If any callbacks are specified, call them.
            feedback(items(item), item + 1, items.Length)
        End If
    Next
End Sub
```

Just below the comment is the line of code that invokes the callback method. It might seem as if I'm calling a function named **feedback** and passing it three parameters. However, there is no function named **feedback**. Again, because it knows that **feedback** is a variable that refers to a delegate object, the compiler generates code to call the delegate object's **Invoke** method. In other words, the compiler sees this:

```
feedback(items(item), item + 1, items.Length)
```

But the compiler generates code as though the source code said this:

```
feedback.Invoke(items(item), item + 1, items.Length)
```

You can verify that the compiler produces code to call the delegate type's **Invoke** method by using ILDasm.exe to examine the code for the **ProcessItems** method. Figure 17-2 shows the IL for the **ItemSet** type's **Process-Items** method. The boxed lines in the figure indicate the instruction that calls **ItemSet.Feedback**'s **Invoke** method. In fact, Visual Basic allows you to write your code explicitly calling the **Invoke** method, if you prefer.

You'll recall that the compiler defined the **Invoke** method when it defined the **Feedback** class. When **Invoke** is called, it uses the private **_target** and **_methodPtr** fields to call the desired method on the specified object. Note that the signature of the **Invoke** method matches the signature of the delegate; that is, because the **Feedback** delegate is a **Sub** method that takes three parameters, the **Invoke** method is also a **Sub** method that takes the same three parameters.

Figure 17-2   ILDasm.exe proves that the compiler emitted a call to the **ItemSet.Feedback** delegate type's **Invoke** method.

Some Delegate History: `System.Delegate` and `System.MulticastDelegate`

Even though the FCL defines the `System.MulticastDelegate` class, `Multicast-Delegate` is actually derived from the `System.Delegate` class (also defined in the FCL), which itself is derived from `System.Object`. When originally designing the .NET Framework, Microsoft engineers felt the need to provide two different types of delegates: single-cast and multicast. `MulticastDelegate`-derived types would represent delegate objects that could be chained together, and `Delegate`-derived types would represent objects that could not be chained together. The `System.Delegate` type was designed as the base type, and this class implemented all the functionality necessary to call back a wrapped method. The `Multicast-Delegate` class was derived from the `Delegate` class and added the ability to create a linked list (or chain) of `MulticastDelegate` objects.

When compiling source code, a compiler would check the delegate's signature and select the more appropriate of the two classes for the compiler-generated delegate type's base class. For the curious, methods with a signature that indicated a return value (`Function` methods) would be derived from `System.Delegate`, and methods that have no return value (`Sub` methods) would be derived from `System.MulticastDelegate`. This made sense because you can get the return value only from the last method called in a linked-list chain.

During the beta testing of the .NET Framework, it became clear that having the two different base types greatly confused developers. In addition, designing delegates this way placed arbitrary limitations on them. For example, many methods have return values that you can ignore in many situations. Because these methods would have a return value, they wouldn't be derived from the `MulticastDelegate` class, preventing them from being combined into a linked list.

To reduce developer confusion, Microsoft's engineers wanted to merge the `Delegate` and `MulticastDelegate` classes together into a single class that allowed any delegate object to participate in a linked-list chain. All compilers would generate delegate classes deriving from this one class. This change would reduce complexity and effort for the .NET Framework team, the CLR team, the compiler team, and for developers out in the field who are using delegates.

Unfortunately, the idea of merging the `Delegate` and `MulticastDelegate` classes came along a bit late in the .NET Framework development cycle, and Microsoft was concerned about the potential bugs and testing hit that would occur if these changes were made. So in version 1 of the .NET Framework, these classes haven't been merged; in a future version of the .NET Framework, I expect that these two classes will be combined into a single class.

Although Microsoft chose to delay the merging of these two classes in the FCL, they were able to modify all the Microsoft compilers. All the Microsoft compilers now generate delegate types derived from the **MulticastDelegate** class all the time. So when I said earlier in this chapter that all delegate types are derived from **MulticastDelegate**, I wasn't lying. Because of this change to the compiler, all instances of delegate types can be combined into a linked-list chain regardless of the callback method's return value.

You might be thinking, "Why do I need to know about all this?" Well, here's why: As you start working more and more with delegates, you'll undoubtedly run across both the **Delegate** and **MulticastDelegate** types in the .NET Framework SDK documentation. I want you to understand the relationship between these two classes. In addition, even though all delegate types you create have **MulticastDelegate** as a base class, you'll occasionally manipulate your types using methods defined by the **Delegate** class instead of the **MulticastDelegate** class. For example, the **Delegate** class has static methods called **Combine** and **Remove**. (I explain what these methods do later.) The signatures for both these methods indicate that they take **Delegate** parameters. Because your delegate type is derived from **MulticastDelegate**, which is derived from **Delegate**, instances of your delegate type can be passed to the **Combine** and **Remove** methods.

Comparing Delegates for Equality

The **Delegate** base class overrides **Object**'s virtual **Equals** method. The **MulticastDelegate** type inherits **Delegate**'s implementation of **Equals**. **Delegate**'s implementation of **Equals** compares two delegate objects to see whether their **_target** and **_methodPtr** fields refer to the same object and method. If these two fields match, **Equals** returns **True**; if they don't match, **Equals** returns **False**. The following code demonstrates:

```
' Construct two delegate objects that refer to the same target/method.
Dim fb1 As New Feedback(AddressOf FeedbackToConsole)
Dim fb2 As New Feedback(AddressOf FeedbackToConsole)

' Even though fb1 and fb2 refer to two different objects, internally
' they both refer to the same callback target/method.
Console.WriteLine(fb1.Equals(fb2))   ' Displays "True"
```

Understanding how to compare delegates for equality is important when you try to manipulate delegate chains, a topic I'll talk about next.

Delegate Chains

By themselves, delegates are incredibly useful. But add in their support for chaining, and delegates become even more valuable. I've already mentioned that each **MulticastDelegate** object has a private field, named **_prev**. This field holds a reference to another **MulticastDelegate** object; that is, every object of type **MulticastDelegate** (or any type derived from **MulticastDelegate**) has a reference to another **MulticastDelegate**-derived object. This field allows delegate objects to be part of a linked list.

The **Delegate** class defines three static methods that you can use to manipulate a linked-list chain of delegate objects.

```
Public Class System.Delegate
  ' Combines the chains represented by head and tail; head is returned.
  ' NOTE: head will be the last delegate called.
  Public Shared Function Combine(ByVal tail As Delegate, _
     ByVal head As Delegate) As Delegate


  ' Creates a chain represented by the array of delegates.
  ' NOTE: entry 0 is the head and will be the last delegate called.
  Public Shared Function Combine(ByVal delegateArray() As Delegate) _
     As Delegate


  ' Removes a delegate matching value's Target/Method from the chain.
  ' The new head is returned and will be the last delegate called.
  Public Shared Function Remove(ByVal source As Delegate, _
     ByVal value As Delegate) As Delegate
End Class
```

When you construct a new delegate object, the object's **_prev** field is set to **Nothing**, indicating that no other objects are in the linked list. To combine two delegates into a linked list, you call one of **Delegate**'s static **Combine** methods:

```
Dim fb1 As New Feedback(AddressOf FeedbackToConsole)
Dim fb2 As New Feedback(AddressOf FeedbackToMsgBox)
Dim fbChain As Feedback = DirectCast([Delegate].Combine(fb1, fb2), Feedback)
' The left side of Figure 17-3 shows what the
' chain looks like after this code executes.

Dim appobj As New App()
Dim fb3 As New Feedback(appobj.FeedbackToFile)
fbChain = DirectCast([Delegate].Combine(fbChain, fb3), Feedback)
' The right side of Figure 17-3 shows what the
' chain looks like after all the code executes.
```

Figure 17-3 shows what the internal representation of delegate chains looks like.

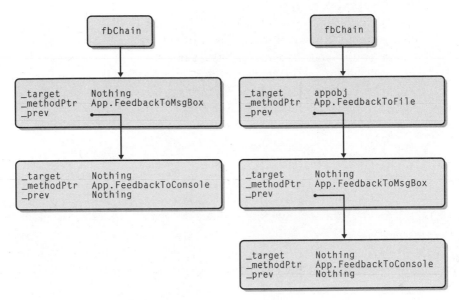

Figure 17-3   Internal representation of delegate chains

You'll notice that the **Delegate** type offers another version of the **Combine** method that takes an array of **Delegate** references. Using this version of **Combine**, you could rewrite the preceding code as follows:

```
Dim fbArray(2) As Feedback
fbArray(0) = New Feedback(AddressOf FeedbackToConsole)
fbArray(1) = New Feedback(AddressOf FeedbackToMsgBox)
Dim appobj As New App()
fbArray(2) = New Feedback(AddressOf appobj.FeedbackToFile)

Dim fbChain As Feedback = DirectCast([Delegate].Combine(fbArray), Feedback)
' The right side of Figure 17-3 shows what the
' chain looks like after all the code executes.
```

When a delegate is invoked, the compiler generates a call to the delegate type's **Invoke** method (as discussed earlier in this chapter). To refresh your memory, my earlier example declared a **Feedback** delegate as follows:

```
Public Delegate Sub Feedback(ByVal value As Object, _
   ByVal item As Int32, ByVal numItems As Int32)
```

This caused the compiler to generate a **Feedback** class that contains an **Invoke** method that looks like this (in pseudocode):

```
Class Feedback
    Inherits MulticastDelegate

    Public Overridable Sub Invoke(ByVal value As Object, _
        ByVal item As Int32, ByVal numItems As Int32)

        ' If there are any delegates in the chain that
        ' should be called first, call them recursively.
        If Not (_prev Is Nothing) Then
            _prev.Invoke(value, item, numItems)
        End If

        ' Call the callback method on the specified target object.
        _target.methodPtr(value, item, numItems)
    End Sub
End Class
```

As you can see, invoking a delegate object causes its previous delegate to be invoked first. When the previous delegate returns, its return value is discarded (if it's a **Function**). After calling its previous delegate, the delegate can then invoke the callback target/method that it wraps. The following code demonstrates.

```
Dim fb1 As New Feedback(AddressOf FeedbackToConsole)
Dim fb2 As New Feedback(AddressOf FeedbackToMsgBox)
Dim fbChain As Feedback = DirectCast([Delegate].Combine(fb1, fb2), Feedback)
' At this point, fbChain refers to a delegate that calls
' FeedbackToMsgBox, this delegate refers to another delegate that
' calls FeedbackToConsole, and this delegate refers to Nothing.

' Now let's invoke the head delegate, which internally invokes
' its previous delegate and so on.
If Not (fbChain Is Nothing) Then fbChain(Nothing, 0, 10)
' NOTE: In the preceding line, fbChain will never be Nothing, but checking a
' delegate reference against Nothing before attempting to invoke it is a
' very good habit to get into.
```

So far, I've shown examples where my delegate type, **Feedback**, is defined as a **Sub** method that doesn't have a return value. However, I could have defined my **Feedback** delegate as follows:

```
Public Delegate Function Feedback(ByVal value As Object, _
    ByVal item As Int32, ByVal numItems As Int32) As Int32
```

If I had, its **Invoke** method would have internally looked like this (again, in pseudocode):

```
Class Feedback
    Inherits MulticastDelegate

    Public Overridable Function Invoke(ByVal value As Object, _
        ByVal item As Int32, ByVal numItems As Int32) As Int32

        ' If there are any delegates in the chain that
        ' should be called first, call them recursively.
        If Not (_prev Is Nothing) Then
            _prev.Invoke(value, item, numItems)
        End If

        ' Call the callback method on the specified target object.
        _Return target.methodPtr(value, item, numItems)
    End Sub
End Class
```

When the head of the delegate chain is invoked, it calls any previous delegate in the chain. However, notice that the previous delegate's return value is discarded. Your application code will receive the return value only from the delegate that is at the head of the chain (the last callback method called).

Now that you know how to build delegate chains, let's look at how to remove a delegate from a chain. To remove a delegate from a linked list, you call the **Delegate** type's static **Remove** method:

```
Dim fb1 As New Feedback(AddressOf FeedbackToConsole)
Dim fb2 As New Feedback(AddressOf FeedbackToMsgBox)
Dim fbChain As Feedback = DirectCast([Delegate].Combine(fb1, fb2), Feedback)
' fbChain refers to a chain of two delegates.

' Invoke the chain: two methods are called.
If Not (fbChain Is Nothing) Then fbChain(Nothing, 0, 10)

fbChain = DirectCast([Delegate].Remove(fbChain, _
    New Feedback(AddressOf FeedbackToMsgBox)), Feedback)
' fbChain refers to a chain with one delegate.

' Invoke the chain: one method is called.
If Not (fbChain Is Nothing) Then fbChain(Nothing, 0, 10)

fbChain = DirectCast([Delegate].Remove(fbChain, _
    New Feedback(AddressOf FeedbackToConsole)), Feedback)

' fbChain refers to a chain of 0 delegates. (fbChain is Nothing.)

' Invoke the chain: 0 methods are called.
If Not (fbChain Is Nothing) Then fbChain(Nothing, 0, 10)
```

This code first builds a chain by constructing two delegate objects and then combining them into a linked list by calling the **Combine** method. The **Remove** method is then called. **Remove**'s first parameter refers to the head of the delegate object chain, and its second parameter refers to the delegate object that is to be removed from the chain. I know it seems strange to construct a new delegate object in order to remove it from the chain. To fully understand why this is necessary requires some additional explanation.

In the call to **Remove**, I'm constructing a new delegate object. This delegate object has its **_target** and **_methodPtr** fields initialized appropriately, and the **_prev** field is set to **Nothing**. The **Remove** method scans the chain (referred to by **fbChain**), checking whether any of the delegate objects in the chain are equal to the new delegate object. Remember that the overridden **Equals** method implemented by the **Delegate** class compares the **_target** and **_methodPtr** fields only and ignores the **_prev** field.

If a match is found, the **Remove** method removes the located delegate object from the chain by fixing up the previous delegate object's **_prev** field. **Remove** returns the head of the new chain. If a match isn't found, **Remove** does nothing (no exception is thrown) and returns the same value that was passed for its first parameter.

Note that each call to **Remove** eliminates only one object from the chain, as the following code demonstrates:

```
Dim fb As New Feedback(AddressOf FeedbackToConsole)
Dim fbChain As Feedback = DirectCast([Delegate].Combine(fb, fb), Feedback)
' fbChain refers to a chain of two delegates.

' Invoke the chain: FeedbackToConsole is called twice.
If Not (fbChain is nothing) then fbChain(...)

' Remove one of the callbacks from the chain.
fbChain = DirectCast([Delegate].Remove(fbChain, fb), Feedback)

' Invoke the chain: FeedbackToConsole is called once.
If Not (fbChain is nothing) then fbChain(...)

' Remove one of the callbacks from the chain.
fbChain = DirectCast([Delegate].Remove(fbChain, fb), Feedback)

' Invoke the chain: 0 methods are called.
If Not (fbChain is nothing) then fbChain(...)
```

Having More Control over Invoking a Delegate Chain

At this point, you understand how to build a linked-list chain of delegate objects and how to invoke all the objects in that chain. All items in the linked-list chain are invoked because the delegate type's **Invoke** method includes code to call the previous delegate (if one exists). This is obviously a very simple algorithm. And although this simple algorithm is good enough for a lot of scenarios, it has many limitations.

For example, the return values of the callback methods are all discarded except for the last one. Using this simple algorithm, there's no way to get the return values for all the callback methods called. But this isn't the only limitation. What happens if one of the invoked delegates throws an exception or blocks for a very long time? Because the algorithm invoked each delegate in the chain serially, a "problem" with one of the delegate objects stops all the other delegates in the chain from getting called. Clearly, this algorithm isn't robust.

For those scenarios in which this algorithm is insufficient, the **Multicast-Delegate** class offers an instance method, **GetInvocationList**, that you can use to call each delegate in a chain explicitly, using any algorithm that meets your needs:

```
Public Class System.MulticastDelegate
    Inherits System.Delegate
    ' Creates a delegate array; each item is a clone from the chain.
    ' NOTE: entry 0 is the tail, which would normally be called first.
    Public Overridable Function GetInvocationList() As Delegate()
End Class
```

The **GetInvocationList** method operates on a reference to a delegate chain and returns an array of references to delegate objects. Internally, **GetInvocation-List** walks the specified chain and creates a clone of each object in the chain, appending the clone to the array. Each clone has its **_prev** field set to **Nothing**, so each object is isolated and doesn't refer to a chain of any other objects.

You can easily write an algorithm that explicitly calls each object in the array. The following code demonstrates:

```vb
Imports System
Imports System.Text

' Define a Light component.
Class Light
    ' This method returns the light's status.
    Public Function SwitchPosition() As String
        Return "The light is off"
    End Function
End Class

' Define a Fan component.
Class Fan
    ' This method returns the fan's status.
    Public Function Speed() As String
        Throw New Exception("The fan broke due to overheating")
    End Function
End Class

' Define a Speaker component.
Class Speaker
    ' This method returns the speaker's status.
    Public Function Volume() As String
        Return "The volume is loud"
    End Function
End Class

Class App
    ' Definition of delegate that allows querying a component's status
    Delegate Function GetStatus() As String

    Shared Sub Main()
        ' Build an array of delegates.
        Dim delegArray(2) As GetStatus
        delegArray(0) = New GetStatus(AddressOf New Light().SwitchPosition)
        delegArray(1) = New GetStatus(AddressOf New Fan().Speed)
        delegArray(2) = New GetStatus(AddressOf New Speaker().Volume)

        ' Declare and initialize the delegate chain.
        Dim getStatus As GetStatus = _
           DirectCast([Delegate].Combine(delegArray), GetStatus)

        ' Show consolidated status report reflecting
        ' the condition of the three components.
        Console.WriteLine(GetComponentStatusReport(getStatus))
    End Sub
```

```vb
' Method that queries several components and returns a status report
Shared Function GetComponentStatusReport(ByVal status As GetStatus) _
    As String

    ' If the chain is empty, there's nothing to do.
    If (status Is Nothing) Then Return Nothing

    ' Use this to build the status report.
    Dim report As New StringBuilder()

    ' Get an array where each element is a delegate from the chain.
    Dim arrayOfDelegates() As [Delegate] = status.GetInvocationList()

    ' Iterate over each delegate in the array.
    Dim getStatus As GetStatus

    For Each getStatus In arrayOfDelegates
        Try
            ' Get a component's status string, and append it to the report.
            report.AppendFormat("{0}{1}{1}", getStatus(), Environment.NewLine)
        Catch ex As Exception
            ' Generate an error entry in the report for this component.
            Dim component As Object = getStatus.Target
            Dim compType As String = ""
            If Not (component Is Nothing) Then
                compType = component.GetType.Name
            End If

            report.AppendFormat( _
                "Failed to get status from {1}{2}{0}    Error: {3}{0}{0}", _
                Environment.NewLine, compType, _
                getStatus.Method.Name, ex.Message)
        End Try
    Next

    ' Return the consolidated report to the caller.
    Return report.ToString()
End Function
End Class
```

When you build and run this code, the following output appears:

```
The light is off

Failed to get status from Fan.Speed
    Error: The fan broke due to overheating

The volume is loud
```

Delegates and Reflection

So far in this chapter, the use of delegates has required that the developer know up front the prototype of the method that is to be called back. For example, if **feedback** is a variable that references a **Feedback** delegate, then to invoke the delegate, the code would look like this:

```
feedback(items(item), item + 1, items.Length)
```

As you can see, the developer must know when coding how many parameters the callback method requires and the types of those parameters. Fortunately, the developer almost always has this information and so writing code like the preceding isn't a problem. In some rare scenarios, however, the developer doesn't have this information at compile time. Fortunately, **System.Delegate** offers a few methods that allow you to create and invoke a delegate when you just don't have all the necessary information about the delegate at compile time. Here are the methods that **Delegate** defines:

```
Public Class System.Delegate
   ' Construct a delType delegate wrapping the specified methodInfo.
   Public Shared Function CreateDelegate(ByVal delType As Type, _
      ByVal mi As MethodInfo) As Delegate

   ' Construct a delType delegate wrapping a type's static method.
   Public Shared Function CreateDelegate(ByVal delType As Type,
      ByVal type As Type, ByVal methodName As String) As Delegate

   ' Construct a delType delegate wrapping an object's instance method.
   Public Shared Function CreateDelegate(ByVal delType As Type,
      ByVal obj As Object, ByVal methodName As String) As Delegate

   ' Construct a delType delegate wrapping an object's instance method.
   Public Shared Function CreateDelegate(ByVal delType As Type,
      ByVal obj As Object, ByVal methodName As String, _
      ByVal ignoreCase As Boolean) As Delegate

   Public Function DynamicInvoke(ByVal args() As Object) As Object
End Class
```

All the **CreateDelegate** methods here construct a new object of a **Delegate**-derived type identified by the first parameter, **delType**. The remaining parameters to **CreateDelegate** determine the callback method that the **Delegate**-derived object is to wrap. You can specify a **MethodInfo** (discussed in Chapter 20), a type's static method by **String**, or an object's instance method by **String**.

The **Delegate**'s instance **DynamicInvoke** method allows you to invoke a delegate object's callback method, passing a set of parameters that you determine at run time. When you call **DynamicInvoke**, it internally ensures that the parameters you pass are compatible with the parameters that the callback method expects. If they're compatible, the callback method is called. If they're not, an exception is thrown. **DynamicInvoke** returns the object that the callback method returned.

The following code shows how to use these methods:

```
Imports System
Imports System.Reflection
Imports System.IO

' Here are some different delegate definitions.
Delegate Function TwoInt32s(ByVal n1 As Int32, ByVal n2 As Int32) As Object
Delegate Function OneString(ByVal s1 As String) As Object

Class App
    Shared Sub Main()
        ' Get arguments passed on the command line.
        Dim args() As String = Environment.GetCommandLineArgs

        If (args.Length < 3) Then
            Dim fileName As String = Path.GetFileNameWithoutExtension( _
                [Assembly].GetEntryAssembly().CodeBase)
            Console.WriteLine("Usage:")
            Console.WriteLine("{0} delType methodName [Param1] [Param2]", _
                fileName)
            Console.WriteLine("   where delType must be TwoInt32s or OneString")
            Console.WriteLine("   if delType is TwoInt32s, " _
                & "methodName must be Add or Subtract")
            Console.WriteLine("   if delType is OneString, " _
                & "methodName must be NumChars or Reverse")
            Console.WriteLine()
            Console.WriteLine("Examples:")
            Console.WriteLine("   {0} TwoInt32s Add 123 321", fileName)
            Console.WriteLine("   {0} TwoInt32s Subtract 123 321", fileName)
            Console.WriteLine("   {0} OneString NumChars ""Hello there""", _
                fileName)
            Console.WriteLine("   {0} OneString Reverse  ""Hello there""", _
                fileName)
            Exit Sub
        End If
```

(continued)

```vb
        ' args(0) is the name of the executable.
        ' args(1) is the delegate type.
        Dim delType As Type = Type.GetType(args(1))
        If delType Is Nothing Then
           Console.WriteLine("Invalid delType argument: {0}", args(1))
           Exit Sub
        End If


        Dim d As [Delegate]
        Try
           ' Create a delegate that points to the specific method.
           ' args(2) is the method name.
           d = [Delegate].CreateDelegate(delType, GetType(App), args(2))
        Catch ex As ArgumentException
           Console.WriteLine("Invalid methodName argument: {0}", args(2))
           Exit Sub
        End Try


        ' Prepare the array containing arguments.
        Dim callbackArgs(args.Length - 4) As Object

        If d.GetType() Is GetType(TwoInt32s) Then
           ' If the method takes two Int32s, retrieve
           ' them by parsing command arguments.
           Try
              Dim a As Int32
              For a = 3 To args.Length - 1
                 callbackArgs(a - 3) = Int32.Parse(args(a))
              Next
           Catch ex As FormatException
              Console.WriteLine("Parameters must be integers.")
              Exit Sub
           End Try

        ElseIf d.GetType() Is GetType(OneString) Then
           ' If the method takes string arguments, copy them from the
           ' args array.
           Array.Copy(args, 3, callbackArgs, 0, callbackArgs.Length)
        End If


        Try
           ' Invoke the delegate dynamically and print the result.
           Dim result As Object = d.DynamicInvoke(callbackArgs)
           Console.WriteLine("Result = {0}", result)
        Catch ex As TargetParameterCountException
           Console.WriteLine("Incorrect number of parameters specified.")
        End Try
     End Sub
```

```vb
' This is the callback method that takes two Int32 parameters.
Shared Function Add(ByVal n1 As Int32, ByVal n2 As Int32) As Object
    Return n1 + n2
End Function

Shared Function Subtract(ByVal n1 As Int32, ByVal n2 As Int32) As Object
    Return n1 - n2
End Function

' This is the callback method that takes one String parameter.
Shared Function NumChars(ByVal s1 As String) As Object
    Return s1.Length
End Function

Shared Function Reverse(ByVal s1 As String) As Object
    Dim chars() As Char = s1.ToCharArray()
    Array.Reverse(chars)
    Return New String(chars)
End Function
End Class
```

Part V

Managing Types

18

Exceptions

In this chapter, I'll talk about a powerful mechanism that allows you to write more maintainable and robust code: *exception handling*. Here are just a few of the benefits offered by exception handling:

- **The ability to keep cleanup code in a localized location, and the assurance that this cleanup code will execute** By moving cleanup code out of an application's main logic to a localized location, the application is easier to write, understand, and maintain. The assurance that the cleanup code runs means that the application is more likely to remain in a consistent state. For example, files will get closed when the code writing to the file can no longer continue what it's doing for whatever reason.

- **The ability to keep code that deals with exceptional situations in a central place** A line of code can fail for many reasons: arithmetic overflow, stack overflow, out-of-memory status, an out-of-range argument, an out-of-range index into an array, and an attempt to access a resource (such as a file) after it has been closed, to name a few. Without using exception handling, it's very difficult, if not impossible, to write code that gracefully detects and recovers from such failures. Sprinkling the code to detect these potential failures into your application's main logic makes the code difficult to write, understand, and maintain. In addition, having code that checks for these potential failures would be a huge performance hit on an application.

    Using exception handling, you don't need to write code to detect these potential failures. Instead, you can simply write your code assuming that the failures won't occur. This certainly makes the code easier to write, understand, and maintain. In addition, the code runs fast. Then you put all your recovery code in a central location. Only if a failure occurs does the exception handling mechanism step in to execute your recovery code.

■   **The ability to locate and fix bugs in the code**   When a failure occurs, the common language runtime (CLR) walks up the thread's call stack, looking for code capable of handling the exception. If no code handles the exception, you receive a notification of this "unhandled exception." You can then easily locate the source code that issued the failure, determine why the failure happened, and modify the source code to fix the bug. This means that bugs will be detected during development and testing of an application and fixed prior to the application's deployment. Once deployed, the application will be more robust, improving the end-user's experience.

When used properly, exception handling is a great tool that eases the burden on software developers. However, if you use it improperly, exception handling can bring much sorrow and pain by hiding serious problems in the code or by misinforming you of the actual problem. The bulk of this chapter is dedicated to explaining how to use exception handling properly.

The Mechanics of Exception Handling

In this section, I'll introduce the mechanics and Visual Basic constructs for using exception handling, but it's not my intention to explain them in great detail. The purpose of this chapter is to offer useful guidelines for when and how to use exception handling in your code. If you want more information about the mechanics and language constructs for using exception handling, see the .NET Framework documentation and your programming language reference. Also, the .NET Framework exception handling mechanism is built using the structured exception handling (SEH) mechanism offered by Windows. SEH has been discussed in many resources, including my own book, *Programming Applications for Microsoft Windows* (4th ed., Microsoft Press, 1999), which contains three chapters devoted to SEH.

The following Visual Basic code shows a standard usage of the exception handling mechanism. This code gives you an idea of what exception handling blocks look like and what their purpose is. In the subsections after the code, I'll formally describe the `Try`, `Catch`, and `Finally` blocks and their purpose and provide some notes about their use.

```
Sub SomeMethod()
    Try
        ' Inside the try block is where you put code requiring
        ' graceful recovery or common cleanup operations.
    Catch e As InvalidCastException
        ' Inside this catch block is where you put code that recovers
        ' from an InvalidCastException (or any exception type derived
        ' from InvalidCastException).
    Catch e As NullReferenceException
        ' Inside this catch block is where you put code that recovers
        ' from a NullReferenceException (or any exception type derived
        ' from NullReferenceException).
    Catch e As Exception
        ' Inside this catch block is where you put code that recovers
        ' from any CLS-compliant exception.

        ' When catching a CLS-compliant exception, you usually rethrow
        ' the exception. I explain rethrowing later in this chapter.
        Throw
    Catch
        ' A Catch statement that doesn't specify a type is identical
        ' to catching System.Exception. In other words, this block is
        ' identical to the block above. If you have both Catch blocks,
        ' as in this example, the code in this block will never execute.

        ' When catching a CLS-compliant exception, you usually rethrow
        ' the exception. I explain rethrowing later in this chapter.
        Throw
    Finally
        ' Inside the finally block is where you put code that
        ' cleans up any operations started within the try block.
        ' The code in this block ALWAYS executes, regardless of
        ' whether an exception is thrown.
    End Try
    ' Code below the finally block executes if no exception is thrown
    ' within the try block or if a catch block catches the exception
    ' and doesn't throw or rethrow an exception.
End Sub
```

This code demonstrates one possible way to use exception handling blocks. Don't let the code scare you—most methods have simply a **Try** block matched with a single **Finally** block or a **Try** block matched with a single **Catch** block. It's unusual to have as many **Catch** blocks as in this example. I put them there for illustration purposes.

The Try Block

A **Try** block contains code that requires common cleanup or exception recovery operations. The cleanup code should be placed in a single **Finally** block. A **Try** block can also contain code that might potentially throw an exception. The exception recovery code should be placed in one or more **Catch** blocks. You create one **Catch** block for each kind of event you think the application can recover from. A **Try** block must be associated with at least one **Catch** or **Finally** block; it makes no sense to have a **Try** block that stands by itself.

The Catch Block

A **Catch** block contains code to execute in response to an exception. A **Try** block can have zero or more **Catch** blocks associated with it. If the code in a **Try** block doesn't cause an exception to be thrown, the CLR never executes any code contained within any of its **Catch** blocks. The thread skips over all the **Catch** blocks and executes the code in the **Finally** block (if one exists). After the code in the **Finally** block executes, execution continues with the statement following the **Finally** block.

The expression appearing after the **Catch** keyword is called an *exception filter*. The exception filter is a type representing an exceptional situation that the developer anticipated and can recover from. In Visual Basic, the type in a **Catch** filter must be **System.Exception** or a type derived from **System.Exception**. For example, the previous code contains **Catch** blocks ready to handle an **Invalid-CastException** (or any exception derived from it), a **NullReferenceException** (or any exception derived from it), or any **Exception** (any type of Common Language Specification [CLS]–compliant exception at all).

Note that **Catch** blocks are searched from top to bottom; place the more specific exceptions (types whose base class is farther from **System.Object**) at the top. Unlike some other compilers (C#, for example), the Visual Basic compiler does not generate an error if more specific **Catch** blocks appear closer to the bottom. The reason the Visual Basic compiler doesn't produce an error is because it allows a **Catch** block to include a sophisticated catch filter via Visual Basic's **When** keyword (discussed later in this chapter).

If an exception is thrown by code executing within the **Try** block (or any method called from within the **Try** block), the CLR starts searching for **Catch** blocks whose filter recognizes the thrown exception. If none of the catch filters accepts the exception, the CLR continues searching up the call stack looking for a catch filter that will accept the exception. If after reaching the top of the call stack no **Catch** block is interested in handling the exception, an unhandled exception results. I'll talk more about unhandled exceptions later in this chapter.

Once it locates an exception filter capable of handling the exception, the CLR executes the code in all **Finally** blocks, starting from the **Try** block whose code threw the exception and stopping with the catch filter that matched the exception. Note that any **Finally** block associated with the **Catch** block that matched the exception is not executed yet. The code in this **Finally** block won't execute until after the code in the handling **Catch** block has executed.

> **Important**   Visual Basic can throw only CLS-compliant exceptions—that is, an exception type derived from `System.Exception`. However, the CLR allows any type of object to be thrown. Some languages, such as C#, allow you to catch non-CLS-compliant exceptions. Unfortunately, Visual Basic doesn't offer this ability. For the record, the .NET Framework Class Library (FCL) never throws any non-CLS-compliant exceptions, and in fact, I've never seen any managed code throw a non-CLS-compliant exception. Of course, if you program in intermediate language (IL) assembly language, you could throw a non-CLS-compliant exception object (such as an `Int32`). Managed Extensions for C++ also allows the developer to throw non-CLS-compliant exceptions. Obviously, any code you write should throw CLS-compliant exceptions only since many managed programming languages don't offer a high degree of support for non-CLS-compliant exception types.

In Visual Basic, a catch filter can specify an exception variable. When an exception is caught, this variable refers to the **System.Exception**-derived object that was thrown. The **Catch** block's code can reference this variable to access information specific to the exception (such as the stack trace leading up to the exception). Although it's possible to modify this object, you shouldn't; consider the object to be read-only. I'll explain the **Exception** type and what you can do with it later in this chapter.

After all the code in **Finally** blocks has executed, the code in the handling **Catch** block executes. This code typically performs some operations to recover from the exception. At the end of the **Catch** block, you have three choices:

- Rethrow the same exception, notifying code higher up the call stack of the exception.

- Throw a different exception, giving richer exception information to code higher up the call stack.

- Let the thread fall out the bottom of the **Catch** block.

Later in this chapter, I'll offer some guidelines for when you should use each of these techniques.

If you choose either of the first two techniques, you're throwing an exception and the CLR behaves just like it did before: it walks up the call stack looking for a catch filter interested in recovering from the exception. If you pick the last technique, when the thread falls out the bottom of the **Catch** block, it immediately starts executing code contained in the **Finally** block, if one exists. After all the code in the **Finally** block executes, the thread drops out of the **Finally** block and starts executing the statements immediately following the **Finally** block. If no **Finally** block exists, the thread continues execution at the statement following the last **Catch** block.

The **Finally** Block

A **Finally** block contains code that's guaranteed to execute. Typically, the code in a **Finally** block performs the cleanup operations required by actions taken in the **Try** block. For example, if you open a file in a **Try** block, put the code to close the file in a **Finally** block:

```
Sub ReadData(ByVal pathname As String)

    Dim fs As FileStream = Nothing
    Try
        fs = New FileStream(pathname, FileMode.Open)
        ' Process the data in the file.
        ⋮
    Catch e As OverflowException)
        ' Inside this catch block is where you put code that recovers
        ' from an OverflowException (or any exception type derived
        ' from OverflowException).
        ⋮
    Finally
        ' Make sure that the file gets closed.
        If Not fs Is Nothing Then fs.Close()
End Sub
```

If the code in the **Try** block executes without throwing an exception, the file is guaranteed to be closed. If the code in the **Try** block does throw an exception, the code in the **Finally** block still executes and the file is guaranteed to be closed, regardless of whether or not the exception is caught. It's improper to put the statement to close the file after the **Finally** block; the statement wouldn't execute if an exception were thrown and not caught, leaving the file open.

A **Try** block doesn't have to have a **Finally** block associated with it at all; sometimes the code in a **Try** block just doesn't require any cleanup code. However, if you do have a **Finally** block, it must appear after any and all **Catch** blocks, and a **Try** block can have no more than one **Finally** block associated with it.

When the thread reaches the end of the code contained in a **Finally** block, the thread simply falls out the bottom of the block and starts executing the statements immediately following the **Finally** block. Remember that the code in the **Finally** block is cleanup code. This code should execute only what is necessary to undo operations initiated in the **Try** block. Avoid putting code that might throw an exception in a **Finally** block. However, if an exception is thrown within a **Finally** block, the world doesn't come to an end—the application isn't terminated, and the exception mechanism continues to work as though the exception were thrown after the **Finally** block. The only potentially serious problem is that statements in the **Finally** block that follow the statement that threw the exception aren't executed: since these statements are typically cleanup instructions, some resources in your applications won't be released correctly, or at least not immediately.

What Exactly Is an Exception?

Over the years, I've run into many developers who think that an exception identifies something that rarely happens: "an exceptional event." I always ask them to define "exceptional event." They respond, "You know, something you don't expect to happen." Then they add, "If you're reading bytes from a file, eventually you'll reach the end of the file. So because you expect this, an exception shouldn't be raised when you reach the end of the file. Instead, the **Read** method should return some special value when the end of the file is reached."

Here's my response: "I have an application that needs to read a 20-byte data structure from a file. However, for some reason, the file contains only 10 bytes. In this case, I'm not expecting to reach the end of the file while reading. But because I'll reach the end of the file prematurely, I'd expect an exception to be thrown. Wouldn't you?" In fact, most files contain structured data. It's rare that applications read bytes from a file and process them one at a time until the end of the file is reached. For this reason, I think it makes more sense to have the **Read** method always throw an exception when attempting to read past the end of a file.

Important   Many developers are misguided by the term *exception handling*. These developers believe that the word *exception* is related to how *frequently* something happens. For example, a developer designing a file `Read` method is likely to say the following: "When reading from a file, you'll eventually reach the end of its data. Since reaching the end will *always* happen, I'll design my `Read` method so that it reports the end by returning a special value; I won't have it throw an exception." The problem with this statement is that it is being made by the developer designing the `Read` method, not by the developer calling the `Read` method.

When designing the `Read` method, it is impossible for the developer to know all the possible situations in which the method gets called. Therefore, the developer can't possibly know how *often* the caller of the `Read` method will attempt to read past the end of the file. In fact, since most files contain structured data, attempting to read past the end of a file is something that *rarely* happens.

Another common misconception is that an "exception" identifies an "error." The term *error* implies that the programmer did something wrong. However, again, it isn't possible for the developer designing the `Read` method to know when the caller has called the method incorrectly for the application. Only the developer calling the method can determine this, and therefore only the caller can decide if the results of the call indicate an "error." So you should avoid thinking, "I'll throw an exception here in my code to report an error." In fact, because exceptions don't necessarily indicate errors, I've avoided using the term *error handling* throughout this entire chapter (except for this sentence, of course).

The preceding note explained what *exception* does not mean. Now I'll describe what it does mean. An *exception* is the violation of a programmatic interface's implicit assumptions. For example, when designing a type, you first imagine the various situations for how the type will be used. Then you define the fields, properties, methods, events, and so on for the type. The way you define these members (property data types, method parameters, return values, and so forth) becomes the programmatic interface to your type.

The interface you define carries with it some implicit assumptions. An exception occurs when an assumption made by your programming interface is violated. Look at the following class definition:

```
Public Class Account
    Public Shared Sub Transfer(ByVal fromAccount As Account, _
        ByVal toAccount As Account, ByVal amount As Decimal)
        ⋮
    End Sub
End Class
```

The **Transfer** method accepts two **Account** objects and a **Decimal** value that identifies an amount of money to transfer between accounts. When calling the **Transfer** method, some obvious assumptions are implied: the **fromAccount** argument refers to a valid **Account**, and the account has enough money in it to subtract the specified amount. Also, it isn't clear from this prototype whether **amount** must be a positive value or whether **amount** can be negative. In addition, what happens if the **fromAccount** argument and the **toAccount** argument refer to the same account? Is it "legal" to transfer money to and from the same account? Also, what if the **amount** argument is outside a specific range set by the class designer? Is it "legal" to transfer an amount of 0?

The answers to the questions posed in the preceding paragraph are baked into **Transfer**'s implementation by the developer of the **Account** class. Ideally, the developer designing this class will clearly document all these assumptions so that developers using the class can implement the calling code in the most efficient way possible and so that few surprises occur at run time. Unfortunately, developers usually find that documentation lacks a description of all the implicit assumptions, causing developers to discover their violations at run time. Hopefully, all these violations will be detected and corrected during the application's test cycle so that no violations occur after the application is deployed and running in the hands of users.

How does a method notify its caller that one of its assumptions has been violated? It throws an exception. After all, an exception is simply a violation of a programming interface's assumptions.

The next point I want you to understand is that violating a programming interface's assumption isn't necessarily a bad thing. In fact, it can be a good thing because exception handling allows you to catch the exception and gracefully continue execution.

Implied Assumptions Developers Almost Never Think About

When accessing any method, developers make several assumptions—assumptions that we hardly ever think about. When we call a method, we assume that there is enough stack space; we assume that there is enough memory for the method's IL code to be JIT compiled into native code; and we assume that no bug will occur within the CLR itself when attempting the call. Although it happens rarely, these assumptions are sometimes violated.

As you write code to catch and deal with exceptions, keep in mind that these assumptions can be violated at any time, causing the CLR itself to throw a `System.StackOverflowException`, a `System.OutOfMemoryException`, or a `System.ExecutionEngineException` exception, respectively. For example, imagine the following method:

```
Sub InfiniteLoop()
    Do: Loop While True
End Sub
```

The loop in the preceding method could execute successfully 1000 times, but on the 1001st time an exception could be thrown. If the CLR needs to perform a garbage collection, it could hijack the calling thread (discussed in Chapter 19) and make it call an internal function, thereby causing a `StackOverflowException` to be thrown.

These three exceptions are unlike most others because they're usually thrown when the CLR is in a catastrophic situation and can't recover gracefully. Depending on the circumstance that causes one of these exceptions, your code might not be able to catch it and your `Finally` blocks might not execute. The following list describes what happens when one of these special exceptions is thrown:

■   `OutOfMemoryException`   This exception is thrown when you try to new up an object and the garbage collector can't find any free memory. In this case, your application code can successfully catch this exception, and `Finally` blocks will execute. This exception is also thrown when the CLR needs some internal memory and none is available. In this case, the CLR displays a message to the console and the process is immediately terminated: your application won't be able to catch this exception,

Implied Assumptions Developers Almost Never Think About   *(continued)*

and your `Finally` blocks won't execute. Since the CLR can't recover gracefully when it runs out of memory internally, you should be careful when creating a server application using the .NET Framework. In particular, you should have a separate watchdog process that respawns the server automatically if it determines that the server has just terminated.

■ `StackOverflowException` The CLR throws this exception when the thread has used all its stack space. Your application can catch this exception, but `Finally` blocks won't execute since they would require additional stack space and none is available. Also, while a `Catch` block might catch this exception (to log some information to help debugging), it should never swallow it. The reason is that the application is in an undefined state now because its `Finally` blocks didn't execute. Any `Catch` block that catches `StackOverflowException` should rethrow it—let the CLR terminate the process. If the stack overflow occurs within the CLR itself, your application code won't be able to catch the `StackOverflowException` exception and none of your `Finally` blocks will execute. In this case, the CLR will connect a debugger to the process or, if no debugger is installed, just kill the process.

■ `ExecutionEngineException` The CLR throws this exception when it detects that its internal data structures are corrupted or if it detects some bug in itself. When the CLR throws this exception, it will connect a debugger to the process; if no debugger is installed, it just kills the process. No `Catch` blocks or `Finally` blocks will be processed when this exception is thrown.

By the way, some other thread could always call `System.Threading.Thread`'s `Abort` method, forcing a `System.Threading.ThreadAbortException` exception to be thrown in a thread. This is another example demonstrating that an exception can get thrown at any time.

When designing a type, first imagine how the type is going to be most commonly used; then design your interface to work well with this usage. Also think about the implicit assumptions that your interface is introducing and throw exceptions when any assumption is violated. If your type is going to be used in lots of different situations, designing an interface that meets all the possible scenarios will be impossible. In this case, you must simply try your best and get feedback from users that you can take into account when designing the next version of your type's interface.

As you develop an application, you might try using a type whose interface isn't ideal for your situation, thereby violating the type's assumptions frequently. Again, this isn't a bad thing because you can catch the exceptions and continue gracefully. For example, you might write an application that builds an index of all files on the user's drives. To build this index, you must open each file and parse its contents. However, some of the files you try to access might be secured, preventing the file from being opened. In this example, the application should expect lots of `System.Security.SecurityException` exceptions to be thrown. Again, don't think that exceptions always indicate a mistake (or an error) on your part—exceptions might be thrown frequently in your application because of the way your application needs to use the types designed by a different developer. Your code can just catch these exceptions and recover from them as appropriate so that your application continues running. However, be aware that a performance penalty occurs while the system searches for a catch filter capable of handling the exception. The fewer exceptions an application throws, the faster it runs.

The `System.Exception` Class

The common language runtime (CLR) allows an instance of any type to be thrown for an exception—from an `Int32` to a `String` and beyond. However, Microsoft decided against forcing all programming languages to throw and catch exceptions of any type. So Microsoft defined the `System.Exception` type and decreed that all CLS-compliant programming languages must be able to throw and catch exceptions whose type is derived from this type. Exception types that are derived from `System.Exception` are said to be CLS-compliant. Visual Basic and many other languages allow your code to throw only CLS-compliant exceptions.

The `System.Exception` type is a very simple type that contains the properties described in Table 18-1.

Table 18-1   **Properties of the** `System.Exception` **Type**

Property	Access	Type	Description
`Message`	Read-only	`String`	Contains helpful text indicating why the exception was thrown. The message should be localized because a user might see this message if the application code doesn't catch the exception or if the application code does catch the exception in order to log it.
`Source`	Read/write	`String`	Contains the name of the assembly that generated the exception.
`StackTrace`	Read-only	`String`	Contains the names and signatures of methods called that led up to the exception being thrown. This property is very useful for debugging.
`TargetSite`	Read-only	`MethodBase`	Contains the method that threw the exception.
`HelpLink`	Read-only	`String`	Contains a URL (such as *file:// C:\MyApp\Help.htm#MyException-Help*) to documentation that can help a user understand the exception.
`InnerException`	Read-only	`Exception`	Indicates the previous exception if the current exception was raised while handling an exception. This field is usually **Nothing**. The **Exception** type also offers a public **GetBaseException** method that traverses the linked list of inner exceptions and returns the originally thrown exception.
`HResult`	Read/write	`Int32`	This protected property is used only for scenarios in which managed code and unmanaged COM code are interoperating. The property is protected because Microsoft wants developers to reduce their dependency on **HRESULT**s. However, if you're using the CLR's interoperability mechanisms, obtaining an **HRESULT** can come in quite handy. If you want to get the value in this protected property, you can pass an **Exception**-derived object to the **System.Runtime.InteropServices.Marshal** type's shared **GetHRForException** method.

FCL-Defined Exception Classes

The .NET Framework Class Library defines many exception types (all ultimately derived from **System.Exception**). The following hierarchy shows the exception types defined in the MSCorLib.dll assembly; other assemblies define even more exception types. (The application used to obtain this hierarchy is shown in Chapter 20.)

```
System.Exception
  System.ApplicationException
    System.Reflection.InvalidFilterCriteriaException
    System.Reflection.TargetException
    System.Reflection.TargetInvocationException
    System.Reflection.TargetParameterCountException
  System.IO.IsolatedStorage.IsolatedStorageException
  System.SystemException
    System.AppDomainUnloadedException
    System.ArgumentException
      System.ArgumentNullException
      System.ArgumentOutOfRangeException
      System.DuplicateWaitObjectException
    System.ArithmeticException
      System.DivideByZeroException
      System.NotFiniteNumberException
      System.OverflowException
    System.ArrayTypeMismatchException
    System.BadImageFormatException
    System.CannotUnloadAppDomainException
    System.ContextMarshalException
    System.ExecutionEngineException
    System.FormatException
      System.Reflection.CustomAttributeFormatException
    System.IndexOutOfRangeException
    System.InvalidCastException
    System.InvalidOperationException
      System.ObjectDisposedException
    System.InvalidProgramException
    System.IO.IOException
      System.IO.DirectoryNotFoundException
      System.IO.EndOfStreamException
      System.IO.FileLoadException
      System.IO.FileNotFoundException
      System.IO.PathTooLongException
    System.MemberAccessException
      System.FieldAccessException
      System.MethodAccessException
      System.MissingMemberException
```

```
        System.MissingFieldException
        System.MissingMethodException
    System.MulticastNotSupportedException
    System.NotImplementedException
    System.NotSupportedException
        System.PlatformNotSupportedException
    System.NullReferenceException
    System.OutOfMemoryException
    System.RankException
    System.Reflection.AmbiguousMatchException
    System.Reflection.ReflectionTypeLoadException
    System.Resources.MissingManifestResourceException
    System.Runtime.InteropServices.ExternalException
        System.Runtime.InteropServices.COMException
        System.Runtime.InteropServices.SEHException
    System.Runtime.InteropServices.InvalidComObjectException
    System.Runtime.InteropServices.InvalidOleVariantTypeException
    System.Runtime.InteropServices.MarshalDirectiveException
    System.Runtime.InteropServices.SafeArrayRankMismatchException
    System.Runtime.InteropServices.SafeArrayTypeMismatchException
    System.Runtime.Remoting.RemotingException
        System.Runtime.Remoting.RemotingTimeoutException
    System.Runtime.Remoting.ServerException
    System.Runtime.Serialization.SerializationException
    System.Security.Cryptography.CryptographicException
        System.Security.Cryptography.CryptographicUnexpectedOperationException
  System.Security.Policy.PolicyException
    System.Security.SecurityException
    System.Security.VerificationException
    System.Security.XmlSyntaxException
    System.StackOverflowException
    System.Threading.SynchronizationLockException
    System.Threading.ThreadAbortException
    System.Threading.ThreadInterruptedException
    System.Threading.ThreadStateException
    System.TypeInitializationException
    System.TypeLoadException
        System.DllNotFoundException
        System.EntryPointNotFoundException
    System.TypeUnloadedException
    System.UnauthorizedAccessException
```

Microsoft's idea was that **Exception** would be the base type for all exceptions and that two other types, **System.SystemException** and **System.ApplicationException**, would be derived from **Exception**.

The CLR throws types derived from **SystemException**. Most of the exceptions derived from **SystemException** (such as **DivideByZeroException**, **InvalidCastException**, and **IndexOutOfRangeException**) signal nonfatal situations that an application might be able to recover from. However, some of the exceptions, such as `StackOverflowException`, are considered fatal. An application shouldn't attempt to recover from these exceptions because it's extremely unlikely that recovery would be successful.

In addition, methods defined by FCL types are also supposed to throw exceptions derived from `SystemException`. For example, all FCL methods validate their arguments before attempting to perform any operations. If an argument doesn't live up to the method's implicit assumptions, an `ArgumentNullException`, `ArgumentOutOfRangeException`, or `DuplicateWaitObjectException` exception is thrown. All these exceptions are derived from `ArgumentException`; this allows an application to catch `ArgumentException` as a convenient way to catch any of the specific argument exception types.

Microsoft's idea for the `ApplicationException` type was that it would be a base type reserved solely for an application's use; that is, Microsoft wouldn't use `ApplicationException` as the base type for any of its own exception types.

If you examine the exception type hierarchy, you'll see that Microsoft's developers didn't exactly follow Microsoft's guidelines. The FCL defines some reflection-related exception types derived from `ApplicationException`. In addition, some exception types, such as `IsolatedStorageException`, are derived directly from `Exception` instead of `SystemException`.

You might think that these "bugs" are bad. However, before you make that judgment, you should wonder about the value of having all the CLR/FCL exception types derived from `SystemException` and all your application exception types derived from `ApplicationException`. Once you start thinking about exception hierarchies, it doesn't take long before you realize that the sole benefit of a hierarchy is to allow code to catch a related set of exception types easily. In other words, it's easier to write code that catches an `ArithmeticException` than it is to catch all the exception types derived from it: `DivideByZeroException`, `NotFiniteNumberException`, and `OverflowException`.

Now, would you ever want to catch all exceptions derived from `System-Exception` versus all exceptions derived from `ApplicationException`? I don't think so. On the other hand, there are times when you'll want to know if any exception is thrown, and you can gain this knowledge easily by catching `System.Exception`. So it does make sense that all exception types are derived from `Exception`; it also makes sense that `DirectoryNotFoundException`, `EndOfStreamException`, `FileLoadException`, and `FileNotFoundException` are derived from `IOException`. However, I don't think there is any value in having the `SystemException` and `ApplicationException` base types in the exception hierarchy. In fact, I think having them is just confusing.

Also, I think that the two special exceptions, `ExecutionEngineException` and `StackOverflowException`, should be in a special hierarchy because they are unlike any other exceptions. Only the CLR itself—never the application code—should be able to throw one of these exceptions because an application can't recover gracefully from any of them.

Defining Your Own Exception Class

When implementing your methods, you might come across scenarios in which you want to throw an exception. For example, I recommend that your nonprivate methods always validate their arguments, and if any argument doesn't live up to your method's implicit assumptions, an exception should be thrown. In this case, I recommend that you throw one of the exception classes already defined in the FCL: `ArgumentNullException`, `ArgumentOutOfRangeException`, or `DuplicateWaitObjectException`.

I strongly suggest that you throw an object of a specific exception class, a class that has no other classes derived from it. For example, don't throw an `ArgumentException` because it's too vague, it could mean any of its three derived types, and it doesn't provide as much information as possible to its catchers. You should never throw `Exception`, `ApplicationException`, or `SystemException`.

> **Note**   Throwing an instance of an exception class that you've defined provides your catch code with the capability to know exactly what happened and to recover in any way it sees fit.

Now let's say that you're defining a method that's passed a reference to an object whose type must implement the `ICloneable` and `IComparable` interfaces. You might implement the method like this:

```
Class SomeType
   Public Sub SomeMethod(ByVal o As Object)
      If (TypeOf o Is ICloneable) And (TypeOf o Is IComparable) Then
         ⋮
      Else
         Throw New MissingInterfaceException(...)
      End If
   End Sub
End Class
```

Because the FCL doesn't define an appropriate exception type, you must define the `MissingInterfaceException` type yourself. Note that by convention the name of an exception type should end with "Exception". When defining this type, you must decide what its base type will be. Should you choose `Exception`, `ArgumentException`, or a different type entirely? I've spent months thinking about this question, but unfortunately, I can't come up with a good rule of thumb to offer you, and here's why.

If you derive `MissingInterfaceException` from `ArgumentException`, any existing code that's already catching `ArgumentException` will catch your new exception, too. In some ways this is a feature, and in some ways it's a bug. It's a feature because any code that wants to catch any kind of argument exception (via `ArgumentException`) now catches this new kind of argument exception (`MissingInterfaceException`) automatically. It's a bug because a `Missing-InterfaceException` identifies a new event that wasn't anticipated when code was written to catch an `ArgumentException`. When you define the `Missing-InterfaceException` type, you might think it's so similar to an `ArgumentException` that it should be handled the same way. However, this unanticipated relationship might cause unpredictable behavior.

On the other hand, if you derive `MissingInterfaceException` directly from `Exception`, the code throws a new type that the application couldn't have known about. Most likely, this will become an unhandled exception that causes the application to terminate. I could easily consider this desired behavior because an implicit assumption was violated and the application never considered a remedy for it. Catching this new exception, swallowing it, and continuing execution might cause the application to run with unpredictable results.

Answering questions like these is one of the reasons that application design is more of an art form than a science. When defining a new exception type, carefully consider how application code will catch your type (or base types of your type), and then choose a base type that has the least negative effect on your callers.

When defining your own exception types, feel free to define your own subhierarchies, if they're applicable to what you're doing. You can define them directly from `Exception` or from some other base type. Again, just make sure that where you're putting the subhierarchy makes sense for your callers. As a general rule, hierarchies should be broad and shallow: exception types should be derived from a type close to `Exception` and should typically be no more than two or three levels deep. If you define an exception type that's not going to be the base of other exception types, then mark the type as `NotInheritable`.

The **Exception** base type defines three public constructors:

- A parameterless (default) constructor that creates an instance of the type and sets all fields and properties to default values.

- A constructor taking a **String** that creates an instance of the type and sets a specific message.

- A constructor taking a **String** and an instance of an **Exception**-derived type that creates an instance of the type and sets a specific message and an inner exception. Unfortunately, there are a lot of **Exception**-derived types in the FCL that don't have this constructor. Microsoft will rectify this oversight in a future version of the .NET Framework.

When defining your own exception type, your type should implement a set of three matching constructors and call the base type's corresponding constructor.

Of course, your exception type will inherit all the fields and properties defined by **Exception**. In addition, you might add fields and properties of your own. For example, the **System.ArgumentException** exception adds a **String** property called **ParamName**. The **ArgumentException** type also defines new constructors (in addition to the three public constructors) that take an extra **String** as a parameter so that the **ParamName** property can be initialized to identify the name of the parameter that violated the method's implicit assumptions.

When an **ArgumentException** is caught, the **ParamName** property can be read to determine exactly which parameter caused the problem. Let me tell you, this is incredibly handy when you're trying to debug an application! If you do add fields to your exception type, make sure you define some constructors that allow the fields to be initialized.

Exception types should always be serializable so that the exception object can be marshaled across an AppDomain or a machine boundary and rethrown in the client's code. Making an exception type serializable also allows it to persist in a log or a database. To make your exception type serializable, you must apply the **SerializableAttribute** custom attribute to the type, and if the type defines any fields of its own, you must also implement the **ISerializable** interface's **GetObjectData** method and special protected constructor, both of which take **SerializationInfo** and **StreamingContext** parameters. The following code shows how to properly define your own exception type:

```
Imports System
Imports System.IO
Imports System.Runtime.Serialization
Imports System.Runtime.Serialization.Formatters.Soap
```

(continued)

```
' Allow instances of DiskFullException to be serialized.
<Serializable()> _
NotInheritable Class DiskFullException
   Inherits Exception

   ' The three public constructors
   Public Sub New()
      MyBase.New() ' Call base constructor.
   End Sub

   Public Sub New(ByVal message As String)
      MyBase.New(message) ' Call base constructor.
   End Sub

   Public Sub New(ByVal message As String, _
      ByVal innerException As Exception)
      MyBase.new(message, innerException)     ' Call base constructor.
   End Sub

   ' Define a private field.
   Private m_diskpath As String

   ' Define a read-only property that returns the field.
   ReadOnly Property DiskPath() As String
      Get
         Return m_diskpath
      End Get
   End Property

   ' Override the public Message property so that the
   ' field is included in the message.
   Public Overrides ReadOnly Property Message() As String
      Get
         Dim msg As String = MyBase.Message
         If Not m_diskpath Is Nothing Then
            msg &= Environment.NewLine & "Disk Path: " + m_diskpath
         End If
         Return msg
      End Get
   End Property

   ' Because at least one field is defined, define the
   ' special deserialization constructor. Because this
   ' class is sealed, this constructor is private. If this
   ' class is not sealed, this constructor should be protected.
   Private Sub New (info as SerializationInfo, _
      context as StreamingContext)
```

```vb
        ' Let the base deserialize its fields.
        MyBase.new(info, context)
        ' Deserialize each field.
        m_diskpath = info.GetString("DiskPath")
    End Sub


    ' Because at least one field is defined,
    ' define the serialization method.
    Overrides Sub GetObjectData(ByVal info As SerializationInfo, _
        ByVal context As StreamingContext)
        ' Serialize each field.
        info.AddValue("DiskPath", m_diskpath)

        ' Let the base type serialize its fields.
        MyBase.GetObjectData(info, context)
    End Sub


    ' Define additional constructors that set the field.
    Public Sub New(ByVal message As String, ByVal diskpath As String)
        Me.New(message)                        ' Call another constructor.
        m_diskpath = diskpath
    End Sub


    Public Sub New(ByVal message As String, ByVal diskpath As String, _
        ByVal innerException As Exception)
        Me.New(message, innerException)     ' Call another constructor.
        m_diskpath = diskpath
    End Sub
End Class


' The following code tests the serialization of the exception.
Class App
    Shared Sub Main()
        ' Construct a DiskFullException object, and serialize it.
        Dim e As New DiskFullException("The disk volume is full", "C:\")
        Dim fs As New FileStream("Test", FileMode.Create)
        Dim f As IFormatter = New SoapFormatter()
        f.Serialize(fs, e)
        fs.Close()

        ' Deserialize the DiskFullException object, and check its fields.
        fs = New FileStream("Test", FileMode.Open)
        e = DirectCast(f.Deserialize(fs), DiskFullException)
        fs.Close()
        Console.WriteLine("Type: {1}{0}DiskPath: {2}{0}Message: {3}", _
            Environment.NewLine, e.GetType(), e.DiskPath, e.Message)
    End Sub
End Class
```

How to Use Exceptions Properly

Understanding the exception mechanism is certainly important; equally important is understanding how to use exceptions wisely. All too often I see library developers catching all kinds of exceptions, preventing the application developer from knowing that a problem occurred. In this section, I offer some guidelines that all developers should be aware of when using exceptions.

> **Important**   If you're a *class library developer*, developing types that will be used by other developers, take these guidelines very seriously. You have a huge responsibility: you're trying to design the type's interface so that its implicit assumptions make sense for a wide variety of applications. Remember that you don't have intimate knowledge of the code you're calling (via delegates, virtual methods, or interface methods). And you don't know what code is calling you. It's not feasible to anticipate every situation in which your type will be used, so don't make any policy decisions. Your code must not decide what is an error; let the caller make this decision. Follow the guidelines in this chapter, or application developers will have a difficult time using the types in your class library.
>
> If you're an *application developer*, define whatever policy you think is appropriate. Following the design guidelines in this chapter will help you discover problems in your code sooner, allowing you to fix them and make your application more robust. However, feel free to diverge from these guidelines after careful consideration. You get to set the policy. For example, application code can get more aggressive about catching exceptions.

You Can't Have Too Many `Finally` Blocks

I think `Finally` blocks are awesome! They allow you to specify a block of code that's guaranteed to execute no matter what kind of exception the thread throws. You should use `Finally` blocks to clean up from any operation that successfully started before returning to your caller or continuing to execute code following the `Finally` block. You also frequently use `Finally` blocks to explicitly dispose of any objects to avoid resource leaking. Here's an example that has all cleanup code (closing the file) in a `Finally` block:

```
Class SomeType
    Sub SomeMethod()

        ' Open a file.
        Dim fs As New FileStream("C:\ReadMe.txt", FileMode.Open)
        Try
            ' Display 100 divided by the first byte in the file.
            Console.WriteLine(100 / fs.ReadByte())
        Finally
            ' Put cleanup code in a Finally block to ensure that
            ' the file gets closed regardless of whether or not an
            ' exception occurs (for example, the first byte was 0).
            fs.Close()
        End Try
    End Sub
End Class
```

Ensuring that cleanup code always executes is so important that many programming languages offer constructs that make coding easier. For example, Visual Basic provides the **SyncLock** statement for dealing with thread synchronization. This statement provides the developer with a simple syntax that causes the compiler to automatically generate **Try** and **Finally** blocks, where the **Finally** block contains the cleanup code.

Don't Catch Everything

A common mistake is to use **Catch** blocks too often and to use them improperly. When you catch an exception, you're stating that you expected this exception, you understand why it occurred, and you know how to deal with it. In other words, you're defining a policy for the application. All too often, I see code like this:

```
Catch e As Exception
    ⋮
```

This code indicates that it was expecting *any* and *all* exceptions and knows how to recover from *any* and *all* situations. How can this possibly be? A type that's part of a class library should never catch all exceptions because there is no way for the type to know exactly how the application intends to respond to an exception. In addition, the type will frequently call out to application code via a delegate or a virtual method. If the application code throws an exception, another part of the application is probably expecting to catch this exception. The exception should filter its way up the call stack and let the application code handle the exception as it sees fit.

You might identify specific places in your code where you want to catch everything that can go wrong and gracefully recover. The temptation is to add a **Catch** block that catches **System.Exception**. As an illustration of what *not* to do, consider the virtual **Equals** method (defined by **System.Object**). This method should return **False** if two objects don't have the same logical value. So if some code tries to compare an **Apple** to an **Orange**, **Equals** should return **False**. Here's how you might (incorrectly) implement **Apple**'s **Equals** method:

```
NotInheritable Class Apple
   Dim c As Color = Color.Red  ' The color of the apple

   Public Overloads Overrides Function Equals(ByVal o As Object) _
      As Boolean
      Dim equal As Boolean = False ' Assume objects aren't equal.

      Try
         ' Cast o to an Apple.
         Dim a As Apple = DirectCast(o, Apple)

         ' Compare the fields of 'Me' and a.
         ' If any fields aren't equal, leave the Try block.
         If Me.c <> a.c Then Exit Try

         ' If all fields have the same value, they're equal.
         equal = True
      Catch e As Exception

      End Try

      Return equal
   End Function
End Class
```

Inspecting this code, you see that attempting to cast **o** to an **Apple** might cause the CLR to throw an **InvalidCastException** exception. In fact, this is the only real exception I can imagine the method throwing. Because the **Invalid-CastException** is the only exception you expect, you might feel that it's OK to catch **Exception** as shown in the code. In fact, you might think that it's OK to catch **Exception** even if anything else were to throw an exception. After all, **Equals** should return **True** or **False**.

However, you shouldn't catch **Exception** here because a **StackOver-flowException** or **OutOfMemoryException** exception could be thrown at any time. Because of the way the previous code is written, **Equals** would catch either of these two exceptions and simply return **False** to its caller. **Equals** is now hiding these fatal problems and allowing the application to continue running with unpredictable results. This situation is certainly not desired! To fix the code, catch `InvalidCastException` instead of `Exception`. An `InvalidCast-Exception` is the only exception that this code knows how to recover from gracefully; all other exceptions are not anticipated by `Equals` and should be allowed to propagate out of the method.

> **Important**   When calling Win32 functions, it would be ludicrous not to check the function's return value to see if the function failed for some reason, allowing the code to continue running as if everything were fine. Writing code that catches all exceptions is equivalent to ignoring a failure and yet, for some reason, developers feel fine doing it. The technique described in this section should really be used only for unhandled exceptions (as described later in this chapter).

Gracefully Recovering from an Exception

Sometimes you call a method knowing in advance some of the exceptions that the method might throw. Because you expect these exceptions, you might want to have some code that allows your application to recover gracefully from the situation and continue running. Here's an example in pseudocode.

```
Public Function CalculateSpreadsheetCell(ByVal row As Int32, _
    ByVal columns As Int32) As String
    Dim result As String
    Try
        result = ...     ' Code to calculate the value of a spreadsheet's cell
    Catch e As DivideByZero
        result = "Can't show value: Divide by zero"
    End Try
    Return result
End Function
```

This pseudocode calculates the contents of a cell in a spreadsheet and returns a string representing the value back to the caller so that the caller can display the string in the application's window. However, a cell's contents might be the result of dividing one cell by another cell. If the cell containing the denominator contains 0, the CLR will throw a `DivideByZeroException` exception. In this case, the method catches this specific exception and returns a special string that will be displayed to the user.

When you catch specific exceptions, fully understand the circumstances that cause the exception to be thrown and know what exception types are derived from the exception type you're catching. Don't catch and handle `System.Exception` because it's not feasible for you to know all the possible exceptions that could be thrown within your `Try` block (especially if you consider `OutOfMemoryException`, `OverflowException`, `StackOverflowException`, or even `ExecutionEngineException`, to name a few).

Backing Out of a Partially Completed Operation When an Unrecoverable Exception Occurs

Usually methods call several other methods to perform a single abstract operation. Some of the individual methods might complete successfully, and some might not. For example, a method that transfers money from one account to another account might first add money to one account and then subtract money from the second account. If the first operation completes successfully but the second operations fails (for any reason), the money must be subtracted from the first account so that the accounts balance.

Here is another, perhaps more meaningful, example: Let's say that you're serializing a set of objects to a disk file. After serializing 10 objects, an exception is thrown. (Perhaps the disk is full or the next object to be serialized isn't marked with the `Serializable` custom attribute.) At this point, the exception should filter up to the caller, but what about the state of the disk file? The file is now corrupt because it contains a partially serialized object graph. It would be great if the application could back out of the partially completed operation so that the file would be in the state it was before any objects were serialized into it. The following code demonstrates the correct way to implement this:

```
Public Sub SerializeObjectGraph(ByVal fs As FileStream, _
   ByVal formatter As IFormatter, ByVal rootObj As Object)

   ' Save the current position of the file.
   Dim beforeSerialization As Int64 = fs.Position

   Try
      ' Attempt to serialize the object graph to the file.
      formatter.Serialize(fs, rootObj)

   Catch   ' Catch all CLS exceptions.
      ' If something goes wrong, reset the file back to a good state.
      fs.Position = beforeSerialization

      ' Truncate the file.
      fs.SetLength(fs.Position)
```

```
' NOTE: The preceding code isn't in a Finally block because
' the stream should be reset only when serialization fails.

' Let the caller(s) know what happened by
' rethrowing the SAME exception.
Throw
        End Try
    End Sub
End Sub
```

To properly back out of the partially completed operation, write code that catches all exceptions. Yes, catch *all* exceptions here because you don't care what kind of error occurred; you need to put your data structures back into a consistent state. After you've caught and handled the exception, don't swallow it—let the caller know that the exception occurred. You do this by rethrowing the same exception. In fact, Visual Basic and many other languages make this easy. Just use Visual Basic's **Throw** keyword without specifying anything after **Throw**, as shown in the previous code.

Hiding an Implementation Detail

In some situations, you might find it useful to catch one exception and rethrow a different exception. Here's an example:

```
Public Function SomeMethod(ByVal x As Int32) As Int32
    Try
        Return 100 \ x
    Catch e As DivideByZeroException
        Throw New ArgumentOutOfRangeException("x", x, "x can't be 0", e)
    End Try
End Function
```

When **SomeMethod** is called, the caller passes in an **Int32** value and the method returns 100 divided by this value. Upon entry into the method, code could check to see whether **x** is 0, and if it is, throw an **ArgumentOutOfRange-Exception** exception at that point. However, this check would be performed every time, and because there is an implicit assumption that **x** is rarely 0, the check would cause a performance hit. So, this method assumes that **x** is not 0 and attempts to divide 100. Now, if **x** does happen to be 0, then the specific **DivideByZeroException** exception is caught and rethrown as an **Argument-OutOfRangeException** exception. Note that the **DivideByZeroException** exception is set as the **ArgumentOutOfRangeException**'s **InnerException** property via the constructor's fourth argument.

> **Important**   In this discussion, I've shown how to catch an exception and throw a different exception. When you use this technique, the new exception should have its inner exception property refer to the original exception. The preceding code demonstrates how you should do this correctly. Unfortunately, that code won't compile. The problem is that many of the FCL exception types don't offer constructors that take an `innerException` parameter. These missing constructors are bugs that Microsoft says they will correct in future versions of the .NET Framework. Personally, I've found these bugs to be quite frustrating, and there is no workaround because the `Exception` type offers no way to set an inner exception.

This technique results in catches similar to those discussed in the earlier section "Gracefully Recovering from an Exception." You catch specific exceptions, you fully understand the circumstances that cause the exception to be thrown, and you know what exception types are derived from the exception type you're catching.

Again, class library developers shouldn't catch `System.Exception` and the like. Doing so means that you're converting all exception types into a single exception type. It discards all meaningful information (the type of the exception) and throws a single exception type that doesn't contain any useful information about what really happened. Without this information, it's much harder for code higher up the call stack to catch and handle a specific exception. Give the code higher up the call stack a chance to catch `System.Exception` or some other exception that's a base type for more specific exceptions.

Basically, the only time to catch an exception and rethrow a different exception is to improve the meaning of a method's abstraction. Also, the new exception type you throw should be a specific exception (an exception that's not used as the base type of any other exception type). Imagine a `PhoneBook` type that defines a method that looks up a phone number from a name, shown in the following pseudocode:

```
Class PhoneBook
    Dim pathname As String  ' pathname for address book file

    ' Other methods go here.

    Public Function GetPhoneNumber(ByVal name As String) As String
```

```
        Dim phone As String
        Dim fs As FileStream = Nothing

        Try
            fs = New FileStream(pathname, FileMode.Open)
            ' ..(Code to read from fs until name is found)
            phone = "..."        ' the phone # found
        Catch e As FileNotFoundException
            ' Throw a different exception containing the name, and
            ' set the originating exception as the inner exception.
            Throw New NameNotFoundException(name, e)
        Catch e As IOException
            ' Throw a different exception containing the name, and
            ' set the originating exception as the inner exception.
            Throw New NameNotFoundException(name, e)
        Finally
            If Not fs Is Nothing Then fs.Close()
        End Try

        Return phone
    End Function
End Class
```

The phonebook data is obtained from a file (versus a network connection or database). However, the user of the **PhoneBook** type doesn't know this. So if the file isn't found or can't be read for any reason, the caller would see a **FileNotFoundException** or **IOException**, which wouldn't be anticipated. In other words, the file's existence and ability to be read is part of the method's implied assumptions. However, there is no way that the caller could have guessed this. So the **GetPhoneNumber** method catches these two exception types and throws a new **NameNotFoundException**.

Throwing an exception still lets the caller know that an implied assumption was violated, and the **NameNotFoundException** type gives the caller an abstracted view of the implied assumption that was violated. Setting the inner exception to **FileNotFoundException** or **IOException** is important so that the real cause of the exception isn't lost; knowing what caused the exception could be useful to the developer of the **PhoneBook** type.

Now let's say that the **PhoneBook** type was implemented a little differently. Assume that the type offers a public **PhoneBookPathname** property that allows the user to set or get the pathname of the file in which to look up a phone number. Because the user is aware that the phone book data comes from a file, I would modify the **GetPhoneNumber** method so that it doesn't catch any exceptions; instead, I let whatever exception is thrown propagate out of the method. Note that I'm not changing any parameters of the `GetPhoneNumber` method but I am changing how it's abstracted to users of the `PhoneBook` type.

Again, let me emphasize that class library developers should follow all the design guidelines mentioned here very carefully. As I said earlier, application developers, however, should always be able to define whatever policy they think is appropriate. Following the design guidelines in this chapter will probably help you discover problems in your code sooner, allowing you to fix them and make your application more robust. Application developers should feel free to diverge from these guidelines after careful consideration. They get to set any policy they think is best; the application code can get more aggressive about catching exceptions, for example.

What's Wrong with the FCL

In this chapter, I've given you my recommendations for working with exceptions. These recommendations are based on conversations with many developers and my own experience writing code for many years. In the previous section, I mentioned that many of the FCL exception types are missing a constructor that allows the inner exception to be set. This is just one type of bug in the FCL. Unfortunately, the FCL contains many more bugs related to exception handling. In this section, my intent is to make you aware of these bugs so that you won't waste as much time as I have trying to figure out what's going on when your code doesn't work quite as you expect.

Microsoft hasn't followed a lot of the guidelines that I describe in this chapter. In fact, quite a bit of Microsoft's code violates Microsoft's own guidelines, a situation that can make working with the FCL difficult at times. The problem is exacerbated by the fact that the FCL documentation doesn't always describe what exceptions a developer can expect or how to recover from them.

The first problem is that Microsoft's FCL code is peppered with `Catch` clauses that intercept and swallow any `System.Exception`-derived exception without rethrowing it to the caller. As I explained previously, these constructs catch and swallow exceptions that shouldn't be caught and swallowed by a class library.

Here's an example: the `System.IO.Directory` and `System.IO.File` types have static `Exists` methods. Both methods return `True` or `False` depending on whether the path argument identifies a directory/file that exists on the user's disk drive.

If anything goes wrong inside these methods, the methods catch `Exception` and return `False` to their caller. The caller has no way to tell whether the exception occurred because the file doesn't exist or whether the caller doesn't have sufficient access to the directory or file. Also, if a **StackOverflowException** or an **OutOfMemoryException** is thrown, **False** is also returned!

The second problem is that Microsoft's FCL code frequently catches an exception and throws a new exception. As explained previously, this can be useful if the new exception provides necessary information, but the FCL often hides what actually happened from the application developer.

For example, the **System.Array** type's **Sort** method sorts an array of objects by calling each object's **CompareTo** method. If the **CompareTo** method throws an exception (any exception), the **Sort** method catches it and throws a new **InvalidOperationException**. This is terrible! It means that your code could throw an exception that your code can never catch. There's no reason for **Array**'s **Sort** method to do this. By the way, **Array**'s **BinarySearch** method also catches any and all exceptions and throws a new **InvalidOperationException**, which is equally as troublesome.

The third problem with the FCL is the way it handles reflection (a topic I'll discuss more in Chapter 20). If you obtain a **MethodInfo** for a method and call its **Invoke** method, the method being invoked could throw an exception. Unfortunately, **MethodInfo**'s **Invoke** method catches any and all exceptions and throws a new **System.Reflection.TargetInvocationException**. For this reason, you can't catch the actual exception thrown by the method you invoked.

Another example of this third problem is that the FCL code frequently catches one exception and throws a new **System.Exception**. Again, useful information is lost because the caller must now catch **Exception** and then figure out what really went wrong.

Here's another problem with the FCL code: the **System.Windows.Forms.DataGrid** control has a public **CurrentCell** property. If your code tries to set the value in the current cell and an exception is thrown, the **DataGrid** control catches all **Exception**-derived exceptions and displays a message box! I couldn't believe this when I discovered it. Not only can you not catch the exception, but the user is also confronted with a message box that your application can't control.

I've run into these and other problems the hard way: writing code to handle what I expected, discovering that my code didn't work right, and then finding out that the FCL code had been swallowing my exceptions. It's my fervent hope that Microsoft will examine the FCL source code and correct it so that it follows the design guidelines set out in this chapter. Experience is the best way to learn which FCL methods will cause you problems.

Performance Considerations

The developer community actively debates the performance of exception handling. My experience is that the benefit of exception handling far outweighs any performance penalties. In this section, I'll address some of the performance issues related to exception handling.

It's difficult to compare performance between exception handling and the more conventional means of reporting exceptions (HRESULTs, special return codes, and so forth). If you write code to check the return value of every method call and filter the return value up to your own callers, your application's performance will be seriously affected. But performance aside, the amount of additional coding you must do and the potential for mistakes is incredibly high. Exception handling is a much better alternative.

Unmanaged C++ compilers must generate code that tracks which objects have been constructed successfully. The compiler must also generate code that, when an exception is caught, calls the destructor for each of the successfully constructed objects. It's great that the compiler takes on this burden, but it generates a lot of bookkeeping code in your application, adversely affecting code size and execution time.

On the other hand, managed compilers have it much easier because managed objects are allocated in the managed heap, which is monitored by the garbage collector. If an object is successfully constructed and an exception is thrown, the garbage collector will eventually deallocate the object. Compilers don't need to emit any bookkeeping code to track which objects are constructed successfully and to ensure that a destructor is called (especially because managed objects are destroyed at a nondeterministic time). Compared to unmanaged C++, this means that less code is generated by the compiler and less code has to execute at run time: your application's performance is better.

Over the years, I've used exception handling in different languages, different operating systems, and different CPU architectures. In each case, exception handling is implemented differently. Each implementation has its pros and cons with respect to performance. Some implementations compile exception handling constructs directly into a method, while other implementations store information related to exception handling in a data table associated with the method—this table is accessed only if an exception is thrown. Some compilers can't inline methods that contain exception handlers, and some compilers won't enregister variables if the method contains exception handlers.

The point is that you can't determine how much additional overhead using exception handling adds to an application. In the managed world, it's even more difficult to tell because your assembly's code can run on any platform that supports the .NET Framework. So the code produced by the JIT compiler to manage exception handling when your assembly is running on an x86 machine will be very different than the code produced by the JIT compiler when your code is running on an IA64 processor or the code produced by the .NET Compact Framework's JIT compiler.

Actually, I've been able to test some of my own code with a few different JIT compilers that Microsoft has internally, and the difference in performance that I've observed has been quite dramatic and surprising. The point is that you must test your code on the various platforms that you expect your users to run on and make changes accordingly. Again, I wouldn't worry about the performance of using exception handling; as I've said, the benefits far outweigh any negative performance impact.

If you're interested in seeing how exception handling impacts the performance of your code, you can use PerfMon.exe or the System Monitor ActiveX control that comes with Windows NT 4, Windows 2000, Windows XP, and the Windows .NET Server product family. The screen in Figure 18-1 shows the exception-related counters that get installed when the .NET Framework is installed.

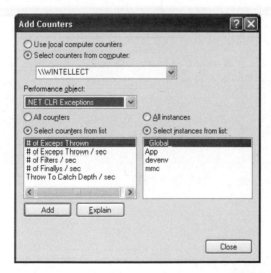

Figure 18-1   PerfMon.exe showing the .NET CLR exception counters

Here's what each counter means:

■   **# Of Exceps Thrown**   Displays the total number of exceptions thrown since the application started. These include both .NET exceptions and unmanaged exceptions that get converted into .NET exceptions. For example, a null pointer reference exception in unmanaged code would get rethrown in managed code as a .NET `System.NullReferenceException` exception; this counter includes both handled and unhandled exceptions. Exceptions that are rethrown would get counted again.

■   **# Of Exceps Thrown/Sec**   Displays the number of exceptions thrown per second. These include both .NET exceptions and unmanaged exceptions that get converted into .NET exceptions. For example, a null pointer reference exception in unmanaged code would get rethrown in managed code as a .NET `System.NullReference-Exception` exception; this counter includes both handled and unhandled exceptions. This counter was designed as an indicator of potential performance problems caused by a large (>100s) number of exceptions being thrown. This counter isn't an average over time; rather, it displays the difference between the values observed in the last two samples divided by the duration of the sample interval.

■   **# Of Filters/Sec**   Displays the number of .NET exception filters executed per second. An exception filter evaluates whether or not an exception should be handled. This counter tracks the rate of exception filters evaluated, regardless of whether or not the exception was handled. As with the preceding counter, this counter isn't an average over time; rather, it displays the difference between the values observed in the last two samples divided by the duration of the sample interval.

■   **# Of Finallys/Sec**   Displays the number of `Finally` blocks executed per second. A `Finally` block is guaranteed to be executed regardless of how the `Try` block was exited. Only the `Finally` blocks that are executed for an exception are counted; this counter doesn't count `Finally` blocks on normal code paths. Again, this counter isn't an average over time; it displays the difference between the values observed in the last two samples divided by the duration of the sample interval.

■   **Throw To Catch Depth/Sec**   Displays the number of stack frames traversed from the frame that threw the .NET exception to the frame that handled the exception per second. This counter resets to 0 when an exception handler is entered, so nested exceptions would show the handler-to-handler stack depth. Again, this counter isn't an average over time; it displays the difference between the values observed in the last two samples divided by the duration of the sample interval.

Catch Filters

When an exception is thrown, the CLR walks up the call stack looking at each **Catch** block's catch filter—the exception type specified after the **Catch** keyword. The following code shows a **Try** block with three **Catch** blocks.

```
Public Sub SomeMethod()
    Try
        ' Do something in here.
    Catch e As NullReferenceException
        ' Handle a null reference exception.
    Catch e As InvalidCastException
        ' Handle an Invalid cast exception.
    Catch e As Exception
        ' Handle any CLS exception.
    End Try
End Sub
```

When compiling this code, the compiler emits a tiny "catch filter funclet" for each **Catch** block contained inside the **SomeMethod** method. When an exception is thrown, the CLR calls the **NullReferenceException** funclet and passes it the object that identifies the thrown exception. The catch filter funclet checks whether the type of the object is a **NullReferenceException** or a type derived from **NullReferenceException**. If there isn't a match, the catch filter funclet returns a special value telling the CLR to continue searching. In my example, the **InvalidCastException** funclet is asked next, followed by the "catch all" filter funclet. If the "catch all" **Catch** block didn't exist, the CLR would continue walking up the call stack.

When a catch filter funclet recognizes the thrown object's type, it returns a special value to inform the CLR. The CLR executes all the **Finally** blocks necessary to unwind and clean up the started operations farther down the call stack. Then the CLR passes execution to the code contained inside the **Catch** block.

In Visual Basic, and many other languages designed for the .NET Framework, a catch filter is simply a data type. The catch filter funclet matches the thrown object's type against the filter's specified type. However, the CLR supports more complex catch filters. Visual Basic, Managed Extensions for C++, and IL assembly language are the only languages that I'm aware of that allow more complex catch filters. Here is the Visual Basic code that demonstrates a complex catch filter:

```
Imports System

Public Module MainMod

    Function HundredDivX(x as Int32) As String
        Try
            x = 100 \ x
            HundredDivX = x.ToString()

            Dim a as Object
            Console.WriteLine(a.ToString())

        Catch e as Exception When x = 0
            HundredDivX = "Problem: x was 0"

        Catch e as Exception
            HundredDivX = "Problem: I don't know what the problem is"

        End Try
    End Function


    Sub Main()
        Console.WriteLine(HundredDivX(0))
        Console.WriteLine(HundredDivX(2))
    End Sub

End Module
```

When you compile and execute this code, you get the following output:

```
Problem: x was 0
Problem: I don't know what the problem is
```

Here's what's happening. **Main** begins executing and calls **HundredDivX**, passing it **0**. Inside **HundredDivX**, **100** is divided by **0**, which causes the CLR to throw a **DivideByZeroException**. Note that you see this exception only if you use the **** operator (integer division): had I used the **/** operator (floating-point division), the division would have returned the value **PositiveInfinity** and the code would have thrown an **OverflowException** when trying to assign the result back to the **Int32** variable.

When the exception is thrown, the CLR calls the first catch filter funclet (generated by the compiler) corresponding to the first `Catch` block. This complex catch filter funclet checks whether the `DivisionByException` object is derived from `Exception`. Because it is, the filter then asks if `x` is `0`, by way of the Visual Basic `When` statement. Because this is also true, the catch filter funclet returns a value telling the CLR that it wants to handle the exception. The CLR now unwinds the stack by executing any `Finally` blocks farther down the call stack. In this example, there aren't any. Once all the `Finally` blocks have executed, execution passes to the code inside the handling `Catch` block. The return string is set to "Problem: x was 0"; the thread falls out of the `Catch` block and then out of the `Try` block; lastly, the thread returns from the method.

Now back inside `Main`, `HundredDivX` is called again, but this time `2` is passed. Inside `HundredDivX`, `100` is divided by `2`, which sets `x` to `50` without causing an exception to be thrown. But then, `a`, a reference to a `System.Object`, is declared and initialized to `Nothing`. Attempting to call `ToString` causes the CLR to throw a `NullReferenceException` exception. The first catch filter funclet examines the type and sees a match. But because `x` is now `50` (not `0`), the catch filter funclet tells the CLR to continue searching.

The CLR checks the second catch filter. Because `NullReferenceException` is derived from `Exception` and because this second catch filter has no `When` statement associated with it, the filter funclet returns a special value telling the CLR that it will handle the exception. Again, the CLR unwinds any `Finally` blocks that might exist and then passes execution to the code inside the active `Catch` block. This block sets the return string to "Problem: I don't know what the problem is". The thread now falls out of the `Catch` block, then out of the `Try` block, and then returns from the method.

Notice from the previous code example how the CLR manages an exception. First, the CLR locates a catch filter that accepts the exception. Then the CLR unwinds the call stack by calling `Finally` blocks. Finally, the CLR passes execution to the code contained inside the handling `Catch` block.

The `When` clause can be useful in several circumstances. For example, you can use it to check properties of the exception object being examined by the `Catch` filter. Consider this code:

```
Sub ProcessFiles(ByVal file1 As String, ByVal file2 As String)
    Dim fs1 As FileStream = Nothing
    Dim fs2 As FileStream = Nothing
    Try
        ' Open the two files.
        fs1 = New FileStream(file1, FileMode.Open)
        fs2 = New FileStream(file2, FileMode.Open)
        ' Process the two files.
        ⋮
```

(continued)

```
Catch e As FileNotFoundException _
   When e.FileName = file1
   Console.WriteLine("Unable to open the first file")
Catch e As FileNotFoundException _
   When e.FileName = file2
   Console.WriteLine("Unable to open the second file")
Catch e As Exception
   Console.WriteLine("An error has occurred")
Finally
   ' Properly close all successfully open files.
   If Not (fs1 Is Nothing) Then fs1.Close()
   If Not (fs2 Is Nothing) Then fs2.Close()
End Try
End Sub
```

The preceding code works because the **FileName** property of the **FileNot-FoundException** object contains the name of the file that caused the exception. Here's another, more efficient way to detect which file caused the problem; I'm using the **When** clause but I don't rely on the **FileName** property. Instead, I use the **currStep** variable to detect where in code the exception was thrown:

```
Sub ProcessFiles(ByVal file1 As String, ByVal file2 As String)
   ' This variable keeps track of what code is executing.
   Dim currStep As Int32 = 0
   Dim fs1 As FileStream = Nothing
   Dim fs2 As FileStream = Nothing
   Try
      ' Open the two files.
      currStep = 1
      fs1 = New FileStream(file1, FileMode.Open)
      currStep = 2
      fs2 = New FileStream(file2, FileMode.Open)
      ' Process the two files.
      currStep = 3
      ⋮
   Catch e As Exception When currStep = 1
      Console.WriteLine("Unable to open the first file")
   Catch e As Exception When currStep = 2
      Console.WriteLine("Unable to open the second file")
   Catch e As Exception
      Console.WriteLine("Error while processing the files")
   Finally
      ' Properly close all successfully open files.
      If Not (fs1 Is Nothing) Then fs1.Close()
      If Not (fs2 Is Nothing) Then fs2.Close()
   End Try
End Sub
```

What Happened to the On Error **Statement?**

Old-time Visual Basic developers might wonder what happened to the **On Error Goto** and **On Error Resume Next** statements, which have been with Visual Basic since its inception—and with Basic well before that. The good news is that these statements are still supported in Visual Basic .NET, so you don't have to rewrite your error recovery code from scratch when porting your applications from previous versions of the language. Even if you aren't porting legacy code to Visual Basic .NET, you might be tempted by two features that old-style statements have and that the **Try/Catch** syntax doesn't have, such as the capability to completely ignore errors (with the **On Error Resume Next** statement) and the capability to resume execution from the statement that caused the error (**Resume**) or the statement after that one (**Resume Next**).

Personally, I think of these statements as abominations. They basically tell the compiler to produce code that keeps the method running no matter what goes wrong. This is equivalent to catching all exceptions, and I've already described earlier in this chapter why this practice should be avoided.

In addition, these statements cause the Visual Basic compiler to generate a lot of IL code, significantly hurting your application's performance. The reason for the additional IL code is that because the CLR doesn't know anything about **On Error** statements, the compiler must emit code that logically wraps each statement in a **Try/Catch** block. If you choose to ease your porting and stick with the old-style **On Error** statement in a procedure, then at the very minimum, you shouldn't propagate the error to the calling procedure with an **Err.Raise** method. This is because the CLR ignores the error number and this statement throws a generic **System.Exception** object. The calling procedure can catch **Exception**, but it won't be able to determine what actually happened. To propogate a meaningful exception object, you should use the **Throw** statement and the new **Err.GetException** function, which returns the exception object that was originally thrown and that the IL emitted by the Visual Basic compiler turned into an error code. This code demonstrates:

```
Function SomeMethod(ByVal x As Int32) As Int32
   On Error GoTo ErrorHandler
   ⋮
   ErrorHandler:
      Select Case Err.Number
         Case 11          ' This means DivisionByZero.
            ' In this case, return 999,999.
            Return 999999
```

(continued)

```
        Case Else
            ' Throw the original exception to the caller.
        Throw Err.GetException()
    End Select
End Function
```

Unhandled Exceptions

As explained in the previous section, when an exception is thrown, the CLR starts searching for a catch filter interested in handling the exception. If no catch filter accepts the exception object, an *unhandled exception* occurs. An unhandled exception identifies a situation that the application didn't anticipate.

When developing an application, you should set a policy for dealing with unhandled exceptions. In addition, it's quite common to have one policy for debug versions of your application and a different policy for release versions. Normally, in a debug version, you want the debugger to start and attach itself to your application so that you can find out exactly what went wrong and correct the code.

For a release version, the unhandled exception is occurring while the user is using the application. The user probably doesn't have the knowledge (or the source code) to debug the application. So the best thing to do is log some information about the unhandled exception and allow the application to recover as gracefully as possible. For a client-side application, a graceful recovery might mean trying to save the user's data and terminating the application. For a server-side application, it might mean aborting the current client's request and preparing for a new client request—normally, an unhandled exception in a server-side application shouldn't terminate the server.

> **Note**   Class library developers shouldn't consider setting a policy for unhandled exceptions. The application developer should have complete control over defining and implementing this policy.

Personally, I like what the Microsoft Office XP applications do when they experience an unhandled exception—even though they're not .NET Framework applications. They save the document that the user was currently editing and then display a dialog box notifying the user that a problem occurred. Figure 18-2 shows such a dialog box for Microsoft PowerPoint.

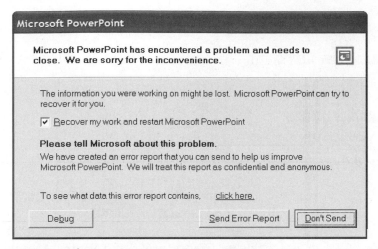

Figure 18-2   Microsoft PowerPoint showing its Unhandled Exception
dialog box

The Send Error Report button allows the user to send an error report to
Microsoft over the Internet. The Recover My Work And Restart Microsoft Power-
Point check box offers the user the option to relaunch the application (after
clicking the Send Error Report or Don't Send button). If the application is
relaunched, it automatically reloads the document that was being edited. If the
machine has a debugger installed, the Debug button appears in the dialog box,
allowing the user to debug the application. Later in this chapter, I'll discuss how
an application can set up a policy similar to Office XP's policy of handling
unhandled exceptions.

Here's another example of a policy that deals with an unhandled exception: When making a request of a remote object or remote service, a thread
(from a thread pool) is awakened to handle the client's request. The server's
code is executed in a **Try** block that has a **Catch** block associated with it that
catches all exceptions. If this **Catch** block catches an exception, the information
about the exception (including a stack trace) is sent back to the client as the
server's response. This is possible because the exception type is serializable, as
described in the "Defining Your Own Exception Class" section earlier in this
chapter.

When the client code detects that an exception was returned from the
server, it deserializes the exception object and throws it. This allows the client
code to catch an exception thrown by the server—very cool indeed! It effectively
hides the AppDomain, process, or machine boundary and allows the client
code to believe that the remote call was made locally.

When thinking about unhandled exceptions, you should know what kind of thread you're dealing with. There are five kinds of threads:

- **Main thread** The thread that executes a console (CUI) or Windows Forms (GUI) application's `Main` method is a managed main thread.

- **Manual threads** Application code can explicitly create threads by constructing a `System.Threading.Thread` object.

- **Pool threads** A lot of features in the .NET Framework take advantage of the thread pool that's built into the CLR. Thread pool threads typically execute code started by methods of the `System.Threading.ThreadPool` class or the `System.Threading.Timer` class. In addition, methods that expose the CLR's asynchronous programming model (such as a delegate's `BeginInvoke` and `EndInvoke` methods) typically complete using a thread pool thread.

- **Finalizer thread** The managed heap has a thread dedicated to executing an object's `Finalize` method when a garbage collection determines the object to be unreachable.

- **Unmanaged threads** Some threads are created without the knowledge of the CLR. Using P/Invoke or COM interoperability, these unmanaged threads can transition into the CLR to execute managed code. Because the CLR itself doesn't create these threads, any unhandled exceptions are thrown outside the CLR and the unmanaged thread code can handle these unhandled exceptions any way it desires; the CLR doesn't get involved.

For all five kinds of threads, you can implement an unhandled exception policy using code similar to the following:

```
Imports System
Imports System.Diagnostics
Imports System.Windows.Forms

Class App
   Shared Sub Main()
      ' Register the MgdUEFilter callback method with the AppDomain
      ' so that it gets called when an unhandled exception occurs.
      AddHandler AppDomain.CurrentDomain.UnhandledException, _
         AddressOf mgdUEPolicy
```

```
    ' The rest of the application code goes here.
    Try
        ' Simulate an exception here for testing purposes:
        Dim o As Object
        o.GetType()      ' throws a NullReferenceException
    Finally
        Console.WriteLine("In finally")
    End Try
End Sub


' //////////////////////////////////////////////////////////////


' The following method is called when an unhandled exception is
' encountered.
Shared Sub MgdUEPolicy(ByVal sender As Object, _
    ByVal e As UnhandledExceptionEventArgs)
    ' This string contains the information to display or log.
    Dim info As String

    ' Initialize the contents of the string.

    If TypeOf e.ExceptionObject Is Exception Then
        Dim ex As Exception = DirectCast(e.ExceptionObject, Exception)
        ' An unhandled CLS-compliant exception was thrown.
        ' Do whatever: you can access the fields of Exception.
        ' (Message, StackTrace, HelpLink, InnerException, etc.)
        info = ex.ToString()
    Else
        ' An unhandled non-CLS-compliant exception was thrown.
        ' Do whatever: all you can call are the methods defined by
        ' Object. (ToString, GetType, etc.)
        info = String.Format("Non-CLS-Compliant exception: " _
            & "Type={0}, String={1}", _
            e.ExceptionObject.GetType(), e.ExceptionObject.ToString)
    End If

#If Debug Then

    ' For debug builds of the application, launch the debugger
    ' to understand what happened and to fix it.
    If Not e.IsTerminating Then
        ' An unhandled exception occurred in a thread pool or a finalizer
        ' thread.
        Debugger.Launch()
```

(continued)

```
        Else

            ' An unhandled exception occurred in a managed thread.
            ' By default, the CLR will automatically attach a debugger,
            ' but you can force it with the following line:
            Debugger.Launch()
        End If

#Else

        ' For release builds of the application, display or log the
        ' exception so that the user can report it back to you.
        If not e.IsTerminating then
            ' An unhandled exception occurred in a thread pool or a finalizer
            ' thread. For thread pool or finalizer threads, you might just
            ' log the exception and not display the problem to the user.
            ' However, each application should do whatever makes the most
            ' sense for it.

        Else

            ' An unhandled exception occurred in a managed thread.
            ' The CLR is going to terminate the application; you should display
            ' and/or log the exception.
            Dim msg As String = _
                String.Format("{0} has encountered a problem and needs " _
                & "to close. We are sorry for the inconvenience.{2}{2}" _
                & "Please tell {1} about this problem.{2}" _
                & "We have created an error report that you can send to " _
                & "help us improve {0}. We will treat this report as " _
                & "confidential and anonymous.{2}{2}" _
                & "Would you like to send the report?", _
                "(AppName)", "(CompanyName)", Environment.NewLine)

            If MessageBox.Show(msg, "AppName", MessageBoxButtons.YesNo) _
                = DialogResult.Yes Then
                ' The user has chosen to send the error report to you.
                ' Send yourself the contents of the info variable and any
                ' additional information you think you'd find useful to
                ' help you correct this problem.

                ' For testing purposes only, I'll display info here:
                MessageBox.Show(info, "Error Report")
            End If
        End If

#End If
    End Sub
End Class
```

During application initialization (in the **Main** method), this code constructs a **System.UnhandledExceptionEventHandler** delegate as a wrapper around the static **MgdUEPolicy** method; this delegate is then registered with the **Unhandled-Exception** event offered by the **System.AppDomain** type. Whenever a thread has an unhandled exception, the CLR will invoke the **MgdUEPolicy** method. If an unmanaged thread has an unhandled exception that was thrown by unmanaged code, the CLR won't invoke the **MgdUEPolicy** method.

For a release build of the application, the code in the **MgdUEPolicy** method should display or log the unhandled exception information (including the stack trace) so that this information can be sent back to the company developing the application. The code could also try to send the exception information over the Internet back to the company (similar to what Office XP applications do) so that the users don't have to spend their own time reporting the problem. The company can then revise the source code so that the next version of the application properly anticipates this exception and responds to it appropriately. For a debug build of the application, the debugger should start up and attach itself to the process so that the developer can determine the reason for the exception and correct the code.

The callback method is considered a catch filter; that is, no deeper catch filter accepted the exception and therefore no **Finally** blocks have executed yet. Also note that the callback method receives a **System.UnhandledException-EventArgs** object. This object has two public, read-only properties, **Exception-Object** (of type **System.Object**) and **IsTerminating** (of type **System.Boolean**). **ExceptionObject** identifies the exception object that was thrown. Note that the type of **ExceptionObject** is **Object**, not **Exception**. The reason is that the object thrown might not be CLS-compliant.

The **IsTerminating** property tells you if the CLR would terminate the application because of this unhandled exception. Normally, for manual threads, pool threads, and the finalizer thread, the CLR swallows any unhandled exceptions and either kills the thread, returns the thread to the pool, or moves on to call the **Finalize** method of the next object. If an unhandled exception occurs in any of these kinds of threads, the **IsTerminating** property will be **False**. Should an application's main thread or an unmanaged thread have an unhandled exception, **IsTerminating** will be **True**.

If you want to debug your application when an unhandled exception occurs in a nonterminating thread, you should place a call to **System.Diagnostics.Debugger** type's static **Launch** method inside the **MgdUEPolicy** method. The sample code demonstrates this.

For a main thread or an unmanaged thread, the system offers to either connect a debugger to the AppDomain or terminate the process. This is why the **IsTerminating** property will be **True**.

Controlling What the CLR Does When an Unhandled Exception Occurs

When a managed thread has an unhandled exception, the CLR examines some settings to determine whether it should launch a debugger. To make this determination, the CLR checks the following registry subkey for the **DbgJITDebugLaunchSetting** value:

HKEY_LOCAL_MACHINE\Software\Microsoft\.NETFramework

If this value exists, its value must be one of those listed in Table 18-2.

Table 18-2 Possible Values of DbgJITDebugLaunchSetting

Value	Description
0	Display a dialog box asking the user whether he would like to debug the process. If the user chooses not to debug the process, the CLR fires the **AppDomain**'s **UnhandledException** event and then, if the exception occurred in the main thread or in an unmanaged thread, terminates the process along with all the AppDomains in it. If no callback methods have registered with **AppDomain**'s **UnhandledException** event and if the process is a CUI application, the CLR displays the stack trace to the console. If the user chooses to debug the application, the CLR spawns a debugger, which will attach itself to the AppDomain. The CLR determines the command line used to spawn the debugger by examining the **DbgManagedDebugger** registry value contained in the same registry subkey.
1	In this case, no dialog box is displayed to the user. The CLR fires the **AppDomain**'s **UnhandledException** event and then, if the exception occurred in the main thread or in an unmanaged thread, terminates the process along with all the AppDomains in it. If no callback methods have registered with **AppDomain**'s **UnhandledException** event and if the process is a CUI application, the CLR displays the stack trace to the console.
2	In this case, no dialog box is displayed to the user and **AppDomain**'s **UnhandledException** event doesn't fire. Instead, the CLR just spawns the debugger attaching it to the application.

By default, the CLR terminates the application or offers to spawn a debugger only for an application's main thread or for an unmanaged thread. For manual threads, pool threads, or finalizer threads, the CLR just swallows the exception and allows the thread to continue running—it doesn't terminate the process.

To help with debugging, you might want to know when an unhandled exception occurs in any thread. To get this information, just set the top three bytes of the `DbgJITDebugLaunchSetting` registry value to 0xFFFFFF. Use 0, 1, or 2 from Table 18-2 for the bottom-most byte.

> **Note**   In my opinion, Microsoft should check the registry value only if no callback method is registered with `AppDomain`'s `UnhandledException` event. Currently, when an unhandled exception occurs, the CLR examines the bottom-most byte of the `DbgJITDebugLaunchSetting` registry value. If this byte contains 0 or 2, the user is presented with the CLR's dialog box or the debugger just starts running—this happens even if the application has registered a callback method with `AppDomain`'s `UnhandledException` event. In the future, I'd like to see the CLR consider an exception unhandled only if no method is registered with `AppDomain`'s `UnhandledException` event.

Unhandled Exceptions and Windows Forms

In a Windows Forms application, the `System.Windows.Forms.Application` class has a static `Run` method that's responsible for the thread's message loop. This loop dispatches window messages to a private method defined by the `System.Windows.Forms.NativeWindow` type. This method simply sets up a `Try/Catch` block, and inside the `Try` block the protected `WndProc` method is called.

If a `System.Exception`-derived unhandled exception occurs while processing a window message, the `Catch` block calls the window type's virtual `OnThreadException` method (passing it the exception object). `System.Windows.Forms.Control` type's implementation of `OnThreadException` ends up calling `Application`'s `OnThreadException`. By default, this method displays a dialog box like the one shown in Figure 18-3.

This dialog box appears when a window procedure has an unhandled CLS-compliant exception, notifying the user that an unhandled exception has occurred and giving the user the option of ignoring the window message and continuing to run or quitting the application. If the user ignores the exception, the application will continue running, but it has probably been corrupted and will behave unpredictably at this point. If the application processes a data file, the user should save the work to a new file.

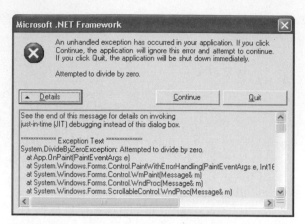

Figure 18-3   An unhandled exception in a window procedure causes Windows Forms to display this dialog box.

Then the user should exit the application and restart it. The user should load the new file once it has restarted and check it to make sure it hasn't been corrupted. If it is corrupted, any new work would have been lost but the user can go back to the original file and make the changes again. If the new file seems OK, the user can continue editing it and at some point delete the original file or keep it as a backup.

You can override the built-in dialog box by defining a method that matches the **System.Threading.ThreadExceptionEventHandler** delegate (defined in the System.dll assembly) and then registering your method with the **Application** type's static **ThreadException** event.

> **Note**   I think it's sad that this event didn't mimic the names and behavior of **AppDomain**'s **UnhandledException** event; that is, **Application**'s event should have been called **UnhandledException** instead of **ThreadException** and it should have used the **UnhandledException-EventHandler** delegate instead.

You might have realized by now that Windows Forms deals only with CLS-compliant exceptions; non-CLS-compliant exceptions continue to propagate outside the thread's message loop and up the call stack. So if you want to display or log both CLS-compliant and non-CLS-compliant exceptions, you must define two callback methods and register one with the **Application** type's **ThreadException** event and register the other with the **AppDomain** type's **UnhandledException** event.

As I explained, the behavior of **NativeWindow**'s internal method is to catch all CLS-compliant exceptions and display a dialog box or call any callback method that you've registered with the **ThreadException** event. However, some situations can change this default behavior. First, if a debugger is attached to your Windows Forms application, any unhandled exception thrown from a window procedure isn't caught and the exception is allowed to propagate up the call stack. Second, if a JIT debugger is installed and if the **jitDebugging** configuration setting is specified in the application's XML .config file, then again, the exception isn't caught and the exception is allowed to propagate up the call stack.

Unhandled Exceptions and ASP.NET Web Forms

ASP.NET executes any of your Web Forms code inside its own **Try** block. If your code throws an unhandled exception, ASP.NET catches the exception and determines how to handle it. ASP.NET offers a few mechanisms that you can use to receive a notification when an unhandled exception occurs. First, you can define a callback method that will get called when a particular Web page experiences an unhandled exception. You register the callback method using the **Error** event offered by the **System.Web.UI.TemplateControl** class; this class is the base class of the **System.Web.UI.Page** and **System.Web.UI.UserControl** classes.

In addition to allowing you to receive notifications of unhandled exceptions for a specific page, ASP.NET also lets you register a callback method that will receive notifications of unhandled exceptions on any page in your Web Forms application. You register the application-wide callback method using the **Error** event offered by the **System.Web.HTTPApplication** class. You typically add this code to your Global.asax file.

ASP.NET also offers tracing options that dump stack traces for unhandled exceptions out to a Web page to help you detect problems and correct your code. For more details on ASP.NET and exceptions, consult the .NET Framework SDK documentation.

Unhandled Exceptions and ASP.NET XML Web Services

For ASP.NET XML Web services, the unhandled exception story is easy. When your XML Web service's method throws an unhandled exception, ASP.NET catches the exception and throws a new **System.Web.Services.Protocols.Soap-Exception** object. A **SoapException** object is serialized into XML, representing a SOAP fault. This SOAP fault XML can be parsed and understood by any machine acting as an XML Web service client. This allows for XML Web service client/server interoperability.

If the client is a .NET Framework client, the SOAP fault XML is deserialized into a **SoapException** object and this new object is thrown in the client's thread. The client code can now catch this exception and proceed any way it chooses. A minor problem is that the **SoapException** object provides no information about the original exception thrown when the XML Web service was executing, at least not directly. However, the message of the original exception is embedded in the **SoapException**'s **Message** property, so you can retrieve additional information about the exception by querying this property.

Exception Stack Traces

As I mentioned earlier, the **System.Exception** type offers a public, read-only **StackTrace** property. An exception filter or a **Catch** block can read this property to obtain the stack trace indicating what events occurred up to the exception. This information can be extremely valuable when you're trying to detect the cause of an exception so that you can correct your code. In this section, I'll discuss some issues related to the stack trace that aren't immediately obvious.

The **Exception** type's **StackTrace** property is magical. When you access this property, you're actually calling into code in the CLR; the property doesn't simply return a string. When you construct a new object of an **Exception**-derived type, the **StackTrace** property is initialized to **Nothing**. If you were to read the property, you wouldn't get back a stack trace; you would get back **Nothing**.

When an exception is thrown, the CLR internally records where the **Throw** instruction occurred. When a catch filter accepts the exception, the CLR records where the exception was caught. If, inside a **Catch** block, you now access the thrown exception object's **StackTrace** property, the code that implements the property calls into the CLR, which builds a string identifying all the methods between the place where the exception was thrown and the filter that caught the exception. Note that a catch filter can't access the stack information because it's not built until after a catch filter accepts the exception.

Important   When you throw an exception, the CLR resets the starting point for the exception; that is, the CLR remembers only the location where the most recent exception object was thrown. The following code throws the same exception object that it caught and causes the CLR to reset its starting point for the exception:

```
Sub SomeMethod()
   Try
      ⋮
   Catch e As Exception
      ⋮
      Throw e   ' The CLR thinks this is where the exception
                ' originated.
End Sub
```

In contrast, if you rethrow an exception object, the CLR doesn't reset the stack's starting point. The following code rethrows the same exception object that it caught, causing the CLR to not reset its starting point for the exception:

```
Sub SomeMethod()
   Try
      ⋮
   Catch e As Exception
      ⋮
      Throw     ' This has no effect on where the CLR thinks
                ' the exception originated.
End Sub
```

In fact, the only difference between these two code fragments is what the CLR thinks is the original location where the exception was thrown.

The string returned from the `StackTrace` property doesn't include any of the methods in the call stack that are above the point where the catch filter accepted the exception object. If you want the complete stack trace from the top of the thread to the exception handler, you can call `System.Environment`'s static `StackTrace` method and merge the two strings.

> **Note** The FCL also offers a `System.Diagnostics.StackTrace` type that defines some properties and methods that allow a developer to programmatically manipulate a stack trace and the frames that make up the stack trace. You can construct a `StackTrace` object using several different constructors. Some constructors build a `StackTrace` object representing the frames from the top of the thread to the point where the object is constructed. Other constructors initialize the frames of the `StackTrace` object using an `Exception`-derived object. Calling `Environment`'s static `StackTrace` property internally constructs a `StackTrace` object by calling the constructor that takes a single `Boolean` parameter; `True` is passed for this parameter. `Environment` then builds a string from the `StackTrace` object's frames.

If the CLR can find debug symbols for your assemblies, then the string returned by `Exception`'s `StackTrace` property or `Environment`'s `StackTrace` property will include source code file pathnames and line numbers. This information is incredibly useful for debugging. Unfortunately, the `System.Diagnostics.StackTrace` type's `ToString` method doesn't support source code file pathnames and line numbers. I hope this bug will be fixed in a future version of the .NET Framework.

Whenever you obtain a stack trace, you might find that some methods in the call stack don't appear in the stack trace. The reason for their absence is that the JIT compiler can inline methods to avoid the overhead of calling and returning from a separate method. Many compilers (including the Visual Basic compiler), offer a **/debug** command-line switch. When this switch is turned on, these compilers embed information into the resulting assembly that tells the JIT compiler not to inline any of the assembly's methods so that stack traces are more complete and meaningful to the developer debugging the code.

> **Note**   The JIT compiler examines the `System.Diagnostics.Debug-gableAttribute` custom attribute applied to the assembly. Your compiler of choice normally applies this attribute automatically. If this attribute has `True` specified for the `DebuggableAttribute` constructor's `isJITOptimizerDisabled` parameter, the JIT compiler won't inline the assembly's methods. Using the Visual Basic compiler's `/debug` switch sets this parameter to `True`. By applying the `System.Runtime.Compil-erServices.MethodImplAttribute` custom attribute to a method, you can forbid the JIT compiler from inlining the method for both debug and release builds. The following method definition shows how to forbid the method from being inlined:
>
> ```
> Imports System.Runtime.CompilerServices
>   ⋮
> Class SomeType
>     <MethodImpl(MethodImplOptions.NoInlining)> _
>     Public Sub SomeMethod()
>        ⋮
>     End Sub
> End Class
> ```

Remoting Stack Traces

If a client makes a request of a server and the server code throws an exception, the exception object can be marshaled back to the client and rethrown in the client's thread. This capability is cool because the client code can simply react to the server-thrown exception the same way that it would react to a client-thrown exception. But what about the stack trace?

Well, the full stack trace is also marshaled back to the client. If the client were to examine the stack trace, the trace would contain all the frames from where the exception was thrown (on the server) to where the exception was caught (on the client). This is another neat capability: developers building distributed applications can easily detect where problems occur and fix them regardless of whether the problem occurred on the client or the server.

Here is how the server's stack trace gets marshaled back to the client. When an `Exception`-derived object is serialized, the stack trace information is serialized as a string. When the object is deserialized, the new `Exception`-derived object saves the string in a private field. From now on, when you request the `StackTrace` property on this new object, the string returned contains the stack from the point where the exception was caught to the point where the new exception object was thrown. Appended to this string is the string from the internal field. In other words, the string returned from the `StackTrace` property contains the complete trace from where the server originally threw the exception to the point where the client catches the exception.

Debugging Exceptions

The Microsoft Visual Studio .NET debugger offers special support for exceptions. To access this support, choose the Debug.Exceptions menu item and you'll see the dialog box shown in Figure 18-4.

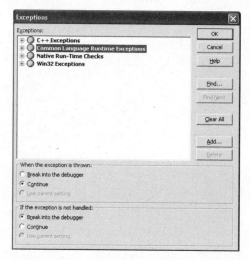

Figure 18-4   Visual Studio .NET Exceptions dialog box showing the different kinds of exceptions

This dialog box shows the different kinds of exceptions that Visual Studio is aware of:

■ **C++ Exceptions**   For working with unmanaged C++ exceptions.

■ **Common Language Runtime Exceptions**   For working with managed exceptions, the focus of this chapter.

■ **Native Run-Time Checks**   For working with a new feature offered by the unmanaged Microsoft Visual C++ compiler. These exceptions are useful only when you're compiling the code with the **/RTC** compiler switch.

■ **Win32 Exceptions**   For working with Windows unmanaged 32-bit exception codes.

For Common Language Runtime Exceptions, expanding the corresponding branch in the dialog box, as in Figure 18-5, shows the set of namespaces that the Visual Studio debugger is aware of.

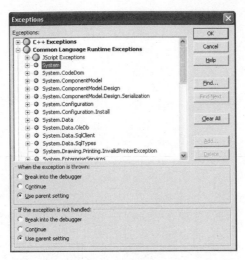

Figure 18-5   Visual Studio .NET Exceptions dialog box showing CLR exceptions by namespace

If you expand a namespace, you'll see all the `System.Exception`-derived types defined within that namespace. For example, Figure 18-6 shows what you'll see if you open the `System` namespace.

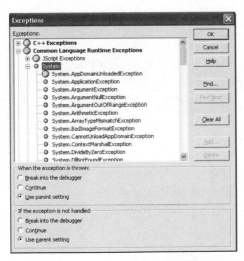

Figure 18-6   Visual Studio .NET Exceptions dialog box showing CLR exceptions defined in the `System` namespace

After selecting an exception type, you can tell the debugger what you want it to do as soon as the exception is thrown:

- **Break Into The Debugger**   Tells the debugger to notify you as soon as the exception is thrown. The CLR hasn't tried to walk up the call stack yet looking for any catch filters. This option is useful if you want to debug your code that catches and handles an exception.

- **Continue**   Tells the debugger not to notify you as soon as the exception is thrown. The CLR will walk up the call stack looking for a catch filter that accepts the exception. If a `Catch` block handles the exception, the debugger will never notify you that the exception occurred. This option is the most common one to select because a handled exception indicates that the application anticipated the situation and dealt with it; the application continues running normally. If no exception filter accepts the exception object, an unhandled exception occurs. In this case, the debugger will notify you of the unhandled exception even if the Continue option is selected.

- **Use Parent Setting**   Tells the debugger to use the setting associated with the parent node in the tree. In my opinion, this setting is meaningless as is. It's unlikely that you'd ever want to choose Break Into The Debugger or Continue for all exception types in a namespace. What Microsoft should have done was show the exception type hierarchy, not the namespace hierarchy. If this dialog box showed the exception type hierarchy, this setting would make some sense: I could choose a setting for `ArgumentException`, and the exception types derived from it (`ArgumentNullException`, `Argument-OutOfRangeException`, and `DuplicateWaitObjectException`) could inherit this setting. This way I could break into the debugger whenever any of these related exception types were thrown.

At the bottom of the dialog box in Figure 18-6, you can tell the debugger how to behave when an unhandled exception is encountered. Here are the options:

- **Break Into The Debugger**   Tells the debugger to notify you that an unhandled exception occurred and allows you to debug the application code. For managed applications, this is by far the most useful option. In fact, this is the only option I'd ever choose.

■   **Continue**   For managed applications, tells the debugger to let the application die. In other words, the debugger won't present you a notification of the unhandled exception; the application will just terminate. When debugging a managed application, this option is useless because you're typically debugging the application in order to fix unhandled exceptions, not to ignore them. However, if you're debugging a script code (in Internet Explorer or some other HTML host), then the script code stops executing, the error is reported to the host, and the host can keep running.

■   **Use Parent Setting**   Tells the debugger to use the setting associated with the parent node in the tree. Again, because the tree shows the namespace hierarchy instead of the type hierarchy, this option isn't that useful.

If you define your own exception types, you can add them to this dialog box by selecting the Common Language Runtime Exceptions node and clicking the Add button. This causes the dialog box in Figure 18-7 to appear.

Figure 18-7   Making Visual Studio .NET aware of your own exception type

In this dialog box, you can enter the fully qualified name of your own exception type. Note that the type you enter doesn't have to be a type derived from **System.Exception**; non-CLS-compliant types are fully supported. If you have two or more types with the same name but in different assemblies, there is no way to distinguish the types from one another. Fortunately, this situation rarely happens.

If your assembly defines several exception types, you must add them one at a time. In the future, I'd like to see this dialog box allow me to browse for an assembly and automatically import all **Exception**-derived types into Visual Studio's debugger. Each type could then be identified by assembly as well, which would fix the problem of having two types with the same name in different assemblies.

In addition, it might be nice if this dialog box also allowed me to individually select types not derived from `Exception` so that I could add any non-CLS-compliant exceptions that I might define. However, non-CLS-compliant exception types are strongly discouraged, so this isn't a must-have feature.

Telling Visual Studio What Kind of Code to Debug

When using Visual Studio to debug an application, you must tell the debugger what kind of code you want to debug. When you attach the Visual Studio debugger to a process, it displays the dialog box shown in Figure 18-8.

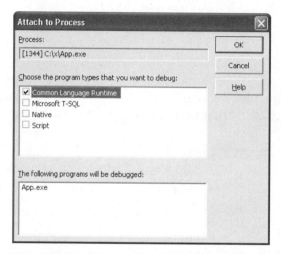

Figure 18-8   Attaching the Visual Studio .NET debugger to a process

Now let me explain what it means to debug the different kinds of code:

■ **Common Language Runtime**   Allows you to debug managed code. The debugger shows managed symbols and stack traces. If this option isn't checked, the debugger won't show any symbols for managed code, making it very tedious to step through managed code.

■ **Microsoft T-SQL**   Allows you to debug T-SQL procedures stored in a SQL server database.

■ **Native**   Allows you to debug unmanaged code. The debugger shows unmanaged symbols and stack traces. If your managed application uses unmanaged code but you don't need to debug the unmanaged code, you should make sure that this option isn't checked. With this option off, single-stepping through the managed portion of your code will be much faster and unmanaged threads aren't suspended when a breakpoint is hit. If a thread is executing unmanaged code, it continues to run.

With this option turned on, detaching the debugger from the process is possible only on Windows XP and Windows .NET Server platforms. With this option turned off, the debugger can detach from a process on any Windows platform.

■   **Script**   Allows you to debug scripting code executing within a host such as Internet Explorer.

The only time you should check both Common Language Runtime and Native is when you're debugging the portions of your code that interoperate between managed and unmanaged code (P/Invoke and COM interoperability). Doing both managed and unmanaged debugging causes single-stepping to be quite slow. In addition, the debugger can't be detached regardless of the version of Windows you're running.

You should also be aware that the debugger sometimes loses control of the application when stepping over a managed/unmanaged transition. In other words, you might try to single step over a transition and the thread might just start running (or possibly hang). Most of the time, stepping over these transitions works fine, but occasionally it doesn't. The loss of control occurs because of decisions made in the CLR team to favor performance over "accurate debugging."

For a Visual Studio project, you can also indicate what kinds of code you want to debug. You do this by displaying the property page dialog box for the project. Figure 18-9 shows the property page for a Visual Basic console application project. Because the project is a Visual Basic project, Visual Studio assumes that you always want to debug managed code. Using this dialog box, I could enable unmanaged code debugging and/or SQL Server debugging.

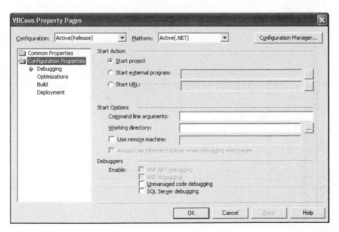

Figure 18-9   Selecting the kind of code I want to debug for my project

19

Automatic Memory Management (Garbage Collection)

In this chapter, I'll discuss how managed applications construct new objects, how the managed heap controls the lifetime of these objects, and how the memory for these objects gets reclaimed. In short, I'll explain how the Microsoft .NET Framework's garbage collector works and various performance issues related to it.

Understanding the Basics of Working in a Garbage-Collected Platform

Every program uses resources of one sort or another, be they files, memory buffers, screen space, network connections, database resources, and so on. In fact, in an object-oriented environment, every type identifies some resource available for a program's use. To use any of these resources requires that memory be allocated to represent the type. The following steps are required to access a resource:

1. Allocate memory for the type that represents the resource by calling the intermediate language's **newobj** instruction, which is emitted when you use the **New** operator in Visual Basic, C#, and other programming languages.

2. Initialize the memory to set the initial state of the resource and to make the resource usable. One of the type's instance constructors is responsible for setting this initial state.

3. Use the resource by accessing the type's instance members (repeating as necessary).

4. Tear down the state of a resource to clean up. I'll address this topic in the section "The Dispose Pattern: Forcing an Object to Clean Up" later in this chapter.

5. Free the memory. The garbage collector is solely responsible for this step.

This seemingly simple paradigm has been one of the major sources of programming errors. How many times have programmers forgotten to free memory when it is no longer needed? How many times have programmers attempted to use memory after it had already been freed?

These two application bugs are worse than most others because you usually can't predict the consequences or the timing of them. For most other bugs, when you see your application misbehaving, you just fix the problem. But these two bugs cause resource leaks (memory consumption) and object corruption (destabilization), making the application perform unpredictably—and at unpredictable times. In fact, there are many tools (such as the Microsoft Windows Task Manager, the System Monitor ActiveX Control, NuMega BoundsChecker from Compuware, and Rational's Purify) specifically designed to help developers locate these types of bugs.

In many development platforms, managing objects properly distracts developers from concentrating on the real problems they're trying to solve. It would be wonderful if some mechanism existed that simplified the mind-numbing memory management task for developers. Fortunately, there is: garbage collection.

Garbage collection completely absolves the developer from having to track memory usage and to know when to free memory. However, the garbage collector doesn't know anything about the resource represented by the type in memory, which means that a garbage collector can't know how to perform step 4 in the preceding list: tear down the state of a resource to clean up. To get a resource to clean up properly, the developer must write code that knows how to properly clean up a resource. The developer writes this code in `Finalize`, `Dispose`, and `Close` methods, as described later in this chapter. However, as you'll see, the garbage collector can offer some assistance here too, allowing developers to skip step 4 in many circumstances.

Also, most types, such as `Int32`, `Point`, `Rectangle`, `String`, `ArrayList`, and `SerializationInfo`, represent resources that don't require any special cleanup. For example, a `Point` resource can be completely cleaned up simply by destroying its **x** and **y** fields maintained in the object's memory.

On the other hand, a type that represents (or wraps) an unmanaged (operating system) resource, such as a file, a database connection, a socket, a mutex, a bitmap, an icon, and so on, always requires the execution of some cleanup code when the object is to be destroyed. In this chapter, I'll explain how to properly define types that require explicit cleaning up, and I'll also show you how to properly use types that offer this explicit cleanup. For now, let's examine how memory is allocated and how resources are initialized.

The common language runtime (CLR) requires that all resources be allocated from a heap called the *managed heap*. This heap is similar to a C-runtime heap except that you never free objects from the managed heap—objects are automatically freed when the application no longer needs them. This, of course, raises the question, "How does the managed heap know when the application is no longer using an object?" I'll address this question shortly.

Several garbage collection algorithms are in practice today. Each algorithm is fine-tuned for a particular environment to provide the best performance. In this chapter, I'll concentrate on the garbage collection algorithm used by the .NET Framework's CLR. Let's start off with the basic concepts.

When a process is initialized, the CLR reserves a contiguous region of address space that initially contains no backing storage. This address space region is the managed heap. The heap also maintains a pointer, which I'll call `NextObjPtr`. This pointer indicates where the next object is to be allocated within the heap. Initially, `NextObjPtr` is set to the base address of the reserved address space region.

The `newobj` intermediate language (IL) instruction creates an object. Many languages (including Visual Basic and C#) offer a `New` operator, which causes the compiler to emit a `newobj` instruction into the method's IL code. The `newobj` instruction causes the CLR to perform the following steps:

1. Calculate the number of bytes required for the type's (and all its base type's) fields.

2. Add the bytes required for an object's overhead. Each object has two overhead fields: a method table pointer and a SyncBlockIndex. On a 32-bit system, each of these fields requires 32 bits, adding 8 bytes to each object. On a 64-bit system, each is 64 bits, adding 16 bytes to each object.

3. The CLR then checks that the bytes required to allocate the object are available in the reserved region (committing storage if necessary). If the object fits, it is allocated at the address pointed to by NextObjPtr and NextObjPtr is advanced past the object and indicates the address where the next object will be placed in the heap. The type's instance constructor is called (passing the memory address of where the object was allocated for the Me parameter), and the newobj IL instruction (or the New operator) returns this address.

Figure 19-1 shows a managed heap consisting of three objects: A, B, and C. If a new object were to be allocated, it would be placed where **NextObjPtr** points (immediately after object C).

NextObjPtr

Figure 19-1   Newly initialized managed heap with three objects constructed in it

By contrast, let's look at how the C-runtime heap allocates memory. In a C-runtime heap, allocating memory for an object requires walking through a linked list of data structures. Once a large enough block is found, that block is split and pointers in the linked-list nodes are modified to keep everything intact. For the managed heap, allocating an object simply means adding a value to a pointer—this is blazingly fast by comparison. In fact, allocating an object from the managed heap is nearly as fast as allocating memory from a thread's stack! In addition, most heaps (like the C-runtime heap) allocate objects wherever they find free space. Therefore, if I create several objects consecutively, it's quite possible that these objects will be separated by megabytes of address space. In the managed heap, however, allocating several objects consecutively ensures that the objects are contiguous in memory.

In many applications, objects allocated around the same time tend to have strong relationships to each other and are frequently accessed around the same time. For example, it's very common to allocate a **FileStream** object immediately followed by a **BinaryWriter** object. Then the application would use the **BinaryWriter** object, which internally uses the **FileStream** object. In a garbage-collected environment, new objects are allocated contiguously in memory, providing performance gains resulting from locality of reference. Specifically, this means that your process's working set will be smaller, and it's also likely that the objects your method is using can all reside in the CPU's cache. Your application will access these objects with phenomenal speed because the CPU will be able to perform most of its manipulations without having cache misses forcing RAM access.

So far, it sounds like the managed heap is far superior to the C-runtime heap because of its simplicity of implementation and its speed. But there's one little detail you should know about before getting too excited. The managed heap gains these advantages because it makes one really big assumption: that address space and storage are infinite. Obviously, this assumption is ridiculous, and the managed heap must employ a mechanism that allows it to make this assumption. This mechanism is the garbage collector. Here's how it works.

When an application calls the **New** operator to create an object, there might not be enough address space left in the region to allocate to the object. The heap detects this lack of space by adding the bytes the object requires to the address in **NextObjPtr**. If the resulting value is beyond the end of the address space region, the heap is full and a garbage collection must be performed.

 Important   What I've just said is an oversimplification. In reality, a garbage collection occurs when generation 0 is full. Some garbage collectors use *generations*, a mechanism whose sole purpose is to improve performance. The idea is that newly created objects are part of a young generation, and objects created early in the application's lifecycle are in an old generation. Separating objects into generations can allow the garbage collector to collect specific generations instead of collecting all the objects in the managed heap. I'll explain generations in more detail later in this chapter. Until then, it's easiest for you to think that a garbage collection occurs when the heap is full.

The Garbage Collection Algorithm

The garbage collector checks to see whether there are any objects in the heap that are no longer being used by the application. If such objects exist, the memory used by these objects can be reclaimed. (If no more memory is available in the heap, then **New** throws an **OutOfMemoryException** exception.) How does the garbage collector know whether or not the application is using an object? As you might imagine, this isn't a simple question to answer.

Every application has a set of *roots*. A single root is a storage location containing a memory pointer to a reference type. This pointer either refers to an object in the managed heap or is set to **Nothing**. For example, all global or static reference type variables are considered roots. In addition, any reference type local variable or parameter variable on a thread's stack is also considered a root. Finally, within a method, a CPU register that refers to a reference type object is also considered a root.

When the JIT compiler compiles a method's IL, in addition to producing the native CPU code, the JIT compiler also creates an internal table. Logically, each entry in the table indicates a range of byte offsets in the method's native CPU instructions, and for each range, a set of memory addresses (or CPU registers) that contain roots. For example, the table could logically look like Table 19-1.

Table 19-1   Sample of a JIT Compiler–Produced Table Showing Mapping of Native Code Offsets to a Method's Roots

Starting Byte Offset	Ending Byte Offset	Roots
0x00000000	0x00000020	Me, arg1, arg2, ECX, EDX
0x00000021	0x00000122	Me, arg2, fs, EBX
0x00000123	0x00000145	fs

If a garbage collection were to start while code was executing between offset 0x00000021 and 0x00000122 in the method, the garbage collector would know that the objects referred to by the **Me** parameter, **arg2** parameter, **fs** local variable, and **EBX** register were all roots and refer to objects in the heap that shouldn't be considered garbage. In addition, the garbage collector can walk up the thread's call stack and determine the roots for all the calling methods by examining each method's internal table. The garbage collector uses other means to obtain the set of roots stored in global and static reference type variables.

When the garbage collector starts running, it makes the assumption that all objects in the heap are garbage. In other words, it assumes that none of the application's roots refer to any objects in the heap. The garbage collector then starts walking the roots, building a graph of all reachable objects. For example, the garbage collector might locate a global variable that points to an object in the heap. Figure 19-2 shows a heap with several allocated objects where the application's roots refer directly to objects A, C, D, and F. All these objects become part of the graph. When adding object D, the garbage collector notices that this object refers to object H and also adds object H to the graph. The garbage collector continues to walk through all reachable objects recursively.

Note   In Table 19-1, notice that the method's `arg1` argument isn't referred to after the CPU instruction at offset 0x00000020. This means that the object `arg1` refers to can be collected anytime after this instruction executes (assuming that there are no other roots in the application that also refer to this object). In other words, as soon as an object becomes unreachable, it is a candidate for collection—objects aren't guaranteed to live throughout a method's lifetime.

However, when an application is running under a debugger or when an assembly contains the `System.Diagnostics.Debuggable-Attribute` attribute with its constructor's `isJITOptimizerDisabled` parameter set to `True`, the JIT compiler extends the life of all variables (value type and reference type) until the end of their scope, which is usually the end of the method. (By the way, Microsoft's Visual Basic compiler offers a `/debug` command-line switch that adds the `DebuggableAttribute` attribute to the assembly, setting the `isJITOptimizerDisabled` parameter to `True`.) This extension prevents a garbage collection from collecting reference objects while executing the code in the scope and is useful when you're debugging your code. It would be very odd if you called an object's method, got the wrong result, and then couldn't even look at the object!

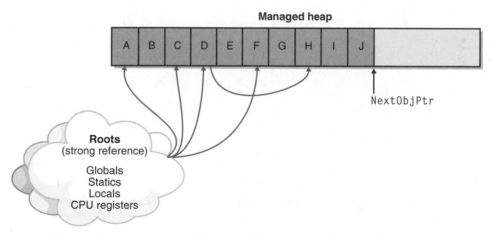

Figure 19-2   Managed heap before a collection

Once this part of the graph is complete, the garbage collector checks the next root and walks the objects again. As the garbage collector walks from object to object, if it attempts to add an object to the graph that it previously added, it can stop walking down that path. This behavior serves two purposes. First, performance is enhanced significantly because the garbage collector doesn't walk through a set of objects more than once. Second, infinite loops are prevented should you have any circular linked lists of objects.

Once all the roots have been checked, the garbage collector's graph contains the set of all objects that are somehow reachable from the application's roots; any objects that aren't in the graph aren't accessible by the application and are therefore garbage. The garbage collector now traverses the heap linearly looking for contiguous blocks of garbage objects (now considered free space). If small blocks are found, the garbage collector leaves the blocks alone.

If large free contiguous blocks are found, however, the garbage collector shifts the nongarbage objects down in memory (using the standard `memcpy` function that C programmers have known for years) to compact the heap. Naturally, moving the objects in memory invalidates all pointers to the objects. So the garbage collector must modify the application's roots so that the roots point to the objects' new locations. In addition, if any object contains a pointer to another object, the garbage collector is responsible for correcting these pointers as well. After the heap memory is compacted, the managed heap's `NextObjPtr` pointer is set to point just after the last nongarbage object. Figure 19-3 shows the managed heap after a collection.

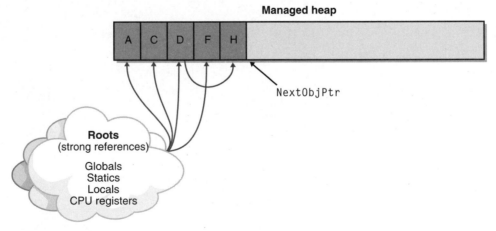

Figure 19-3 Managed heap after a collection

As you can see, a garbage collection generates a considerable performance hit, which is the major downside of using a managed heap. But keep in mind that garbage collections occur only when generation 0 is full, and until then, the managed heap is significantly faster than a C-runtime heap. Finally, the CLR's garbage collector offers some optimizations that greatly improve the performance of garbage collection. I'll discuss these optimizations later in this chapter, in the "Generations" and "Other Garbage Collector Performance Issues" sections.

As a programmer, you should take away a couple important points from this discussion. To start, you no longer have to implement any code that manages the lifetime of objects your application uses. And notice how the two bugs described at the beginning of this chapter no longer exist. First, it's not possible to leak objects because any object not accessible from your application's roots can be collected at some point. Second, it's not possible to access an object that is freed because the object won't be freed if it's reachable, and if it's not reachable, your application has no way to access it.

The following code demonstrates how objects are allocated and managed:

```
Class App
   Shared Sub Main()

      ' ArrayList object created in heap; a is now a root.
      Dim a As New ArrayList()

      ' Create 10,000 objects in the heap.
      Dim x As Int32
      For x = 0 To 9999
         a.Add(New Object())     ' Object created in heap
      Next

      ' Right now, a is a root (on the thread's stack). So a is
      ' reachable and the 10,000 objects it refers to are reachable.
      Console.WriteLine(a.Count)

      ' After a.Count returns, a isn't referred to in the code and is no
      ' longer a root. If another thread were to start a garbage collection
      ' before the result of a.Count were passed to WriteLine, the 10,001
      ' objects would have their memory reclaimed.
      Console.WriteLine("End of method")
   End Sub
End Class
```

Finalization

At this point, you should have a basic understanding of garbage collection and the managed heap, including how the garbage collector reclaims an object's memory. Fortunately for us, most types only need memory to operate. For example, the `Int32`, `Point`, `Rectangle`, `String`, and `ArrayList` types are really just types that manipulate bytes in memory. However, some types require more than just memory to be useful.

The `System.IO.FileStream` type, for example, needs to open a file and save the file's handle. Then the type's `Read` and `Write` methods use this handle to manipulate the file. Similarly, the `System.Threading.Mutex` type opens a Windows mutex kernel object and saves its handle, using it when the `Mutex`'s methods are called.

Any type that wraps an unmanaged resource, such as a file, network connection, socket, mutex, and so on, must support *finalization*. Finalization allows a resource to gracefully clean up after itself when it is being collected. Basically, the type implements a method named `Finalize`. When the garbage collector determines that an object is garbage, it calls the object's `Finalize` method (if it exists). The `Finalize` method is usually implemented to call `CloseHandle`, passing in the handle of the unmanaged resource. Because `FileStream` defines a `Finalize` method, every `FileStream` object is guaranteed to have its unmanaged resource freed when the managed object is freed. If a type that wraps an unmanaged resource fails to define a `Finalize` method, the unmanaged resource won't be closed and will be a resource leak that exists until the process terminates, at which point the operating system will reclaim the unmanaged resources.

The following `OSHandle` type demonstrates how to define a type that wraps an unmanaged resource. When the garbage collector determines that the object is garbage, it calls the `Finalize` method, which in turn calls the Win32 `CloseHandle` function, ensuring that the unmanaged resource is freed. The `OSHandle` class can also be used for any unmanaged resource that is freed by calling `CloseHandle`. If you're working with some unmanaged resource that requires a different function to clean it up, you'll have to modify the `Finalize` method accordingly.

```
Public NotInheritable Class OSHandle

    ' This field holds the Win32 handle of the unmanaged resource.
    Private handle As IntPtr

    ' This constructor initializes the handle.
```

```
Public Sub New(ByVal handle As IntPtr)
   Me.handle = handle
End Sub

' When garbage collected, the Finalize method, which
' will close the unmanaged resource's handle, is called.
Protected Overrides Sub Finalize()
   Try
      CloseHandle(handle)
   Finally
      MyBase.Finalize()
   End Try
End Sub

' Public method that returns the value of the wrapped handle
Public Function ToHandle() As IntPtr
   Return handle
End Function

' Private method called to free the unmanaged resource
<System.Runtime.InteropServices.DllImport("Kernel32")> _
Private Shared Function CloseHandle(ByVal handle As IntPtr) As Boolean
   End Function
End Class
```

When an **OSHandle** object is garbage collected, the garbage collector will call its **Finalize** method. This method will perform any required cleanup operations and then call the base type's **Finalize** method so that it has a chance to perform any cleanup that the base type finds necessary. The call to the base type's **Finalize** method is inside a **Finally** block. This ensures that it gets called even if **OSHandle**'s cleanup code throws an exception for some reason. In this example, **System.Object**'s **Finalize** method gets called. **Object**'s **Finalize** method does nothing except return, so you could omit the exception handling code and the call to **MyBase.Finalize** from the preceding code to improve performance without losing any "correctness."

To create an instance of the **OSHandle** object, you'd first have to call a Win32 function that returns a handle to an unmanaged resource, such as **CreateFile, CreateMutex, CreateSemaphore, CreateEvent, socket, CreateFile-Mapping**, and so on. Then you'd use Visual Basic's **New** operator to construct an instance of **OSHandle**, passing the Win32 handle to the constructor. Sometime in the future, the garbage collector will determine that this object is garbage. When that happens, the garbage collector will see that the type has a **Finalize** method and will call the method, allowing **CloseHandle** to close the unmanaged resource. Sometime after **Finalize** returns, the memory occupied in the managed heap by the **OSHandle** object will be reclaimed.

When designing a type, it's best if you avoid using a `Finalize` method, for several reasons:

■ Finalizable objects get promoted to older generations, which increases memory pressure and prevents the object's memory from being collected at the time when the garbage collector determines the object is garbage. In addition, all objects referred to directly or indirectly by this object get promoted as well. (I'll talk about generations and promotions later in this chapter.)

■ Finalizable objects take longer to allocate because pointers to them must be placed on the finalization list (which I'll discuss in the "Finalization Internals" section a little later).

■ Forcing the garbage collector to execute a `Finalize` method can hurt performance significantly. Remember, each object is finalized. So if I have an array of 10,000 objects, each object must have its `Finalize` method called.

■ A finalizable object can refer to other (finalizable and nonfinalizable) objects, prolonging their lifetime unnecessarily. In fact, you might want to consider breaking a type into two different types: a lightweight type with a `Finalize` method that doesn't refer to any other objects (just like the `OSHandle` type shown earlier) and a separate type without a `Finalize` method that does refer to other objects.

■ You have no control over when the `Finalize` method will execute. The object might hold on to resources until the next time the garbage collector runs.

■ The CLR doesn't make any guarantees as to the order in which `Finalize` methods are called. For example, let's say an object contains a pointer to another object, which I'll call the inner object. The garbage collector has detected that both objects are garbage. Let's further say that the inner object's `Finalize` method gets called first. Now, the outer object's `Finalize` method is allowed to access the inner object and call methods on it, but the inner object has been finalized and the results can be unpredictable. For this reason, Microsoft strongly recommends that `Finalize` methods do not access any inner, member objects. The dispose pattern, which I'll cover later in this chapter, offers a way to clean up an object where this restriction doesn't apply.

If you determine that your type must implement a `Finalize` method, make sure that the code executes as quickly as possible. Avoid all actions that would block the `Finalize` method, including any thread synchronization operations. Also, if you let any exceptions escape the `Finalize` method, the CLR swallows the exception and continues calling other objects' `Finalize` methods.

> **Note**   By far, the most common reason to implement a `Finalize` method is to free an unmanaged resource that the object itself owns. In fact, during finalization, you should avoid writing code that accesses other managed objects or managed `Shared` (static) methods. You should avoid accessing other managed objects because the object's type can implement a `Finalize` method, which might get called first, putting the object in an unpredictable state. You should avoid calling any managed `Shared` (static) methods because these methods can internally access objects that have been finalized, first causing the behavior of the `Shared` (static) method to be unpredictable.

`Finalize` methods can also be used for other purposes. Here's a class that causes the computer to beep every time the garbage collector performs a collection.

```
Public NotInheritable Class GCBeep
    Protected Overrides Sub Finalize()
        ' We're being finalized, beep.
        MessageBeep(-1)

        ' If the AppDomain isn't unloading, create a new object
        ' that will get finalized at the next collection.
        ' I'll discuss IsFinalizingForUnload in the next section.
        If Not AppDomain.CurrentDomain.IsFinalizingForUnload() Then
            Dim gcb As New GCBeep()
        End If
    End Sub

    <System.Runtime.InteropServices.DllImport("User32.dll")> _
    Private Shared Function MessageBeep(ByVal uType As Int32) As Boolean
    End Function
End Class
```

To use this class, you just need to construct one instance of the class. Then whenever a garbage collection occurs, the object's `Finalize` method is called, which calls **MessageBeep** and constructs a new **GCBeep** object. This new **GCBeep** object will have its **Finalize** method called when the next garbage collection occurs. Here's a sample program that demonstrates the **GCBeep** class:

```
Class App
    Shared Sub Main()
        ' Constructing a single GCBeep object causes a beep to
        ' occur every time a garbage collection starts.
        Dim gcb As New GCBeep()

        ' Construct a lot of 100-byte objects.
        Dim x As Int32
        For x = 0 To 9999
            Console.WriteLine(x)
            Dim b(100) As Byte
        Next
    End Sub
End Class
```

Also be aware that a type's **Finalize** method is called even if the type's instance constructor throws an exception. So your **Finalize** method shouldn't assume that the object is in a good, consistent state. The following code demonstrates.

```
Imports System.IO

Class TempFile
    Dim filename As String = Nothing
    Public fs As FileStream

    Public Sub New(ByVal filename As String)
        ' The following line might throw an exception.
        Dim fs As New FileStream(filename, FileMode.Create)

        ' Save the name of this file.
        Me.filename = filename
    End Sub

    Protected Overrides Sub Finalize()
        ' The right thing to do here is to test filename
        ' against Nothing because you can't be sure that
        ' filename was initialized in the constructor.
        If Not filename Is Nothing Then
            File.Delete(filename)
        End If
    End Sub
End Class
```

Alternatively, you could write the code as follows:

```
Imports System
Imports System.IO

Class TempFile
    Dim filename As String = Nothing
    Public fs As FileStream

    Public Sub New(ByVal filename As String)
        Try
            ' The following line might throw an exception.
            Dim fs As New FileStream(filename, FileMode.Create)

            ' Save the name of this file.
            Me.filename = filename
        Catch
            ' If anything goes wrong, tell the garbage collector
            ' not to call the Finalize method. I'll discuss
            ' SuppressFinalize later in this chapter.
            GC.SuppressFinalize(Me)

            ' Let the caller know something failed.
            Throw
        End Try
    End Sub

    Protected Overrides Sub Finalize()
        ' No if statement is necessary now because this code
        ' executes only if the constructor ran successfully.
        File.Delete(filename)
    End Sub
End Class
```

What Causes Finalize Methods to Get Called

Four events cause an object to have its **Finalize** method called:

- **Generation 0 is full**   This event is by far the most common way for **Finalize** methods to be called because it occurs naturally as the application code runs, allocating new objects.

- **Code explicitly calls System.GC's static Collect method**   Code can explicitly request that the CLR perform a collection. Although Microsoft strongly discourages such requests, at times it might make sense for an application to force a collection. (I'll talk about this later in the chapter.)

- **The CLR is unloading an AppDomain**   When an AppDomain unloads, the CLR considers nothing in the AppDomain to be a root and calls the `Finalize` method for all objects that were created in the AppDomain. I'll discuss AppDomains in Chapter 20.

- **The CLR is shutting down**   When a process is gracefully terminating, it tries to shut down the CLR gracefully as well. At this point, the CLR considers nothing in the process to be a root and calls the `Finalize` method for all objects in the managed heap.

The CLR uses a special, dedicated thread to call `Finalize` methods. For the first, second, and third events, if a `Finalize` method enters an infinite loop, this special thread is blocked and no more `Finalize` methods can be called. This is a very bad situation because the application will never be able to reclaim the memory occupied by finalizable objects—the application will leak memory for as long as it runs.

For the fourth event, each `Finalize` method is given approximately 2 seconds to return. If a `Finalize` method doesn't return within 2 seconds, the CLR just kills the process—no more `Finalize` methods are called. Also, if it takes more than 40 seconds to call all objects' `Finalize` methods, then again, the CLR just kills the process.

> **Note**   These timeout values were correct at the time I wrote this text, but Microsoft might change them in the future.

Code in a `Finalize` method can construct new objects. If this happens during CLR shutdown, the CLR continues collecting objects and calling their `Finalize` methods until no more objects exist or until the 40 seconds have expired.

Recall the `GCBeep` type presented earlier in this chapter. If a `GCBeep` object is being finalized because of the first or second event, a new `GCBeep` object is constructed. This is OK because the application continues to run, assuming that more collections will occur in the future. However, if a `GCBeep` object is being finalized because of the third or fourth event, a new `GCBeep` object shouldn't be constructed because this object would be created while the AppDomain was unloading or the CLR was shutting down. If these new objects were created, the CLR would have a bunch of useless work to do because it would continue to call `Finalize` methods.

To prevent the construction of new GCBeep objects, GCBeep's Finalize method contains a call to AppDomain's IsFinalizingForUnload method. This method returns True if the object's Finalize method is being called because of the AppDomain unloading. This solution works for AppDomain unloading, but what about CLR shutdown?

To know whether the CLR is shutting down, Microsoft added the HasShutdownStarted read-only property to the System.Environment class. GCBeep's Finalize method should be reading this property and shouldn't be constructing a new object when the property returns True. Unfortunately, GCBeep's Finalize method doesn't do this. Why not? The reason GCBeep's Finalize method doesn't read this property is that the property is inaccessible! A Microsoft developer made a mistake and implemented the property as an instance property, but the Environment class has only a private constructor, preventing you from creating an instance of it. So there's no way to access this property—what a bad bug! I hope Microsoft will fix this in a future version of the .NET Framework Class Library (FCL).

There is no real workaround for this problem. GCBeep's Finalize method does construct new objects during CLR shutdown. The new objects are continuously finalized, and after 40 seconds, the CLR gives up and terminates the process.

Finalization Internals

On the surface, finalization seems pretty straightforward: you create an object; when the object is collected, the object's Finalize method is called. But once you dig in, finalization is more complicated than this.

When an application creates a new object, the New operator allocates the memory from the heap. If the object's type defines a Finalize method, a pointer to the object is placed on the *finalization list* just before the type's instance constructor is called. The finalization list is an internal data structure the garbage collector controls. Each entry in the list points to an object that should have its Finalize method called before the object's memory can be reclaimed.

Figure 19-4 shows a heap containing several objects. Some of these objects are reachable from the application's roots, and some are not. When objects C, E, F, I, and J were created, the system detected that these objects' types defined Finalize methods and added pointers to these objects to the finalization list.

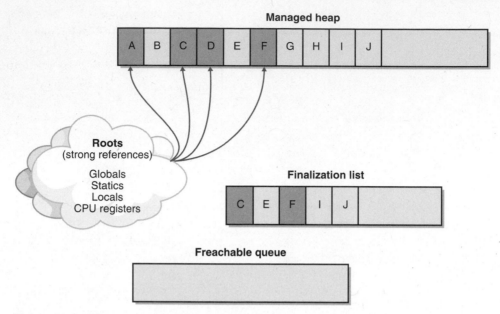

Figure 19-4 The managed heap showing pointers in its finalization list

> **Note** Even though `System.Object` defines a `Finalize` method, the CLR knows to ignore it; that is, when constructing an instance of a type, if the type's `Finalize` method is the one inherited from `System.Object`, the object isn't considered finalizable. One of the derived types must override `Object`'s `Finalize` method.

When a garbage collection occurs, objects B, E, G, H, I, and J are determined to be garbage. The garbage collector scans the finalization list looking for pointers to these objects. When a pointer is found, the pointer is removed from the finalization list and appended to the *freachable queue*. The freachable queue (pronounced "F-reachable") is another of the garbage collector's internal data structures. Each pointer in the freachable queue identifies an object that is ready to have its `Finalize` method called. After the collection, the managed heap looks like Figure 19-5.

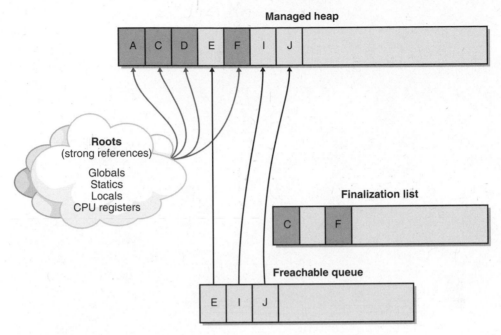

Figure 19-5   The managed heap showing pointers that moved from the finalization list to the freachable queue

In this figure, you see that the memory occupied by objects B, G, and H has been reclaimed because these objects didn't have a **Finalize** method that needed to be called. However, the memory occupied by objects E, I, and J couldn't be reclaimed because their **Finalize** methods haven't been called yet.

A special high-priority CLR thread is dedicated to calling **Finalize** methods. A dedicated thread is used to avoid potential thread synchronization situations that could arise if one of the application's threads was used instead. When the freachable queue is empty (the usual case), this thread sleeps. But when entries appear, this thread awakens, removes each entry from the queue, and calls each object's **Finalize** method. Because of the way this thread works, you shouldn't execute any code in a **Finalize** method that makes any assumptions about the thread that's executing the code. For example, avoid accessing thread local storage in the **Finalize** method.

The interaction between the finalization list and the freachable queue is fascinating. First I'll tell you how the freachable queue got its name. Well, the "f" is obvious and stands for "finalization": every entry in the freachable queue should have its `Finalize` method called. But the "reachable" part of the name means that the objects are reachable. To put it another way, the freachable queue is considered a root just as global and static variables are roots. So if an object is on the freachable queue, the object is reachable and is *not* garbage.

In short, when an object isn't reachable, the garbage collector considers the object garbage. Then when the garbage collector moves an object's entry from the finalization list to the freachable queue, the object is no longer considered garbage and its memory can't be reclaimed. At this point, the garbage collector has finished identifying garbage. Some of the objects identified as garbage have been reclassified as not garbage: in a sense, the object has been *resurrected*. The garbage collector compacts the reclaimable memory, and the special CLR thread empties the freachable queue, executing each object's `Finalize` method.

The next time the garbage collector is invoked, it sees that the finalized objects are truly garbage because the application's roots don't point to it and the freachable queue no longer points to it. The memory for the object is simply reclaimed. The important point to get from all of this is that two garbage collections are required to reclaim memory used by objects that require finalization. In reality, more than two collections might be necessary because the objects get promoted to another generation (which I'll explain later). Figure 19-6 shows what the managed heap looks like after the second garbage collection.

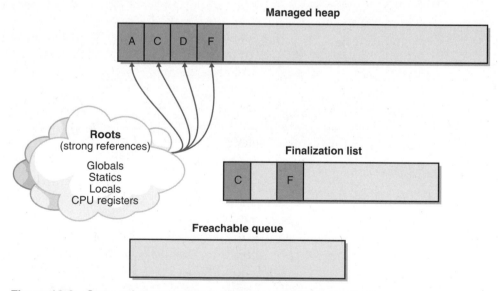

Figure 19-6 Status of managed heap after second garbage collection

The Dispose Pattern: Forcing an Object to Clean Up

The `Finalize` method is incredibly useful because it ensures that unmanaged resources aren't leaked when managed objects have their memory reclaimed. However, the problem with the `Finalize` method is that you have no guarantee when it will be called, and because it isn't a public method, a user of the class can't call it explicitly.

The capability to deterministically dispose of or close an object is frequently useful when you're working with unmanaged resources such as mutexes and bitmaps; this capability is even more useful when you're working with files and database connections. For example, you might want to open a database connection, query some records, and close the database connection—you don't want the database connection to stay open until the next garbage collection occurs, especially because the next garbage collection could occur hours or even days after you retrieve the database records.

Types that offer the capability to be deterministically disposed of or closed implement what is known as the *dispose pattern*. The dispose pattern defines conventions that a developer should adhere to when defining a type that wants to offer explicit cleanup to a user of the type. In addition, if a type implements the dispose pattern, a developer using the type knows exactly how to explicitly dispose of the object when it's no longer needed.

> **Note**   Any type that defines a `Finalize` method should also implement the dispose pattern as described in this section so that users of the type have a lot of control. However, a type can implement the dispose pattern and not define a `Finalize` method. For example, the `System.IO.BinaryWriter` class falls into this category. I'll explain the reason for this exception in the section "An Interesting Dependency Issue" later in this chapter.

Earlier, I showed you the `OSHandle` type. That version of the code implemented a `Finalize` method, so the unmanaged resource that the object wrapped was closed when the object was collected. However, a developer using an `OSHandle` object had no way to explicitly close the unmanaged resource—the unmanaged resource got closed only when the object got garbage collected.

The following code shows a new and better version of the `OSHandle` class. This new version implements the well-defined dispose pattern.

```vb
Imports System

' Implementing the IDisposable interface signals users of
' this class that it offers the dispose pattern.
Public NotInheritable Class OSHandle
    Implements IDisposable

    ' This field holds the Win32 handle of the unmanaged resource.
    Private handle As IntPtr

    ' This constructor initializes the handle.
    Public Sub New(ByVal handle As IntPtr)
        Me.handle = handle
    End Sub

    ' When garbage collected, this Finalize method, which
    ' will close the unmanaged resource's handle, is called.
    Protected Overrides Sub Finalize()
        Dispose(False)
    End Sub

    ' This public method can be called to deterministically
    ' close the unmanaged resource's handle.
    Public Sub Dispose() Implements IDisposable.Dispose
        ' Because the object is explicitly cleaned up, stop the
        ' garbage collector from calling the Finalize method.
        GC.SuppressFinalize(Me)

        ' Call the method that actually does the cleanup.
        Dispose(True)
    End Sub

    ' This public method can be called instead of Dispose.
    Public Sub Close()
        Dispose()
    End Sub

    ' The common method that does the actual cleanup.
    ' Finalize, Dispose, and Close call this method.
    ' Because this class is sealed, this method is private.
    ' If this class weren't sealed, this method would be protected
    ' and overridable.
    Private Sub Dispose(ByVal disposing As Boolean)
        ' Synchronize threads calling Dispose/Close simultaneously.
```

```
        SyncLock Me
            If disposing Then
                ' The object is being explicitly disposed of/closed, not
                ' finalized. It is therefore safe for code in this If
                ' statement to access fields that reference other
                ' objects because the Finalize method of these other objects
                ' hasn't yet been called.

                ' For the OSHandle class, there is nothing to do in here.
            End If

            ' The object is being disposed of/closed or finalized.
            If IsValid Then
                ' If the handle is valid, close the unmanaged resource.
                ' NOTE: Replace CloseHandle with whatever function is
                ' necessary to close/free your unmanaged resource.
                CloseHandle(handle)

                ' Set the handle field to some sentinel value. This precaution
                ' prevents the possibility of calling CloseHandle twice.
                handle = InvalidHandle
            End If
        End SyncLock
    End Sub

    ' Public property to return the value of an invalid handle,
    ' NOTE: Make this property return an invalid value for
    ' whatever unmanaged resource you're using.
    Public ReadOnly Property InvalidHandle() As IntPtr
        Get
            Return IntPtr.Zero
        End Get
    End Property

    ' Public method to return the value of the wrapped handle
    Public Function ToHandle() As IntPtr
        Return handle
    End Function

    ' Public properties to return whether the wrapped handle is valid
    Public ReadOnly Property IsValid() As Boolean
        Get
            Return Not handle.Equals(InvalidHandle)
        End Get
    End Property
```

(continued)

```
Public ReadOnly Property IsInvalid() As Boolean
    Get
        Return Not IsValid
    End Get
End Property


' Private method called to free the unmanaged resource.
<System.Runtime.InteropServices.DllImport("Kernel32")> _
Private Shared Function CloseHandle(ByVal handle As IntPtr) As Boolean
End Function
End Class
```

This **OSHandle** code is hardly trivial: a lot of code is necessary to support the dispose pattern, and this class just wraps a simple unmanaged resource. The good news is that this class is almost all you'll ever need; that is, if you're designing a type that wraps an unmanaged resource, you can pretty much take the **OSHandle** code and copy it directly into your own project as is. In fact, it would be great if Microsoft had incorporated this class into the FCL itself.

Now let me explain what all this code does. First, the **OSHandle** type implements the **System.IDisposable** interface. This interface is defined in the FCL as follows:

```
Public Interface IDisposable
    Sub Dispose()
End Interface
```

Any type that implements this interface is stating that it adheres to the dispose pattern. Simply put, this means that the type offers a public, parameterless **Dispose** method that can be explicitly called to free the resource wrapped by the object. Note that the memory for the object itself is *not* freed from the managed heap's memory; the garbage collector is still responsible for freeing the object's memory, and there's no telling exactly when this will happen.

> **Note**   You might notice that this **OSHandle** type also offers a public **Close** method. This method simply calls **Dispose**. Some classes that offer the dispose pattern also offer a **Close** method for convenience; but the dispose pattern doesn't require this method. For example, the **System.IO.FileStream** class offers the dispose pattern, and this class also offers a **Close** method. Programmers find it more natural to "close" a file rather than "dispose of" a file. However, the **System.Threading.Timer** class doesn't offer a **Close** method even though it adheres to the dispose pattern.

The parameterless **Dispose** and **Close** methods should both be public and nonvirtual. However, because the **Dispose** method is implementing a method of an interface, the method is virtual by default. So the best you can do is seal the **Dispose** method by not marking it as **Overridable** (which can be used only if the class isn't **NotInheritable**).

So now you know of three ways to clean up an **OSHandle** object: a programmer can write code to call **Dispose**, a programmer can write code to call **Close**, or the garbage collector can call the object's **Finalize** method. The cleanup code is the same no matter which option you choose, so it's placed in a separate, private, nonvirtual method, which is also called **Dispose**; but this **Dispose** method takes a **Boolean** parameter, **disposing**.

This **Dispose** method is where you put all the cleanup code. In the **OSHandle** example, the method simply calls the Win32 **CloseHandle** function and changes the **handle** field to an invalid value. Setting the field to an invalid value ensures that the handle isn't closed multiple times; because the parameterless **Dispose** and **Close** methods are public, application code could call them multiple times. And because multiple threads can call these methods simultaneously, the Boolean **Dispose** method uses Visual Basic's **SyncLock** statement to ensure that the code in the method is thread-safe.

When an object's **Finalize** method is called, the **Dispose** method's **disposing** parameter is **False**. This tells the **Dispose** method that it shouldn't execute any code that references other managed objects. Imagine that the CLR is shutting down, and inside a **Finalize** method, you attempt to write to a **FileStream**. This might not work because the **FileStream** might have already had its **Finalize** method called.

On the other hand, when **Dispose** or **Close** is called, the **Dispose** method's **disposing** parameter will be set to **True**. This indicates that the object is being explicitly disposed of, not finalized. In this case, the **Dispose** method is allowed to execute code that references another object (such as a **FileStream**); because you have control over the program's logic, you know that the **FileStream** object is still open.

By the way, if the **OSHandle** class were not marked **NotInheritable**, the Boolean **Dispose** method would be implemented as a protected virtual method instead of a private nonvirtual method. Any class that derives from **OSHandle** would implement the Boolean **Dispose** method only; it wouldn't implement the parameterless **Dispose** or **Close** method, and it wouldn't implement a **Finalize** method. The derived class would simply inherit the implementation of all these methods.

> **Important** You need to be aware of some versioning issues here. If, in version 1, a base type doesn't implement the IDisposable interface, it can never implement this interface in a later version. If the base type were to add the IDisposable interface in the future, all the derived types wouldn't know to call the base type's methods and the base type wouldn't get a chance to clean itself up properly. Likewise, if, in version 1, a base type implements the IDisposable interface, it can never remove this interface in a later version because the derived type would be trying to call methods that no longer existed in the base type.

In fact, if the derived class didn't have any cleanup to do itself, it wouldn't have to do anything with respect to the dispose pattern. But if the derived class did need to do some cleanup, it would just override the virtual Boolean **Dispose** method. In this method, you would write code to do the necessary explicit cleanup and then call the base class's Boolean **Dispose** method. Before we can derive from **OSHandle**, we must make it inheritable and change the scope of a few of its members from **Private** to **Protected**. Finally, we must ensure that the **Dispose** method that takes an argument can be overridden. Here's the new version of the **OSHandle** class. (Changes have been highlighted in boldface.)

```
' Implementing the IDisposable interface signals users of
' this class that it offers the dispose pattern.
Public Class OSHandle
    Implements IDisposable

    ' This field holds the Win32 handle of the unmanaged resource.
    Private handle As IntPtr

    ' This constructor initializes the handle.
    Public Sub New(ByVal handle As IntPtr)
        Me.handle = handle
    End Sub

    ' When garbage collected, this Finalize method, which
    ' will close the unmanaged resource's handle, is called.
    Protected Overrides Sub Finalize()
        Dispose(False)
    End Sub

    ' This public method can be called to deterministically
    ' close the unmanaged resource's handle.
```

```
Public Sub Dispose() Implements IDisposable.Dispose
   ' Because the object is explicitly cleaned up, stop the
   ' garbage collector from calling the Finalize method.
   GC.SuppressFinalize(Me)

   ' Call the method that actually does the cleanup.
   Dispose(True)
End Sub

' This public method can be called instead of Dispose.
Public Sub Close()
   Dispose()
End Sub

' The common method that does the actual cleanup.
' Finalize, Dispose, and Close call this method.
' Because this class isn't NotInheritable, this method is protected.
Protected Overridable Sub Dispose(ByVal disposing As Boolean)
   ' Synchronize threads calling Dispose/Close simultaneously.
   SyncLock Me
      If disposing Then
         ' The object is being explicitly disposed of/closed, not
         ' finalized. It is therefore safe for code in this If
         ' statement to access fields that reference other
         ' objects because the Finalize method of these other objects
         ' hasn't yet been called.

         ' For the OSHandle class, there is nothing to do in here.
      End If

      ' The object is being disposed of/closed or finalized.
      If IsValid Then
         ' If the handle is valid, close the unmanaged resource.
         ' NOTE: Replace CloseHandle with whatever function is
         ' necessary to close/free your unmanaged resource.
         CloseHandle(handle)

         ' Set the handle field to some sentinel value. This precaution
         ' prevents the possibility of calling CloseHandle twice.
         handle = InvalidHandle
      End If
   End SyncLock
End Sub

' Public property to return the value of an invalid handle.
' NOTE: Make this property return an invalid value for
' whatever unmanaged resource you're using.
```

(continued)

```
         Public ReadOnly Property InvalidHandle() As IntPtr
            Get
               Return IntPtr.Zero
            End Get
         End Property

         ' Public method to return the value of the wrapped handle
         Public Function ToHandle() As IntPtr
            Return handle
         End Function

         ' Public properties to return whether the wrapped handle is valid
         Public ReadOnly Property IsValid() As Boolean
            Get
               Return Not handle.Equals(InvalidHandle)
            End Get
         End Property

         Public ReadOnly Property IsInvalid() As Boolean
            Get
               Return Not IsValid
            End Get
         End Property


         ' Private method called to free the unmanaged resource
         <System.Runtime.InteropServices.DllImport("Kernel32")> _
         Protected Shared Function CloseHandle(ByVal handle As IntPtr) As Boolean
         End Function
      End Class
```

Here's an example of a class that overrides the **OSHandle** class:

```
Class SomeType
   Inherits OSHandle

   ' This field holds the Win32 handle of the unmanaged resource.
   ' This handle is used by this derived type only and is not the
   ' same handle the base type uses.
   Private handle As IntPtr

   Public Sub New(ByVal handleSomeType As IntPtr, ByVal handleBase as IntPtr)
      Me.handle = handleSomeType
      MyBase.New(handleBase)
   End Sub

   Protected Overloads Overrides Sub Dispose(ByVal disposing As Boolean)
      ' Synchronize threads calling Dispose/Close simultaneously.
```

```
        SyncLock Me
          Try
            If disposing Then
                ' The object is being explicitly disposed of/closed, not
                ' finalized. It is therefore safe for code in this If
                ' statement to access fields that reference other
                ' objects because the Finalize method of these other
                ' objects hasn't been called.

                ' For this class, there is nothing to do in here.
            End If

            ' The object is being disposed of/closed or finalized.
            If IsValid Then
                ' If the handle is valid, close the unmanaged resource.
                ' NOTE: Replace CloseHandle with whatever function is
                ' necessary to close/free your unmanaged resource.
                CloseHandle(handle)

                ' Set the handle field to some sentinel value. This precaution
                ' prevents the possibility of calling CloseHandle twice.
                handle = InvalidHandle
            End If

          Finally
            ' Let the base class do its cleanup.
            Dispose(disposing)
          End Try
        End SyncLock
      End Sub
End Class
```

Another noteworthy part of this code is the call to GC's static **Suppress-Finalize** method inside the parameterless **Dispose** method. You see, if code using an **OSHandle** object explicitly calls **Dispose** or **Close**, the object's **Finalize** method shouldn't execute. For if **Finalize** did execute, **CloseHandle** would be called multiple times. The call to GC's **SuppressFinalize** turns on a bit flag associated with the object referred to by **Me**. When this flag is on, the CLR knows not to move this object's pointer from the finalization list to the freachable queue, preventing the object's **Finalize** method from being called. When the garbage collector determines the object to be garbage, its memory is simply reclaimed.

Using a Type That Implements the Dispose Pattern

Now that you know how a type implements the dispose pattern, let's take a look at how a developer uses a type that offers the dispose pattern. Instead of talking about the **OSHandle** class, let's talk about the more common **System.IO.FileStream** class. The **FileStream** class offers the ability to open a file, read bytes from the file, write bytes to the file, and close the file. Internally, the **FileStream** class is implemented identically to the **OSHandle** class except that its constructor calls the Win32 **CreateFile** function and the result is saved in the private handle field. The **FileStream** class also offers several additional properties (such as **Length**, **Position**, **CanRead**, **Handle**, and so on) and methods (such as **Read**, **Write**, **Flush**, and so on).

Let's say you want to write some code that creates a temporary file, writes some bytes to the file, and then deletes the file. You might start writing the code like this:

```
Imports System
Imports System.IO

Class App
    Shared Sub Main()
        ' Create the bytes to write to the temporary file.
        Dim bytesToWrite() As Byte = {1, 2, 3, 4, 5}

        ' Create the temporary file.
        Dim fs As New FileStream("Temp.dat", FileMode.Create)

        ' Write the bytes to the temporary file.
        fs.Write(bytesToWrite, 0, bytesToWrite.Length)

        ' Delete the temporary file.
        File.Delete("Temp.dat")     ' Throws an IOException
    End Sub
End Class
```

Unfortunately, if you build and run this code, it might work, but most likely it won't. The problem is that the call to **File**'s static **Delete** method requests that Windows delete a file that is open. And so, **Delete** throws a **System.IO.IOException** exception with the following string message: "The process cannot access the file "Temp.dat" because it is being used by another process."

Be aware that in some cases, the file might actually get deleted! If another thread somehow caused a garbage collection to start after the call to **Write** and before the call to **Delete**, the **FileStream** object would get its **Finalize** method called, which would close the file and allow **Delete** to work. The likelihood of this situation is extremely rare, however, and the previous code will fail more than 99 percent of the time.

Fortunately, the **FileStream** class implements the dispose pattern, allowing me to modify the source code to explicitly close the file. Here's the corrected source code:

```
Imports System
Imports System.IO

Class App
    Shared Sub Main()
        ' Create the bytes to write to the temporary file.
        Dim bytesToWrite() As Byte = {1, 2, 3, 4, 5}

        ' Create the temporary file.
        Dim fs As New FileStream("Temp.dat", FileMode.Create)

        ' Write the bytes to the temporary file.
        fs.Write(bytesToWrite, 0, bytesToWrite.Length)

        ' Explicitly close the file when done writing to it.
        DirectCast(fs, IDisposable).Dispose()

        ' Delete the temporary file.
        File.Delete("Temp.dat")     ' Throws an IOException
    End Sub
End Class
```

The only difference here is that I've added a call to **FileStream**'s **Dispose** method. The **Dispose** method calls the Boolean **Dispose** method, which calls **CloseHandle**; Windows closes the file. Now, when **File**'s **Delete** method is called, Windows sees that the file isn't open and successfully deletes it.

Note that the **FileStream** object still exists in the managed heap, so you could still call methods on the object. Eventually, the garbage collector will run and determine that the **FileStream** object is garbage. At this point, the garbage collector would normally call its **Finalize** method, but because the **Dispose** method called GC's **SuppressFinalize** method, the **Finalize** method won't be called—the object's memory will just be reclaimed.

Note   The previous code casts the **fs** variable to an **IDisposable** before calling **Dispose**. Most classes that implement the dispose pattern won't require this cast. However, for a **FileStream** object, the cast is required because Microsoft's developers implemented the **Dispose** method as an explicit interface method implementation (as described in Chapter 15). I felt that this was a poor decision because it just makes things more complex without adding any value. In general, you should use privately defined interface methods only when you have multiple methods with the same name. Because **Dispose** and **Close** are different method names, I think that they should be publicly available and that no casting should be required.

Because the **FileStream** class also offers a public **Close** method, you could write the earlier code as follows with identical results:

```
Imports System
Imports System.IO

Class App
    Shared Sub Main()
        ' Create the bytes to write to the temporary file.
        Dim bytesToWrite() As Byte = {1, 2, 3, 4, 5}

        ' Create the temporary file.
        Dim fs As New FileStream("Temp.dat", FileMode.Create)

        ' Write the bytes to the temporary file.
        fs.Write(bytesToWrite, 0, bytesToWrite.Length)

        ' Explicitly close the file when done writing to it.
        fs.Close()

        ' Delete the temporary file.
        File.Delete("Temp.dat")     ' Throws an IOException
    End Sub
End Class
```

> **Note**   Again, remember that the **Close** method isn't officially part of the dispose pattern: some types will offer it and some won't.

Keep in mind that calling **Dispose** or **Close** simply gives the programmer a way to force the object to do its cleanup at a deterministic time; these methods have no control over the lifetime of the memory used by the object in the managed heap. This means that you can still call methods on the object even though it has been cleaned up. The following code calls the **Write** method after the file is closed, attempting to write more bytes to the file. Obviously, the bytes can't be written, and when the code executes, the second call to the **Write** method throws a **System.ObjectDisposedException** exception with the following string message: "Cannot access a closed file."

```
Imports System
Imports System.IO

Class App
    Shared Sub Main()
        ' Create the bytes to write to the temporary file.
        Dim bytesToWrite() As Byte = {1, 2, 3, 4, 5}

        ' Create the temporary file.
        Dim fs As New FileStream("Temp.dat", FileMode.Create)

        ' Write the bytes to the temporary file.
        fs.Write(bytesToWrite, 0, bytesToWrite.Length)

        ' Explicitly close the file when done writing to it.
        DirectCast(fs, IDisposable).Dispose()

        ' Try to write to the file after closing it.
        ' The following line throws an ObjectDisposedException.
        fs.Write(bytesToWrite, 0, bytesToWrite.Length)

        ' Delete the temporary file.
        File.Delete("Temp.dat")     ' Throws an IOException
    End Sub
End Class
```

No memory corruption has occurred here because the memory for the **FileStream** object still exists; it's just that the object can't successfully execute its methods after it is explicitly disposed.

> **Important**   When defining your own type that implements the dispose pattern, be sure to write code in all your methods to throw a **System.ObjectDisposedException** exception if the object has been explicitly cleaned up. The **Dispose** and **Close** methods should never throw an **ObjectDisposedException** exception if called multiple times, though; these methods should just return (as shown earlier in the **OSHandle** type).

Accounting for Exceptions When Using the Dispose Pattern

The previous code examples show how to explicitly call a type's Dispose or Close method. If you decide to call either of these methods explicitly, I highly recommend that you place the call in an exception handling **Finally** block. This way, the cleanup code is guaranteed to execute. So it would be better to write the previous code example as follows:

```vb
Imports System
Imports System.IO

Class App
    Shared Sub Main()
        ' Create the bytes to write to the temporary file.
        Dim bytesToWrite() As Byte = {1, 2, 3, 4, 5}

        ' Create the temporary file.
        Dim fs As FileStream = Nothing
        Try
            fs = New FileStream("Temp.dat", FileMode.Create)
```

```
            ' Write the bytes to the temporary file.
            fs.Write(bytesToWrite, 0, bytesToWrite.Length)
        Finally
            ' Explicitly close the file when done writing to it.
            If Not fs Is Nothing Then
                DirectCast(fs, IDisposable).Dispose()
                ' Delete the temporary file.
                File.Delete("Temp.dat")  ' This always works now.
            End If
        End Try
    End Sub
End Sub
```

Adding the exception handling code is the right thing to do, and you must have the diligence to do it.

An Interesting Dependency Issue

The `System.IO.FileStream` type allows the user to open a file for reading and writing. To improve performance, the type's implementation makes use of a memory buffer. Only when the buffer fills does the type flush the contents of the buffer to the file. A `FileStream` supports the writing of bytes only. If you want to write more complex data types (such as an `Int32`, a `Double`, a `String`, and so on), you can use a `System.IO.BinaryWriter` as demonstrated in the following code:

```
Dim fs As New FileStream("DataFile.dat", FileMode.Create)
Dim bw As New BinaryWriter(fs)
bw.Write("Hi there")

' The following call to Close is what you should do.
bw.Close()
' NOTE: BinaryWriter.Close closes the FileStream. The FileStream
' shouldn't be explicitly closed in this scenario.
```

Notice that the `BinaryWriter`'s constructor takes a reference to a `FileStream` object as a parameter. Internally, the `BinaryWriter` object saves the `FileStream`'s reference. When you write to a `BinaryWriter` object, it internally buffers the data in its own memory buffer. When the buffer is full, the `Binary-Writer` object writes the data to the `FileStream`.

When you're done writing data via the `BinaryWriter` object, you should call `Dispose` or `Close`. Both of these methods do exactly the same thing: cause the `BinaryWriter` object to flush its data to the `FileStream` object and close the `FileStream` object. When the `FileStream` object is closed, it flushes its buffer to disk just prior to calling the Win32 `CloseHandle` function.

> **Note**   You don't have to explicitly call `Dispose` or `Close` on the `FileStream` object because the `BinaryWriter` calls it for you. However, if you do call `Dispose/Close` explicitly, the `FileStream` will see that the object has already been cleaned up—the methods do nothing and just return.

What do you think would happen if there were no code that explicitly called `Dispose` or `Close`? Well, at some point, the garbage collector would correctly detect that the objects were garbage and finalize them. But the garbage collector doesn't guarantee the order in which the `Finalize` methods are called. So if the `FileStream` got finalized first, it would close the file. Then when the `BinaryWriter` got finalized, it would attempt to write data to the closed file, throwing an exception. If, on the other hand, the `BinaryWriter` got finalized first, the data would be safely written to the file.

How was Microsoft to solve this problem? Making the garbage collector finalize objects in a specific order would have been impossible because objects could contain references to each other and there would be no way for the garbage collector to correctly guess the order in which to finalize these objects. Here is Microsoft's solution: the `BinaryWriter` type doesn't implement a `Finalize` method. This means that if you forget to explicitly close the `BinaryWriter` object, data is guaranteed to be lost. Microsoft expects developers to see this consistent loss of data and fix the code by inserting an explicit call to `Close/Dispose`.

Weak References

When a root points to an object, the object can't be collected because the application's code can reach the object. When a root points to an object, a *strong reference* to the object is said to exist. However, the garbage collector also supports *weak references*. Weak references allow the garbage collector to collect the object but also allow the application to access the object. It all comes down to timing.

If only weak references to an object exist and the garbage collector runs, the object is collected, and when the application later attempts to access the object, the access will fail. On the other hand, to access a weakly referenced object, the application must obtain a strong reference to the object. If the application obtains this strong reference before the garbage collector collects the object, the garbage collector can't collect the object because a strong reference to the object exists.

Confused? Let's examine some code to clarify what all this really means:

```
Sub SomeMethod()
    ' Create a strong reference to a new Object.
    Dim o As New Object()

    ' Create a strong reference to a short WeakReference object.
    ' The WeakReference object tracks the Object's lifetime.
    Dim wr As New WeakReference(o)

    o = Nothing    ' Remove the strong reference to the object.

    o = wr.Target
    If o Is Nothing Then
        ' A garbage collection occurred and Object's memory was reclaimed.
    Else
        ' A garbage collection did not occur and I can successfully
        ' access the Object using o.
    End If
End Sub
```

Why might you want to use weak references? Well, some data structures are easy to create but require a lot of memory. For example, you might have an application that needs to know all the directories and files on the user's hard drive. You can easily build a tree that reflects this information and, as your application runs, refer to the tree in memory instead of accessing the user's hard disk. This greatly improves the performance of your application.

The problem is that the tree could be extremely large, requiring quite a bit of memory. If the user starts accessing a different part of your application, the tree might no longer be necessary but could be wasting valuable memory nonetheless. You could give up the reference to the tree's root object, but if the user switches back to the first part of your application, you'll need to reconstruct the tree again. A weak reference allows you to handle this scenario easily and efficiently.

When the user switches away from the first part of the application, you can create a weak reference to the tree's root object and give up all strong references. If the other subcomponent's memory load is low, the garbage collector won't reclaim the tree's objects. When the user switches back to the first component, the application attempts to obtain a strong reference to the tree's root object. If successful, the application doesn't have to traverse the user's hard drive again.

The `System.WeakReference` type offers two public constructors:

```
Public Sub New(ByVal target As Object)
Public Sub New(ByVal target As Object, ByVal trackResurrection As Boolean)
```

The `target` parameter identifies the object that the `WeakReference` object should track. The `trackResurrection` parameter indicates whether the `WeakReference` object should track the object after its `Finalize` method has been called. Usually, `False` is passed for the `trackResurrection` parameter, and the first constructor creates a `WeakReference` that doesn't track resurrection.

For convenience, a `WeakReference` that doesn't track resurrection is called a *short weak reference*; a `WeakReference` that does track resurrection is called a *long weak reference*. If an object's type doesn't offer a `Finalize` method, short and long weak references behave identically. I strongly recommend that you avoid using long weak references. Long weak references allow you to resurrect an object after it has been finalized and the state of the object is unpredictable.

Once you've created a weak reference to an object, you usually set the strong reference to the object to `Nothing`. If any strong reference remains, the garbage collector will be unable to collect the object.

To use the object again, you must turn the weak reference into a strong reference. You accomplish this by simply querying the `WeakReference` object's `Target` property and assigning the result to one of your application's roots. If the `Target` property returns `Nothing`, the object was collected. If the property doesn't return `Nothing`, the root is a strong reference to the object and the code can manipulate the object. As long as the strong reference exists, the object can't be collected.

Weak Reference Internals

From the preceding discussion, it should be obvious that `WeakReference` objects don't behave like other object types. Normally, if your application has a root that refers to an object, and that object refers to another object, both objects are reachable and the garbage collector can't reclaim the memory either object is using. However, if your application has a root that refers to a `WeakReference` object, the object referred to by the `WeakReference` object isn't considered reachable and can be collected.

To fully understand how weak references work, let's look inside the managed heap again. The managed heap contains two internal data structures whose sole purpose is to manage weak references: the short weak reference table and the long weak reference table. These two tables simply contain pointers to objects allocated within the managed heap.

Initially, both tables are empty. When you create a **WeakReference** object, an object isn't allocated from the managed heap. Instead, an empty slot in one of the weak reference tables is located; short weak references use the short weak reference table, and long weak references use the long weak reference table.

Once an empty slot is found, the value in the slot is set to the address of the object you want to track—the object's pointer is passed to the **WeakReference**'s constructor. The value returned from the **New** operator is the address of the slot in the weak reference table. Obviously, the two weak reference tables aren't considered part of an application's roots or the garbage collector wouldn't be able to reclaim the objects the tables point to.

Here's what happens when the garbage collector runs:

1. The garbage collector builds a graph of all the reachable objects. I already explained how the garbage collector does this.

2. The garbage collector scans the short weak reference table. If a pointer in the table refers to an object that isn't part of the graph, then the pointer identifies an unreachable object and the slot in the short weak reference table is set to **Nothing**.

3. The garbage collector scans the finalization list. If a pointer in the list refers to an object that isn't part of the graph, then the pointer identifies an unreachable object and the pointer is moved from the finalization list to the freachable queue. At this point, the object is added to the graph because the object is now considered reachable.

4. The garbage collector scans the long weak reference table. If a pointer in the table refers to an object that isn't part of the graph (which now contains the objects pointed to by entries in the freachable queue), then the pointer identifies an unreachable object and the slot is set to **Nothing**.

5. The garbage collector compacts the memory, squeezing out the holes left by the unreachable objects. Note that the garbage collector sometimes decides not to compact memory if it determines that the amount of fragmentation isn't worth the time to compact.

Once you understand the logic behind how the garbage collector works, it's easy to understand how weak references work. Querying the **WeakReference**'s **Target** property causes the system to return the value in the appropriate weak reference table's slot. If **Nothing** is in the slot, the object was collected.

A short weak reference doesn't track resurrection. This means that the garbage collector sets the pointer to **Nothing** in the short weak reference table as soon as the garbage collector has determined the object to be unreachable. If the object has a **Finalize** method, the method hasn't been called yet, so the object still exists. If the application accesses the **WeakReference** object's **Target** property, then **Nothing** will be returned even though the object still exists.

A long weak reference tracks resurrection. This means that the garbage collector sets the pointer to **Nothing** in the long weak reference table when the object's storage is reclaimable. If the object has a **Finalize** method, the **Finalize** method has been called and the object was not resurrected.

Resurrection

I'm sure you'd agree that finalization is fascinating. And there's even more to it than what I've already described. You'll notice that when an object requiring finalization is considered dead, the garbage collector forces the object back to life so that its **Finalize** method can be called. Then after its **Finalize** method is called, the object is permanently dead. To summarize: an object requiring finalization dies, lives, and then dies again. This very interesting phenomenon is called *resurrection*. Resurrection, as its name implies, allows an object to come back from the dead.

The act of preparing to call an object's **Finalize** method is a form of resurrection. When the garbage collector places a reference to the object on the freachable queue, the object is reachable from a root and has come back to life. Eventually, the object's **Finalize** method is called, no roots point to the object, and the object is dead forever after. But what if an object's **Finalize** method executed code that placed a pointer to the object in a global or static variable, as demonstrated in the following code?

```
Class SomeType
   Protected Overrides Sub Finalize()
      Application.ObjHolder = Me
   End Sub
End Class

Class Application
   Public Shared ObjHolder As Object      ' Defaults to Nothing
      ⋮
End Class
```

In this case, when the object's **Finalize** method executes, a reference to the object is placed in a root and the object is reachable from the application's code. This object is now resurrected, and the garbage collector won't consider the object to be garbage. The application is free to use the object—but you must remember that the object *has* been finalized, so using it can cause unpredictable results. Also keep in mind that if **SomeType** contained fields that referenced other objects (either directly or indirectly), all objects would be resurrected because they are all reachable from the application's roots. However, be aware that some of these other objects might also have had their **Finalize** method called.

> **Note**   Any type you define might at some point be resurrected out of your control; that is, an object of your type might have members accessed after your **Finalize** method has been called. In an ideal world, you might consider adding code that checks to see whether your **Finalize** method has already executed and handle the member access gracefully, perhaps by throwing an appropriate exception. In practice, however, you'd have to write a lot of very tedious code, and I'm not aware of any type that has been implemented to handle this situation gracefully.
>
>   If some other piece of code sets **Application.ObjHolder** to **Nothing**, the object is unreachable. Eventually, the garbage collector will consider the object to be garbage and will reclaim the object's storage. The object's **Finalize** method won't be called because no pointer to the object exists on the finalization list.

As cool as resurrection sounds, there are very few good uses of it, and you should really avoid using it if possible. When developers do use resurrection, they usually want the object to gracefully clean itself up every time it dies. To make this possible, the **GC** type offers a static method named **ReRegisterFor-Finalize**, which takes a single parameter: a reference to an object. The following code is a better version of the code shown earlier:

```
Class SomeType
   Protected Overrides Sub Finalize()
      Application.ObjHolder = Me
      GC.ReRegisterForFinalize(Me)
   End Sub
End Class
```

When the **Finalize** method is called, it resurrects the object by making a root refer to the object. The **Finalize** method then calls **ReRegisterForFinalize**, which appends the address of the specified object (**Me**) to the end of the finalization list. When the garbage collector detects that this object is unreachable (sometime in the future), it will move the object's pointer to the freachable queue and the **Finalize** method will get called again.

This example shows how to create an object that constantly resurrects itself and never dies—but you don't usually want objects to do this. It's far more common to conditionally set a root to reference the object inside the **Finalize** method.

> **Note**   Make sure that you call **ReRegisterForFinalize** no more than once per resurrection or the object will have its **Finalize** method called multiple times. The reason is that each call to **ReRegisterFor-Finalize** appends a new entry to the end of the finalization list. When an object is determined to be garbage, all these entries move from the finalization list to the freachable queue, calling the object's **Finalize** method multiple times.

Designing an Object Pool Using Resurrection

Here's a great scenario that really shows the value of resurrection. Let's say that you want to create a pool of **Expensive** objects. These objects are expensive because they take a lot of time to construct. For performance reasons, the application is going to construct a bunch of **Expensive** objects during startup and then reuse them over and over again during the lifetime of the application.

The code to manage a pool of **Expensive** objects would look like this:

```
Imports System
Imports System.Collections

' Instances of this class are expensive to construct.
Class Expensive

    ' This Shared Stack field contains references
    ' to the objects available in the pool.
    Private Shared pool As New Stack()

    ' This Shared method returns an object from the pool.
    Public Shared Function GetObjectFromPool() As Expensive
        ' If the pool is empty, force a collection in an effort to get
        ' some unreachable Expensive objects back into the pool.
        If pool.Count = 0 Then
```

```
        ' The following two methods are discussed in this chapter's
        ' "Programmatic Control of the Garbage Collector" section.
        GC.Collect()
        GC.WaitForPendingFinalizers()
      End If

      ' If the pool is still empty, then we'll construct a new
      ' object, which will add itself to the pool.
      If pool.Count = 0 Then
         Dim Expensive As New Expensive()
      End If

      ' Get a reference to an object in the pool, and
      ' remove the object from the pool.
      Return DirectCast(pool.Pop, Expensive)
   End Function

   ' This constructor creates an object and adds it to the pool.
   Private Sub New()
      ' It takes a long time to construct this object.
      ⋮
      ' After the object is constructed, it adds itself to the pool.
      pool.Push(Me)
   End Sub

   ' Finalize is called when the application no longer needs this object.
   Protected Overrides Sub Finalize()
      Dim ShutDown As Boolean
      ShutDown = AppDomain.CurrentDomain.IsFinalizingForUnload

      ' Uncomment the line below after Microsoft fixes the
      ' System.Environment's HasShutdownStarted property bug
      ' (as described earlier in this chapter).
      ' ShutDown = ShutDown Or Environment.HasShutdownStarted

      ' If the application isn't shutting down,
      ' add the object back into the pool.
      If Not ShutDown Then
         ' Call ReRegisterForFinalize so that the object will
         ' get added back to the pool after subsequent uses.
         GC.ReRegisterForFinalize(Me)

         ' Add the object back into the pool.
         pool.Push(Me)
      End If
   End Sub
End Class
```

(continued)

```
Class App
   Shared Sub Main()
      ⋮
      ' When you need an object, grab one out of the pool.
      ' (Repeat as necessary.)
      Dim e As Expensive = Expensive.GetObjectFromPool()
      ' The application can now use e.
      ⋮
   End Sub
End Class
```

The **Expensive** type has a private shared **System.Collections.Stack** field, which is used to manage the available objects in the pool. This field, called **pool**, is a root and refers to the set of **Expensive** objects—none of which can be collected.

When the application needs to work with an object, it calls **Expensive**'s shared **GetObjectFromPool** method. This method first checks to see whether any objects are waiting in the pool. If the pool is empty, the method forces a garbage collection to occur so that any unreachable **Expensive** objects are finalized and returned to the pool. If the pool is still empty after the forced collection, a new **Expensive** object is constructed and added to the pool. Ultimately, **GetObjectFromPool** returns a reference to an object in the pool and removes the reference from the **Stack**. The application can now use the object.

At some point in the future, the application will no longer hold a reference to the object and a garbage collection will occur, causing the **Expensive** object to be finalized. When the object's **Finalize** method is called, it adds the reference to the object back into the pool, resurrecting the object and preventing the garbage collector from reclaiming the object's memory. In addition, the **Finalize** method calls **GC**'s **ReRegisterForFinalize** method, passing it a reference to the object. At some point in the future, this object will be given to the application again. Sometime later, the application will give up its reference to the object and the garbage collector will collect it again. Because **ReRegisterForFinalize** was called, the **Finalize** method will again execute and add the object back into the pool so that it can be used again.

When the application shuts down (or when the AppDomain is being unloaded), the CLR calls the **Finalize** methods for all the objects remaining in the heap. When **Expensive** objects are finalized, **ReRegisterForFinalize** shouldn't be called because doing so would create an infinite loop (that the CLR would forcibly terminate after 40 seconds). So when the application is shutting down, **Expensive**'s **Finalize** method calls the AppDomain object's **IsFinalizingForUnload** property. If this property returns **True**, the objects aren't reregistered for finalization and they're not added back into the pool—they are allowed to die and have their memory reclaimed.

The code also shows how to call **Environment**'s **HasShutdownStarted** property so that proper cleanup occurs when the application is shutting down. Unfortunately, this property can't be called because of the bug mentioned earlier in this chapter. If you wanted to use this technique today, you'd have to devise an alternate mechanism to inform **Expensive**'s **Finalize** method that the application is shutting down. As you can see, resurrection offers an easy and efficient way to implement object pooling.

Generations

As I mentioned near the beginning of the chapter, generations is a mechanism within the CLR garbage collector whose sole reason for being is to improve an application's performance. A *generational garbage collector* (also known as an *ephemeral garbage collector*, though I don't use this latter term in this book) makes the following assumptions:

- The newer an object is, the shorter its lifetime will be.

- The older an object is, the longer its lifetime will be.

- Collecting a portion of the heap is faster than collecting the whole heap.

Numerous studies have demonstrated the validity of these assumptions for a very large set of existing applications, and these assumptions have influenced how the garbage collector is implemented. In this section, I'll describe how generations work.

When initialized, the managed heap contains no objects. Objects added to the heap are said to be in generation 0. Stated simply, objects in generation 0 are newly constructed objects that the garbage collector has never examined. Figure 19-7 shows a newly started application that has had five objects allocated (A through E). After a while, objects C and E become unreachable.

Generation 0

Figure 19-7   A newly initialized heap containing some objects; all in generation 0. No collections have occurred yet.

When the CLR initializes, it selects a threshold size for generation 0, say, 256 KB. (The exact size is subject to change.) So if allocating a new object causes generation 0 to surpass its threshold, a garbage collection must start. Let's say that objects A through E occupy 256 KB. When object F is allocated, a garbage collection must start. The garbage collector will determine that objects C and E are garbage and will compact object D so that it is adjacent to object B. The objects that survive the garbage collection (objects A, B, and D) are said to be in generation 1. Objects in generation 1 have been examined by the garbage collector once. The heap now looks like Figure 19-8.

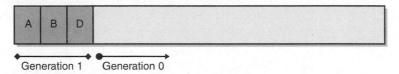

Figure 19-8   After one collection: generation 0 survivors are promoted to generation 1; generation 0 is empty.

After a garbage collection, generation 0 contains no objects. As always, new objects will be allocated in generation 0. Figure 19-9 shows the application running and allocating objects F through K. In addition, while the application was running, objects B, H, and J became unreachable and should have their memory reclaimed at some point.

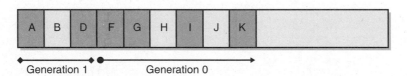

Figure 19-9   New objects are allocated in generation 0; generation 1 has some garbage.

Now let's say that attempting to allocate object L would put generation 0 over its 256-KB threshold. Because generation 0 has reached its threshold, a garbage collection must start. When starting a garbage collection, the garbage collector must decide which generations to examine. Earlier, I said that when the CLR initializes, it selects a threshold for generation 0. Well, it also selects a threshold for generation 1. Let's say that the threshold selected for generation 1 is 2 MB.

When starting a garbage collection, the garbage collector also sees how much memory is occupied by generation 1. In this case, generation 1 occupies much less than 2 MB, so the garbage collector examines only the objects in generation 0. Look again at the assumptions that a generational garbage collector makes. The first assumption is that newly created objects have a short lifetime.

So generation 0 is likely to have a lot of garbage in it, and collecting generation 0 will therefore reclaim a lot of memory. The garbage collector will just ignore the objects in generation 1, which will speed up the garbage collection process.

Obviously, ignoring the objects in generation 1 improves the performance of the garbage collector. However, the garbage collector improves performance more because it doesn't traverse every object in the managed heap. If a root or an object refers to an object in an old generation, the garbage collector can ignore any of the older objects' inner references, decreasing the amount of time required to build the graph of reachable objects. Of course, it's possible that an old object refers to a new object. To ensure that these "old" objects are examined, the garbage collector uses a mechanism internal to the JIT compiler that sets a bit when an object's reference field changes. This support lets the garbage collector know which old objects (if any) have been written to since the last collection. Only old objects that have had fields changed need to be examined to see whether they refer to any new objects in generation 0.

> **Note**   Microsoft's performance tests show that it takes less than 1 millisecond on a 200-MHz Pentium to perform a garbage collection of generation 0. Microsoft's goal is to have garbage collections take no more time than an ordinary page fault.

A generational garbage collector also assumes that objects that have lived a long time will continue to live. So it's likely that the objects in generation 1 will continue to be reachable from the application. Therefore, if the garbage collector were to examine the objects in generation 1, it probably wouldn't find a lot of garbage and it wouldn't be able to reclaim much memory. So collecting generation 1 is likely to be a waste of time. If any garbage happens to be in generation 1, it just stays there. The heap now looks like Figure 19-10.

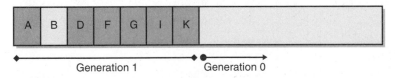

Figure 19-10   After two collections: generation 0 survivors are promoted to generation 1 (growing the size of generation 1); generation 0 is empty.

As you can see, all the generation 0 objects that survived the collection are now part of generation 1. Because the garbage collector didn't examine generation 1, object B didn't have its memory reclaimed even though it was unreachable at the time of the last garbage collection. Again, after a collection, generation 0 contains no objects and is where new objects will be placed. In fact, let's say that the application continues running and allocates objects L through O. And while running, the application stops using objects G, L, and M, making them all unreachable. The heap now looks like Figure 19-11.

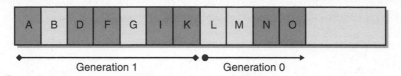

Figure 19-11 New objects are allocated in generation 0; generation 1 has more garbage.

Let's say that allocating object P causes generation 0 to pass its threshold, causing a garbage collection to occur. Because the memory occupied by all the objects in generation 1 is less than 2 MB, the garbage collector again decides to collect only generation 0, ignoring the unreachable objects in generation 1 (objects B and G). After the collection, the heap looks like Figure 19-12.

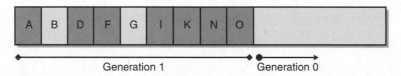

Figure 19-12 After three collections: generation 0 survivors are promoted to generation 1 (growing the size of generation 1 again); generation 0 is empty.

In Figure 19-12, you see that generation 1 keeps growing slowly. In fact, let's say that generation 1 has now grown to the point where all the objects in it occupy 2 MB of memory. At this point, the application continues running (because a garbage collection just finished) and starts allocating objects P through S, which fill generation 0 up to its threshold. The heap now looks like Figure 19-13.

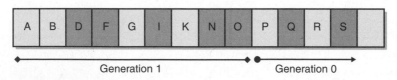

Figure 19-13 New objects are allocated in generation 0; generation 1 has more garbage.

When the application attempts to allocate object T, generation 0 is full and a garbage collection must start. This time, however, the garbage collector sees that the objects in generation 1 are occupying so much memory that generation 1's 2-MB threshold has been reached. Over the several generation 0 collections, it's likely that a number of objects in generation 1 have become unreachable (as in our example). So this time, the garbage collector decides to examine all the objects in generation 1 and generation 0. After both generations have been garbage collected, the heap now looks like Figure 19-14.

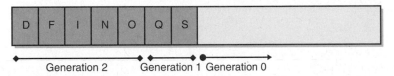

Figure 19-14   After four collections: generation 1 survivors are promoted to generation 2, generation 0 survivors are promoted to generation 1, and generation 0 is empty

Like before, any objects that were in generation 0 that survived the garbage collection are now in generation 1; any objects that were in generation 1 that survived the collection are now in generation 2. As always, generation 0 is empty immediately after a garbage collection and is where new objects will be allocated. Objects in generation 2 are objects that the garbage collector has examined at least twice. There might have been several collections, but the objects in generation 1 are examined only when generation 1 reaches its threshold, which usually requires several garbage collections of generation 0.

The managed heap supports only three generations: generation 0, generation 1, and generation 2; there is no generation 3. When the CLR initializes, it selects thresholds for all three generations. As I mentioned earlier, the threshold for generation 0 is about 256 KB, and the threshold for generation 1 is about 2 MB. The threshold for generation 2 is around 10 MB. Again, the threshold sizes are selected to improve performance. The larger the threshold, the less frequently a garbage collection will occur. And again, the performance improvement comes because of the initial assumptions: new objects have short lifetimes, and older objects are likely to live longer.

The CLR's garbage collector is a self-tuning collector. This means that the garbage collector learns about your application's behavior whenever it performs a garbage collection. For example, if your application constructs a lot of objects and uses them for a very short period of time, it's possible that garbage collecting generation 0 will reclaim a lot of memory. In fact, it's possible that the memory for all objects in generation 0 can be reclaimed.

If the garbage collector sees that there are very few surviving objects after collecting generation 0, it might decide to reduce the threshold of generation 0 from 256 KB to 128 KB. This reduction in the allotted space will mean that garbage collections occur more frequently but will require less work for the garbage collector, so your process's working set won't grow much. In fact, if all objects in generation 0 are garbage, then a garbage collection doesn't have to compact any memory; it can simply set `NextObjPtr` back to the beginning of generation 0 and the garbage collection is done. This is a fast way to reclaim memory!

> **Note** The garbage collector works extremely well with ASP.NET Web Forms and XML Web service applications. For ASP.NET applications, a client request comes in, a bunch of new objects are constructed, the objects perform work on the client's behalf, and the result is sent back to the client. At this point, all the objects used to satisfy the client's request are garbage. In other words, each ASP.NET application request causes a lot of garbage to be created. Because these objects are unreachable almost immediately after they're created, each garbage collection reclaims a lot of memory. This keeps the process's working set very low, and the garbage collector's performance is phenomenal.

On the other hand, if the garbage collector collects generation 0 and sees that there are a lot of surviving objects, not a lot of memory was reclaimed in the garbage collection. In this case, the garbage collector will grow generation 0's threshold to something like 512 KB. Now, fewer collections will occur, but when they do, a lot more memory should be reclaimed.

Throughout this discussion, I've been talking about how the garbage collector dynamically modifies generation 0's threshold after every collection. But the garbage collector also modifies the thresholds of generation 1 and generation 2 using similar heuristics. When these generations get garbage collected, the garbage collector again sees how much memory is reclaimed and how many objects survive. Based on the garbage collector's findings, it might grow or shrink the thresholds of these generations as well to improve the overall performance of the application.

Programmatic Control of the Garbage Collector

The **System.GC** type allows your application some direct control over the garbage collector. For starters, you can query the maximum generation supported by the managed heap by reading the **GC.MaxGeneration** property. Currently, this property always returns 2.

You can also force the garbage collector to perform a garbage collection by calling one of the following two shared methods (defined by the **GC** type):

```
Sub Collect (ByVal Generation As Int32)
Sub Collect()
```

The first method allows you to specify which generation to collect. You can pass any integer from 0 to **GC.MaxGeneration** inclusive. Passing 0 causes generation 0 to be collected, passing 1 causes generations 1 and 0 to be collected, and passing 2 causes generations 2, 1, and 0 to be collected. The version of the **Collect** method that takes no parameters forces a full collection of all generations and is equivalent to calling

```
GC.Collect(GC.MaxGeneration)
```

Under most circumstances, you should avoid calling any of the **Collect** methods; it's best just to let the garbage collector run on its own accord and fine-tune its generation thresholds based on actual application behavior. However, if you're writing a CUI or GUI application, your application code "owns" the process and the CLR in that process. For these application types, you *might* want to force a garbage collection to occur at certain times.

For example, it might make sense for your application to force a full garbage collection of all generations after the user saves a data file. I'd also imagine Internet browsers performing a full collection each time a page is unloaded. You might also want to force a garbage collection when your application is performing other lengthy operations. The basic idea here is to hide the time required by a collection when your application is doing something that's already time-consuming. In the three scenarios just described, the user will never feel a garbage collection because the time is overshadowed by the other work the application is doing.

The **GC** type also offers a **WaitForPendingFinalizers** method. This method simply suspends the calling thread until the thread processing the freachable queue has emptied the queue, calling each object's **Finalize** method. In most applications, it's unlikely that you'll ever have to call this method. Occasionally, though, I've seen code like this:

```
GC.Collect()
GC.WaitForPendingFinalizers()
GC.Collect()
```

This code forces a garbage collection. When the collection is complete, the memory for objects that don't require finalization is reclaimed. But the objects that do require finalization can't have their memory reclaimed yet. After the first call to **Collect** returns, the special, dedicated finalization thread is calling **Finalize** methods asynchronously. The call to **WaitForPendingFinalizers** puts the application's thread to sleep until all **Finalize** methods have been called. When **WaitForPendingFinalizers** has returned, all the finalized objects are now truly garbage. At this point, the second call to **Collect** forces another garbage collection, which reclaims all the memory that was occupied by the now finalized objects.

Finally, the **GC** class offers two Shared methods that allow you to determine which generation an object is currently in:

```
Function GetGeneration(ByVal obj As Object) As Int32
Function GetGeneration(ByVal wr As WeakReference) As Int32
```

The first version of **GetGeneration** takes an object reference as a parameter, and the second version takes a **WeakReference** reference as a parameter. The value returned will be between **0** and **GC.MaxGeneration** inclusive.

The following code will help you understand how generations work. The code also demonstrates the use of the **GC** methods just discussed.

```
Imports System
Imports System.Collections

Class GenObj
   Protected Overrides Sub Finalize()
      Console.WriteLine("In Finalize method")
   End Sub
End Class

Class App
   Shared Sub Main()
      Console.WriteLine("Maximum generations: {0}", GC.MaxGeneration)

      ' Create a new GenObj in the heap.
      Dim o As Object = New GenObj()

      ' Because this object is newly created, it is in generation 0.
      Console.WriteLine("Gen {0}", GC.GetGeneration(o))     ' 0

      ' Performing a garbage collection promotes the object's generation.
      GC.Collect()
      Console.WriteLine("Gen {0}", GC.GetGeneration(o))      ' 1
```

```
    GC.Collect()
    Console.WriteLine("Gen {0}", GC.GetGeneration(o))      ' 2

    GC.Collect()
    Console.WriteLine("Gen {0}", GC.GetGeneration(o))      ' 2 (max)


    o = Nothing    ' Destroy the strong reference to this object.

    Console.WriteLine("Collecting Gen 0")
    GC.Collect(0)                          ' Collect generation 0.
    GC.WaitForPendingFinalizers()          ' Finalize is NOT called.

    Console.WriteLine("Collecting Gen 1")
    GC.Collect(1)                          ' Collect generation 1.
    GC.WaitForPendingFinalizers()          ' Finalize is NOT called.

    Console.WriteLine("Collecting Gen 2")
    GC.Collect(2)                          ' Same as Collect()
    GC.WaitForPendingFinalizers()          ' Finalize IS called.
  End Sub
End Class
```

Building and running this code yields the following output:

```
Maximum generations: 2
Gen 0
Gen 1
Gen 2
Gen 2
Collecting Gen 0
Collecting Gen 1
Collecting Gen 2
In Finalize method
```

Other Garbage Collector Performance Issues

Earlier in this chapter, I explained the garbage collection algorithm. However, I made a big assumption during that discussion: that only one thread is running. In the real world, it's likely that multiple threads will be accessing the managed heap or at least manipulating objects allocated within the managed heap. When one thread sparks a garbage collection, other threads must not access any objects (including object references on its own stack) because the garbage collector is likely to move these objects, changing their memory locations.

So when the garbage collector wants to start a garbage collection, all threads executing managed code must be suspended. The CLR has a few different mechanisms that it uses to safely suspend threads so that a garbage collection can be done. The reason there are multiple mechanisms is to keep threads running as long as possible and to reduce overhead as much as possible. I don't want to get into all the details here, but suffice it to say that Microsoft has done a lot of work to reduce the overhead involved with doing a garbage collection. And Microsoft will continue to modify these mechanisms over time to ensure efficient garbage collections in the future.

When the CLR wants to start a garbage collection, it immediately suspends all threads in the process that have ever executed managed code. The CLR then examines each thread's instruction pointer to determine where the thread is executing. The instruction pointer address is then compared with the JIT compiler–produced tables in an effort to determine what code the thread is executing.

If the thread's instruction pointer is at an offset identified by a table, the thread is said to have reached a *safe point*. A safe point is a place where it's OK to suspend the thread until a garbage collection completes. If the thread's instruction pointer isn't at an offset identified by an internal method table, then the thread isn't at a safe point and the CLR can't perform a garbage collection. In this case, the CLR *hijacks* the thread: the CLR modifies the thread's stack so that the return address points to a special function implemented inside the CLR. The thread is then resumed. When the currently executing method returns, this special function will execute, suspending the thread.

However, the thread might not return from its method for quite some time. So after the thread resumes execution, the CLR waits about 250 milliseconds for the thread to be hijacked. After this time, the CLR suspends the thread again and checks its instruction pointer. If the thread has reached a safe point, the garbage collection can start. If the thread still hasn't reached a safe point, the CLR checks to see whether another method has been called; if one has, the CLR modifies the stack again so that the thread is hijacked when it returns from the most recently executing method. Then the CLR resumes the thread and waits another few milliseconds before trying again.

When all the threads have reached a safe point or have been hijacked, the garbage collection can begin. When the garbage collection is completed, all threads are resumed and the application continues running. The hijacked threads return to the method that originally called them.

In addition to the mechanisms mentioned earlier (generations, safe points, and hijacking), the garbage collector offers some additional mechanisms that improve the performance of object allocations and collections.

> **Note** This algorithm has one small twist. If the CLR suspends a thread and detects that the thread is executing unmanaged code, the thread's return address is hijacked and the thread is allowed to resume execution. However, in this case, the garbage collection is allowed to start even though the thread is still executing. This isn't a problem because unmanaged code isn't accessing objects on the managed heap unless the objects are *pinned*. A pinned object is one that the garbage collector isn't allowed to move in memory. If a thread currently executing unmanaged code returns to managed code, the thread is hijacked and is suspended until the garbage collection has completed.

Synchronization-Free Allocations

On a multiprocessor system running the workstation (MSCorWks.dll) or server (MSCorSvr.dll) version of the execution engine, generation 0 of the managed heap is partitioned into multiple memory arenas, one arena per thread. This allows multiple threads to make allocations simultaneously so that exclusive access to the heap isn't required.

Scalable Parallel Collections

On a multiprocessor system running the server version of the execution engine (MSCorSvr.dll), the managed heap is split into several sections, one per CPU. When a garbage collection is initiated, the garbage collector has one thread per CPU; each thread collects its own section in parallel with the other threads. Parallel collections work well for server applications where the worker threads tend to exhibit uniform behavior. The workstation version of the execution engine (MSCorWks.dll) doesn't support this feature.

Concurrent Collections

On a multiprocessor system running the workstation version of the execution engine (MSCorWks.dll), the garbage collector has an additional background thread that collects objects concurrently, while the application runs. When a thread allocates an object that pushes generation 0 over its threshold, the garbage collector first suspends all threads and then determines which generations to collect. If the garbage collector needs to collect generation 0 or 1, then it proceeds as normal. However, if generation 2 needs collecting, the size of generation 0 grows beyond its threshold to allocate the new object and the application's threads are resumed.

While the application threads are running, the garbage collector has a normal priority background thread that builds the graph of unreachable objects. This thread competes for CPU time with the application's threads, causing the application's tasks to execute more slowly; however, the concurrent collector runs only on multiprocessor systems, so you shouldn't see much of a degradation. Once the graph is built, the garbage collector suspends all threads again and decides whether or not to compact memory. If the garbage collector decides to compact memory, then memory is compacted, root references are fixed up, and the application's threads are resumed—this garbage collection takes less time than usual because the graph of unreachable objects has already been built. However, the garbage collector might decide not to compact memory; in fact, the garbage collector favors this approach. If you have a lot of free memory, the garbage collector won't compact the heap; this improves performance but grows your application's working set. When using the concurrent garbage collector, you'll typically find that your application is consuming more memory than it would compared with the nonconcurrent garbage collection.

To summarize, concurrent collection makes for a better interactive experience for users and is therefore best for interactive CUI or GUI applications. For some applications, however, concurrent collection will actually hurt performance and will cause more memory to be used. When testing your application, you should experiment with and without concurrent collection and see which approach gives the best performance and memory usage for your application.

You can tell the CLR not to use the concurrent collector by creating a configuration file (as discussed in Chapter 2 and Chapter 3) that contains a **gcConcurrent** element for the application. Here's an example of a configuration file:

```
<configuration>
   <runtime>
     <gcConcurrent enabled="false"/>
   </runtime>
</configuration>
```

You can also use the Microsoft .NET Framework Configuration administrative tool to create an application configuration file containing the **gcConcurrent** element. To do this, open Control Panel, select Administrative Tools, and then invoke the Microsoft .NET Framework Configuration tool. In the tool, go to the Applications node in the left-hand tree pane and add an application or select an existing application. Then right-click on the application and select Properties. The dialog box shown in Figure 19-15 will appear.

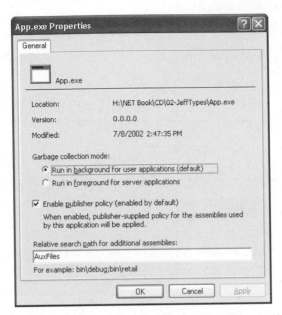

Figure 19-15   Configuring an application to use the concurrent garbage collector using the Microsoft .NET Framework Configuration administrative tool

The radio buttons under the Garbage Collection Mode selection set the `gcConcurrent` element's `enabled` attribute to `true` or `false`, respectively.

Large Objects

There is one more performance improvement that you might want to be aware of. Any objects that are 85,000 bytes or more in size are considered to be *large objects*. Large objects are allocated from a special large object heap. Objects in this heap are finalized and freed just like the small objects I've been talking about. However, large objects are never compacted because it would waste too much CPU time shifting 85,000 byte blocks of memory down in the heap.

Large objects are always considered part of generation 2, so you should create large objects only for resources that you need to keep alive for a long time. Allocating short-lived large objects will cause generation 2 to be collected more frequently, which will hurt performance.

All of these mechanisms are transparent to your application code. To you, the developer, it appears as if there is just one managed heap; these mechanisms exist simply to improve application performance.

Monitoring Garbage Collections

When you install the .NET Framework, it installs a set of performance counters that offer a lot of real-time statistics about the CLR's operations. These statistics are visible via the PerfMon.exe tool or the System Monitor ActiveX control that ships with Windows. The easiest way to access the System Monitor control is to run PerfMon.exe and select the + toolbar button, which causes the Add Counters dialog box shown in Figure 19-16 to appear.

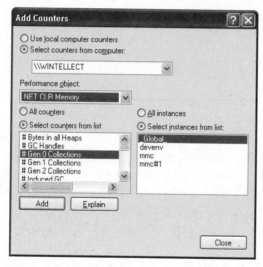

Figure 19-16   PerfMon.exe showing the .NET CLR memory counters

To monitor the CLR's garbage collector, select the .NET CLR Memory performance object. Then select a specific application from the instance list box. Finally, select the set of counters that you're interested in monitoring and press the Add button followed by the Close button. At this point, the System Monitor will graph the selected real-time statistics. For an explanation of a particular counter, select the desired counter and press the Explain button.

20

CLR Hosting, AppDomains, and Reflection

In this chapter, I'll discuss three main topics that really show off the incredible value provided by the Microsoft .NET Framework. In particular, I'll explain how many of Microsoft's existing application and server products intend to leverage the common language runtime (CLR) in the future. You'll see that your investment in learning the .NET Framework today will certainly pay off down the line. I'll also talk about *AppDomains*, a mechanism offered by the CLR to reduce memory usage and improve system performance. And finally, I'll discuss *reflection*, a mechanism that allows you to design dynamically extensible applications that your types or another party's types can easily enhance.

Metadata: The Cornerstone of the .NET Framework

By now, it should be obvious to you that metadata is the cornerstone technology of the .NET Framework development platform. Metadata describes a type's fields along with its methods. Metadata is what allows a type developed in one programming language to be consumed by code developed in a completely different programming language. In addition, the garbage collector uses metadata to determine what objects are reachable; the metadata indicates what other objects an object can refer to. Development tools, such as Microsoft Visual Studio's editor, use metadata to provide IntelliSense and other help-related assistance. And, of course, metadata is used to serialize and deserialize objects so that they can be persisted to disk or sent over the network. In fact, this ability to use metadata to easily serialize and deserialize objects over the wire is what makes building XML Web services with the .NET Framework child's play.

Throughout this book, I've been using the ILDasm.exe tool that ships with the .NET Framework SDK. This tool parses the metadata contained inside a managed module or assembly and shows the metadata information in human-readable format. The act of examining metadata is called *reflection*; in other words, ILDasm.exe reflects over the module's or assembly's metadata and shows the results to the user.

Reflection is an incredibly powerful tool for developers. Reflection allows developers to build dynamically extensible applications. For example, anyone can produce a type and package it in an assembly. However, if that type follows certain rules, the Visual Studio .NET Windows Forms and Web Forms designers can integrate the type (component) into the designers. Visual Studio can add the type to the Toolbox window, and when an instance of the type is dropped on a form, the Properties window will show the properties that are exposed by the type. This rich level of integration and the ease with which it's produced are unparalleled in earlier technologies such as Win32 and COM. In this chapter, I'll demonstrate how to use reflection to accomplish this level of integration.

A method can use reflection to alter its behavior based on facts learned about another piece of code. You saw an example of this in Chapter 13. If an enumerated type has an instance of the `System.FlagsAttribute` applied to it, then calling `ToString` on an instance of the enumerated type causes the value to be treated as a bit flag instead of a single numeric value. In fact, reflection is really what custom attributes are all about.

Using reflection, a method can alter its behavior based on its caller. For example, it's possible to implement a method that performs a certain operation when called from code in the same assembly. The same method could perform slightly different operations when called from code outside the assembly. The possibilities are endless.

Before getting too deep into reflection, you need to become familiar with CLR hosting and AppDomains. So I'll spend some time addressing these topics before delving back into reflection to explain how all this fits together.

CLR Hosting

The .NET Framework runs on top of Microsoft Windows. This means that the .NET Framework must be built using technologies that Windows understands. For starters, all managed module and assembly files must use the Windows portable executable (PE) file format and be either a Windows EXE file or a dynamic-link library (DLL).

When developing the CLR, Microsoft implemented it as a COM server contained inside a DLL; that is, Microsoft defined a standard COM interface for the CLR and assigned GUIDs to this interface and the COM server. When you install the .NET Framework, the COM server representing the CLR is registered in the Windows registry just like any other COM server. If you want more information about this topic, refer to the MSCorEE.h C++ header file that ships with the .NET Framework SDK. This header file defines the GUIDs and the unmanaged **ICor-RuntimeHost** interface definition.

Any Windows application can host the CLR. However, you shouldn't create an instance of the CLR COM server by calling **CoCreateInstance**; instead, your unmanaged host should call the **CorBindToRuntimeEx** function (prototyped in MSCorEE.h). The **CorBindToRuntimeEx** function is implemented in the MSCorEE.dll, which is usually found in the C:\Windows\System32 directory. This DLL is called the *shim*, and its job is to determine which version of the CLR to create; the shim DLL doesn't contain the CLR COM server itself.

You see, version 1.0 of the .NET Framework comes with two versions of the CLR COM server. The MSCorWks.dll file contains the workstation version; this version is tuned to offer better performance in single-processor, workstation environments. The MSCorSvr.dll file contains the server version, which is tuned to offer better performance in multiprocessor, server environments. In the future, Microsoft will be producing new versions of the CLR, and these can be installed on a user's hard disk as well.

When **CorBindToRuntimeEx** is called, its parameters allow the host to specify which version of the CLR it would like to create. The version information indicates workstation vs. server as well as a version number. **CorBindToRuntimeEx** uses the specified version information and gathers some additional information of its own (such as how many CPUs are installed in the machine and which versions of the CLR are installed) to decide which version of the CLR to load—the shim might not load the version that the host requested.

By default, the shim examines the managed executable file and extracts the information indicating what version of the CLR the application was built and tested with. However, an application can override the default by placing entries in its XML configuration file (as described in Chapter 2 and Chapter 3). The following sample XML configuration file shows how an application can tell the shim to load a particular CLR version:

```
<configuration>
   <startup>
      <requiredRuntime version="v1.0.0.0" safemode="true"/>
   </startup>
</configuration>
```

After examining this information, the shim loads the corresponding CLR version. If **safemode** is set to **false** (the default), the shim loads the most recently installed version of the CLR that is compatible with the version the application wants.

Microsoft determines which versions of the CLR are compatible with other versions by creating some registry settings. You can see the CLR version policy settings by examining the values under the following registry subkey:

```
HKEY_LOCAL_MACHINE\Software\Microsoft\.NETFramework\Policy
```

You should never modify any of the values under this registry subkey; when you install a new version of the .NET Framework, the setup program will modify these settings based on Microsoft's compatibility testing.

The `CorBindToRuntimeEx` function returns a pointer to an unmanaged `ICorRuntimeHost` interface (also defined in MSCorEE.h). The hosting application can call methods defined by this interface to initialize the CLR. The host can also call methods telling the CLR what assembly to load and what method to start executing. The section "Loading the Common Language Runtime" in Chapter 1 explains how all this works for managed console and Windows Forms applications.

AppDomains

When the CLR COM server is loaded into a Windows process, it initializes. Part of this initialization is to create the managed heap that all reference objects get allocated in and garbage collected from. In addition, the CLR creates a thread pool usable by any of the managed types whose assemblies are loaded into the process. While initializing, the CLR also creates an *AppDomain*. An AppDomain is a logical container for a set of assemblies. The first AppDomain created when the CLR initializes is called the *default AppDomain*; this AppDomain is destroyed only when the Windows process terminates.

> **Note**   In version 1 of the .NET Framework, no more than one CLR COM server object can exist in a Windows process, and this CLR COM server object can't be destroyed until the hosting process terminates; that is, `CorBindToRuntimeEx` creates an instance of a CLR COM server and returns a pointer to an `ICorRuntimeHost` interface. Calling the `AddRef` and `Release` methods on this interface has no effect. In addition, a single host process can create only one instance of a CLR COM server. If a single host process calls `CorBindToRuntimeEx` multiple times, the same `ICorRuntimeHost` pointer is returned every time.

In addition to the default AppDomain, a host can instruct the CLR to create additional AppDomains. Moreover, code in a managed assembly can also tell the CLR to create additional AppDomains. Three characteristics of AppDomains make them useful:

- **AppDomains are isolated from one another** An AppDomain can't see the objects created by a different AppDomain. This enforces a clean separation because code in one AppDomain can't have a direct reference to an object created in a different AppDomain. This isolation allows AppDomains to easily be unloaded from a process.

- **AppDomains can be unloaded** The CLR doesn't support the ability to unload a single assembly. However, you can tell the CLR to unload an AppDomain and all the assemblies currently contained in it.

- **AppDomains can be individually secured and configured** When created, an AppDomain can have *evidence* applied to it. Evidence is a security-related feature that determines the maximum rights granted to assemblies running in the AppDomain. More common, however, is that an AppDomain will have a security policy applied to it using `AppDomain`'s `SetAppDomainPolicy` method. In addition, the `System.AppDomainSetup` class allows you to set and query an AppDomain's settings. These configuration settings are used to fine-tune how the CLR locates and loads assemblies. These settings include the following:

  - ❏ `ApplicationName` A friendly string name used to identify an AppDomain.

  - ❏ `ApplicationBase` A directory where the CLR will look to locate assemblies.

  - ❏ `PrivateBinPath` A set of directories where the CLR will look to locate weakly named assemblies.

  - ❏ `ConfigurationFile` The pathname of a configuration file containing rules that the CLR will use to locate assemblies. The file also contains remoting settings, Web applications settings, and more.

  - ❏ `LoaderOptimization` A flag telling the CLR whether to treat loaded assemblies as domain-neutral or single-domain.

Important   It would be dangerous to run multiple unmanaged applications in a single process. The reason is that the different applications have access to each other's data and code, making it all too easy for one application to corrupt another application. However, this isn't a concern with managed code because the managed IL code is type-safe and the IL code is verified, making it impossible for code in one AppDomain to corrupt code in another AppDomain. Of course, an administrator could turn off verification and allow the managed code to make calls to unmanaged functions. If an administrator does this, all bets are off and AppDomain corruption is entirely possible.

Figure 20-1 shows a single Windows process that has one CLR COM server running in it. This CLR is managing two AppDomains. Each AppDomain has its own loader heap, which maintains a record of which types have been accessed since the AppDomain was created. Each type in the loader heap has a method table, and each entry in the method table points to JIT-compiled x86 code if that method has been executed at least once.

In addition, each AppDomain has some assemblies loaded into it. AppDomain #1 (the default AppDomain) has three assemblies: MyApp.exe, TypeLib.dll, and System.dll. The TypeLib.dll assembly consists of three modules: TypeLib.dll (which contains the manifest), FUT.netmodule, and RUT.netmodule. AppDomain #2 has three single-module assemblies loaded into it: Wintellect.dll, System.dll, and Microsoft.dll.

By default, an assembly is loaded once per AppDomain; that is, the System.dll assembly is actually loaded into both AppDomain #1 and AppDomain #2. This means that the information about the System.dll assembly is reconstructed in each AppDomain's loader heap. Even the JIT-compiled code for the methods defined by System.dll's types exists twice in this process's address space. The advantage of this is that an AppDomain can be completely unloaded from the process without affecting any other AppDomain.

Some assemblies are expected to be used by several AppDomains. The best example is MSCorLib.dll, which is a single-module assembly created by Microsoft. This assembly contains `System.Object`, `System.Int32`, and all the other types that are so integral to the .NET Framework. This assembly is automatically loaded when the CLR initializes, and all AppDomains share the types in this assembly. To reduce resource usage, MSCorLib.dll is loaded in an App-Domain-neutral fashion; that is, the CLR maintains a special loader heap for assemblies that are loaded in a domain-neutral fashion. Assemblies loaded this way can't be unloaded until the process terminates.

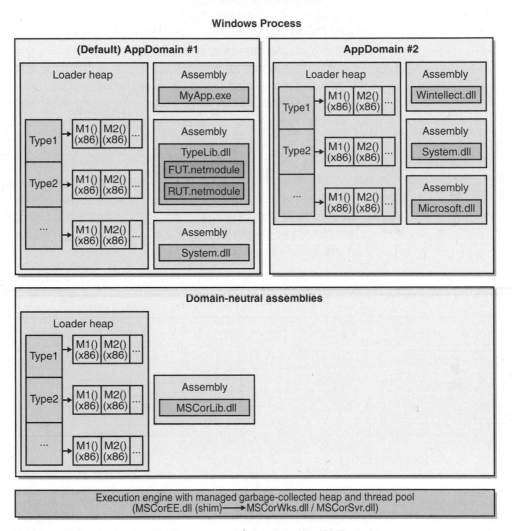

Figure 20-1   A single Windows process hosting the CLR and two AppDomains

Accessing Objects Across AppDomain Boundaries

Code in one AppDomain can communicate with types and objects contained in another AppDomain. However, the access to these types and objects is only through well-defined mechanisms. Most types are marshaled by value across AppDomain boundaries. In other words, if an object is constructed in one App-Domain and a reference to this object is passed to another AppDomain, the CLR must first serialize the object's fields into a block of memory. This block of memory is then passed to the other AppDomain, which deserializes the block to produce a new object. The destination AppDomain uses the reference to this new object. The destination AppDomain has no access to the original AppDo-main's object. For objects to be remoted by value, the object's type must have the `System.Serializable` custom attribute applied to it.

> **Note**   Deserializing an object causes the CLR to load the type's assembly if necessary. If the CLR can't locate the assembly using the destination AppDomain's policies (for example, the AppDomain can have a different AppBase directory), the object can't be deserialized and an exception will be thrown.

Types that are derived from `System.MarshalByRefObject` can also be accessed across AppDomain boundaries. However, access to the object is accomplished by reference rather than by value. Let's say that an AppDomain has an object created in it whose type is derived from `MarshalByRefObject`. When a reference to this object is passed to a destination AppDomain, the CLR actually creates an instance of a proxy type in the destination AppDomain, and a reference to this proxy object is what code in the destination AppDomain will use. The original object and its fields remain in the original AppDomain. The proxy object is a wrapper that knows how to call instance methods on the orig-inal object in the original AppDomain. Again, the destination doesn't have direct access to the original AppDomain's object.

Obviously, accessing objects across AppDomain boundaries has some performance costs associated with it. When possible, you should avoid manip-ulating objects across AppDomain boundaries. A one-to-one correspondence doesn't exist between threads and AppDomains. When a thread in one AppDo-main calls a method in another AppDomain, the thread transitions between the two AppDomains. This means that method calls across AppDomain boundaries are executed synchronously. However, at any given time, a thread is considered to be in just one AppDomain. You can call `System.Threading.Thread`'s static `GetDomain` method to obtain a reference to the `System.AppDomain` object to identify the AppDomain that the thread is currently executing in.

When unloading an AppDomain, the CLR knows which threads are in the AppDomain, and the CLR forces a `ThreadAbortException` exception in the threads so that they unwind out of the AppDomain. Once the threads have left the AppDomain, the CLR can invalidate all proxy objects that refer to objects in the unloaded AppDomain. At this point, any calls to methods using an invalid proxy will cause a `System.AppDomainUnloadedException` exception to be thrown because the original object no longer exists.

The AppDomainRunner sample application discussed in this chapter's "Explicitly Unloading Assemblies: Unloading an AppDomain" section demonstrates how to marshal an object by reference across an AppDomain boundary.

AppDomain Events

I want to briefly mention that each AppDomain exposes a number of events that can be incredibly useful. Table 20-1 lists the events that your code can register interest in.

Table 20-1   AppDomain Events

Event Name	Description
`AssemblyLoad`	This event is fired every time the CLR loads an assembly into the AppDomain. The handler receives a `System.Reflection.Assembly` object identifying the loaded assembly.
`DomainUnload`	This event is fired just before the AppDomain is unloading. This event isn't fired when the process containing the AppDomain is terminating.
`ProcessExit`	This event is fired just before the process terminates. This event is fired only for the default AppDomain; any other AppDomain that registers interest in this event won't receive a notification.
`UnhandledException`	This event is fired when an unhandled exception occurs in an AppDomain. This event is covered in Chapter 18.
`AssemblyResolve`	This event is fired when the CLR can't locate an assembly required by the AppDomain. The handler receives a string identifying the name of the missing assembly.

(continued)

Table 20-1   AppDomain Events   *(continued)*

Event Name	Description
ResourceResolve	This event is fired when the CLR can't locate a resource required by the AppDomain. The handler receives a string identifying the name of the missing resource.
TypeResolve	This event is fired when the CLR can't locate a type required in one of the AppDomain's assemblies. The handler receives a string identifying the name of the missing type and can tell the CLR what type to use by returning a reference to a **Type** object. Frequently, the handler decides what **Type** object to return based on the client's location or operating system.

Applications and How They Host the CLR and Manage AppDomains

So far, I've talked about hosts and how they load the CLR, AppDomains, and how the host can tell the CLR to create and unload AppDomains. To make the discussion more concrete, I thought I'd describe some common hosting and AppDomain scenarios. In particular, I'll explain to you how different application types host the CLR and how they manage AppDomains.

Console and Windows Forms Applications

When invoking a managed console or Windows Forms application, the shim examines the CLR header information contained in the application's assembly. The header information indicates what version of the CLR was used to build and test the application. The shim uses this information to determine which CLR COM server to create. After the CLR loads and initializes, it again examines the assembly's CLR header to determine which method is the application's entry point (**Main**). The CLR invokes this method, and the application is now up and running.

As the code runs, it accesses other types. When referencing a type contained in another assembly, the CLR locates the necessary assembly and loads it into the same AppDomain. Any additionally referenced assemblies also load into the same AppDomain. When the application's **Main** method returns, the default AppDomain unloads and the Windows process terminates.

> **Note** By the way, you can call System.Environment's static Exit method if you want to shut down the Windows process, including all its AppDomains. Exit is the most graceful way of terminating a process because it first calls the Finalize methods of all the objects on the managed heap and then releases all the unmanaged COM objects held by the CLR. Finally, Exit calls the Win32 ExitProcess function.

It's possible for a console or Windows Forms application to tell the CLR to create additional AppDomains in the process's address space. However, these application types rarely ever use or require multiple AppDomains.

ASP.NET Web Forms and XML Web Services Applications

ASP.NET is an ISAPI DLL (implemented in ASPNet_ISAPI.dll). When a client requests a URL handled by the ASP.NET ISAPI DLL, ASP.NET creates what is called a *worker process* (ASPNet_wp.exe). A worker process is a Windows process that hosts a CLR COM server.

When a client makes a request of a Web application, ASP.NET determines if this is the first time a request has been made. If it is, ASP.NET tells the CLR to create a new AppDomain for this Web application; each Web application is identified by its virtual root directory. ASP.NET then tells the CLR to load the assembly that contains the type exposed by the Web application into this new AppDomain, creates an instance of this type, and starts calling methods in it to satisfy the client's Web request. If the code references more types, the CLR will load the required assemblies into the Web application's AppDomain. By the way, strongly named assemblies (such as System.Web.dll) are loaded in a domain-neutral fashion to conserve operating system resources.

When future clients make requests of an already running Web application, ASP.NET doesn't create a new AppDomain; instead, it just uses the existing AppDomain, creates a new instance of the Web application's type, and starts calling methods. The methods will already be JIT compiled into native code, so the performance of processing all subsequent client requests is excellent.

If a client makes a request of a different Web application, ASP.NET tells the CLR to create a new AppDomain. This new AppDomain is typically created inside the same worker process as the other AppDomains. This means that many Web applications run in a single Windows process, which improves the efficiency of the system overall. Again, the assemblies required by the different Web application are loaded into its own AppDomain.

Microsoft Internet Explorer

When you install the .NET Framework, it installs a MIME filter (MSCorIE.dll) that gets hooked into Internet Explorer versions 5.01 and later. This MIME filter handles downloaded content marked with a MIME type of "application/octet-stream" or "application/x-msdownload". When the MIME filter detects a managed assembly being downloaded, it calls the `CorBindToRuntimeEx` function to create a CLR COM server; this makes Internet Explorer's process a host.

The MIME filter is in control of the CLR and ensures that all assemblies from one Web site are loaded into their own AppDomain. This allows an administrator to treat assemblies downloaded from different Web sites in different ways, say, trusting assemblies from one Web site but not those from another. This also allows assemblies used by one Web application to be unloaded when the user surfs to a different Web application.

"Yukon"

The next version of Microsoft SQL Server (code-named "Yukon") is an unmanaged application because most of its code is still written in unmanaged C++. During initialization, however, "Yukon" will create a CLR COM server. "Yukon" allows stored procedures to be written in any managed programming language (C#, Visual Basic, Smalltalk, and so on). These stored procedures will run in their own AppDomain that has special evidence applied to it prohibiting the stored procedures from adversely affecting the database server. "Yukon" can instruct the CLR to load just the desired assembly and to call methods in that assembly that will execute under the necessary security restrictions.

This functionality is absolutely incredible! It means that developers will be able to write stored procedures in the programming language of their choice. The stored procedure can use strongly typed data objects in its code. The code will also be JIT compiled into native code when executed, instead of interpreted. And developers can take advantage of any types defined in the .NET Framework Class Library (FCL) or in any other assembly to help them. The result is that our job becomes much easier and our applications perform much better. What more could a developer ask for?

In the future, productivity applications such as word processors and spreadsheets will also allow users to write macros in any programming language they choose. These macros will have access to all the assemblies and types that work with the CLR. They will be compiled, so they will execute fast, and, most important, these macros will run in a secure AppDomain so that users don't get hit with any unwanted surprises.

The Gist of Reflection

As you know, metadata is a bunch of tables. When you build an assembly or a module, the compiler you're using creates a type definition table, a field definition table, a method definition table, and so on. The FCL's `System.Reflection` namespace contains several types that allow you to write code that reflects over (or parses) these metadata tables. In effect, the types in this namespace offer an object model over the metadata contained in an assembly or a module.

Using these object model types, you can easily enumerate all the types in a type definition metadata table. Then for each type, you can obtain its base type, what interfaces it implements, and what flags are associated with the type.

Additional types in the `System.Reflection` namespace allow you to query the type's fields, methods, properties, and events by parsing the corresponding metadata tables. You can also discover any custom attributes (covered in Chapter 16) that have been applied to any of the metadata entities. With this information, you could build a tool very similar to Microsoft's ILDasm.exe.

Important   The types in the `System.Reflection` namespace allow you to query definition metadata tables. No types are offered that allow you to query reference metadata tables. Nor do the reflection types offer the capability to read a method's IL code. The ILDasm.exe tool parses the file's bytes directly to obtain this information. Fortunately, the file format for managed modules and assemblies is public. In fact, this file format is being standardized by the ECMA technical committee. So if you're writing an application that wants to query reference metadata tables or get the IL bytes from a managed method, you'll have to write code that manually parses the file's format because reflection doesn't offer you this capability.

In addition, some definition metadata information isn't obtainable via reflection. For example, there's no way to determine the default value for optional arguments (a feature offered in Visual Basic). Microsoft will address these "holes" in the reflection types in future versions of the .NET Framework.

Finally, you should be aware that some of the reflection types and some of the members defined by these types are designed specifically for use by developers who are producing compilers for the CLR. Application developers don't typically use these types and members. The .NET Framework documentation doesn't explicitly point out which of these types and members are for compiler developers rather than application developers, but if you realize that not all reflection types and their members are for everyone, the documentation can be less confusing.

In reality, very few applications will need to use the reflection types. Reflection is typically used for class libraries that need to understand a type's definition in order to provide some rich functionality. For example, the FCL's serialization mechanism uses reflection to determine what fields a type defines. The serialization formatter can then obtain the values of these fields and write them into a byte stream for sending across the Internet. Similarly, Visual Studio's designers use reflection to determine which properties should be shown to developers when laying out controls on their Web Forms or Windows Forms at design time.

Reflection is also used when an application needs to load a specific type from a specific assembly at run time to accomplish some task. For example, an application might ask the user to provide the name of an assembly and a type. The application could then explicitly load the assembly, construct an instance of the type, and call methods on the type. This usage is conceptually similar to calling Win32's **LoadLibrary** and **GetProcAddress** functions. Binding to types and calling methods in this way is frequently referred to as *late binding*. (*Early binding* is when the types and methods an application uses are determined at compile time.)

The remainder of this chapter contains sample applications, all of which use reflection. Each application demonstrates a different use of reflection and addresses topics that you'll need to know about to use reflection effectively and efficiently.

Reflecting Over an Assembly's Types

Reflection is frequently used to determine what types an assembly defines. The Reflector sample code (which can be downloaded from *http://www.Wintellect.com/*) demonstrates how to do this:

```
Imports System
Imports System.Reflection

Class App
   Shared Sub Main()
      ' Notice that Assembly is a Visual Basic keyword.
      Dim assem As [Assembly] = [Assembly].GetExecutingAssembly()
      Reflector.ReflectOnAssembly(assem)
   End Sub
End Class

Public Class Reflector
   Public Shared Sub ReflectOnAssembly(ByVal assem As [Assembly])
      WriteLine(0, "Assembly: {0}", assem)

      ' Find modules.
      ' Notice that Module is a Visual Basic keyword.
      Dim m As [Module]
      For Each m In assem.GetModules
         WriteLine(1, "Module: {0}", m)
```

```
        ' Find types.
        Dim t As Type
        For Each t In m.GetTypes
            WriteLine(2, "Type: {0}", t)

            ' Find members.
            Dim mi As MemberInfo
            For Each mi In t.GetMembers
                WriteLine(3, "{0}: {1}", mi.MemberType, mi)
            Next
        Next
    Next
    End Sub


    Private Shared Sub WriteLine(ByVal indent As Int32, _
        ByVal format As String, ByVal ParamArray args() As Object)
        Console.WriteLine(New String(" "c, 3 * indent) & format, args)
    End Sub
End Class


Class SomeType
    Public Class InnerType
    End Class

    Public SomeField As Int32
    Private Shared goo As String

    Private Sub SomeMethod()
    End Sub

    Private Property SomeProperty() As TimeSpan
        Get
            Return New TimeSpan()
        End Get
        Set(ByVal Value As TimeSpan)
        End Set
    End Property

    Public Shared Event SomeEvent As System.Threading.ThreadStart
End Class
```

In **Main**, the application calls **System.Reflection.Assembly**'s static **GetExecutingAssembly** method. This method determines which assembly contains the method that's making the call and returns a reference to this **Assembly** object. This reference is then passed to the **Reflector** type's static **ReflectOnAssembly** method. This method displays the full name of the assembly and then calls **GetModules**, which returns an array of **System.Reflection.Module** classes. Each element in the array identifies a module that is part of the assembly.

A loop then enumerates over each module in the assembly. In the loop, the module's name is displayed and then **GetTypes** is called. **GetTypes** returns an array of **System.Type** elements; each element identifies a type defined within the assembly's module. A loop then iterates over each type. In this loop, the type's name is displayed and then **GetMembers** is called. This method returns an array of **System.Reflection.MemberInfo** elements, where each element identifies a member (constructor, method, field, property, event, or nested type) of the type.

In the Reflector application, the **SomeType** type exists purely for demonstration purposes. This type defines a bunch of different members showing what you can expect when reflecting over metadata. If you build and run the Reflector application, you'll see the following output:

```
Assembly: Reflector, Version=0.0.0.0, Culture=neutral, PublicKeyToken=null
   Module: Reflector.exe
      Type: App
         Method: Int32 GetHashCode()
         Method: Boolean Equals(System.Object)
         Method: System.String ToString()
         Method: Void Main()
         Method: System.Type GetType()
         Constructor: Void .ctor()
      Type: Reflector
         Method: Int32 GetHashCode()
         Method: Boolean Equals(System.Object)
         Method: System.String ToString()
         Method: Void ReflectOnAssembly(System.Reflection.Assembly)
         Method: System.Type GetType()
         Constructor: Void .ctor()
      Type: SomeType
         Field: Int32 SomeField
         Method: Int32 GetHashCode()
         Method: Boolean Equals(System.Object)
         Method: System.String ToString()
         Method: Void add_SomeEvent(System.Threading.ThreadStart)
         Method: Void remove_SomeEvent(System.Threading.ThreadStart)
         Method: System.Type GetType()
         Constructor: Void .ctor()
         Event: System.Threading.ThreadStart SomeEvent
         NestedType: SomeType+InnerType
      Type: SomeType+InnerType
         Method: Int32 GetHashCode()
         Method: Boolean Equals(System.Object)
         Method: System.String ToString()
         Method: System.Type GetType()
         Constructor: Void .ctor()
```

Here you see that the assembly is called **Reflector**, it has a version of 0.0.0.0, and it has no specific culture associated with it. In addition, notice that there is no public key token associated with the assembly, making this a weakly named assembly instead of a strongly named assembly. This assembly consists of just one module: Reflector.exe. This module defines four types: **App**, **Reflector**, **SomeType**, and **SomeType+InnerType** (**SomeType**'s nested type). For each type, you see the members defined by the type. Because **SomeType** defines a variety of members, its members are the most interesting.

You'll notice that only publicly defined members are shown in the preceding output. I'll explain how to obtain all the public and nonpublic members when I get to binding flags (coming up shortly).

Reflecting Over an AppDomain's Assemblies

The Reflector sample is a good introduction to reflection because it shows how to reflect over an assembly's metadata. At times, however, you might want to reflect over all the assemblies contained within an AppDomain. To demonstrate how to reflect over all the assemblies in an AppDomain, I took the Reflector sample application and made a small change to the **Main** method. Here's the new **Main** method (nothing else has changed):

```
Shared Sub Main()
    Dim assem As [Assembly]
    For Each assem In AppDomain.CurrentDomain.GetAssemblies
        Reflector.ReflectOnAssembly(assem)
    Next
End Sub
```

In this version of **Main**, **System.AppDomain**'s static **CurrentDomain** property is called. This property returns a reference to an **AppDomain** object that identifies the AppDomain containing the calling code. Then the **AppDomain** object's **GetAssemblies** method is called, which returns an array of **System.Reflection.Assembly** elements—one element for each assembly loaded into the App-Domain at the time **GetAssemblies** is called.

At this point, a loop iterates over the array of assemblies, calling **Reflector**'s static **ReflectOnAssembly** method for each one. This version of the Reflector application shows all the assemblies in the AppDomain, all the modules that make up each assembly, all the types defined by each module, and all the members defined by each type.

If you build and run this version of the Reflector sample application, you'll see that two assemblies are shown in the output: MSCorLib.dll and Reflector.exe. Because MSCorLib.dll defines over 1400 types, the output produced by this application is much too long to reprint in this book.

Reflecting Over a Type's Members: Binding

In the Reflector application, a type's members are obtained by calling the **Type** object's **GetMembers** method. **Type** actually offers two versions of the **GetMembers** method. The first overload takes no parameters. This version returns the type's publicly defined static and instance members only. The second overload of **GetMembers** takes a single parameter: an instance of a **System.Reflection.BindingFlags** enumerated type. Table 20-2 shows the relevant symbols defined by the **BindingFlags** enumerated type.

Table 20-2   Search Symbols Defined by the BindingFlags **Enumerated Type**

Symbol	Value	Description
Default	0x00	A placeholder for no flags specified. Use this flag when you don't want to specify any of the flags in the remainder of this table.
IgnoreCase	0x01	Search using case-insensitivity.
DeclaredOnly	0x02	Only search members on the declared type. (Ignore inherited members.)
Instance	0x04	Search instance members.
Static	0x08	Search shared (static) members.
Public	0x10	Search public members.
NonPublic	0x20	Search nonpublic members.
FlattenHierarchy	0x40	Search shared (static) members defined by base types.

Earlier, I pointed out that Reflector's output doesn't include a type's private members. You can specify exactly which members the **GetMembers** method should return by passing the desired **BindingFlags** when calling this method.

To reflect over the nonpublic members of a type, I've modified the original Reflector sample application again. In this version, I've now told **GetMembers** to return all public and nonpublic, and shared (static) and instance members that are declared by the type itself. Any members inherited from a base type are not displayed. Here's what the new code to call **GetMembers** looks like. (Nothing else in the source code has changed.)

```
Dim bf As BindingFlags = BindingFlags.DeclaredOnly Or _
   BindingFlags.NonPublic Or BindingFlags.Public Or _
   BindingFlags.Instance Or BindingFlags.Static
Dim mi As MemberInfo
For Each mi In t.GetMembers(bf)
   WriteLine(3, "{0}: {1}", mi.MemberType, mi)
Next
```

Here, **bf** is initialized to a set of flags, indicating that I want to iterate over the type's public and nonpublic, and shared (static) and instance members. Furthermore, the **DeclaredOnly** flag indicates that I only want to iterate over the members that the type defines—not any of the members that the type inherits. Once **bf** is initialized, it is passed to the **GetMembers** method, which now knows exactly what members I'm interested in processing.

After making the above change to the Reflector source code, building and running the new version of this application yields the following output:

```
Assembly: Reflector, Version=0.0.0.0, Culture=neutral, PublicKeyToken=null
   Module: Reflector.exe
      Type: App
         Method: Void Main()
         Constructor: Void .ctor()
      Type: Reflector
         Method: Void ReflectOnAssembly(System.Reflection.Assembly)
         Method: Void WriteLine(Int32, System.String, System.Object[])
         Constructor: Void .ctor()
      Type: SomeType
         Field: Int32 SomeField
         Field: System.Threading.ThreadStart SomeEventEvent
         Field: System.String goo
         Method: Void add_SomeEvent(System.Threading.ThreadStart)
         Method: Void remove_SomeEvent(System.Threading.ThreadStart)
         Method: Void SomeMethod()
         Method: System.TimeSpan get_SomeProperty()
         Method: Void set_SomeProperty(System.TimeSpan)
         Constructor: Void .ctor()
         Property: System.TimeSpan SomeProperty
         Event: System.Threading.ThreadStart SomeEvent
         NestedType: SomeType+InnerType
      Type: SomeType+InnerType
         Constructor: Void .ctor()
```

Explicitly Loading Assemblies

So far, I've shown you how to reflect on the assemblies that are loaded into an AppDomain. Knowing how to do this is useful, but you must remember that the CLR decides when to load an assembly: the first time a method is called, the CLR examines the method's IL code to see what types are referenced. The CLR then loads all the assemblies that define the referenced types. If a required assembly is already available in the AppDomain, the CLR knows not to load the assembly again.

But let's say you want to write an application that counts the number of types that implement a particular interface. To accomplish this, you'd have to implement a method that references at least one type in each assembly you want loaded. Then you'd have to call this method to force the CLR to load all the assemblies that define these types. Once the assemblies are loaded, you can use the reflection methods already discussed.

This isn't the most ideal way to write this application. Instead, you'd like to have a way to explicitly load assemblies into your AppDomain so that you can reflect over their types. The technique I'm about to describe is similar to using Win32's **LoadLibrary** function.

The **System.Reflection.Assembly** type offers three static methods that allow you to explicitly load an assembly: **Load**, **LoadFrom**, and **LoadWithPartialName**. (Each method offers several overloaded versions.) Of the three methods, I highly recommend that you use **Load** whenever possible and avoid **LoadFrom** and **LoadWithPartialName**.

The **Load** method takes an assembly identity and loads it. By assembly identity, I mean an assembly name, a version, a culture, and a public key token, if the assembly is strongly named. If the assembly is weakly named, the identity is just the name of the assembly (without a file extension). **Load** uses the same algorithm that the CLR uses to implicitly load an assembly. If a strongly named assembly is specified, **Load** causes the CLR to apply policy to the assembly and look for the assembly in the global assembly cache (GAC) followed by the application's base directory and private path directories. If you call **Load** passing a weakly named assembly, **Load** doesn't apply policy to the assembly and the CLR won't look in the GAC for the assembly. In either case, if the specified assembly can't be found, a **System.IO.FileNotFoundException** exception is thrown.

Assembly's static **LoadFrom** method works differently. When calling **LoadFrom**, you pass the pathname of an assembly file (including the file's extension) and the CLR will load the exact assembly file you specify. The string that you pass to **LoadFrom** can't contain any strong-name information; that is, the string can't include version, culture, or public key information. The CLR doesn't apply any policy to the file you specify, and the CLR doesn't search for the file. If the file doesn't exist at the specified path, a **System.IO.FileNotFoundException** exception is thrown.

The last static method that loads an assembly is **LoadWithPartialName**. You should never use this method because an application won't know for sure what version of an assembly it is loading. The method exists only to help some customers who were using some behavior offered by the .NET Framework during its beta cycle; this behavior was later removed because of its unpredictability.

For those of you who care, here's how **LoadWithPartialName** works. When calling this method, you pass an assembly identity, which includes the assembly's name (without file extension), and you can optionally pass version, culture, and public key token information. When calling `LoadWithPartialName`, the CLR first checks the application's XML configuration file looking for a `qualifyAssembly` element. If this element exists, it tells the CLR how to map a partial assembly identity to a fully qualified assembly identity—the CLR will now use its normal rules to locate the assembly. If no `qualifyAssembly` element exists, the CLR searches in the AppBase and private bin path directories looking for an assembly with the specified name. If a matching assembly is found, the assembly is loaded.

If no matching assembly is found, the CLR looks in the GAC using the portions of the assembly's identity specified by the caller. If the culture or public key information wasn't specified, the behavior of `LoadWithPartialName` is undefined and you're not guaranteed to load any particular assembly. However, if only the version wasn't specified, `LoadWithPartialName` loads the assembly from GAC that has the highest version number.

Important   Some developers notice that `System.AppDomain` offers a `Load` method. Unlike `Assembly`'s static `Load` method, AppDomain's `Load` method is an instance method that allows you to load an assembly into the specified AppDomain. This method was designed to be called by unmanaged code, and it allows a host to inject an assembly into a specific AppDomain. Managed code developers generally shouldn't call this method. Here's why.

When AppDomain's `Load` method is called, you pass it a string that identifies an assembly. The method then applies policy and searches the normal places—the user's disk or codebase references—looking for the assembly. Recall that an AppDomain has settings associated with it that tell the CLR how to look for assemblies. To load this assembly, the CLR will use the settings associated with the specified AppDomain, not the calling AppDomain.

However, AppDomain's `Load` method returns a reference to an assembly. Because the `System.Assembly` class isn't derived from `System.MarshalByRefObject`, the assembly object must be marshaled by value back to the calling AppDomain. But the CLR will now use the calling AppDomain's settings to locate the assembly and load it. If the assembly can't be found using the calling AppDomain's policy and search locations, a `FileNotFoundException` exception is thrown. This behavior is usually undesirable and is the reason you should avoid AppDomain's `Load` method.

Loading Assemblies as "Data Files"

Imagine a user has installed some utility application on her hard drive. The utility consists of two assemblies: SomeTool.exe (the main application's assembly file) and Component.dll (an assembly file containing some components that SomeTool.exe uses). These two assemblies are installed as follows:

```
C:\SomeTool\SomeTool.exe
C:\SomeTool\Component.dll
```

Let's further suppose that the user has an assembly that she wants to process using SomeTool.exe. The assembly file to be processed happens to be named Component.dll and resides in the following location:

```
C:\Component.dll
```

Now, let's say that the user executes the following command line:

```
C:\>C:\SomeTool\SomeTool.exe C:\Component.dll
```

SomeTool.exe's **Main** method starts running and calls **Assembly.LoadFrom**, passing the command-line argument indicating the assembly that the tool is to process. The CLR loads the C:\Component.dll assembly. Now let's say that **Main** calls some other method that references an object defined in the C:\SomeTool\Component.dll assembly. What do you think should happen? Should the CLR realize that an assembly named Component.dll is already loaded in the AppDomain and just use this assembly? Or should the CLR realize that the C:\Component.dll assembly file was loaded "as a data file" and wouldn't normally have been loaded into the AppDomain?

The CLR can't assume that the Component.dll file loaded from C:\ is the same Component.dll file that is in C:\SomeTool because the two assembly files can define completely different types and methods. You'll be glad to hear that the CLR does the right thing here: it loads C:\SomeTool\Component.dll into the AppDomain, and the code in SomeTool.exe will access types and methods defined in the correct assembly.

Here's how this works. Internally, when **Assembly**'s **LoadFrom** method is called, the CLR opens the specified file and extracts the assembly's version, culture, and public key token information from the file's metadata. Then the CLR internally calls **Load**, passing all this information. **Load** applies all the policy information and searches for the assembly. If a matching assembly is found, the CLR compares the full pathname of the assembly file specified by **LoadFrom** with the full pathname of the assembly file found by **Load**. If the pathnames are the same, the assembly is considered to be a normal part of the application. If the pathnames are different or if **Load** doesn't find a matching file, the assembly is considered a "data file" and isn't considered a normal part of the application.

When the CLR needs to find a dependency of an assembly loaded via `LoadFrom`, the CLR goes through the regular probing logic, and if it can't find the dependent assembly in any of those locations, it looks in the directory where the referring assembly was found (and in any subdirectory whose name matches that of the dependent assembly).

Earlier, I mentioned that you should always use `Load` and avoid using `LoadFrom` whenever possible. One reason is that `LoadFrom` is much slower than `Load` because it calls `Load` internally, which has to apply policy and scan several disk locations. Another reason is that an assembly loaded with `LoadFrom` is treated like a "data file," and if your AppDomain does load two identical assembly files from different paths, you're wasting a lot of memory and also hurting run-time performance. Calling `Load` ensures that performance is as good as it can be and that an assembly isn't loaded more than once into an AppDomain.

Whenever you're about to place a call to `LoadFrom`, think about your application and try to figure out a way to change it so that `Load` will work instead. Of course, there will be times when `Load` simply won't do and using `LoadFrom` is necessary (such as in the SomeTool.exe example). Certainly, if you can't use `Load`, use `LoadFrom` instead—just be careful.

Building a Hierarchy of Exception-Derived Types

The ExceptionTree sample application (source code shown below) displays all classes that are ultimately derived from `System.Exception`. However, I wanted to examine types in several assemblies to produce this tree. To accomplish this, the application must explicitly load all the assemblies whose types I want to consider. This is the job of the application's `LoadAssemblies` method. After loading all the assemblies, the application gets an array of all the AppDomain's assemblies. Then I get an array for all types defined in each assembly.

For each type, I check its base type by querying `Type`'s `BaseType` property. If the `Type` returned is `System.Exception`, this type is an exception type. If the `Type` returned is `System.Object`, the type isn't an exception type. If the `Type` returned isn't either of these types, I check the base type's type recursively until I find `Exception` or `Object`.

The following code is for the ExceptionTree application. The output from this application is shown in Chapter 18 (page 424), so I won't display it here.

```
Imports System
Imports System.Text
Imports System.Reflection
Imports System.Collections
```

(continued)

```vb
Class App
    Shared Sub Main()
        ' Explicitly load the assemblies that I want to reflect over.
        LoadAssemblies()

        ' Initialize the counters and the exception type list.
        Dim totalTypes, totalExceptionTypes As Int32
        Dim exceptionTree As New ArrayList()

        ' Iterate through all assemblies loaded in this AppDomain.
        Dim a As [Assembly]
        For Each a In AppDomain.CurrentDomain.GetAssemblies

            ' Iterate through all types defined in this assembly.
            Dim t As Type
            For Each t In a.GetTypes

                totalTypes += 1

                ' Ignore type if not a public class.
                If t.IsClass Or t.IsPublic Then

                    ' Build a string of the type's derivation hierarchy.
                    Dim typeHierarchy As New StringBuilder(t.FullName, 5000)

                    ' Assume that the type isn't an Exception-derived type.
                    Dim derivedFromException As Boolean = False

                    ' See if System.Exception is a base type of this type.
                    Dim baseType As Type = t.BaseType
                    Do Until baseType Is Nothing Or derivedFromException
                        ' Append the base type to the end of the string.
                        typeHierarchy.Append("-")
                        typeHierarchy.Append(baseType)

                        derivedFromException = baseType Is GetType(Exception)
                        baseType = baseType.BaseType
                    Loop

                    ' No more bases and not Exception-derived, so try next type.
                    If derivedFromException Then

                        ' I found an Exception-derived type.
                        totalExceptionTypes += 1

                        ' For this Exception-derived type, reverse the order
                        ' of the types in the hierarchy.
                        Dim h() As String = typeHierarchy.ToString().Split("-"c)
                        Array.Reverse(h)
```

```vb
            ' Build a new string with the hierarchy in order
            ' from Exception -> Exception-derived type.
            ' Add the string to the list of Exception types.
            exceptionTree.Add(String.Join("-", h, 1, h.Length - 1))
         End If

      End If
   Next

   ' Sort the Exception types together in order of their hierarchy.
   exceptionTree.Sort()

   ' Display the Exception tree.
   Dim s As String
   For Each s In exceptionTree
      ' For this Exception type, split its base types apart.
      Dim x() As String = s.Split("-"c)

      ' Indent based on the number of base types,
      ' and then show the most derived type.
      Console.WriteLine(New String(" "c, 3 * x.Length) + _
         x(x.Length - 1))
   Next
   Next

   ' Show the final status of the types considered.
   Console.WriteLine()
   Console.WriteLine("---> Of {0} types, {1} are " & _
      "derived from System.Exception.", totalTypes, totalExceptionTypes)
   Console.ReadLine()
End Sub

Shared Sub LoadAssemblies()
   Dim assemblies() As String = { _
      "System,                    PublicKeyToken={0}", _
      "System.Data,               PublicKeyToken={0}", _
      "System.Design,             PublicKeyToken={1}", _
      "System.DirectoryServices,  PublicKeyToken={1}", _
      "System.Drawing,            PublicKeyToken={1}", _
      "System.Drawing.Design,     PublicKeyToken={1}", _
      "System.EnterpriseServices, PublicKeyToken={1}", _
      "System.Management,         PublicKeyToken={1}", _
      "System.Messaging,          PublicKeyToken={1}", _
      "System.Runtime.Remoting,   PublicKeyToken={0}", _
      "System.Security,           PublicKeyToken={1}", _
      "System.ServiceProcess,     PublicKeyToken={1}", _
      "System.Web,                PublicKeyToken={1}", _
      "System.Web.RegularExpressions, PublicKeyToken={1}", _
```

(continued)

```
            "System.Web.Services,             PublicKeyToken={1}", _
            "System.Windows.Forms,            PublicKeyToken={0}", _
            "System.Xml,                      PublicKeyToken={0}" _
            }

    Dim EcmaPublicKeyToken As String = "b77a5c561934e089"
    Dim MSPublicKeyToken As String = "b03f5f7f11d50a3a"

    ' Get the version of the assembly containing System.Object.
    ' I'll assume the same version for all the other assemblies.
    Dim version As Version = _
        GetType(System.Object).Assembly.GetName().Version()

    ' Explicitly load the assemblies that I want to reflect over.
    Dim a As String
    For Each a In assemblies
        Dim AssemblyIdentity As String = String.Format(a, _
            EcmaPublicKeyToken, MSPublicKeyToken) & _
            ", Culture=neutral, Version=" & version.ToString
        [Assembly].Load(AssemblyIdentity)
    Next
    End Sub
End Class
```

Explicitly Unloading Assemblies: Unloading an AppDomain

The CLR doesn't support the ability to unload an assembly. Instead, you can unload an AppDomain, which causes all the assemblies contained within it to be unloaded. Unloading an AppDomain is very easy: you just call **AppDomain**'s static **Unload** method, passing it a reference to the **AppDomain** you want unloaded.

> **Note**   As I mentioned previously, assemblies that are loaded in a domain-neutral fashion can never be unloaded from an AppDomain. To "unload" these assemblies, the process must be terminated.

The AppDomainRunner sample application demonstrates how to create a new AppDomain, use a type in it, and then unload the AppDomain along with all its assemblies. The code also shows how to define a type that can be marshaled by reference across AppDomain boundaries. Finally, it shows what happens if you attempt to access a marshal-by-reference object that used to exist in an AppDomain that's been unloaded.

```vb
Imports System
Imports System.Reflection
Imports System.Threading

Class App
    Shared Sub Main()
        ' Create a new AppDomain.
        Dim ad As AppDomain = AppDomain.CreateDomain("MyNewAppDomain", _
            Nothing, Nothing)

        ' Create a new MarshalByRef object in the new AppDomain.
        Dim mbrt As MarshalByRefType = DirectCast( _
            ad.CreateInstanceAndUnwrap( _
            [Assembly].GetCallingAssembly.FullName, _
            "MarshalByRefType"), MarshalByRefType)

        ' Call a method on this object. The proxy remotes
        ' the call to the other AppDomain.
        mbrt.SomeMethod(Thread.GetDomain().FriendlyName)

        ' I'm done using the other AppDomain, so
        ' I'll unload it and all its assemblies.
        AppDomain.Unload(ad)

        ' Try to call a method on the other AppDomain's object.
        ' The object was destroyed when the AppDomain was unloaded,
        ' so an exception is thrown.
        Try
            mbrt.SomeMethod(Thread.GetDomain().FriendlyName)
            ' The following line should NOT be displayed.
            Console.WriteLine("Called SomeMethod on object in other AppDomain.")
            Console.WriteLine("This shouldn't happen.")
        Catch e As AppDomainUnloadedException
            ' I'll catch the exception here, and the
            ' following line should be displayed.
            Console.WriteLine( _
                "Fail to call SomeMethod on object in other AppDomain.")
            Console.WriteLine("This should happen.")
        End Try
    End Sub
End Class

' This type is derived from MarshalByRefObject.
Public Class MarshalByRefType
    Inherits MarshalByRefObject

    ' This instance method can be called via a proxy.
    Public Sub SomeMethod(ByVal sourceAppDomain As String)
```

(continued)

```
' Display the name of the calling AppDomain and my AppDomain.
' NOTE: The application's thread has transitioned between AppDomains.
Console.WriteLine("Code from the '{0}' AppDomain", sourceAppDomain)
Console.WriteLine("called into the '{0}' AppDomain.", _
    Thread.GetDomain().FriendlyName)
    End Sub
End Class
```

If you build and run this application, you'll see the following output:

```
Code from the 'AppDomainRunner.exe' AppDomain
called into the 'MyNewAppDomain' AppDomain.
Fail to call SomeMethod on object in other AppDomain.
This should happen.
```

Obtaining a Reference to a `System.Type` Object

Reflection is most commonly used to learn about types or to manipulate objects using information that is typically known only at run time, not at compile time. Obviously, this dynamic exploring and manipulation of types and objects comes at a performance hit, so you should use it sparingly. In addition, a compiler can't help you locate and fix programming errors related to type safety when you're using reflection.

The `System.Type` type is your starting point for doing type and object manipulations. `System.Type` is an abstract base type derived from `System.Reflection.MemberInfo` (because a `Type` can be a member of another type). The FCL provides a few types that are derived from `System.Type`: `System.RuntimeType`, `System.Reflection.TypeDelegator`, some types defined in the `System.Reflection.Emit` namespace, `EnumBuilder`, and `TypeBuilder`. Aside from the few classes in the FCL, Microsoft doesn't expect to define any other types that derive from `Type`.

> **Note**   The `TypeDelegator` class allows code to dynamically subclass a `Type` by encapsulating the `Type`, allowing you to override some of the functionality while having the original `Type` handle most of the work. In general, the `TypeDelegator` type isn't useful. In fact, Microsoft isn't aware of anyone actually using the `TypeDelegator` type for anything.

Of all these types, the `System.RuntimeType` is by far the most interesting. `RuntimeType` is a type that is internal to the FCL, which means that you won't find it documented in the .NET Framework documentation. The first time a type is accessed in an AppDomain, the CLR constructs an instance of a **RuntimeType** and initializes the object's fields to reflect (pun intended) information about the type.

Recall that **System.Object** defines a method named **GetType**. When you call this method, the CLR determines the specified object's type and returns a reference to its **RuntimeType** object. Because there is only one **RuntimeType** object per type in an AppDomain, you can use equality and inequality operators to see whether two objects are of the same type:

```
Function AreObjectsTheSameType(ByVal o1 As Object, _
    ByVal o2 As Object) As Boolean
    Return o1.GetType Is o2.GetType
End Function
```

In addition to calling **Object**'s **GetType** method, the FCL offers several more ways to obtain a **Type** object:

- The **System.Type** type offers several overloaded versions of a static **GetType** method. All versions of this method take a **String**. The string must specify the full name of the type (including its namespace), and compiler primitive types (such as Visual Basic's **Integer**, **Long**, **Boolean**, and so on) aren't allowed. If the string is simply the name of a type, the method checks the calling assembly to see whether it defines a type of the specified name. If it does, a reference to the appropriate **RuntimeType** object is returned.

  If the calling assembly doesn't define the specified type, the types defined by MSCorLib.dll are checked. If a type with a matching name still can't be found, **Nothing** is returned or a **System.TypeLoad-Exception** exception is thrown, depending on which **GetType** method you call and what parameters you pass to it. The .NET Framework documentation fully explains this method.

  You can pass an assembly qualified type string, such as "System.Int32, mscorlib, Version=1.0.3300.0, Culture=neutral, PublicKey-Token=b77a5c561934e089", to **GetType**. In this case, **GetType** will look for the type in the specified assembly (loading the assembly if necessary).

- The **System.Type** type offers the following instance methods: **Get-NestedType** and **GetNestedTypes**.

- The **System.Reflection.Assembly** type offers the following instance methods: **GetType**, **GetTypes**, and **GetExportedTypes**.

■   The **System.Reflection.Module** type offers the following instance methods: **GetType**, **GetTypes**, and **FindTypes**.

Many programming languages also offer an operator that allows you to obtain a **Type** object from a type name. When possible, you should use this operator to obtain a reference to a **Type** instead of using any of the methods in the preceding list because the operator generally produces faster code. In Visual Basic, the operator is named **GetType**. The following code demonstrates how to use it:

```
Sub SomeMethod()
   Dim t As Type = GetType(MyType)
   Console.WriteLine(t.ToString)        ' Displays "MyType"
End Sub
```

I compiled this code and obtained its IL code using ILDasm.exe. I'll explain what's going on in the annotated IL code here:

```
.method public instance void  SomeMethod() cil managed
{
  ' Code size       23 (0x17)
  .maxstack  1
  .locals init ([0] class [mscorlib]System.Type t)

  ' Look up the MyType metadata token, and place a "handle" to
  ' the internal data structure on the stack.
  IL_0000: ldtoken    MyType

  ' Look up the RuntimeTypeHandle, and put a reference to
  ' the corresponding RuntimeType object on the stack.
  IL_0005: call       class [mscorlib]System.Type
      [mscorlib]System.Type::GetTypeFromHandle(
          valuetype [mscorlib]System.RuntimeTypeHandle)

  ' Save the RuntimeType reference in the local variable t.
  IL_000a: stloc.0

  ' Load the reference in t on the stack.
  IL_000b: ldloc.0

  ' Call the RuntimeType object's ToString method.
  IL_000c: callvirt   instance string [mscorlib]System.Type::ToString()

  ' Pass the String to Console.WriteLine.
  IL_0011: call       void [mscorlib]System.Console::WriteLine(string)

  ' Return from the method.
  IL_0016: ret
} ' end of method App::SomeMethod
```

The `ldtoken` IL instruction has a metadata token specified as an operand. The `ldtoken` instruction causes the CLR to look for the internal data structure representing the specified metadata token. If an internal data structure for this metadata token doesn't exist, the CLR will create it on the fly. A "handle" to this internal structure, represented as a `System.RuntimeTypeHandle` (a value type), is then pushed on the virtual stack. This "handle" is really the memory address of the internal data structure, but you should never access these internal structures directly.

Now `System.Type`'s static `GetTypeFromHandle` method is called. This method takes the "handle" and returns a reference to the `RuntimeType` object for the type. The rest of the IL code just saves the `RuntimeType` reference in the variable `t` and then calls `ToString` on `t`; the resulting string is passed to `Console.WriteLine` and the method then returns.

> **Note**   The `ldtoken` IL instruction allows you to specify a metadata token representing an entry in the type definition/reference table, the method definition/reference table, or the field definition/reference table. Keep in mind that Visual Basic's `GetType` operator accepts only the name of a type defined in the module or a type referenced in another module; you can't specify a field or method name.

It's extremely rare that you'd ever need to obtain a "handle" for a field or method, which is why most compilers won't offer operators that emit an `ldtoken` instruction that has a field or method metadata token. Field and method "handles" are most useful to compiler writers, not to application developers. If you're interested in field handles, however, see the `System.RuntimeFieldHandle` type and `System.Reflection.FieldInfo`'s static `GetFieldFromHandle` method and instance `Handle` property. For method handles, see the `System.Runtime-MethodHandle` type and `System.Reflection.MethodBase`'s static `GetMethodFrom-Handle` method and instance `MethodHandle` property.

Once you have a reference to a `Type` object, you can query many of the type's properties to learn more about it. Most of the properties, such as `IsPublic`, `IsSealed`, `IsAbstract`, `IsClass`, `IsValueType`, and so on, indicate flags associated with the type. Other properties, such as `Assembly`, `AssemblyQualifiedName`, `FullName`, `Module`, and so on, return the name of the type's defining assembly or module and the full name of the type. You can also query the `BaseType` property to obtain the type's base type, and a slew of methods will give you even more information about the type.

The .NET Framework documentation describes all the methods and properties that **Type** exposes. Be aware that there are a lot of them. For example, the **Type** type offers about 45 public instance properties. This doesn't even include the methods and fields that **Type** also defines. I'll be covering some of these methods in the next section.

> **Note** By the way, if you need to obtain a **Type** object that identifies a reference to a type, you can call one of the **GetType** methods, passing the name of the type suffixed with an ampersand, as demonstrated in the following code:
>
> ```vb
> Imports System
> Imports System.Reflection
>
> Class App
>    Shared Sub Main()
>        ' Get the array of SomeMethod's parameters.
>        Dim p() As ParameterInfo = _
>            GetType(App).GetMethod("SomeMethod").GetParameters()
>
>        ' Get a reference to a type that identifies a String reference.
>        Dim stringRefType As Type = Type.GetType("System.String&")
>
>        ' Is SomeMethod's first parameter a String reference?
>        Console.WriteLine(p(0).ParameterType Is stringRefType)' "True"
>    End Sub
>
>    ' You get identical results if 'ref' is changed to 'out' here:
>    Public Sub SomeMethod(ByRef s As String)
>        s = Nothing
>    End Sub
> End Class
> ```

Reflecting Over a Type's Members

Fields, constructors, methods, properties, events, and nested types can all be defined as members within a type. The FCL contains a type named **System.Reflection.MemberInfo**. The various versions of the Reflector sample application discussed earlier in this chapter used this type to demonstrate how to discover what members a type defines. Table 20-3 shows several properties and methods offered by the **MemberInfo** type. These properties and methods are common to all type members.

Table 20-3   **Properties and Methods Common to All MemberInfo-Derived Types**

Member Name	Member Type	Description
Name	**String** property	Returns a **String** representing the member.
MemberType	**MemberTypes** (enum) property	Returns the kind of member (field, constructor, method, property, event, type (non-nested type), or nested type.
DeclaringType	**Type** property	Returns the **Type** that defines the member.
ReflectedType	**Type** property	Returns the **Type** that was used to obtain this member.
GetCustomAttributes	Method returning an **Object** array	Returns an array in which each element identifies an instance of a custom attribute applied to this member. Custom attributes can be applied to any member.
IsDefined	Method returning a **Boolean**	Returns **True** if at least one instance of the specified custom attribute is applied to the member.

Most of the properties mentioned in Table 20-3 are self-explanatory. However, developers frequently confuse the **DeclaringType** and **ReflectedType** properties. To fully understand these properties, let's define the following type:

```
Class MyType
    Public Overrides Function ToString()
        Return "Hi"
    End Function
End Class
```

What would happen if the following line of code executed?

```
Dim members() As MemberInfo = GetType(MyType).GetMembers()
```

The **members** variable is a reference to an array in which each element identifies a public member defined by **MyType** and any of its base types, such as **System.Object**. If you were to query the **DeclaringType** property for the **Member-**

Info element identifying the **ToString** method, you'd see **MyType** returned because **MyType** declares or defines a **ToString** method. On the other hand, if you were to query the **DeclaringType** property for the **MemberInfo** element identifying the **Equals** method, you'd see **System.Object** returned because **Equals** is declared by **System.Object**, not by **MyType**.

The **ReflectedType** property always returns **MyType** because this was the type specified when **GetMembers** was called to perform the reflection. If you look up the **MemberInfo** type in the .NET Framework documentation, you'll see that it is a class derived immediately from **System.Object**. Figure 20-2 shows the hierarchy of the reflection types.

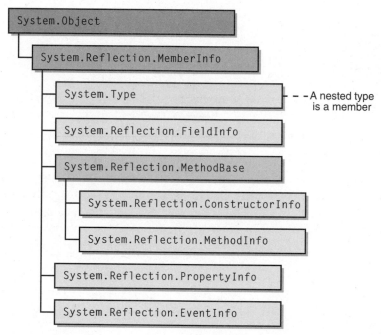

Figure 20-2 Hierarchy of the reflection types

> **Note** Don't forget that **System.Type** is derived from **MemberInfo** and therefore, **Type** also offers all the properties shown in Table 20-3.

Each element of the array returned by calling **GetMembers** is a reference to one of the concrete types in this hierarchy. While **Type**'s **GetMembers** method returns all the type's members, **Type** also offers methods that return specific member types. For example, **Type** offers **GetNestedTypes**, **GetFields**, **GetConstructors**, **GetMethods**, **GetProperties**, and **GetEvents**. These methods all return arrays where each element is a **Type**, **FieldInfo**, **ConstructorInfo**, **MethodInfo**, **PropertyInfo**, or **EventInfo**, respectively.

Figure 20-3 summarizes the types used by an application to walk reflection's object model. From an AppDomain, you can discover the assemblies loaded into it. From an assembly, you can discover the modules that make it up. From an assembly or a module, you can discover the types that it defines. From a type, you can discover its nested types, fields, constructors, methods, properties, and events.

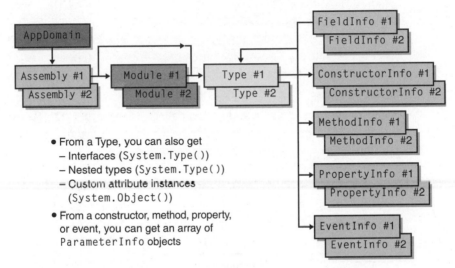

Figure 20-3   Types an application uses to walk reflection's object model

Creating an Instance of a Type

Once you have a reference to a **Type**-derived object, you might want to create an instance of this type. The FCL offers several mechanisms to accomplish this.

■ **System.Activator's CreateInstance methods**   This class offers several overloads of a static **CreateInstance** method. When you call this method, you can pass either a reference to a **Type** object or a **String** that identifies the type of object you want to create. The versions that take a type are simpler. You get to pass a set of arguments to the type's constructor and the method returns a reference to the new object.

The versions of this method in which you specify the desired type with a string are a bit more complex. First, you must also specify a string identifying the assembly that defines the type. Second, these methods allow you to construct a remote object if you have remoting options configured properly. Third, these versions don't return a reference to the new object. Instead, they return a `System.Runtime.Remoting.ObjectHandle` (which is derived from `System.MarshalByRefObject`).

An `ObjectHandle` is a type that allows an object created in one AppDomain to be passed around to other AppDomains without forcing the assembly that defines the type to be loaded into these AppDomains. When you're ready to access the object, you call `ObjectHandle`'s `Unwrap` method. Only when `Unwrap` is called does the assembly that contains the type's metadata get loaded. If the assembly can't get loaded, `Unwrap` throws a `System.Runtime.Remoting.RemotingException` exception. Note that `Unwrap` must be called before the object's lifetime expires; this is 5 minutes by default.

- **System.Activator's `CreateInstanceFrom` methods**   The `Activator` class also offers a set of static `CreateInstanceFrom` methods. These methods behave just like the `CreateInstance` method except that you must always specify the type and its assembly via string parameters. The assembly is loaded into the calling AppDomain using `Assembly`'s `LoadFrom` method (instead of `Load`). Because none of these methods takes a `Type` parameter, all the `CreateInstanceFrom` methods return a reference to an `ObjectHandle`, which must be unwrapped.

- **System.AppDomain's methods**   The AppDomain type offers four instance methods that construct an instance of a type: `CreateInstance`, `CreateInstanceAndUnwrap`, `CreateIntanceFrom`, and `CreateInstanceFromAndUnwrap`. These methods work just like `Activator`'s methods except that methods are instance methods allowing you to specify which AppDomain the object should be constructed in. The methods that end with `Unwrap` exist for convenience so that you don't have to make an additional method call.

- **System.Type's `InvokeMember` instance method**   Using a reference to a `Type` object, you can call the `InvokeMember` method. This method locates a constructor matching the parameters you pass and constructs the type. The type is always created in the calling AppDomain and a reference to the new object is returned. I'll discuss this method in more detail later in this chapter.

■ **System.Reflection.ConstructorInfo's Invoke instance method**
Using a reference to a **Type** object, you can bind to a particular constructor and obtain a reference to the constructor's **ConstructorInfo** object. Then you can use the reference to the **ConstructorInfo** object to call its **Invoke** method. The type is always created in the calling AppDomain, and a reference to the new object is returned. I'll also discuss this method in more detail later in this chapter.

> **Note**   The CLR doesn't require that value types define any constructors. However, this is a problem because all the mechanisms in the preceding list construct an object by calling its constructor. To fix this problem, Microsoft "enhanced" some of **Activator's** **CreateInstance** methods so that they can create an instance of a value type without calling a constructor. If you want to create an instance of a value type without calling a constructor, you must call the version of the **Create-Instance** method that takes a single **Type** parameter or the version that takes **Type** and **Boolean** parameters.

The mechanisms just listed allow you to create an object for all types except for arrays (**System.Array**-derived types) and delegates (**System.Multi-castDelegate**-derived types).

To create an array, you should call **Array**'s static **CreateInstance** method (several overloaded versions exist). The first parameter to all versions of **Create-Instance** is a reference to the **Type** of elements you want in the array. **Create-Instance**'s other parameters allow you to specify various combinations of dimensions and bounds.

To create a delegate, you should call **Delegate**'s static **CreateDelegate** method (several overloads exist). The first parameter to all versions of **Create-Delegate** is a reference to the **Type** of delegate you want to create. **CreateDel-egate**'s other parameters allow you to specify which instance method of an object or which static method of a type the delegate should wrap.

Calling a Type's Method

The easiest way to call a method is to use **Type**'s **InvokeMember** method. This method is quite powerful in that it lets you do lots of stuff. There are several overloaded versions of **InvokeMember**. I'll discuss the one that has the most parameters; the other overloads simply pick defaults for certain parameters, making them easier to call.

```
Class Type
    Public Function InvokeMember( _
        ByVal name As String, _              ' Name of member
        ByVal invokeAttr As BindingFlags, _  ' How to look up members
        ByVal binder As Binder, _            ' How to match members and arguments
        ByVal target As Object, _            ' Object to invoke member on
        ByVal args() As Object, _            ' Arguments to pass to method
        ByVal culture As CultureInfo) _      ' Culture used by some binders
        As Object
    ⋮
End Class
```

When you call **InvokeMember**, it looks at the type's members for a match. If no match is found, a **System.MissingMethodException** exception is thrown. If a match is found, **InvokeMember** calls the method. Whatever the method returns is what **InvokeMember** returns back to you. If the method is a **Sub** (has no return value), **InvokeMember** returns **Nothing**. If the method you call throws an exception, **InvokeMember** catches the exception and throws a new **System.Reflection.TargetInvocationException** exception. The **TargetInvocationException** object's **InnerException** property will contain the actual exception that the invoked method threw. Personally, I don't like this behavior. I'd prefer it if **InvokeMember** didn't wrap the exception and just allowed it to come through.

Internally, **InvokeMember** performs two operations. First, it must select the appropriate member to be called—this is known as *binding*. Second, it must actually invoke the member—this is known as *invoking*.

When you call **InvokeMember**, you pass a string as the **name** parameter, indicating the name of the member you want **InvokeMember** to bind to. However, the type might offer several members with a particular name. After all, there might be several overloaded versions of a method, or a method and a field might have the same name. Of course, **InvokeMember** must bind to a single member before it can invoke it. All the parameters passed to **InvokeMember** (except for the **target** parameter) are used to help **InvokeMember** decide which member to bind to. Let's take a closer look at these parameters.

The **binder** parameter identifies an object whose type is derived from the abstract **System.Reflection.Binder** type. A **Binder**-derived type is a type that encapsulates the rules for how **InvokeMember** should select a single member. The **Binder** base type defines abstract virtual methods such as **BindToField**, **BindToMethod**, **ChangeType**, **ReorderArgumentArray**, **SelectMethod**, and **SelectProperty**. Internally, **InvokeMember** calls these methods using the **Binder** object passed via **InvokeMember**'s **binder** parameter.

Microsoft has defined an internal (undocumented) concrete type, named `DefaultBinder`, which is derived from `Binder`. This `DefaultBinder` type ships with the FCL, and Microsoft expects that almost everyone will use this binder. When you pass `Nothing` to `InvokeMember`'s `binder` parameter, it will use the `DefaultBinder`. `Type` offers a public read-only property, `DefaultBinder`, that you can query to obtain a reference to a `DefaultBinder` object should you want one for some reason.

If you're concerned about `DefaultBinder`'s rules, you must define your own `Binder`-derived type and pass an instance of this type via `InvokeMember`'s `binder` parameter. Sample source code for a simple `Binder`-derived type can be obtained by downloading the code associated with this book from *http://www.Wintellect.com/*.

When a binder object has its methods called, the methods will be passed parameters to help the binder make a decision. Certainly, the binder is passed the name of the member that is being looked for. In addition, the binder's methods are passed the specified `BindingFlags` as well as the types of all the parameters that need to be passed to the member being invoked.

Earlier in this chapter, I showed a table (Table 20-2) that described the following `BindingFlags`: `Default`, `IgnoreCase`, `DeclaredOnly`, `Instance`, `Static`, `Public`, `NonPublic`, and `FlattenHierarchy`. The presence of these flags tells the binder which members to include in the search.

In addition to these flags, the binder examines the number of arguments passed via `InvokeMember`'s `args` parameter. The number of arguments limits the set of possible matches even further. The binder then examines the types of the arguments to limit the set even more. However, when it comes to the argument's types, the binder applies some automatic type conversions to make things a bit more flexible. For example, a type can define a method that takes a single `Int64` parameter. If you call `InvokeMember` and for the `args` parameter pass a reference to an array containing an `Int32` value, the `DefaultBinder` considers this a match. When invoking the method, the `Int32` value will be converted to an `Int64` value. The `DefaultBinder` supports the conversions listed in Table 20-4.

Table 20-4   Conversions That `DefaultBinder` Supports

Source Type	Target Type
Any type	Its base type
Any type	The interface it implements
Char	UInt16, UInt32, Int32, UInt64, Int64, Single, Double
Byte	Char, UInt16, Int16, UInt32, Int32, UInt64, Int64, Single, Double

(continued)

Table 20-4 **Conversions That** DefaultBinder **Supports** *(continued)*

Source Type	Target Type
SByte	Int16, Int32, Int64, Single, Double
UInt16	UInt32, Int32, UInt64, Int64, Single, Double
Int16	Int32, Int64, Single, Double
UInt32	UInt64, Int64, Single, Double
Int32	Int64, Single, Double
UInt64	Single, Double
Int64	Single, Double
Single	Double
Nonreference	By reference

There are two more **BindingFlags** that you can use to fine-tune the **DefaultBinder**'s behavior. These are described in Table 20-5.

Table 20-5 BindingFlags **Used with** DefaultBinder

Symbol	Value	Description
ExactBinding	&H010000	The binder will look for a member whose parameters match the types of the arguments passed. This flag can be used only with the **DefaultBinder** type because a custom binder would be implemented to select the appropriate member. Note that binders are free to ignore this flag. In fact, when the **DefaultBinder** type doesn't find a match, it doesn't fail; it considers a match where the passed parameter can be coerced to a compatible type without loss of precision.
OptionalParamBinding	&H040000	The binder will consider any member whose count of parameters matches the number of arguments passed. This flag is useful when there are members whose parameters have default values and for methods that take a variable number of arguments. Only **Type**'s **InvokeMember** method honors this flag.

InvokeMember's last parameter, **culture**, is also used for binding. However, the **DefaultBinder** type completely ignores this parameter. If you define your own binder, you could use the **culture** parameter to help with argument type conversions. For example, the caller could pass a **String** argument with a value of "1,23". The binder could examine this string, parse it using the specified **culture**, and convert the argument's type to a **Single** (if the culture is "de-DE") or continue to consider the argument a **String** (if the culture is "en-US").

At this point, I've gone through all **InvokeMember**'s parameters related to binding. The one parameter I haven't discussed yet is **target**. This parameter is a reference to the object whose method you want to call. If you want to call a type's static method, you should pass **Nothing** for this parameter.

The **InvokeMember** method is a very powerful method. It allows you to call a method (as I've been discussing), construct an instance of a type (basically by calling a constructor method), and get or set a field. You tell **InvokeMember** which of these actions you want to perform by specifying one of the **Binding-Flags** in Table 20-6.

For the most part, the flags in Table 20-6 are mutually exclusive—you must pick one and only one when calling **InvokeMember**. However, you can specify both **GetField** and **GetProperty**, in which case **InvokeMember** searches for a matching field first and then for a matching property if it doesn't find a matching field. Likewise, **SetField** and **SetProperty** can both be specified and are matched the same way. The binder uses these flags to narrow down the set of possible matches. If you specify the **BindingFlags.CreateInstance** flag, the binder knows that it can select only a constructor method.

Table 20-6 **BindingFlags** Used with **InvokeMember**

Symbol	Value	Description
InvokeMethod	&H0100	Tells **InvokeMember** to call a method
CreateInstance	&H0200	Tells **InvokeMember** to create a new object and call its constructor
GetField	&H0400	Tells **InvokeMember** to get a field's values
SetField	&H0800	Tells **InvokeMember** to set a field's value
GetProperty	&H1000	Tells **InvokeMember** to call a property's get accessor method
SetProperty	&H2000	Tells **InvokeMember** to call a property's set accessor method

> **Important** With what I've told you so far, it would seem that reflection makes it easy to bind to a nonpublic member and invoke the member, allowing application code a way to access private members that a compiler would normally prohibit the code from accessing. However, reflection uses code access security to ensure that its power isn't abused or exploited.
>
> When you call a method to bind to a member, the method first checks to see whether the member you're trying to bind to would be visible to you at compile time. If it would be, the bind is successful. If the member wouldn't normally be accessible to you, the method demands the `System.Security.Permissions.ReflectionPermission` permission, checking to see whether the `System.Security.Permissions.ReflectionPermissionFlags`'s `TypeInformation` bit is set. If this flag is set, the method will bind to the member. If the demand fails, a `System.Security.SecurityException` exception is thrown.
>
> When you call a method to invoke a member, the method performs the same kind of check that it would when binding to a member. But this time, it checks whether the `ReflectionPermission` has `ReflectionPermissionFlag`'s `MemberAccess` bit set. If the bit is set, the member is invoked; otherwise, a `SecurityException` exception is thrown.

Bind Once, Invoke Multiple Times

`Type`'s `InvokeMember` method gives you access to all a type's members. However, you should be aware that every time you call `InvokeMember`, it must bind to a particular member and then invoke it. Having the binder select the right member each time you want to invoke a member is time-consuming, and if you do it a lot, your application's performance will suffer. So if you plan on accessing a member frequently, you're better off binding to the desired member once and then accessing that member as often as you want.

You bind to a member (without invoking it) by calling one of the following `Type`'s methods: `GetFields`, `GetConstructors`, `GetMethods`, `GetProperties`, `GetEvents` methods, or any similar method. All these methods return references to objects whose type offers methods to access the specific member directly. Table 20-7 summarizes the types and what methods you call to access the member.

Table 20-7   Types Used to Bind to a Member

Type	Member Description
FieldInfo	Call GetValue to get a field's value. Call SetValue to set a field's value.
ConstructorInfo	Call Invoke to construct an instance of the type.
MethodInfo	Call Invoke to call a method of the type.
PropertyInfo	Call GetValue to call a property's get accessor method. Call SetValue to call a property's set accessor method.
EventInfo	Call AddEventHandler to call an event's add accessor method. Call RemoveEventHandler to call an event's remove accessor method.

The **PropertyInfo** type represents a property's metadata information only (as discussed in Chapter 10); that is, **PropertyInfo** offers **CanRead**, **CanWrite**, and **PropertyType** read-only properties. These properties indicate whether a property is readable or writeable and what data type the property is. **PropertyInfo** has a **GetAccessors** method that returns an array of **MethodInfo** elements: one for the get accessor method (if it exists), and one for the set accessor method (if it exists). Of more value are **PropertyInfo**'s **GetGetMethod** and **GetSetMethod** methods, each of which returns just one **MethodInfo** object. **PropertyInfo**'s **GetValue** and **SetValue** methods exist for convenience; internally, they get the appropriate **MethodInfo** and call it.

The **EventInfo** type represents an event's metadata information only (as discussed in Chapter 11). The **EventInfo** type offers an **EventHandlerType** read-only property that returns the **Type** of the event's underlying delegate. **EventInfo** also has **GetAddMethod** and **GetRemoveMethod** methods, which return the appropriate **MethodInfo**. **EventInfo**'s **AddEventHandler** and **RemoveEventHandler** methods exist for convenience; internally, they get the appropriate **MethodInfo** and call it.

When you call one of the methods listed in the right column of Table 20-7, you're not binding to a member; you're just invoking the member. You can call any of these methods multiple times, and because binding isn't necessary, the performance will be pretty good.

You might notice that **ConstructorInfo**'s **Invoke**, **MethodInfo**'s **Invoke**, and **PropertyInfo**'s **GetValue** and **SetValue** methods offer overloaded versions that take a reference to a **Binder**-derived object and some **BindingFlags**. This would lead you to believe that these methods bind to a member. However, they don't.

When calling any of these methods, the **Binder**-derived object is used to perform type conversions such as converting an **Int32** argument to an **Int64** so that the already selected method can be called. As for the `BindingFlags` parameter, the only flag that can be passed here is `BindingFlags.SuppressChange-Type`. Like the `ExactBinding` flag, binders are free to ignore this flag. However, `DefaultBinder` doesn't ignore this flag. When `DefaultBinder` sees this flag, it won't convert any arguments. If you use this flag and the arguments passed don't match the arguments expected by the method, an `ArgumentException` exception is thrown.

Usually when you use the `BindingFlags.ExactBinding` flag to bind to a member you'll specify the `BindingFlags.SuppressChangeType` flag to invoke the member. If you don't use these two flags in tandem, it's unlikely that invoking the member will be successful unless the arguments you pass happen to be exactly what the method expects. By the way, if you call `MemberInfo`'s `InvokeMethod` to bind and invoke a member, you'll probably want to specify both or neither of the two binding flags.

The following sample application demonstrates the various ways to use reflection to access a type's members. The code shows how to use `Type`'s `InvokeMember` to both bind and invoke a member. It also shows how to bind to a member, invoking it later.

```
' Modify the following line to test,
' bind, and invoke as separate steps.
#Const BindAndInvokeTogether = True


Imports System
Imports System.Reflection
Imports System.Threading


' This class is used to demonstrate reflection. It has a
' a field, a constructor, a method, a property, and an event.
Class SomeType
   Dim someField As Int32
   Public Sub New(ByRef x As Int32)
      x *= 2
   End Sub

   Public Overrides Function ToString() As String
      Return someField.ToString
   End Function

   Property SomeProp() As Int32
      Get
         Return someField
      End Get
      Set(ByVal Value As Int32)
         If Value < 1 Then
```

```vbnet
                Throw New ArgumentOutOfRangeException("value", value, _
                    "value must be > 0")
            End If
            someField = Value
        End Set
    End Property

    Public Event SomeEvent As ThreadStart

End Class

Class App
    Shared Sub Main()
        Dim t As Type = GetType(SomeType)

        Dim bf As BindingFlags = BindingFlags.DeclaredOnly Or _
            BindingFlags.Public Or BindingFlags.NonPublic Or _
            BindingFlags.Instance

#If BindAndInvokeTogether Then

        ' Construct an instance of the type.
        Dim args() As Object = {12}      ' Constructor arguments
        Console.WriteLine("x before constructor called: {0}", args(0))
        Dim obj As Object = t.InvokeMember(Nothing, _
            bf Or BindingFlags.CreateInstance, Nothing, Nothing, args)
        Console.WriteLine("Type: {0}", obj.GetType().ToString)
        Console.WriteLine("x after constructor returns: {0}", args(0))

        ' Read from and write to a field.
        t.InvokeMember("someField", bf Or BindingFlags.SetField, _
            Nothing, obj, New Object() {5})
        Dim v As Int32 = CType(t.InvokeMember("someField", _
            bf Or BindingFlags.GetField, Nothing, obj, Nothing), Int32)
        Console.WriteLine("someField: {0}", v)

        ' Call a method.
        Dim s As String = DirectCast(t.InvokeMember("ToString", _
            bf Or BindingFlags.InvokeMethod, Nothing, obj, Nothing), String)
        Console.WriteLine("ToString: {0}", s)

        ' Read from and write to a property.
        Try
            t.InvokeMember("SomeProp", bf Or BindingFlags.SetProperty, _
                Nothing, obj, New Object() {0})
        Catch e As TargetInvocationException
            If Not e.InnerException.GetType Is _
                GetType(ArgumentOutOfRangeException) Then Throw
```

(continued)

```vb
            Console.WriteLine("Property set catch.")
        End Try

        t.InvokeMember("SomeProp", bf Or BindingFlags.SetProperty, _
            Nothing, obj, New Object() {2})
        v = CType(t.InvokeMember("SomeProp", _
            bf Or BindingFlags.GetProperty, Nothing, obj, Nothing), Int32)
        Console.WriteLine("SomeProp: {0}", v)

        ' NOTE: InvokeMember doesn't support events.

#Else

        ' Construct an instance.
        Dim ctor as ConstructorInfo = t.GetConstructor(New Type() _
            { Type.GetType("System.Int32&") })
        Dim args() As Object = { 12 }        ' Constructor arguments
        Console.WriteLine("x before constructor called: {0}" , args(0))
        Dim obj As Object = ctor.Invoke(args)
        Console.WriteLine("Type: {0}" , obj.GetType().ToString)
        Console.WriteLine("x after constructor returns: {0}" , args(0))

        ' Read from and write to a field.
        Dim fi as FieldInfo = obj.GetType().GetField("someField", bf)
        fi.SetValue(obj, 33)
        Console.WriteLine("someField: {0}" , fi.GetValue(obj))

        ' Call a method.
        Dim mi as MethodInfo= obj.GetType().GetMethod("ToString", bf)
        Dim s as String= DirectCast(mi.Invoke(obj, Nothing), String)
        Console.WriteLine("ToString: {0}" , s)

        ' Read from and write to a property.
        Dim pi As PropertyInfo = obj.GetType().GetProperty( _
            "SomeProp", GetType(Int32))
        Dim m as MethodInfo
        For each m in pi.GetAccessors
            Console.WriteLine(m)
        Next
        Try
            pi.SetValue(obj, 0, Nothing)
        Catch e As TargetInvocationException
            If Not e.InnerException.GetType() Is _
                GetType(ArgumentOutOfRangeException) Then Throw
            Console.WriteLine("Property set catch.")
        End Try
```

```
    pi.SetValue(obj, 2, Nothing)
    Console.WriteLine("SomeProp: {0}", pi.GetValue(obj, Nothing))

    ' Add and remove a delegate from the event.
    Dim ei As EventInfo = obj.GetType().GetEvent("SomeEvent", bf)
    Console.WriteLine("AddMethod: {0}", ei.GetAddMethod)
    Console.WriteLine("RemoveMethod: {0}", ei.GetRemoveMethod)
    Console.WriteLine("EventHandlerType: {0}", ei.EventHandlerType)

    Dim ts As New ThreadStart(AddressOf Main)
    ei.AddEventHandler(obj, ts)
    ei.RemoveEventHandler(obj, ts)

#End If
    End Sub
End Class
```

If you build and run this code with **BindAndInvokeTogether** defined as **True**, you'll see the following output:

```
x before constructor called: 12
Type: SomeType
x after constructor returns: 24
someField: 5
ToString: 5
Property set catch.
SomeProp: 2
```

Notice that **SomeType**'s constructor takes an **Int32** reference as its only parameter. The previous code shows how to call this constructor and how to examine the modified **Int32** value after the constructor returns.

If you build and run the previous code without **BindAndInvokeTogether** defined as **False**, you'll see the following output:

```
x before constructor called: 12
Type: SomeType
x after constructor returns: 24
someField: 33
ToString: 33
Void set_SomeProp(Int32)
Int32 get_SomeProp()
Property set catch.
SomeProp: 2
AddMethod: Void add_SomeEvent(System.Threading.ThreadStart)
RemoveMethod: Void remove_SomeEvent(System.Threading.ThreadStart)
EventHandlerType: System.Threading.ThreadStart
```

Reflecting Over a Type's Interfaces

To obtain the set of interfaces that a type inherits, you can call **Type**'s **Find-Interfaces**, **GetInterface**, or **GetInterfaces** method. All these methods return **Type** objects that represent an interface.

Determining which members of a type implement a particular interface is a little complicated because multiple interface definitions can all define the same method. For example, the **IBookRetailer** and **IMusicRetailer** interfaces might both define a method named **Purchase**. To get the **MethodInfo** objects for a specific interface, you call **Type**'s **GetInterfaceMap** instance method. This method returns an instance of a **System.Reflection.InterfaceMapping** (a value type). The **InterfaceMapping** type defines the four public fields listed in Table 20-8.

Table 20-8   Public Fields Defined by the InterfaceMapping **Type**

Field Name	Data Type	Description
TargetType	Type	This is the type that was used to call **GetInterfaceMapping**.
InterfaceType	Type	This is the type of the interface passed to **GetInterfaceMapping**.
InterfaceMethods	MethodInfo array	An array in which each element exposes information about an interface's method.
TargetMethods	MethodInfo array	An array in which each element exposes information about the method that the type defines to implement the corresponding interface's method.

The **InterfaceMethods** and **TargetMethods** arrays run parallel to each other; that is, **InterfaceMethods(0)** identifies a **MethodInfo** object that reflects information about the member as defined in the interface. **TargetMethods(0)** identifies a **MethodInfo** object that reflects information about the interface's member as defined by the **TargetType**.

```vb
Imports System
Imports System.Reflection

' Define two interfaces for testing.
Public Interface IBookRetailer
    Inherits IDisposable
    Sub Purchase()
    Sub ApplyDiscount()
End Interface
Public Interface IMusicRetailer
    Sub Purchase()
End Interface

' This class implements two interfaces defined by this
' assembly and one interface defined by another assembly.
Class MyRetailer
    Implements IBookRetailer, IMusicRetailer

    Public Sub Purchase()
    End Sub
    Public Sub Dispose() Implements IDisposable.Dispose
    End Sub
    Sub IBookRetailer_Purchase() Implements IBookRetailer.Purchase
    End Sub
    Public Sub ApplyDiscount() Implements IBookRetailer.ApplyDiscount
    End Sub
    Sub IMusicRetailer_Purchase() Implements IMusicRetailer.Purchase
    End Sub
End Class

Class App
    Shared Sub Main()
        ' Find the interfaces implemented by MyRetailer where
        ' the interface is defined in your own assembly. This
        ' is accomplished using a delegate to a filter method
        ' that you create and pass to FindInterfaces.
        Dim t As Type = GetType(MyRetailer)
        Dim interfaces() As Type = t.FindInterfaces( _
            New TypeFilter(AddressOf App.TypeFilter), _
            [Assembly].GetCallingAssembly().GetName())
        Console.WriteLine("MyRetailer implements the following " _
            & "interfaces (defined in this assembly):")

        ' Show information about each interface.
        Dim i As Type
```

(continued)

```
      For Each i In interfaces
         Console.WriteLine()
         Console.WriteLine("Interface: {0}", i)

         ' Get the type methods that map to the interface's methods.
         Dim map As InterfaceMapping = t.GetInterfaceMap(i)
         Dim m As Int32
         For m = 0 To map.InterfaceMethods.Length - 1
            ' Display the interface method name and which type
            ' method implements the interface method.
            Console.WriteLine("   {0} is implemented by {1}", _
               map.InterfaceMethods(m), map.TargetMethods(m))
         Next
      Next
   End Sub


   ' This filter delegate method takes a type and an object, performs
   ' some check, and returns True if the type is to be included
   ' in the array of returned types.
   Shared Function TypeFilter(ByVal t As Type, _
      ByVal filterCriteria As Object) As Boolean
      ' Return True if the interface is defined in the same
      ' assembly identified by filterCriteria.
      Return t.Assembly.GetName.ToString() = filterCriteria.ToString()
   End Function
End Class
```

Reflection Performance

In general, using reflection to invoke a method or access a field or property is slow, for several reasons:

- Binding causes many string comparisons to be performed while looking for the desired member.

- Passing arguments requires that an array be constructed and that the array's elements be initialized. Internally, invoking a method requires that the arguments be extracted from the array and placed on the stack.

- The CLR must check that the parameters being passed to a method are of the correct number and type.

- The CLR ensures that the caller has the proper security permission to access the member.

For all these reasons, it's best to avoid using reflection to access a member. If you're writing an application that will dynamically locate and construct types, you should take one of the following approaches:

■   Have the types derive from a base type that is known at compile time. At run time, construct an instance of the type, place the reference in a variable that is of the base type (casting if your language requires it), and call virtual methods defined by the base type.

■   Have the type implement an interface that is known at compile time. At run time, construct an instance of the type, place the reference in a variable that is of the interface type (casting if your language requires it), and call the methods defined by the interface. I prefer this technique over the base type technique because the base type technique doesn't allow the developer to choose the base type that works best in a particular situation.

■   Have the type implement a method whose name and prototype match a delegate that is known at compile time. At run time, construct an instance of the type and then construct an instance of the delegate type using the object and the name of the method. Then call the method via the delegate as you desire. This technique is the most work of the three and quickly becomes a lot more work if you need to call more than one of the type's methods. Also, calling a method via a delegate is slower than calling a type's method or an interface method directly.

When you use any of these three techniques, I strongly suggest that the base type, interface, or delegate type be defined in its own assembly. This will reduce versioning issues. For more information about how to do this, see the section "Designing an Application That Supports Plug-In Components" on page 350 of Chapter 15.

Index

Send feedback about this index to *mspindex@microsoft.com*.

Symbols and Numbers

!= symbol in C#, 220
Of Exceps Thrown counter, 444
Of Exceps Thrown/Sec counter, 444
Of Filters/Sec counter, 444
Of Finallys/Sec counter, 444
& concatenation operator, 267–68
& (ampersand) in a GetType method, 560
/ division operator, 127
/ operator (floating-point division), 446
@ sign, prepending a response file, 91
[] (square brackets) in C#, 365
[] syntax in C#, 243
\ operator (integer division), 446
^ operator, 127
^ symbol, exclusive OR (XOR) in C# vs. exponent in
    Visual Basic, 220
+ symbol in C#, 220
<> (angle brackets), custom attributes in, 365
<> operator
  comparing primitive types, 172
  comparing strings in Visual Basic, 270
<> symbol in Visual Basic, 220
= operator
  comparing primitive types, 172
  comparing strings in Visual Basic, 270
() operator, 241
() parentheses, allowing in strings, 298
1-byte type ID, 372
6-byte x86 stub functions, 11, 12
16-bit characters, 303
16-bit Unicode code values, 261, 301
32-bit PE file format, 12
64-bit PE file format, 12

A

abbreviated delegate syntax, 387
Abort method, 421
abstract attribute in C#, 187, 189
Abstract CLR term, 187, 189
accessibility modifiers, 185–86
accessor methods, 236
Activator class, 564
add_, prepending to an event's name, 251
add accessor method, 253

Add An Application To Configure link, 72
Add Counters dialog box in PerfMon.exe, 528
add instruction in the CLR, 144
Add method of ArrayList, 154
Add Reference dialog box in Visual Studio .NET, 56
AddEventHandler method, 571
AddHandler statement, 254
/addmodule switch of the Visual Basic compiler, 52, 53
add.ovf instruction in the CLR, 144
AddressOf operator, 253, 387
AdjustToUniversal symbol, 300
administrative control
  advanced, 104–9
  allowing over applications, 68
administrators, creating machine-wide policies, 71
ADO.NET, 24
/Adv switch of ILDasm.exe, 43
advanced administrative control, 104–9
aggressive casting, 129, 130
AL.exe tool
  building satellite assemblies, 65–66
  command-line switches, 61–62
  incrementing assembly version numbers, 64
algorithms, intellectual property protection for, 14
alias for a single type or namespace, 136
allocations, synchronization-free, 525
AllowMultiple property of AttributeUsageAttribute class,
  369–70
AL.utility, 57–58
AmbiguousMatchException exception, 374
ampersand (&), suffixing the name of a type in a
  GetType method, 560
angle brackets < >, placing custom attributes in, 365
Any symbol for a NumberStyles' bit combination, 299
APL programming language, combining with other
  languages, 13
AppDomain boundaries, accessing objects across, 536–37
AppDomain type, instance methods offered by, 564
AppDomainRunner sample application, 554–56
AppDomains, 22, 529, 532–35
  accessing a single string object from multiple, 277
  characteristics of, 533
  corruption possible with verification turned off, 534
  creating for Web applications, 539

Jeffrey Richter

Jeffrey Richter is a cofounder of Wintellect (*http://www.Wintellect.com/*), a training, design, and debugging company dedicated to helping companies produce better software faster. Jeff has written many books, including *Programming Applications for Microsoft Windows* (Microsoft Press, 1999), *Programming Server-Side Applications for Microsoft Windows 2000* (Microsoft Press, 2000), and *Applied Microsoft .NET Framework Programming* (Microsoft Press, 2002). Jeff is also a contributing editor for MSDN Magazine, for which he has written several feature articles and is the .NET columnist. Jeff also speaks at various trade conferences worldwide, including VSLive!, WinSummit, and Microsoft's TechEd and PDC.

Jeff has consulted for many companies, including AT&T, DreamWorks, General Electric, Hewlett-Packard, IBM, and Intel. Jeff's code has shipped in many Microsoft products, among them Visual Studio, Microsoft Golf, Windows Sound System, and various versions of Windows, from Windows 95 to Windows XP and the Windows .NET Server Family. Since October 1999, Jeff has consulted with the .NET Framework team and has used the .NET Framework to produce the XML Web service front end to Microsoft's very popular TerraServer Web property (*http://www.TerraService.net*).

On the personal front, Jeff holds both airplane and helicopter pilot licenses, though he never gets to fly as often as he'd like. He is also a member of the International Brotherhood of Magicians and enjoys showing friends sleight-of-hand card tricks from time to time. Jeff's other hobbies include music, drumming, and model railroading. He also enjoys traveling and the theater. He lives near Bellevue, Washington, with his wife, Kristin, and their cat, Max. He doesn't have any children yet, but he has the feeling that kids may be a part of his life soon.

Francesco Balena

Francesco Balena began his software studies in the late 1970s and had to fight for a while against huge IBM mainframes and tons of punched cards while he waited for the PC to be invented. From those good old days—when the word *megabyte* made little sense and *gigabyte* was pure blasphemy—he has retained the taste for writing the most efficient and resource-aware code possible.

Kathleen Atkins

In more recent years, Francesco became a contributing editor and member of the Technical Advisory board of *Visual Studio Magazine* (formerly *Visual Basic Programmer's Journal*), for which he writes feature articles and columns, and editor-in-chief of *Visual Basic Journal*, the Italian licensee of *Visual Studio Magazine*. He's the author of *Programming Microsoft Visual Basic 6* (Microsoft Press, 2000) and *Programming Microsoft Visual Basic .NET* (Microsoft Press, 2002). Francesco teaches the Visual Basic .NET courses for Wintellect (*www.wintellect.com*) in the United States and Europe and is a regular speaker at developer conferences such as VBITS, SQL2TheMax, WinDev, and WinSummit. He is the founder of the popular VB-2-The-Max site (*www.vb2themax.com*), where you can find hundreds of articles, tips, and routines.

Francesco is the lead author of VBMaximizer, an add-in for Visual Basic 6 that has won an award from readers of *Visual Studio Magazine*; he is currently working on VSMaximizer for Visual Studio .NET. He has been appointed Microsoft's MSDN Regional Director for Italy and is cofounder of Code Architects, an Italian company that specializes exclusively in .NET programming, training, and consulting.

Francesco lives in Bari, Italy, with his wife, Adriana, and his son, Andrea, but spends a lot of his time abroad. In his previous life, he had a lot of good times playing his alto sax with big bands and jazz combos until he found that computer programming can be just as fun and doesn't require that he be awake and blowing until 4 a.m. each and every night. Only later he realized that—to write code and meet deadlines—he couldn't go to sleep before 4 a.m. anyway, but it was too late to change his mind. He has recently joined Band On The Runtime and plays with musicians of the caliber of David Chappell, Don Box, and Ted Pattison.

Helicopter's Dual Tachometer

The dual tachometer on a helicopter displays revolutions per minute (RPM) ranges for the engine on the left side and for the main rotor on the right. Colored arcs on each side indicate safe (green), caution (yellow), and prohibited (red) ranges. For example, a green arc on the left shows the engine's safe range, while a green arc on the right indicates the main rotor's safe range. Yellow arcs above and below the green range on the right mean the rotor can also be operated, if necessary, either above or below the normal safe range. This allows the pilot a much larger range of RPMs while *autorotating*—using the main rotor to slowly descend if the engine fails or if the tail rotor fails, requiring engine shutdown. A yellow range on the right shows where the tail rotor and main rotor sometimes resonate dangerously together, indicating that the pilot should accelerate and decelerate rapidly through this range during startup and shutdown.

At Microsoft Press, we use tools to illustrate our books for software developers and IT professionals. Tools very simply and powerfully symbolize human inventiveness. They're a metaphor for people extending their capabilities, precision, and reach. From simple calipers and pliers to digital micrometers and lasers, these stylized illustrations give each book a visual identity, and a personality to the series. With tools and knowledge, there's no limit to creativity and innovation. Our tagline says it all: *The tools you need to put technology to work.*

The manuscript for this book was prepared and galleyed using Microsoft Word. Pages were composed by Microsoft Press using Adobe FrameMaker+SGML for Windows, with text in Garamond and display type in Helvetica Condensed. Composed pages were delivered to the printer as electronic prepress files.

Cover Designer:	Methodologie, Inc.
Interior Graphic Designer:	James D. Kramer
Principal Compositor:	Elizabeth Hansford
Interior Artist:	Michael Kloepfer
Principal Proofreader:	Lisa Pawlewicz
Indexer:	Richard Shrout

Programming Visual Basic .NET
Starring Francesco Balena

Everything new and experienced VB developers need to know to leverage the power of Visual Basic .NET and ease the transition from previous versions.

Who should attend: Visual Basic 6.0 developers migrating to Visual Basic .NET; programmers who never used Visual Basic but wish to learn Visual Basic .NET.

Topics: Language syntax changes; object-oriented programming; working with data; advanced language features; threading; regular expressions; assemblies; reflection; interoperability; Windows Forms; ADO.NET; Web Forms; Web services.

Prerequisites: Working knowledge of the BASIC language and its syntax.

Length: 5 days.

Wintellect.com

For the latest in .NET articles and code samples as well as tips, newsletters and course materials, check out our website at www.wintellect.com.

Programming the .NET Framework with C#
Starring Jeffrey Richter, Jason Clark & Brent Rector

A highly detailed, no-holds-barred introduction to the platform and it's programming models, with special emphasis on understanding the Common Language Runtime and .NET Framework Class Library -- all in C#.

Who should attend: Developers looking for a broad but detailed overview of .NET who wish to explore its architecture, learn about the types of applications that it supports, and get first-hand experience programming the new platform.

Topics: Platform architecture; assemblies; types and type members; automatic memory management (garbage collection); the .NET Framework Class Library; reflection; threading; Web Forms; Windows Forms; Web services; interoperability.

Prerequisites: Understanding of basic object-oriented programming concepts.

Length: 5 days.

Programming ADO.NET
Starring Dino Esposito

An in-depth look at data access in the world of .NET.

Who should attend: Developers new to the platform whose applications will interact with back-end databases such as Microsoft SQL Server; experienced .NET developers who wish to enrich their knowledge of ADO.NET.

Topics: ADO.NET architecture; reading and viewing data; managed providers; updating data; server-side data binding; advanced DataGrids; XML and DataSets; XML navigation and transformation; Web services; exposing data to clients.

Prerequisites: Understanding of basic object-oriented programming concepts; familiarity with database design fundmentals.

Length: 4 days.

Programming ASP.NET
Starring Jeff Prosise & John Lam

Learn to write cutting-edge Web applications and Web Services by combining the richness of the .NET Framework with the easy-to-use programming model of ASP.NET.

Who should attend: Developers new to .NET whose primary focus is writing applications that run on the Web; ASP developers migrating to ASP.NET.

Topics: Essential Web programming concepts; C# and the Common Language Runtime; the .NET Framework Class Library; Web Forms; Web controls; user controls; custom controls; ADO.NET; XML; ASP.NET application architecture; ASP.NET security; Web Services; error handling and debugging; scalability and performance.

Prerequisites: Reading knowledge of HTML; understanding of basic object-oriented programming concepts.

Length: 5 days.

Debugging .NET Applications
Starring John Robbins

Write managed code that works right the first time, brought to you by the Bugslayer himself.

Who should attend: Developers with 6 months or more of .NET experience who wish to enrich their knowledge of the Framework and use that knowledge to become expert debuggers.

Topics: Platform architecture; exception handling; .NET debuggers; debugging with Visual Studio.NET; advanced debugging concepts and practices; debugging ASP.NET Web applications and Web services; debugging multithreaded .NET applications; performance tuning.

Prerequisites: Working knowledge of the .NET Common Language Runtime.

Length: 3 days.

Learn More About the Microsoft .NET Framework

Visit Francesco Balena's *www.vb2themax.com* to browse a huge collection of tips, ready-to-use code routines, utilities, original articles, and unabridged chapters from dozens of Visual Basic and .NET books. You'll also find a searchable list of the best articles that have appeared in all major developer magazines since 1996 and an index of the most useful Microsoft Knowledge Base articles. You can also subscribe to Francesco's newsletter to receive a new Visual Basic .NET tip each week right in your mailbox.

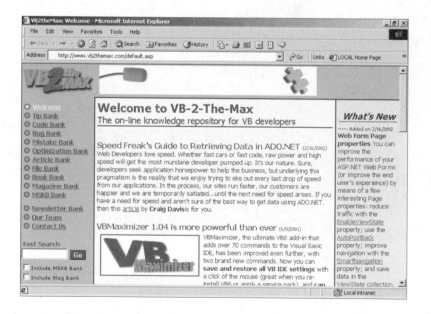

Everything you need to know to develop in
Visual Basic .NET

U.S.A. **$59.99**
Canada $86.99
ISBN: 0-7356-1375-3

Building on the success of the earlier version of this popular book, this core reference is designed to equip both beginning and veteran developers with the comprehensive instruction and code details they need to get up to speed in the Web-enabled Microsoft® Visual Basic® .NET environment. The book demonstrates best practices for porting and reusing existing Visual Basic code in the .NET environment, as well as exploiting the object-oriented capabilities of the new version. It includes extensive code samples plus the complete text of the previous edition as well as this book on CD-ROM!

Graduate

to the next generation of Visual Basic

at your own pace

with the proven
Microsoft Step by Step method.

This primer is the fast way for any developer—new or experienced—who uses Microsoft® Visual Basic® to begin creating professional applications for the Microsoft .NET platform. The best-selling author shows you in easy-to-understand chapters how to unleash all the power of the new, Web-integrated version of Visual Basic. Learn core skills for programming in Visual Basic .NET at your own pace with the proven, modular, Microsoft STEP BY STEP training format. Select just the chapters you need—with expert code, optimization tips, advice, and samples straight from the experts.

U.S.A. **$39.99**
Canada $57.99
ISBN: 0-7356-1374-5

Microsoft®
microsoft.com/mspress

Get a **Free**
*e-mail newsletter, updates,
special offers, links to related books,
and more when you*

register on line!

Register your Microsoft Press® title on our Web site and you'll get a FREE subscription to our e-mail newsletter, *Microsoft Press Book Connections*. You'll find out about newly released and upcoming books and learning tools, online events, software downloads, special offers and coupons for Microsoft Press customers, and information about major Microsoft® product releases. You can also read useful additional information about all the titles we publish, such as detailed book descriptions, tables of contents and indexes, sample chapters, links to related books and book series, author biographies, and reviews by other customers.

Registration is easy. Just visit this Web page and fill in your information:

http://www.microsoft.com/mspress/register

Microsoft®

Proof of Purchase

Use this page as proof of purchase if participating in a promotion or rebate offer on this title. Proof of purchase must be used in conjunction with other proof(s) of payment such as your dated sales receipt—see offer details.

Applied Microsoft® .NET Framework Programming in Microsoft® Visual Basic® .NET

0-7356-1787-2

CUSTOMER NAME

Microsoft Press, PO Box 97017, Redmond, WA 98073-9830